The Essential Guide to Telecommunications

4th Edition

Annabel Z. Dodd

Prentice Hall Professional Technical Reference
Upper Saddle River, NJ · Boston · Indianapolis · San Francisco
New York · Toronto · Montreal · London · Munich · Paris · Madrid
Capetown · Sydney · Tokyo · Singapore · Mexico City

The publisher offers excellent discounts on this book when ordered in quantity for bulk purchases or special sales, which may include electronic versions and/or custom covers and content particular to your business, training goals, marketing focus, and branding interests. For more information, please contact:

U. S. Corporate and Government Sales
(800) 382-3419
corpsales@pearsontechgroup.com

For sales outside the U. S., please contact:

International Sales
international@pearsoned.com

Visit us on the Web: www.phptr.com

Library of Congress Catalog Control Number: 2005924225

ISBN 0-13-148725-6
Text printed in the United States on recycled paper at R.R. Donnelley in Crawfordsville, Indiana.
Second printing, December 2005

To Bob, Judy, Nancy, Laura, Steve, Ross,
Elizabeth, Julia, Gabriel, and Michael

The Essential Guide to Telecommunications

4th Edition

Prentice Hall PTR
Essential Guide Series

THE ESSENTIAL GUIDE TO DATA WAREHOUSING

Agosta

THE ESSENTIAL GUIDE TO WEB STRATEGY FOR ENTREPRENEURS

Bergman

THE ESSENTIAL GUIDE TO TELECOMMUNICATIONS, FOURTH EDITION

Dodd

THE ESSENTIAL GUIDE TO WIRELESS COMMUNICATIONS APPLICATIONS, SECOND EDITION

Dornan

THE ESSENTIAL GUIDE TO INTERNET BUSINESS TECHNOLOGY

Honda & Martin

THE ESSENTIAL GUIDE TO NETWORKING

Keogh

THE ESSENTIAL GUIDE TO DIGITAL SET-TOP BOXES AND INTERACTIVE TV

O'Driscoll

THE ESSENTIAL GUIDE TO KNOWLEDGE MANAGEMENT: E-BUSINESS AND CRM APPLICATIONS

Tiwana

THE ESSENTIAL GUIDE TO SEMICONDUCTORS

Turley

THE ESSENTIAL GUIDE TO COMPUTING: THE STORY OF INFORMATION TECHNOLOGY

Walters

THE ESSENTIAL GUIDE TO RF AND WIRELESS, SECOND EDITION

Weisman

ADDITIONAL PRAISE FOR *THE ESSENTIAL GUIDE TO TELECOMMUNICATIONS*

"From starting entrepreneurs to industry veterans, employees from all kinds of network communications companies have found this primer to be an excellent reference book and interesting reading . . . the best way to keep current on evolving technology."

—Carol J. Meier, Executive Director, Massachusetts
Network Communications Council

"With jargon-free definitions, clear schematic drawings, and its steady narrative drive, The Essential Guide to Telecommunications *is a reassuring testament to the human ability to comprehend and communicate at some fundamental level even the most bewildering technology."*

—David Warsh, Editor, Economic Principals.com

"I find this book very useful for my graduate students in business and economics to become familiar with an up-to-date explanation of modern telecommunications."

—Jerry Hausman, McDonald Professor of Economics, MIT

"Annabel Dodd has distilled down the essential elements of digital communications and cogently translated the technobabble of the telecommunications revolution. This fine new edition of her book explains how Internet Protocol-based broadband networks will affect consumers, companies, and communities as the inexorable march of digital technologies continues . . . ."

—Congressman Edward J. Markey, Ranking Member
Subcommittee on Telecommunications, Trade and
Consumer Protection

"Annabel Dodd's Guide is an excellent source of technical information that's understandable to people who never studied engineering. I use it regularly."

—Jon Van, technology reporter, *The Chicago Tribune*

"The Essential Guide to Telecommunications is probably one of the most useful and well-written books on our telecom bookshelf. Annabel Z. Dodd does a great job in capturing a snapshot of the current telecom industry. Even those with little or no technical training should be able to understand the text. This is the perfect book for salespeople who want to learn more about the products and services they are selling, or for those who just want to keep up to date on the latest in telecom technology."

—William Van Hefner, President, Vantek Communications, Inc.

"As a technology management consultant, I am often required to have hands-on knowledge on a wide range of technology topics. Whenever I need quick and accurate information on telecommunications technology, I turn to The Essential Guide to Telecommunications. *I find it to be a very valuable reference."*

—Lumas Kendrick, Jr., Kendrick Technology Associates

"The Essential Guide to Telecommunications *is a fine guide to the field, readable by anyone, useful to everyone. As a first guide to the field, as a reference, and as a commentary on the history and strategy of telecommunications, it is simply superb."*

—Andrew Allentuck, Review Editor, Globetechnology,
THE GLOBE AND MAIL, Toronto

"People who enjoy a straightforward view of the ever-changing world of high technology will like this book. I did."

—William Sherry, Product Specialist,
Messaging & Mobility Applications, Avaya

"Ms. Dodd continues to provide an excellent and thorough text on the telecommunications industry. As in her previous editions, she presents a good balance of technical- and business-related information that is readily understandable by anyone with an interest in this key component of today's business environment. In her new edition, she has captured many of the recent changes in this dynamic field that will affect every company in the years ahead. I strongly recommend her book to anyone who wants a better understanding of telecommunications."

—Joe McGrath, Vice President,
Information Technologies, Sepracor Inc.

"After reading The Essential Guide to Telecommunications, *I regret that there is not an Oscar given to authors. ANI, DNIS, ILEC, MMDS—Are you familiar with all of these terms? If you are, then you move to the front of the class. If you are not, then you're among 90 percent of the population that might just be missing out on some of the latest technological advancements that can significantly impact your business and increase your bottom line. It pays to read Dodd's book and gain an insight in this fast-changing field."*

—Brad Tuttle, Chief Operating Officer, ITV Direct Inc.

"This book is an excellent resource to understand the technologies used in the data and telecommunications industry. Dodd brings together the descriptions, standards, and history to not only answer "what" but also "why." In particular, those new to the industry will appreciate the clear language and broad scope."

—Brent D. Stewart, Course Director, Global Knowledge

"I have used this book in my classes on Internet and telecommunications policy for years, and each edition is always the best and most thorough explanation of these complex topics. And I always tell my students to keep this book handy as a basic reference on issues that will undoubtedly be part of their careers in the future."

—Gary Chapman, LBJ School of Public Affairs,
University of Texas at Austin

Contents

Part II
Industry Overview and Public Networks

3 Industry Overview *111*

Part III
Advanced Technologies, Cable TV Networks, and the Internet

Part IV
Wireless Service

8 Mobile Services   *387*

Preface

The September 11, 2001 attacks on the World Trade Center and the Pentagon and the 2004 Asian tsunami poignantly highlighted the importance of mobile telephones. People in doomed airplanes said goodbye to loved ones, families contacted each other, and emergency workers relied on cell phones. Mobile wireless technology is more than a way for governments, the military, and individuals to stay in touch during emergencies. For many, it is a way of life, a way to stay connected at all times of day whether by text messaging or by voice.

The Essential Guide to Telecommunications, Fourth Edition examines mobile networks as well as the landline networks that support and connect wireless networks and the Internet worldwide. It discusses technological and business issues and the multi-national carriers that manage our largest networks. In addition, it provides real-life examples of how consumers, small and medium sized organizations, and enterprise customers use technologies and the critical factors that influence customers' and carriers' adoption of new technology.

The significance of a strong telecommunications infrastructure on the economy and on international trade is widely recognized and has prompted attention from governments worldwide. *The Essential Guide to Telecommunications* reviews regulatory issues that are of concern to carriers and governments. It explores the role of regulations in promoting innovation and competition and robust networks critical to national security. In addition, regulatory rulings are examined in light of their impact on customer segments and carriers.

The Essential Guide to Telecommunications presents profiles of industry sectors, including cable TV providers, incumbent telephone companies, wireless carriers, Voice over IP providers, and competitive local exchange carriers. It explores strategies carriers deploy to gain a competitive edge and the network technologies used to further these strategies. In addition to looking at the architecture of wireless networks, the book depicts networks based on Internet protocol (IP) as well as traditional circuit switched and signaling systems that tie networks together and link applications to networks. It also explores how IP networks are connected to other carriers' IP networks and to public switched telephone networks. It also explains new wireless services and compares the differences and similarities between technologies, such as Zigbee, Bluetooth, and Radio Frequency Identification (RFID) in terms of the technological differences as well as the ways these technologies are used.

In addition to wireless services and the structure of carriers' networks, *The Essential Guide to Telecommunications* analyzes equipment and technologies used in enterprises and in homes. It explains how converged telephone systems are used—their architecture and the connection to applications such as speech recognition, instant messaging, and multimedia messaging. Along with explanations of technology are examples of applications and historical highlights. How the industry evolved and how the technology changed is explained.

The language and significance of important telecommunications technologies are explored. This is not intended to be a deeply technical book. Rather, it is an overview of technologies and an explanation of the structure of the telecommunications industry. The Fourth Edition includes quotes and interviews with staff at key organizations, who express their views of how technologies, the Internet, and regulations have impacted and will continue to influence the industry.

This book is intended for nontechnical people who work in the field of telecommunications, teach at and attend classes at educational institutions, and those responsible for the administration of telecommunications services for their organizations. The intended audience includes regulatory staff, salespeople, attorneys, researchers, marketing personnel, human resources professionals, project managers, telecommunications managers, and high-level administrators.

Acknowledgments

Thanks to the many people who took the time to speak with me and to share views acquired from years of experience in telecommunications. Staff at the following companies were enormously helpful: Judy Reed Smith at Atlantic-ACM; Marian Croak at AT&T Corporation; Rachel Lamont, Wayne Miyamoto, and Bill Sherry at Avaya Communications; Tom Case at Boston Scientific Corporation; Paul Scheib at Children's Hospital Boston; Tony DiBenedetto and Joe Williams at Cisco Systems; Marty Dugan at Comverse; Ted Messmer at Corning Cable Systems; Michael Saurbaugh at Corning Federal Credit Union; Dan Estes at Cox Communications; Sascha Meinrath at CU Wireless Network; David Cole at DFC Intelligence; Scott Nelson at Gartner, Inc; Joseph Heinen at Genesys Telecommunications; Brent D. Stewart at Global Knowledge; Scott Stull at iBiquity Digital Corporation; Madelyn Smith at IPWireless; Brad Tuttle at ITV Direct, Inc.; Jerry Watts at ITC^DeltaCom; Kendrick Lumas at Kendrick Technology Associates; Bill Rebello at Lifeline Systems Inc.; Peter Eggimann at Metropolitan 911 Board (MN); Jeff Walker at Motorola Broadband; Greg Mycio at New Paradigm Resources Group; Mark Fletcher and Michael J. McDonough III at Nortel Networks; Richard Packer at R. Packer Electrical Services, Inc.; Lisa Ahlman and Bob Walters at SBC Communications Inc.; Will Biedron at Stargus, Inc.; Stephan Beckert at TeleGeography/PriMetrica, Inc.; Jeff Kaplan at THINKstrategies; and Kathleen McCarthy at the town of Framingham, Massachusetts.

Thanks also to the following for their time and valuable insights: David Diamond, vice president, operations at Amperion Incorporated; Tom A. Anschutz, principal member technical staff at BellSouth; Matthew Pittinsky, chairman at Blackboard Inc.; Dixon Doll, cofounder and managing general partner at Doll Capital Management; Tom Starr, president and chairperson DSL Forum Board of Directors and senior member of technical staff at SBC; Kurt Melden, chief scientist, and John Riedel, vice president of business development at Juniper Networks; Antonio Carro

Marina, cofounder and vice chairman at Jazztel plc; Craig Farrill, CEO at Kodiak Networks; Brough Turner, Sr. VP and chief technology officer at NMS Communications; Robert Weir, vice president information services, and Mark Hildebrand, director of enterprise systems at Northeastern University; Peter Fannon, vice president, technology policy and regulatory affairs at Panasonic/Matsushita Electric Corporation of America; John Hoffman, chief executive officer at Roamware; Bob McIntyre, corporate senior vice president, chief technical officer at Scientic-Atlanta, Inc.; Dan Bricklin, founder at Software Garden; Mike Hluchyj, founder and chief technology officer at Sonus Networks; Brent Petersen, senior vice president of marketing and communications at USDTV; and Greg Evans, VP of services and access technologies at Verizon Communications.

Experts from the following associations provided information: Mike Schwartz at CableLabs; Patrick Pearlman, deputy consumer advocate at the Consumer Advocate Division of the Public Service Commission of West Virginia; Brad Ramsay, general counsel and director - policy department at the National Association of Regulatory Utility Commissioners.

Colin Crowell, Massachusetts Congressman Edward Markey's aide for telecommunications, was an inestimable help for updates on regulatory issues. Walt Tetschner, president of Tern Systems in Acton, Massachusetts, provided background and statistics about speech recognition and unified messaging services. Fred Goldstein, principal at Ionary Consulting, provided information on competitive local exchange carriers and regulatory issues. Joseph Lawrence, senior director, global technology marketing, and Ravi Kalavakunta, senior manager, global technology marketing, at Qualcomm provided updates on mobile standards and technologies. Thanks to my acquisitions editors Catherine Nolan, Mary Franz, and especially Mike Meehan, who started it all.

Thanks also to my daughter, Nancy Dodd, principal at Nancy Dodd Research; Joe McGrath, vice president information technologies, and Susan Truesdale, director networking and telecommunications at Sepracor, Inc.; and Peter McGowan, m-g marketing. I couldn't have written this book without the support and help of all these people.

Special thanks to my husband, Bob, for his perceptive comments. Bob read every chapter multiple times. He provided the keen insights and asked the tough questions I've come to expect based on his observations for my first three editions.

About the Author

Annabel Z. Dodd teaches courses on wireless mobile services and data communications in the graduate program of Northeastern University's School of Professional and Continuing Studies. She has been an adjunct professor in the Master of Science in Technology Management program at the State University of New York at Stony Brook, where she taught in a joint program with The Institute of Industrial Policy Studies, Seoul, South Korea. In addition, the Fundación de la Innovación Bankinter, selected her to participate in their Future Trends Forum in Madrid in 2004. Formerly in marketing at New England Telephone and Telecommunications Manager at Dennison Manufacturing Company, now Avery Dennison, she consults with major corporations and institutions and gives seminars to organizations worldwide. The Massachusetts Network Communications Council honored her as the Professor of the Year 2000. *The Essential Guide to Telecommunications* has been translated into eight languages worldwide since its first Edition, which was published in 1997. More information can be found at her Web site, www.doddontheline.com.

Part I

Fundamentals and Voice Over IP

1 Basic Concepts

In this chapter:

Basics matter; new products and services are often developed using technologies that have been available for many years. Continual improvements in these basic tools have led to important innovations. For example, advances in compression spurred developments in downloading music and digital entertainment.

Apple Computer's iTunes service is made possible because the music is compressed, made smaller. Compression squeezes large amounts of data into smaller "pipes," something like putting data into a trash compactor. In addition, compression makes it possible for video to use less of a network's capacity when it is transmitted. Cable and satellite TV operators compress and digitize television signals to expand the number of channels for premium movies and video-on-demand that can be carried over existing network facilities.

Multiplexing is an enabling technology for innovative services in broadband wireless and landline networks. Multiplexing is a way to carry information more efficiently on networks. However, unlike compression, it does not shrink data. Rather, it enables multiple devices and sources of traffic to share telecommunications paths. It uses existing fiber-optic, wireless media, and copper cabling to carry an ever-increasing amount of entertainment, voice traffic, and information from multiple sources. With multiplexing, a small number of fiber-optic cables can support entire office parks. Telephone companies no longer bear the expense of laying many strands of copper cabling to support each building in an office park.

Multiplexing and compression could not have made such dramatic breakthroughs without the transition from analog to digital services. Digital signals are clearer, have fewer errors, take up less space, and can be transmitted at higher speeds than analog signals. Digital cable television can carry ten times the number of channels as analog cable television. Moreover, digital TV is spurring the sale of new home entertainment centers to take advantage of surround-sound audio and movie-theater-quality video on some types of digital television sets.

Standardized protocols enabled many changes in how corporations conduct business and consumers communicate. Protocols define how devices and networks communicate with each other. For example, a suite of protocols, transmission control protocol/Internet protocol (TCP/IP), spells out rules for sending voice, images, and data across the Internet and in corporate networks. Corporations and small businesses that initially used the Internet for casual e-mail are now putting important business processes on internal networks and on the Internet. "Open," widely understood Internet protocols like TCP/IP leave networks vulnerable to hackers when they are poorly implemented. Specific protocols such as secure socket layer (SSL) have been developed to protect public and private networks from external threats.

Computers are no longer the standalone entities they were initially. Nor are local area networks like the early local area networks that were isolated within departments to share expensive printers or to meet specialized needs such as finance departments' requirements for accounting packages. Technology that was first developed to connect diverse internal networks to exchange information and e-mail messages within a building and then on campuses now is used to link corporate main offices and remote sales and manufacturing sites. Wide area networks (WANs) link sites *between* metropolitan areas; metropolitan area networks (MANs) link locations *within* metropolitan areas.

Government regulations have added to the amount of traffic and the security requirements on networks. For example, the Sarbanes-Oxley Act of 2002 not only requires that public firms retain more financial documents for longer periods; in addition, internal processes and controls are liable to be audited by the government. Moreover, healthcare institutions need to comply with Health Insurance Portability and Accountability Act of 1996 (HIPPA) rules. HIPPA mandates that healthcare providers protect patient records from snoopers. The result is that LAN networks and devices need to securely handle, store, and back up larger amounts of traffic.

THE TRANSITION TO DIGITAL ....

The transition from analog to digital networks is a major factor in the economic and technical forces that changed telecommunications dramatically in the twentieth and twenty-first centuries. The analog format, which was designed for lower volumes of voice traffic, is inadequate for the large amounts of voice, data, music, and video images carried on our cellular, public telephone, Internet, and cable TV networks.

Analog Signals—Slower, More Prone to Errors

Analog services are slower and more prone to errors than digital service. Analog signals take the form of waves that are more complex to re-create than digital off and on bits. This is one reason speeds on analog lines are slower than those on digital links. Analog signals also lose strength over shorter distances than digital signals and therefore require more equipment to boost their strength. However, boosting the strength of analog signals introduces impairments such as static in voice calls and blurry images in television signals as they travel farther from transmitters.

Impairments on Analog Services— Electrical Interference

Analog telephone signals are analogous to water flowing through a pipe. Rushing water loses force as it travels through a pipe. The farther it travels in the pipe, the more force it loses and the weaker it becomes. Similarly, an analog signal weakens as it travels over distances, whether it is sent over copper, coaxial cable, or through the air as a radio or microwave signal. The signal meets resistance in the media (copper, coaxial cable, air) over which it is sent, causing the signal to fade. In voice conversation, the voice will sound softer. This is referred to as *attenuation*.

In addition to becoming weaker, analog signals react to electrical interference, or "noise," on the line. Power lines, lights, and electric machinery all inject noise in the form of electrical energy into the analog signal. In voice conversations, noise on analog lines is heard as static.

To overcome resistance and boost the signal, an analog wave is periodically strengthened with a device called an *amplifier*. In analog services, the amplifier that strengthens the signal cannot tell the difference between the electrical energy present in the form of noise and the actual voice, video, or data signals. Thus, the noise as well as the signal is amplified. The last mile of cable TV systems in neighborhoods where the cable connects to homes is usually made up of coaxial cabling. In this analog portion, signals are amplified every half a mile. In these systems, amplifying the signal also amplifies the noise. Thus, the television signals are amplified more often as they travel farther from the cable providers' equipment, more noise is introduced, and TV reception becomes blurrier. In analog systems, people who live farther from their providers have poorer quality TV reception, but they can generally still see the images.

Frequency on Analog Services—Wavelengths

Analog signals move down telephone lines as electromagnetic waves, wavelengths. A *wavelength* is a complete cycle, as illustrated in Figure 1.1. It starts at a zero point of voltage, goes to the highest positive part of the wave, down to the negative voltage portion, and then back to zero. Frequency is expressed in cycles per second, the number of times per second that a wave oscillates, or swings back and forth, in a complete cycle from its starting point to its endpoint.

The higher the frequency, the more cycles of a wave are transmitted in a period of time. This is because the higher the number of waveforms sent, the more data the line can carry. Thus, higher frequencies have more capacity because each wavelength carries voice or data information. *Modulation*, the process of varying characteristics such as amplitude (height), frequency, and phase (shape) of wavelengths, also impacts carrying capacity. Advanced modulation schemes enable wavelengths to carry, for example, 16 bits per wavelength. New wireless services that use advanced modulation are being developed for broadband wireless Internet access.

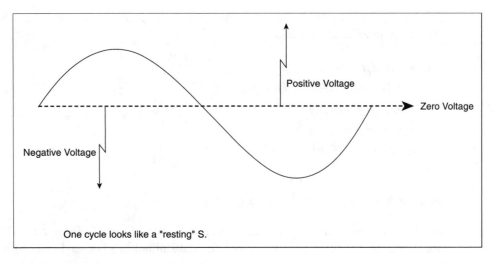

Figure 1.1
One cycle of an analog wave, 1 hertz (Hz).

This speed or frequency is stated in hertz (Hz). For example, a wavelength that oscillates, or swings back and forth, 10 times per second has a speed of 10 hertz (Hz) or cycles per second.

Analog frequencies are expressed in the following abbreviated forms:

- kilohertz or kHz = thousands of cycles per second

  Voice is carried in the frequency range of .3kHz to 3.3kHz, or 3000Hz.

- megahertz or MHz = millions of cycles per second

  Analog cable TV signals are carried in the frequency range of 54MHz to 750MHz.

- gigahertz or GHz = billions of cycles per second

  Most analog microwave towers operate at between 2GHz and 12GHz.

Digital Signals

It wasn't until the 1960s that carriers started taking advantage of the superiority of digital service when they used T-1 links between telephone company central offices. T-1 enabled telephone companies to save on the cost of outside cabling by packing

24 voice channels on two pairs of copper cabling. Digital signals have the following advantages over analog signals:

- Higher speeds
- Clearer video and audio quality
- Greater capacity
- Fewer errors
- More reliability

Binary Bits—On and Off Signals

Instead of waves, digital signals are transmitted in the form of binary bits. The term *binary* means that there are two values for transmitted bits: on and off. On bits are depicted as ones and off bits as zeroes in programming and binary notations. For data transmitted on copper cabling, on bits are represented by positive voltage and off bits by the absence of voltage. In fiber-optic cabling, on bits are represented by light pulses and off bits by the absence of light pulses.

Fewer Errors, Higher Speeds, Additional Reliability

It is faster to re-create binary digital ones and zeros than more complex analog wavelengths. Whereas the highest speed projected for analog dial-up modems is 33,600 bits per second when sending data, digital routers operate at terabit-per-second speeds. A *terabit* is equal to a thousand gigabits; 2,000,000,000,000 bits per second equals two terabits per second.

Digital signals can be re-created more reliably than analog waves. Both analog and digital signals are subject to impairments: They lose strength, fade over distance, and are susceptible to interference such as noise. However, digital signals travel farther before fading. Thus, less equipment is needed to boost the signals.

Fewer pieces of equipment translate to lower maintenance and installation costs. At every point that a signal fades, amplifiers or regenerators are required. Each amplifier is a place for a possible failure. For example, water can leak into a telephone company's manhole, or the amplifier itself might fail. Organizations that use digital lines such as T-1 often experience only one or two brief failures in an entire year. High reliability results in lower maintenance costs for telephone companies.

Moreover, digital signals can be "repaired" more cleanly than analog signals. Figure 1.2 illustrates that when a digital signal loses strength and fades over distance, equipment regenerates the signal and discards the noise and static. The noise is not, as in an analog signal in Figure 1.2, regenerated. In digital transmissions, where

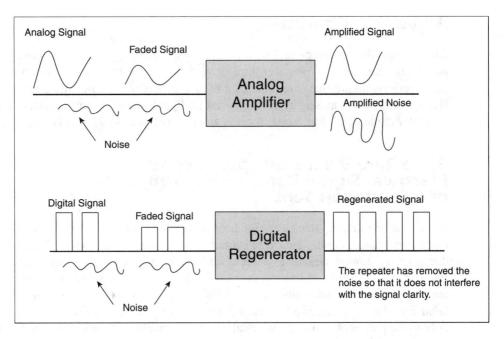

Figure 1.2
Noise amplified on the analog line, eliminated   on digital service.

noise is discarded, garbling occurs less frequently; thus, there are fewer errors in the communication.

ADDING MEANING TO SIGNALS— CODES AND BITS..

Computers communicate with each other using specialized codes made up of bits. Without these standardized codes, computers would not be able to interpret bits into consistent words in, for example, e-mail messages. Computers can "read" each other's on and off binary bits when these bits are arranged in a standard, predefined series of on and off bits.

People use the terms "bits," "baud rate," and "bytes" interchangeably. Their meanings, however, differ significantly. The signaling speed on analog lines is the *baud rate*, the number of times per second a cycle is completed. The baud rate is measured differently than bits per second. *Bits per second* are the actual number of bits sent in a given time from point A to point B.

A Byte = A Character

Bits organized into groups of 7 or 8 bits are bytes. Each byte is a character, piece of punctuation, or space. Computer hard drive capacity tends to be measured in bytes, but speeds on digital lines are measured in the number of bits transmitted per second. Bytes stored on computer drives are stored in digital form. To summarize, a byte is a character made up of 7 or 8 bits. A bit is an on or off electrical pulse or light pulse.

Baud Rate Versus Bits per Second— Electrical Signal Rates Versus Amount of Information Sent

A *baud* is one analog electrical signal or wavelength. One cycle of an analog wave equals one baud. A complete cycle starts at zero voltage, goes to the highest voltage, down to the lowest negative voltage, and back to zero voltage, the resting S in Figure 1.1. A 1,200-baud line means that the analog wave completes 1,200 cycles in one second. A 2,400-baud line carries 2,400 complete cycles in one second. The term *baud rate* does not indicate the amount of information sent on these waves. It refers only to the number of analog electrical signals—wavelengths or cycles per second.

The public switched telephone network (PSTN) runs at only 2,400 bauds per second. To achieve greater capacity, modem manufacturers design modems capable of carrying more than one bit on each analog wave. Thus, a 9,600-bit-per-second (bps) modem sends 4 bits of data on each analog wave (9600 ÷ 2400 = 4). It is correct to state that the 9,600bps modem runs at 2,400 baud but carries 9,600 bits per second. It still uses a 2,400-baud line.

Baud rate refers to analog, not digital, transmission services. Digital services transmit information as on or off electrical signals in the case of copper wires, and on or off light pulses on fiber-optic lines. On digital services, 56,000-bit-per-second lines can carry 56,000 bits in one second. The speed is 56Kbps, or 56 kilobits per second.

Codes—Adding Meaning to Bits

All computers use codes so that they can translate bits into meaningful language. The main code, American Standard Code for Information Interchange (ASCII), is used in English-language personal computers. The international version of ASCII is known as the International Reference Alphabet (IRA). IBM minis and mainframes use a different code, the Extended Binary Coded Decimal Interexchange Code (EBCDIC).

Distant computers can read simple e-mail messages because they are both in ASCII. American Standard Code for Information Interchange is a 7-bit code. Each character is made up of 7 bits. ASCII is limited to 128 characters. Most PCs now use extended ASCII, which supports 8-bit codes. These characters include all of the upper- and lowercase letters of the alphabet, numbers, and punctuation such as !, ", and : (see Table 1.1).

Table 1.1   Examples of ASCII Code

Character	ASCII Representation
!	0100001
A	1000001
m	1101101

The limited number of ASCII characters, 128 or 256, results in ASCII not including formatting characters such as underlining, tabs, and columns. Specialized word processing and spreadsheet programs supplement ASCII with formatting and proprietary features such as columns. This is why Microsoft Word documents, for example, need to be "translated" when they are opened in a WordPerfect program. The translation converts Microsoft Word code to WordPerfect code.

In addition, specialized, non-ASCII formatting for tabs, tables, and columns in e-mail messages requires specialized formatting. For example, the Hypertext Markup Language (HTML) and Rich Text Format (RTF) in Microsoft Outlook's e-mail program support this formatting. HTML is the *markup language* used on the World Wide Web. Markup languages specify how characters should be formatted. In Hypertext Markup Language, brackets <> surround text with formatting commands. For example, <bold> tells the e-mail program to bold characters. Other commands in HTML are for linking Web addresses included in e-mail messages to particular Web sites or for adding italics, graphics such as smiley faces, or bulleted text.

MEASURING SPEED AND CAPACITY ....

In telecommunications, bandwidth refers to capacity. Bandwidth is expressed differently in analog and digital transmissions. The capacity of analog media, such as coaxial cable, is referred to as *frequency*. The bandwidth of an analog service is the difference between the highest and lowest frequency within which the medium carries traffic. For example, in the early 1980s when the government gave spectrum (a range of frequencies) rights to local telephone companies for analog cellular service, it gave it to them in the range of 894MHz to 869MHz. It gave them 25MHz (894 – 869 = 25) of spectrum. Analog cable TV in the United States uses 6MHz for each channel carried. The greater the difference between the highest and lowest frequency, the higher the capacity or bandwidth supported.

For digital services such as ISDN, T-1, and ATM, speed is stated in bits per second. Simply put, it is the number of bits that can be transmitted in one second. T-1 has a bandwidth of 1.54 million bits per second. Bandwidth or hertz can be expressed in many ways. Some of these include

- T-1 North American and Japanese circuits have a bandwidth of 1.54 million bits per second, or 1.54 megabits per second (Mbps).
- E-1 European standard circuits have a bandwidth of 2.048 million bits per second, 2.048 megabits per second, or 2.048Mbps.
- Some ATM systems have the capacity for 13.22 billion bits per second, or 13.22 gigabits per second (Gbps).
- One thousand gigabits is called 1 terabit; 10 terabits per second = 10,000,000,000,000 bits per second.

The letter C for *concatenated* is sometimes added to high-speed designations used on optical networks. Concatenated means multiple streams from the same source—such as video—travel together so there are no interruptions in video transmissions that share a multiplexed fiber path with traffic from other sources. To the people watching the video, the images appear as a single stream of video.

Broadband Service—Multiple Data Streams

The International Telecommunication Union (ITU), a standards organization based in Geneva, Switzerland, refers to broadband services as those that generally have the following functionality:

- Operate at higher than 1.54 or 2 megabits per second
- Carry full-motion video, such as that in corporate video conference systems but not as high a quality as broadcast television
- Support multiple streams of traffic simultaneously

The definition of broadband has evolved over time. Broadband originally referred to internal, high-speed, local area networks such as Wang Laboratories' WangNet™. This coaxial-cabling-based network transported signals concurrently from multiple personal computers within facilities. One early definition of broadband referred to networks such as cable TV networks in which multiple streams of television channels are transmitted simultaneously. The definition of broadband differs within the industry. An example of this evolution is shown in Table 1.2.

For example, DSL modems carry data over the same lines used for voice. Cable TV neighborhood networks transport Internet access along with television and voice traffic. The ITU points out that because compression enables slower-speed networks to transmit images, music, and video at higher quality than previously, speed is not always indicative of broadband capabilities. (See the following section for information on compression.) The ITU notes that countries with more wireless than wired telephones concentrate their focus on wireless services to provide widespread broadband Internet access.

Broadband services are characterized as being transported on larger pipes. Just as more water fits into a wider pipe, broadband services carry more information than narrowband lines such as those for analog voice. Some experts define broadband services as those at T-3 and higher speeds. Table 1.2 offers a comparison of broadband and narrowband services.

Table 1.2 Broadband and Narrowband Services

Narrowband	Broadband
T-1 at 1.54Mbps Twenty-four voice or data conversations on fiber optics, infrared, microwave, or two pairs of wire.	*Analog broadcast and cable TV services—use 6MHz per channel* Multiple television channels broadcast, each using 6MHz of capacity.
Analog telephone lines at 3,000Hz Plain old telephone service (POTS) modems used for Internet access.	*Digital broadcast, satellite, and cable TV* Four to ten channels of programming carried on 6MHz of bandwidth. Newer, digital high definition TV (HDTV) offers enhanced clarity over analog TV.
BRI ISDN at 144Kbps Two paths for voice or data, each at 64Kbps. One path for signals at 16Kbps.	*Mobile data networks* Advanced wireless networks that enable users to access data at 144 kilobits per second and above speeds.
	T-3 at 44.7 megabits per second (equivalent to 28 T-1 circuits) A way of transmitting 672 conversations over fiber optics or digital microwave.

IMPROVING UTILIZATION—COMPRESSION AND MULTIPLEXING ....

Compression and multiplexing improve efficiency on wireless and wireline networks. Compression shrinks the data, and multiplexing combines data from multiple sources onto a single path.

Compression—Shrinking Data to Send More Information

Just as a trash compactor makes trash smaller so that more refuse can be packed into a garbage barrel, compression makes data smaller so that more information can be packed into networks. It is a technique to add more capacity on telephone lines, cable TV networks, the Internet, advanced cellular networks, and airwaves used for broadcasts. Advances in compression have enormous potential to make cable modems, DSL services, and cellular networks adequate for movies, games, music, and downloading graphics such as JPEG and PowerPoint images.

In addition, enterprise customers use compression as one way to add capacity to their internal networks and to the links between their sites. For example, instead of upgrading to higher-speed lines to other branch offices, they may add hardware with software that compresses traffic before it is transmitted to the branch office. At the remote site, a device decompresses the voice and data back to its original format.

In video, compression works by transmitting only the changed image, not the same image over and over. For example, in a videoconference, nothing is transmitted after the initial image of a person until that person moves or speaks. Fixed objects such as walls, desks, and background are not repeatedly transmitted. The device performing the compression, the *codec*, knows that discarding minor changes in the image won't noticeably distort the viewed image.

Throughput—User Information Transmitted

Throughput is the actual amount of useful data sent on a transmission. Improvements in throughput increase the amount of data transmitted in a given amount of time over, for example, DSL or cable modems. Compression increases throughput without changing the actual speed of the line. For instance, a song that is compressed may be downloaded in just a few seconds rather than a minute or two. Users often send large graphics attachments in compressed formats; this makes the files smaller and quicker to send. They use compression software such as Stuffit. However, the network's speed has not changed. The file has been squeezed into a smaller format at the sending end and put back into a larger format by the receiver's compatible software.

When compression is used with text and facsimile, data to be transmitted is reduced by removing white spaces and redundant images and by abbreviating the most frequently appearing letters. When modems equipped with compression transmit text, repeated letters are abbreviated into smaller codes. For example, the letters E, T, O, and I appear frequently in text. Compression sends shortened versions of these letters with 3 bits rather than the entire 8 bits for each letter. Thus, a page of text might be sent using 1,600 bits rather than 2,200 bits. With facsimile, compression removes white spaces from pictures and only transmits the images.

Compression Standards = Interoperability

There are many types of compression methods. A device called a codec (short for coder-decoder) encodes text, audio, video, or images using a mathematical algorithm. For compression to work, both the sending and receiving ends must use the same compression method. The sending end looks at the data, voice, or image. It then compresses it using a mathematical algorithm. The receiver decodes the transmission. Compression on devices such as modems and video teleconferencing from various manufacturers can interoperate when both devices use agreed-upon compression standards.

More powerful personal computers as well as improvements in compression have increased the use of streaming audio and video over the Internet. Further improvements in compression make streaming audio and graphics viable for slower-speed cellular devices. RealNetworks, Inc. makes its decoding compression and player software available free or at minimal costs to consumers. The strategy is to make its software so prevalent among consumers that software developers will purchase RealNetworks' server products to create content such as Web ads and other graphics in Web pages. See Table 1.3 at the end of this chapter for compression standards.

MPEG Standards—Compressing Audio and Video

The International Telecommunications Union (ITU) formed the Moving Picture Experts Group (MPEG) in 1991 to develop compression standards for playback of video clips and digital TV. MPEG-3 also came to be used for streaming audio. MPEG and proprietary streaming media compression schemes are asymmetrical. It takes more processing power to encode at the Internet, satellite TV, broadcaster, or cable TV provider than to decode an image at the customer. Streaming compression algorithms assume that the end user will have less processing power to decode transmissions than the developers and broadcasters that encode the video and audio. A newer standard, MPEG-4, is designed for multimedia files and television and is able to compress files to use four times less capacity than MPEG-2.

Some applications require better resolution than supplied by asymmetric compression software. Radiology departments for viewing images, firefighters for viewing forest fires images beamed from airplanes, and the FBI for fingerprint viewing are examples that might use symmetric compression software.

Streaming—Listening and Viewing Without Downloading

Streaming, an important feature of browsers, is different than downloading. When text, music, or graphics are downloaded, the entire file must be downloaded before it can be viewed or played. When music is streamed, callers listen to the music but cannot store it to listen to it later. Downloading actually stores the music files on a listener's computer hard drive.

Streaming speeds up transmission of video, images, and audio over the Internet. When graphics and text are sent to an Internet user's browser, the text can be viewed as soon as it reaches the PC. The graphics, which take longer to be viewed, are filled in as they are received.

Compressing and Digitizing Speech

Speech, audio, and television are analog in their original form. Before they are transmitted over digital landline or wireless networks, codecs compress (encode) them and convert them to digital. Codecs sample speech at different heights (amplitude) along the sound wave and convert it to a one or a zero. At the receiving end, decoders convert the ones and zeros back to sound or video waves. With compression, codecs do not have to sample every height on the sound wave to achieve high-quality sound. For example, they skip silence or predict the next sound based on the previous sound. Thus, fewer bits per second are transmitted to represent the speech. Codecs are located in cellular handsets, telephones, high definition TV transmitters, set-top boxes, televisions, IP telephones, and radios. Codecs also compress voice in speech recognition and voice mail systems.

Multiplexing—Let's Share

Multiplexing combines traffic from multiple voice or data devices into one stream so that it can share a telecommunications path. Like compression, multiplexing enables companies and carriers to send more information on cellular airwaves and telephone networks. However, unlike compression, multiplexing does not alter the actual data sent. Multiplexing equipment is located in long distance companies, in local telephone companies, and at end user premises. It is used with both analog and digital services. Examples of multiplexing over digital facilities include T-1, fractional T-1, E-1, E-3, T-3, ISDN, and ATM. See Figure 1.3.

The oldest multiplexing techniques were devised by AT&T for use with analog voice services. The goal was to make more efficient use of the most expensive portion of the public telephone network, the outside wires used to connect homes and telephone offices to each other. This analog technique was referred to as *frequency division multiplexing*. Frequency division multiplexing divides the available range of frequencies among multiple users. It enabled multiple voice and later data calls to

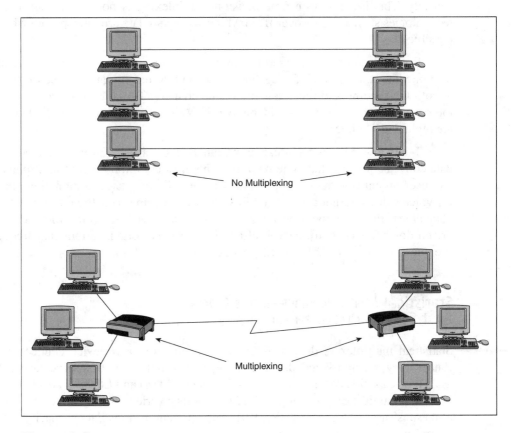

Figure 1.3
Multiplexing.

share paths between central offices. Thus, AT&T did not need to provide a cable connection for each conversation. Rather, multiple conversations could share the same wire between telephone company central offices.

Time Division Multiplexing—Higher Capacity with Digital Multiplexing

Time division multiplexing is a digital multiplexing scheme that saves capacity for each device or voice on a telephone call. Once a connection is established, capacity is saved even when the device is not sending information. For example, if a call is put on hold, no other device can use this spare capacity. Small slices of silence with thousands of calls in progress in carriers' networks result in high amounts of unused capacity. This is the reason time division multiplexing is not as efficient as newer technologies such as Voice over IP, in which voice and data are interspersed whenever possible.

Both T-1 and T-3 use time division multiplexing. T-3 carries 672 conversations over one line at a speed of 45 megabits per second. A matching multiplexer is required at both the sending and receiving end of the channel. T-3 is used for very large customers and Internet service provider networks. At telephone companies, higher speeds are replacing T-3 lines.

T-1 is lower in cost and capacity than T-3. T-1 allows 24 voice, video, and/or data conversations to share one path. It is the most common form of multiplexing at end user organizations. T-1 applications include linking organization sites together for voice calls, Internet access, and links between business customers and telephone companies. Price competition among carriers and manufacturing efficiencies have driven down T-1 costs to make it affordable for small organizations that frequently use one T-1 circuit for both Internet access and voice calling.

Statistical Multiplexing—First Come, First Served Prioritization

Statistical multiplexers do not guarantee capacity for each device connected to it. Rather, they transmit voice, data, and images on a first come, first serve basis as long as there is capacity. Asynchronous transfer mode (ATM) and Ethernet are examples of statistical multiplexing techniques. ATM supports a variety of classes of services. One of these is variable bit rate (VBR). VBR traffic is sent over available capacity not used for traffic with a higher priority.

Statistical multiplexers support more devices than time division multiplexers because they don't need to save capacity when a device is not active. Carriers can sell aggregated Internet access equal to higher speeds than the ports on their network. For example, Internet service providers may sell 250 megabits of Internet access supported by a 155MBps ATM multiplexer.

INTEROPERABILITY—PROTOCOLS AND ARCHITECTURES...

Protocols enable like devices to communicate with each other by providing a common set of rules. Standardized protocols for wireless local area networks (LANs) have made the convenience of affordable wireless services available to more homes and smaller businesses than ever before. (See Chapter 9, "Wi-Fi, Wireless Broadband, Sensor Networks, and Personal Area Networks," for wireless LANs.)

Protocols—A Common Set of Rules

Protocols are key enablers for all types of communications, including the proliferation of affordable Internet access. Devices communicate over the Internet using a suite of protocols called TCP/IP. For example, the IP, or Internet protocol, portion of TCP/IP allows portions of messages called datagrams to take different routes through the Internet. The datagrams are assembled into one message at the receiving end of the route. Other protocols, such as Bluetooth, make possible wireless communications among devices located within 33 feet of each other.

The following are examples of protocol functions:

- Who transmits first?
- Which network sent this packet?
- In a network with many devices, how is it decided whose turn it is to transmit?
- How is it determined if an error has occurred?
- Which applications is this message allowed to access?
- What is this packet's priority?
- If there is an error, does the entire transmission have to be re-sent or just the portion with the error?
- How is data packaged to be sent, one bit at a time or one block of bits at a time? How many bits are in each block? Should data be put into envelopes called packets?

Protocol structures impact speed, cost, and efficiency. The following protocols illustrate this point:

- *Secure sockets layer (SSL).* Encrypts (scrambles) communications between a user's browser and Web pages so that only the authorized server (computer containing the electronic commerce application) can read credit card information. It also provides authentication—are you who you say you are? Users know if a site uses SSL by the locked padlock displayed on their screens during transactions.

- *Session initiation protocol (SIP).* SIP is a signaling protocol used to set up phone calls in some Voice over IP telephone systems that convert voice into packets in data networks. As the session initiation protocol is adopted uniformly, it is hoped that feature-rich telephones and applications from many manufacturers can be intermixed in telephone systems. The expectation is that this will drive down the cost of multibutton telephones for Voice over IP systems. SIP is also used to set up real time audio conferences, videoconferences, and instant-messaging sessions.

Architectures—How Devices Fit Together in a Network

Architectures define how computers are tied together. The main goal of architectures is to enable dissimilar protocols and computer networks to communicate. During the 1970s, the International Organization for Standardization developed an architecture, Open System Interconnection (OSI), to provide the means for devices from multiple vendors to interoperate. OSI is based on the earlier four-layer suite of protocols, TCP/IP.

Although OSI was not widely implemented because of its complexity, it has had a profound influence on telecommunications. It laid the foundation for the concept of open communications among multiple manufacturers' devices. The basic concept of OSI is that of layering. (See Table 1.4 at the conclusion of this chapter.) Groups of functions are broken up into seven layers, which can be changed and developed without having to change any other layer. LANs, public networks, and the Internet's TCP/IP suite of protocols are based on a layered architecture.

The Internet suite of protocols, TCP/IP, corresponds to the functions in Layers 3 and 4 of the OSI model. These functions are addressing, error control, and access to the network. The TCP/IP suite of protocols provides a uniform way for diverse devices to communicate with each other from all over the world. It was developed in the 1970s by the U.S. Department of Defense and was provided at no charge to end users in its basic format. Having a readily available, standard protocol is a key ingredient in the spread of the Internet.

In layered architectures or protocol suites, when transmitting, layers communicate with the layer immediately below them. Only Layer 1 actually transmits to the network. On the receiving end, Layer 1 receives the data and sends it to Layer 2, which then reads the Layer 2 protocol before sending the message to the next higher layer, and so on to the application layer.

TYPES OF NETWORKS—LANS, MANS, AND WANS...

The difference between LANs, MANs, and WANs is the distance over which devices can communicate with others. (See Table 1.5 at the end of this chapter.) As the name implies, a local area network is local in nature. It is owned by one organization and is located in a limited geographic area, most commonly a single building. In large organizations, LANs can be linked together within a complex of buildings on a campus. These organizations often refer to their linked LANs as their network (see Figure 1.4). Devices such as computers linked together within a city or metropolitan area are part of a metropolitan area network (MAN). Similarly, devices that are linked together between cities are part of a wide area network (WAN).

LANs—Local Area Networks

A discrete LAN is typically located on the same floor or within the same department of an organization. LANs first appeared in 1980. The initial impetus for tying PCs together was to share costly peripherals such as high-speed printers. Users exchange files and e-mail, access the Internet, and share resources over local area networks (LANs). Examples of devices within LANs are shared printers, PCs, alarm devices, factory automation gear, quality-control systems, shared databases, voice mail, telephone systems, factory and retail scanners, and security monitors.

Network operating systems control access to the LAN where resources such as files, printers, and security applications are located. Microsoft Windows 2000 and Advanced Server, and Novell NetWare are client-server-based LAN network operating systems.

LAN network operating systems (NOS) software is located on specialized computers called file servers connected to the LAN. In addition, LAN operating system client software is located on each device, such as PCs and printers connected to the LAN. Access to file servers can be limited by password to only approved users (clients). Most operating systems in use today are built on the client-server model. Clients (PCs) request services such as printing and access to databases. Applications such as print and e-mail servers run access to services (such as printers and databases).

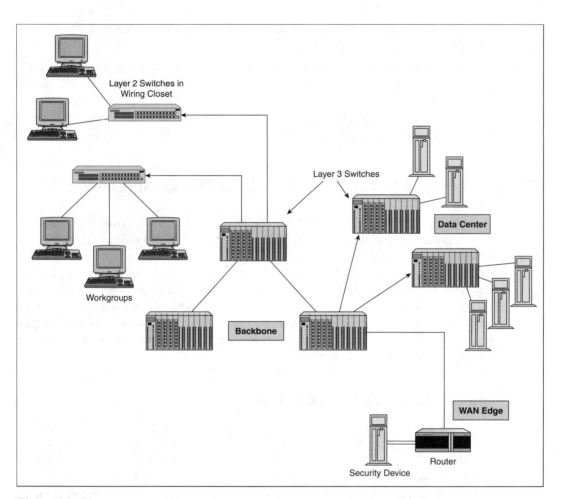

Figure 1.4
LAN architecture.

The Ethernet Protocol—Within LANs

Ethernet, which is based on the 802.3 standard approved by the Institute of Electrical and Electronics Engineers (IEEE), is used by devices such as personal computers to access the LAN and to retrieve packets carried on the LAN. Each device on an Ethernet local area network has a medium access control (MAC) address. Wi-Fi and other 802.11-type wireless LANs also use Ethernet to access the LAN. But the version used on wireless networks operates a little differently. (See Chapter 9 for wireless LAN networks.) For the most part, devices are connected to a LAN by twisted pair cabling that is similar to but sometimes of a higher quality than cabling used for business telephones. (Media options are covered in Chapter 2, "VoIP Systems, Circuit Switched PBXs, and Cabling.")

TCP/IP Protocols—Communications Between Networks

Whereas Ethernet is a way for individual packets to access LANs and retrieve packets from local networks, TCP/IP is used to tie LANs together and to route packets between networks. As the need arose to tie LANs together for e-mail and file sharing, compatibility between LANs from different manufacturers became a problem. The TCP/IP suite of protocols became a popular choice for overcoming these incompatibilities and for managing the flow of information on LANs. NetBEUI is another high-level protocol that manages communications between devices on a LAN. It is an early protocol based on IBM's NetBIOS protocol. It is used primarily for devices in smaller, departmental LANS.

Bridges and routers were developed to send data between LANs. Routers send packets to individual networks based on their Internet protocol (IP) address. IP addresses are assigned to individual networks.

LAN and WAN Devices—Higher Speeds, Lower Prices

LAN and WAN gear handle more traffic in carrier and enterprise networks than ever before. Early LANs operated at 10 megabits per second. New backbone LAN switches typically operate at gigabit (billion bit per second) speeds and are connected to each other with fiber-optic rather than unshielded twisted pair (copper) cabling. In addition, connections on Layer 2 and Layer 3 switches run at *wire speed*. Wire speed refers to switches able to forward packets equal to the full speed of their ports. Ports are the interfaces to which cabling is connected. Wire speed is achieved with powerful switch processors, the computers that look up addresses and forward packets.

Lower equipment prices are making LANs feasible for small businesses and residences. One factor in lower prices is the fact that many devices are based on standards so that manufacturing costs have been driven lower.

The major challenges in managing local area networks are keeping networks secure from hackers and virus free. The fact that networks operate on common protocols that hackers understand makes it easier for these hackers to create malicious software with embedded code capable of corrupting and destroying files. The embedded code often takes over computers and uses them to send malicious code to hundreds of other computers, thus wreaking havoc on networks.

The Impact of High-Bandwidth Applications

LANs no longer carry mostly "bursty" traffic such as brief e-mail messages for which early LANs were designed. New applications consist of traffic with a longer duration and shorter pauses between packets for other devices to transmit. The following are some examples:

- Large graphical attachments such as PowerPoint files.

- Server farms, centralized locations in corporations' or carriers' networks with groups of servers containing large databases and backup copies of databases.

- Daily backups to databases of entire corporate electronic files.

- Web downloads of long, continuous streams of images, audio, and video files.

- Voice mail, call center, and voice traffic.

- Web access typified by users with four or more pages open concurrently. Each open Web page is a session, an open communication with packets traveling between the user and the Internet.

MANAGING WEB PAGES—LAYER 4 SWITCHES, ACCELERATORS, AND DEEP PACKET INSPECTION

The images people click on and the Web addresses they type in when they browse the Internet send them to specific Web pages. The Web pages are at sites owned by medium and large businesses, government offices, and educational and healthcare institutions. They are also located at sites that host Web pages for small and medium-sized businesses and large enterprises that don't want to dedicate resources to managing their own Web pages. Hosting companies include carriers such as AT&T, MCI, Sprint, and SAVVIS Communications Corporation, which purchased Cable & Wireless USA, Inc. (Purchases of AT&T by SBC Communications and MCI by Verizon Communications have been announced.)

MANAGING WEB PAGES—LAYER 4 SWITCHES, ACCELERATORS, AND DEEP PACKET INSPECTION (CONTINUED)

The actual Web pages that people view when they browse the Internet are located on clusters of computers called   Web server farms. The Web servers communicate with application servers that store applications for business processes such as purchases and surveys conducted online. When someone is making a purchase online, he or she is using software on these application servers. The application server, in turn, may be pulling information about the product or user from large enterprise applications such as those offered by Oracle or PeopleSoft. Databases used by these applications are located in storage networks.

Hosting sites use Layer 4 switches,   also known as content switches, to improve the up time (availability) of Web server farms. They also make these sites more efficient by balancing traffic among the servers in which Web pages are located. For example, they send traffic either in a round robin, predetermined fashion or to the server or port that has been idle the longest.

Layer 4 switches look deeper into packets so that they can send them to particular ports on servers. Layer 3 switches only look at the packet's IP address, which identifies the network. They keep track of which Web servers are up and which are out of service. They monitor each session for the duration of the connection. They can take servers out of service without disrupting transactions or Web surfing. For example, if someone is in the middle of making a purchase when the server he or she is connected to goes down, he or she is transferred to a different server seamlessly without losing data already entered for the transaction. This is because the Layer 4 switch has stayed on the "call" to manage it.

Next-generation Layer 7 switches provide deep packet inspection to improve security on Web traffic. Deep packet inspection looks deeper into the packet than Layer 4 switches to learn which application is being used. They look at bits in the packet, the "signature," that indicate which application is associated with the packet. It can determine, for example, if the packet is used for an Oracle, PeopleSoft, or Microsoft application. Specialized cards in the switch decrypt, or unscramble, data as it enters the Web site and re-encrypt data sent to the user. Software companies that develop these applications need to share information with vendors that produce Layer 7 switches so that they can recognize "signature" arrangements of bits for particular applications.

continues

MANAGING WEB PAGES—LAYER 4 SWITCHES, ACCELERATORS,
AND DEEP PACKET INSPECTION (CONTINUED)

Another new development is accelerators   that are installed on separate computers called appliances   and that use compression to make files
smaller so that they take less time to be transmitted to end users. This
enables sites to handle more traffic without adding capacity because
browsing and viewing graphics and video tie up Web sites for shorter
amounts of time when they are accelerated (compressed).

In addition to the preceding equipment that increases Web sites'
robustness and efficiency, large organizations often have backups offsite
or locally of their entire Web server farm, Web   application server, and
databases.

Hubs and Bridges

Hubs and bridges were deployed in the 1980s and the 1990s. Using hubs reduced the
cost of cabling in LANs. Bridges were used to link local area networks that used the
same protocols or a limited number of different protocols together.

Hubs—Largely Replaced by Switches

Hubs were developed to enable devices on LANs to be linked together by twisted pair
copper wire instead of the heavier, thicker coaxial cable that was used in early LANs.
Coaxial cable is expensive to install and move and requires more space in dropped
ceilings and conduit. Hubs operate as "repeaters." Each device repeats each message
to the next device on the network, and the device to which the message is addressed
takes it off the network.

With a hub, each node or device is wired back to the hub in a star pattern. The
hub creates a star design, or topology. (Topology is "the view from above"—in the
case of hubs, each device is connected to a central device, the hub.) Prior to hubs, each
device in a LAN was wired to another device in a "bus" arrangement. In the bus topology, if one PC is out of service or if there is a break in the cable, other nodes (devices
attached to the LAN) are affected. By employing a hub, a device can be moved or
taken out of service if it is defective without affecting other devices on the LAN.
A hub is located in the wiring closet of each floor within a building.

Layer 2 switches have generally replaced hubs because of hubs' limitations:

- Only one device at a time can communicate on each LAN.

- Each message is sent to every node (device attached to the LAN).
- Hubs can't accommodate the multimedia services on today's networks. Although speeds are 10 megabits, actual throughput, user information transmitted, is much less because of retransmissions and collisions that occur when multiple nodes attempt to transmit simultaneously.

Bridges—Less Flexible Than Routers and Switches

Bridges became available in the 1980s as a way to connect a small number of LANs together. Bridges provide one common path over which multiple LANs can be connected together. For example, if an organization has two locations in different cities that need to exchange data, a bridge can be used. Bridges also are used as a way to reduce LAN congestion. The bridge can connect two different departments so that each departmental LAN is not congested with interdepartmental traffic. Bridges most often connect two LANs with like protocols such as an Ethernet LAN to an Ethernet LAN. There are more sophisticated bridges that connect an IBM token ring network to an Ethernet LAN.

As LANs proliferated and router prices dropped, people turned to more powerful and feature-rich routers and switches rather than bridges.

Layer 2 Switches—Connections to the Desktop

Layer 2 devices store and forward packets and filter packets so that they need not be broadcast to all users. Devices on LANs such as PCs, workstations, and printers are connected to Layer 2 switches located in each floors' wiring closet.

Networks that use switches

- Are faster than those with hubs
- Don't broadcast every message to each user
- Are simpler to manage than routers because each device's address does not need to be maintained in the switch memory (see the section on routers below)
- Provide more bandwidth per device than hubs

Some Layer 2 switches are *non-blocking*. They have enough capability so that each device can communicate at the same time up to the full speed of the port to which they are connected. For example, a switch capable of forwarding packets at 100 million bits per second would be non-blocking if 10 users were connected to the switch and each could concurrently forward 10 million packets per second ($10 \times 10,000,000 = 100,000,000$).

Layer 2 switches are located either in work groups where they are connected to a group of 24 or 48 or so users or in wiring closets serving a few hundred users. The number of nodes (devices) connected to a switch depends on the switch's speed and the users' requirements.

Virtual LANs—A Way to Segregate Devices

A virtual local area network (VLAN) is made up of devices, such as personal computers and wireless telephones, whose addresses are programmed as a group in Layer 2 switches to give them higher capacity or special privileges or to segregate them from the rest of the corporate network for higher security. They are programmed as a separate LAN but are sometimes connected to the same switch as other devices. Voice over Internet protocol telephones that send voice as packets over networks and wireless LAN devices are often programmed into their own virtual LANs. These devices allow only certain types of equipment, such as other telephones, to communicate with them. Some computers are put into virtual LANs so that they can access secure files such as healthcare records.

Layer 3 Switches—Also Known As Switching Routers

Layer 3 switches are faster and more complex to install and maintain than Layer 2 switches. A Layer 3 switch has connections to multiple Layer 2 switches, and each port has routing capability. If a link to one switch is down, the Layer 3 switch can send traffic via another link. Layer 3 switches generally are located in wiring closets (connecting hundreds of users) or LAN data centers (connecting many wiring closets or buildings together). Most enterprises use Layer 3 switches to connect traffic on the LAN or campus backbone.

Because of increased traffic on corporate local area networks, most new Layer 3 switches support 1 gigabit and 10 gigabit speeds. In addition, they tend to be larger than Layer 2 switches. They are housed in chassis (cabinets). Chassis look like refrigerators. They have multiple or single carriers (shelves) with blades (circuit packs) positioned vertically in slots (see Figure 1.5). Many Layer 2 switches are rack mounted with horizontally positioned blades. Rack-mounted equipment is 19 inches wide and is housed in equipment racks with other LAN devices.

Routers—To Access the Internet and Carry Internet Traffic

In enterprise and home networks, routers connect LANs to the Internet, to carriers' networks, and to other corporate sites. Internet-based routers in carriers' networks forward packets over the least congested paths, also called *hops* because packets "hop" from router to router to reach their destination. To illustrate, a user may send two

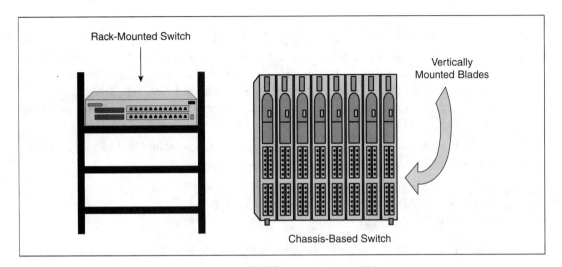

Figure 1.5
Rack-mounted and chassis-based switches.

messages from Chicago to Los Angeles. The first message might travel via Alaska and the second via Texas. Because of congestion and the route taken, the second message might arrive before the first one. A major advantage of routers is their capability to forward differing protocols from varied departmental local area networks. It is important to note that routers do not translate application protocols. A UNIX computer cannot read a Microsoft Windows word processing document. The router merely transports differing LAN protocols in corporate and carrier networks.

Router capabilities include

- *Queuing.* If the path the data takes is congested, the router can hold the data in a queue until capacity is available.
- *Path optimization.* The sending router selects the best available path by checking routing tables contained within the router.
- *Priority routing.* Some routers contain protocols that let them assign priority to packets with particular types of headers.

Intelligence inherent in routers leads to a major disadvantage: Routers are complex to install and maintain. Every router in an organization's network must have up-to-date address tables. Each device on a LAN is called a node and has an address. For example, if a printer or PC is moved from one LAN to another, the router table must be updated or messages will not reach that device. New routers are faster because they do not look up each packet's address in the CPU's memory. Routers check the routing table for the first packet's address and then store the address in chips on a card or a module.

Blades

Routers contain circuit boards located in slots within the router. Circuit boards are often referred to as *blades* when they are dense—for example, when they have many ports (connections). Specialized blades are available for wide area network T-1 and T-3 connections. (See Chapter 5, "VPNs and Specialized Network Services," for T-1 and T-3.) Blades may also be firewalls, hardware, and software used to block hacker access to internal networks. Blades are also used in switches.

The functions of congestion control, routing, sequencing, and receipt acknowledgment make routers network Layer 3 devices.

Home LANs—Sharing High-Speed Internet Access

According to statistics released in April 2004 by the Pew Internet & American Life Project, 34% of U.S. residential broadband users have home networks, 21% use wired home networks, and 13% use wireless products such as Wi-Fi. (See Chapter 9 for wireless home networks.) In addition, Pew found that 6% of dial-up users have home networks. Home networks enable residents to share DSL and cable modem Internet access, printers, and multimedia files such as television and movies among multiple computers. The following factors have led to a growth of home networks:

- Lower broadband Internet access prices are spurring purchase of DSL and cable modem connections.
- The availability of less-complex setup procedures for home networks.
- Decreases in router costs.
- More powerful PCs with larger memories to handle Web and music files downloaded from the Internet.
- The desire by users for e-mail and Internet access at home.
- Lower-cost PCs so that families can purchase separate computers for parents and children.
- The requirement for people who work from home full time or part time to access files remotely using high-speed Internet access.

Although often slower and less complex, home networks are created along the same line as corporate networks. Hubs and switches (built into home routers) connect devices together via cabling or wireless media. Routers provide shared access for all PCs to high-speed Internet connections. Equipment on home LANs includes PCs, switch/routers, media centers with movies and television shows, printers, and scanners. Each computer and printer connected to the LAN needs an Ethernet card for connection to a cable that is plugged into the switch/router. If the computer is in another room, the PC is plugged into an RJ-45 data jack from which unshielded twisted pair cabling is run to the switch/router. RJ-45 jacks are similar to jacks that analog phones plug into except that they have four wires (two pair) instead of the one pair used for analog phone service.

To share high-speed DSL or cable modem service, users purchase switch and router functions in one "box" from vendors such as LinkSys, 3Com, and NETGEAR for Windows and Xsense for Macintosh computers (see Figure 1.6). In addition to cabling, computer software needs to be installed on personal computers as well as wireless and coaxial-cabling-based networks, running data and multimedia is possible through a home's electrical wiring using a standard called HomePlug. HomePlug service for the most part augments wireless home networks in instances in which the wireless network coverage does not extend to another floor or porch. With HomePlug hardware, users plug their router into a 4-inch by 2-inch device that is plugged into a wall outlet. In the distant room, a computer is plugged into another 4-inch by 2-inch device that is also plugged into an electrical outlet. The top speed on HomePlug is 14 megabits per second.

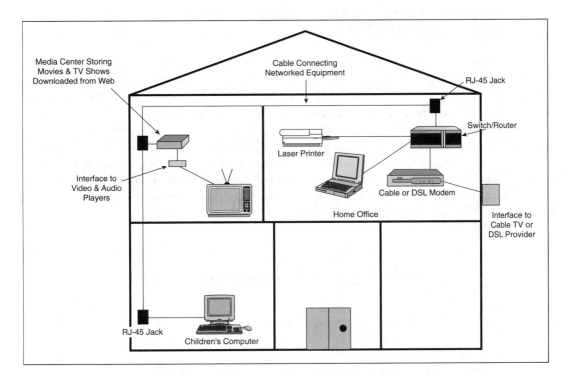

Figure 1.6
Home LAN .

The biggest challenge to implementing home networks is making them secure against viruses that are inadvertently downloaded when people open e-mail attachments and from hackers that access files on peoples' computers that are on and connected to broadband networks. Home users often purchase routers equipped with firewall software to keep out hackers and antivirus software that they install on their computers and keep updated with the latest antivirus updates.

Poor customer support is a major impediment to the implementation of home networks. Customers often require help from router companies, friends, and the MIS staff where they work to set up their networks.

Most carriers that sell high-speed Internet access to consumers are concerned about home LANs that generate large amounts of traffic with applications such as on-line games and song sharing, also referred to as peering. Some cable companies and DSL providers charge higher fees to customers who generate large amounts of traffic. The growing residential adoption of broadband is adding traffic to Internet backbones and edge networks operated by carriers such as Level 3, SBC, Sprint, and MCI.

MANs—Metropolitan Area Networks . . .
Links Within Cities

Metropolitan area networks, or MANs, are connections between local area networks within a city or within a large campus. Campus MANs are spread out over many blocks of a city. Examples of MANs are those at large hospitals and university complexes. For example, a hospital in downtown Boston keeps its x-rays and medical records in a nearby section of the city. Instead of trucking records and x-rays between the two sites, the hospital leases high-capacity telephone lines to transmit records and images. The connections between these two sites are metropolitan area networks. These links can be leased from a telephone company or constructed by the organization. They operate over fiber-optic, copper, or microwave-based media. They also include the same services mentioned for WANs, such as Gigabit Ethernet, T-3, and T-1.

WANs—Wide Area Networks . . .
Links Between Cities

The term "WAN" refers to connections between locations over long distances via telecommunications links. For example, a warehouse in Alabama connected to a sales office in Massachusetts by a T-1 line is a wide area network (WAN) connection. In contrast to a local area network, a WAN is not contained within a limited geographical location. The variety of WAN connections available is complex. Selection of an appropriate WAN service depends on the amount of traffic between locations, the quality of service needed, the price, and the compatibility with the organization's computer systems. WAN technologies and WAN vendors are reviewed in Chapter 6, "Entertainment, Cable TV, and Last-Mile Fiber Systems." These include ISDN, T-1, T-3, ATM, and frame relay.

Instead of complex WANs, many organizations now have high-speed connections either to the Internet or to carriers instead of directly to other corporate locations. Carriers manage the security and transmission of their customers' telecommunications in virtual private network (VPN) arrangements. (See Chapter 5 for VPNs.)

Higher Speed Services for LAN Traffic

Not only is the nature of LAN traffic changing but the number of applications is growing.

- Gigabit Ethernet is a high-speed Ethernet protocol. It requires fiber-optic cabling or Level 6 unshielded twisted pair because of its high speeds. Level 6 cabling is built to higher standards of performance than Level 3 and Level 5 cabling. (See Chapter 2 for media.) Gigabit Ethernet is used for connections on backbone enterprise networks and servers in data centers. New Layer 3 switches operate at gigabit speeds.

- Fibre channel protocols are used for gigabit speed, highly reliable short-distance access to devices such as disks, graphics equipment, video input/output devices, and storage devices that hold massive amounts of data. Backing up corporate files is an important fibre channel application. Fewer overhead bits for tasks such as error control and addressing are included in the fibre channel protocol, which uses a device's input/output interface to communicate directly with switches. Enterprise system connection (ESCON) is another storage-oriented protocol.

- *MPLS (multiprotocol label switching)* is used in switches and routers to speed up networks and provide type-of-service instructions. Bits representing the address are placed in the router's short-term cache memory. In MPLS, short, fixed-length "labels" tell the router how to route each packet so that the router does not have to examine the entire header of each packet after the first point in the carrier's network. The router merely looks at the label in its short-term memory for routing instructions. Multiprotocol label switching also provides networks with the capability to treat packets differently if they are voice or video packets. For example, voice and video can have tags that classify them with a higher priority than data bits.

Carrier and Internet Service Provider Networks

Customers access the network edge via cellular devices, cable modems, DSL modems, or plain old telephones. The network edge, the point where customer lines are connected to carriers' networks, sends traffic to the network core. Major carriers have backbone networks over which their greatest concentration of voice, data, and video traffic travels. Backbone networks consist of fiber-optic cabling connected by high-speed routers and switches. Carriers' backbone networks span multiple states. Incumbent telephone companies such as SBC carry high concentrations of traffic in metropolitan area backbones, within large cities, and between suburban and rural locales.

Carrier backbone networks are starting to look more alike. Carriers such as cellular providers and former Bell telephone companies that in earlier decades supported a higher percentage of voice services relied on voice switches and T-1 and T-3 lines. They had separate networks for data services. Much of the equipment suited mostly for voice is still in place, but carriers are planning and starting to implement converged, unified networks appropriate for data as well as voice.

Convergence is occurring at a faster pace in the core rather than at the edge. This is because more services are needed at the edge such as billing and prioritizing traffic, which tend to make edge devices more complex, requiring more features. In core or backbone devices, speed, reliability, and brute strength are needed. In addition, there are more edge devices, so the cost to upgrade the edge is higher. There is more equipment to upgrade and more features to program at the edge.

Reliability, quality of service, and security in public networks have always been important for public safety and emergency communications. However, terrorist threats, added vulnerability to hackers and worms, and more critical applications from enterprise, government, and healthcare institutions have heightened these concerns and raised the bar on performance. Carriers need to carry more types of traffic faster.

Enterprise and residential customers have used the Internet and various data networks for years. However, customers are adding more critical applications to networks, and additional residential customers are using broadband access. Networks need to scale, or grow larger to accommodate this growth.

An added pressure carriers are facing is price competition. To keep their own costs low and stay price competitive, they are looking at operating one network for voice, frame relay, and data instead of multiple networks. The thought is that one network costs less to build and support than two or three networks. For carriers, keeping costs low and reliability high is a vital challenge. In particular, if the one network crashes, all customers lose all services on the carrier's network.

Vendors that sell edge and core routers include Juniper Networks, Cisco Systems, and Avici Systems.

MINIMIZING RISKS WHEN ADOPTING NEW TECHNOLOGY

Availability and reliability are key selection criteria for carriers when they purchase equipment. Carriers that upgrade networks to take advantage of new technology need to determine how these systems will perform and the viability of manufacturers that supply them.

Reliability refers to how often a device operates without failing. Carriers typically require NEBS Level 3 compliance on equipment they purchase. NEBS stands for Network Equipment Building System. Bellcore (now Telcordia), the former R&D arm of the Regional Bell Operating Companies, developed NEBS standards. The standards include compliance with thermal, electrical, redundancy, and earthquake-resistance tests. Carriers often test reliability in their own labs by subjecting vendor equipment to fire, water, and other conditions to see how the equipment stands up.

In evaluating vendor performance, some carriers check whether vendors are TL9000 certified. TL9000 is a way to audit vendor processes. It includes ISO 9001, an international standard for internal quality management, plus other measurements specifically for telecommunications suppliers. For example, TL9000 looks at the formal process a vendor has in place for corrective action if equipment it manufactures fails. TL9000 metrics apply to hardware, software, and service providers.

Availability refers to how long it takes to repair equipment, or having the equipment in service even though part of it is not working. For example, if ports are inoperable, the other ports should be available to route calls normally handled by the inoperable ports. In the same vein, backup central processing units (CPUs) should be able to automatically take over if the main CPU goes down.

Core Routing— In Carrier Networks . . . Speed, Reliability, and Capacity

Requirements for routers built for carriers are more complex than for routers built for enterprise customers. Routers made primarily for carriers need higher reliability, scalability, and security than those built primarily for enterprises. All routers hold network addresses (prefixes) in their routing tables. Whereas enterprise routers may have thousands of addresses, carrier routers often hold 250,000 Internet protocol (IP) addresses for customers worldwide. Core routers require complex memory to store so many network addresses. In addition, they tend to be larger, with multiple cabinets (chassis) seamlessly connected to each other and operating as a single router.

Routers geared to the carrier market often operate at *terabit* speeds, trillions of bits per second (1,000,000,000,000). The switching fabric is often made up of super computing platforms with hundreds of routers in a single device. If any one of the computers associated with a router fails, the router still functions and uses the input/output ports associated with the remaining computers.

Individual ports, each supporting one connection, often operate at OC-192, which equals 10,000 million bits per second (10 gigabits per second). Juniper Network has plans to introduce routers that support OC-768, 40 billion bits per second (40 gigabits) ports.

Juniper Network core routers are based on application-specific integrated circuit (ASIC) processors for high performance. ASICs are specialized chips built with the capability of many chips integrated within them. Advances in computers, such as memory and connectors, have benefited routers that need to check addresses and forward packets at consistently high speeds.

Implications of More Voice and Video

With more voice and video now on carriers' backbones, routers are required to differentiate between different types of traffic. They do this via protocols such as multiprotocol label switching (MPLS). There is also development and interoperability with asynchronous transfer mode (ATM) traffic. This enables IP networks to carry this traffic while preserving quality of service specified in ATM for traffic such as voice and video. (See Chapter 6 for information on ATM.)

Carrying voice and video has implications on reliability and speed. To ensure reliability and speed, Cisco is introducing a router based on a massively parallel computer and chips with 188 32-bit processors. All of these requirements plus the need to meet stringent reliability and redundancy specifications in the event of disasters such as fire and earthquakes result in higher router prices. The large research and development investments needed to support these efforts also add to higher per-port costs compared to routers made for the enterprise market.

Carrier Edge Routers—Security, Billing, and Filtering

Edge routers connect enterprises to carriers' networks. They are located at the edge of carrier networks. Edge routers aggregate large numbers of relatively slow circuits from end users at T-1 (1.54 megabits per second), T-3 (44 megabits per second), and OC-3 (155 megabits per second) speeds and send them to core routers at higher speeds of OC-12 (622 megabits), OC-48 (2.5 gigabits), and OC-192 (10 gigabits). See Figure 1.7. Connections between core and edge routers are hierarchical in nature, similar to connections between Layer 2 and Layer 3 switches in LANs.

Edge Routers—Slower, More Services Provided

Edge routers are slower than core routers. They also provide more services because they connect directly to customers as opposed to core routers that transmit to other

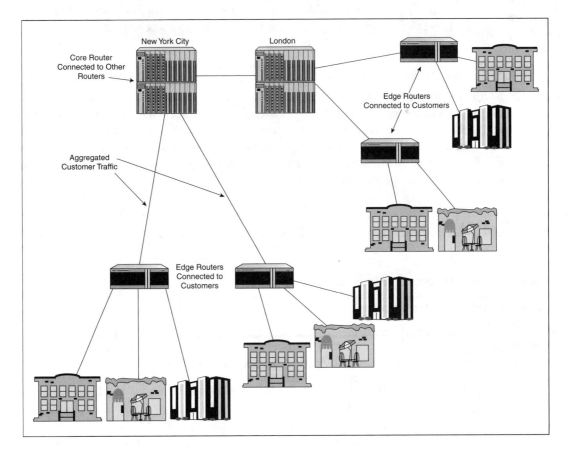

Figure 1.7
Edge and core routers.

core routers and to edge routers. Edge routers furnish services such as filtering, billing, VPN service, rate limiting, and traffic shaping.

- *Filters* are used to block traffic to sites such as those that are pornographic, music peering, or possibly personal shopping related for enterprises that don't want their employees to use the Internet for personal use.
- *Rate limiting* enables carriers to equip their routers with T-3, 44.5-megabit ports but to sell services of more than 44.5 megabits because it assumes that not everyone will use the service to its full capacity. To illustrate, it might sell 36 T-1s, which equals 55.44 megabits (36×1.54), 10.9 megabits more than the port's capacity of 44.5 megabits.
- *VPN service* furnishes security and remote access to enterprise customers. (See Chapter 5 for VPNs.)
- *Traffic classification* enables routers to distinguish between voice and data. This enables voice to be prioritized so that people don't hear delays, which impairs the quality of their calls.

Security—The Biggest Challenge

Security is the biggest challenge for edge routers. Edge routers block spam and monitor networks to keep them free from attacks. Routers keep lists that need frequent updates of sites used to launch attacks against carriers' networks. They can shut off residential customers who unknowingly download a worm and can send the customers to an Internet site that explains what has occurred and how to fix their computer so that it does not infect the carrier's network.

APPENDIX ....

Table 1.3 Appendix: Compression Standards and Their Descriptions

Compression Standard	Description
MNP 5	Microcom Network Protocol compression protocol developed by Microcom for modems. Provides 2:1 compression.
V.42bis	Data compression protocol for modems. Provides 4:1 compression.

Table 1.3 *Appendix: Compression Standards and Their Descriptions*   (continued)

Compression Standard	Description
H.320	A family of standards for video adopted by the ITU (International Telecommunications Union). Quality is not as high as proprietary video compression algorithms. Most video codecs employ both proprietary and standard compression algorithms. The proprietary compression is used to transmit to another "like" video units, and the standard algorithm is used when conferencing between differing brands.
H.323	A family of standards for video adopted by the ITU for sending video over packet networks. Microsoft Corporation and Intel Corporation adopted the standard in 1996 for sending voice over packet networks. It is installed on Windows-based PCs and is used to packetize and compress voice when callers with PCs make calls from their computers over the Internet. See Chapter 5.
G.726	A family of standards for video adopted by the ITU (International Telecommunications Union). Quality is not as high as proprietary video compression algorithms. Most video codecs employ both proprietary and standard compression algorithms. The proprietary compression is used to transmit to another "like" video unit, and the standard algorithm is used when conferencing between differing brands.
IBOC	In-band on-channel broadcasting uses airwaves within the current AM and FM spectrum to broadcast digital programming. IBOC is based on the Perceptual Audio Coder (PAC). There are many sounds that the ear cannot discern because they are masked by louder sounds. PAC discerns and discards these sounds that the ear cannot hear and that are not necessary to retain the quality of the transmission. This results in transmission with 15 times fewer bits. PAC, the Perceptual Audio Coder, was first developed at Bell Labs in the 1930s.
JPEG	Joint Photographic Experts Group is a compression standard used mainly for photographs. The International Standards Organizations (ISO) and the International Telecommunications Union (ITU) developed JPEG.

continues

Table 1.3 Appendix: Compression Standards and Their Descriptions   (continued)

Compression Standard	Description
MPEG-2	A Moving Picture Experts Group standard approved in 1993 for coding and decoding video and television images. MPEG-2 uses past images to predict future images and color, and it transmits only the changed image. For example, the first in a series of frames is sent in a compressed form. The ensuing frames send only the changes. A frame is a group of bits representing a portion of a picture, text, or audio section.
MPEG-3	Moving Picture Experts Group 3 is Layer 3 of MPEG-1. MPEG-3, also referred to as MP3, is a compression standard for streaming audio. MPEG-3 is the compression algorithm used to download audio files from the Internet. For example, some Internet e-commerce sites allow people with compression software to download samples of music so that they can decide if they want to purchase a particular CD.
MPEG-4	Moving Picture Experts Group 4 is a standard used mainly for streaming and downloading compressed video and television. It is four times more efficient than MPEG-2.

Table 1.4 Appendix: OSI Layers

OSI Layer Name and Number	Layer Function
Layer 1: Physical Layer	*Layer 1* is the most basic layer.
	Layer 1 defines the type of media—for example, copper, wireless, or fiber optics and how devices access media.
	Repeaters used to extend signals over fiber, wireless, and copper are Layer 1 devices. Repeaters in cellular networks extend and boost signals inside buildings and in subways so that people can use their cellular devices in these locations. In tall buildings, antennas on rooftops transmit signals over fiber or copper to small repeaters with antennas on each floor.

Table 1.4 Appendix: OSI Layers (continued)

OSI Layer Name and Number	Layer Function
Layer 2: Data Link Layer	Ethernet, also known as 802.3, is a *Layer 2* protocol. It provides rules for error correction and access to LANs.
	Layer 2 devices have addressing information analogous to Social Security numbers. They are random but specific to individuals.
	Frame relay is a Layer 2 protocol used to access carrier networks from enterprises.
Layer 3: Network Layer	*Layer 3* is known as the routing layer. It is responsible for routing traffic between networks using IP (Internet protocol) network addresses, and it has error-control functions.
	Layer 3 is analogous to a local post office routing an out-of-town letter by ZIP code, not looking at the street address. Once an e-mail message is received at the distant network, a Layer 2 device looks at the address and delivers the message.
Layer 4: Transport Layer	*Layer 4* protocols enable networks to differentiate between types of content.
	Layer 4 devices route by content. They are also known as content switches. For example, video or voice transmissions over data networks might receive a higher priority or quality of service than e-mail, which can tolerate delay.
	TCP (transmission control protocol) is a Layer 4 protocol.
	Filters in routers that check for computer viruses by looking at additional bits in packets perform a Layer 4 function.
Layer 5: Session Layer	*Layer 5* manages the actual dialog of sessions. Encryption that scrambles signals to ensure privacy occurs in Layer 5.
	H.323 is a Layer 5 protocol that sends signals in packet networks to set up and tear down; for example, video and audio conferences.
Layer 6: Presentation Layer	*Layer 6* controls the format or how the information looks on the user's screen.
	Hypertext Markup Language (HTML), used to format Web pages and some e-mail messages, is a Layer 6 standard.

continues

Table 1.4 Appendix: OSI Layers (continued)

OSI Layer Name and Number	Layer Function
Layer 7: Application Layer	*Layer 7* includes the application itself plus specialized services such as file transfers or print services. Hypertext transfer protocol (HTTP) is a Layer 7 protocol.

Table 1.5 Appendix: LAN, MAN, and WAN Terms and Devices

LANs, MANs, WANs, and More	Definition
LAN (local area network)	A group of devices, such as computers, printers, and scanners, that can communicate with each other within a limited geographic area such as a floor, department, or small cluster of buildings.
MAN (metropolitan area network)	Networks that can communicate with each other within a city or a large campus area covering many city blocks.
WAN (wide area network)	A group of data devices, usually LANs, that communicate with each other between multiple cities.
Hub	The wiring center to which all devices, printers, scanners, PCs, and so forth are connected within a segment of a LAN. Hubs enable LANs to be connected to twisted pair cabling instead of coaxial cable. Only one device at a time can transmit via a hub. Higher-speed switches have replaced hubs in most organizations.
Backbone	Wiring running from floor to floor in single buildings and from building to building within campuses. A backbone connects switches in different wiring closets to each other. Backbones support high concentrations of traffic in carrier and enterprise networks.
Bridge	Bridges usually connect LANs using the same type of protocol together. They have limited intelligence and generally only connect a few LANs together. Bridges were in limited use as of the early 1990s when the price of routers dropped.

Table 1.5 Appendix: LAN, MAN, and WAN Terms and Devices   (continued)

LANs, MANs, WANs, and More	Definition
Layer 2 switch (also called switching hub)	Layer 2 switches, located in wiring closets, are bridges that allow multiple simultaneous transmissions within a single LAN. Layer 2 switches provide a dedicated connection during an entire transmission.
Layer 3 switch (also known as routing switch)	Layer 3 switches have the capability to route traffic across the LAN backbone. They are more complex to manage than Layer 2 switches, but they can use alternate paths if one path is out of service. They are located in data centers and link wiring closets and buildings within a campus.
Layer 4 switch (also known as content switches)	Layer 4 switches are located at hosting sites and corporate and government sites that host their own Web pages. Layer 4 switches connect Web traffic to the desired Web pages by looking at the universal resource locator (URL), the Web address from which each packet was transferred to their site.
Router	Routers carry traffic between LANs, from enterprises to the Internet, and across the Internet. They are more complex than switches because they have routing tables with addresses and perform other functions. Routers select the best available path over which to send data.
Server	A centrally located computer with common departmental or organizational files such as personnel records, e-mails, sales data, price lists, student information, and medical records. Servers are connected to Layer 2 or 3 switches. Access to servers can be restricted to authorized users only.
VLAN (virtual local area network)	A virtual local area network is made up of devices, usually personal computers or Voice over IP devices, whose addresses are programmed as a group in Layer 2 switches. This segregates them from the rest of the corporate network so that all devices in the same VLAN can be given a higher priority or level of security. They are programmed as a separate LAN but are physically connected to the same switch as other devices.

2 VoIP Systems, Circuit Switched PBXs, and Cabling

In this chapter:

For the first time in over 30 years, the basic structure of business telephone systems is changing dramatically. Telephone system technology evolved from mechanical switching to electronic processing. Electronic systems, which were all based on proprietary computer platforms, were initially analog and later digital. Starting in the late 1990s, systems began appearing using the voice over Internet Protocol (VoIP) on common computer platforms. These represent a major shift in technology.

Early telephone systems, first developed in 1877, were manual. An operator was required to "patch" calls together by plugging each end of a cord into a jack on a switchboard. In 1891, undertaker Almon B. Strowger invented the electromechanical switch to avoid having switchboard operators listen in on his calls. The electromechanical automatic dial switch (also known as "step-by-step") used electrical pulses to complete calls without operator intervention for local calls. Customer dialing of toll calls was not trialed until 1951 when the mayor of Englewood, NJ called the mayor of Alameda, CA without operator assistance. Analog systems based on computer-stored program control became available in the 1960s, and digital switches were introduced in the 1960s with gradual adoption in the 1970s. Computerization of telephone systems vastly increased reliability by eliminating mechanical moving parts and decreased space requirements in central offices and customer equipment rooms.

Using all of the preceding switches, carriers and customers operated separate networks for voice and data. In the 1980s, various vendors introduced ways to integrate data into their PBXs, but these schemes all failed to gain acceptance because of costs, slow speeds, and complexity. IP telephony-based systems for carrying voice on data networks were first introduced in the 1990s. They are gradually gaining acceptance.

Telephone systems, PBXs, key systems, and Centrex services provide business customers with connections to the public network and to staff at other sites. They also enable employees to call each other without paying telephone company usage fees. Traditionally, these systems have been based on circuit switching. Circuit switches save a dedicated path for each ongoing call. This results in excellent call quality. Moreover, circuit switched systems are extremely reliable.

However, add-ons to circuit switched systems are expensive. Each manufacturer uses proprietary signaling techniques to connect electronic telephones, voice mail, and call center equipment to their systems. Therefore, the only digital phones that work on these systems are those made by each system's own manufacturer. Moreover, if organizations add voice mail or call center equipment from other providers, the manufacturer has to modify its equipment for each manufacturer's unique telephone system signaling. Thus, customers are locked into either using peripherals from the telephone system manufacturer or risk using add-ons that don't always work quite right or have fewer features because of signaling incompatibilities.

Organizations are adopting or trialing Voice over IP for branch offices and new sites. Other companies are testing them in lab environments or purchasing hybrid systems with both VoIP and circuit switched capabilities. They know that VoIP is the wave of the future and that manufacturers are putting all of their research efforts into these new platforms rather than into traditional, circuit switched systems.

Telephone systems based on Voice over Internet Protocol digitize analog voice, compress it, and put it into packets (similar to envelopes). An important point is that this format, the Internet Protocol (IP), is compatible with existing data networks. Therefore, voice can travel on the same infrastructure as data and video. It can, moreover, be installed, monitored, and programmed by the same staff that oversees organizations' data networks. It is envisioned that this will result in staffing synergies with attendant labor savings. In addition, the same staff that manages voice and data at headquarters will be able to provide ongoing management for sites such as sales offices, warehouses, and manufacturing locations. Another important advantage of voice over telephony is geographic independence. Staff members can receive calls to their main extension at their home office, branch office, or hotel when traveling.

In addition, as the signaling protocols used in VoIP systems mature, it is hoped that enhanced software for applications such as voice mail, multi-featured telephones, speech recognition, and call center capabilities will work seamlessly on all telephone systems. When this happens, prices for these peripherals will fall, and customers will have the choice of purchasing applications and telephones from multiple manufacturers, all of whose services and equipment interoperate.

The hesitation of some organizations to move to Voice over Internet Protocol (VoIP) centers first and foremost on security and reliability. Organizations still depend on voice services for important business functions even though an increasing number of transactions are conducted via the Internet and e-mail. These enterprises are cautious about putting all of their voice as well as data and video on one network in case it crashes or is attacked successfully by hackers. Furthermore, some organizations don't feel that their data networks are robust enough to support voice, which requires more consistent quality than most data transmissions. Finally, the cost of upgrading infrastructure to support Voice over IP and the cost to replace working telephone systems are barriers to purchases.

Automatic call distributors (ACDs) route incoming calls to contact center agents based on criteria such as the agent that has been idle the longest. (The terms "call center" and "contact center" are used interchangeably because many call centers are contacted by e-mail and chat as well as telephone calls.) If an agent is not available, the automatic call distributor holds the call in a queue, and the caller hears a message such as, "Please hold for our next available agent." ACDs are sold as part of key systems, Centrex and PBXs, and as standalone systems for large contact centers. ACDs provide sophisticated reports to help companies determine correct staffing levels and the number of outside telephone lines. In an effort to increase call center agent productivity, some companies are adding software to enable the same agents to handle outgoing calls, e-mail messages, and Internet chat as well as incoming telephone calls.

Speech recognition, another productivity enhancement for contact centers, is growing as a way to make it easier to access information without speaking with an agent. Airline schedules, stock quotes, and directory assistance are easier and faster to use with speech recognition rather than cumbersome menus using touch-tone buttons on telephones. Corporate directories are also faster to access via speech recognition. Callers merely say the department or employee name they wish to reach. However, speech recognition sales are hampered by high prices.

The desire for mobility within campuses and buildings is driving wireless voice capabilities within enterprises, particularly hospitals, universities, and warehouses. Just as consumers expect to be able to use their cordless home phones from anywhere within their house, so too do corporate employees. One-number service is available where calls to a corporate extension simultaneously ring an employee's cellular phone. Moreover, wireless phones equipped with caller ID enable users to screen calls and respond to important clients and internal staff on a timely basis when they are away from their desk.

Improvements in fiber-optic cabling and optical electronics have had a major impact on network capabilities. The growth of the Internet and the increase in traffic carried would not have been possible without dense wavelength division multiplexing (DWDM), which enables a single pair of fiber cabling to carry up to 160 channels of traffic. The prices of these electronics and the connectors used in fiber cabling have decreased in the past three years. In addition, a new, lower cost fiber multiplexing technique, coarse wavelength division multiplexing (CWDM), is a multiplexing technology that enterprises and carriers deploy to connect corporate sites to public networks and to bring the capacity of fiber closer to residential neighborhoods. CWDM carries up to eight channels of traffic on one fiber pair.

TELEPHONE SYSTEMS—VOICE OVER IP, PBXs, AND CENTREX SYSTEMS ....

Without a PBX or key system, commercial organizations would need to rent an individual telephone line from each phone to the telephone company's equipment. PBXs and key systems use a "pool" of telephone trunks (lines) from their sites to local phone companies. A *trunk* is a high-capacity path between a telephone system and a central office. Trunks also link central offices. In this way, 100 or so users share a pool of about 10 phone trunks. This eliminates fees for calls between people in the same office and decreases costs for telephone lines. Until the late 1990s, telephone systems were based on proprietary signaling. Newer telephone systems are based on Internet Protocol standards.

What Is a Private Branch Exchange (PBX)?

A PBX is an onsite telephone system that connects organizations to other people in their establishment and to people outside of their company. PBXs are private switches located within an enterprise. Central office switches are public, located at telephone company premises. Both types of switches set up connections between people and between devices for the duration of a telephone call.

Both central office switches and PBXs eliminate the need to wire each telephone to every other telephone. Rather, each telephone is wired to the PBX. In the case of the central office, each residence or business PBX is wired to the nearest central office switch. PBXs can be based on circuit switching. These are also referred to as traditional or proprietary switches. Telephone systems based on Voice over Internet Protocol (VoIP) are PBXs.

IP PBXS FOR THE ENTERPRISE ....

Traditional proprietary PBXs and key systems, such as Avaya, Nortel, and Toshiba systems, carry circuit switched voice. Circuit switching saves a path in the network for the entire duration of a call. Converged phone systems use Voice over IP (VoIP) technology to convert analog voice to digital bits, compress voice, and put the compressed, digitized bits into "envelopes of data" called *packets*. Data and voice packets share the same local area network (LAN) infrastructure as that used for businesses' data traffic. Moreover, packets from multiple sources can be sent on the same "path" during short pauses between messages. Because voice is sensitive to delays caused by traffic congestion, packets with voice are often prioritized.

For converged telephone systems that use local area network (LAN) infrastructure, the following issues are critical:

- The LAN must have enough capacity for both voice and data.
- Voice needs to be compressed (made smaller) to travel over the wide area network (WAN) and the LAN.
- Information technology staff that previously handled only voice or only data services must be educated to understand each other's terminology and technology.
- Corporate networks must be continually monitored to ensure voice quality.
- The system must be secure from hackers.

Vendors of IP-based telephone systems include the following:

- Avaya Communications
- Cisco Systems, Inc.
- Nortel Networks
- Compagnie Financiére Alcatel
- Mitel Networks
- Siemens ICN
- 3Com

Other manufacturers are Altigen; ShoreTel, Inc.; Interactive Intelligence, Inc.; EADS Telecom; Nexspan System; Pingtel Corporation; and Vertical Networks, Inc. (now part of Artisoft Inc.).

Impetus for Change

The main forces behind organizations' purchases of IP telephony systems are

- The desire to support applications such as call centers and messaging uniformly across campuses, between remote offices and at international locations, without purchasing expensive gear or costly links between sites.
- The means to enable teleworkers and sales staff who travel to make and receive phone calls using the same features and phone numbers as when they are in their office.
- The ability to administer remote telephone systems from a central site.
- The desire to keep up with technology so that new systems won't be obsolete in a short time. Most manufacturers are concentrating their research and development on Voice over IP telephone systems.

Architecture of IP-Based Systems . . . How the Pieces Fit Together

In traditional time division multiplexing telephone systems switching, call setup and teardown and ports connected to telephones and trunks all fit into one cabinet or series of cabinets connected by fiber. In contrast, in most IP telephony systems, call-processing software is separate from switching and other functions (see Figure 2.1). In addition, IP telephones are wired to Layer 2 switches located in wiring closets, not to the IP telephone system.

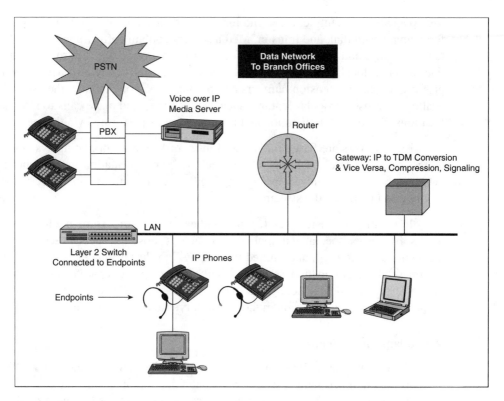

Figure 2.1
A hybrid system with circuit switched PBX and Voice over IP capabilities   .

IP systems are made up of the following components:

- Media servers
- Media gateways
- Hybrid systems
- Links between traditional PBXs and IP systems
- Connections to branch offices

Media Servers—Voice As an Application on the LAN

Media servers perform call processing, meaning they send instructions about setting up calls. (Servers are specialized computers containing applications such as e-mail or

Web pages.) For example, they send instructions for features such as three-party conferencing, speed dial, and transfer. Media servers contain software with all of the system, trunking, and station features. For instance, they specify the trunks over which international, local, and interstate calls should be routed. They also have lists of user profiles, meaning extension numbers and permissions. For example, they specify who is allowed to use particular features such as voice mail and place calls to international locations. System administration and programming is performed via the media server.

Most servers are based on UNIX, Linux, or Windows operating systems. Operating systems control basic operations such as how information gets on and off the network, how it's organized in memory, and the administrative interface for staff to monitor and maintain the system.

In addition to basic voice features and call processing, some media servers also hold software for specialized applications such as those for speech recognition, contact centers, voice mail, and unified messaging. In other instances, these applications are on separate application servers. Whether they are in separate servers or in the media server, any device connected to the corporate LAN, even those at remote locations, can be given permission in the media server to access these applications.

Redundant Media Servers

For redundancy in case the main Voice over IP media server crashes, many IP phone systems are equipped with two servers. If one fails, the other one automatically takes over processing calls. In addition, media servers at different sites can provide redundancy to each other. If the server at one site fails, traffic is sent over the data network to the backup site. This assumes that the link to the remote site has adequate capacity to support this additional traffic. If the entire network fails at one site, the telephone company would have to be notified to forward calls to the backup location.

Media Gateways—Protocol Translation and Signaling

Media gateways contain digital signal processors (DSPs) that compress voice traffic to make it smaller so that it can be carried more efficiently. DSPs also convert analog voice to digital and vice versa and put the voice signals into packets compatible with LAN networks. In addition, media gateways are equipped with circuit packs with ports for connections to traditional circuit switched analog and T-1 trunks. They also contain ports for analog telephones. In a pure IP telephone system, the gateways are connected to the public telephone network, and the DSPs perform the IP-to-circuit-switched conversions to make IP telephone system calls compatible with the public network.

In addition, media gateways are responsible for managing some security, monitoring call quality, and detecting and transmitting off-hook conditions, touch tone, dial tone, busy signals, and ring-no-answer conditions. In organizations using 802.11 Wi-Fi for wireless Voice over IP, the gateway is responsible for traffic between the wireless internal network, the wired IP voice service, and the public switched telephone network. The signals for Voice over IP such as ringing, call setup, and touch-tone are carried in separate channels from voice calls.

Layer 2 and Layer 3 switches transmit voice and data within the enterprise. Unlike circuit switched traditional analog and digital telephones, each IP telephone does not require a port on a circuit pack in the telephone system's cabinet. Rather they require a connection to the Layer 2 switch that sends calls within departments or on the same floor. Layer 2 switches send traffic to Layer 3 switches when it is destined to other floors, buildings, and external locations. (Refer to Chapter 1, "Basic Concepts," for more information on Layer 2 and Layer 3 switches.)

Hybrid Systems—Combining IP and Circuit Switched Capabilities

Some organizations purchase hybrid phone systems that support both IP and circuit switched telephony. The rationale for hybrid systems includes the wish to do the following:

- Install specialized systems, such as voice mail, audio conferencing equipment, and call center services at headquarters, to use at multiple sites. This often makes it affordable to run sophisticated telephone system adjuncts at all locations. With centralized systems, training and maintenance are simplified, and features such as voice mail broadcasts function across the organization.

- Equip new branch offices or replace old phone systems at remote offices with an IP phone system that IT staff can manage along with the data network.

- Test Voice over IP in small departments or offices before moving to Voice over IP for larger locations.

- Save money on voice calls between offices by carrying voice as IP packets on in-place data networks linking offices.

In addition to the preceding lists, some organizations purchase new telephone systems but don't want to rely on a total Voice over IP solution in the event of a denial of service attack or viruses that makes a network or endpoint unavailable to users. A hybrid system lets organizations use IP telephones in some departments or buildings in a campus and migrate to IP in other areas later. Moreover, having some telephones separate from the data network means they will still have voice service if the data network crashes.

The most common way to upgrade traditional circuit switched phone systems to hybrid systems capable of supporting IP telephony is to replace the processor on the circuit switched system with a server-based processor. The server is directly connected to the PBX with fiber-optic cabling. Circuit switched components communicate with the IP phones previously listed via the organization's local area network. The corporate wide area and metropolitan area network connect remote offices to headquarters. Refer to Figure 2.1 for hybrid system components.

Links Between Traditional PBXs and IP Systems

Some organizations purchase an IP telephone system for a new site. They may, for example, have a Nortel traditional PBX at their main office and a Cisco or 3Com IP phone system at a different site. They connect the two telephone systems together so that they can call each other using four or five digits. The goal is to make it simple for users in the same organization to call each other. A common way to achieve this is by linking the systems together using an integrated services digital network (ISDN) line. ISDN is similar to T-1. However, ISDN carries signals such as called party and calling party in a control channel, which is separate from the channels that carry voice. These separate signaling channels enable the phone system to interpret signals such as busy signals, ring-no-answer indicators, and calling party number and handle traffic more appropriately.

Connections to Branch Offices

The capability to connect IP telephone systems to each other over existing data networks is a major motivating factor in purchasing IP telephone systems. In addition to carrying packetized voice, these networks carry signals for centralized voice mail, unified messaging, and call center applications. For example, call center signals may indicate that all agents are busy and that calls should be sent to another site. Signals may also indicate the level of traffic at sites so that calls are distributed to alternate sites based on traffic volumes or the number of agents logged into the system.

Often, customers with private lines, frame relay service, or multiprotocol labeling system (MPLS) networks between their locations use these connections for IP voice as well as data. (Frame relay and MPLS networks connect locations together via

ONE HOSPITAL'S EXPERIENCES WITH VOICE OVER IP

A large hospital in a major metropolitan area installed a Cisco   Systems Voice over IP platform in a new office building a few city blocks from their main hospital building. The new offices are used for research functions. The hospital selected Cisco's Voice over IP solution as a way to use a converged technology platform that could be deployed in the future for new facilities and possibly for wireless Voice over IP. Moreover, the hospital felt that it would have more control and knowledge of how to manage and program a Voice over IP platform than a proprietary telephone system.

A system integrator was hired to manage the implementation. However, the integrator had limited technical knowledge on the Cisco Voice over IP platform. Therefore, the hospital called in Cisco directly, which quickly solved the echo problem on calls. The hospital found that virus protection and keeping up with new patches, required for protection against viruses, without bringing down voice services, was difficult. The biggest challenges were convincing the data staff about the criticality of voice service and training the voice staff on data terms used in IP networks. To meet the challenge of ensuring adequate quality on their LAN, they use network management software tools to monitor packet loss, quality of service, routers, firewalls, and virtual LANs. The hospital hasn't saved any money on moves, additions, and changes. However, administrative tasks are simpler than on their circuit switched telephone system. They don't want to risk using Voice over IP for mission critical clinical areas.

carrier networks; see Chapter 5, "VPNs and Specialized Network Services.") Customer calls answered in a central location can be transferred over these data links along with data traffic.

The most important issue in extending Voice over IP between sites is making sure that the local area network and the links between locations are engineered with enough capacity to support voice. Often the data connections are upgraded for more capacity to handle voice traffic. The upgrade is less costly than separate T-1s for voice and individual voice mail and contact center systems per site. Often enterprises upgrade their Layer 3 switches as well as their wide area networks (WANs) for additional bandwidth.

Voice Over IP for Calls Between Locations—Circuit Switched PBXs at the Sites

Often organizations first use IP telephony to combine voice and data traffic between sites. This is particularly true of organizations with locations in different countries. For example, they may have worldwide headquarters in London and regional headquarters in the United States. To save money on international calling, they install an IP card in their telephone systems or in their routers. The IP card converts voice to digital and vice versa, compresses and decompresses voice, and puts the voice in packets at the sending end and takes it out of the packet format at the receiving end (see Figure 2.2). This can be accomplished with a proprietary PBX based on circuit switched technology. Some router cards and PBXs can monitor data network connections between sites and fall over to the public switched telephone network if the wide area data network is congested.

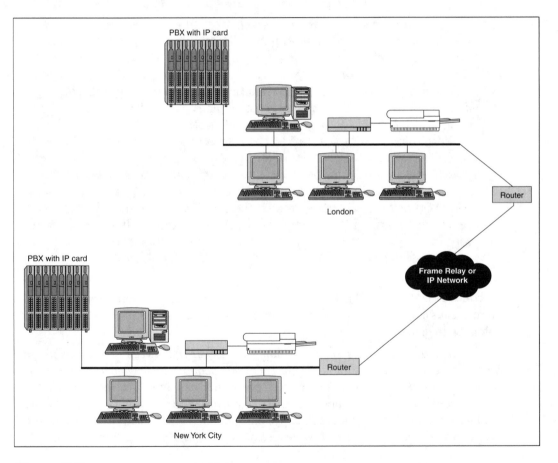

Figure 2.2
Circuit switched PBXs connected to a data network for Voice over IP traffic   .

IP Telephony for Small Organizations and Branch Offices—A System in a Box

IP telephone systems designed for small to medium-size businesses have essentially all of the features and functionality of larger systems, including provisions for redundant key components. However, because they support fewer users, in many systems, the server, gateway, and switching components fit into a single rack-mountable device or small cabinet (see Figure 2.3). Cisco system's small IP PBX fits inside a router.

When IP telephone systems are installed in small branch offices, the branch sometimes makes all of its outgoing calls through headquarters using a wide area network link and receives incoming calls through local phone lines. In these systems, there is generally a backup in case the link to headquarters is down. If this occurs, the system automatically falls over to local telephone lines for outgoing calls.

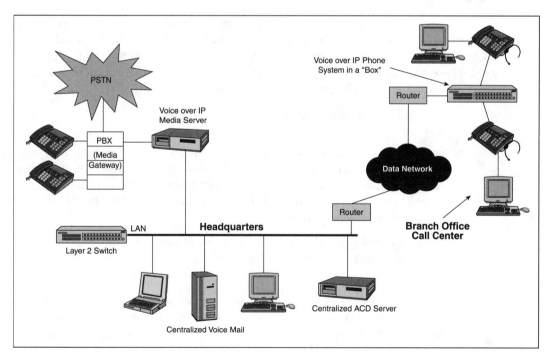

Figure 2.3
Connection to a branch office Voice over IP telephone system.

Small organizations frequently purchase IP telephone systems from system integrators, professionals that design the system, manage the implementation, and program new data systems for customers. They may also add applications such as audio conferencing and unified messaging from various suppliers.

Voice Quality and Security

Deploying corporate networks that are robust enough to support voice is a key ingredient in the success of new Voice over Internet Protocol systems. Faster digital signaling process chips that digitize voice and compress it into smaller chunks have made sending quality voice over data networks feasible. Voice is not like data. It needs to be sent in real time. Impairments such as delay and packet loss caused by network congestion are not noticeable for much of data traffic. However, these impairments noticeably degrade voice quality. Thus, network capacity is critical for sustaining voice quality.

Keeping networks secure is a difficult, ongoing challenge. Security needs to be installed in Voice over IP system servers, all of the Layer 2 and Layer 3 switches, the routers, and firewalls. In particular, many Voice over IP systems use common protocols. These protocols are wide open in the sense that many hackers know how they work and put a great deal of effort into finding their vulnerabilities.

Quality and security are impacted by the following:

- Engineering capacity in the enterprise network to support voice. If there is congestion, the network will discard packets, and voice quality will be degraded. Quality of service (QoS) solutions that mark and prioritize voice are important to ensure minimal delays for acceptable voice quality. See below for voice quality measurements.

- Compressing voice at an adequate rate. Sampling more bits per second results in better voice quality because more bits are used for each utterance. For instance, compressing speech at 64,000 bits per second yields better quality than compressing it at 8,000 bits per second.

- Vulnerability to viruses. Viruses are malicious programs. Some attempt to disrupt normal computer and network operation by duplicating themselves on multiple computers. Once a virus has infected a computer, it sends out many messages to other computers on the network in an attempt to find vulnerable computers. Organizations subscribe to security monitoring services, such as those offered by Microsoft and Symantec, to receive patches that prevent attacks from newly discovered viruses.

- Applying the patch quickly enough before major damage occurs is a challenge. The fix needs to be tested and then installed on every PC and server. Each computer and server with the new patch must be taken offline and rebooted. Taking servers offline to apply patches is a major challenge because the process disrupts business functions that rely on servers.

- Using VoIP PBX vendors that quickly certify Microsoft patches.

- *Worms* are like viruses except that they are programmed to start infecting computers or other devices on networks at a predetermined future date. These time-release worms are also referred to as bots.

In addition to the preceding, *proxy servers* authenticate callers to make sure they are who they say they are before they are sent to their destination. Proxy servers serve as intermediaries between callers and applications or endpoints, telephones, and other devices connected to the LAN. They are commonly used with the session initiation protocol (SIP) for audio and video conferencing.

Virtual Local Area Networks— Separation for Special Treatment

Organizations program voice telephony as a separate virtual local area network (VLAN). VLANs are groups of devices programmed in Layer 2 switches for special treatment in enterprise networks. They are not grouped together in physical networks. Rather, they are "virtual" networks that act as if they were separate LANs. Components of voice systems are programmed together to decrease delay, use common protocols, and control types of devices able to communicate with IP telephones.

Virtual local area networks provide special treatment for IP endpoints when they do the following:

- Tag voice packets via 802.1P protocols. This prioritizes packets to improve availability by decreasing delay. The tag distinguishes voice packets and indicates that only one router, not intermediate routers or Layer 3 switches, looks at routing information. The one router marks and classifies these packets based on 802.1p. Tagging protocols such as 802.1P are used for multimedia and conferencing services as well.

- Shield endpoints from hackers by allowing only certain types of packets through firewalls to reach them. They accomplish this with policies for firewall logical ports dedicated to voice traffic. Logical firewall ports are ports defined in software, not actual physical ports.

Voice Quality Measurements—Awareness of Voice Requirements

One of the consequences of installing Voice over IP systems is that the "voice" sides of information technology departments are learning the lingo and technology of measuring voice quality on data networks. In addition, staffs that manage data networks are becoming aware of the criticality of voice. They are developing a cognizance of the impact on voice services of congestion when they add new applications. They also note lost voice service when they take down the network for maintenance or new installations.

Staff use network management tools that entail quality of service assessments to monitor the following factors in voice quality:

- *Packet loss* refers to the network dropping packets when there is congestion. Packet loss results in uneven voice quality. Voice conversations "break up" when packet loss is too high.

- *Latency* refers to delays when voice packets transverse the network. Latency is measured in milliseconds. It results in long pauses within conversations and clipped words.

- *Jitter* is uneven latency and packet loss resulting in noisy calls that contain pops and clicks or crackling sounds.

- *Echo*, hearing your voice repeated, is often caused when voice is translated from a circuit switched format to the IP format. This is usually corrected by special echo-canceling devices.

Barriers to Acceptance of Voice over IP

Factors delaying acceptance of local-area-network-based phone systems are

- *Political factors and unfamiliarity with new technology.* Communications barriers, lack of knowledge about new technology, and power struggles are significant impediments to acceptance of new technology.

- *Reliability.* Not all users are confident that they can duplicate PBX and key system reliability on LAN-connected systems. Moreover, they are alarmed about "putting all their eggs in one basket." With separate PBX and data services, if the data network crashes, they still have voice. For this reason, they often try out Voice over IP in branch offices, labs, or particular departments. They keep critical departments and core functions on traditional PBXs.

- *Cost of infrastructure upgrades.* In large enterprise organizations, costs can be high to upgrade cabling, add power over Ethernet, enlarge data closets for new switches, and add bandwidth to networks that link sites. (Power over Ethernet is a way to power IP phones from the wiring closet rather than at each telephone.) Category 5 or above cabling is required for IP telephony. (See below for Copper Cabling Standards.) However, they are not always sure they can achieve an adequate return on investing in IP telephony.

- *A lack of adequate cost savings.* Organizations located at a single site with adequate telephone systems often see no driving need to replace their phone system. Some organizations with older systems upgrade installed-base phone systems by moving to a hybrid system so they can keep many of their cards and cabinets but obtain IP functionality where needed. See above for Hybrid Systems.

IP-based telephone systems have had more initial acceptance by small or startup firms that want to use their data wiring for both telephone and computer connections and thus build their network infrastructure to support voice as well as data. In addition, many small startup firms don't have legacy, older, proprietary systems. They can start from scratch with new technology.

Endpoints—IP Telephones Connected to Layer 2 Switches

IP telephones are often referred to as endpoints. In computer networks, endpoints refer to devices connected to the network that can originate or terminate traffic. Video conferencing devices, IP telephones, and personal computers are examples of endpoints. They serve as the end or beginning point of a communications session.

On IP-based systems, multi-featured IP telephones are connected to ports in Layer 2 switches on local area networks rather than to ports on the IP telephone system. Computers and phones often share the same jack and cabling to the Layer 2 switch. In this scenario, the user's personal computer is plugged into a data outlet on the back of the telephone and the telephone is plugged into the nearest RJ-45 data jack, a type of jack that data devices plug into to connect to networks.

For greater redundancy and a dedicated path to the Layer 2 switch, the PC and the telephone can each use a separate RJ-45 jack, cabling, and port on the Layer 2 switch. This requires additional hardware and an extra cable run from the telephone to the Layer 2 switch. In either case, voice, video, and data share the fiber cabling and ports on Layer-3 switches that transmit traffic between floors and buildings. This is the enterprise backbone.

IP Endpoints—Telephone Selection Complexity and Interoperability

PBX telephones represent about a third of the cost of a new telephone system. Selecting the right telephones is a particular challenge when technology changes. Information technology staff must learn to evaluate new types of phones and a myriad of features. To add to the complexity, choices will increase as the technology matures and telephones from different manufacturers become interoperable on multiple IP voice systems.

Session initiation protocol (SIP) is a signaling standard made up of a number of protocols that define a uniform way to set up phone calls, audio conferences and video conferences, and features on phones so that telephones from different manufacturers operate as designed. As manufacturers work toward uniform implementation of SIP, the number of phones from which to choose will grow, and competition will lead to lower-priced phones.

IP Endpoints—Softphones and Directories

IP PBXs support analog phones, IP feature phones, and softphones. *Softphones* are software installed on computers that let people use their computer as a telephone.

Softphones enable employees to use their PC for telephone calls. See Figure 2.4. Features such as hold buttons, caller ID, and message waiting alerts appear on their PC screen. The advantages of softphones are savings on telephone hardware and increased mobility for users. If the softphone is on a laptop, staff can use the softphone anywhere on the corporate network or remotely if remote access is enabled. Mobile employees such as salespeople often use hardware-based phones at the office and softphones when they work from hotels or home offices.

Voice quality on softphones will be degraded by hardware problems such as poor-quality speakers or headsets or slow processors. In addition, while a PC is downloading a large file, voice quality can suffer. If the PC crashes, people lose voice as well as data.

Many manufacturers integrate softphones with collaboration software and with instant messaging containing presence indicators. Instant messaging is the ability to

Collaborative software enables users to look at the same file on their screen while on an audio conference call or simply speaking together on the telephone. The softphone may also contain or link to corporate directories via application programming interfaces (APIs) that translate between the directory and the endpoint. For example, the screen on the softphone may be used to search existing lightweight directory access protocol (LDAP) compliant directories, such as Outlook™, for a particular name or department phone number. The directory can also be used to easily set up conference calls by merely clicking on each name to add it to the conference and for speed dialing. *LDAP* is a directory protocol that describes a uniform way of organizing information in directories.

IP Phones—Large Screens and Directories

High-end IP-hardware-based telephones are computer based with features found on personal computers. Some have large color screens and Web-based displays. Many can be used to access corporate directories and to provide visual indication of e-mail messages and presence. *Presence* is an indicator that another user is available to take calls or participate in e-mail chats.

Phones with Web-based displays are capable of displaying Internet pages pushed to the phone from proxy servers. The proxy server formats Web content so that Web sites formatted in display protocols such as HTML are displayed on IP endpoints. Users select items on their display phones that they wish to view. These requests are sent to the proxy server, which obtains the information from the Web and pushes it to the endpoint. In addition, third-party developers are creating applications for IP telephones. For example, an application for vertical industries such as hotels lets people order tickets, get weather information, and rent DVDs from a large screen on an IP telephone.

Power over Ethernet—Efficient Power Distribution and Backup

Every IP telephone in an IP telephone system needs its own electrical power. To avoid the expense and labor of providing local electricity to each set at installation, most organizations power telephones via the Layer 2 switch located in the wiring closet, to which their phone is connected. This ensures that all phones are connected to a UPS and survive power interruptions. It also avoids the problem of making sure everyone's phone is near an electrical outlet, is plugged in, and has an electrical cord. To bring power to groups of endpoints, organizations use 802.3af, the Institute of Electrical and

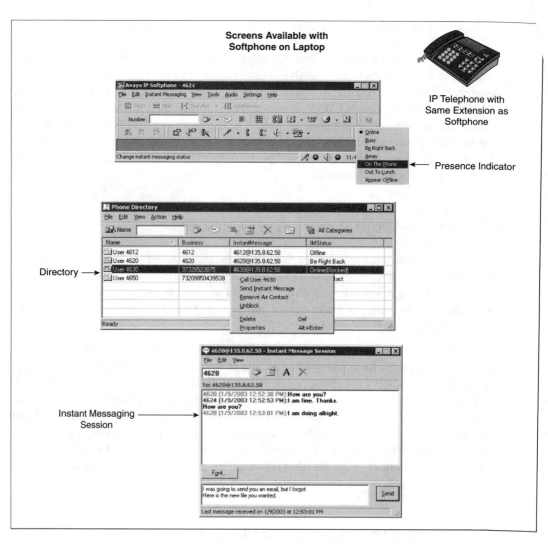

Figure 2.4
Courtesy of Avaya, 2005. Voice over IP softphone with the same extension number as the desk telephone .

exchange e-mail in near real time without typing in an address. Users merely select an icon representing the user to whom the message is intended and click submit after typing the message. Presence indicators let users know when someone within their community of users is available for real-time or near real-time messaging. People click on icons in their e-mail software to indicate their availability.

Electronics Engineers, Inc. (IEEE) standard known as *Power over Ethernet* that defines how power can be carried from the Layer 2 switch to the endpoint using the same cabling that transmits voice and data. Battery backups and generators are deployed in wiring closets where switches support mission-critical telephones or attendant consoles. Power over Ethernet is also used to power corporate wireless Wi-Fi antennas and base stations. (See Chapter 9, "Wi-Fi, Wireless Broadband, Sensor Networks, and Personal Area Networks," for corporate wireless networks.)

PBX Trunks—Switch-to-Switch Connectivity

PBXs are connected to telephone company central offices by trunks that carry calls between the PBX and the telephone company. Depending on the volume of calls generated by the staff, eight to ten users can share each channel (path) within a trunk. Most companies now use T-1 or PRI ISDN trunks. Instead of having 24 separate pairs of wires, the T-1 can carry 24 incoming and/or outgoing calls on two pairs of wire or on fiber-optic cable. Each PRI trunk also has 24 channels, but one is reserved for signals such as dial tone and dialed numbers. Fiber-optic cables have the capability to carry multiple trunks. Large organizations that support busy call centers may have T-3 trunks. These carry 672 simultaneous calls and are equal to the capacity of 28 T-1s. In most of these cases, the PBX is equipped with backup analog trunks or additional T-1s in case of failure of their T-1 or T-3 trunks. Each trunk is wired to a port located on a circuit pack in the telephone system's cabinet.

Demarcation—The Location at Which Telcos Wire Trunks

The local telephone company brings telephone lines into buildings and wires them to interfaces. The interface is called a *jack* or a *punch-down block*. Each outside line is punched down (wired) to the connecting block. Jacks that hold one line are called *RJ11c* jacks. The RJ stands for registered jack. These are the jacks found in most homes. The *RJ21x*, which holds 25 lines, is the interface to which local telephone companies wire multiple outside lines in businesses. The RJ21x jack is a point from which telephone lines and trunks can be tested. For instance, if there is a question with a repair problem as to where the problem lies, the telephone company can test its trunk to the RJ21x jack, and the PBX vendor can test service between the PBX and the interface. The RJ21x jack is the demarcation point between the telephone company line and the inside wiring (see Figure 2.5). Individual T-1 lines terminate at data jacks (RJ48 jacks) at customer premises. This is the point where telephone companies test the T-1 if there is an outage.

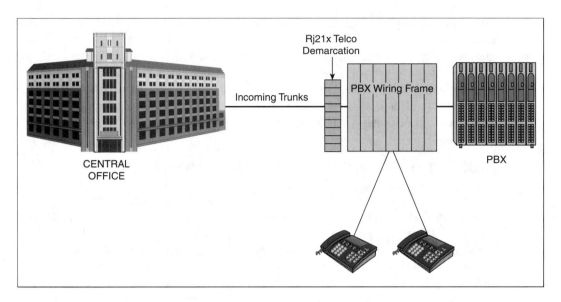

Figure 2.5
PBX trunks from the telephone company to the demarcation.

Circuit Switched PBXs—Proprietary Platforms

PBXs that use circuit switching are also referred to as proprietary PBXs. Each manufacturer uses proprietary signaling to link telephone and trunk lines to the central processing unit. Features and peripherals such as contact center software also operate on proprietary signaling. In PBXs that support a single building, the components are generally housed in one unit. The main components of a PBX are as follows:

- The central processing unit and circuit packs for dial tone, touch tone, and other signals

- Ports connected to trunks for incoming and outgoing calls

- Ports to each telephone and often the voice mail system as well

Thus, the main computer that runs the system and the software for the features, as well as the equipment used to connect internal callers and external callers and telephones, are in one unit or multiple connected cabinets that function as one unit.

The two market leaders in proprietary PBXs are Avaya Communications (formerly part of Lucent Technologies) and Nortel Networks. Companies with smaller market shares are Siemens, NEC, and Mitel Networks. Other suppliers include Alcatel, Fujitsu, Ericsson, and Hitachi. Alcatel is the largest provider of PBXs in Europe.

PBX Telephones—Screens and Feature Buttons

Prices of user-friendly phones with feature buttons such as hold, transfer, conference, and LCDs (liquid crystal displays) have dropped to the point where they are affordable for more employees. The LCDs on these proprietary digital sets often display the name and/or extension number of the person calling, and context-sensitive instructions on how to use features and corporate directories. This has made it easier for people to use more of the telephone system's features. Telephone systems also support analog telephones, generally for low usage common areas such as halls, elevators, and cafeterias. All analog telephones work on all PBXs. However, each manufacturer supports its own proprietary digital telephones, which results in higher prices for digital sets. In traditional telephone systems each telephone is wired to a port in the telephone system's main cabinet.

Centrex—Telephone Company Supplied Service

In contrast to PBXs, where the switching equipment is located on organizations' sites, Centrex switching equipment is part of the telephone company's central office.

The original motivation for Centrex, which was first implemented in 1965, was much the same as the motivation behind such automated services as voice mail and speech recognition today. Organizations wanted to save money on operators, administration, and space. Centrex provided these savings by eliminating the requirement for onsite switching equipment, enabling calls to bypass the operator and go directly to end users, letting users place calls without operator assistance by identifying the extension that made each call.

In the last decade, for other than multi-site, large organizations, Centrex failed to gain deep market penetration because onsite telephone systems were more feature rich and flexible. According to Datapro Research Corporation's 1986 report "An Overview of Centrex Service," prior to 1982, 70% of businesses with over 1,000 lines used Centrex. In contrast, *Business Communications Review* found that by the year 2002 the Centrex installed base of Centrex/PBX was 18.1% of businesses with over 401 lines and only 10.2% of medium-size organizations. By 2003, the Centrex installed base grew 1.8% because of the advent of IP Centrex. The Telecommunications Industry Review published the *Business Communications Review* statistics in *TIA's 2004 Telecommunications Market Review and Forecast.* (See the next several sections for IP Centrex.)

Where Centrex Is Used

Centrex is used by organizations with buildings spread out across a campus. Centrex provides connections between these sites so that enterprises do not need to obtain rights of way for cable connections, purchase wireless infrastructure, or lease expensive telephone lines from the phone company to connect buildings separated by public streets. Campus-type environments include those for

- Hospitals
- Cities and towns
- Universities
- Large businesses with buildings spread out over a metropolitan area

Telephone companies have also marketed Centrex to organizations with fewer than 100 employees as a way for small companies to have someone else manage their system.

IP Centrex—Phone Companies Hosting Voice Over IP

IP Centrex is also referred to as hosted IP, hosted PBX, hosted VoIP, managed Voice over IP service, and managed services for voice. Incumbent telephone companies such as SBC offer it as a strategy to stem the loss of traditional Centrex service to IP-based telephone systems. Centrex service to large universities, municipal governments, and financial institutions with buildings scattered throughout cities is a lucrative source of revenue to incumbent telephone companies such as Qwest and BellSouth. However, many institutions are considering and some have purchased IP telephone systems to replace or supplement their Centrex systems. The very Centrex feature, geographic flexibility, that appeals to organizations that needs transparent calling between sites is available with Voice over IP PBXs.

IP Centrex has a similar architecture to on-site Voice over IP systems. However, the system server and switching components are located at the provider's site rather than at the customer. IP Centrex traffic is carried over high-speed telephone links between the provider and the customer. Like hybrid on-site Voice over IP systems, IP Centrex can be added for certain departments or telecommuters, and the rest of the organization can retain their circuit switched Centrex services or telephone system.

When telecommuters use IP Centrex, voice traffic is carried over the remote worker's DSL or cable modem service. To date, BellSouth, Qwest, and SBC offer IP Centrex. Verizon Communications has stated its intention to offer IP Centrex. In addition, both Covad Communications and Level 3 Communications offer IP Centrex directly to end users and on a wholesale basis through other carriers. Covad acquired its IP Centrex technology through its purchase of GoBeam and Level 3 through its purchase of Telverse.

Direct Inward Dialing—Bypassing the Operator for Incoming Calls

Direct inward dialing (DID) is a feature that routes incoming calls directly to a PBX or key system extension without operator intervention. DID was a major innovation when it was first available in the 1980s because it enabled non-Centrex PBX extensions to receive calls during the day and after-hours without attendant assistance. DID is now affordable for small and large organizations because the service can be carried on existing T-1 trunks used for incoming and outgoing voice calls. Small organizations combine their voice traffic and Internet access service on their T-1 trunks. (See Chapter 6, "Entertainment, Cable TV, and Last Mile Fiber Systems," for T-1.)

As Figure 2.6 illustrates, direct inward dialing service is made up of "software" telephone numbers. Each number is not assigned a specific trunk; rather, a few hundred DID numbers are able to share 24 T-1 slots (paths). Depending on the traffic requirements at the site, there generally is one path per eight to ten DID numbers. When DID calls reach it, the central office looks at the digits dialed and identifies the call as belonging to a particular organization. The central office passes the last three or four digits of the dialed number to the organization's key system or PBX. The on-site telephone system reads the digits and sends the call directly to the correct telephone.

In the case of a T-1 failure, calls can be routed on back-up individual analog or T-1 lines.

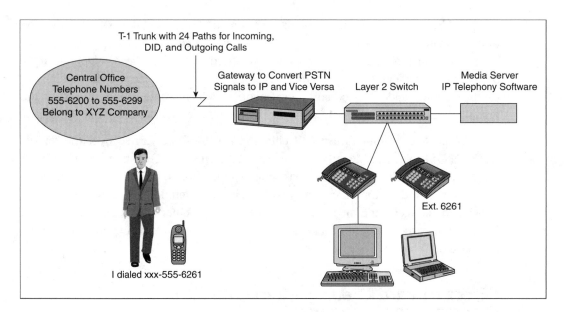

Figure 2.6
Direct inward dialing (DID) carried on a T-1 trunk to an IP-based telephone system.

Key Systems—Multi-featured for Smaller Organizations

Key systems are telephone systems designed for smaller organizations. Although there are some technical differences in the way they handle calls, new key systems have all of the features and most of the functionality of private branch exchanges. Key systems generally serve the under-70-users-per-site market.

The major difference between key systems and PBXs is the connection between the central office and the key system. Key systems are loop start and PBXs are ground start. With a ground-start PBX, a trunk is seized or grounded by the PBX or central office before a call is transmitted between the two locations. With a loop-start key system, if a path is available, the call is sent either to the key system from the central office or to the public network from the key system. The central office does not seize the telephone line between the customer location and the central office before the call is sent. Analog home phones also are loop start, which is why a person can pick up the handset to make a call and find that someone calling them is already on the phone even though the telephone has not rung. Glare occurs when incoming and outgoing calls are made simultaneously on a loop start line.

On a key system, dial tone is derived from the central office. A person making an outside call on a key system does not have to dial an access code such as "9."

Pressing an outside line button on a key system telephone signals the central office that the end user wants to make or receive a telephone call. This is the reason key systems have an outside line button to make or receive outside calls and an intercom button for internal calls.

In PBXs, the PBX provides the dial tone to the user. Users dial an access code, usually "9," to make an outside call. The PBX responds to a lifted handset by sending a dial tone to the end user and then requesting that a trunk to the central office be "grounded" or seized to make a telephone call.

Hybrid PBX/Key Systems

Large key systems are generally "hybrid" systems with features of both PBXs and key systems. They can be installed as either key systems with outside lines, or PBXs with grounded trunk connections to the central office and the requirement to dial an access code such as "9" to make outside calls. When they are installed as key systems, users are not required to dial an access code such as "9" to make an outside call. Hybrid systems often overlap in size with PBXs and range in size from 50 to 125 telephones. They provide most of the functionality of a PBX.

Limited Range Cordless Phones

Many PBX and key system suppliers provide lower priced "home type" or proprietary 900-megahertz (MHz), 2.4-gigahertz (GHz), or 5.8GHz wireless phones. These phones only work within range of the antenna in the phone and the phone's base unit. The 900MHz, 2.4GHz, and 5.8GHz phones have a range of about 100 to 125 feet, depending on building conditions.

Wireless Options for PBXs

Mobility within enterprises is compelling, particularly in organizations such as warehouses and hospitals where staff are rarely at a fixed location. Moreover, certain departments, such as security, maintenance, and IT, have highly mobile staff. Wireless telephones enable workers to be reached (and interrupted!) at all times if they take their phones with them and turn them on. The mobile feature that is generating enormous interest, particularly among salespeople, is the ability to be contacted at both cell phones and wired phones by people that call an office number. In addition, IP telephony holds the potential for delivering affordable wireless in-building solutions. See Chapter 9 for wireless Voice over IP service in 802.11 networks.

In-Building Wireless—Connections to Circuit Switched Phone Systems

Wireless solutions that work with traditional phone systems have been available since the mid-1990s. Wireless in-building service has been particularly popular in hospitals to reach nurses and other mobile staff. SpectraLink has the largest installed base of these systems. Symbol Technologies also provides in-building wireless systems. Telephone system manufacturers such as Nortel and Avaya sell mainly third-party, non-PBX manufacturers' wireless systems that operate with their PBXs. SpectraLink incorporates proprietary signaling made available by PBX manufacturers into its control units. This enables wireless phones to use wired desk phone features from manufacturers such as Avaya, Siemens, and Nortel.

These features include

- Hold buttons
- Speed-dial buttons that enable abbreviated dialing of frequently called numbers
- LCD screens to show the name of the person calling
- Message waiting lights for voice mail

The structure of in-building wireless systems resembles cellular service described in Chapter 8, "Mobile Services." Whereas base stations in cellular networks are connected to mobile switching offices, the base station, and its attendant antenna on in-building systems are connected to the PBX. In third-party systems like SpectraLink's, a control unit sits between the telephone system and the base station to translate the PBX's proprietary signals to those that can be interpreted by the wireless handset and vice versa. Base stations and antennas are located on every floor where wireless service is available (see Figure 2.7). Like cellular systems, base stations hand off calls to other antennas and base stations as workers move around the building. Because in-building base stations cover smaller areas, their coverage areas are referred to as picocells. *Picocell* refers to very small cell size.

One-Number Dialing to Reach a Cell Phone and Desk Phone

So that employees can receive office calls when they are out of the office, many IP and traditional proprietary telephone systems offer a feature in which calls to desk phones

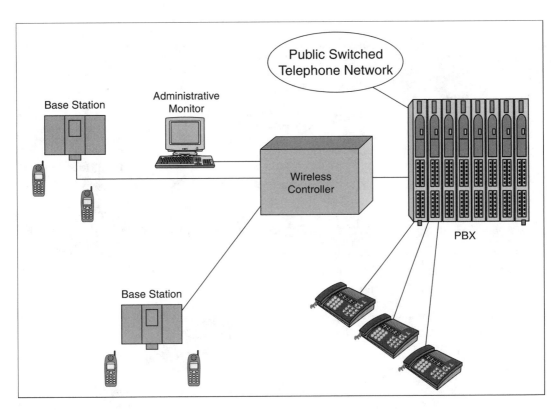

Figure 2.7
In-building wireless service .

also ring cell phones. In essence, the cell phone becomes an extension of the PBX. Every time the desk phone is called, both the cell phone and the desk phone ring. The displays on the cell phone and the desk phone indicate the calling party's phone number and name if available from the carrier used by the caller (see Figure 2.8).

These cell phone extensions of the PBX are applications in the PBX. Some of them require external servers and others only require software installed in the PBX. They require integrated services digital network (ISDN) telephone links to the landline carrier. ISDN is similar to T-1; however, it has a separate signaling channel. The signaling channel carries the called party number in the separate channel so that the PBX can treat calls to users with cellular extensions in a special way. The application on the server or software contains the cellular telephone number associated with each PBX extension on the service. This tells the system which cellular device to ring simultaneously with the wired extension. Alcatel, Avaya, Ericsson, Nortel, and Siemens offer variations on this service.

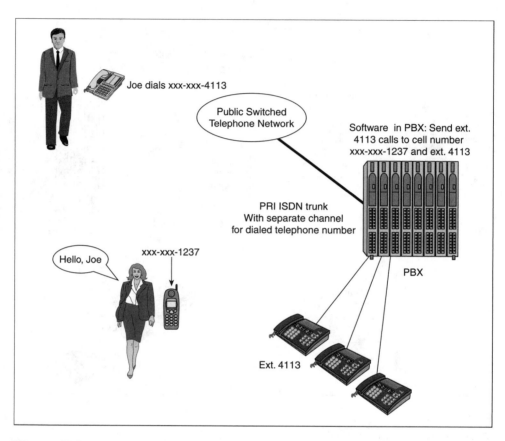

Figure 2.8
One-number wireless service in conjunction   with a PBX.

ADVANCED APPLICATIONS FOR TELEPHONE SYSTEMS ....

Private branch exchange (PBX) and key system vendors depend on profits from adjunct services and maintenance contracts. New Voice over Internet Protocol telephone systems are spurring system sales, but the heated competition keeps margins low. Vendors derive much of their profits in the following areas:

- Maintenance contracts on telephone systems

- Moves, adds, and changes of installed-base telephone equipment

- Upgrades to the hardware and software of existing telephone systems

- Feature telephones with built-in speakerphones, feature buttons, and liquid crystal displays
- Wireless telephones for PBX and key systems
- Peripheral devices such as voice mail, automatic call distributors, and call accounting systems.

Call Accounting—Billing Internal Departments

Due to decreasing long distance costs, sales of call accounting systems, which track calls made by individual users, are declining. They are, however, still used to allocate costs to individual departments. They also indicate the amount of traffic on each telephone line or trunk so that organizations can determine when there are too many or too few outside telephone lines. A large amount of traffic during weekends or nights might indicate that hackers are using the system to make free long distance calls.

Call accounting systems, also called *station message detail recording (SMDR)* and *call detail recording (CDR)*, generally are installed on PCs. The PC is connected through a serial port to the telephone system. An alternative to onsite call accounting systems is the use of service bureaus to collect calling statistics.

Organizations use call accounting reports to do the following:

- Charge time spent on calls back to clients
- Charge calls equitably back to the appropriate internal department
- Determine by traffic spikes if hackers are making long distance calls
- Note possible trunk outages when particular trunks show no traffic
- Create internal directories
- Make sure agents in credit departments are making the required number of collections calls

Call accounting systems are often connected to corporate intranets. (Intranets use Web technology for internal and trusted partner access to information.) Connections to intranets enable department managers to download reports in spreadsheet formats if they want to see the calls that their staff made.

Call Detail Recording for Carriers— Generating Data for Billing

Carriers need accurate records of calls for which they bill customers and other carriers that use their network. Call detail recording in carriers' networks is referred to as

automated message accounting (AMA). Specifications for information to include on call detail reports are available from standards organizations such as Telcordia. Wireless and wireline carriers use equipment to generate reports sorted by, for example, billing telephone numbers for billing purposes. They identify carriers that use their network by trunk groups assigned to the carrier and by the carrier identity code (CIC) assigned to each carrier.

In the event of billing disputes between carriers, call detail records provide backup support that types of traffic were actually carried. For example, local traffic is rated differently than long distance. The call detail record (CDR) shows each call's destination and origination. Call detail systems are also programmed to code-enhanced services such as voice mail, audio conferencing, call forwarding, and caller ID so that they can be billed appropriately. There are also formats for tracking, sorting, and collecting data services such as frame relay.

Equipment to store and sort call detail records is located at central offices that connect callers to networks. As networks change from circuit switched traditional voice networks to IP-based structures, billing for calls will become more centralized with servers supporting multiple switching centers. Call detail equipment is connected both to switches and to billing systems that generate actual bills.

Voice Mail—Storing and Retrieving Messages

Voice mail systems are changing from those first installed in the 1980s on proprietary hardware platforms. Most large systems that support multiple locations are still on these platforms. However, small systems are PC-based or integrated as cards in a telephone system. Large telephone system providers such as Avaya, Cisco, Toshiba, and Nortel supply the majority of voice mail systems so that customers have support from one vendor for their phone and their messaging system.

Most new voice mail systems include unified messaging capabilities. Voice mail manufacturers are promoting unified messaging to boost sales and upgrades of voice mail. Unified messaging systems enable users to receive voice mail, e-mail, and fax messages from a personal computer or a touch-tone telephone. The Telecommunications Industry Association (TIA) in *TIA's 2004 Telecommunications Market Review and Forecast* cites year 2003 sales of vanilla voice mail systems at $2.25 billion compared to $3.1 billion in 1999. Corporations invested in upgrades and new systems in the late 1990s to make systems compatible with the year-2000 new date format, meaning 2004 rather than just 04. Voice mail sales have been flat since then.

Voice Mail Components

The following components make up voice mail systems:

- *Central processing unit (CPU).* The CPU is responsible for the overall operation of the unit. It executes the application software and operating software that is located in the CPU.
- *Codecs.* These devices convert analog voice to digital signals and digital signals back to analog. Most systems compress voice and take the pauses out of conversations to store voice mail messages on the hard drive more economically.
- *Software.* The software distinguishes one system's features from another system's—for example, the capability to automatically hear the time at which a message was left rather than having to dial a 7 to hear the time it was left.
- *I/O cards.* These printed circuit boards provide the connections between the telephone system and voice mail system. There are usually four ports per board. Each port enables one person to leave or pick up a voice mail message. I/O ports also are used for the receipt and transmission of facsimile messages on systems with voice mail as well as fax mail.
- *Speech recognition cards.* These are specialized cards and software that recognize spoken commands. Speech recognition can also be software based.
- *Other system components.* These include serial ports, high-speed buses, power supplies, hard drives to store messages, and tape and disc drives for system backups.

Automated Attendants—Using Machines to Answer Phones

Automated attendants are used as adjuncts to company operators. An automated attendant is programmed to answer all calls, certain calls to particular telephone lines or departments, or after-hour calls. Here is an example:

> *"Thank you for calling ABC Company. If you know your party's extension, you may dial it now. For sales, press 1. For customer service, press 2."*

The first automated attendant, manufactured by Dytel, was installed in 1984 to help companies answer calls during peak times. They found, for example, that during slow times such as 8:00 a.m. to 10:00 a.m., operators had too much idle time. However, during the busy hours, operators could not keep up with the call volume. When they were first introduced, automated attendant systems grew in popularity faster than voice mail systems. It was immediately apparent to customers that these systems saved money on labor.

Automated attendants are no longer separate systems. They are software features of voice mail systems. Automated attendant functionality also can be purchased as a feature of telephone systems, in which case the functionality is located on a circuit packet within the PBX cabinet.

Speech Recognition—Voice-Activated Dialing to Make Automated Attendants More User Friendly

Speech recognition, also referred to as voice-activated dialing, significantly improves the way automated systems handle incoming calls. It eliminates the long menus on automated attendants that callers find annoying and cumbersome. For example, when someone calls a company with a speech recognition system, instead of hearing the following: "Thank you for calling ABCdotcom. Please dial the extension number of the person you wish to reach. Dial 411 for a company directory or press 6 for a department listing." They might hear this:

> *"Thank you for calling ABCdotcom. Please say the name of the person or department you wish to reach."*

Employees who are traveling or driving don't have to look up telephone extensions or know how to spell a name to use spell-by-name directories. They simply say the name of the person they want to reach as soon as the system answers.

Organizations that use these systems create a database of names and their associated extensions, often importing existing internal directories into the database. When the speech recognition software recognizes the name spoken, it checks the database for the telephone number. It then either asks the caller if its recognition is correct or transfers the call. When the ScanSoft system isn't sure of its recognition, it says, "I think you said Sally Jones. Is that correct?" If the system has a high degree of confidence that the name is correct, it repeats the name and transfers the call.

The systems use speech synthesis or prerecorded spoken names when they say, for example, "I don't understand that name." Speech synthesis translates written names from text to speech. ScanSoft, Phonetic Systems, LocusDialog, and Nuance sell products directly to end users and through partners. For the most part, speech recognition is added on to new or upgraded systems. High prices are a big factor in the slow adoption of speech recognition in voice mail systems. New voice mail systems offer voice recognition access to voice mail—for example, to play messages—as well as voice-activated dialing in conjunction with automated attendants. Speech recognition also is used to access users' calendars and collaboration software for cell phone or e-mail addresses.

Unified Messaging Integration of Voice Mail, Fax Mail, and E-mail

Unified messaging, also referred to as unified communications, is an optional feature of voice mail systems. It provides the capability to retrieve fax, e-mail, and voice mail messages from a single device such as a PC or a touch-tone telephone. The most important advantage of unified messaging is the ability of people that travel to have the convenience of checking only one source for messages. In addition, retrieving messages from PCs gives users the ability to prioritize messages and listen to the most important ones first. It eliminates the need to hear all voice mail messages before getting to the critical ones. These systems can also store incoming facsimile messages on the voice mail system's hard drive.

According to *TIA's 2004 Telecommunications Market Review and Forecast*, 22% of corporations have unified messaging, and 2003 sales were $1.5 billion. However, the TIA report stated that unified messaging is available to only 3% of employees at these organizations. Complex installation and a lack of employee desire for the features result in low penetration. For the most part, mobile employees use unified messaging.

When users access messages from a touch-tone phone, text-to-speech software converts e-mail to speech for callers and reads their e-mail messages to them. Employees access messages through e-mail software on their personal computers. Unified messaging systems need to be compatible with e-mail programs such as Microsoft Exchange and Lotus Notes. Systems typically also support e-mail retrieval from within browsers so that remote workers can retrieve messages from their personal computer and listen to them via the PC's microphone.

Unified Messaging Systems on the LAN

In unified messaging systems, voice mail and fax messages are stored in the voice mail server that is connected both to the LAN and to the on-premises telephone system's voice mail. Gateway software translates the voice mail and fax messages so that they are compatible with the e-mail. When unified messaging is used with voice-over-IP-based telephone systems, it communicates with the voice server and e-mail over the LAN cabling and data switches.

Unified messaging systems add voice mail and facsimile traffic to the LAN. To reduce the bandwidth (that is, capacity) required to transmit voice mail and facsimile over LANs, voice mail vendors compress the messages. Compression reduces both bandwidth used and hard drive space needed on the e-mail and voice mail servers.

Multi-application Platforms in Carrier Networks

Currently, most wireline and wireless carriers offer voice mail but not services such as unified messaging that have the potential to earn them extra revenue. Because of the proprietary nature of traditional time division multiplexing central offices, it has been costly to add peripheral devices that are compatible with proprietary central office equipment from different manufacturers. Carriers are hoping to purchase new, lower cost, multi-application platforms based on standard protocols. These can be linked to Voice over IP-based central offices and also communicate with carriers' signaling systems, billing systems, and operation support systems to update billing records and maintenance systems.

Services that carriers are considering or starting to implement to generate revenue include the following:

- Unified messaging.

- Video mail integration with short messaging service (short text messages on cellular phones). Video mail with which people can see video stills of the person with whom they exchange short messages. They might also exchange stills of shoes they are considering purchasing in a department store or stills from a construction site.

- Access to portals such as AOL and Yahoo! so that customers can exchange short messages and e-mail chats with buddies and others via their mobile phone. They will have an indication on their phone if someone is available to chat.

- Audio conferencing via the Internet, mobile phones, and landline phones.

- "Follow me" service (one number to reach people wherever they are).

- Network-based storage of calendars and address books that are accessible from landline, cellular, and Internet-based devices.

(See Chapter 7, "The Internet," for e-mail chats and Chapter 8, "Mobile Services," for short messaging service.)

Companies such as Comverse Network Systems, Unisys Corporation, Iperia, Inc., Lucent, Nortel Networks, and Cisco Systems sell unified messaging and voice mail to telephone companies, cellular carriers, Internet service providers (ISPs), and service bureaus.

Unified Messaging for Carriers— in Hybrid Networks with IP and TDM Systems

Just as enterprises are upgrading their networks to support Voice over IP, carriers are also adding Voice over IP to their traditional time division multiplexed (TDM) networks. They hope to lower their costs by purchasing applications based on open-standards-based platforms.

Instead of having all of the components of these systems in one "box" (cabinet), the goal is to use modular pieces that can be added to or modified using equipment from competitive suppliers. The following devices need to interoperate on both IP and circuit switched networks:

- *Application servers* containing features and issuing commands—for example, send this instant message to abc@ISP.com
- *Signaling gateways* that translate signals from the public switched network protocol (SS7) into IP packets and vice versa
- *Media servers* using standards-based protocols to convert application streams to IP streams, generate touch-tone, play announcements, and convert IP protocols to a format for storage in message storage devices
- *Media gateways* that convert IP packets to those compatible with the public switched telephone network and vice versa
- *Message storage* that stores media for particular applications, such as speech files associated for video mail and voice mail, video files for video mail, and instant messaging files

Carriers are in the process of building and designing IP networks, but standards bodies have not finalized specifications for all of the IP protocols. As IP networks and protocols evolve and become standardized and mature, carriers hope to be able to "pick and choose" among applications and equipment from multiple vendors without being locked into products from only one supplier. They also hope to be able to modify services by, for example, adding capacity to any one of the preceding devices without changing or upgrading the rest of their equipment. The main goal is to lower the cost of adding revenue-producing applications that interoperate with existing infrastructure without costly upgrades.

Speech Recognition

According to Walt Tetschner, president of consultancy Tern Associates in Acton, Massachusetts, "The challenge for companies selling speech recognition is convincing purchasers that callers will have a better experience with speech recognition than listening to layers of menus and punching numbers using touch tone to reach an agent or department."

Speech Recognition Applications

The most widely sold applications for speech recognition are to support self-service database lookups via integrated voice response systems (IVRs). *Integrated voice response* systems enable callers to access information on computers via either touch-tone or speech commands. They promote self-service in call centers by enabling people to look up information such as bank balances without speaking to a live agent. The airline industry relies on speech recognition for callers to check flight schedule information. The integrated voice response unit in which speech recognition is embedded is linked to a database with scheduling information.

Speech recognition for directory assistance is used by a growing number of carriers to save on operator expense. When callers speak the name of the business or person they want to call, the telephone company's computer "speaks" it back to them. Many carriers now support directory assistance by first recording the name and location of the telephone number requested. An operator then greets the caller, looks up the number and directs the computer to speak the number requested to the caller. With speech recognition, no operator is required. The IVR system speaks the phone number to the caller after checking the directory database. Tellme Networks and Phonetic Systems are leaders in speech recognition systems for directory assistance services.

Overall sales of speech recognition are still low. According to Voice Information Associates, a market research firm in Acton, Massachusetts, only 159,500 ports of speech recognition were sold worldwide in 2004. Systems are expensive, and customers are not confident that they will attain an adequate return on their investment. This may change if Microsoft's announced intention to sell lower-priced speech recognition servers results in lower-priced offerings.

LocusDialog (now part of ScanSoft), Avaya Inc., Nortel Networks, and Phonetic Systems are the leading suppliers of speech recognition platforms for messaging systems. Most of these platforms use speech recognition software developed by Nuance Communications, Microsoft Corporation, and ScanSoft, Inc.

Speech recognition systems are used in the following:

- Telephone companies to save on directory assistance operators' salaries.

- Internal directories to cut down on the number of employees calling internal operators for extension numbers.

- Call centers to increase the number of customers who opt to use "self-service" rather than speak with an agent.
- Cellular telephones so that people can speak the name of the person they are dialing rather than remember the speed dial number while they are driving. This is referred to as speech-assisted dialing.
- Automated attendants in enterprise organizations such as financial services companies with many remote salespeople and first-time callers.

Applications such as prescription renewals in which people enter only numeric data work fine utilizing touch-tone without speech recognition. Entering touch numbers from a telephone is straightforward. However, when call centers need to capture a complex mix of numbers and letters, speech recognition is faster, more accurate, and more convenient.

HOW SPEECH RECOGNITION WORKS

Speech recognition works by first detecting and then capturing spoken words (utterances). It converts the captured utterances to a digital representation of the words after removing background noises. Capturing the speech and digitally representing it is done by digital signal processors (DSPs), which are high-speed specialized computer chips. The speech recognition software then breaks up the sounds into small chunks, which are easier to define than larger pieces of sound.

Next, the software compares various properties of the chunks of sound to large amounts of previously captured data. Based on these comparisons, the speech is assigned probabilities of matching particular phonemes. (Phonemes are most basic sounds such as "b" and "aw.") The software then compares phonemes with possible user responses contained in a database. The software puts together several likely responses made up of phonemes and vocabulary in the speech recognition software.

Faster computer processors are a key factor in improvements in speech recognition. Computers perform the digitization and comparisons in milliseconds. They also take into account gender differences and regional accents. Systems contain different databases of expected responses based on the application. A corporate directory has a different speech database than one for airline scheduling or lost luggage applications.

continues

How Speech Recognition Works (continued)

The following are some important improvements in speech-recognition:

- *Speaker independence.* Current systems recognize words from the general population. They are speaker independent. Previous systems needed users to "train" the system to recognize words.

- *Barge in.* Users who call frequently can interrupt system prompts and say commands or department names as soon as the system answers the phone.

- *Continuous speech.* Systems can pick out keywords when callers are speaking naturally. If a caller says, "I think I'd like my e-mail," the system picks out the word e-mail from the sentence.

VoiceXML—Linking Speech to Databases

Voice extensible Markup Language (VoiceXML) is a markup programming language. A markup language contains tags that tell how code is to be processed. Just as HTML adds tags to format Web pages, VoiceXML essentially tells integrated voice response systems what actions to take based on callers' responses to menus. It is a standard for using tags with audio prompts to describe call flow and dialog in speech recognition applications.

VoiceXML is used to create speech recognition interfaces to the Internet and to contact centers for cellular phones, landline phones, and wireless personal digital assistants. VoiceXML tags contain fields denoting actions such as if (<if>) transfer this call. The tags also identify prompts and fields that contain links that transfer calls based on callers' spoken commands. For example, depending on the application, the actions might be to look up one of the following:

- A stock price

- A directory number

- The status of an order

Speech Application Language Tags (SALT) is a Microsoft backed extension of XML. It is compatible with Web languages and lets developers insert voice tags into existing applications.

ACDs—INCREASING CALL CENTER EFFICIENCY ......

Automatic call distributors (ACDs) were created in the 1980s to substitute expensive in-person sales calls with lower cost phone calls and to provide more efficient, centralized customer service and technical support centers. Departments that used the telephone for sales calls were referred to as telemarketing departments. Automatic call distributors consist of hardware and software to manage incoming and outgoing communications with agents, particularly where there are more calls than people to answer them. Importantly, ACDs provide statistics on utilization of agents and telecommunications lines serving ACD groups. New ACDs give customer service agents the ability to respond to e-mail, facsimile, online chat, and Internet inquiries seamlessly along with telephone calls.

The main theory behind grouping agents into "pools" is that large groups of agents can handle more calls than the same number of agents organized into small groups without overflow of calls between groups. This is analogous to the U.S. Post Office using one long line for postal clerks rather than an individual line for each postal clerk. With one line (queue) for all postal workers, a clerk will be available more quickly from the pool, and the same number of clerks will help more people within a given amount of time than separate lines for each clerk.

Automatic call distributors (ACDs) perform the following functions:

- Route incoming calls to the agent that has been idle the longest.
- Route incoming calls to the appropriate agent group based on the telephone number dialed or by the customer's telephone number.
- If all agents are busy, either hold the call in a queue, route the call to an alternative group of agents, or give the caller the option to leave a voice mail message.
- Route e-mail, chat requests, and facsimile messages to agents in the same queue with incoming telephone calls.
- Dial outbound calls for agents when they have no incoming calls to answer.
- Transfer calls to call centers in any country or part of the world with adequate telecommunications facilities. Cities can be selected based on criteria such as labor availability, lower agent wages, or complementary time zones.

Callers to ACDs can recognize when they reach an ACD if they hear a message such as

"Please hold and the next available agent will take your call."

Automatic call distribution systems are sold as standalone systems and as add-on software and hardware for PBXs and key systems. The vendor with the largest installed base of standalone systems is Aspect Communications. These systems are aimed at large contact centers such as those in the airline and financial services industries. Nortel Networks and Avaya Communications have the largest installed base of PBX-based systems. Most key systems now offer ACD functionality. In addition, there are software packages on the market that provide ACD functionality through links to onsite telephone systems.

ACDs Linked to IP Telephone Systems

As the number of Voice over IP telephone systems grows, the availability of ACDs as a LAN software application will become more common. These applications will cost less than proprietary systems linked to traditional telephone systems. When IP telephony vendors implement signaling such as the session initiation protocol (SIP) uniformly, ACD systems won't need special signaling links to each type of proprietary telephone system. Signals indicate conditions such as the status of agents—for example, idle or busy or the level of telephone traffic.

ACD Functions Located in Carriers' Networks

ACD call-routing functionality is available from telephone companies as well as with onsite equipment. Network-based services generally are adjuncts to customer premises systems. Network-based call routing enhances functionality without requiring end users to purchase more sophisticated hardware or software for intersite routing. They offer a way to seamlessly route and transfer calls between sites. Network-based services route calls based on the following:

- Options callers select from a "menu" of selections ("press 1 for sales," etc.)
- The amount of traffic already sent to each location
- Parameters such as the time of day or day of the week, such as "send all calls to the west coast after 5:00 p.m. on the east coast"
- The availability of agents and trunks at each center

Selections from Menus in Carriers' Networks— Dialed Number Identification Service (DNIS)

Carriers send the three or four dialed number identification service (DNIS) digits associated with each menu selection to the onsite ACD to which the toll-free number dialed is directed. The DNIS digits identify the caller's selection so that the onsite equipment can accurately route callers to the selected group of agents. For example, DNIS digits 6611 may be associated with customer service, and DNIS digits 6622 may be associated with sales. Telephone companies generally charge enterprises a combination of a fixed fee to store menus and a usage fee for every menu selection accessed per month. Toll-free usage charges apply as well.

Contact Center Productivity— Measurements and Enhancements

Because call centers handle e-mail and chat in addition to voice calls, they are often referred to as contact centers. Contact centers are under increasing pressure to

- Justify the number of agents hired
- Increase productivity
- Improve the quality of customer service to retain and attract customers
- Manage the costs of network connections so that service is adequate but expenses are reasonable

It's a particular challenge to improve customer service when under pressure to cut labor expenses by using fewer agents. In addition, call center staff are well aware that, to save money, enterprises have closed call centers in Europe and the United States and relocated centers to Latin America, India, the Philippines, and other countries with lower labor rates.

In addition, the United States government has started a Do Not Call Registry in which, if requested, all organizations except nonprofits, banks, federal credit unions, and federal savings and loan associations may not "cold call" consumers listed on the registry who have not contacted them or been customers for 18 months. These are additional pressures on contact centers to increase efficiency.

The following are some tools available to contact centers to meet productivity goals:

- ACD reports that measure agent and network utilization
- Integrated voice response systems that provide links to computers that respond to repeat questions without agent intervention
- Speech recognition to increase self-service rates in contact centers
- Universal queues to handle e-mail, chat, and outbound and inbound telephone calls more efficiently
- Automated e-mail response systems for common e-mail requests

ACD Statistics Downloaded to PCs

Reports on real-time status of calls are the lifeblood of an ACD and are closely monitored by contact center management. Management uses these statistics to plan network design and analyze staffing requirements.

PCs connected to local area networks (LANs) download ACD statistics from automatic call distributors. Once the information is downloaded, it can be put into a spreadsheet program for sorting, long-term storage, and analysis. These statistics are organized into reports that do the following:

- Provide real-time status of incoming and outgoing ACD calls and agents on ACD supervisors' PC screens.

- Indicate usage on individual trunks so that managers will know if they have the correct number of lines and if all of the lines are operating properly and actually carrying calls.

- Show the number of calls associated with each toll-free number to indicate the response rate generated by particular ads. For example, radio, television, Internet, and print campaigns use specific toll-free numbers.

- Disclose the number of outbound calls connected and the number of e-mail and chat messages handled per agent.

- Determine the number of abandoned calls; a high number of abandoned calls is an indication that the call center is understaffed.

- Alert supervisors to unusually high or low call volumes so that staffing can be adjusted accordingly.

Customer Relationship Management (CRM)— A Customer-Centric Strategy

Customer relationship management (CRM) is a customer-centric strategy to make information about customers' past transactions accessible across the organization. CRM can comprise many elements including sales automation with automated proposals and brochures available to representatives. CRM also includes marketing tools that, for example, track the impact of direct mail, e-mail, and Internet-based campaigns. In addition, customer service with links to billing, payment status, purchase histories, open issues, and universal queues are considered part of customer relationship management. The largest provider of CRM software is Siebel Systems. Others include SAP AG, Amdocs Ltd. through its acquisition of Clarify, Oracle, and PeopleSoft, Inc.

Customer relationship management solutions are often complex, expensive undertakings and not all organizations are convinced that the returns justify the expense. Scott Nelson, vice president, distinguished analyst at Gartner, Inc., estimates that by mid-2004 40% of companies in North America and Europe have undertaken a significant implementation of automation of sales, marketing, or customer service. Few have systems that cut across all of these areas. He further states that the Internet has speeded up transactions and raised customer expectations. "Customers expect all companies to be as good as any experience they've had in all industries." For example, they expect all retailers to replicate the positive experiences they've had at Amazon and Lands End.

Integrated Voice Response Units— Self Service in Contact Centers

Voice response units (VRUs) provide information to callers based on touch-tone or spoken commands they use to query computers. For example, people call their bank or credit card company to find out their balance or to learn if a payment has been received. They enter their account number and personal identification number when prompted by an electronic voice. The voice response unit "speaks" back the requested information.

Companies justify the expense of speech recognition and voice response units because they need fewer people to speak with live agents. (The terms "integrated voice response" and "voice response" are used interchangeably.)

Voice response units (see Figure 2.9) enable organizations to provide round-the-clock information to callers without having to pay overtime wages. Manufacturers of voice response systems are Edify, InterVoice-Brite, Phillips through its purchase of Voice Control Systems, Syntellect, and Periphonics, which is owned by Nortel Networks. The following are examples of short, simple transactions in which voice response technology is used:

- Cable television, to select pay-per-view movies
- Newspapers, to enable subscribers to stop and start papers for vacations and report no delivery of newspapers
- Mutual fund companies, for trades and account balances
- Airlines (those with speech recognition capability), for callers to hear flight information
- Organizations, so that employees can learn about health and pension benefits
- Universities, for registration and grade reporting

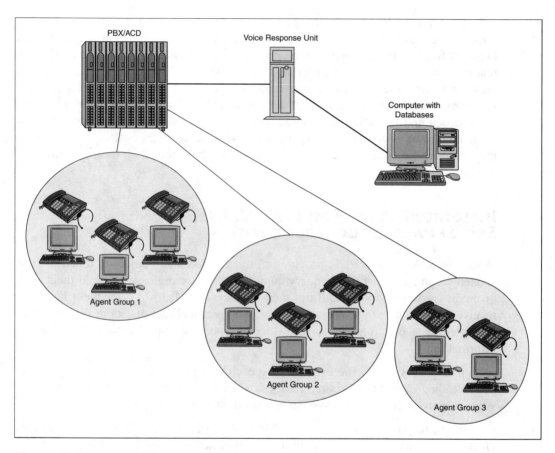

Figure 2.9
Integrated voice response system linked to a   computer and an ACD.

Speech Recognition in Contact Centers—Increase Self-Service Rates

In an effort to increase the self-service success rate, many call centers are adding speech recognition to their integrated voice response platforms to make them more user friendly and faster to navigate. For example, financial services companies ask callers to speak the name of the stock or mutual for which they would like a quote. Toll-free directory services likewise ask callers to speak the name of the company for which they require a toll-free number. Local telephone companies use speech recognition so that customers can easily obtain billing information.

Voice portals connect to or are part of integrated voice response systems. They contain speech dialogues, which are scripts written using VoiceXML. (Refer to the section on VoiceXML earlier in this chapter.)

Computer Telephony Integration (CTI)— Routing Callers More Intelligently

Computer telephony integration (CTI) was first available in the late 1980s. CTI software is referred to as *middleware* because it translates signals between telephone systems and computers so that they can coordinate routing calls and account information to agents. CTI software must be customized for each different telephone system. Genesys Labs has more than 80 versions of CTI customized for different telephone systems. CTI enables the following:

- Routing calls to agents based on the caller's telephone number or digits he or she enters into integrated voice response systems, such as an account number along with the customer's transaction history

- Notifying the organization's computers to send the customer's record to the agent handling the call

- Transferring the customer's record and information on the agent's screen along with calls between representatives

The motivation for installing these usually expensive systems is to save agent time. Having the account information on the screen, a "screen pop," when the telephone call arrives saves 10 to 20 seconds per call. It is also a way to connect other ACD systems to proprietary telephone systems.

The caller's identification can be delivered to an ACD in two different ways:

- Directly from the telephone carrier when the call is received on trunks that capture callers' phone numbers. This functionality is called *automatic number identification (ANI)*.

- From voice response systems in which callers are asked to enter, for example, their account number.

The IVR sends the account information or telephone number to the computer, which sends account information to the PC of the agent who receives the call. All of the communications between the network and the computer, and the computer and the telephone system are translated by the CTI links. Both the ACD and the computer are connected to the LAN. Software in the CTI application is called an *application programming interface (API)*. APIs are an interface or "middleware" between unlike devices.

Universal Queues—Managing E-mail, Chat, and Inbound and Outbound Telephone Calls

Universal queues provide contact centers with the capability to respond to and manage customer contacts in the form of e-mail, telephone calls, and chat.

Contact centers need to find ways to do the following:

- Confirm Internet-originated orders and repair reports
- Perform customer service (such as returns, credits, exchanges) for Internet inquiries
- Use document sharing to guide customers through Web pages and filling out online forms including customer satisfaction surveys
- Send an outbound call dialed by an autodialer to an agent who is not active on a call
- Conduct text-based chats with online customers in real time

Universal queues provide one integrated queue and management reports for e-mail, fax messages, voice calls, and chat messages. Figure 2.10 illustrates a configuration using queue management software linked to e-mail servers and ACDs. Universal queue applications from organizations other than the ACD manufacturer are linked to the ACD using CTI software.

Because of the different skills involved in writing versus talking to customers, most organizations use a particular set of agents to respond to e-mail and chat and other agents for inbound and outbound phone calls. However, having software from one vendor allows enterprises to manage and analyze service levels using one set of reports. Real-time and historical reports monitor and track calling and response time. If they are integrated with back-office systems, they can track revenue per transaction. In addition, at certain times of day, e-mail traffic can overflow to agents that handle mostly telephone calls.

On new IP-based ACD systems, the middleware used is based mainly on Java programming language applets. An applet is a small application. The advantage of Java is that it was designed for the Web with the goal of being able to run on any computer operating system. At this time, IP-based ACD and telephone systems still run proprietary signaling. Therefore, the Java telephony application programming interface (JTAPI) still needs to be customized per system with which it interfaces.

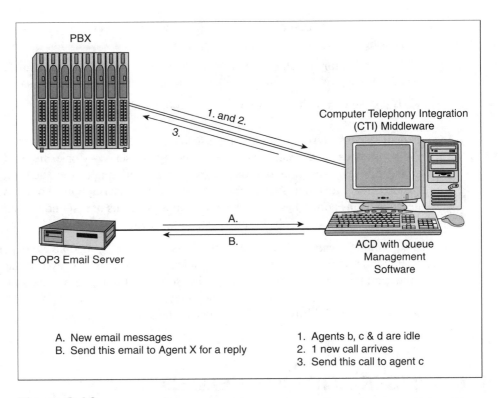

Figure 2.10
Queue management software linked to an e-mail server   and PBX.

A. New email messages
B. Send this email to Agent X for a reply

1. Agents b, c & d are idle
2. 1 new call arrives
3. Send this call to agent c

E-mail Response Management Software

E-mail response management software can be used independently or as part of universal queue software. E-mail response management software installed on organizations' servers routes e-mail messages to agents by topic, subject, and content or, if appropriate, automatically responds to the e-mail. Natural language software for written language is capable of interpreting and extracting concepts in e-mail messages. It can link phrases in a meaningful way. Egain Communications Corporation, Genesys Labs, KANA Software, and Primus Knowledge Solutions supply e-mail management software.

E-mail response management systems do the following:

- Route e-mail to a representative trained on the topic in the subject line, sender line, and e-mail content
- Create reports based on the number of messages received, by message subject, date, and content

- Create reports based on response times to answer e-mail and chat messages

- Respond automatically to the e-mail based on a natural language analysis of the intent of the e-mail as well as keywords included in the message

- Track the number of e-mail messages replied to by each agent

E-mail response systems communicate with e-mail servers in near real time, every 15 or 30 seconds using the same protocol as the e-mail server—for example, POP3, MAPI, and SMTP. They pull out messages to managed mailboxes such as those addressed to generic functions such as info@company.com, techsupport@company.com, and sales@company.com. They route them to groups of agents or respond to them with an automatic reply based on subject, message, and content.

In a similar manner, Web chat pulls messages sent by people who perhaps selected a contact me now button on the organization's Web site. They use the same protocol to pull the messages as that on the chat server. With both the e-mail and Web chat software, a CTI (or in the case of IP telephony, a JTAPI) interface provides information on agent availability and skill level to handle the chat session or e-mail message.

MEDIA: FIBER AND UNSHIELDED TWISTED PAIR COPPER ....

The copper, coaxial cable, fiber optics, and airwaves that carry voice, multimedia, and data traffic are referred to as media. Characteristics of media have a direct bearing on the speed, accuracy, and distance at which traffic can be carried. For example, thin copper wiring carries data more slowly than thicker, higher quality copper. Fiber carries vastly more traffic than copper. It is used for high-speed Internet, local area networks, and carrier networks.

Unshielded twisted pair (UTP) is the most prevalent medium used to link computers, printers, and servers in corporate networks to wiring closets on the same floor. This is referred to as the horizontal plant. Fiber, which is more expensive to install than twisted pair, is generally used in high-traffic areas such as connections between wiring closets, floors (the risers), and buildings in campuses.

Fiber exhibits superior performance because it is a non-electric medium. Because it is non-electric it does not, as copper does, act like an antenna and pick up noise and interference. Systems that improve the capacity of fiber are called *wavelength division multiplexing.* Two types of wavelength division are *dense wavelength division multiplexing (DWDM)* and *coarse wavelength division multiplexing (CWDM).*

Impairments on Copper Cabling— Electrical Properties

Copper cabling's electrical properties are the key factors that limit its performance by creating resistance and interference. Resistance causes signals to weaken the farther they are transmitted. This is why signals on copper cabling in the outside network need to be boosted on cable runs of over about one and a half miles.

Interference from signals such as copiers, magnetic sources, manufacturing devices, and radio stations can introduce noise into the transmission. It is not uncommon for office and residential users to complain that they can hear a nearby radio station's programming on their telephone calls.

Within homes and businesses, crosstalk is another example of "leaking" electrical transmissions. In homes with two lines, a person speaking on one line often can hear the faint conversation on the other line. Current from one pair of wires has "leaked" into the other wire. One way in which copper cabling is protected from crosstalk and noise introduced from nearby wires is by twisting each separately insulated copper wire of a two-wire pair. Noise induced into one wire of the twisted pair cancels an equal amount of noise induced in the other wire of the pair. Twisted pair copper cabling is used from

- Telephone sets to PBX common equipment
- Telephone sets to key systems common equipment
- PCs to the wiring closet of a LAN
- Homes to the nearest telephone company equipment

Structured Cabling Standards—To Uniformly Support Higher Speeds on Copper Cabling

Cabling standards have been created to support ever-higher speeds, to carry multimedia traffic, and to ensure that organizations can purchase cabling and connectors from diverse manufacturers whose products interoperate with each other. Each cabling standard includes defined tests that should be performed when cabling is installed to make sure that the cable and all the connectors perform up to the specifications.

Every new standard is compatible with all lower standards. Thus, applications that operated over lower category cabling systems are able to operate on higher categories as well. The biggest problems organizations have with cabling systems are that they are not always installed and tested properly to meet cabling standards. This results in either lower-than-expected data rates or inconsistent reliability.

Each of the standards in the following section is for a structured cabling system. They specify not only cabling but also all of the connections including jacks (outlets), plugs, and cross-connects in wiring closets. *Cross-connects* in wiring closets provide outlets on each floor where cabling from individual devices is connected. The floor cabling, referred to as the horizontal plant, is connected to the riser plant, cabling between floors. It is also connected to other buildings within a campus in the building's main wiring closet. Standards also specify the network interface card (NIC) in printers and computers to which a cable connects the device to the jack (outlet).

Prior to publication of higher category standards, manufacturers make their own pre-standard version of cabling systems available. The Telecommunications Industry Association/Electronics Industry Association (TIA/EIA) rates twisted pair cabling and connection components used inside buildings.

Copper Cabling Standards—Categories

The following sections describe common cabling systems standards.

Category 5 Unshielded Twisted Pair—Speeds up to 100 Megabits

In 1992, standards were published for Category 5 unshielded twisted pair for data transmitted at 100 megabits per second (Mbps). Category 5 is the most common twisted pair cabling used within buildings for data, and it consists of four pairs, eight wires of unshielded copper wires. Category 5 is commonly referred to as Cat 5. Category 3 unshielded twisted pair is rated as suitable for voice transmission.

Category 5e Unshielded Twisted Pair— One Gigabit at Short Distances

Category 5e was approved in May 2001. It is an enhanced version of Category 5 cabling for unshielded twisted pair. It was developed in response to the need for higher-speed gigabit services on enterprise internal networks. Cat 5e supports higher speeds because the cabling and connectors are manufactured to higher standards. For example, there are more twists per inch in the cabling than that specified for Category 5.

Category 6 Unshielded Twisted Pair

The TIA/EIA approved Category 6 cabling in June 2002 and specified that it can carry data at gigabit speed for a distance of 100 meters (328 feet). At shorter distances, it handles 10-gigabit applications. Category 6 cabling costs about 30% more than Category 5e cabling. Category 6 products achieve higher speeds because of the following improvements:

- A higher twist rate and heavier cabling
- More precise testing specifications for impairments such as crosstalk and jitter, which is uneven electrical changes
- A metallic screen around the entire cable to protect it from ambient noise
- Insulation material (usually plastic strips) placed between each of the four pairs to reduce crosstalk between the wires (see Figure 2.11)
- Higher quality connectors such as jacks and patch panels

Category 7—To Support 10 Gigabit-Per-Second Speeds

Standards boards are considering Category 7 standards for even higher performance on twisted pair copper cabling at longer distances. Category 7 may specify an overall metal foil shield around the entire cable plus shielding around each pair of wires. Components and connectors would be required that accommodate this shielding.

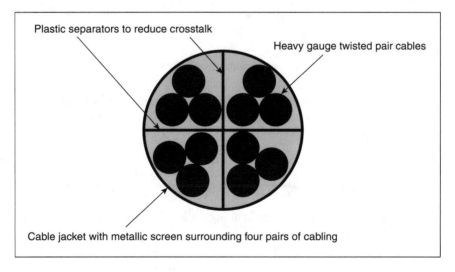

Figure 2.11
Cross section of Category 6 cabling.

Fiber-Optic Cabling—
High Capacity, Decreasing Costs

Because it is non-electric, fiber can be run in areas without regard to interference from electrical equipment. Signals are transmitted in the form of off and on light pulses similar to a flashlight. The following are some benefits of fiber:

- *Security.* Fiber is resistant to taps and does not emit electromagnetic signals; therefore, to tap into fiber strands, the strands have to be physically broken and listening devices spliced into the break. These splices are easily detected.

- *Small size.* Less duct space is required; individual strands of fiber are the diameter of a length of hair. Duct size is significant under city streets where underground conduit is often filled with old copper cables.

- *High bandwidth.* Fiber is suitable for high-speed transmission services in carriers' backbones.

- *Low attenuation.* Less fading or weakening of signals over distances means fewer amplifiers are needed to boost the signals.

- *The absence of sparking hazards.* There is less danger of fire in flammable areas.

- *Low weight.* Single conductor fiber weighs nine times less than coaxial cable.

The following are some disadvantages of fiber-optic cabling:

- More care is required in handling fiber. Fiber is not as flexible as twisted pair in bending around corners, and specifications for fiber connections are more exacting.

- Local power is required when fiber is brought into buildings from telephone companies or to the curb in residential areas. This adds a point of vulnerability in the event of a power outage.

- Specialized technicians paid at higher levels are required to work with and test fiber cabling.

Individual organizations often use fiber cabling

- For the riser between floors within a building portion of their networks. The extra labor expense of laying fiber, however, is usually not justified to individual users and devices on LANs.
- In campus environments, for cable runs between buildings.

Although some telephone companies have announced plans to deploy fiber to homes, most telephone networks use fiber everywhere except the last mile connection to residential and small and some medium-size business customers. Because of the drop in costs for fiber and fiber components, some telephone companies now bring fiber to premises in new developments because of its capability to support video as well as voice and data.

Telephone companies also use fiber because they can lay fewer strands of fiber in less space than heavier copper, which requires many more pairs to achieve the same capacity as fiber-optic cabling. Moreover, signals can travel farther, in the range of 60 miles, on fiber without the use of amplifiers to strengthen a faded signal. The requirement for fewer amplifiers translates into lower maintenance costs: There are fewer amplifiers to break down.

Other places that carriers use fiber are between the following:

- Central offices in local telephone company networks
- Telecommunications providers and enterprises
- Offices and neighborhood wire centers
- Cellular towers and mobile central offices
- Cellular networks and landline networks
- Continents via undersea cables, such as the cable between Asia and India
- Cable TV headends and neighborhood coaxial cable wire centers (see Figure 2.12)
- Electric utility networks and power stations

Fiber-optic cabling is made of ultra-pure strands of glass. It carries on and off light pulses over the central core of the fiber. The narrower the core, the faster and farther a light signal can travel without errors and repeaters. The cladding surrounding the core keeps the light contained within the core to prevent the light signal from *dispersing* (that is, spreading over time with wavelengths reaching their destination at different times). Finally, there is a coating that protects the fiber from environmental hazards such as rain, dust, scratches, and snow.

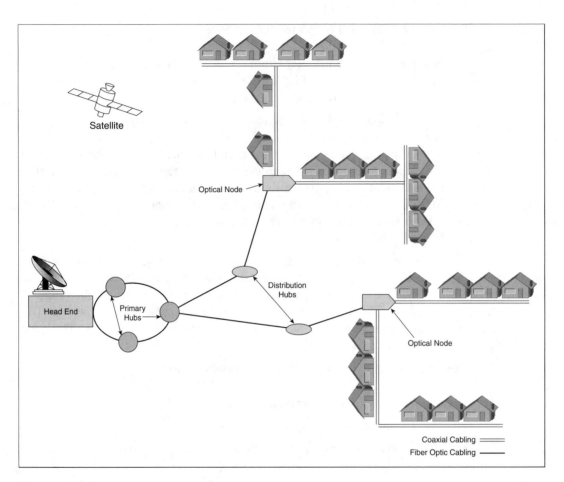

Figure 2.12
Fiber optics in cable TV networks.

Single-Mode Fiber—Smaller Is Faster and More Expensive

There are two main types of fiber: single mode and multimode. Single-mode fiber is smaller, more expensive, and supports higher speeds than multimode fiber. Single-mode fiber is the diameter of a strand of hair. Single-mode fiber-optic cabling is used mainly in carrier networks and in undersea cabling.

The fact that single-mode fiber carries light pulses faster than multimode fiber can be explained by the geometric rule: A straight line is the shortest distance between two points. Light travels faster in a straight line than if it zigzags along a path. These zigzag paths also cause the signals to attenuate, lose power, and fade over shorter distances. Similarly, the small core of single-mode fiber keeps the light signal from bouncing across the diameter of the core of the fiber. Thus, the light signal travels faster and has less attenuation than if it had a more "bouncy" ride through the core.

Because it travels in a straighter line, the light pulses go farther without attenuation, or weakening. Thus, fewer repeaters are needed to boost the signal. Single-mode fiber can be run for 60 miles without the use of a repeater. In contrast, signals on copper cabling needs to be repeated after approximately 1.5 miles. This is the reason telephone companies originally used fiber for outside plant (cabling) with cable runs longer than 2 kilometers, or 1.24 miles.

The main factor in the increased expense of single-mode fiber is the cost to manufacture more exact connectors for patch panels and other devices. The core is so small that connections and splices need to be done in a more precise manner than with multimode fiber. If fiber connections on single-mode fiber do not match cores exactly, the light will not be transmitted from one fiber to another. It will leak or disperse out of the core at the splice. A *splice* is a connection between cables.

Multimode fiber has a wider core than single-mode fiber. Because of its wider core, signals travel a shorter distance before they require amplification. In addition, fewer channels can be carried per fiber pair when it is multiplexed because the signals disperse, spreading more across the fiber core. Multimode fiber is used mainly for LAN backbones between buildings on campuses and between floors of buildings.

Another factor in the expense of installing fiber cabling systems is the lack of standardization of connectors for fiber cabling systems. Different manufacturers require specialized tools and connectors for their fiber systems. Two of the main connectors are the *Straight Tip (ST)* and the *Subscriber Connector (SC)*. Another is the *Small Form Factor (SFF)* connector. Each type of connector requires specialized tools for installation.

Dense Wavelength Division Multiplexing (DWDM)

Dense wavelength division multiplexing is a multiplexing technique that enables single strands of fiber to carry multiple channels of voice, video, and data. The importance of dense wavelength division multiplexing (DWDM) cannot be exaggerated. It is a key technology for enabling carriers to add capacity without laying more fiber. It is an important part of the infrastructure for voice, high-speed data, and video.

Early implementations of dense wavelength division multiplexing (DWDM) carried eight channels over a single strand of fiber. New multiplexers now handle 160 channels. The larger capacity achieved over a single pair of fiber-optic cabling is a key factor in the drastically lowered cost of bandwidth.

DWDM provides the following additional advantages:

- Lower costs to upgrade networks because multiplexed speeds of up to 10 gigabits per channel can be achieved by changing electronics but reusing old fiber cabling (newer fiber supports higher speeds)
- Space savings in service providers' networks because less amplifying equipment is required
- Lower ongoing maintenance expenses in carriers' networks because less equipment is required

Dense wavelength division multiplexers work like prisms, separating out colors into different beams that are carried on the fiber. Dense wavelength division multiplexing divides the light stream into multiple frequencies called *colors*. Each color or shade is carried at a different frequency. In addition, *passbands*, unused channels of frequency between channels, ensure that signals in different channels don't interfere with each other. (Refer to Chapter 1 for an explanation of frequencies.) Individual wavelengths also are called *lambdas*.

Coarse Wavelength Division Multiplexing—A Lower-Cost Way to Expand Fiber Capacity

Coarse wavelength division multiplexing (CWDM) is a lower-cost fiber-optic multiplexing set of standards approved by the International Telecommunications Union (ITU). It is used to carry up to eight channels of voice, data, and video over one pair of fiber-optic cabling at 1.25-gigabit-per-second speeds. It is one way that cable TV operators add capacity for video-on-demand, Internet access, and Voice over IP service in high-usage neighborhoods. Whereas dense wavelength division multiplexing is used in core, backbone, and metropolitan networks on longer cable runs, coarse wavelength division multiplexing is used in the portions of the network closer to customers, the last mile or access network for shorter cable runs.

Some large customers lay their own fiber or lease dark fiber from providers to connect buildings in metropolitan areas. They use coarse wavelength division multiplexing (CWDM) from vendors such as Cisco, which includes multiplexing gear in switches and routers so that customers can derive multiple 1.25-gigabit channels on a single fiber pair. One application for CWDM in organizations is for major hospitals that connect storage area networks (SANs) containing MRIs and other diagnostic images, clinical research files, and patient records to radiology and clinical offices over large metropolitan areas.

Coarse wavelength division multiplexing components cost less than dense wavelength division multiplexing to manufacture because requirements are less precise.

Therefore, each transmitter and receiver costs less than those used per channel in dense wavelength division multiplexing. In addition, coarse wavelength division multiplexing is passive. The optical lenses in CWDM require no electricity to filter out channels of light, each of which carries a separate stream of voice, video, or data.

Coarse Wavelength Division Multiplexing in Cable TV Networks—Maximizing Dark Fiber

CWDM is used to maximize the available dark fiber and avoid the labor-intensive effort of laying new fiber. *Dark fiber* is unused fiber installed in outside networks without gear such as transmitters, receivers, and multiplexers connected to it. Coarse wavelength division multiplexing is an option for cable providers who want to add capacity but are running out of dark fiber.

In cable TV networks, up to 1,000 homes share the bandwidth of coaxial cabling strung in neighborhoods. However, these networks become congested as cable operators add Internet access, video-on-demand, and Voice over IP services. To increase capacity, operators might divide a 1,000-home network into four networks of 250 homes each or two network clusters of 500 homes each.

They do this by adding electronics to dark fiber. This fiber is then referred to as *lit fiber*. The fiber pairs are located between fiber distribution hubs. Distribution hubs extend fiber closer to customers and are terminated at optical nodes. Optical nodes are connected to coaxial cabling. At optical nodes, transmitters and receivers convert light signals to electrical signals compatible with the coax and vice versa. If there is a shortage of dark fiber, coarse wavelength division multiplexing is added between fiber hubs and optical nodes so that one fiber pair can serve multiple nodes, clusters of homes (see Figure 2.13).

To increase their customer base, cable TV operators offer telecommunications service over fiber connections to large and medium commercial organizations such as government buildings, hospitals, and universities. To bring fiber to enterprises, they lay new fiber from a splice in their fiber to the customer. Coarse wavelength division multiplexing enables a splice (connection) at one fiber pair to feed fiber to up to eight commercial sites.

Wavelength Division Multiplexing (WDM) Components

Connecting fiber to copper lines requires converters called transmitters and receivers to convert electrical signals to light pulses. Each channel of light requires its own

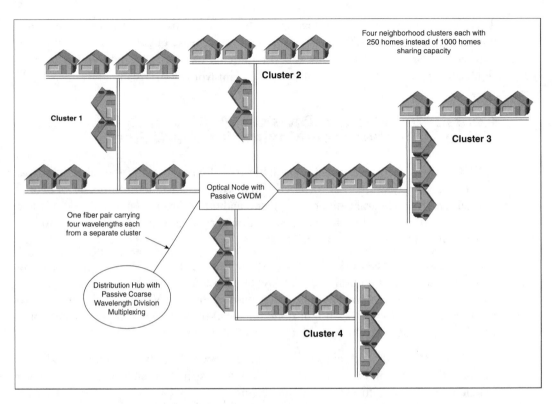

Four neighborhood clusters each with
250 homes instead of 1000 homes
sharing capacity

Cluster 2

Cluster 1

Cluster 3

Optical Node with
Passive CWDM

One fiber pair carrying
four wavelengths each
from a separate cluster

Distribution Hub with
Passive Coarse
Wavelength Division
Multiplexing

Cluster 4

Figure 2.13
Coarse wavelength division multiplexing (CWDM) in cable TV networks.

receiver and transmitter. Transmitters also are called light source transducers. Transmitters in fiber-optic systems are either light emitting diodes or lasers:

- Light-emitting diodes (LEDs) cost less than lasers.

  LEDs are commonly used with multimode fiber.

- Lasers provide more power.

  Less amplification, or boosting, is needed over long distances.

  One laser is required per wavelength.

At the receiving end, the light detector transducers (receivers) that change light pulses into electrical signals are either positive intrinsic negatives (PINs) or avalanche photodiodes (APDs). LEDs and PINs are used in applications with lower bandwidth and shorter distance requirements. Once a length of fiber is in place, upgrades in multiplexing technology enable the embedded fiber to carry additional channels at higher speeds.

Amplifiers and Regenerators

Amplifiers and regenerators are key components of DWDM networks. Amplifiers boost the signals, and multiplexers combine light from multiple sources onto a single strand of fiber.

- Optical amplifiers are spaced approximately 60 miles apart from each other with single-mode fiber. The amplifier boosts the signal, which loses strength as it travels over distances. (In a voice conversation, voice signals sound softer when they lose strength and need to be amplified.) With optical amplifiers, optical signals don't have to be converted back to electrical signals to be regenerated. This eliminates the need for equipment to convert the light signals to electrical signals and vice versa.

- Regenerators are placed approximately every 1,500 miles. They *multiplex* (combine) and *demultiplex* (separate out) the optical signals. The signals are converted from optical to electrical signals for functions such as electrical clocking, noise removal, and error checking. The multiplexers concatenate the signals, a technical term for putting the signals into the correct sequence so that they appear as one continuous stream. Concatenation is used in video and voice to avoid disruptions.

The increased capacity of DWDM is one factor in the bandwidth glut that now exists in carriers' backbone, city-to-city networks. The benefit is that prices on these routes are continuing to decline.

Appendix

Table 2.1   Protocols and Services for Speech Recognition and VoIP

Protocol or Service	Description
	802.1pq is used to tag certain virtual LAN traffic to indicate that it is part of a special group. For example, it might tag voice packets to segregate voice packets for special treatment and monitoring. It also contains bits that identify the packet's priority level.
CoS	Class of service provides priority to particular types of traffic. For example, voice or video can be designated with higher priority than voice mail.

continues

Table 2.1   Protocols and Services for Speech Recognition and VoIP   (continued)

Protocol or Service	Description
DoS	Denial of service attacks occur when hackers attempt to disrupt communications by bombarding endpoints or proxies with packets.
G.711	G.711 is used to compress voice at 64,000 bits per second plus a 6- to 21-kilobit header for Voice over IP services. It produces good voice quality but uses more network capacity than other compression techniques. This technique requires 60 milliseconds to process and "look ahead" (check the route).
G.723.1	G.723.1 is a compression protocol that uses small packets with 6.3-kilobit-per-second compression. Small packets are more efficient than large ones in terms of bandwidth use. With the header, total bandwidth is about 16 kilobits per second. Introduces some delay but less than G.711.
G.729	G.729 is a voice compression standard used in Voice over IP. It compresses voice from 64,000 bits per seconds to 8,000 bits per second. The header brings the total bandwidth to about 18,000 bits per second.
H.323	A family of signaling standards for multimedia transmissions over packet networks adopted by the International Telecommunications Union (ITU). Microsoft Corporation and Intel Corporation adopted the standard in 1996 for sending voice over packet networks. H.323 includes standards for compressing calls and for signaling. It has higher overhead than the newer signaling protocol, SIP.
Presence theft	The impersonation of a legitimate IP telephone or other device by a hacker.
Proxy server	A proxy server screens communications between endpoints to ensure that the called and calling parties are who they say they are and that no virus will be sent. For example, a proxy server might sit between a Voice over IP server and external devices that request an audio conference or videoconference session. This is referred to as intermediating sessions. Proxy servers are also used between IP telephones and the Internet.

Table 2.1 Protocols and Services for Speech Recognition and VoIP   (continued)

Protocol or Service	Description
RTP	Realtime transport protocol is an Internet Engineering Task Force (IETF) standardized protocol for transmitting multimedia in IP networks. RTP is used for the "bearer" channels, the actual voice, video, and image content. SIP is commonly used for the signaling to set up and tear down sessions.
SCCP	Skinny client control protocol is a Cisco proprietary signaling protocol for sending signals between devices in Cisco telephone systems. It is also referred to as Cisco Skinny.
SIP	Session initiation protocol establishes sessions over IP networks such as those for telephone calls, audio conferencing, click-to-dial from the Web, and instant message exchanges between devices. It is also used to link IP telephones from different manufacturers to SIP-compatible IP telephone systems. It is used in landline and mobile networks.
QoS	Quality of service guarantees a particular level of service. To meet these guarantees, service providers or IT staff members allocate bandwidth for certain types of traffic.

Part II

Industry Overview and Public Networks

3 Industry Overview

In this chapter:

The Modified Final Judgment, also known as Divestiture, deregulated long distance services via a Justice Department–negotiated antitrust settlement with AT&T. The 1984 Divestiture, which was approved by Judge Harold Green, separated AT&T from the local Bell Operating Companies (BOCs). It was enacted to ensure that local telephone companies provided the same quality connections to AT&T's competitors, other interexchange carriers, as they offered AT&T. These connections spurred competition in long distance services by ensuring smooth transport of calls between long distance networks and local homes and businesses. Divestiture further mandated that AT&T's 22 former local Bell Operating Companies be merged into seven newly created Regional Bell Operating Companies (RBOCs).

Following Divestiture, interexchange carriers competed for long distance service, but the government limited local calling to the Bell telephone companies because it felt that it was not technologically feasible for competitors to build facilities on the large scale required to serve the millions of local customers. Local competition in telecommunications emerged in the late 1980s in the form of competitive access providers. Competitive access providers (CAPs) initially provided fiber-optic links between customers in major metropolitan areas and interstate long distance providers. These links connected long distance vendors to local customers to avoid the hefty access fees charged by local telephone companies to long distance carriers. Having fiber-optic links in place in major metropolitan areas enabled CAPs to expand their offerings. They became competitive local exchange carriers (CLECs) and started offering additional services, leveraging their investment in fiber-optic cabling.

The Telecommunications Act of 1996 allowed all telephone carriers, utilities, and cable TV companies to sell both local and long distance calling. It also deregulated cable television. Prior to the Telecommunications Act, in most states, interexchange carriers (IXCs) such as AT&T, MCI, and Sprint were allowed to sell only long distance services, and local telephone companies were restricted to local services. When Congress passed the Telecommunications Act, many legislators thought competition would promote development of new high-speed services. Long distance carriers lobbied for the Telecommunications Act in hopes of expanding sales of local services. Bell telephone companies lobbied for passage as a way to offer long distance and data services on an interstate basis. In contrast to Divestiture, the Telecommunications Act of 1996 did not mandate that the local telephone companies form separate companies to supply connections to companies that competed with them. Rather, the RBOCs were expected to provide discounted access to their competitors. This has been a major factor inhibiting competition for local service.

Following passage of the Telecommunications Act of 1996, the seven RBOCs decreased in number to four. Interexchange carrier Qwest purchased US West, and all the others except BellSouth formed mergers with each other. In addition, SBC and Verizon each purchased large, independent, incumbent telephone companies. Verizon bought the largest independent telephone company, GTE, and SBC bought Southern New England Telecommunications (SNET). SNET was the incumbent telephone company in Connecticut. (Independent phone companies are incumbent telephone companies not previously owned by the Bell system.)

In the years immediately following passage of the Telecommunications Act, CLECs emerged as the most viable competitors to the RBOCs. They sell data services, Internet access, and local toll calling to business and residential customers, although most of their sales are to business customers. Competitive local exchange carriers mainly route calls over facilities that they buy at a discount from local telecommunications companies and also over their own fiber-optic and wireless facilities. They have, in essence, become a combination of local exchange carrier (LEC), interexchange exchange carrier, and data communications providers. Interestingly, when RBOCs sell service outside of their home territories, they are considered CLECs. SBC's subsidiary SBC IP, which sells Voice over IP, is an example of this.

In attempts to weaken the Telecommunications Act, the Regional Bell Operating Companies challenged various aspects in the courts. Until 2004, the courts denied the validity of these challenges. In 2004, the U.S. Circuit Court for Washington, D.C. struck down most of the FCC's most recent ruling on discounts applied to interconnecting to RBOC networks. They also struck down individual state utility commissions' authority to set many discounted rates. The circuit court ordered the FCC to issue new rules on these discounts. The new rulings weakened CLECs by increasing costs to lease facilities from incumbents. Most CLECs are currently operating at a loss.

Losses on the regulatory front as well as low prices and shrinking profit margins for long distance services were major factors in AT&T's and MCI's decisions to be acquired. The announced purchases of AT&T by SBC and MCI's likely purchase by Verizon will give these Regional Bell Operating Companies instant national sales forces and a worldwide infrastructure capable of carrying enterprise voice and data traffic and providing services such as Internet access and Web page hosting. Competition for Internet access, local lines, and long distance services will in the future be between providers that offer wireless as well as wireline access to broadband networks.

The viability of Voice over IP, improvements in wireless coverage, and new technology over utilities' fiber infrastructure hold promise for more choices for residential and commercial customers. This competition, now in its infancy, from different technologies is called intermodal competition. In particular, cable TV providers are expected to be a formidable force because of their large customer base and high-capacity cabling to homes. In addition, new forms of wireless technology will enable fixed and mobile high-speed Internet access and local services.

Events described here illustrate the enormous influence that regulatory issues have on the industry. However, currently regulations often apply differently to cable

TV, Voice over IP, wireless, and wireline services. Creating consistent rulings that protect national interest in a strong infrastructure and that also promote fair competition is critical. Supporting industry growth is a major challenge that impacts residential and enterprise customers, carriers, and economic development.

THE BELL SYSTEM AFTER THE 1984 DIVESTITURE ...

Prior to 1984, AT&T had a near monopoly on local and long distance telephone service in the United States. The first major competitive drive against AT&T was launched in the 1960s by MCI, which utilized microwave to provide voice and data service. Microwave enabled MCI to offer service without the labor-intensive task of laying cable. In 1984, the Divestiture ruling officially sanctioned competition for long distance.

Divestiture of the Bell System from AT&T in 1984

Divestiture, also known as the Modified Final Judgment, mandated the separation of AT&T from its 22 local telephone companies, but local telephone service remained a monopoly. Prior to 1984, the Bell system consisted of 22 local Bell telephone companies that were owned by AT&T. *Customers had one point of contact for all of their telecommunications requirements.* AT&T did all of the following:

- Sold local, interstate, and international long distance
- Manufactured and sold central office switches, customer premises telephone systems, electronics, and consumer telephones
- Provided yellow and white page telephone directories

Long distance carriers such as MCI and Sprint only carried traffic between states. They had no lines to individual homes and businesses. They depended on connections that they leased from local Bell telephone companies to carry calls from their equipment to customers. Without these connections, they not could reach their customers. Access to AT&T's local telephone companies by competitive carriers such as Sprint is illustrated in Figure 3.1.

By 1974, so many complaints had been filed with the Justice Department by long distance competitors about lack of cooperation in supplying connections to local phone companies that the Justice Department filed an antitrust suit against AT&T. The Justice Department dropped the suit in 1982 in return for AT&T's agreement to develop a plan to divest itself of its local phone companies. AT&T ironically chose to keep the long

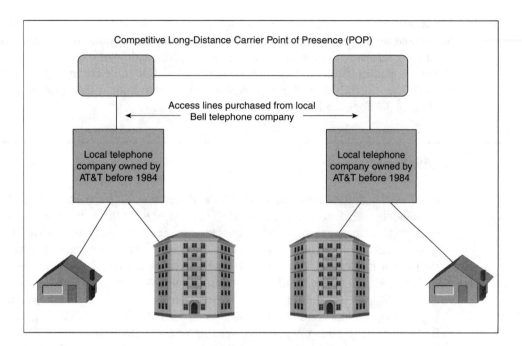

Figure 3.1
Interconnection for local access .

distance portion of their organization, which they saw as more lucrative, and spun off their 22 local telephone companies, which were organized into seven Regional Bell Operating Companies (RBOCs):

- Ameritech (now part of SBC Communications)
- Bell Atlantic (now part of Verizon Communications)
- BellSouth
- NYNEX (now Verizon Communications)
- Pacific Telesis (now part of SBC Communications)
- Southwestern Bell Communications (now SBC Communications)
- US West (now Qwest Communications International Inc.)

After Divestiture, the seven Regional Bell Operating Companies (RBOCs) retained the Bell logo and the right to sell local and toll service within local areas. They also retained the lucrative white and yellow page directory markets. However, they were denied the right to manufacture equipment or sell interstate long distance. A centralized organization, Bellcore, owned jointly by the RBOCs, was formed. This centralized organization had two functions: It was a central point for National Security and Emergency Preparedness, and it was a technical resource for the local telephone companies. Bellcore has since been renamed Telcordia Technologies, Inc. and in 1997 was purchased by Science Applications International Corporation (SAIC). See Figure 3.2 for each RBOC's territory.

LATAs Defined

In 1984, in conjunction with Divestiture, the Justice Department created local access and transport areas (LATAs) . LATAs define the contiguous geographic areas in which local Bell telephone companies were allowed to sell local and long distance services. Interexchange carriers and competitive local exchange carriers (CLECs) carried calls between the 197 LATAs. Local exchange carriers were allowed to carry calls within LATAs. States with small populations, such as Maine, Alaska, and Wyoming, are made up of one LATA. Thus, Qwest (formerly US West), the Bell company serving Wyoming, was allowed to provide long distance to all sites within Wyoming. California has eleven LATAs, and New York State has eight. Calls between LATAs in California were handed off to interexchange carriers, as were those between LATAs in New York State.

Now that RBOCs have Federal Communications Commission (FCC) permission to sell inter-LATA long distance, much of the concept of LATAs has lost its significance except for billing. Telephone companies often rate their intrastate *intra*-LATA and intrastate *inter*-LATA calls differently.

The Decline of AT&T

AT&T, which at one time was the largest corporation in the world, suffered revenue declines and failed purchases following Divestiture up to the time of its proposed purchase by SBC. SBC is made up largely of AT&T's former subsidiaries.

The Further Breakup of AT&T

At Divestiture, AT&T retained the right to manufacture and sell telephone and central office systems and to sell interstate and international long distance. AT&T kept Western Electric manufacturing and Bell Labs, its research arms. AT&T sold its switching and

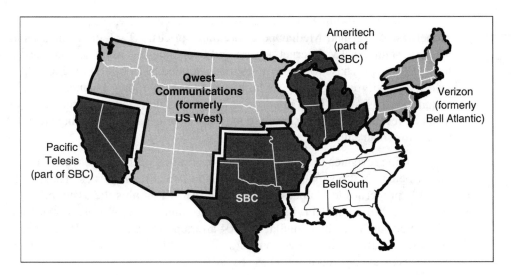

Figure 3.2
Regional Bell Operating Company territories.

data equipment to businesses and telephone companies through separate sales forces. However, it started competing for local service against its own telephone company customers in the late 1980s through its purchase of competitive access provider (CAP) Teleport. (See the section on CAPs later in this chapter.)

In 1996, to protect its central office sales and avoid being perceived as a competitor to its largest customers, AT&T spun off its customer premises, carrier sales, and manufacturing businesses. The new company was called Lucent Technologies. Lucent kept Bell Labs and Western Electric and the central office, networking, and customer premises equipment (CPE) divisions. AT&T also spun off NCR in 1996, the failing computer systems and services business it had purchased in 1991. In September 2000, Lucent spun off its customer premises business to newly formed Avaya Inc.

AT&T's Forays into Wireless and Cable TV and Its Subsequent Purchase

AT&T, which had originally developed and implemented cellular mobile service in 1984, entered cellular service by purchasing Craig McCaw's cellular assets. It bid for spectrum from the U.S. government and purchased spectrum from others as well. It spun off AT&T Wireless to raise capital for its other ventures and to create value for shareholders. AT&T Wireless had consistently outperformed other portions of AT&T.

In the mid-1990s AT&T invested heavily in cable TV, purchasing the cable TV properties of TCI and MediaOne at premium prices. AT&T envisioned using these assets for bundled TV, Internet access, and telephone service. The combined costs of upgrades and purchase for these investments totaled $115 billion by 2000. AT&T also invested heavily in upgrading its high-speed backbone long distance network. In the meantime, losses at AT&T piled up as customers defected to competitors and long distance revenues dropped sharply due to lower prices and increasing substitution of e-mail for voice calling.

Falling revenues in its long distance operations were a major factor in AT&T no longer being able to support the debt levels in its cable properties. Thus, AT&T sold its cable properties to Comcast in 2002 for $41 billion plus the assumption by Comcast of $25 billion of debt. Its former wireless unit, AT&T Wireless, made an agreement to be purchased by Cingular in 2004 after operating at a loss. By 2005, operating at a loss and after consecutive rounds of staff layoffs and additional customer defections, AT&T announced its purchase by SBC.

Independent Telephone Companies— Mostly in Rural Areas

In addition to the RBOCs, there are close to 1,270 independent telephone companies. The four largest are Sprint, ALLTEL, Citizens Communications Corporation, and CenturyTel. (Sprint is an interexchange carrier, a wireless carrier, and an independent telephone company.) Following its announced purchase of Nextel, Sprint stated its intention to spin off its local phone company. Most independent telephone companies are in rural areas such as northern Maine and parts of California. According to the Federal Communications Commission's December 21, 2004 report *Trends in Telephone Service*, as of December 2002, independent telephone companies supply dial tone to 14% of the telephone lines in the United States.

Independent telephone companies sell all of the same services that RBOCs sell. Unlike provisions affecting the ROBCs, the Telecommunications Act of 1996 did not prohibit them from selling interstate long distance or cable TV and wireless services from within their territories. However, they are required to offer cable TV and wireless services through separate subsidiaries.

Interestingly, during the slowdown in telecommunications that impacted the rest of the industry in the early 2000s, most independents, while not growing, were stable. They received steady revenue streams of government subsidies and had little competition from other wireline carriers that didn't see a payback in investing in sparsely populated areas.

Rural telephone companies receive federal subsidies through the Universal Service Fund that compensates carriers for building facilities in areas with few customers

per central office switch and low-income areas. (See the section on the Universal Service Fund later in this chapter.) Rural carriers are reimbursed because the lines between the telephone company and customers are longer, serve fewer customers, and are thus more expensive to build and maintain and generate less revenue. Universal service subsidies enable telephone companies to keep prices comparable to those for basic dial tone in urban areas.

Independent telephone companies also receive a steady stream of revenue from long distance carriers in the form of access fees. Interexchange carriers pay access fees to local exchange carriers for carrying their calls between the long distance network and local customers. (See the section on access fees later in this chapter.) Access fees are set at higher than cost to subsidize local telephone service. According to Citizens Communications Corporation's year-end 2003 Form 10-K, 24% of their incumbent local exchange carrier (ILEC) revenue came from federal and state subsidies and access fees. However, due to federal legislation, access fees paid to incumbent telephone companies are decreasing. Some of these reductions have been offset by end-user fees in the form of subscriber line charges for each local line. In addition, access fees are decreasing due to fewer long distance calls because of substitution of wireless, e-mail, and Voice over IP traffic.

THE EMERGENCE OF LOCAL COMPETITION PRIOR TO 1996 ....

The idea that it was economically and technically feasible to compete for local telephone service, as well as long distance, gradually took hold starting in the late 1980s and early 1990s. It was fostered by technological improvements in fiber-optic cabling, wireless technologies, and lowered costs for switches. Improvements in signaling technology also played a role in lowering the cost of provisioning telephone service. Sophisticated signaling systems link single databases containing applications such as billing and messaging to multiple switches so that carriers don't have to maintain, for example, a separate billing system for each switch.

Competitive Access Providers (CAPs) to Bypass Access Fees

Customers' and carriers' desire for lower-priced local access and egress (exit) was a major factor in the development of local competition. The first local service competitors were competitive access providers (CAPs), which emerged in the 1980s and in the early 1990s. CAPs provided access to long distance at lower prices than the Bell Operating Companies (BOCs). They transported calls to and from interexchange carriers to customers mainly in large cities.

The cost to carry the local access portion, access and egress (exit), was paid by interexchange carriers to local telephone companies and was passed on to consumers. In 1984, access charges amounted to 5.24 cents of the 32 cents per-minute average cost of long distance. BOCs typically received a third of their revenue from business customers, a third from residential customers, and a third from access fees paid by interexchange carriers, of which AT&T was the largest. Because of these access fees, AT&T was the Bell telephone companies' largest customer.

CAPs were the first carriers to use fiber-optic cabling to transport calls from business customers (initially, primarily financial institutions in large cities) to interexchange carriers' points of presence (POPs), bypassing access fees. A *point of presence* is the location in a metropolitan area where a long distance company has its switch. T-1 between customers and POPs enabled institutions to eliminate (bypass) per-minute access fees charged by the Bell telephone companies to interexchange carriers and passed on to end users. T-1 carries 24 channels of voice and/or data calls on two pairs of copper cable or one pair of fiber cabling (see Figure 3.3).

IDENTIFYING CARRIERS—CIC CODES

The North American Numbering Plan Administrator assigns four-digit carrier identification codes (CICs) to every wireline and wireless carrier. CIC, which is pronounced *kick*, identifies carriers for billing and routing purposes. Carriers often transport each other's traffic because no carrier has coverage everywhere. The CIC code identifies the carrier associated with each call so that carriers can bill each other various fees for carrying each other's traffic.

AT&T's main CIC code is 0288, MCI's is 0222, and Sprint's is 0333. Local telephone companies automatically insert CIC codes based on the carrier the customer chooses for their long distance service. However, callers can also select a carrier manually by dialing a CIC code preceded by the carrier access code 101. For example, someone dialing 1010222 before they dial a long distance number will have his or her call routed on MCI's network.

The CIC code format was changed in 1998 from three digits to four digits. This increased the number of CIC codes from 999 to 9999. Thus, MCI's CIC code changed from 222 to 0222. According to the FCC, as of the first quarter of 2004, 2,452 CIC codes were in use. Many carriers have multiple CIC codes, some assigned previously to businesses they purchased and some for subsidiaries or particular lines of business.

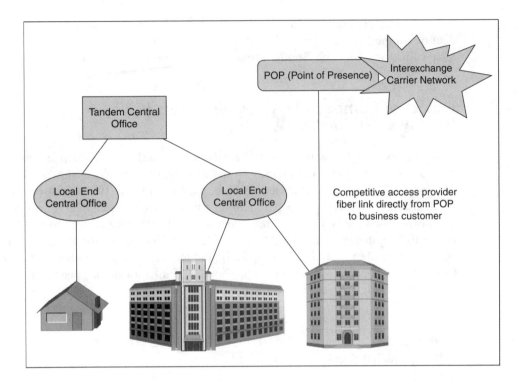

Figure 3.3
Alternative access link to a long distance provider, bypassing the   local
telephone company.

Uneven Competition for Local Telephone Service Throughout the U.S.

Prior to 1996, competitive access providers (CAPs) such as Metropolitan Fiber Systems, later purchased by WorldCom (now called MCI), and Teleport Communications Group, purchased by AT&T, as well as long distance giants AT&T, Sprint, and MCI sold local telephone service. However, market penetration of these services was low, 0.7% by December 1995. Local telecommunications was, for the most part, regulated by state public utility commissions.

Each state allowed incumbent local telephone companies different levels of monopolistic control of local and intra-LATA toll calling. As state utility commissions opened intra-LATA toll calling, interexchange carriers and competitive access providers (CAPs) heavily promoted ways that customers could use their services for local toll calling by dialing 101 plus a CIC code. This is referred to as *dial around*. A great deal of competitive activity took place in California because of its 25% share of the local calling marketplace. Southern states had little competitive activity.

Impact of Competitive Access Providers (CAPs)—Fiber and T-1 Availability

Competition from CAPs in the 1980s motivated the Bell and independent telephone companies to lay fiber more quickly in large cities, directly to customers' buildings. The local telephone companies at this time, the early to mid-1980s, transported calls from customer premises on copper cabling, which is less reliable than fiber. Competition also pushed the Bells to shorten intervals and lower prices for high-speed digital access to long distance carriers. Thus, the telephone companies made digital T-1 connections over fiber available more quickly and at lower costs than they had planned. Competition from alternative access providers was a factor in the speed of upgrading the Bells' cabling from copper to fiber.

The Transition from CAPs to Competitive Local Exchange Carriers (CLECs)

Competitive access providers became competitive local exchange carriers in the 1990s when they branched out from providing bypass, which is access to long distance on their facilities, and started selling connections to the Internet, data networks within metropolitan areas, and local calling services using the fiber networks they had installed for bypass.

They initially entered the interexchange business by constructing fiber-optic links between major metropolitan areas in the East and West Coast corridors. For example, once Los Angeles and San Francisco had fiber within the cities, the next step was to link these two locations with fiber for the purpose of selling long distance. The same is true for New York City to Washington, D.C. These high-capacity fiber-optic lines carried data as well as voice services. In routes other than those with the heaviest traffic, they routed traffic over other carriers' networks.

Collocation—CLEC Switches in RBOC Central Offices

On September 17, 1992, the FCC allowed the local Bell telephone companies, at their discretion, to open up competition by permitting collocation and virtual collocation.

The Telecommunications Act of 1996 *mandated* that Bell companies provide collocation services. With *collocation*, competitors install their own central office switch or other equipment in the same building as the local telephone company's switch. This gives competitors access to Bell telephone company lines for egress and/or termination of telephone calls from the competitors' customers. *Egress* is the exit of traffic from the customer that initiates the call.

Cream-Skimming—Concentrating on Profitable Markets

When competition for local telecommunications began, CLECs concentrated their initial sales efforts in highly populated metropolitan areas. They saw a high-profit potential in areas such as downtown New York City, where one fiber run had access to thousands of customers in a single skyscraper. This concept is known as "cream-skimming." Cream was skimmed from lucrative markets. There is more potential for profit when an investment in new technology reaches thousands of potential customers in a concentrated area. CLECs competed in part by setting their prices lower than incumbent local exchange carriers.

The Critical Nature of Facilities

While framers of the Telecommunications Act of 1996 envisioned cable TV, commercial mobile services, and utilities as viable competition, the industry initially focused most of its attention on CLECs. In states where rates to lease Bell networks decreased, many CLECs used resale as their primary strategy. The 2004 circuit court ruling jeopardized discounted connections to Bell equipment and made this strategy no longer feasible.

As other technologies mature and regulatory rulings make reliance on Bell facilities a poor choice, the industry is directing attention to competition between facilities-based providers. The focus is increasingly on wireless, cable TV, and utilities' use of their own fiber as well as Voice over IP technology that operates on existing broadband facilities. (See Chapter 4, "VoIP, the Public Switched Telephone Network, and Signaling," for information on Voice over IP network services.) These services depend for the most part on upgrading, adding to, and modifying rather than completely rebuilding infrastructure to reach customers. In the case of wireless service, cabling is not needed to each premise.

Factors Leading to Passage of the Telecommunications Act of 1996

The framers of telecommunications reform hoped that the Telecommunications Act of 1996 would increase choices for local services for residences, small businesses, and large organizations. Demand for passage of the Telecommunications Act of 1996 had been building up in Congress for many years, and Congress had attempted in the early 1990s to pass reform bills. The Republican congressional leadership that took office in 1995 wanted to deregulate cable TV and broadcasting. Through intense lobbying by RBOCs and long distance companies, a compromise was struck. The Telecommunications Act promised to open interexchange competition to Bells after they proved they had opened their networks to competition.

It was envisioned that the growth of competition for local telephone service would encourage advancements and business opportunities for entrepreneurs. After the 1984 Divestiture, interexchange carriers had an incentive, in the form of competition, to add innovative services. They offered data services such as frame relay, ATM, and virtual private data networks and new toll-free services not available at that time from incumbent local telephone companies.

The following were important factors in pushing passage of the Telecommunications Act of 1996:

- A desire in Congress to allow competition for local telecommunications services (the "information superhighway") uniformly in all of the states
- A government effort to make access to high-capacity telecommunications services universal and affordable
- Improvements in fiber-optic and signaling technologies
- The Bell telephone companies' lobbying efforts for permission to enter interstate long distance and manufacturing
- The interexchange carriers' push for entry into the local calling market
- Cable TV and utilities' desire to enter new markets
- Viability of wireless services as a substitute for wired local telephone lines

Wireless Services for Local Exchange Service—Spectrum Auctions

In 1993, President Bill Clinton mandated that auctions be held for frequencies within the higher, personal communications services (PCS) airwaves. Frequencies in each metropolitan area would be awarded to the five highest bidders, with some awards given to minority and small businesses. This was seen, in addition to adding to the federal coffers, as a way to open up competition to cellular service providers. It was thought that this would drive down the cost of wireless services to the point where people would use their cellular phones for local calling. Prior to the auctions, there were only two cellular carriers in each metropolitan area, a subsidiary of the incumbent Bell telephone company and one other provider, selected by lottery from eligible carriers. These early cellular carriers were given free spectrum.

THE TELECOMMUNICATIONS ACT OF 1996 ....

The Telecommunications Act of 1996 opened up local telephone service to interexchange carriers, cable television operators, utilities, wireless operators, and new entities that wanted to offer telecommunications services. Section 271 of the Telecommunications Act specified that each of the former Bell telephone companies would be allowed to sell interstate and international telecommunications services and manufacture and sell customer premises equipment once each state in their territory was shown to have local competition. Each state's regulatory agency and the Justice Department were to assess whether the incumbent telephone company had met the guidelines for connecting competitors to its network. The Federal Communications Commission made its final rulings following these assessments.

Qwest (for Arizona) was the final RBOC to receive FCC approval to sell interstate and international service in December 2003, seven years after passage of the Telecommunications Act.

More detail on the Telecommunications Act of 1996, including local number portability, is included in the Appendix section at the end of this chapter.

Universal Service Fund—
Affordability and Availability

The commitment to affordable universal telephone service was established in 1913 when AT&T was given a monopoly for building a nationwide public switched telephone network in exchange for providing affordable, universal service to all residential consumers. The Telecommunications Act of 1996 expanded universal service. Every interstate carrier, cell phone company, and paging company must pay a percentage of its interstate and international revenues to the fund. Voice over IP providers are exempt from Universal Service Fund contributions because they are not currently regulated as telecommunications companies. The contribution percentage is adjusted quarterly based on the fund's projected needs and revenues. The third quarter of 2004 percentage was set at 8.9%. State commissions may also create funds for universal service.

The purpose of the Universal Service Fund (USF) is to provide schools, rural healthcare facilities, low-income consumers, high-cost-to-reach areas (for example, rural areas), and libraries telecommunications services at reasonably comparable rates charged for similar services in urban areas. The portion of the Universal Service Fund that applies to schools and libraries is known as the E-rate. The E-rate subsidizes Internet access and infrastructure costs needed for high-speed Internet access. In 2000, subsidies were extended to Native American reservations.

With the exception of the E-rate and subsidies to rural health care providers, the Universal Service Fund covers only basic dial tone, not broadband services for high-speed Internet access. President George W. Bush has recommended that, by 2007, all Americans have access to affordable broadband technology. To date, no regulations or rulings have been enacted to ensure universal, affordable broadband availability.

POST TELECOMMUNICATIONS ACT OF 1996 DEVELOPMENTS...

Implementation of the Telecommunications Act of 1996 was hampered by RBOC legal challenges. Furthermore, implementation and order-placing snafus hindered competitors that wanted to sell service using incumbents' facilities.

FCC Rulings, Legal Challenges, and Progress Toward Deregulation

The Telecommunications Act of 1996 mandated that the very organizations that compete with new entrants, the RBOCs, must supply connections and services for competitors. Thus, conflicts erupted in pricing for and arranging for resale and connections to Bell resources. It is no surprise that these issues were contested in court. (See Table 3.5 in the Appendix at the end of this chapter.)

Enforcement of provisions and details of implementation of the Telecommunications Act were left, for the most part, to the FCC. Its rulings on wholesale rates and its rights to set rates were challenged by the state public utilities, local telephone companies, and independent telephone companies. State public utilities contended that the 1934 Communications Act granted state utilities the prerogative of setting resale and wholesale discounts in their states. In a major blow to CLECs, in March 2004, the United States Court of Appeals for the District of Columbia struck down an FCC order on the availability of unbundled network element (UNE) discounts for CLEC connections to RBOC facilities. UNE discounts mandated that RBOCs use replacement costs rather than original cost when setting lease rates. Replacement rates are lower than those based on original cost of equipment.

FCC Enforcement of Access to Local Networks after Bells Gain In-Region Long Distance

The Telecommunications Act of 1996 granted the FCC post-approval enforcement powers to monitor Bell Operating Company (BOC) adherence to rules providing access to central office and other Bell facilities (unbundled network elements) at fair rates. A Bell Operating Company refers to the 22 local entities that are now part of the Regional Bell Operating Companies.

Following final approval by the end of 2003 for the Bells to provide long distance service everywhere in the United States, no RBOC state entity has been stripped of its authority to provide long distance service.

IMPACT OF THE TELECOMMUNICATIONS ACT OF 1996 ....

According to the United States Telephone Association booklet *Phone Facts 1998,* the local telecommunications market was $96 billion in 1997. At that time, RBOCs and independents had a 97.7% market share of local lines. In the latest period analyzed, June 2003, CLECs had a 14.7% share of local lines. These statistics do not reflect the fact that the two largest CLECs, AT&T and MCI, will be purchased by Regional Bell Operating Companies, greatly reducing CLEC penetration once the acquisitions are finalized. According to the FCC, 38% of CLECs' lines and 22% of incumbents' lines served medium and large businesses, institutional customers, and government customers in 2003. SBC's planned purchase of AT&T and Verizon's announced purchase of MCI will increase these RBOCs' share of large business lines.

The Telecommunications Act initially spurred new investment in equipment and services. Capital investments decreased after 2001, and many providers went out of business due to the high cost of building infrastructure, the cost and delays associated with connecting to incumbent facilities, unfavorable regulatory rulings, and low retail prices offered in response to competitive bids. However, small businesses have particularly benefited from increased competition, which triggered widespread affordable, high-speed Internet access. However, regulatory decisions, high startup costs, and low margins for competitive services have greatly reduced the impact of the Telecommunications Act. The major impact of the Telecommunications Act is the entrance of cable operators into telecommunications services.

STATE OF THE INDUSTRY . . . KEY SEGMENTS ....

The major segments of the telecommunications industry are wireless mobile operators, cable multiple service operators (MSOs), and incumbent telephone companies.

Regional Bell Operating Companies (RBOCs) Post-1996 Mergers

The flurry of merger announcements in 2005 between AT&T, MCI, and RBOCs will, if the mergers are approved, result in RBOCs having even more industry clout. RBOCs are also referred to as incumbent local exchange carriers (ILECs). Verizon and SBC are the largest local telephone companies in the United States. Between them, they control 61% of the local lines as well as a major percentage of the long distance market and Internet access market. The four Regional Bell Operating Companies are as follows:

- *Verizon Communications* was formed when Bell Atlantic purchased GTE, the largest independent telephone company. At the time, GTE had more access lines than Qwest. Bell Atlantic had previously purchased NYNEX, whose territory covered New England and New York State. Verizon, the largest incumbent telephone company, is the majority owner of Verizon Wireless, and Vodafone is the minority owner with 45%. Verizon Wireless accounts for 40% of revenues. In 2005, Verizon announced its intention to purchase MCI.

- *SBC*, formerly Southwestern Bell Communications, is the second-largest incumbent local exchange carrier. It purchased Pacific Telesis and Ameritech as well as former independent telephone company Southern New England Telephone Company of Connecticut (SNET). It merged its wireless assets with those of BellSouth to form Cingular Wireless, and Cingular purchased AT&T Wireless in 2004. In 2005, SBC announced it would purchase AT&T. If approved, this merger will make SBC the largest telephone company in the United States. Cingular is the largest mobile carrier.

- *BellSouth* is the third-largest local exchange carrier. Its territory is made up of nine southern states. BellSouth owns 40% and SBC 60% of Cingular Wireless. BellSouth is expanding its broadband facilities in hopes of attracting enterprise customers and adding video on demand for residential customers.

- *Qwest Communications International Inc.* was formed when long distance carrier Qwest purchased US West. It covers 14 western states, not including California and Nevada. Qwest resells cellular service via resale on other carriers' networks. Its fiber-optic long distance business incurs large annual losses and has left Qwest with a large debt and interest expense on the debt. Qwest has been the subject of shareholder lawsuits and investigations by the Securities and Exchange Commission and the Justice Department.

Incumbent Local Exchange Carriers (ILECs)

The RBOCs, the four largest incumbents, have enormous regulatory influence and economic clout in the telecommunications industry. Their combined annual revenues make up close to half the revenue of the entire telecommunications market in the United States, including wireless, broadband cable, DSL modem service, local, long distance, and international services (see Table 3.1). The RBOCs' main strengths lie in their skills in influencing regulatory bodies, their engineering expertise, and their sheer economic size.

Table 3.1   Annual Combined RBOC Statistics[1] (Dollar amounts are in millions)

	2003	2002	2001
Total employees	491,569	533,288	580,469
Total revenue	$145,518	$148,253	$153,281
Net income*	$16,998	–$27,413	$4,241
Total capital invested	$22,359	$26,363	$43,505
Capital invested by largest CLECs[2]	$3,895	$4,150	$17,017
Number of CLECs in survey	62 CLECs	66 CLECs	120 CLECs
Total industry revenue[3]	$303,614	$297,767	$305,188

* Reflects Qwest net losses of $38,468m in 2002 and $5,603m in 2001

[1]*Source: RBOC annual reports.*

[2]*Source: New Paradigm Resources Group, Inc.*

[3]*Source: FCC statistics, which include CLECs and wireless carriers.*

Since 2001, the number of local access lines in service at each RBOC has declined. Much of this decline can be attributed to the substitution of DSL and cable modem service for users' second phone lines and the use of wireless phones for long distance. Many families use wireless "buckets of minutes" plans that negate the need for a second line for teenagers and children. In addition, each Bell has lost local lines to competitive local exchange carriers. The RBOCs have captured a large share of the residential and small business long distance market and are now marketing long distance and data services to large enterprises. However, profits on long distance are lower than profits for local telephone lines.

RBOCs are making up for losses in local service by increased sales of DSL, reductions in the size of their work force, and increases in wireless subscribers. They're also attempting to retain their customer base by offering bundles of wireless, DSL Internet access, long distance, and local service and reselling satellite television service. BellSouth, Qwest, and Verizon resell satellite DirecTV service, and SBC resells EchoStar service. The RBOCs provide billing, marketing, and customer service, and the satellite companies do the actual installation and transmission.

The satellite offerings are a response to cable TV's triple-play array of entertainment, telephone, and Internet access. It is also recognition that future revenues may be derived from interactive services such as video-on-demand. The RBOCs have announced plans to build fiber to customer premises or deeper into neighborhoods. They are also researching ways to provide two-way video over copper so that they can offer entertainment on their own networks. They are raising capital for these upgrades in part by attempting to sell lines in rural areas of their networks and by selling investments in international wireless and wireline carriers.

They also hope to capture a larger share of the enterprise and government nationwide data networking business. To do this, they are building extensive interstate fiber networks based on IP protocols. Many of them lease rights to fiber and add their own multiplexing equipment. The term for these long-term leases is *Indefeasible Right of Use (IRU)*. IRUs are analogous to condo ownership. Another carrier arranges for rights of way and lays the fiber. The carrier that purchases the IRU has the sole right to use the fiber it has leased. Just as a condo owner adds furniture and carpeting, the carrier that leases the fiber adds equipment to the fiber strands and monitors traffic on it.

The RBOCs have higher labor expenses than much of the industry due to the fact that the landline side of their operations is unionized. However, their large customer base is an enormous strength in marketing new offerings. They promote new services and plans in bill inserts and telemarketing campaigns that are no longer available to competitors barred by "Do Not Call" regulations from calling people that register on the federal government's Do Not Call registry. These "Do Not Call" regulations do not apply to corporations calling their own customers.

HOW TELEPHONE NUMBERS ARE ASSIGNED FOR WIRELINE, WIRELESS, AND VOICE OVER IP PROVIDERS

The North American Numbering Plan Administration assigns telephone numbers to state-certified wireline carriers in each state. Wireless carriers also receive numbers from the North American Number Plan Administration. However, they don't need to register on a state-by-state basis because the FCC, not individual states, licenses them to offer service. Carriers such as Vonage, Broadview Networks, and SBC for their IP services are required to obtain telephone numbers from local exchange carriers (LECs) in each state. The LECs can be either the incumbent or a competitor to the incumbent. The reason for this requirement is that VoIP is not defined at this time as a telecommunications service. Thus, VoIP carriers or the department and subsidiaries within carriers that offer VoIP must enter into agreements with a licensed carrier to obtain local telephone numbers in each state in which they wish to offer Voice over IP service. SBC IP has asked the FCC for a waiver of the requirement to obtain numbers from other carriers. In their own territory, they receive numbers from their parent, SBC. However, when they offer VoIP outside of their home territory, they have to enter agreements with other LECs. Prior to the announced merger with SBC, AT&T objected to SBC IP's request for a waiver, saying this would be unfair to other VoIP providers.

The North American Numbering Plan Administration assigns numbers in blocks of 1,000. This is called the *number pooling system of allotting numbers* because pools of 1,000 unused numbers are created. Prior to the year 2000, numbers were assigned to carriers in blocks of 10,000. This resulted in wasted numbers because many smaller carriers who did not use up all of their numbers could not share them with other carriers. To further conserve numbers, in 2000, the FCC mandated that phone companies must first use up 60% of their assigned phone numbers before being given new ones. As of June 30, 2004, that percentage increased to 75%.

Agents

Agents act as independent representatives for carriers. The Regional Bell Operating Companies started agent programs as a way to lower the cost of selling services to small businesses. Many agents offered interstate and local data services to their customers as an adjunct to sales of telephone and data systems. Agents are certified and receive some training from the telephone companies they represent. They receive a monthly commission on the telephone services they sell, but customers receive bills and customer service support directly from the carrier. Long distance carriers and CLECs also use agents.

Retail outlets are agents for cellular providers. Staples is an agent for Sprint PCS and Nextel. It is also an agent for prepaid cellular from Cingular and Tracphone. Radio Shack is an agent for Verizon Wireless and Sprint PCS.

Resellers

Like agents, resellers do not own network infrastructure. Unlike agents, however, they do provide billing and customer service for their customers. In addition, unlike agents, they market the service under their own brand. Resellers sell wireline service such as data services (for example, T-1, T-3, and other high-speed services), calling cards, Internet access, local, long distance, Voice over IP, and international calling. They also resell cellular service. For example, Qwest resells Sprint PCS wireless service.

Resellers purchase services at discounts, mark them up, and often offer them at below retail cost. Resellers offer services carried on networks owned by Regional Bell Operating Companies, MCI, AT&T, Sprint, Global Crossing, Level 3, and other carriers worldwide.

TRUTH IN BILLING—TAXES, FEES, AND SURCHARGES

According to the FCC, as of 2002, taxes, 911 costs, and universal service fees make up 38% of consumers' local monthly telephone charges. In addition to these charges, long distance and wireless carriers impose a variety of fees on consumers' and enterprises' monthly phone bills. The surcharges carriers have tacked onto telephone bills increase the cost of telephone service and make it confusing for consumers and commercial organizations to compare costs between competing carriers. The National Association of State Utility Consumer Advocates (NASUCA) , a 43-state organization of consumer advocates, filed a request on March 30, 2004 asking the FCC to prohibit long distance and wireless carriers from imposing surcharges unless such fees are (1) mandated or authorized by federal, state, or local government and (2) conform to the amount authorized by government.

TRUTH IN BILLING—TAXES, FEES, AND SURCHARGES (CONTINUED)

The following charges are added to bills in addition to monthly usage and line charges:

- Taxes such as local, state, and federal taxes assessed by legislative bodies and sent directly to the government by carriers.

- Regulatory fees mandated by the FCC and paid to carriers:

  - Universal Service Fund fees described earlier for high-cost rural and nonrural areas, healthcare providers, educational institutions, and libraries.

  - Subscriber line charges (SLCs) used to recover the cost of access lines between long distance and local exchange carriers. SLCs are intended to replace the lower access fees that local telcos charge long distance carriers for carrying their calls.

  - E911 and local number portability charges to subsidize the cost of upgrading equipment to provide these services.

- Carrier assessments that are not mandated by federal, state, or local government. Wireline and wireless carriers charge fees that range from 41 cents to $4.95 monthly and label them variously as Federal Programs Cost Recovery, Regulatory Cost Recovery Fee, Regulatory Assessment Fee, Carrier Cost Recovery Charge, and Regulatory Fee.

According to NASUCA, most carrier assessments cover nothing more than the carrier's costs of doing business and should be folded into per-minute charges or monthly fixed charges so that consumers can more easily compare prices between carriers. In 1999, the FCC issued a "Truth-in-Billing" order that prohibits carriers from switching customers' long distance company on an unauthorized basis (slamming), adding unauthorized services to customers' bills (cramming), and utilizing confusing billing practices. However, the National Association of State Utility Consumer Advocates contends that the FCC's order did not cover most carrier assessments appearing on consumers' bills today and that the assessments confuse and mislead consumers since, for example, they are not advertised in conjunction with low usage or calling plan rates. NASUCA also believes that the carrier assessments frustrate Congress's goal of a competitive telecommunications market because inefficient carriers can recover their greater operating costs through surcharges while continuing to advertise, and offer, comparatively low rates.

Wholesale Carriers—Carrier-to-Carrier Sales

Carriers sell services directly to end users as well as to other telephone companies. For some carriers, such as Level 3, wholesale is the major part of their business; for others, such as the RBOCs, AT&T, Sprint, and MCI, it either is a way to sell spare capacity on their networks or is the result of regulatory requirements. There are many types of wholesale models in telecommunications. For example, CLECs swap and/or sell fiber routes to each other in metropolitan areas where they either have a need for fiber or have overcapacity. Sprint sells wholesale long distance, 911, and directory services to cable TV providers Time-Warner Cable, USA Companies, and Mediacom Communications Corporation. The cable operators, in turn, use these services in conjunction with their Voice over IP telephone service. Wholesale services that carriers sell include the following:

- Prepaid card platforms for wireline and wireless calling
- Signaling System 7 for cellular and wireline carriers
- Interstate fiber-optic routes
- International, cross-border calls to mobile phones
- Fiber runs between central offices in metropolitan areas and in rings throughout cities
- Equipment to carry Voice over IP traffic
- Dark fiber that has no electronics connected to it
- Directory assistance service
- Audio conferencing service
- The local lines from homes and businesses to central offices
- Ports on central office switches for carriers who don't have their own switches
- Internet access
- Data services

Because of fiber build-outs in long interstate routes and metropolitan areas, prices for fiber capacity have dropped to the point where the wholesale price for T-3 in the metro area is often only $500 per month. Metropolitan fiber drops are still costly to bring from the rings to enterprise and mid-size customer sites because of trenching, right of way, and labor expense. Even so, the impact of this additional infrastructure is the higher availability and affordability of high-speed data services such as SONET and Gigabit Ethernet for enterprises. (See Chapter 5, "VPNs and Specialized Network Services," for discussions of SONET, T-3, and Gigabit Ethernet.) These data services are used for disaster recovery, site-to-site connectivity, and Internet access.

Because of the glut of fiber and increased competition, revenues for wholesale switched voice services are declining.

CLECS—A DWINDLING INDUSTRY SEGMENT..........

Competitive local exchange carriers (CLECs) compete against incumbent telephone companies and each other for local, long distance, Internet access, and data services. However, competitive local exchange carriers (CLECs) lost key regulatory battles and have decreasing revenue as a result of price competition, and many operate at a loss. In a final blow to CLECs as a key industry segment, SBC announced an agreement to purchase AT&T, and Verizon announced an agreement to purchase MCI. AT&T and MCI are the two largest CLECs and sell the largest share of corporate and government long distance and data services.

CLECs—Local, Data, and Long Distance Services

Large, facilities-based competitive local exchange carriers' (CLECs) main strengths are in the following:

- Breadth of their infrastructure
- International data offerings
- Large enterprise, commercial sector, and government customer base
- Complex data network offerings

AT&T, MCI, and Sprint own more of their own interstate network than any other carrier in the United States. (See Table 3.2 later in this chapter for North American wireline carriers.) AT&T, MCI, Sprint, and other large CLECs have the lion's share of corporate, nonprofit, and government long distance and data customers.

Like cable TV and incumbent telephone companies, long distance companies are exploring and developing services to replace shrinking revenues, margins, and decreased long distance traffic, which is now considered a commodity. According to telecommunications strategic consulting and market research firm Atlantic ACM, total interexchange long distance revenues shrank from $102 billion in 1999 to $86.3 billion in 2003. Combined factors of improved technology, increased competition, and elimination of long distance revenue to subsidize local service has caused marked decreases in average revenue per minute for interstate and international calls. The following figures, restated in 2002 dollars and reported by the Federal Communications

Commission's Industry Analysis Division, illustrate the declining per-minute costs of interstate and international long distance:

- 1930 $2.96
- 1984   56¢
- 1999   15¢
- 2002   9¢

In addition, scores of customers have replaced long distance with e-mail. Because of dwindling margins and the high cost of connecting to incumbent local exchange carriers to reach customers, long distance carriers for the most part have stopped promoting long distance to residential customers as a standalone product. When they do offer long distance to consumers and small businesses, it is part of a bundled package with local service. Total minutes of outbound and toll-free calling is shrinking due to substitution of e-mail and implementation of the Do Not Call registry by the Federal Trade Commission. The Do Not Call registry, in particular, resulted in large decreases in outbound traffic generated by call centers.

CLECs are evaluating and starting to offer Voice over Internet Protocol-based services. They see this as a lower-cost way to provide service. Because residential and small business VoIP offerings operate over DSL and cable modem lines, these services are less dependent on connections to ILECs. In addition, access fees currently don't apply on the portion of Voice over IP traffic that bypasses the public switched telephone network, the portion carried from the end users' broadband connection to the network. See the discussion later in this chapter on access fees and local loop leasing, including unbundled network elements (UNEs) from the RBOCs.

Pending Purchases of AT&T and MCI— The Impact of Consolidation

The decisions by SBC to purchase AT&T and Verizon to purchase MCI are directly related to their desire for a worldwide presence and a foothold in enterprise and government sales. In an interview with the *Wall Street Journal*, SBC CEO Edward Whitacre, Jr. discussed his organization's strategy in pursuing a merger:

> *"The telecommunications industry is taking the logical next step in its evolution. Companies that want to compete coast-to-coast and around the world are combining to create the size, scale, and product scope needed to be effective."*

The preceding quote appeared in the February 15, 2005 page one article "After a Year of Frenzied Deals, Two Telecom Giants Emerge" by Almar Latour. It is a reflection of the worldwide nature of telecommunications. Large enterprises expect carriers to support both their domestic and international telecommunications needs. Verizon and SBC are desirous of adding large enterprises to their customer base. These customers spend large sums of money and require less support per dollar of revenue than do residential customers, each of whom requires a monthly bill, repair service, and customer service. Thus, the RBOCs are gearing up to encroach into competitors' data networking and enterprise long distance business.

By early 2005, the RBOCs had made steady gains in adding long distance customers. The RBOCs had also taken steps to form national sales forces to offer service to enterprises. However, for the most part, their long distance customers were residential and small business customers or organizations such as hospitals and universities that have mainly in-state voice and data networks. In addition to their enterprise customer base, the large CLECs have an advantage of being able to provide a single bill that covers nationwide services rather than generating different bills for each part of the country. They also have nationwide marketing and sales forces, and AT&T and MCI have worldwide IP-based data networks as well.

By combining forces with AT&T and MCI, SBC and Verizon will have interstate, international, and local connections needed for Internet access, long distance, and many data communications connections. They will have completed their strategy, begun when they started lobbying for passage of the Telecommunications Act of 96, of being major contenders for nationwide as well as local services.

Interestingly, they already have 25% to 40% of total long distance revenue through the fees they charge long distance carriers to connect to transport traffic to local customers. Because there was never any serious competition for these local connections, the former Bells were able to keep these prices higher than those for interstate services. Having a lock in many areas on local connections to the Internet will give the incumbents with both local access and broadband long-haul networks a tremendous advantage. Integrating these former competitors with their different corporate cultures will be a major challenge.

Impact of Consolidation on Consumers and Business Customers

These industry consolidations will result in fewer choices for consumers for local and long distance service. The main alternative to incumbent telephone companies will be cable operators, whose voice offerings are becoming more widely available. However, having two main options, cable operators and former Bells, does not generally lead to price decreases. In particular, the presence of fewer competitors may keep broadband service costly. Because Voice over IP depends on relatively costly broadband connections, low-income consumers may have less access to lower cost, more innovative VoIP service. In addition, if the trend of less regulatory oversight continues, cable operators and incumbent telephone companies may have the option of cutting off access to competitors such as Vonage or charging high fees for access to incumbents' broadband links needed for VoIP service. For example, SBC implemented a service called Tiptop that levies higher fees to VoIP providers than other traditional carriers to connect to their network for sending Vonage-originated traffic to SBC customers. The service triggered criticism by the FCC, which said it would not tolerate incumbents charging high prices that might hurt rivals.

However, as cellular service matures, it will gradually replace more landline service for voice service, giving residential customers another option for voice telephony. In addition, wireless may also become acceptable for broadband-speed Internet access. But this is still very much a future.

Enterprise customers who expected to have offerings from incumbents as well as CLECs for long distance services will find no increase in the number of choices. Actually, because of regulatory changes, offerings from smaller CLECs will become more costly, and options will decrease. Moreover, in the short term, these mergers may mean lower levels of service. Once these mergers are approved, integrating operation and support systems for billing, maintenance, and installation will be a massive undertaking and may lead to service snafus. Unlike consumer bills, large companies often have custom contracts that require complex billing arrangements. These are already complex to administer, and many enterprises spend enormous amounts of time working with suppliers to correct billing errors. Mergers may exacerbate these problems. In addition, corporate customers will have the added confusion of dealing with staff changes when sales and customer service departments are combined.

In the long run, the industry may benefit from a slimmed down structure with fewer customers divided up among a more limited number of carriers. Moreover, over the next decade, new, lower cost, fixed wireless technologies may be viable and available for high-speed Internet access and voice services. In addition, cable multiple service operators (MSOs) have stated their intention and are starting to offer services to business customers. If newly consolidated incumbent telephone companies keep prices high, this will leave more opportunities for new competitors and lower cost access technologies. See Chapter 9, "Wi-Fi, Wireless Broadband, Sensor Networks, and Personal Area Networks," for information regarding wireless broadband access.

Shrinking Numbers of Competitors— Financial Turmoil

The Association for Local Telecommunications Services (ALTS) listed 410 CLECs in its 2001 directory. By November 2004, Chicago-based research firm New Paradigm Resources Group, Inc. announced there were only 63 CLECs in the United States. Many of the surviving entities have filed for bankruptcy or reduced the scope of their operations. WorldCom (now MCI) and Global Crossing filed for bankruptcy in 2002. The MCI filing was the largest bankruptcy in history. The number of carriers is also shrinking due to mergers. Investors have paid rock-bottom prices to purchase carriers in bankruptcy or near bankruptcy. For example, IDT bought WinStar, Teligent, and STAR Telecommunications. IDT paid $55 million for bankrupt WinStar, which had previously spent $5 billion on equipment for fixed wireless service.

Between 2000 and May 2003, 600,000 people lost their jobs in the telecommunications industry in the United States. This statistic appeared in the May 12, 2003 online article "Feet to the Fire" by Mairin Burns in *Investment Dealers' Digest (IDD)*. In addition to jobs, hundreds of thousands of people lost their entire pension and huge portions of savings they had invested in companies that subsequently filed for bankruptcy. The investment community lost billions of dollars of equity in telecommunications companies. To cite one example, Cincinnati Bell purchased interexchange carrier IXC Communications for $3.2 billion in 1999 and sold it for $108.5 million to Cequel III (owned by Corvis) in 2003. According to the *Washington Post*'s July 23, 2002 article "WorldCom Files Record Bankruptcy Case" by Christopher Stern and Carrie Johnson, WorldCom's bankruptcy resulted in a loss of $180 billion in stock value from its peak in 1999. Many carriers have emerged debt-free from bankruptcy. However, shareholders, creditors, and pension holders lost billions of dollars.

What Went Wrong?

Too many competitors, mismanagement, and high costs, as well as overcapacity in interstate fiber networks, were key factors in the industry shakeout. Moreover, competitors often underestimated the costs and difficulties in attracting sufficient customers to cover the ongoing capital required to build infrastructure and provide marketing, billing, and customer service. Competitive local exchange carriers also underestimated the Regional Bell Operating Companies' enormous lobbying clout, which resulted in their ability to influence the FCC and particularly Congress to pass regulations favoring incumbents. Because of the large number of competitors, prices dropped dramatically, making it difficult to cover operating expense from revenue. Finally, in the early days after passage of the Telecommunications Act of 1996, acquiring connections to incumbent facilities often took longer than expected and resulted in implementation snafus, followed by customer defections.

Moreover, the Circuit Court of Washington, D.C. overturning of the FCC's Triennial Review Order on leasing discounts resulted in competitors essentially losing the regulatory battle against incumbent local exchange carriers. (See "Regulatory Issues" later in this chapter.) The FCC's implementation of new rules dramatically increases costs to lease incumbents' facilities and decreases the viability of resale. Unfortunately, for the years that discounts were in place, many CLECs built whole strategies around using these services to sell bundles of Internet access, local calling, and long distance to residential and small business customers. Many competitors are refocusing their strategy around Voice over IP and, in the future when the technology matures, wireless technologies such as WiMAX to reach customers independent of Bell local loop facilities. (See Chapter 9 for a discussion of wireless broadband access.)

INTERMODAL COMPETITION—CABLE TV, WIRELESS, AND UTILITIES.....................................

Intermodal competition is competition between services based on different media and technology. Challenges to incumbents based on wireless, cable TV, and Internet protocol (IP) technologies are examples of intermodal competition. Competition from cable TV operators, which are introducing voice service using Voice over Internet Protocol, is in early stages but is expected to grow quickly. According to the National Cable & Telecommunications Association 2003 Year-End Industry Overview, by the end of the third quarter of 2003, cable TV operators supplied only 2.5 million of the approximately 183 million local lines in service. Most of these early implementations use circuit switched rather than IP technology. Wireless providers will also pose competitive threats as the quality, technology, and reach of their networks improve. However, utilities, some of which will offer Internet access over their fiber networks, will likely serve smaller niche markets in rural areas and developing nations. Table 3.2, shown later, lists the major wireline carriers in North America.

Cable TV Multiple Service Operators (MSOs)—Wired to the Max

According to consulting firm Kagan Research LLC, as of December 2003, cable systems are available to 95% of occupied homes that have television service. Infrastructure capable of supporting multimedia service gives cable operators a formidable head start in selling a mix of "triple-play" services: television, telephony, and Internet access. Cable companies hope to increase their share of local telephone customers by implementing Voice over IP. They are attracted to the lower cost of implementing

VoIP. In addition, because VoIP compresses voice, removes silences, and puts voice into packets that are interleaved with data and TV signals, it uses less capacity than traditional circuit switched telephony, which requires dedicated bandwidth. This leaves more capacity on cable operators' fiber and coaxial cable infrastructure for advanced service such as movies and television on demand.

Like RBOCs, cable operators have an enormous customer base, hefty monthly cash flows, billing expertise, and vast networks. However, they are losing television subscribers to satellite companies. According to media research firm Kagan Research LLC, in the first six months of 2004, cable operators lost about 300,000 customers. Satellite operators started gaining market share when they won the right to offer local programming in 1999. Cable operators, who until recently had no real competition, have raised prices consistently, to the dismay of cost-conscious consumers who are turning to lower cost satellite TV.

Cable multiple service operators (MSOs), all of whom spent large sums of money to upgrade their facilities for Internet access, interactive video, and recently for voice telephony, have plans to market more of their services to small and medium-size businesses. In many cases, their networks are already in place near businesses. All that is required is new fiber from the cable network to the customer premises.

According to Reuters' online story "U.S. Cable Rates Rose 5.2 pct in Latest Year-FCC" dated January 28, 2004, the four largest cable operators, Charter Communications, Comcast Corporation, Cox Communications, and Time-Warner Inc. serve about 50.5% of the cable TV market.

Mobile Wireless Services

As data speeds, coverage, capacity, and quality improve, mobile wireless service providers will become important competitors to landline service. In the midst of revenue declines and layoffs in landline companies, the mobile wireless market experienced increases in total revenue, capital investment, and number of employees. Moreover, in November 2003, local number portability was extended to allow subscribers to change their landline numbers to their wireless phone. This increased the likelihood of substitution of wireless phones for landlines. Mobile wireless is also evolving as a way to access the Internet.

However, cellular networks need to improve their coverage, capacity, and data speeds to increase the number of customers who use wireless as their only voice service or as their Internet access. Cellular operators have the enormous advantage of not needing to lay cable to every customer they serve. Although they don't have the burden of laying fiber to each customer, they do face large infrastructure expense.

These improvements require upgrades or replacements at the 162,986 cell sites in the United States that the FCC's May 2004 *Trends in Telephone Service* reported are in service. A cell site consists of the antenna and equipment that manages the traffic within the cell site's coverage area. In addition, upgrading mobile networks often requires adding new cell sites and purchasing rights to additional spectrum (air waves). In 2003, the Cellular Telecommunications Internet Association reported that wireless providers invested $19 billion in capital improvements.

Cellular providers, in response to competition from nationwide competitors, lowered their prices and earned reduced average revenue per minute (ARPU) on voice services. However, sales of data services such as short messaging service, e-mail access by corporate customers, and downloadable ring tones have started to reverse the trend of lower revenue per user. A challenge for carriers is lowering churn, customers changing wireless carrier. Churn costs carriers billions of dollars annually because of the cost to activate and deactivate service. The five largest carriers lose between 1.7% and 3.3% of their customers per quarter.

It is possible that industry consolidation will reduce price competition and improve margins. Until mid-2004, there were six nationwide cellular carriers. In 2004, Cingular purchased AT&T Wireless, and in January 2005, Sprint announced its agreement to merge with Nextel, leaving four nationwide carriers when the Sprint merger is completed. Verizon Wireless and T-Mobile are the other two nationwide mobile carriers. According to the Cellular Telecommunications Internet Association, as of June 2004, there were 170 million wireless mobile subscribers. There are 183 million landlines.

Utilities—The Third Pipe

Because electric utilities have enormous fiber-optic networks, which they use for signaling, they are potential competitors for high-speed Internet access and voice telephone service. Some subsidiaries of utilities offer wholesale service to other carriers. For example, they sell dark fiber to cellular companies who use it to connect their antennas to mobile switches. Some utilities are considering a technology called broadband over power lines (BPL) to provide retail telecommunications services. BPL is being offered in 18 states to a limited number of customers on a mainly trial basis. In addition, Current Communications offers it in a joint venture with energy company Cinergy near Cincinnati, Ohio. The Federal Communications Commission has termed broadband over power lines a potential "third pipe" (in addition to cable and DSL modems) for rural areas that sometimes have no broadband service for consumers and in which Internet access available for businesses is expensive. Lack of affordable Internet access hampers rural and sparsely developed areas from keeping and attracting commercial development.

In addition to existing fiber networks, utilities have expertise in billing and customer service and lists of customers to whom they can market services. Moreover, technology that helps them retain business and consumer customers in their coverage area benefits their overall business. Utilities that implement BPL may have the added benefit of using the technology internally to read meters, be notified of outages, and generally manage their network of power grids.

Broadband over power lines (BPL) overcame a regulatory hurdle in October 2004 with an FCC ruling. The FCC had been looking at whether BPL signals interfere with other services, including ham radios and emergency services, offered by the Federal Emergency Management Association (FEMA). In its ruling, the FCC stated that it will allow a small amount of interference in conjunction with the BPL service. However, it restricted the service in areas such as around airports and near Coast Guard stations where the interference might interfere with public safety. The FCC set up a system to monitor interference.

Municipally Controlled Utilities in Telecommunications

According to the American Public Power Association, 14.3% of customers in the United States get their power from publicly owned utilities, utilities that are departments of city governments or created by city governments with government controlled boards. Five hundred seventy of these public utilities offer some type of broadband service in their mainly rural areas. A February 12, 2004 article by Tim Kridel "Supremes Mull Municipal Broadband," which appeared in *Light Reading*, quoted Render, Vanderslice & Associates, "In 2003, municipalities and public utility districts made up 32% of the fiber-to-the-home market and have accounted for the single largest builds."

In March 2004, the Supreme Court ruled that states can block or limit telecommunications sales by municipalities. Thirteen states have various barriers to entry, including taxes and special regulatory approval requirements. Missouri has banned municipalities from telecommunications except those already in place. The RBOCs actively lobbied in states against municipalities providing broadband. The ruling did not impact cable TV and Internet services, both of which are not now classified as telecommunications services.

Previous Utility Telecommunications Losses

Many utilities, attracted by growth in telecommunications, entered telecommunications in the 1990s and lost millions of dollars. Examples include Enron, Williams, and Westar Energy. Montana Power & Light, which sold telecommunications on a wholesale basis, sold its utility business in 2001, changed its name to Touch American, and entered the retail market. Touch America purchased Qwest's long distance assets in

Qwest's 14-state region, and later Qwest and Touch American sued each other over billing and other issues. Touch America lost its court case, filed for bankruptcy, and was purchased by Canadian telecommunications firm 360networks. Like failed CLECs, utilities underestimated the level of competition and swift drop in retail prices and overestimated the number of customers they would attract to cover infrastructure and ongoing operational costs.

Table 3.2   Major North American Wireline Carriers

Carrier	Primary Businesses	Background
AboveNet, Inc.	Metropolitan fiber rings	Formerly Metromedia Fiber Network, emerged from bankruptcy in September 2003. Owns largest independently provided metropolitan fiber network. It's in 13 U.S. cities and Europe. Sells high-speed data services to retail customers and carriers on its metropolitan networks. Offers backup data storage at its data centers. Craig McCaw through Fiber, LLC has a large stake in AboveNet.
Adelphia Communications Corporation	Multiple service operator (MSO) Cable TV	Adelphia provides cable TV service to 5.3 million subscribers. It is currently in bankruptcy. Adelphia's founder John Rigas and his son were convicted of criminal fraud charges by the federal government. Comcast is purchasing 2 million and Time Warner is purchasing 3.3 million of Adelphia's customers.
Aliant Inc.	Canadian incumbent local exchange carrier (ILEC) and wireless provider	Service provided in New Brunswick, Newfoundland, Labrador, and Nova Scotia. Provides wireline as well as wireless service. BCE owns 53%.
ALLTEL Corporation	Independent ILEC Cellular provider	ALLTEL is the sixth largest LEC in the United States with over 3 million local lines in 15 states. It sells cellular service and in 2002 purchased CenturyTel's cellular operations. It is a CLEC in some states outside of its home territory.

Table 3.2   Major North American Wireline Carriers   (continued)

Carrier	Primary Businesses	Background
AT&T	CLEC Data network services Internet backbone Hosting	The number-one long distance provider with the largest nationwide network and an extensive international network. Its consumer division markets only Voice over IP and DSL services. Signed a merger agreement with SBC.
BCE Inc.	Canadian ILEC Mobile wireless Interexchange fiber network	Canada's largest telecom company. Owns Bell Canada, Bell Mobility, and satellite organizations. It has stakes in broadcasting, newspaper, and portal firms and owns 360networks' fiber network. Until 2000, it had a stake in equipment supplier Nortel Networks.
Broadview Networks	CLEC	New York City–based provider of voice and data services to small and medium-size businesses in the northeastern and mid-Atlantic United States. Purchased Network Plus of Massachusetts, which had filed for Chapter 11. Merged with CLEC BridgeCom Holdings in 2005.
CenturyTel Inc.	Independent ILEC Interstate fiber network Cable TV	CenturyTel is the eighth largest local exchange carrier in the United States. It also owns an interstate fiber network. CenturyTel purchased local lines in rural areas from Verizon. Its services are scattered over 20 states in mostly rural and some suburban areas. It also sells cable TV service.
Charter Communications	MSO Cable TV	Charter is the third largest cable TV multiple system operator (MSO). Paul Allen, a cofounder of Microsoft, is the majority owner of Charter. It was established through the purchase of smaller cable TV operators.

continues

Table 3.2 Major North American Wireline Carriers   (continued)

Carrier	Primary Businesses	Background
Citizens Communications Company	Independent ILEC CLEC	A former utility, Citizens, is the seventh largest independent telephone company. It operates under the Frontier brand. It purchased the Frontier lines from Global Crossing and other lines from GTE (now Verizon). It owns CLEC Electric Lightwave. Citizens is for sale.
Comcast Corporation	MSO Cable TV TV networks	Comcast is the largest MSO cable TV operator in the United States with 21.5 million subscribers. It purchased AT&T's cable properties, TCI and MediaOne. Comcast owns Outdoor Life Network, game network G4techTV, The Golf Channel, and E! Entertainment Television.
Corvis Corporation	CLEC Wholesale fiber Optical network manufacturing	Sells voice and data service mainly to enterprises. Purchased CLEC Focal Communications and fiber network provider Broadwing, previously owned by Cincinnati Bell. Corvis manufactures the optical networking equipment used by Broadwing.
Covad Communications Group, Inc.	CLEC Hosted IP Wholesale and retail DSL	Covad installs DSL equipment in Bell offices. Large CLECs resell its DSL service. Purchased Voice over IP provider GoBeam. Covad offers Voice over IP to resellers as well as directly to small and medium-size business customers. Emerged from bankruptcy in 2001.
Cox Communications	MSO Cable TV Video on demand	Cox Communications is the fourth largest multiple system operator cable TV in the United States. It owns video-on-demand provider IN DEMAND and has a 25% ownership in Discovery Communications. Its parent company, Cox Enterprises, owns newspapers, radio and television stations, and auto auction organizations. It has announced its intention to become a private company.

Table 3.2 Major North American Wireline Carriers (continued)

Carrier	Primary Businesses	Background
Equant N.V.	International data Hosting	International, Netherlands-based data network services carrier. Offers international data connectivity, Web hosting, and network design services to global companies. France Telecom owns Equant.
Global Crossing Ltd.	Undersea cables Retail and wholesale telecommunications	International carrier in the United States, Europe, and Asia. Global Crossing filed for bankruptcy in 2002. The SEC and the Justice Department investigated it for questionable accounting and business practices. Now owned by Singapore Technologies' Telemedia (ST Telemedia). Bought and later sold independent ILEC Frontier.
IDT Corporation	CLEC IP wholesaler Prepaid calling cards	Sells retail and wholesale IP and traditional long distance services as well as prepaid calling. Purchased bankrupt carriers Winstar, Teligent, ICG Communications, and Star Telecoummications. Has a stake in Voice over IP provider Net2Phone.
ITC^ DeltaCom, Inc.	Regional CLEC Wholesale fiber	Largest CLEC in southern and southeastern United States. Owns fiber network provider BTI Telecom. DeltaCom sells to retail customers and provides wholesale capacity to other carriers. Emerged from Chapter 11 bankruptcy.
Level 3 Communications, Inc.	Wholesale fiber Undersea cable Software distribution	Sells wholesale voice and data service on its IP-based fiber rings in North America and Europe as well as undersea in the Atlantic ocean. Purchased most of bankrupt Genuity, parts of which it then sold. Derives 50% of its revenue from its software distributors, CorpSoft and Software Spectrum. Owns 24% of cable TV competitor RCN.

continues

Table 3.2 Major North American Wireline Carriers (continued)

Carrier	Primary Businesses	Background
MCI, Inc.	CLEC Internet backbone Hosting Data service Wholesale	Second largest long distance provider in the United States. Operates in 200 countries worldwide. Changed its name to MCI following bankruptcy as WorldCom. WorldCom grew by purchasing the largest competitive access providers (CAPs), MFS and Brooks Fiber, as well as MCI, WilTel, IDB, and Metromedia Communications. It expanded its data services via purchases of Web hosting company Digex and Internet backbone provider UUNET. Has agreed to be purchased by Verizon Communications.
McLeodUSA Incorporated	CLEC	A facilities-based CLEC that operates in 25 states in the western and midwestern United States. Emerged from bankruptcy in 2002. Investment firm Forstmann Little owns a controlling interest. McLeodUSA sold its directory business and data services units to raise capital.
RCN Corporation	Cable TV overbuilder Long distance Dial-up Internet	Largest overbuilder in the United States. (An overbuilder competes with cable TV operators by running fiber to its cable TV customers.) Filed a plan to emerge from bankruptcy. Level 3 owns 23% and Paul Allen's Vulcan Investments 16%. Offers service in metropolitan Boston, Chicago, Los Angeles, New York, Philadelphia, San Francisco, and Washington, D.C.
Rogers Communications Inc.	Canadian MSO cable TV Mobile wireless	Rogers is the largest cable TV provider in Canada, operating mainly in the eastern sections of Canada. It also owns 45% of Rogers Wireless. Rogers' media unit owns radio stations, 2 TV stations, magazines, and 270 video stores.

Table 3.2   Major North American Wireline Carriers   (continued)

Carrier	Primary Businesses	Background
Shaw Communications Inc.	Canadian MSO cable TV Satellite TV	Shaw is Canada's second largest cable TV operator, with franchises in the western parts of Canada. It offers satellite TV through its Canadian Satellite Communications company.
Sprint Corporation	Retail and wholesale long distance Mobile wireless Internet backbone Independent ILEC	Sprint is the third largest long distance company in revenue and third largest wireless provider. Sprint operates a large Internet backbone. It owns 17% of ISP EarthLink and 50% of Virgin Mobile, USA, which resells Sprint PCS wireless service in the United States. It has announced its intention to spin off its local phone company. It has announced its purchase of Nextel.
Telefonos de Mexico, known as Telmex	Mexican ILEC Mobile wireless	Telmex is the incumbent telephone company in Mexico. It has stakes in many Latin American wireline and wireless carriers. It is majority owned by Carlos Slim Helu.
TELUS Corporation	Canadian ILEC Mobile wireless CLEC	Second largest telecom company in Canada and the incumbent LEC in British Columbia and Alberta. Owns TELUS Mobility. Will become the largest carrier in Canada if successful in its bid for wireless provider Microcell. TELUS is a facility-based CLEC in eastern and central Canada.
Time-Warner Cable	MSO cable TV ISP	Time-Warner Cable is the second largest multiple system operator in the United States. It owns ISP Road Runner, which it uses in conjunction with its Internet access for e-mail and Internet services. Its parent media conglomerate Time-Warner owns America Online, HBO, Warner Brothers, Turner Broadcasting, TNT, *Time* magazine, and Time-Warner Books.

continues

Table 3.2 Major North American Wireline Carriers   (continued)

Carrier	Primary Businesses	Background
Time-Warner Telecom Inc.	CLEC Wholesale fiber	Sells wholesale fiber capacity to wireline and wireless carriers and retail long distance to small and medium-size businesses in 22 states. Time Warner owns 44%.
VarTec Telecom, Inc.	Long distance, wireless, and DSL reseller CLEC	Started out in 1989 as a 10-10 "dial-around" provider. Later purchased long distance reseller Excel Communications. It resells long distance, DSL, and wireless service. Its subsidiary eMeritus is a facilities-based CLEC. Large, privately owned carrier with 2003 sales of $1.3 billion.
Vonage Holdings Corporation	Voice over IP	Sells Voice over IP to residential customers and small businesses that access the service over cable and DSL modems. In January 2005, Vonage announced it had 390,000 customers.
XO Communications, Inc.	CLEC	XO is a facilities-based CLEC that operates fiber rings in metropolitan areas and a national fiber network. It serves some customers via fixed wireless. It operates in 21 states. Investor Carl Icahn invested in the company when it emerged from bankruptcy in 2003. It purchased Allegiance Telecom in 2004. XO was originally called NEXTLINK when Craig McCaw founded it.

REGULATORY ISSUES ....

Regulatory rules are critical factors in the success or failure of carriers. They impact pricing, billing practices, and decisions on whether to build or lease network infrastructure. The following is a quote from BellSouth's 2003 annual report:

"Our future operations and financial results will be substantially influenced by developments in a number of federal and state regulatory proceedings. Adverse results in these proceedings could materially affect our revenues, expenses, and ability to compete effectively against other telecommunications carriers."

Unbundled Network Elements (UNEs)— Competitors Leasing Parts of RBOCs' Networks

When the Telecommunications Act of 1996 was enacted, Congress felt that it was not economically feasible for the RBOCs' rivals to build all their own facilities. They therefore mandated that incumbents like SBC make their local networks available at replacement cost plus a reasonable profit to competitors such as MCI and AT&T. Replacement cost discounts are known as Telric, total element long-run incremental cost. Telric calculations were used to price *unbundled network elements* (*UNEs*) and UNE-P for unbundled network element platforms. Unbundled network elements included the local copper loop from the incumbent to the customer, high-speed lines between the CLEC and the incumbent central office, RBOC central office switch ports connected to local loops, operator services, and signaling services to link central offices to, for example, billing systems.

Many competitive local exchange carriers including MCI, Sprint, and AT&T often leased entire platforms, UNE-P, at a discount rate to offer service without building facilities. Some CLECs used this strategy primarily for residential service, and others built their whole business around the resale of UNE-P. Other CLECs built their own facilities in areas where they had concentrations of business customers and used UNE-P in other areas.

Telric Rates—Total Element Long-Run Incremental Cost

The FCC specified that unbundled network element discounts were to be based on the cost to replace facilities rather than the original cost to build them. Because of technological advancements and lower manufacturing costs, the use of Telric to calculate leasing rates resulted in the former Bells often leasing equipment to competitors at prices below their original cost.

Elimination of Most UNE Fees

In March 2004, the United States Court of Appeals for the District of Columbia struck down the FCC's February 20, 2003 Triennial Review Order. The Triennial Review Order had mandated that individual state utility commissions rule on pricing and availability of UNE discounts when competitors lease facilities to reach residential and small business customers. The Triennial Review Order also gave states the right to decide on UNE pricing and availability for various services provided to large and medium-size enterprise customers by CLECs. Rates and availability were to be based on the viability of competition in each state.

The Court of Appeal's March 2004 ruling struck down state authority and ordered the FCC to develop nationwide pricing rules for competitive access to incumbent facilities such as central office switch ports, local loops, and high capacity T-1 (1.54 megabits), T-3 (44 megabits), and optical carrier (155 million bits per second and higher) lines.

To the disappointment of competitive carriers, the FCC and the Justice Department did not appeal the circuit court's ruling to the Supreme Court. The circuit court's ruling will end most of the deep discounts available to competitors in metropolitan areas under the unbundled network element (UNE) pricing. The FCC did spell out a limited number of conditions where eliminating UNE rules impairs competition.

The Impact of Higher Leasing Rates

In the weeks following the FCC and the Justice Department's decision not to appeal the circuit court's ruling, nine CLECs announced major layoffs. Five of the nine either went out of business or declared bankruptcy. AT&T announced that it stopped marketing public switched telephone service to consumers. As a result of the circuit court's decision, costs for carriers without their own local central office switches, fiber networks, and local lines will increase dramatically. As the FCC finalizes rates, more CLECs have decreased the range of their offerings or ceased operations entirely.

According to the FCC's May 2004 *Trends in Telephone Service*, as of June 2003, CLECs own about one-fourth, or 6.3 million, of the local loop facilities over which they sell services. This figure exaggerates the number of premises served by CLEC facilities. According to the FCC's Industry Analysis and Technology Division, each T-1 and T-3 high capacity trunk is counted as multiple lines. The division assumes that each trunk uses a percentage of their 24 or 672 channels for voice. For the most part, CLECs depend on incumbents' local loops to reach customers. In addition, the two largest CLECs, AT&T and MCI, owned many of the 6.3 million lines cited above. They will both soon be purchased by Regional Bell Operating Companies that will then own these facilities.

Small businesses will feel the biggest impact of these changes. According to the Small Business Administration, 29% of small businesses in metropolitan areas use CLECs. The FCC set rules in December 2004 spelling out conditions under which T-1 and T-3 UNE rates can be phased out. The capability for RBOCs to phase out UNE discounts apply to about 47 metropolitan central offices for T-1 and about 100 for T-3. The FCC has also ordered that discount access to central office ports be phased out. This will impact the over half of the CLECs who use UNE-P for most of their offerings.

Local loops that competitors lease from incumbents are referred to as UNE-L for unbundled network element loop (see Figure 3.4 for UNE-L). Analog local loops have not been impacted so far by FCC rulings. However, as RBOCs build out fiber closer to customers, these analog loops will disappear. The FCC has ruled that former Bells do not have to share fiber facilities they build within 500 feet of customers. Thus, where fiber replaces copper or is within 500 feet of customers, local loops will not be available to competitors. UNE-L makes it more feasible for competitors to invest in central office switches and fiber facilities between switches because it leaves in place a way for CLECs to economically extend service to small and medium-size customers. The CLECs are expected to appeal the FCC December 2004 ruling in court.

Where UNE-L is not available, consumers and small and medium-size businesses will have to rely on emerging technologies for competitive choices. These choices include intermodal options previously discussed and possibly new fixed wireless substitutions for local loops such as WiMAX (see Chapter 9 for a discussion of

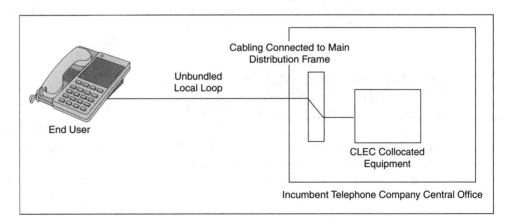

Figure 3.4
A local loop leased by a CLEC.

WiMAX). To date, these wireless services are not widely available. However, cable offerings will become more readily available to businesses.

According to an August 2004 interview with Jerry Watts, ITC^DeltaCom vice president of government and industry affairs and president of CompSouth, a trade association of 19 carriers serving customers in the southeast:

> *"Relative to the circuit court decision's ultimate impact on the industry, at this point, it's too early to tell. There are many issues still undecided. Some of those decisions have to do with jurisdictional issues. For example, how much jurisdiction do state commissions retain relative to the establishment of replacement rates for Telric UNEs that are discontinued? I'm still disappointed and amazed that the Bush administration did not appeal the court's order and was willing to essentially let the D.C. circuit court rewrite the Telecom Act.*
>
> *The most troublesome thing is the potential impact on the availability of the UNE-Platform at cost-based Telric rates. The vast majority of competitive carriers' lines serving small business and residential customers are UNE-P lines that the carriers purchase from the various Bell companies. If, in fact, this order results in these no longer being available, then I think there will be a pretty dramatic impact on the ability of a lot of smaller carriers to compete. Our company is a substantially facilities-based company, and UNE-P is just a piece of our market strategy that we use for some residential and small business offerings. We use high-capacity loops and transport to connect customers to our switches, and these UNE's are also being reviewed. I hope that we get some rational policy from the FCC when they make final rules."*

Regulating Cable Modems— Cable, Information, or Telecommunications Services?

Three possible regulatory classifications for cable modems are as information, as cable, or as telecommunications services. Cable modems are currently regulated as an information service. However, DSL modem service is regulated as a telecommunications service. This puts DSL service at a disadvantage.

Services classified as telecommunications service must do the following:

- Provide enhanced 911 services so that the emergency answering agency receives the caller's telephone number, which is associated with an address in the agency's database.
- Contribute to federal and state Universal Service Funds.
- Allow competitors access to their networks for services to competitors' customers.
- Open their networks to the FBI for court-ordered surveillance under Communications Assistance for Law Enforcement Act (CALEA).
- Provide privacy to subscribers by not revealing customers' information to other companies. Information can be revealed to telcos' affiliates unless customers choose to "opt out."
- Report major outages to the FCC.

The issue of whether cable modem service should be classified as a cable service (and be subject to local franchise fees), a telecommunications service, or an information service has been the subject of a series of court cases. In October 2003, the U.S. Court of Appeals for the Ninth Circuit ruled that the FCC should classify cable broadband as a telecommunications service, not as an information service. This ruling has not been implemented, and the Federal Communications Commission along with the Justice Department is expected to appeal the ruling to the Supreme Court.

Currently, cable operators do provide access to Voice over IP competitors, including AT&T, Vonage, Skype, and Net2phone. This enables cable modem customers to use these companies' Voice over IP over their cable modem connections. Some cable operators also allow ISPs such as EarthLink to access their networks and sell competing Internet service provider services such as e-mail to cable modem customers. If the Supreme Court upholds the Ninth Circuit Court ruling that cable modems are telecommunications services, cable operators will be required to open their networks to competition. Regardless of the ruling, the FCC has stated that it intends to require cable operators and Voice over IP suppliers to open their networks for surveillance as required in the 1994 Communications Assistance for Law Enforcement Act (CALEA).

Voice Over IP—Regulatory Issues

In February 2004, the FCC ruled that voice calls carried from personal computer to personal computer are information services and thus are not subject to common carrier regulations. However, Voice over IP calls from personal computers to telephones connected to the public switched network are currently considered telecommunications services. However, the FCC is reviewing these rules. The FCC does allow states to provide Voice over IP customers protection against fraud and other state laws governing marketing, advertising, and other business practices.

In another ruling, in November 2004, the FCC further ruled that Voice over IP traffic should be regulated as an interstate service at the national, not the state, level because it's not always clear where calls originate or terminate. This makes it less cumbersome for VoIP providers, as they will not be required to obtain state-by-state approval to offer service. The FCC did state that VoIP providers are required to provide emergency 911 services equivalent to that provided by incumbent telephone companies.

Regulatory issues are still very much up in the air. The commission has stated that it will look at whether VoIP should be classified as an information or telecommunications service later. It also stated its intention to address in 2005 VoIP providers' obligations to pay access fees and contribute to universal service fees. Currently, information services are exempt from these fees. Also not addressed yet is the issue of states' rights to tax Internet phone service. This is likely to be addressed by Congress.

More regulatory uncertainty was created when public utility commissions in California and Minnesota appealed the FCC's November 2004 decision to two different appeals courts. The courts can accede to the FCC's decision or strike it down. In the event that it strikes it down, the FCC may appeal to the Supreme Court. The states expressed concerns about losing state-imposed access fee subsidies used for poor and rural areas. They are also concerned about regulation on the national level of local 911 capabilities.

Access Fees—A Shift in Balance Between Local and Long Distance Costs

Carriers pay access fees to local telephone companies for transporting long distance traffic to and from local customers. The FCC sets access fees for interstate traffic, and state utility commissions set access fees for intrastate traffic. Access fees are designed to recover local exchange carriers' (LECs') variable costs for originating and terminating long distance calls. Historically, intrastate access fees tended to be higher than cost as a way to subsidize local service so that telephone companies could keep rates for residential customers affordable.

Rules promulgated by the FCC on May 7, 1997 lowered access fees by $18.5 billion over five years. This action shifted costs to residential and business users in the form of higher monthly subscriber line charges (SLCs). The decrease in access fees is one factor in lower long distance rates and the resultant cost shifts to consumers in the form of subscriber line charges.

Traffic Exempt from Access Fee Rules— Voice Over IP and Wireless

Access fees for toll traffic do not currently apply to Voice over IP calls that originate and terminate on the Internet. Nor do access fee regulations apply to wireless carriers. Rather, wireless carriers are required to negotiate contracts with each carrier to which they connect so that the wireline carrier is able to cover its costs for transmitting calls between wireless networks and the public switched telephone network.

If Voice over IP service remains exempt from access fees, the RBOCs will lose an important source of access fee revenue. According to an April 14, 2004 online article "S&P Cautions Bells on VOIP" in *Light Reading* by Justin Hibbard, RBOCs derive 22% of their revenues from access fees.

Reciprocal Compensation—Access Fees for Carrying Local Traffic

Carriers pay each other reciprocal compensation fees for terminating and originating local traffic. The FCC ruled in April 2001 that Internet-bound dial-up traffic, largely from incumbent carriers to CLECs, is interstate information access and is not eligible for reciprocal compensation. Rather than eliminating the fees entirely, they were dramatically reduced over a two-year period at transitional rates. Prior to this ruling, many CLECs received a large portion of their revenue in the form of reciprocal compensation for terminating dial-up traffic to Internet service providers.

Access Fee Reform—Making Access Fees Simple to Administer and Fair

In 2001, the FCC released a Notice of Proposed Rulemaking about establishing a unified intercarrier compensation plan to include wireless, local, and Internet-based services as well as wireline voice traffic. The FCC has stated that its goal in reforming access fees is to have one system of access fees regardless of technology. The FCC announced that it is considering eliminating all access fees that carriers pay each other for terminating and originating traffic to each other's customers. The FCC termed this approach bill and keep. With *bill and keep*, carriers recoup the costs of originating and terminating traffic from their own customers rather than from other carriers.

Bill and keep will transfer more costs to end users in general. It will impact rural customers the most. Rural telephone companies depend on higher-than-national-average access fees as well as universal service fees to subsidize their high costs of providing telephone service. They are concerned that a major decrease in access fees will force them to raise prices for basic dial tone.

Industry groups convened to reach agreement on access fee reforms have to date failed to reach a consensus. Dissatisfaction with bill and keep occurs among carriers who don't send each other a roughly equivalent amount of traffic. Incumbent local exchange carriers are concerned that bill and keep will raise their costs by decreasing access fees, making them less competitive. The National Association of Regulatory Utility Commissions feels states should continue to have a key role in determining intrastate access fees. They do agree that local phone companies should charge a single rate to terminate any type of traffic, including wireless, Voice over IP, and circuit switched calls to consumers.

GAMING THE ACCESS FEE SYSTEM

To make up for decreasing margins,   lower revenue, and increased competition, some carriers in recent years have attempted to "game" the access fee system to either save money or earn extra revenue using access fee schemes.

For example:

- In one lawsuit, AT&T accused MCI of disguising interstate traffic as local so that calls from MCI customers to AT&T would incur lower access charges.

- In another lawsuit, one CLEC accused another CLEC of charging unlawful access fees for toll-free traffic that originated at wireless carriers who are not entitled to federal access fees.

- In another plan, CLECs collocate information service providers' audio conference equipment at their central office switch site. A large part of the revenue they receive for conference calling is derived from access fees they charge interexchange carriers to terminate the audio conferencing traffic. When customers call a telephone number connected to the conference equipment, the local CLEC charges access fees to the customers' interexchange carrier for terminating the calls.

APPENDIX ....

Table 3.3 Major Features of the Telecommunications Act

The Telecommunications Act of 1996 outlined provisions by which competitors were to be allowed to lease and resell portions of incumbent telephone company networks so that they could compete without installing brand new infrastructure in cities and metropolitan areas. Parts of the Telecommunications Act apply also to cable TV providers and broadcasters.	
Bell Company entry into inter-LATA service	The first step in the process was state utility commission approval. The FCC, with feedback from the Justice Department, then granted final permission for the Bell companies to sell in-region long distance.
Approval to enter long distance—the 14-point checklist	Each Bell had to have signed agreements with facilities-based carriers that use predominately their own switches and cabling for carrying customers' calls, unless no facilities-based carrier had requested interconnection. The 14-point checklist spelled out requirements for interconnection agreements.

Table 3.4 Regulatory Highlights

Landmark Acts and Court Rulings	Summary of Acts and Rulings
The Federal Communications Act of 1934	Congress created the Federal Communications Commission and gave it the authority to regulate interstate telephone, radio, and telegraph companies.
The 1956 Consent Decree	The Justice Department allowed AT&T to keep its monopoly but restricted it to common carrier functions. The Consent Decree mandated that any patents developed by Bell Labs, then AT&T, be licensed to all applicants requesting them. This led to microwave technology's availability to MCI and the ability of competitive carriers to build long distance networks.
The 1969 MCI Case	The Federal Communications Commission ruled that MCI, then known as Microwave Communications Inc., could connect its equipment to the public network provided that the network was not harmed. This decision opened the CPE market to AT&T rivals such as Rolm and Executone.

continues

Table 3.4   Regulatory Highlights (continued)

Landmark Acts and Court Rulings	Summary of Acts and Rulings
The 1982 to 1983 Modified Final Judgment	The Justice Department, in agreement with AT&T and with approval by Judge Harold H. Greene, agreed to a settlement that • Divested the then 22 Bell Operating Companies (BOCs) from AT&T • Prohibited BOCs from inter-LATA long distance, sale of CPE, and manufacturing • Mandated that the local exchange companies provide equal access (dial 1) from end users to all interexchange carriers
The 1984 Divestiture	The terms spelled out in the Modified Final Judgment were implemented on January 1, 1984. The 22 Bell telephone companies were merged into seven Regional Bell Operating Companies (RBOCs). The RBOCs were allowed to sell local and toll calling within the 197 defined local or LATA areas. They also retained the yellow pages. AT&T kept manufacturing, inter-LATA, and international toll calling.
The Telecommunications Act of 1996	Decreed that cable TV companies, electric utilities, broadcasters, interexchange carriers, and competitive access providers could sell local and local toll calling.
	Allowed local competitors interconnection to and resale of local telephone companies' facilities.
	Set fees for interconnection services at the LECs'* costs plus a reasonable profit.
	Set fees for resale at LECs' costs.
	Allowed Bell companies to immediately provide out-of-region long distance.
	Allowed Bell companies to provide inter-LATA toll calling and manufacturing in their regions under FCC approval or by February 1999, whichever is earlier.

Table 3.4 Regulatory Highlights (continued)

Landmark Acts and Court Rulings	Summary of Acts and Rulings
	Dictated that FCC approval depends on the incumbent LECs meeting conditions of a 14-point checklist of opening its regions for competition.
FCC 2001—Deregulation of devices connected to the public switched network	The FCC will no longer set specifications for modems, phones, and fax machines connected to the public network. This will be turned over to a private agency. The FCC will continue to set standards for wireless devices.
January 2004—Supreme Court restricted phone lawsuits	The Supreme Court ruled that RBOCs cannot be sued under federal antitrust law over claims that they are not opening their networks to competition.

The term "incumbent LEC," or "local exchange carrier," refers to the Bell Operating Companies and independent local exchange carriers.

Table 3.5 FCC Rulings and Legal Challenges to the Telecommunications Act of 1996

Date	Decision or Action
June 27, 1996	The FCC spelled out rules on service provider portability. It stated that customers must be able to keep their telephone numbers when they change carriers. It also stated they must be able to keep "smart" features such as call waiting when they change carriers.
August 8, 1996	The FCC set rules for calculating the wholesale fees that BOCs could charge competitors for network elements. It also identified seven pieces of the network that must be leased to rivals. The discounts were in the 17% to 25% range. Access fees to wireless companies were reduced by $1 billion annually.
September 12, 1996	The FCC allowed utilities whose lines cross state boundaries into telecommunications.
October 15, 1996	The U.S. Court of Appeals for the Eighth Circuit stayed (denied) the FCC's jurisdiction in setting interconnection and wholesale pricing at the local level. Stayed the FCC's August 8, 1996 ruling.

continues

Table 3.5 FCC Rulings and Legal Challenges to the Telecommunications Act
of 1996 (continued)

Date	Decision or Action
October 11, 1996	Justice Clarence Thomas refused to lift the October 15, 1996 stay by the Eighth Court of Appeals. Federal regulators had asked that the ruling be overturned.
November 11, 1996	The FCC appealed Justice Thomas's ruling. The Supreme Court upheld the Eighth Circuit's October 15, 1996 stay on the FCC's ability to set pricing guidelines.
May 7, 1997	The FCC lowered access fees, the fees interexchange carriers charge to transmit and receive calls from the local networks, by $1.7 billion the first year and $18.5 billion over five years. The FCC also raised end-user line charges by $2.75 for each business line and $1.50 for a second home phone line to pay for subsidies for schools and libraries mandated by the Telecommunications Act of 1996.
July 1997	The Eighth Circuit Court of Appeals suspended the FCC's pricing rules.
October 1997	The Eighth Circuit Court of Appeals suspended FCC authority and rules on procedures for interconnection to local networks.
December 31, 1997	The U.S. District Court excluded October's ban of SBC's and US West's entry into long distance. After long distance companies, the FCC, and the Justice Department appealed, the judge delayed implementation of this ruling.
January 19, 1999	The Supreme Court upheld the constitutionality of the Telecommunications Act of 1996 not to allow the baby Bells into in-region long distance before they open their networks to rivals. US West, SBC, and Bell Atlantic had argued that they were singled out because the Telecommunications Act did not apply to GTE, Frontier, and Southern New England Telephone Company.

Table 3.5 FCC Rulings and Legal Challenges to the Telecommunications Act of 1996 (continued)

Date	Decision or Action
January 25, 1999	The Supreme Court upheld the FCC's authority to implement the Telecommunications Act of 1996 but directed the Eighth Circuit Court of Appeals to approve the FCC's national pricing plans and allowed exemptions of independent telephone companies to rules of the Telecommunications Act. If a network element is available elsewhere, the Bells should not be required to make it available to competitors (for example, Internet access, voice mail, or high-speed data lines). This effectively reversed the Eighth Circuit Court of Appeals' suspension of FCC jurisdiction of interconnection to local networks.
July 1999 and January 2001	The Eight Circuit Court of Appeals struck down FCC rules for how Bell telephone companies set fees for network elements they rent to CLECs. This ruling would have resulted in higher fees for CLECs. However, the FCC appealed to the Supreme Court, which stated that it would rule on the issue in 2001. The Court also stated it would rule on whether CLECs can rent packages of services if they request them rather than only individual pieces as now required.
September 1999	The FCC increased the number of unbundled network elements the Bells are required to provide competitors. The most important of these is the right for competitors to share the same Bell lines for voice phone service for DSL Internet access service. (See Chapter 5 for DSL service.)
January 2001	The U.S. Court of Appeals struck down an FCC rule that absolved SBC from making connections to data services such as DSL to competitors if the incumbent sold these data services through a separate subsidiary. It appears that instead of a separate subsidiary, SBC will be required to sell data service through a separate division that will be required to lease connections to competitors.
February 2001	On his last day of office, William E. Kennard, the outgoing chairman of the FCC, ruled that Bells must share local loops for voice and DSL when they are made up of a mix of fiber and copper as well as all copper, as is often the case.
May 2002	The Supreme Court ruled that telephone companies can challenge state utility agencies in federal courts on rates that state utility commissions set for leasing network and services to competitors.

To date, service provider and service portability are mandated.

Table 3.6   Four Types of Telephone Number Portability

Service provider portability	An end user's ability to keep his or her telephone number when changing carriers within the same rate center. The method approved by the FCC to accomplish service provider portability is local routing number (LRN). With LRN, every central office switch is assigned a 10-digit number. These switch numbers, or LRNs, reside in network databases. All telephone calls trigger a "dip" into a database to determine to which central office a call should be routed.
Location portability	Keeping a telephone number when moving to another rate center.
	Rate centers are the points within exchanges used to determine toll rates. Location portability is not mandated. It is thought that implementation of location portability will be driven by customer demand. The capability for large businesses to keep their telephone numbers when they move is significant. Voice over IP, covered in Chapter 4, enables customers to keep their telephone number at various locations.
Service portability	Keeping a telephone number when changing from wireline to wireless service.
	Service provider portability, which was phased in beginning November 2003, allows users to keep their telephone numbers when they change to wireless providers for their home telephone service or when they move their wireless number to their landline service.
One number for life portability	Keeping a telephone number regardless of location or service used.
	This opens up the possibility for out-of-area geographic portability between towns and states as well as between carriers. This is the case with toll-free 800, 888, 866, and 877 calling. These numbers are assigned to customers regardless of their location. No date is set or mandated for one number for life portability.

4 VoIP, the Public Switched Telephone Network, and Signaling

In this chapter:

Carriers worldwide are in the early stages of a major shift toward deployment of single networks capable of carrying voice, data, and entertainment traffic. Carriers with older technology support separate networks for voice, data, and video. The shift to newer, IP-based technology is most pronounced where carriers are building new networks. China is an example in which carriers are expanding the reach of networks using the IP protocol for legs of their network. The prime drivers for the transition to IP are the lower cost to operate a single network and the promise of adding revenue-producing services at lower costs.

Although carriers know how to carry high-quality voice on their private IP packet networks, they are still developing ways to send IP traffic to each other without first going through the public switched telephone network. They rely on gateway devices to make unlike protocols compatible with each other. They are also developing ways to standardize how they bill each other for packetized voice carried between networks. An additional challenge is their lack of control over the voice quality on other providers' DSL and cable TV facilities over which their customers' VoIP packets travel.

While Voice over IP for residential customers is growing, most households are still cautious about adopting it. To be accepted as a mainstream service for residential customers, certain limitations need to be overcome. More VoIP providers need to find a way to easily support all of a home's telephones. Cable TV providers do this by dispatching an installer, but other providers for the most part just tell users to plug their main telephone, which supports cordless handsets as extensions, into the VoIP equipment. Providers also need to be able to give customers the capability to support two simultaneous calls. This is important in the small business home office market (SOHO) and other homes that need multiple lines.

Many providers, including some RBOCs, CLECs, and Sprint, focus their Voice over IP product on business customers. Even Vonage, known for its residential service, states that 20% of its customer base consists of small businesses. The higher-revenue enterprise customer is attractive to providers. In addition, medium and large enterprises can use in-place T-1 (1.54 megabits per second) and T-3 (45 megabits bits per second) data links for voice traffic directly to carriers' equipment. This gives the carrier control of quality from the customer all the way through the carrier's network.

Cross-border traffic, traffic carried between countries, is a leading application for IP. Carriers use Voice over IP to save money on fax and debit card traffic and increasingly for voice calling. Quality on this traffic is fine because of the abundance of capacity in most long distance routes. Table 4.1 indicates the trend on international traffic that crosses borders. On domestic routes in the core, long distance portion of networks, more and more traffic is also carried in IP and other types of packets.

Instant messaging, and online gaming services carry Voice over IP using a different method than the RBOCs, CLECs, and cable TV providers. They use variations of the peer-to-peer services previously offered by companies such as Gnutella and KaZaA that let users download free music from each other's computers. Peer-to-peer models are proprietary, and their computer-to computer communications operate over closed communities of users. For a fee, some of them let users call people on the public switched telephone network. Skype is an example of a carrier that uses peer-to-peer technology.

These technologies highlight the fact that voice is a commodity service or part of a package with other applications. Voice is often free in, for example, instant messaging services. Providers are hoping to make up for these declining revenues in voice traffic with advanced voice mail, conference calling, and video calling. They're working with developers and hope to discover new, profitable services.

A major strength of the public switched network is its capability to connect users worldwide. Much of the capability to bill carriers for this traffic and enhancements such as toll-free calling between countries was enabled by Signaling System 7, which is used, with variations, worldwide. When it was implemented in the 1980s, it was the basis for much of the automation in maintaining equipment and the resultant ability to reduce the technician staffing levels.

Increased competition, hopes for new applications, and the potential for network efficiencies are causing carriers and manufacturers to concentrate their development efforts on Voice over IP.

Table 4.1 International Cross Border VoIP and PSTN Traffic Summary, 1998–2003

	1998	1999	2000	2001	2002	2003	CAGR*
VoIP Traffic (millions of minutes)	150	1,655	5,954	10,147	18,045	24,519	177%
PSTNTraffic** (millions of minutes)	93,000	108,000	132,027	146,095	155,165	166,615	12%
VoIP Share of International Traffic	0.2%	1.5%	4.3%	6.5%	10.4%	12.8%	

*Cumulative average growth rate
**Public switched telephone network
From: TeleGeography 2004
Source: PriMetrica, Inc.

CONVERGENCE IN PUBLIC NETWORKS ....

Carriers now use converged technology primarily in core, backbone portions of their networks to carry customer traffic more efficiently. As the technology matures and more features are added to edge equipment closer to customers, more carriers will use converged platforms for all of their traffic. Although user acceptance is growing, there are impediments to carrier and user implementation of the technology that are gradually being overcome.

Circuit Switching—Network Inefficiencies and Convergence

Although carriers increasingly add IP equipment when they replace their voice switches, the majority of voice traffic is still carried in circuit switched networks. A *circuit* is a physical path for the transmission of voice, image, or data. The ITU (International Telecommunications Union) defines circuit switching as follows:

> *"The switching of circuits for the exclusive use of the connection for the duration of a call."*

When a person or a modem dials a call, the network sets up a path between the caller and the dialed party. Importantly, the path is available exclusively for the duration of the call. The path is not shared. Natural pauses in conversation and data transmission are not used for other voice or data calls. Capacity is reserved in the network for the entire duration of the transmission. When the call is ended, the path is released and becomes available for another phone call. This exclusivity causes wasteful utilization of network capacity.

The Rationale for Convergence

The Internet protocol (IP) does not have this limitation. Packets from other sources fill pauses in one conversation. For example, when a call is on hold, network capacity is used for other traffic. Moreover, technical advances have improved the quality of voice and video carried on packet networks. In addition, costs for routers, hard drives, and fiber optics have decreased.

An additional rationale is the capability to deploy and maintain a single network for voice, data, and video. As margins decrease, carriers no longer want to support multiple networks. Furthermore, revenue-producing applications can be added at lower costs to converged networks than to those that use older circuit switches based on equipment with proprietary signaling. As Voice over IP protocols become increasingly standardized, custom interfaces between switches and applications will increasingly become unnecessary.

Impediments to Adoption—Training, Embedded Assets, User Adoption, and Fear of the Unknown

Similar forces holding back implementation of Voice over IP in enterprises affect carriers. Most incumbent carriers have existing voice networks based on circuit switched technology that are not fully depreciated. As switches used in these networks become manufacturer-discontinued with decreasing maintenance support and less spare part availability, carriers will migrate to new technology.

Training workforces on new technology and evaluating new equipment also holds back implementations. Skills needed to program, implement, and monitor a network based on new architecture are different than those used on circuit switch equipment. Rather than purchasing VoIP infrastructure and training staff, many carriers rely on other carriers' networks. For example, equipment at their site sends VoIP traffic to other carriers that carry their VoIP traffic.

In addition, many providers initially took a wait-and-see approach to learn how well new gear functioned in other networks and the financial stability of new manufacturers. When next-generation VoIP gear was first introduced, many new companies were formed to develop and manufacture Voice over IP gear, and it was not clear which of them would survive over the longer term. Carriers now recognize that Voice over IP is going to be the platform of the future.

Finally, while voice over broadband offers many features not available on traditional local lines, there are key features missing. These are listed later in this chapter and include E911, the capability to use the telephone in blackouts, and compatibility with alarm lines. As the service matures, many of these issues will be resolved. However, they do currently hold back user acceptance. Like carriers, many customers are interested in the service but are taking a wait-and-see approach.

VoIP Networks—Putting the Pieces Together

Cable TV, wireless mobile, and traditional local exchange carriers use common Internet protocol (IP) core and edge IP network components when they upgrade their networks to IP. The major difference in these networks is how customers reach the edge of the network, fixed line, wireless, or cable TV service. Various manufacturers and industry segments use different terms to describe components. CableLabs, the central research and development organization supported by cable TV operators, calls media servers *media resource function (MRF)*.

These devices are as follows:

- *Softswitches* process calls (issue commands on setting up and ending calls), communicate with billing systems, and act as an overall network control point.

- *Media gateways* switch calls and translate protocols between different networks and between public network trunks such as T-1 and T-3 trunks and IP networks.

- *Media servers* generate touch-tone, play announcements, and contain some features such as three-way calling.

- *Application servers* contain complex applications such as unified messaging (the capability to receive voice mail, e-mail, and fax messages on personal computers) and large audio conferencing systems.

See Figure 4.1 for Voice over IP architecture. Peer-to-peer services provided by Buzzfon P2P, Free World Dialup, GloPhone, Peerio, and Skype use a different architecture that is discussed in the sections that follow.

Softswitches—Standards-Based Platforms for Call Control

Softswitches are the "traffic cops" in Internet protocol (IP) networks that carry voice, fax, and video traffic. Some carriers—for example, AT&T—refer to their softswitch function as their call control element. Softswitches perform some of the tasks of central office switches used in circuit switched networks. However, unlike switches used in circuit switched networks, they are built on standard computer processors and use standards-based protocols. Because they are built on common platforms, programmable switches cost less than traditional, proprietary central office switches. Like IP PBXs (refer to Chapter 2, "VoIP Systems, Circuit Switched PBXs, and Cabling") in enterprises, the switching and control functions are separate.

Softswitches perform the following call processing and control functions:

- Send messages to the border element with instructions on where to send the call. (See the following sections for information regarding border elements.)

- Check to see which services the caller is entitled to use, such as voice mail or conference calling.

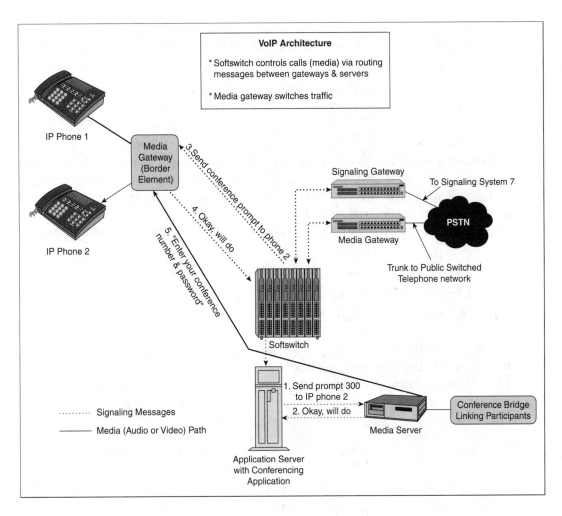

Figure 4.1
Application and architecture in an IP network, courtesy of NMS Communications Corp.

- Communicate with billing systems.
- Send a message to the network setting up a path between the caller (media) and endpoint (the called party).
- Stay alert and watchful during calls for new commands, such as touch-tone signals requesting to add a third party to the call or disconnect the call.

- Send messages to media servers (see subsequent sections for information on media servers) to play announcements such as "The telephone number you called is no longer in service."

- Send messages to process calls—for example, end (tear down) this call, use this IP address for this call, receive the call on this IP address.

Softswitches with standard protocols interface more easily to network-based applications such as unified messaging, speech recognition, and network-based systems for call centers when these systems are also based on standard protocols. Proprietary central office switches require costly interfaces to applications to translate signaling between applications and the switch. Major softswitch manufacturers include Lucent Technologies, Nortel Networks, Siemens AG, Sonus Networks, and Tekelec.

THE EMERGENCE OF IP INSTEAD OF ATM FOR NEXT-GENERATION VOICE NETWORKS

Prior to 1995, the prevailing notion was that asynchronous transfer mode (ATM) and Internet protocol (IP) were competitive technologies. IP at that time was considered a "best effort" service because IP-based networks indiscriminately discarded packets if there was congestion. There was no standardized protocol to identify and prioritize video and voice. It was thought that best effort would not be acceptable to carriers. Thus, at that time, ATM's ability to create virtual connections and to prioritize voice and video so that packets were not dropped and quality was acceptable gave ATM an important advantage.

In addition to being able to prioritize voice and video, ATM was faster, running at speeds of 155 and 622 megabits per second. Local area networks using Ethernet were limited to 10 megabits per second, and IP used between networks was also slower than ATM. Thus, at that time, when carriers wanted to upgrade their networks, they used ATM. For example, to speed up its Internet backbone, WorldCom (now MCI) invested millions of dollars in the late 1990s for ATM gear for its UUNET data network subsidiary.

However, ATM was complex to install and expensive. Although there was a push for ATM in LANs, initially on campus backbones, ATM was too costly to deploy to the desktop. Thus, ATM became used primarily in carrier and large enterprise backbone networks.

THE EMERGENCE OF IP INSTEAD OF ATM FOR NEXT-GENERATION VOICE NETWORKS (CONTINUED)

Because of the speed and quality-of-service advantages, established telecom vendors and most new softswitch developers initially based their next-generation voice switch architecture on ATM rather than IP. Meanwhile, improvements in routers and faster speeds on IP networks were making IP networks more suitable for voice. Importantly, the TAG protocol (now MPLS) developed by Cisco was maturing. This protocol marked packets so that voice and video could be prioritized. This capability let IP packet flows be handled similarly to ATM virtual connections, which treat various types of traffic differently. Also, IP speeds improved from 10 megabits per second to 100 megabit per second and then gigabit (1,000,000,000 bits per second) speeds.

These improvements in speed and service qualities, along with the fact that enterprise endpoints are already compatible with IP, led the founders of Sonus Networks to choose IP for their next-generation, softswitch-based voice infrastructure architecture in 1997. This gave Sonus a head start over competitors who initially developed platforms based on ATM, losing time and previously invested development money when they switched gears to IP.

Hybrid IP and Circuit Switched Networks— Softswitches As Tandem Office Replacements in the Core

Local exchange carriers, for the most part, first installed softswitches in long-haul backbone (core) networks rather than as replacements for end-office switches that connect directly to end users. Because toll switches, also called tandem switches in North America and transit switches in Europe, do not have connections to end users, they don't need the complex features found in local or edge central offices connected to customers in last-mile access networks. Early softswitches often did not have the many features required at end offices. Therefore, they were installed in backbone telephone company networks where their primary functions were to set up and tear down the large number of calls between central offices.

Softswitches cost less than purchasing new proprietary tandem switches, and using them as tandem replacements gave telephone companies an opportunity to try softswitches from a variety of manufacturers. It also added capacity to existing fiber because packetizing and compressing traffic increased capacity on fiber routes previously used by circuit switches. Gateway hardware and software converts SS7 signals between the IP portion of backbone networks and the time division multiplexing (TDM) local portions to IP packets.

Application Servers—Voice Mail, ACDs, Speech Recognition

Application servers are computer-based platforms that contain advanced applications such as multiparty audio conference systems, unified messaging, network-based call center software, and speech recognition. Because both softswitches and application servers use signaling protocols that are becoming standardized, adding new capabilities to IP networks is less complex and costs less than adding proprietary platforms with these features to circuit switched networks. This is the result of a different type of protocol conversion being needed to interface with each model of circuit switch.

Softswitches send messages to application servers, for example, requesting a 25-person conference. The application server then retrieves a script from a separate document server that contains application code with instructions.

Document server instructions are written in either voice extensible markup language (VXML) or speech application language tags (SALT) code that instruct the application to go to certain uniform resource locators (URLs). The application server uses these instructions to execute (carry out) actions in real time. Refer to Chapter 2 for VXML and SALT (developed by Microsoft), which are markup languages with Web type instructions. They base their instructions on touch-tone or speech commands.

A separate application or media server is not needed for each softswitch. If they have adequate capacity, application and media servers can support multiple softswitches from remote locations.

Feature Servers—Adjuncts to Softswitches

Some softswitches depend on feature servers to provide traditional end-office functions. (Feature servers are essentially application servers.) There are various types of partnerships between feature server manufacturers and softswitch suppliers. These include resale and original equipment (OEM) agreements. With an OEM agreement, the switch manufacturer puts its own label on the feature servers. Other partnerships include joint marketing and sales efforts. However, with all of these agreements, the partners arrange testing in labs and guarantee that the systems will interoperate using compatible signaling such as session initiation signaling (SIP). There are also partnerships between feature server manufacturers and suppliers of terminal adapters, IP telephones, and gateways. The two major suppliers of feature servers are Sylantro Systems and Broadsoft, Inc.

The following are some of the functionalities that feature servers provide:

- Call waiting
- Caller ID
- Speed dialing
- Automatic callback
- Hosted IP Centrex
- Last call return
- Three-way calling
- Follow me/find me (calls reaching people wherever they are)
- 411 directory and 911 emergency notification services

Feature servers are also used to add VoIP functionality to traditional local office central switches. Two examples are hosted PBXs for large and medium-size enterprises and IP Centrex for small business customers. Centrex provides telephone system functionality to business customers via equipment at carriers' sites. These IP capabilities let employees receive and make telephone calls on their office telephone number when they are away from the office without requiring the enterprise to invest in an IP PBX (refer to Chapter 2).

Media Server—Generating Ring Tones and Announcements

Media servers do the following:

- Receive and respond to touch-tone and voice commands such as voice mail commands and speech-activated dialing.
- Play announcements and prompts such as "All circuits are busy."
- Generate Voice over IP packets from voice mail applications.
- Transcode voice streams (convert voice mail messages to digital IP packets and vice versa). (Transcoders modify traffic to make it compatible with other types of networks.)
- Record audio such as voice mail messages.
- Generate ring tones, busy signals, and dial tone.

Application servers instruct media servers as to which announcement to play. For example, "Play message at www.xxxx.xxx." Small applications such as three-way conferencing often reside on media servers, but large, multiparty conference systems are usually on separate servers. Media servers are based on operating systems such as Linux and often use Pentium processors, which perform the digital signal processing in software without DSP chips.

The signaling gateway at the edge of the network sends signals based on caller input about voice mail and other applications and ring tones to the softswitch. The softswitch decides whether to invoke a media server or an application server or direct the call to an endpoint (called party).

Currently, many application servers use media servers supplied by the same company that supplies the application server. Carriers are hoping that, in the future, they will save money by using media servers based on standard protocols that interoperate with most application servers. In this way, carriers can upgrade or change applications without buying new media servers. Media servers are starting to support streams of pictures as well as voice. In the future, they will support music and other types of multimedia streams.

Media Gateways (Border Elements)— Switching and Interoperability Between Networks

Media gateways are hardware and software devices located at the edge of IP networks. They convert unlike protocols to protocols compatible with networks that send traffic to each other. Another name for media gateways is *border elements*. Media gateways receive traffic from customers and other networks and switch packets through IP networks based on instructions from softswitches. Gateways are used at *peering* locations, interconnection points where carriers pass traffic between each other. Higher-level gateways at peering sites between IP networks that have additional functions such as security and address translation are sometimes referred to as *network border switches* or *session border controllers*.

Media gateways convert between the following:

- Packets from residential consumers' broadband links and IP networks to ensure compatibility.

- IP networks' signaling and Signaling System 7 (SS7) so that IP networks and circuit switched networks can transmit signaling messages to each other. (This functionality is built into signaling gateways.)

- T-1 and T-3 public switched telephone type trunks and IP networks. (This functionality is built into trunking gateways.)

- IP networks using different versions of the same protocols or different protocols.
- Enterprise networks and carriers' IP networks.

One element that reduces the cost of supporting Voice over IP is the fact that each port on a media gateway supports multiple customers because customers don't all communicate at the same time. Traditional circuit switches dedicate a port to each customer's telephone line. Border elements are based on commercial services platforms running Sun Solaris, Linux, or Microsoft Windows operating systems.

Digital Signal Processors (DSPs)—Real-Time Packetizing, Compression, and Conversion

Digital signal processors (DSPs) are used in media servers, media gateways, speech recognition, and wireless telephone handsets. DSPs compress voice and video (shrink the number of bits required), perform the digital-to-analog and analog-to-digital voice conversions, and packetize voice and video in real-time speeds so that they are acceptable over IP networks. This process is referred to as *transcoding*. DSPs also perform echo cancellation. They cancel unwanted noise caused by echo. Digital signal processors (DSPs) are special-purpose microprocessors on pieces of silicon to execute instructions. These powerful processors may be specialized to perform a small number of repetitive tasks such as transcoding (converting) voice. DSP vendors include Texas Instruments, Philips Semiconductor, and Analog Devices.

Peer-to-Peer Music, Instant Messaging, Online Games, and VoIP

Peer-to-peer services operate in a decentralized mode without softswitches to control signaling and communications. Peer-to-peer technology captured public attention when services from companies such as Napster, Gnutella, and KaZaA were deployed to enable people to share free music over the Internet. Peer-to-peer technology has been updated and is now used as an alternative technology for Voice over IP. Major carriers, including AT&T, Level 3, RBOCs, CLECs, and cable TV operators that deploy Voice over IP, rely on softswitch architecture. Instant messaging and online gaming are peer-to-peer applications that also support VoIP.

Computer-to-Computer Voice Traffic

Computer-to-computer calling requires that users download free proprietary software from providers and that they have sound cards in their personal computers or personal digital assistants. They can plug telephones, headsets, or microphones into their PCs. Alternatively, callers can speak directly into their laptops when they travel if they don't have headsets or external telephones available.

Peer-to-Peer—Proprietary Technology

Skype introduced peer-to-peer architecture for Voice over IP without central servers. Skype Technologies SA claims to carry more Voice over IP minutes worldwide than any other provider. It has approximately 10 million users in 210 countries. Peer-to-peer providers keep their costs low by utilizing a "flat" architecture without central control, such as softswitches or servers to manage traffic and signaling between devices. Rather, they use the intelligence in customers' endpoints to send calls (media) between users. Newer providers have emerged that also use peer-to-peer technology. These include Buzzfon P2P, Dingotel, Free World Dialup, Popular Telephony's Peerio offering, and Voiceglo's GloPhone. Most of these providers offer public switched telephone network (PSTN) to computer as well as computer-to-computer calling. Skype's computer-to computer customers must pay an extra fee to reach the PSTN.

Skype customers download free specialized software from Skype.com. When they log into Skype from their endpoint, which can be personal computers, personal digital assistants (PDAs) like PocketPC,or Wi-Fi handsets, Skype authenticates them (verifies that they are who they say they are) and performs encryption (scrambles their data so that it is secure from hackers). The endpoint then downloads a client certificate that lets other Skype users know who they are. The Skype computer then drops out of the communications. When peer-to-peer software is running on a computer, a window, similar to an instant message window, opens, letting users see which of their buddies is logged in.

Peer-to-peer networks operate by constantly sending lots of "pings," made up of small packets, between endpoints searching for peers or content servers. Skype uses supernodes, customers' computers that communicate with and are aware of the best possible route for packets. Developers using software licensed from content distribution network Joltid are creating applications that will be made available to Skype customers. One licensing arrangement is with Siemens. Siemens has developed a cordless phone with Skype software. The phone can be used to make both Skype calls and PSTN calls. Skype resells equipment such as USB-compatible headsets and handsets that are able to connect to ports on customers' computers. Skype has stated that it intends to sell services such as advanced voice mail and video mail and to increase the endpoints compatible with its downloadable software such as additional personal digital assistants and cellphones.

Niklas Zennstrøm and Janus Friis, who developed the music file-sharing software KaZaA, founded Skype. KaZaA was a peer-to-peer file-sharing system that enabled users to obtain free music from each other.

Connections to Other Networks

Peer-to-peer free services enable customers to communicate computer to computer on the Internet, without going through any public networks. Customers that want to call people connected to the public switched telephone network, mobile networks, or other Voice over IP networks generally purchase a low-priced service from their providers. Rather than bill for these services, for the most part, these services generally require that users prepay via credit card.

Peer-to-peer providers sign termination agreements with carriers to connect to public switched telephone network (PSTN) tandem central offices and IP networks. Rather than arranging their own connections to other networks, they rely on other carriers. For example, Skype has termination agreements with Colt, iBasis, Level 3, and Teleglobe. Skype pays these carriers to send calls to central office switches. Skype sends session initiation protocol (SIP) traffic to these carriers who convert Skype traffic to protocols compatible with networks to which they connect. The Skype service is outgoing only because customers don't have telephone numbers to which they are able to receive PSTN calls.

VoIP in Instant Messaging (IM) and Online Gaming

Voice over Internet protocol calling is embedded in most instant messaging and many online games, which use the Internet and peer-to-peer technology. Millions of customers use these systems for voice communications. Instant messaging, which provides the capability to have real-time text messaging, uses peer-to-peer service to determine if a "buddy" is available to chat. Most instant messaging services from AOL, Microsoft, and Yahoo! support voice as well as text messaging.

Microsoft's XBox Live online gaming service and Sony's PlayStation 2 offer VoIP on their for-fee services. Players with headsets speak to each other while participating in games. According to "Not Your Parents' Phone System" by Kevin Werbach, published August 25, 2004 in *Tech Central Station*, Microsoft's service has over one million customers for its multiplayer game, and Yahoo!'s Japanese affiliate is the world's largest voice over broadband provider. It has more than 3.6 million subscribers. Werbach makes the point in his article that voice calling in the future will be less of a standalone application and more of a service embedded in other applications.

Connections Between Carriers— IP Peering and Circuit Switched

Networks that carry Voice over IP packets have connections to circuit switched networks and to other IP networks to complete calls between their customers.

IP Networks Connected to Circuit Switched Networks

When a Vonage or Net2Phone user calls someone with plain old telephone service (POTS), the call travels from the IP network to the PSTN. The IP network uses trunking gateways to transcode packets to a format compatible with the public network and sends them to the called party's telephone company over PSTN trunks from their network to the local telco.

Carriers make arrangements with mainly local exchange carriers to terminate trunks with them. The incumbent completes the call to its own customer or sends it to a competitive local exchange carrier's (CLEC) customer. These trunks between providers are often optical carrier 3 (OC-3) at 155 megabits or T-3 at 44 megabits circuits.

A signaling gateway translates between IP signaling protocols and signaling system 7, which is used on the public switched telephone network. Signaling performs call setup and teardown, address translations, maintenance functions, database lookups for advanced features, and billing functions.

Peering—IP Networks Connected to IP Networks

IP networks exchange traffic at peering locations (see Figure 4.2). For example, AT&T, for its residential Voice over IP offering, needs to receive and send data to its customers over their last mile broadband cable modem and DSL services. AT&T has direct peering arrangements for this with large cable operators. IP carriers that exchange traffic with each other directly rather than through the circuit switched network avoid access and other interconnect fees.

Security, routing via softswitches, traffic policing, and network address translations take place at peering sites.

- *Security.* Firewalls and security software and hardware check messages to ensure against denial of service attacks that can overwhelm networks with millions of messages. They also check for phreaking, which is illicit use of the network where people try to access networks to make free calls.

- *Routing via softswitches.* The softswitch looks up databases on received packets and directs border elements on where to send packets.

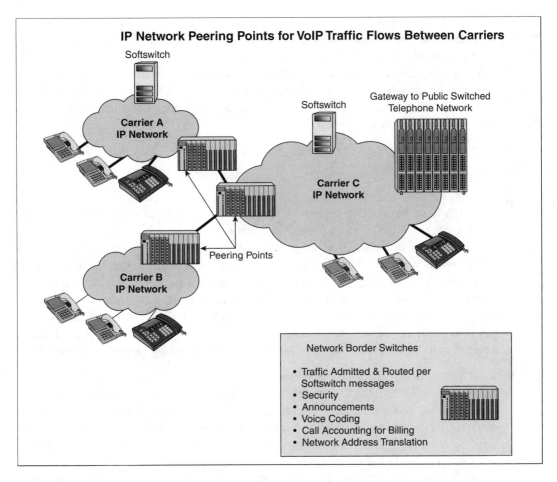

IP Network Peering Points for VoIP Traffic Flows Between Carriers

Softswitch

Carrier A
IP Network

Softswitch

Gateway to Public Switched
Telephone Network

Carrier C
IP Network

Peering Points

Carrier B
IP Network

Network Border Switches

- Traffic Admitted & Routed per
  Softswitch messages
- Security
- Announcements
- Voice Coding
- Call Accounting for Billing
- Network Address Translation

Figure 4.2
Peering in packet networks, courtesy   of Sonus Networks.

- *Traffic policing.* This refers to tracking packets received from carriers and tagging them when more than the agreed amount is received. Tagging traffic enables carriers to identify and bill each other for packets they carry.

- *Translating telephone numbers into IP addresses.* Carriers access databases and use the ENUM standard to translate phone numbers to individuals' IP addresses, also referred to as universal resource identifiers (URIs).

- *Network address translation (NAT).* NAT translates external IP addresses to internal IP addresses and vice versa. Carriers use different internal and external IP addresses to conserve public addresses and to shield IP addresses from outside sources.

Carriers such as Peer 1, headquartered in Canada, and MCI have neutral peering facilities. Multiple carriers locate gateways and routers at neutral peering facilities to exchange traffic. Neutral refers to the fact that carriers that use this peering facility can send traffic over routes from a choice of carriers connected to the facility. For example, a carrier using Peer 1's neutral peering site can exchange traffic with or lease routes from Bell Canada or MCI in addition to Peer 1. Peering sites are a possible source of delay in packet networks.

Voice Quality

Although IP networks drop packets or retransmit them on other routes if there is congestion, prioritization of voice packets over data packets greatly decreases the number of voice packets dropped. Dropped packets can result in choppy voice or video, called "clipping." Because carriers overbuilt long-haul fiber network in the telecommunications boom of the late 1990s, on many of these routes, packet loss is not a problem. However, congestion is more of an issue in metropolitan fiber networks and, in particular, on the last mile between the customer and the telephone company equipment. It can also occur at peering sites where carriers exchange traffic if there is inadequate equipment to handle traffic spikes. (See the section on peering earlier in this chapter.)

Voice quality in packet networks is improving, but it is still not as consistent as that in the public switched network. Carriers that send traffic on their own networks are better able to control quality than those that use the public Internet. However, even carriers that use their own private IP networks can experience congestion on the last-mile cable modem and DSL networks from incumbent broadband carriers. These links don't provide packet prioritization for traffic between customers' routers and other carriers' edge devices. Thus congestion on this leg can negatively impact call quality for carriers who transport voice on their own IP long-haul networks but use last-mile connections from incumbent broadband providers.

The following are key protocols used for sending mixed media (voice, pictures, data, and video) in packet networks:

- Signaling protocols:
  - Session initiation protocol (SIP) is used between endpoints for negotiating features. SIP is important in features such as instant messaging and buddy lists because it indicates when users are available. SIP is used when carriers exchange IP traffic with each other and also in enterprise networks.

- Media gateway control protocol (MGCP) looks up phone numbers dialed and directs media gateways to create connections using identified port numbers and IP addresses. It informs destination gateways of incoming phone calls. Some carriers use MGCP rather than SIP.

- H.323 is an older suite of protocols for setting up and sending calls over IP networks. Most networks and endpoints are transitioning to SIP, which is more straightforward with fewer variations and parameters to set.

- Multiprotocol label switching (MPLS) reduces latency. The first MPLS router (an "edge router") tags packets based on destination address. Subsequent routers forward packets based on a small number of tags rather than having to look up addresses in routing tables. This is faster than looking up each table.

- Realtime transport protocol (RTP) carries the actual media (voice and video). RTP identifies packet content—that is, voice and video—so that it can be prioritized. It also determines if packets are lost.

Calling 911—VoIP Versus Circuit Switched

The Wireless Communication and Public Safety Act of 1999 established 911 as the universal emergency number throughout the United States. The Act mandated that all landline carriers connect callers who dial 911 to the appropriate local emergency dispatch center. It also mandated that the FCC develop a plan for wireless providers to transition to enhanced 911. (Dialing 911 accesses enhanced 911 on public network calls.) However, rules on enhanced 911 have not been developed for VoIP traffic.

- *911*. A common telephone number that users dial to reach emergency reporting and dispatching personnel.

- *Enhanced 911 (E911)*. The capability for agents who answer 911 calls to receive callers' phone numbers and locations. If a caller dials 911 and is too debilitated to state his address, emergency responders will know how to reach him.

- *Public safety answering point (PSAP)*. A group of agents who answer and dispatch 911 and E911 calls for their town, county, or cluster of towns.

When people in the United States and Canada dial 911 from traditional public switched telephones, their calls are answered at a public safety answering point (PSAP). The display on the PSAP employee's telephone set indicates the caller's name and telephone number. The caller's address and emergency service numbers for police, fire, and medical services are displayed on their computer. Each E911-equipped public safety answering point has links to redundant databases that it uses to populate agents' PC screens with callers' addresses. Telephone companies, including incumbent local exchange carriers and CLECs, send 911 calls and caller ID over redundant special telephone lines between tandem central office switches and public safety answering points (see Figure 4.3). Tandem central offices do not have lines to end users, only to other central offices and, in this case, to public safety answering points. (See the following section for tandem central offices.)

Most Voice over IP providers—for example, Vonage, Verizon for its VoIP service, and AT&T—provide 911 but not E911. With 911, the PSAP receives the call but no address information appears on its computer screen (see Figure 4.4).

911 for VoIP—Arrangements That Dial 10-Digit Numbers to Reach the PSAP

When most Voice over IP customers dial 911, their provider uses the Ethernet address associated with the customer's terminal adapter to determine the customer's local

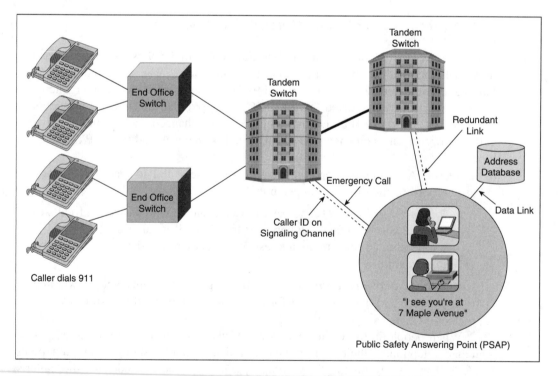

Figure 4.3
E911 call to a public safety answering point.

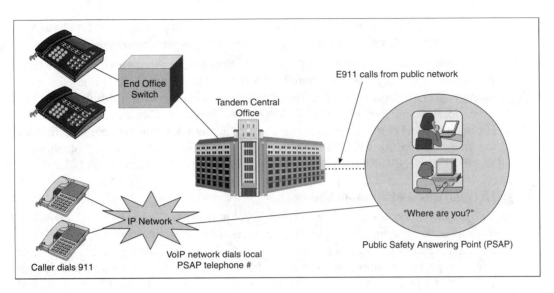

E911 calls from public network

End Office
Switch

Tandem Central
Office

IP Network

"Where are you?"

Public Safety Answering Point (PSAP)

VoIP network dials local
PSAP telephone #

Caller dials 911

Figure 4.4
911 call to a public safety answering point without enhanced 911 (E911).

public safety answering point (PSAP). This information is in databases maintained by companies such as Intrado. The Voice over IP provider's softswitch then dials the PSAP's ten-digit telephone number. These are local telephone numbers that are supposed to be answered 24 hours a day. They are separate from the special lines between PSAPs and tandem switches used for E911.

This isn't a foolproof system. For example, town administrators change these numbers, not realizing that they are being used for 911 calls. Most towns' police departments have answering points in their headquarters. Outside of metropolitan areas, counties or multiple towns pool their resources and run joint PSAPs. If a number in the database is incorrect for any reason, callers may reach police administrative departments who tell them to call 911. Other calls might be routed to voice mail after-hours if an incorrect number is in the 911 databases.

VoIP E911 Within Customers' Geographic Region

Some Voice over IP carriers are starting to deploy E911 that is more reliable than dialing the public safety answer point's ten-digit telephone number. This improved scenario is similar to that used in Figure 4.3. However, carriers connect to the tandem offices from softswitches rather than from legacy-type central office end offices.

Rather than invest in their own links to tandem offices, VoIP carriers such as cable companies use a service from a wholesale provider such as Level 3 that resells connections to tandem offices for E911 on a wholesale basis. Level 3 refers to its service as direct trunking.

However, to work correctly, this arrangement requires that people dial 911 from the address that they have registered with their VoIP carrier. It also does not work properly when people use a telephone number associated with a different city (for example, someone living in Arkansas but using a New York City phone number). This is because the tandem switch looks up the originating telephone number to determine the correct PSAP to which to send the call. VoIP provider Packet8 and others offer E911 to their retail customers. Some charge an extra monthly fee for E911.

E911 for VoIP—Mobility and Security

Two major hurdles for establishing E911 in conjunction with Voice over IP are mobility and authentication. Residential customers who use, for example, DeltaThree, Packet8, Net2Phone, Vonage, or AT&T, can take their terminal adapters with them when they travel or move and receive calls remotely. If they don't notify their provider, their 911 calls dialed from remote locations are sent to the PSAP associated with the terminal adapter's local address in the provider's database.

Many manufacturers are working on the mobility issue. One model involves capturing the IP address of the router nearest to the customer in the carrier's network. The idea is to update databases used by PSAPs in real time.

Authentication is a challenge in this plan. For example, many Voice over IP customers know how to *spoof* their Ethernet address. Spoofing refers to disguising, hiding, or changing a device's address through software on personal computers. Manufacturers are working on ways to authenticate addresses so that databases can be updated in real time in a trusted fashion so that, for instance, hackers with hidden identities don't wreak havoc on emergency response centers by, for example, sending false fire alarms into 911 centers.

EMERGENCY NUMBERS AROUND THE WORLD

There is not one standard telephone number that people dial worldwide to reach emergency providers. In addition, some countries have different numbers for mobile phones, fire, police, and ambulance services. For example, Hong Kong uses 999 for emergencies for landline phones and 112 for cellular emergency calls. The first emergency number was 999, used in London in 1937.

The following is a partial list of emergency numbers:

EMERGENCY NUMBERS AROUND THE WORLD (CONTINUED)

Country or area	Emergency Number
Argentina	101
Australia	000
Brazil	190
China	110, 119, 120
Columbia	123
England	999
European Union	112
Iceland	0112
Israel	100
Jamaica	119
Japan	110
Mexico	060 or 080
Moscow, Russia	051
New Zealand	111
Philippines	117
Poland	997
Romania	961
South Africa	112

Resale—Voice Over IP on Other Carriers' Equipment and Network

Rather than purchasing and managing their own facilities, some IP providers send their customers' voice calls over infrastructure or portions of infrastructure that they lease from other providers. This lowers initial capital outlays and obviates the need for smaller carriers to gain expertise and hire staff knowledgeable about IP. Carriers may also outsource billing and order processing. Voice over IP providers often lease the following facilities from other carriers for their Voice over IP facilities:

- *Collocation.* Vonage, for example, leases space for servers at sites maintained by Peer 1 Networks. Collocation sites have fire suppression, theft protection, backup power generators, plus duplicate power sources from multiple utilities. For even more reliability, some providers place redundant servers at more than one collocation site.

- *Termination.* Carriers such as Level 3 and Teleglobe resell connections from their networks to local exchange carriers' tandem central offices on a worldwide basis. (The tandem central offices then switch traffic to the designated local central office.)

- *IP softswitch infrastructure.* Some cable providers and others use softswitches, media gateways, and application servers in other carriers' networks. For example, they use AT&T's and Net2Phone's softswitch infrastructure for their Voice over IP service.

- *Media gateway.* Other cable providers have their own softswitches and application servers but use media gateways managed by other carriers to transfer calls to cable operators' own softswitches.

- *Provisioning, customer acquisition, and customer service.* Instead of training employees for customer service or order processing (provisioning) and investing resources to attain customers, carriers such as Charter Cable outsource these functions to someone such as Accenture.

Outsourcing—The Role of IP

Because labor is the highest call center expense, organizations often subcontract portions of their call center activities, such as non-technical customer service, to areas of the world where hourly labor rates are lower. Voice over IP reduces the cost to relocate call centers in remote countries. Links between the remote site and the main call center often use data networks based on IP as well as backup private lines.

These connections are arranged with international carriers such as AT&T, Equant, and MCI that supply private lines or virtual private networks (VPNs) to large enterprise organizations. Private lines are connections dedicated to a single customer. VPNs are connections shared by multiple customers with features of private connections. (See Chapter 5, "VPNs and Specialized Network Services," for private lines and VPNs.) Calls to toll-free numbers are often distributed by the main automatic call distribution (ACD) at main locations over international connections to remote call centers. Equipment at the remote sites is often based on Voice over IP at the remote site. For additional information, refer to Chapter 2.

VOICE OVER BROADBAND FOR RESIDENTIAL CONSUMERS ....

CLECs, cable TV operators, and incumbent telephone companies sell residential VoIP service. Skype has a major Voice over IP customer base worldwide, with primarily computer-to-computer, proprietary offerings based on peer-to-peer networking. AT&T, Net2Phone, and Vonage currently have the largest open standards VoIP base of customers in the United States. However, cable TV operators, with their preponderance of broadband customers, could be formidable competitors. In addition, Regional Bell Operating Companies have expanded DSL availability and are poised to take a larger share of residential and business VoIP customers. Additional VoIP players include Primus, Packet8, and VoicePulse. Smaller CLECs offer Voice over IP primarily to business customers.

Voice Over IP Service in Homes

Voice over IP customers can order service through providers' Web sites. In these instances, the provider mails out the equipment (a terminal adapter) and cables. Customers can also sign up for service and purchase the equipment at retail outlets. In either case, personal Web page software downloaded to customers' personal computers has billing information, access to voice mail messages, and features such as clicking to set up a conference call or find me/follow me.

Terminal Adapters, Router and Hub Combos

Terminal adapters transcode (compress, packetize, and convert analog voice streams to digital and vice versa) voice. Some terminal adapters (TAs) also prioritize voice as it travels through the cable or DSL modem. This enables the modem to handle voice as it travels before data packets so that personal computer traffic does not cause delays in voice packets as they access the network. These packets are not prioritized on last-mile networks unless they are from the broadband supplier's customer. In addition to transcoding and prioritizing voice, the terminal adapter registers with the provider's network. This lets the provider know the user is logged onto the network.

Terminal adapters generally have two Ethernet ports and one or two telephone jacks. The cable or DSL modem plugs into one Ethernet port, and a router/hub or (if there is just one computer) the PC plugs into the other Ethernet port (see Figure 4.5).

Some terminal adapters are multifunctional. For example, Cisco manufactures Linksys and Cisco ATA terminal adapters, which are combination wireless router and hub devices. Verizon Communications offers an all-in-one device with a DSL modem,

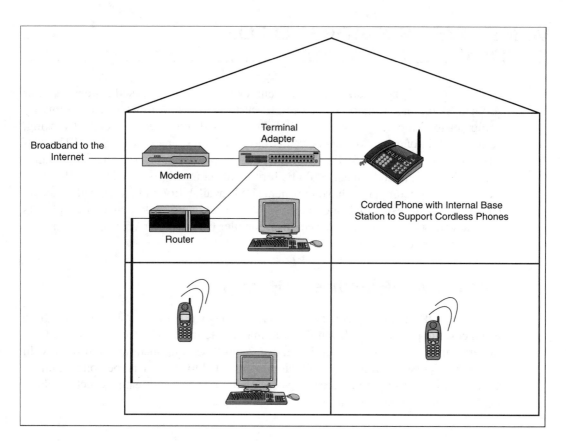

Figure 4.5
A home connection of Voice over IP over DSL or cable modem service.

Wi-Fi router, cordless telephone base station, TA, unified messaging software, and large screen.

Features—Bundles and Portability

Voice over broadband for residential customers is still used primarily by early adopters. There are close to 183 million phone lines in the United States. In contrast, industry consultant Yankee Group predicts there will be 800,000 Voice over IP users by year end 2004 as reported in the August 26, 2004 *The Wall Street Journal Online* article "A Price War Hits Internet Calling" by Shawn Young. However, VoIP is expected to grow, and the number of circuit switched lines in service is decreasing.

Many customers hear of VoIP by word-of-mouth from friends and are attracted by the low prices, bundles of features, ease of use in activating features via personal Web pages, and geographic portability. People who travel can make and receive calls using their terminal adapter and a personal computer. They have geographic portability. In addition, customers can request telephone numbers for cities in other area codes. This would enable someone in New York City to make a local call to reach someone in Nebraska who had a New York City telephone number.

Current Limitations—The Decreasing Criticality of Voice

Many people who use voice over their broadband connections use it as their second line or depend on their cellular phone for most of their calls and are not overly concerned with VoIP's existing shortcomings. Moreover, people depend less on their telephone as they use more e-mail. Thus, for many customers, landline telephone service is not as critical as it once was. As the offerings mature, many of these limitations will be eliminated.

Current limitations include the following:

* E911 is inconsistent or not available.
* People lose their phone service when they lose electricity, although some carriers automatically forward calls to a predesignated alternative number during power outages.
* VoIP telephone numbers may not be listed in directory assistance.
* Some do not work with operators that accept TTY (Teletype) input from deaf callers, place the call for deaf people, and type spoken messages back to the hard-of-hearing person.
* Only one or two telephones can be plugged into terminal adapters. Customers with multiple phones must use cordless ones that support multiple handsets or arrange their own cabling.
* Most services aren't compatible with TiVo-type digital video recorders, alarms, or modems for programming and account updates for satellite television service.

Cable Operators' Offerings—Wired to Every Telephone; No Mobility

Cable operators are starting to offer telephone service to their customers using Voice over IP with technical specifications designed by their central research and development organization, CableLabs. Time-Warner Cable dubs its VoIP service digital telephone service. The main difference between the cable offerings and those of most other service providers is that the terminal adapter is installed at the demarcation point where the coaxial cable enters homes. Rather than mailing the terminal adapter to customers, a technician installs it and connects it to the copper cabling that runs to each telephone. This ensures that all telephones are connected to cable's telephone service.

However, the terminal adapter is not intended to be portable. Because customers don't typically take their terminal adapters with them when they travel, they can't make and receive calls remotely.

A Free Ride for Competitors—Possible Fees or Slowdowns

Currently, cable multiple system operators (MSOs) do not charge fees to VoIP providers that use their last-mile facilities to carry customers' VoIP traffic. This could change as these volumes increase. One possibility is that cable operators might slow down traffic from providers such as Vonage unless they pay to use these facilities. They don't currently do that, but the possibility exists.

Currently, cable MSOs are regulated as information providers and not as telecommunications for their Internet access service. Regional Bell Operating Companies (RBOCs), however, are regulated as telecommunications carriers. This leaves cable broadband operators free of regulations that require Regional Bell Operating Companies to allow other providers to connect to their networks. Congress and the FCC are examining these differences, and they may change so that both types of providers are regulated in a uniform manner.

Manufacturers such as P-Cube (now owned by Cisco) supply gear that lets cable companies examine packet headers to determine traffic types such as video and voice. This enables cable operators to manage traffic and charge differently for heavy users or carriers that use their connections for voice over broadband.

Customer Acquisition—Agents, Retail Outlets, and Amazon.com

The cost to acquire customers is the biggest marketing expense facing VoIP providers. To expand their customer base economically, VoIP providers sell through retail and other online sites in addition to their own Web sites. AT&T sells through retail giant Best Buy and online retailer Amazon.com. (AT&T has announced an agreement to be purchased by SBC.) Vonage sells through Staples and Radio Shack and other retail online and "bricks and mortar" outlets.

These are agent arrangements in which the retail or online provider receives a one-time fee. The VoIP provider performs the billing and customer service.

Billing for VoIP Service—Credit and Prepaid

Providers typically save money by not issuing bills directly to customers. Rather, they often bill credit cards one month in advance. Some providers also use prepaid debit billing for features not included in the monthly feature package such as international calling, extra telephone numbers, and directory assistance calls. These carriers may require a minimum balance in the debit account to cover services for the following billing cycle.

However, providers do make call logs and details of services billed-for available on the software that customers download on their personal computer. For example, customers can use the personal Web pages associated with their account to view the calls they've made and the premium services for which they are billed.

DOCUMENT SHARING AND ONLINE WEBCONFERENCING ....

Webconferencing software, also referred to as document sharing, uses the Internet to enable institutions to share files with employees, customers, and vendors and to hold online conferences. Some systems use the public switched telephone network for the audio portion of the conference and a document-sharing program so that conference participants can all view the same PowerPoint™ slides. As Voice over IP matures and becomes more accepted in corporate networks, more users will conduct both the audio and visual portion of conference calls on IP networks.

Webconferencing to Share Documents

Webconferencing systems enable organizations to train end users, sell products, and review presentations without the expense of traveling. These document-sharing products are used for the following:

- Sharing Web pages and forms such as credit applications with customers as they browse the Web
- Sharing documents during meetings
- Distance-based learning, seminars, and training

Webconferencing, also referred to as collaboration and document-sharing software, is used to train people at remote locations. At the same time that customers, staff, or students are viewing documents on their computers, they also can be speaking on a conference call. For instance, a trainer at headquarters can explain to the organization's salespeople how a new software package that tracks their sales and commissions works. On most of the systems, users can type text messages to the instructor or chat online.

Online meeting software is used also as a sales tool. Inside salespeople use it to make presentations and hold audio conferences with potential customers. To enter a conference, users log into a uniform resource locator (URL) Internet address. The URL connects the callers to the host's server from which the presentation is sent.

Call centers use document sharing to help customers navigate their Web sites. For example, an inside salesperson can "push" (that is, transmit) Web pages to customers who are simultaneously speaking with him and browsing the Web. Finally, companies push forms such as mortgage applications for customers to fill out interactively.

Vendors of these types of software systems include Cisco Systems, Act Teleconferencing, Centra Software, InterCall, Microsoft, Raindance Communications, Inc., and WebEx Communications Inc. In addition, Sprint, AT&T, and MCI offer Webconferencing. (Mergers are pending between SBC, AT&T, and Verizon Communications and MCI.) The systems include document-sharing software with Java-based software installed on customers' PC-based servers. Java is used because it has the capability to be downloaded only as needed to users, which are referred to as clients. On systems that work on http-compliant software, a Java collaboration script is downloaded to clients. The Java script repeatedly polls the central site from the client PC to see if information in the form of a Web address (uniform resource locator [URL]) is available. When it finds the address, the Java script pulls the document at the URL to the participant's computer.

THE PUBLIC SWITCHED TELEPHONE NETWORK ....

Although certainly mobile wireless and Voice over IP are the wave of the future and are used for increasing amounts of traffic, the public switched network still carries the majority of voice traffic. However, parts of the public switched telephone network (PSTN), mostly in the long haul, do use packet switching.

Components of Local Calls

The following are ingredients of local calling:

- *Transport*. The lines from homes or businesses to the central office and trunks, high capacity lines between central offices.

- *Switching*. The central office switch directs calls to their destination. It also has links to billing and enhanced feature systems such as voice mail and caller ID.

- *Terminating transport*. The transmission of the call to its end site, or destination.

- *Signaling*. Signals in the network include telephone number dialed, busy signals, ringing, and the diagnostic signals generated by carriers for repair and maintenance of the network.

Transport, termination, and switching functions are illustrated in Figure 4.6.

Because of declining revenues and total minutes of use associated with landline telephone service, capital investments in the public switched telephone networks are minimal and being shifted to wireless and VoIP infrastructure.

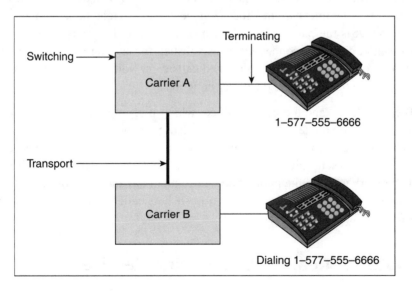

Figure 4.6
Components of local calls.

SWITCHED SERVICES—LOCAL AND LONG DISTANCE CALLING.....................................

The public switched telephone network is analogous to a network of major highways originally built by a single organization but added to and expanded by multiple organizations. Traffic enters and exits these highways (backbone networks) from multiple "ramps" built by still more carriers (for example, the incumbent local telephone companies, cable TV providers, and competitive local exchange carriers [CLECs]). Increasingly, multimodal traffic using different technologies—such as wireless, 802.11, and Voice over IP sources—also interfaces with the PSTN as more customers use alternative services to call people on the PSTN.

AT&T constructed the "highway" system that is the basis of the public switched network in the United States. Prior to the 1984 Divestiture, AT&T set standards via its research arm, Bell Laboratories (now part of Lucent Technologies), such that all central office switches and all lines that carried calls met prescribed standards. As a result of these standards, anyone with a telephone can talk to anyone else. Dialing, ringing, routing, and telephone numbering are uniform.

The International Telecommunications Union (ITU) defines switching as "the establishment, on demand, of an individual connection from a desired inlet to a desired outlet within a set of inlets and outlets for as long as is required for the transfer of information." The inlets are the lines from customers to telephone company equipment. The outlet is the party called, the connection from the central office switch to the customer. A circuit or connection is established for as long as desired within the network until one party hangs up. Switched calls carry voice, data, video, and graphics. They operate on landline and cellular networks.

The mobile or landline central office, which performs the switching function, routes calls based on the telephone number dialed. Switches use route selection tables and databases in the Signaling System 7 (SS7) network to select the most efficient route over which to send each call. Signaling System 7, described later in this chapter, is a data network used by the public network to maintain and monitor the network, to provide access to databases with information such as callers' carriers, and to activate special features such as caller ID.

Attributes of Real-Time Switching Services

Unlike e-mail and voice mail, cellular, voice over broadband, facsimile, and voice traffic are switched in real time based on digits dialed.

Addressing—With Dual Tone Multifrequency (DTMF)

Telephone calls are routed to destinations based on the number dialed. This is the *addressing function*. The PSTN, cellular networks, and Voice over IP networks route calls based on digits customers dial. For the most part, addressing signals are sent as control signals, separate from voice signals.

Telephones using circuit switched landline connections send dual tone multifrequency (DTMF) tones over the network. DTMF tones are also referred to as touch tone. At the central office, these tones or frequencies are decoded to address signals.

In cellular networks, users first dial the number they want to reach and then press Send. The telephone number is sent as digital bits within packets to the mobile switching office.

In the Voice over IP world, the addressing function uses IP addresses to identify users. Carriers translate telephone numbers to IP addresses.

Peer-to-peer Voice over IP services don't use these dialing conventions because generally they don't have phone numbers. Rather people "click" to dial from their computer screen.

In the North American Numbering Plan (NANP), which covers the United States, Canada, and the Caribbean, three-digit area codes are assigned to metropolitan areas. *Exchanges,* the next three digits of a phone number, are assigned to a rate center, and the last four digits, the line number, are assigned to a specific business or residential customer. A *rate center* is a geographic area defined by incumbent telephone companies as rated for local calling. Rate centers are also defined for toll calling.

In the rest of the world, each country has country codes, city codes, and user numbers. The digits of each vary in length: Country codes and city codes are one to three digits long, and numbers assigned to users generally are five to ten digits long. There is no uniform worldwide numbering pattern.

Availability—On Demand

Voice and data calls are initiated by picking up the handset or by instructing a modem to dial a call. The service is available "on demand." However, callers might find that on peak traffic days, such as Mother's Day, callers receive a "fast busy" signal. Extreme weather conditions such as blizzards often result in a high number of people working from home and using modems for long stretches of time. This can result in a strain on carriers' network capacity and "fast busies" on call attempts.

In contrast to circuit switched networks that deny access when network capacity has been reached, IP networks degrade service. Degraded service results in latency, delays in voice and/or data traffic.

Immediate Access

If capacity is available, service is instantaneous. When someone dials a telephone number, he or she expects the call to be completed immediately. As previously noted, extreme conditions can eliminate the immediate capacity expected by users. Natural disasters, unusual demand, and human error all impact availability.

Carriers build in redundant power sources, remote alarm monitoring, backup systems, multiple fiber paths to central offices in case of a fiber cut, and hurricane-proofing in central offices to ensure continuous telephone service. Customers take for granted immediate telephone service, which carriers take great efforts to provide.

Postalized Rates—Flat Rate Plans

In the past, calls to distant locations cost more than calls to, for example, nearby states. The cost of long distance service is no longer consistently distance sensitive. Most carriers have flat 3¢ to 5¢ per-minute rate plans. This is known as *postalized pricing.* Just as a first class letter costs the same to mail next door or 2,000 miles away, calls often cost the same whether to a friend across the state or to a relative across the country. Once a carrier's high-speed network is in place, it costs the carrier no more to send a call 2,000 miles than 400 miles. Capacity is available and carriers want to fill their "pipes."

Store-and-Forward Switching— Nonsimultaneous Sending and Receiving

The storage and transfer of messages such as voice mail, recorded announcements, data, and facsimile in a non-real-time fashion is known as *store-and-forward switching.* Store-and-forward switching does not require both sender and receiver to be available at the time of transmission. Moreover, the network can hold the message and retry multiple times until the receiving equipment is available. Stored messages can be transferred at off-peak times to minimize network idle time, which also avoids network overload during busy times. For example, political organizations record "get out the vote" announcements and send them to lists of voters at preprogrammed times. Pharmacies send "your prescription is ready" announcements to customers.

"THE LAST MILE" OR ACCESS NETWORKS ....

The portion of the public network from the central office to the end user's location is the *access network,* or "*last mile,*" as illustrated in Figure 4.7. A major bottleneck of analog services exists in the copper cabling to residential and small businesses from the telephone company central office or digital loop carrier. Digital loop carriers convert electric signals to optical signals and vice versa.

Cable modem service is provided over the last mile. Cable modems operate on hybrid fiber coaxial (HFC) cable infrastructure (see Chapter 6, "Entertainment, Cable TV, and Last-Mile Fiber Systems"). Fiber runs from the cable company's facility to

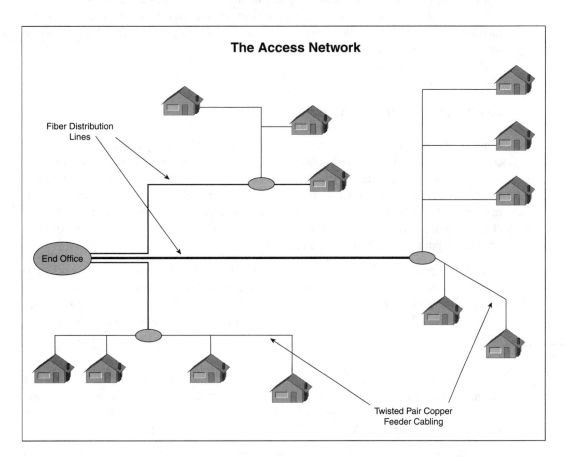

Figure 4.7
The last-mile access portion of incumbent local exchange carrier networks.

the neighborhood. Coaxial cable usually is used to connect each residential customer to the network. Cable modems are a nonswitched, always-on data communications and Internet access service. Cable TV companies have invested huge amounts of money to convert their cabling from one-way-only cable TV service to two-way systems for cable modems, video on demand, and telephone service.

In contrast to the last mile in residential areas, the vast majority of which are made up of twisted pair copper, competitive local exchange carriers and incumbent telephone companies lay fiber to their large business customers. The expense of supplying fiber cable to office and apartment buildings with multiple tenants can be spread across many customers.

The decreasing cost of fiber-optic cabling technologies and competition from cable TV providers has led Verizon Communications and SBC to start deploying fiber optics to homes or near homes. Their goal is to sell entertainment services over these facilities. It is hoped that the expense of new fiber using newer technologies will be offset by sales of video on demand and other services. See Chapter 5 for passive optical networks technology.

End and Tandem Central Offices

Central offices switch calls between end users. There are two types of central offices: end and tandem offices in public switched telephone networks. *Tandem offices,* also referred to as toll and transit offices, do not have connections to end users. They have trunks to other carriers, other tandem offices, and end offices. They provide the connections for central office traffic to other central offices, and central office to interexchange carriers' (IXCs') switches (see Figure 4.8). These switches carry high volumes of calls on paths called trunks.

End central offices connect directly to business, commercial, and residential customers as well as to tandem offices. Long distance carriers connect to tandem offices. They also are referred to as *Class 4 switches*. End offices are sometimes referred to as *Class 5 switches*. The volume of calls between end offices and customers, and between end offices and tandem offices, is lower than on trunks between tandem offices.

Competitive local exchange carriers (CLECs) also have tandem- and end-office functionality in their switches. However, both functions are often installed into one switch because of the smaller size of CLECs. CLECs sometimes locate their switches in incumbents' central offices. This is referred to as collocation.

The end office-to-customer portion of networks is the access or last-mile portion of the network.

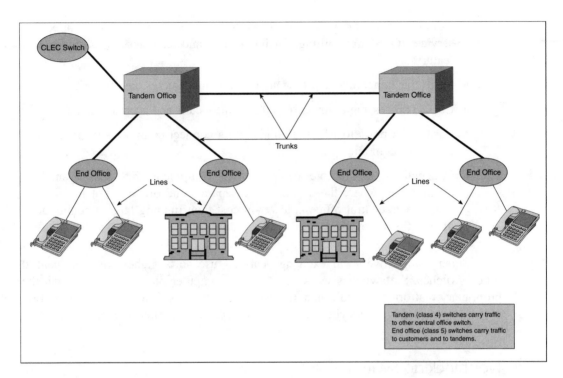

Tandem (class 4) switches carry traffic to other central office switch.
End office (class 5) switches carry traffic to customers and to tandems.

Figure 4.8
Tandem and end offices and connection to a competitive local exchange carrier's central office switch .

Hardware in central offices includes the following:

- Line cards with a port for each telephone line. (Only end offices have line cards because tandem offices have no connections to end users.)

- Trunk cards with a port for each trunk connected to a tandem or end office (that is, T-3, T-1, E-1, OC-3, and E-3 ports).

- Cards and software for Centrex service. (Centrex service is key system or PBX-like service served from a central office [see Chapter 2].)

- Connections to the Signaling System 7 (SS7) network to support enhanced features such as voice mail and caller ID (see the discussion of SS7 later in this chapter).

- Administration software with links to carriers' operation and support service (OSS) for billing, maintenance, and changes to customer's features.

- Cards that generate touch-tone signals, announcements, and ringing.

- Central processing units (CPUs) that control calls and access to features.

- Cards with ports to which administrators connect computers to program features and monitor the switch.

- Connections for remote central office equipment that serves small communities where the expense of a separate end office is not justified. The remote central office is lower in cost than running large amounts of fiber to the remote town.

Some competitive local exchange carriers use softswitches for their central office switches. Softswitches work on standard computer platforms rather than the proprietary platforms of traditional switches and often cost less than those based on proprietary signaling. Softswitches were discussed earlier in this chapter.

Nonblocking Switches

In both the voice and data world, switches in which everyone served by the switch can be on their phone or data device simultaneously are called *nonblocking switches.* Carriers originally designed their networks with the assumption that, at any given time, not every telephone user will be on a telephone call and that most calls do not tie up the carriers' and local telephone companies' networks for long periods of time. Designing central office switches so that not everyone can make calls at the same time saves money on central office equipment. There is generally one path for every four to six users in central office class 5 (end-office) switches.

PBXs Compared to Central Office Switches— Capacity and Reliability

PBXs and central offices have the same functionality. This is true for softswitches as well as proprietary central offices and PBXs. Both enterprise and carrier switches establish paths for calls, connect to systems for billing purposes, arrange ringing tones and announcements, and control the setup and teardown of calls. However, carrier class switches are generally larger and are built to higher standards of reliability. Carriers also arrange for more stringent power backup in the event of blackouts.

Digital Loop Carrier Systems—Fiber Optics and Copper Cabling in the Last Mile

Digital loop carriers (DLCs) are used to economically bring fiber closer to customers. When telephone companies first started using fiber, they used it rather than copper where distances between customers and central office switches were longer than 1.5 miles. This is because signals on copper deteriorate and need to be boosted at these distances. Rather than put amplifiers on the analog copper cabling, carriers ran fiber to the neighborhood and terminated it in digital loop carriers (see Figure 4.9). This eliminated repair problems on amplifiers and noise introduced when amplifiers boosted the noise as well as the signal as it lost strength on distances over 1.5 miles. Fiber is more reliable, requires less maintenance than copper, and does not require

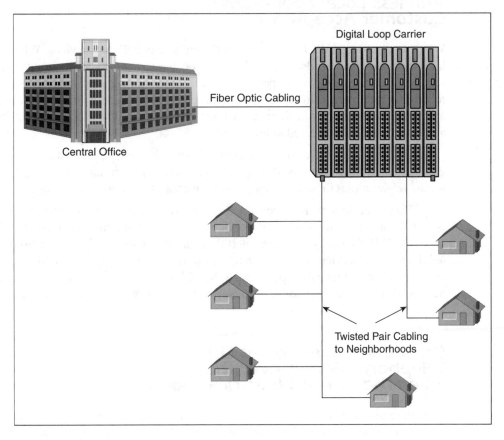

Figure 4.9
Digital loop carriers.

amplifiers in the local loop. With the decreasing cost of electronics for DLC equipment, incumbent telephone companies now use fiber on shorter runs also.

Digital loop carrier systems have multiplexing and demultiplexing functionality. At the central office, traffic is combined into high-speed, up to 155 megabit, optical carrier-level 3 (OC-3) streams. The digital loop carrier separates out, demultiplexes the traffic, and sends it to end users in analog format on twisted pair copper cabling. It also converts the optical pulses to electrical signals and vice versa. Most digital loop carriers support plain old telephone service (POTS), T-1, E-1, and integrated services digital network (ISDN) (see Figure 4.9). See Chapter 5 for T-1, E-1, and ISDN.

New next-generation DLCs also support digital subscriber line (DSL), high-speed Internet access service.

Wireless Local Loop—Low Customer Acceptance

Wireless local loop (WLL) services are different than cellular services. Whereas cellular users use their handsets from different locations, wireless local service is a fixed service. It operates between specified, fixed points. Antennas placed on customers' roofs send radio signals to vendors' antennas and receivers. Carriers that use wireless local loop technology run fiber from their central office switches to neighborhood antennas or antennas located at hub sites.

Customer distrust of the technology, higher than expected costs, and technical glitches caused wireless local loop services sold by WinStar, XO, and Advanced Radio Telecom (ART) to fail to catch on with enough customers to be profitable.

These services were based on local multipoint distribution service (LMDS), originally intended for cable TV services and multipoint multichannel distribution service (MMDS). LMDS operates at 100 megabits per second. Multipoint multichannel distribution service (MMDS) operates on lower frequencies than LMDS and supports speeds of 10 megabits per second. See Chapter 9, "Wi-Fi, Wireless Broadband, Sensor Networks, and Personal Area Networks," for newer, high-capacity, fixed wireless services such as WiMax.

Broadband over Power Lines— Telephone Signals over the Same Fiber That Carries Electrical Signals

The attraction of using utilities' power lines for broadband Internet access and Voice over IP is the wide availability and thus relatively low cost to deploy service. Broadband over power lines is also aimed at enabling utilities to use their own fiber lines to monitor devices from utilities' network operating centers (NOCs). The NOCs could read meters remotely, monitor devices used to distribute and generate electricity, and detect electricity thefts. Broadband over power lines (BPL) would in essence create a private data network for utilities using the same fiber that utilities own for carrying signals.

The Structure of Utility Networks—The Grid

Electric utilities send power to customers over a hierarchical network using different voltages. *Voltage* refers to the level of pressure pushing electric signals. It is analogous to rushing water. Higher voltages use greater pressure, like turning a garden hose on high. Low voltages have less pressure, like lowering the spray of water from the hose. Voltage is not a measure of the quantity of electricity. The following is an overview of electric utility networks.

- *Transmission* lines carry the highest voltage signals from the main generator, which creates electricity, to substations.

- *Substations* convert electricity received from transmission lines to lower voltages and distribute it to an average of 5,000 homes over medium-voltage lines.

- *Transformers* in neighborhoods convert electricity to low voltages and send it to homes, apartment buildings, and businesses. In the United States, transformers support four or five homes. In Europe, they support 400 to 500 homes. Transformers look like large cans on poles.

- The *distribution network*, also referred to as feeder lines, is made up of lines carrying medium- and low-voltage electricity from the substation to customers.

- The power line *grid* consists of transmission and distribution lines, the lines that carry or transport electricity.

Telecommunications Signals over Utility Lines—An Emerging Technology for VoIP and Broadband

Broadband over power lines is an emerging technology that carries telecommunications signals over medium-voltage distribution lines in residential and commercial neighborhoods. BPL equipment enters the electric grid at substations. An equipment cabinet typically contains a router blade (circuit pack) and, depending on the service, a wireless device to send the signal to the medium voltage lines. The router sends signals to the Internet over power companies' spare fiber. These systems function on both overhead and underground distribution fiber (see Figure 4.10).

Couplers use electromagnetic energy to induce (transfer) voltage onto the electrical lines. Induction refers to the transfer of signals from one source to another. The

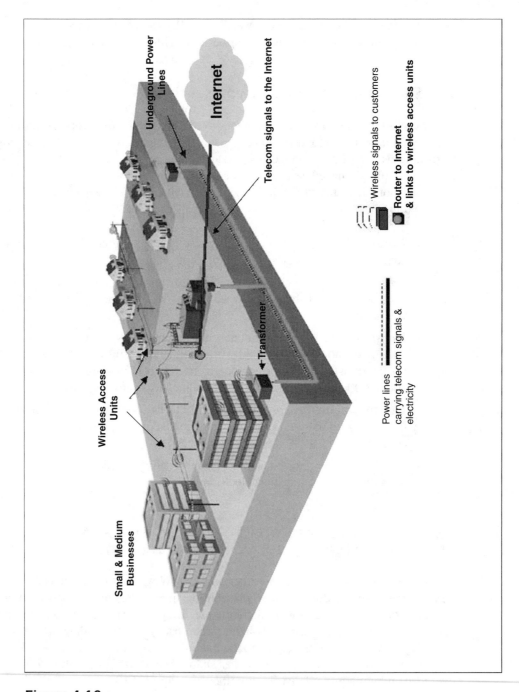

Figure 4.10
Broadband over power lines; figure courtesy of Amperion, Inc.

signals are carried at different frequencies than electric signals. This ensures that telecommunications signals don't interfere with electrical signals. Broadband over power lines is now possible because all of the BPL manufacturers have figured out a way to bypass insulation barriers in transformers. Amperion uses Wi-Fi wireless technology, and the others use patented processes over wires. Amperion has stated its intention to upgrade from Wi-Fi to the more robust WiMAX in the future when the standard is stable. (See Chapter 9 for more on WiMAX and Wi-Fi.) In addition, manufacturers use various repeaters and/or amplifiers to boost signals when they fade and devices to manage security.

The Last 100 Yards and Inside Homes and Businesses

There are two models of broadband over power lines. One version, used by Amperion, Inc., uses Wi-Fi wireless technology for the last hundred yards from the nearest transformer to the home. In this model, the customer uses a wireless modem/router inside the home to connect to the Amperion service. Amperion thus bypasses the transformer by going directly from the medium-voltage line to customers (see Figure 4.10).

The other type does not use wireless for the last hundred yards. Ambient Corporation, Current Technologies, and Main.net PLC transport signals over electric lines all the way into customers' homes. They provide couplers that transfer signals from medium-voltage to low-voltage signals without going through a transformer. In these examples, BPL customers use a power-line modem, also called a bridge, to convert electrical current to Ethernet signals compatible with home networks. The power-line modems are plugged into standard electric outlets and use the HomePlug standard for carrying telecommunications signals over power lines inside homes. Consumers plug their computers or routers into the HomePlug bridge.

These models are used with some variation for apartment buildings and commercial facilities as well as homes. For example, the service may enter the building over medium-voltage lines rather than low-voltage lines. They use various techniques including inside electrical wires to carry signals to individual businesses or floors in apartment buildings.

Who Sells BPL?

Broadband over power line manufacturers sell directly to electric service providers and more often to competitive local exchange carriers (CLECs), also termed broadband over power line value added resellers (BPL VARs). When the manufacturer sells to a CLEC, the CLEC does the marketing and billing and arranges installation of its equipment with the utility. This enables the CLEC to bypass incumbent local exchange carriers for interconnections to end users.

The biggest opportunity for BPL is internationally in developing countries such as India, China, Africa, South America, and the Middle East. In many of these countries, electrical lines are available to a majority of homes. Fixed-line telephone service is not. It is thought that even where these countries establish cellular service, electric utilities' fiber can be used to carry signals from wireless providers to the Internet using broadband over power line technology.

Currently, for most manufacturers, the majority of installations are in the United States. However, because of the growing availability of cable and DSL modem service, many feel there is limited potential in developed countries.

Regulatory Issues Regarding Limiting Interference

All electrical signals produce radio frequency interference (RFI). They radiate energy that can interfere with nearby signals that use the same portion of the airwaves (spectrum). BPL services operate on low power frequencies of up to 50 MHz (50 million cycles per second). The Federal Emergency Management Association (FEMA) as well as ham radios and others use these frequencies and want assurances that BPL will not interfere with their signals.

The FCC, which regulates use of spectrum, is reviewing Section 15 rules for unlicensed equipment and has stated its intention to modify Section 15 rules so that BPL equipment and other systems use techniques to mitigate (lessen) interference. The FCC has certified that BPL providers operate under existing Section 15 rules. In addition, BPL providers use various techniques to ensure that their signals do not interfere with other services using the same unlicensed spectrum.

The FCC has stated its support of BPL as a possible "third pipe" in addition to cable and DSL service for broadband Internet access because of the universal availability of power lines. They are particularly interested in BPL for underserved and rural areas. To date, the FCC has not addressed how broadband over power lines will comply with universal service, disabilities access, Communications Assistance for Law Enforcement Act (CALEA), E911, and subsidization of telecommunications service by revenue from utilities' main services. (See Chapter 2 for CALEA and universal service. E911 was covered earlier in this chapter.)

Carrier Hotels—Interconnecting Carriers and Providing Secure Space for Equipment

Carrier hotels are locations where network service providers locate their switches and routers and connect to each others' networks.

Rather than construct their own buildings to house their switches, carriers lease space in carrier hotels. They place their equipment in cages in the carrier hotel. Locked wire cages surround the equipment and access to the equipment is available only to the carrier that owns the equipment. Leasing space in carrier hotels saves network providers the expense of providing the following:

- Physical security against break-ins
- Access to large amounts of power
- Access to backup power
- Backup generators
- Dual air conditioning systems
- Uninterrupted power supplies
- Fire detection and fire suppression equipment
- Alarming to fire departments and police departments
- Staff to plan and maintain the facilities
- Construction of earthquake-resistant facilities

"Carrier hotels" also are called *collocation facilities*. Carriers in these facilities also lease fiber for connections to other POPs and incumbent local telephone companies. Incumbent local telephone companies and large carriers such as AT&T generally have their own facilities, points-of-presence (POPs), and central offices in which they house their gear. Network service providers use fiber connections between carrier hotels and incumbents' central offices over which they transmit traffic to incumbents.

The Public Network and National Security

Governments consider telecommunications a necessary service. It's a vital national security and business resource and is regulated accordingly. The Federal Communications Commission (FCC) monitors the reliability of major carriers' networks but not the Internet. Earthquakes, equipment thefts, software glitches, and power disturbances have all interrupted telephone service. Because of the importance of wireless service in national disasters, the FCC now requires that mobile carriers also report major outages.

Backup, redundancy, and power failure are major factors in planning for telecommunications. However, because of the large number of cell sites and cell towers required, arranging power backup in wireless networks is more costly than in landline networks. The blackout that affected large portions of the eastern and midwestern United States and sections of Canada in mid-August 2003 left many customers without cell service.

Terrorism Threats and Emergency Preparedness Versus Decreasing Margins

Securing public networks and the Internet from terrorism, cable cuts, and natural disasters is costly. However, carriers are facing lower prices for services, narrow and sometimes disappearing profit margins, and intense competition. They don't always have the resources to provide sustainability and capacity in times of disasters. The government is funding some initiatives for compatibility between wireless services used by different emergency responders so that, for example, fire and police departments can communicate wirelessly with each other. Landline services and most commercial cellular operators, for the most part, have not received subsidies.

Issues facing carriers include building backup wireless routes between critical switches and public safety answering points (PSAPs), boosting security against hackers and terrorists at peering sites where carriers exchange IP traffic, and plain old user errors by staff.

Electrical Requirements for Digital Loop Carriers—Implications on Sustainability

Prior to the use of digital loop carriers (DLCs), telephone companies supplied low-voltage, direct-current electrical power for telephone service on the copper cabling that carries telephone signals. The power was carried from the central office to customers, and each central office was equipped with generators and backup batteries. Thus, during disasters when commercial power was lost, telephones still functioned.

However, with digital loop carriers, power needs to be supplied from each DLC to the customer. This is a problem because there are many more digital loop carriers than central office switches. BellSouth alone has 65,000 digital loop carriers, each of which has battery backup but not all have a generator. During the 2004 series of hurricanes in Florida, BellSouth used trucks to deliver generators to DLCs in areas without power. Even so, 775,000 subscribers in Florida, 13% of the customer base, lost telephone service for some amount of time during Hurricane Frances. Most of the outages were due to power failures. No central office switch failed.

End-to-End Telephone Service

Callers take for granted the capability to reach people on different long distance networks. For instance, MCI subscribers assume they can reach AT&T subscribers. This was not always the case. During the early years of the telecommunications industry, 1893 to 1907, people frequently needed two telephones: one phone for people served by The Bell Telephone Company, for example, and another telephone to reach people in a town served by an independent telephone company.

Independent and Bell telephone company networks were not connected to each other at this time. AT&T articulated the strategy of end-to-end telephone service in its 1910 annual report. The public switched telephone network grew out of this concept. The federal government granted AT&T a monopoly on telephone service in return for AT&T's providing end-to-end, affordable telephone service.

Interconnections Between Carriers—Transport

Interexchange carriers rent lines that connect their points of presence (POPs) to local telephone central offices. They use these lines to transport traffic between their POP and local telephone companies. Interexchange carriers select incumbents as well as competitive local exchange carriers (CLECs) for this local transport. In some areas where there is more than one carrier with a local network, the interexchange carrier selects a carrier to access local customers based on pricing and coverage.

Pay Now, Call Later—Prepaid Cards

Debit cards were first used in Europe, where credit is not a ready option for calling, in 1976. They were introduced in the United States in the late 1980s where they are used mainly for landline long distance services and mobile wireless services. With debit cards, people without access to credit or without their own telephone service can purchase telephone calling. Users pay for the card in advance and are allowed a set amount of time or calling units. With mobile wireless service, callers pay in advance and receive a telephone along with a set number of minutes.

The cards gained popularity in the United States initially as a way for people without telephones or credit to make telephone calls. However, they only make up a fraction of the United States' total $292 billion (in 2002) telecommunications revenue. According to consulting firms Atlantic-ACM and Wilkofsky Gruen Associates, total prepaid telephone revenues were $7.7 million in 2002 and $9.3 million in 2003. The prepaid card statistics were in *TIA's 2004 Telecommunications Market Review and Forecast* published by the Telecommunications Industry Association.

In Europe, a majority of mobile wireless users, particularly young people, depend on prepaid calling. Many of these callers depend on mobile phones as their only phone. Immigrant populations in all areas of the world represent a particularly high percentage of prepaid customers, as they don't have ready access to credit. They often use debit cards for international calls back to their original home.

A troubling use of prepaid calling is in conjunction with planning terrorist attacks. There have been numerous reports in the press and by governments worldwide stating that known terrorists used prepaid services because of their anonymity. Prepaid services were used in conjunction with the 9/11 World Trade Center attack, the March 11, 2004 bombings at the Madrid subway, and the Oklahoma City bombings. Many countries such as Japan now require identification of people that purchase prepaid telecom.

continues

PAY NOW, CALL LATER—PREPAID CARDS (CONTINUED)

Debit cards are sold directly by carriers, resellers, sales agents, distributors, and retail outlets. The debit card industry is a "layered" industry with different segments selling the cards, promoting the cards, handling the administration and billing aspects, and actually carrying the calls. For example, many of the local Bell telephone companies merchandise the cards themselves but outsource the processing of calls to alternate operator service (AOS) providers, which buy bulk long distance from carriers at wholesale prices.

The "prompts" callers hear when they use debit cards (for example, "Please enter the PIN number on the back of your card") are generated on the carrier or prepaid company's integrated voice response (IVR) platforms (see Figure 4.11). Integrated voice response equipment also lets users know how many minutes they have left on their card. IVR platforms are often located at carriers' sites. Much of the international prepaid traffic is carried as IP traffic to reduce costs.

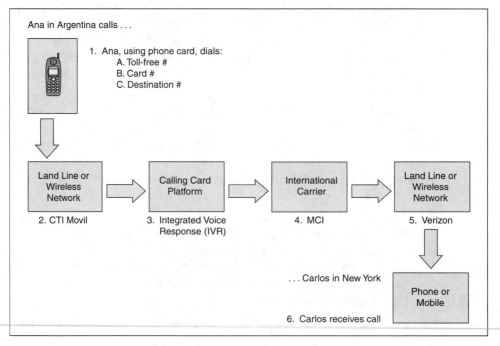

Figure 4.11
Call flow for prepaid service.

SIGNALING—THE GLUE THAT HOLDS THE PSTN TOGETHER ....

Signaling system 7 (SS7) is used for billing, monitoring, links to advanced features, and for carriers to exchange traffic with each other. When IP networks send calls to the public switched telephone number, they interface with SS7. The public network owes much of its reliability, advanced features, and interoperability to signaling.

Overview of Signaling—Uniform Signaling Developed by AT&T

Signaling is used to process every switched call on the public switched network and the public cellular network. The caller dials a number and hears progress tones such as dial tone, ringing, busy signals, or reorder tones. These are all signaling tones carried on signaling links in the PSTN. In addition to tones, callers might hear digital messages telling them that the number they dialed is not in service or has been changed.

When they were introduced and later upgraded, signaling innovations represented a major improvement in the public network's capabilities. They not only enable carriers to manage their networks more efficiently, but they also provide the means for the introduction of profitable, new services.

Signaling innovations led to the following:

- A platform for new, network-based services such as fax-on-demand, prepaid calling cards, and voice mail.
- Toll-free 800, 877, and 888 number portability between carriers (the capability for an organization to retain its toll-free numbers when changing carriers).
- Local number portability, which allows users to keep their telephone number when they change telephone provider.
- Improved network reliability.
- ISDN integrated services digital network is a way to carry 2 or 23 voice and data channels over the same cables. The signals are carried in a separate channel on the same cable.
- Lucrative "smart" services such as caller ID, call trace, call return, and call waiting.

In addition, signaling is the backbone for interconnection between cellular, global wireless, and multiple carriers' networks. AT&T established the architecture of the signaling network in conjunction with Bell Labs in the 1970s. Prior to the 1984 divestiture, AT&T owned all of the 22 Bell Operating Companies (BOCs). It had the necessary control of the public network that enabled it to set a standard that was followed across the country and later adopted by the international community.

A SIGNALING TUTORIAL

Signaling is the process of sending information between two parts of a network to control, route, and maintain a telephone call. For example, lifting the handset of a telephone from the receiver sends a signal to the central office, "I want to make a phone call." The central office sends a signal back to the user in the form of a dial tone, indicating the network is ready to carry the call.

The three types of signals are as follows:

- *Supervisory signals*. Supervisory signals monitor the busy or idle condition of a telephone. They also are used to request service. They tell the central office when the telephone handset is lifted (off-hook requesting service) or hung-up (on-hook in an idle condition).

- *Alerting signals*. These are bell signals, tones, or strobe lights that alert end users that a call has arrived.

- *Addressing signals*. These are touch tones or data pulses that tell the network where to send the call. A computer or person dialing a call sends addressing signals over the network.

Signals can be sent over the same channel as voice or data conversation or over a separate channel. Prior to 1976, all signals were sent over the same path as voice and data traffic. This is called in-band signaling. In-band signaling resulted in inefficient use of telephone lines. When a call was dialed, the network checked for an available path and tied up an entire path through the network before it sent the call through to the distant end. For example, a call from Miami to Los Angeles tied up a path throughout the network after the digits were dialed but before the call started.

Prior to the proliferation of voice mail, between 20% and 35% of calls were incomplete due to busy signals, network congestion, and ring-no-answers. Therefore, channels that could be used for telephone calls were used to carry in-band signals such as those for incomplete calls, dial tone, and ringing. Multiplying this scenario by the millions of calls placed resulted in wasted telephone network facilities.

A SIGNALING TUTORIAL (CONTINUED)

In addition to tying up telephone facilities, in-band signaling sets up calls more slowly than out-of-band signaling. To illustrate, the time between dialing an 800 call and hearing ring-back tones from the distant end is the call setup part of the call. *Call setup* includes dialing and waiting until the call is actually established.

The Basis for Intelligent Networks

Common channel interoffice signaling, also known as out-of-band signaling, evolved into the basis for intelligent networks. Routing instructions, database information, and specialized programs are stored in computers in the carriers' networks and are accessible over out-of-band signaling links.

Beginning in the late 1970s, the public network evolved from purely carrying voice and data calls to a vehicle with intelligence, greater capacity, and faster recovery from equipment failure. The impetus to upgrade the network came from AT&T's desire to manage and add capacity to the network more cost effectively. This upgrade laid the foundation for new services such as enhanced 800 services, prepaid calling cards, roaming in cellular networks, ISDN, call forwarding, three-way calling, and call waiting.

Separate, out-of-band signaling networks are the basis for intelligent routing and access to applications in IP networks as well as public switched telephone networks. Just as the PSTN uses SS7, IP networks are moving to session initiation protocol (SIP) as the common platform for call setup, teardown, and setup for features such as audio and videoconferences.

Signaling System 7—Lowering Costs and Increasing the Reliability of Public Networks

In Signaling System 7 (SS7) protocol, routing intelligence is located in lower-cost, computer-based peripherals rather than in central office switches. For example, powerful parallel processing computers hold massive databases with information such as routing instructions for toll-free and 900 calls. One processor with its database supports multiple central office switches (see Figure 4.12). In this case, each central office switch is not required to maintain sophisticated routing information. The expense of the upgrade is shared among many central offices.

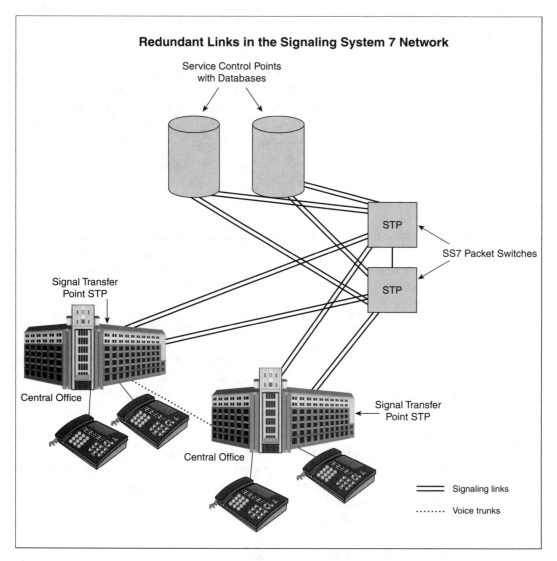

Figure 4.12
Common channel signaling— separate links for signaling and voice traffic.

The significance of advancements in signaling technology should not be underestimated. When network problems are detected, alerts are sent over the signaling network to centralized network operation centers (NOCs) where technicians see visual indications of alarms on wall-mounted, computerized displays. Moreover, sections of carrier networks can be quickly reconfigured from commands sent by centralized network control centers over signaling channels rather than by technicians located at each central office.

Common channel signaling efficiencies are achieved by having one signaling link support multiple voice and data transmissions. The fact that one signaling link supports many trunks (high-speed links between telephone switches) highlights the requirement for reliability. If one signaling link crashes, many trunks are out of service. Redundancy is an important consideration in the design of carriers' signaling networks. (See Figure 4.12 for an illustration of redundant signaling links.)

SS7 is a data communications network capable of sending more complex messages than the limited in-band tones that notified the network when calls were completed, how they were addressed, and so forth. The first implementation of an early version of out-of-band-signaling enabled AT&T to eliminate operators for calling card validation. With common channel interoffice signaling (CCIS), authorization for calling card calls is done automatically by checking the telephone company databases, called *line information databases (LIDBs)*. Line information databases contain all valid telephone and calling card numbers. An operator is not required to check a computer database to determine if the calling card number is valid. Instead, the central office sees from the number dialed that the call was made from a calling card. It then initiates a call to the LIDB to determine the validity of the calling card.

MCI first implemented SS7 in its network in April 1988. SS7 enabled it to halve call setup time on calls over its Philadelphia/Los Angeles route. Freeing up voice paths from signaling enabled carriers to pack more calls on their existing network paths.

Features in Carriers' Networks—Multiswitch Support

In both IP networks and circuit switched networks, specialized processors contain applications on computers that can be located at separate locations than the central office switches. In addition, single applications are able to support multiple central office switches through signaling links. Thus, adding upgrades through the signaling network provides additional functionality to multiple central offices without the cost of upgrading multiple applications or switches.

Examples of features available on networks with common channel signaling include

- Voice-activated dialing for calling cards, car phones, and home phone lines supported by speech recognition systems in the network
- Load balancing by call volume (for example, 50% of the calls sent to California and 50% to the call center in Iowa)

Signaling in Mobile Wireless Networks

Cellular networks use SS7 technology to support roaming. Every cellular provider has a database called the *home location register (HLR)* where complete information is kept about each subscriber. They also have a *visitor location register (VLR)*, which keeps temporary records for callers who are visiting from other areas. When a cellular subscriber roams, each visited system exchanges SS7 messages with the "home" system. The home system also marks its home location register so that it knows where to send calls for its customers that are roaming.

As cellular providers upgrade their networks to support higher data rates and more capacity, new signaling services will need to be implemented. For example, general packet radio services (GPRS), which is being implemented for higher speed data services, requires GPRS Roaming Exchange. GPRS Roaming Exchange standardizes addressing, security, and call routing between networks.

Signaling System 7—Links Between Carriers

A major value of Signaling System 7 (SS7) is its capability to enable all carriers to work in concert with each other. It is a standard protocol approved by the International Telecommunications Union (ITU). Global billing, toll-free and 900 services, and international roaming for wireless calls all are dependent on SS7.

SS7 is used, with variations, on a global basis. As with many standards, implementation of SS7 differs among countries. For example, the United States, Canada, Japan, and parts of China implemented the American National Standards Institute (ANSI) version of SS7. Europe implemented the European Telecommunications Standards Institute (ETSI) version. Parts of the world also use an International Telecommunications Union (ITU) version of SS7.

Gateways translate these various SS7 protocols so that international carriers can understand each other's signaling. This enables central office switches to communicate, for instance, with Chinese and European SS7 implementations.

SS7 Components

SS7 components include the following:

- *Packet switches*. Signal transfer points that route signals between databases and central offices
- *Service switching points*. Software and ports in central offices that enable switches to query databases
- *Service control points*. Specialized databases with billing and customer feature information

See Figure 4.12 for an overview of these SS7 components. Not all carriers own and operate their SS7 networks. They may, for example, use SS7 networks from companies such as Illuminet (part of VeriSign, Inc.). Carriers that use Illuminet have links from their central office to the Illuminet signal transfer points.

Signal Transfer Points (STPs)—Packet Switches

Signal transfer points are packet switches that route signals between central offices and specialized databases. Messages are sent between points on the SS7 network in variable-length packets with addresses attached. (Think of the packets as envelopes of data containing user information such as the called and calling telephone number, error correction information, and sequencing numbers so that the correct packets or envelopes are grouped together in the correct order at the receiving end.) Signal transfer switches read only the address portion of the packets and forward the messages accordingly.

Service Switching Points (SSPs)— Central Office Queries, Data Dips

Service switching points convert the central office query from the central office "machine language" to SS7 language. They enable central offices to initiate queries to databases and specialized computers in the SS7 network. Service switching points are software capable of sending specialized messages to databases and ports connected to the S77 network. For example, when a toll-free call is dialed, SSPs set up a special query to a toll-free database (the service control point) to determine the local telephone number associated with the toll-free number and the carrier responsible for routing it. This is referred to as performing a *data dip*.

Service Control Points (SCPs)— Databases

Service control points hold specialized databases with routing instructions for each call based on the calling party and/or the called party. For example, service control points tell the network to which carrier to route an 800 call. Services such as network-based voice mail, fax applications, and voice-activated dialing are located on service control points or intelligent peripherals.

5 VPNs and Specialized Network Services

In this chapter:

Improved, lower-priced technology plus business and consumer wishes for higher-speed broadband connections are resulting in growing availability of faster, high-capacity network access. Enterprise customers are requesting higher-speed access to providers' networks, to the Internet, and to other sites. In addition, carriers are interested in selling consumers high-bandwidth applications, including interactive games and video on demand along with chat and Voice over IP. Cable multiple system operators (MSOs) and incumbent telephone companies have invested billions to make their networks capable of supporting these services.

Regional Bell Operating Companies and independent telephone companies worldwide have embarked on efforts to compete with MSO broadband offerings. To accomplish this, they are deploying fiber-optic cabling at the edge, also called the last mile, of their networks. They are spending billions of dollars to extend fiber closer to customers. They will offer faster Internet access, voice, and television on infrastructure composed of all fiber or of fiber plus twisted pair cabling the last few thousand feet to the customer.

Some small, independent telephone companies and Verizon Communications are bringing fiber all the way to customers' premises. Other telephone companies are terminating fiber networks in neighborhoods and making plans to use improved DSL on short copper cabling runs between the fiber and the customer. These new flavors of DSL support video over short distances on twisted pair copper. However, because of its superiority and declining costs, telephone companies will lay fiber to more consumers and businesses for their broadband voice, Internet access, and television offerings.

When residential customers first used dial-up and then broadband connections to the Internet, they expected delays and uneven response times for browsing. However, when they watch movies and use the Internet for voice, their expectations change. If DSL is to become a viable broadband wireline option for movies and television, it will have to deliver the same quality as that provided on cable TV. These networks will need to support high speeds that are sustainable continuously for long periods. This is more complex than sending high-bandwidth information for short peak periods where lower-priority traffic can be sent between peaks. This requires upgrades in the metropolitan and core networks as well as over the last-mile access connections to customers.

Most large telephone companies have built long-haul networks based on Internet protocol (IP) capable of transporting video from content providers. However, upgrading metropolitan networks is more complex. This is because there is more gear in the metropolitan portion of networks, nearer customers. Gigabit Ethernet is a key technology for supporting video in metropolitan areas.

Gigabit Ethernet is based on the same protocol Ethernet used in enterprise networks. It is capable of reaching 1000 megabits (1 gigabit) per second to 10 gigabits per second in carrier networks. It operates on fiber-optic cabling. In carrier and cable TV networks, Ethernet aggregates traffic from many customers and sends it to central office equipment or to core networks.

Gigabit Ethernet service is available to large enterprises as well as carriers. Many of the providers who initially promoted Ethernet failed because of the expense of laying fiber the last few miles to customers. Currently, incumbent telephone companies that want to increase their nationwide offerings, specialized providers, and some long distance companies such as MCI are promoting gigabit services. Enterprises use the service in the metropolitan area to transmit corporate databases to back up data centers that safeguard files in the event of a disaster. They also use Gigabit Ethernet to access the Internet and virtual private networks and for connections to other corporate sites in the metropolitan area.

Dedicated services, also called private lines, are fixed paths between locations whose capacity is not shared by any other organization. Establishments have the use of these paths 24 hours a day, 7 days a week. Users pay a flat monthly fee. In addition to connecting two sites together, private lines are used to connect many sites together in a variety of configurations using many different lines between multiple locations. This is done so that if one path fails, data can be sent on other lines.

However, dedicated lines are expensive and complex to manage, particularly if they connect many locations. For these reasons, many companies are choosing carrier-managed, value-added virtual private networks (VPNs). Virtual private networks are "virtually" private. They have many of the features of private networks; however, many customers share the capacity, and carriers manage reliability and some of the security. Frame relay, multiprotocol label switching (MPLS), and other protocols are used to access VPNs and to carry traffic through the network.

VPNs are widely used for remote access by employees, branch offices, and business partners. Most organizations rely on Internet protocol security (IPSec) that is more complex to use and implement than the newer secure socket layer (SSL). However, changing to SSL requires upgrades to enterprise equipment for security and protection from hackers.

T-1 and higher-speed T-3 and their European counterparts, E-1 and E-3, are widely used worldwide. As the technology has matured, prices have decreased to the point where T-1 is affordable to small companies. All of these services carry voice, data, and video. They are the most commonly used technologies for Internet access and access to long distance networks. ISDN is not as prevalent as T-1 and T-3. It is used mainly by enterprises for videoconferencing and to receive incoming callers' telephone numbers. The PRI flavor of ISDN has the same speed as T-1; however, 23 of its channels carry user voice and data, and the twenty-fourth is used for signaling: dial tone, ringing, caller ID, and so forth.

Enterprises use ATM mainly for private lines. However, ATM is more complex to administer and program than other, newer network technologies. These newer technologies for wide area and metropolitan networks are based on Ethernet and IP. Carriers use ATM in their metropolitan and core networks. However, they are migrating to faster and more efficient ways to transport data such as Gigabit Ethernet and IP-based networks.

SONET is an interesting example of a service that was initially affordable only to carriers but is now used by enterprises as well. SONET multiplexers send voice and data over fiber-optic cabling. The fiber cabling can be configured in dual rings. If one of part of the ring crashes, traffic is sent over the backup ring. SONET is used widely in carrier networks. Enterprises lease SONET service mainly for disaster recovery in case their main central office crashes or the fiber to their main central office is cut. If either of these things occurs, traffic is sent over the backup fiber to the alternate central office or to the main central office.

A summary of digital network services is listed in Table 5.1.

Table 5.1   An Overview of Specialized Digital Network Services

Network Service	Places Typically Used	How Used
T-1: 24 voice or data channels 1.54 megabits per second	Commercial organizations	Internet access, connections to long distance and local telephone companies for voice and data, private lines between company sites
E-1: 30 voice or data channels, 2 megabits per second plus one channel for signaling and one for framing and remote maintenance		Each channel = 64 kilobits per second
T-3: 672 voice or data channels	Very large organizations	Access to long distance companies, Internet access, high-speed private lines between company sites, connections to other carriers
E-3: 480 voice or data channels	Local exchange carriers (LECs) and small ISPs	The European version of T-3

Table 5.1 An Overview of Specialized Digital Network Services   (continued)

Network Service	Places Typically Used	How Used
BRI ISDN: Two voice or data channels and one signaling channel	Residential customers; mainly in Europe and Asia Organizations	Internet access, voice calling Videoconferencing
PRI ISDN: 23 voice/data channels and one signaling channel in the United States 30 voice/data channels and one signaling channel in Europe	Business and commercial customers	Call centers, videoconferencing, voice and data links to local and long distance providers; PRI ISDN has different speeds in the United States and Europe
Digital subscriber lines (DSL): 128 kilobits per second (Kbps) to 44 megabits per second (Mbps)	Residential consumers, small and medium-size businesses Telecommuters	Internet access, television Remote access to corporate files and e-mail
Frame relay	Medium to large commercial customers	56Kbps to 45 megabits per second access to data networks for LAN-to-LAN communications and Internet access; mostly data but some voice
Gigabit Ethernet 1 megabit per second to 10 gigabit (Gb) over fiber	Medium to large commercial customers Carrier networks and cable TV networks	Access to the Internet, connections to storage area networks, and LAN-to-LAN connections; data only To aggregate traffic in metropolitan networks and send it as a single stream to central offices or cable headends

continues

Table 5.1   An Overview of Specialized Digital Network Services   (continued)

Network Service	Places Typically Used	How Used
Asynchronous transfer mode (ATM): Up to 2.5 gigabits per second	Telephone companies	Switches voice, video, and data traffic on high-usage network backbone routes over fiber; carries frame relay traffic in carriers' core networks
	Enterprises	Private lines
Synchronous optical network (SONET): Up to 129,000 channels on fiber-optic cable	Carrier networks Enterprises	Multiplexes voice and data traffic onto fiber optic rings; access to long distance carriers, backup central offices, and data centers

VIRTUAL PRIVATE NETWORKS—REMOTE ACCESS AND INTEROFFICE CONNECTIONS ....

A virtual private network (VPN) is any arrangement that provides connections between offices, remote workers, and the Internet without requiring dedicated lines, also referred to as private networks between sites. The term "virtual" refers to the fact that these VPNs provide the features of private lines; they are virtually private.

Frame relay is an early virtual private network technology used initially for connecting local area networks at different sites without the expense of dedicated private lines to each location. Frame relay is now used for Internet access as well.

Rationale for Virtual Private Networks Between Offices

Organizations use virtual private networks to save money on renting and managing private lines between sites. Private lines, also referred to as dedicated services, are circuits used only by the organization that leases them monthly. (For more information, see the section "Dedicated, Private Lines" later in this chapter.) In contrast, virtual private networks use shared circuits (electronic paths between points) within carriers' networks. Carriers benefit by not having to dedicate as much infrastructure to single customers.

In addition, VPN installation intervals, the time between ordering service and implementations, are shorter than for new private lines, which take weeks to engineer. Thus, customers with existing virtual private networks can quickly add locations. The biggest delays revolve around new access lines, if they are not already in place between the customer and the VPN provider. If links to the carrier are in place, sites can be added in a matter of days using spare capacity on these links.

VPNs enable businesses to avoid administering growth and day-to-day maintenance of private networks. Adding capacity to a virtual private network is simpler than adding higher-speed, dedicated lines and new hardware to each site of a private network. The customer only needs higher-speed access lines from its building to the carrier's network (see Figure 5.1). The carrier is responsible for making sure there is capacity in the network for the customer's applications.

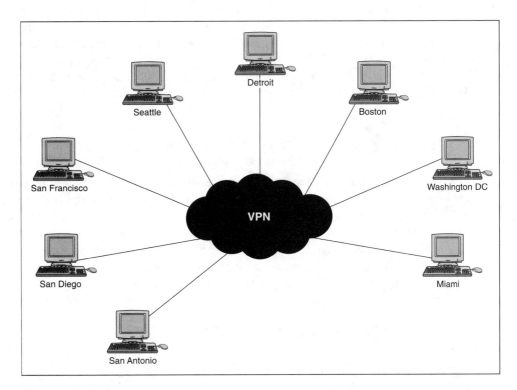

Figure 5.1
A virtual private network with access lines from branches nationwide.

Large organizations often have a mix of private lines for routes with the highest amount of voice and data traffic and virtual private network (VPNs) services for routes with less voice and data traffic.

Productivity Away from the Office— VPNs for Remote Access

In many organizations, employees assume that they will have the tools to be as productive (or more productive) away from the office as in the office. Organizations frequently supply salespeople and other remote workers with laptop computers that enable them to work offsite. Employees remotely access e-mail messages, place orders, check order status, and check inventory levels from the road and from home computers. With the growth of Voice over IP, some employees also receive phone calls directed to their office extensions on their laptops or pocket PCs.

Without a virtual private network, employees dial into remote access equipment consisting of modem banks at corporate headquarters to access e-mail or other applications using toll-free numbers billed to the corporation. Organizations rack up thousands of dollars in toll-free charges. In addition, calls are frequently dropped and speeds are slow. Moreover, these dial-in remote access arrangements do not support cable or DSL modems.

Access to Corporate Files—VPNs for Intranet Service

Intranets use Internet protocols and browser technology to provide employees with access to corporate information. An Intranet icon is on users' computers. When they click on this icon, they can browse among corporate sites to find information such as templates to create sales proposals, corporate directories, and information on benefits that have been made available to them. With VPN service, staff at remote offices or home offices click on an icon on their computer and access the Intranet in the same manner they would if they were locally connected to files.

Virtual Private Network Technology

Improvements in routing and security protocols and increased capacity in the Internet led to the capability of IP networks to differentiate different types of corporate traffic and to improvements in secure remote access. The following are newer virtual private network services carried on IP networks:

- **VPNs for Site-to-Site Communications Within Organizations:**
  - **Multiprotocol label switching (MPLS) VPNs** provide any site–to–any site connectivity. This is referred to as meshed service. MPLS service is more flexible than frame relay to configure and is more suitable for intersite voice traffic. MPLS VPN traffic is carried separately from public Internet traffic to guarantee levels of service.
  - **IP VPNs** are for site-to-site data communications using the public Internet and mixing Internet traffic with site-to-site e-mail and other applications with Internet protocol security (IPSec). IPSec creates a tunnel for each packet. The tunnel hides the destination IP address by surrounding it with a different address. IPSec also scrambles data by encrypting it.
- **Secure access on VPNs for Remote Access:**
  - **Internet protocol security (IPSec)** requires client software on computers. The IPSec protocol establishes a secure, encrypted link to a security device at the carrier or the enterprise. This is referred to as tunneling.
  - **Secure socket layer (SSL) security** is a newer VPN access method. Access is embedded in browsers so that organizations aren't required to install special client software in each user's computer.

IP VPN and MPLS offerings enable carriers to migrate traffic to their existing IP networks rather than older networks designed to carry frame relay traffic.

Multiprotocol Label Switching (MPLS) VPNs— Everyone-to-Everyone Links

When customers sign up for MPLS virtual private network service, they give their provider a list of the Internet protocol (IP) addresses associated with each site they want included in the VPN. The carrier uses this list to define a closed group of users allowed to communicate with each other using the VPN service.

Classes of Service—To Prioritize Particular Traffic

The customer chooses from a list of four or five classes of service. These classes of service are used to define the priority given to traffic for each class. For example, there may be two or three classes for data, one for voice, and another (the most expensive) for video. Voice and video have higher priorities than data. Some organizations use the lowest priced class of service for most data and higher-priced classes of service for database lookups. Often customers choose MPLS for its capability to treat voice differently than data. They initially use the network exclusively for data but plan to add voice traffic at a later time. For example, they want a network in place that enables them to do the following in the future:

- Create worldwide voice mail functionality such as broadcasting lists made up of staff at diverse sites
- Hold audio conferences
- Send call center traffic to remote sites based on time-of-day or staffing levels
- Transmit voice calls between international and domestic sites

Electronic Tags on MPLS packets

Multiprotocol label switching attaches electronic tags to packets. Routers read the tags and assign levels of priority. The tags also enable routers to forward packets more quickly because they don't have to look up addresses in tables for each packet.

Most carriers offer *service level agreements (SLAs)* for an additional fee in conjunction with MPLS VPNs. These agreements offer guarantees on issues like the following:

- Uptime, the percentage of time that the service operates.
- Latency, the amount of delay in milliseconds between when packets are sent and when they are received. This is important for voice and video.
- Restoral time per failure.
- Packet loss.
- Access line (the line from the customer to the carrier) uptime.

Carriers that don't meet these service level agreements generally give agreed-upon credits to customers.

Service Components

Customers that order MPLS use *access lines* between their network and the carrier. These lines are typically T-1, 1.54 megabits per second or less. Most customers have a separate access line for MPLS traffic and a different line for their Internet traffic. They feel their MPLS traffic is from trusted sources at branches. The public Internet traffic requires higher levels of security.

They also specify the following:

- A *port speed* at the provider's point of presence, often at a lower speed than their access line, perhaps 1 megabit.

- A *committed access rate (CAR)*—also referred to as *committed data rate (CDR), and committed information rate (CIR)*. The *bandwidth charge* is the fee charged by many carriers for guaranteeing a particular speed between the carrier's edge and the carrier's high-speed core network. Some carriers charge a higher rate for international traffic. These speeds vary from 64 kilobits to 44 megabits (T-3).

- *Access charge* for the circuit connecting the customer to the provider's network.

- They can "burst" send data at up to the speed of the port and access line they lease.

- Service level agreements.

- Classes of service; classes with a lower priority cost less than those with a higher priority. See the earlier section, "Multiprotocol Label Switching (MPLS) VPNs," for classes of service.

Managed Service—Providers Monitor Onsite Routers

Customers have the option of managing their own router or paying their provider to manage it. Carrier management of the router is referred to as *managed service*. With managed service, carriers monitor the router 24 hours per day, 7 days a week for service disruptions, denial of service attacks indicated by unusual traffic levels, and viruses. For medium-size companies, it may cost less to depend on a pool of specially trained provider technicians than to train and hire their own technical staff for these functions. As part of the service, carriers provide activity reports that track the level of traffic so that customers can ensure there is adequate capacity.

MPLS Advantages for Carriers—Revenue Sources and Administrative Efficiency

Carriers are eager to migrate customers to MPLS to save money on administration and as a platform for new services. Administratively, carriers have the capability to add classes of service for higher-priced voice and videoconferencing. These changes can be made in real time by programming requested modifications. Making changes to frame relay service is more complex because each path between sites must be programmed separately. (See the section later in this chapter on frame relay.) Other potential sources of revenue for carriers are hosting, and access to hosted data storage (backup storage of customer files on the network).

However, carriers still have investments in asynchronous transfer mode (ATM) network infrastructure that is not fully depreciated. The transition to MPLS as the single network will take place gradually.

VPNs for International Connectivity

Many businesses use MPLS or frame relay for data communications between sales offices, manufacturing, and distribution centers in other countries. For connections between the MPLS intercontinental network and the remote branch, the VPN provider contracts with a local telephone company in the distant country. If there is a repair problem with the local access line, the VPN provider contacts the local telephone company to resolve the problem. The VPN provider manages the intercountry portion of the network. In some areas of the world—for example, in parts of Eastern Europe and Africa—these connections bypass the poor quality on the public switched telephone network. T-1 and lower speeds are available in most parts of the world. However, lead times between placing the order and installation is longer in some areas. These can be from 90 to 120 days.

Carriers often refer to sites where their equipment is located as points of presence (POPs). To reach the MPLS VPN network, lines are run from customer premises to carriers' access points. NTT, BT, AT&T, Infonet, MCI, Sprint, and Equant all offer intercontinental service.

IPSec VPNs—Public Internet-Based VPNs for Intersite Connections

Some organizations save money by using the public Internet for VPN service rather than MPLS VPN or frame relay service. Companies using the public Internet mix intracompany and public Internet traffic on the same access lines. They provide their own security, usually IPSec as described in the next section, as well as firewalls and antivirus software. Alternatively, they contract with their carrier to manage their security devices, which are onsite or at the carriers' POPs.

While the public Internet does not guarantee speeds, companies are finding that providing a high-speed access line gives them adequate site-to-site service at a lower price than frame relay and MPLS VPNs. This is because many Internet backbone providers overbuilt their networks, expecting a larger increase in traffic than occurred. Moreover, the costs for T-1 and T-3 have been decreasing, making them affordable for many more organizations.

Network-Based IPSec VPNs—Over Carriers' Private IP Networks

These IPSec VPN-based services operate over carriers' private IP networks instead of the public Internet. The carrier provides security in its network. It encapsulates (creates tunnels around) packets routed between its points of presence (POPs).

Both of these IPSec VPN-type offerings don't offer the classes of service for voice and video. In addition, they don't provide service level agreements with statistics on traffic levels and network reliability. Customers are responsible for monitoring traffic flows through their own routers.

IPSec VPNs—Complex Administration, Client Software

With IPSec VPNs, users click on client software installed on their computers to launch remote access. The client software is a special program containing IPSec security. It can be used with dial-up or broadband access. When it's used with dial-up service, the computer modem dials into the network provider's nearest bank of Internet modems and associated security. Security software at the provider issues prompts for usernames, passwords, and token ID numbers if they're used.

As indicated in Figure 5.2, customers with broadband cable or DSL service log onto the public Internet. From there, dial-in and broadband traffic are routed to their provider's private Internet and then to the T-1 or other dedicated line connected to their corporation. For an additional monthly fee, carriers manage a customer's onsite router or switch and security such as a firewall and virus scanning devices.

IPSec Virtual Private Network for Remote Access

To support VPN remote access, IT staff distribute software to each person's computer or laptop. In addition, the help line answers calls from employees who need assistance. A shortcoming is that employees can only access their e-mail when they have their computers with the client software with them. This service does not work at public computers such as those at airports or Internet cafes.

IPSec establishes a secure connection between the corporate local area network and the remote user by scrambling and tunneling the bits and hiding the IP header in each packet. This ensures privacy. Tunneling prevents hackers from learning corporate LAN IP addresses. To stop remote users from passing viruses from the Internet to corporate networks, the client software will often not function if there is an open connection to the Internet while the user is logged in remotely.

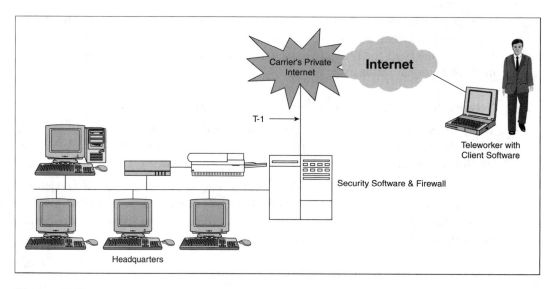

Figure 5.2
IPSec virtual private network for remote access.

VPN Aggregation and Outsourcing for IPSec Remote Access

Some organizations that support hundreds or even thousands of remote access employees worldwide use network aggregators, also referred to as virtual network operators, to manage their remote access. A network aggregator makes agreements with carriers worldwide, including those at hotels and airports, so that customers have Wi-Fi wireless, cellular, and landline access through one provider. The virtual network operator runs a clearinghouse that performs billing settlements. In essence, the aggregator pays network operators a fee and bills the corporation, which receives only one bill.

Users receive the aggregator's client software, which establishes a session with the aggregator when it is activated. The aggregator passes the transmission on to the corporate firewall and security server after authenticating the user and checking that he or she has up-to-date firewall and virus-protection software.

Using an aggregator means the enterprise does not have to make agreements with multiple carriers and Wi-Fi operators for worldwide remote access. In addition, aggregators supply another level of security. Some companies use aggregators for people who work from home as well as those who travel. These arrangements also use client software and therefore have the same user interface issues as the IPSec VPN service. Network aggregators include iPass, Fiberlink, and GoRemote International Communications, Inc.

Secure Socket Layer (SSL)—VPNs Accessed from Browsers

The attraction of secure socket layer (SSL) virtual private network service is that the service works from within standard browsers on laptops, desk computers, and personal digital assistants such as Pocket PCs. This makes virtual private networks easier to use, with less administrative support required from information technology (IT) staff. The business or commercial enterprise is not required to supply special software to each laptop computer used for remote access. The simplified login results in fewer user logon errors.

Secure sock layer virtual private networks is a newer technology. According to a Frost & Sullivan study, in 2003, worldwide spending for IPSec gear was $2 billion. For SSL, it was $89.7 million for the same period. Tim Greene reported this in *Network World Fusion* on July 26, 2004 in an article "SSL Making Strides Against IPSec VPNs."

Simplified access and improvements in SSL are expected to spur growth. Employees using SSL-type security can only access applications such as e-mail supported by the SSL gear. Software in SSL *appliances* is adapted to enable access to particular applications. An appliance is a specialized computer dedicated to a particular task. For example, SSL VPN appliances from companies such as Neoteris, Inc. (pending acquisition by NetScreen), Nortel Networks, F5, and Aventail Corp. supply security and remote access for secure socket layer virtual private network users. These appliances prompt users for their names, passwords, and (if used) token number. They apply encryption and a secure tunnel and allow or deny access to enterprise applications. They have other features such as scanning users' PCs and automatically downloading software patches to computers that don't have the latest security corrections loaded.

Because SSL is a higher-level security protocol, it has the benefit of allowing or denying access to particular applications based on privileges granted to classes of employees. As it is possible for remote computers to pass viruses to corporate networks, some SSL appliances have the capability to scan remote computers for antivirus software and operating systems with the latest security patches. Other appliances have the capability to wipe out passwords and corporate data from computers used for remote access. This eliminates the possibility of computers in public areas, such as kiosks, storing and passing on private information and passwords.

Security—Firewalls, Protection Against Viruses, and Other Attacks

A *firewall* is a device or set of devices at carriers, enterprises, and homes that screens incoming and internal traffic to prevent hackers' access to files. Firewalls are designed to keep out hackers by allowing only designated users to access networks. In organizations' networks, firewall software is installed on routers and on remote access switches called VPN gateways. Organizations that use carriers' firewall protection have onsite firewall protection as well.

Firewalls use various techniques including *address filtering,* which looks at a user's IP address and accepts or rejects messages based on the IP address. Important applications might contain their own firewalls for extra protection. Firewalls can also restrict communications to certain addresses. New firewalls can also filter by port. In addition, they can be programmed to recognize applications and content. Acting as an agent for and screening traffic for applications is referred to as *intermediation* or *proxy-type* functions.

Because employees use their laptops at home to surf the Web and then bring them into work, corporations monitor internal transmissions as well as communications from the Internet. The goal is to avoid contamination from these laptops.

Firewalls don't protect against viruses and other threats. Corporations often subscribe to security services that keep them posted about new software attacks, monitor their networks for unusual amounts or types of traffic, and download protection against new types of attacks.

Token ID Security—To Verify Identification

Token identification, which adds an additional layer of user authentication in addition to passwords, is used in most remote access services. Tokens are small devices that can be attached to peoples' key rings (fobs), and they generate new six- to eight-digit numbers every 60 seconds. When prompted, users type in the token-generated number. These numbers are generated by a combination of factory set matching numbers in the user's device and a central server combined with the time. To be authenticated, the number the user types in must match that generated by the central computer. RSA is the leading supplier of token IDs. Competitors include Secure Computing, Aladdin Knowledge Systems, SafeNet, and VeriSign.

If a person's password is stolen, the hacker will not be able to access the network unless he or she has the token as well as the password.

FRAME RELAY—A SHARED WIDE AREA NETWORK SERVICE.................................

First implemented in 1992, frame relay is a public network offering that enables customers to transmit data between LANs at multiple locations (see Figure 5.3). It also is

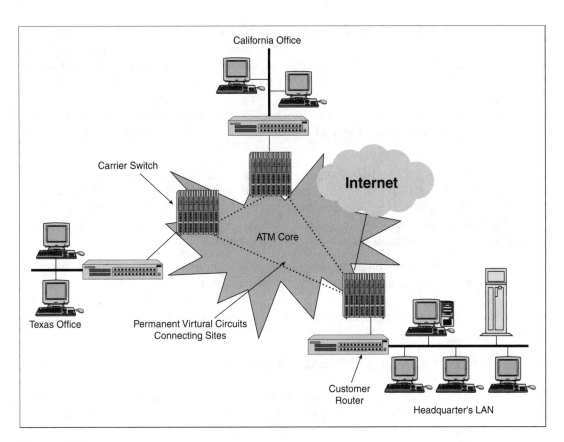

Figure 5.3
Frame relay network permanent virtual circuits (PVCs) between branches and with links to the Internet.

used to access the Internet. Frame relay was first promoted as a lower-priced substitute for private lines. By using frame relay, organizations do not have to plan, build, and maintain their own duplicate paths to each of their sites. Multiple users share the frame relay networks. It is offered by local and long distance telephone companies.

Frame relay's requirement of defining links between sites in advance, which can be cumbersome for large organizations that want to connect each site to every other site, is leading some companies to choose MPLS VPNs. Falling prices on MPLS service and frame relay's unsuitability for voice are other reasons organizations are starting to migrate to MPLS. However, frame relay is still a popular, cost-effective choice for organizations.

Access to Frame Relay—56 Kilobits to T-3

The line that connects each customer to the frame relay network is called an access line. It provides access from the user's router to the frame relay network. Each site that uses the frame relay service leases a circuit, a telephone line, from its equipment to a port on the frame relay switch. Access line speeds vary from 56Kbps to subrate T-1 speeds (that is, 128, 156, and 384Kbps and T-1 all the way up to T-3, 44 megabits per second).

Sites at different locations in the same organization can be configured with access lines at different speeds. Some frame relay vendors also offer dial-up (for example, ISDN) access to their networks, most often as a backup to their dedicated access in case the dedicated access lines to the frame relay network fail. Higher-speed access lines cost more than lower-speed ones.

To save money on access lines, smaller customers share their T-1 lines for voice and frame relay access. For example, 18 channels of the 24 T-1 channels may be connected to the telephone system for voice traffic. The other six channels carry frame relay traffic to the network service provider's frame relay port.

Frame Relay to Access Other Networks

Frame relay is an access technology in which customers' packets are put into frames. In addition to LAN-to-LAN connectivity, it is used to access the following types of networks:

- Frame relay networks that carry traffic on asynchronous transfer mode (ATM) switches

- MPLS virtual private networks

- The public Internet

Equipment on customer premises that converts Ethernet local area network packets into frames is called a frame relay access device (FRAD). It is often a card within the router. Each frame has bits called the flag, telling the network when the user data (frame) starts and when it ends. There also are addressing and destination bits in the frame for billing and routing purposes so that the frame relay provider knows where to route and bill each frame.

Customers' frames are sent to ports on the carrier's network. Routers at the carrier's central office convert the customer data to a format compatible with the carrier's network and send it to the core network.

Frame Relay Service—Permanent Virtual Circuits and Committed Information Rate

Frame relay service is priced at fixed monthly fees based on the following elements, plus the cost of the access line used to connect each site to the carrier's frame relay equipment:

- **The permanent virtual circuit (PVC)** is a logical, predefined path or link through a carrier's network. For example, if San Francisco and Tucson sites need to exchange data, the carrier defines a permanent virtual circuit between these two locations. PVCs are priced at fixed monthly fees.

- **The frame relay port is the entry point**, on a frame relay provider's switch, to the frame relay network. Multiple permanent virtual circuits can use one port. Ports are available in variable speeds such as T-1, 56Kbps, 256Kbps, and 512Kbps.

- **The committed information rate (CIR)** is the minimum number of bits per second, perhaps half the capacity of the port, that the customer is guaranteed to be able to send from each site. Some customers save money by using low committed information rates. Customers can "burst," send data at the maximum speed of their frame relay port, if bandwidth is available.

Voice on Frame Relay— Instead of Private Lines

Some customers replace private lines with frame relay networks to carry voice traffic between sites. Voice is compressed so that it requires less bandwidth. Customers either add separate permanent virtual circuits for voice or upgrade their committed information rates for extra capacity. For large organizations, defining separate permanent virtual circuits is cumbersome. It is also costly. Moreover, it does not guarantee quality on the access line between the customer and the frame network. These frames do not have fields capable of indicating priority levels.

Because of the quality issue, some customers do not use frame relay for customers' calls, only for employee-to-employee calls. If the frame relay network becomes congested, voice quality can be degraded because packets are dropped or delayed even with higher committed information rates.

The desire to add voice between sites is another factor in customers' migration to MPLS because of this extra expense to upgrade frame relay service and the lack of prioritization on the access line. This is particularly true for larger organizations that want to send customer traffic between sites.

REPLACING PRIVATE LINES WITH FRAME RELAY FOR DISASTER RECOVERY AND COST SAVINGS

An energy company that generates fossil fuel formerly leased 125 private lines from their control center to each power plant. The private lines carried signals for monitoring and controlling equipment at the plants. To save money, the utility changed its leased-line network to frame relay service. In addition to saving money on private lines, it was no longer responsible for network reliability. It previously had to keep track of the circuit identification numbers for each local and interoffice channel on 125 lines. It also had to work with carriers and equipment vendors to determine if problems were in the equipment or lines. Now the frame relay provider tracks reliability on each access line and on the backbone network, which transports the traffic.

Redundancy in the event of a disaster was an important factor in the selection of frame relay. The September 11, 2001 attacks at the World Trade Center in New York City highlighted the need for backup to the main control center in the event of a terrorist attack. Moreover, natural disasters such as hurricanes, operator error, and fire can also cause a control center to fail.

As part of its disaster-recovery plan, the utility has a permanent virtual circuit (PVC) from each plant to the control center plus PVCs from each plant to two backup locations. The permanent virtual circuits are paths defined in the carrier's network between particular sites. In the event of a disaster, remote monitoring and control is automatically switched to a backup center. Implementing an analogous disaster-recovery plan using private lines would have entailed adding router ports and combination channel service unit/data service units (CSU/DSUs) at each site. In addition, two new private lines from each site to the backup control centers would have been needed. (See the following section on private lines.) CSU/DSUs are digital modems, which are required on digital lines such as T-1s and T-3s.

DEDICATED, PRIVATE LINES ....

Dedicated services, also known as private lines, are similar to having two tin cans and a string between sites. The "string" and "tin cans" are for the exclusive use of the organization that leases them. The "string" portion is the medium over which the voice or data transmission is sent. The medium is generally copper, microwave, or fiber optics. The "tin cans" are the devices, such as a telephone, modem, or digital modem, that enable sites to transmit data, voice, or video between locations.

The number of costly private lines used by commercial organizations is decreasing. They are being replaced by virtual private networks (VPNs), which are less costly to maintain and have lower monthly lease rates. However, large enterprises, utilities, and financial services organizations still use high-speed private lines for high-speed, secure communications.

Dedicated Services—Wide and Metropolitan Area Networks

Dedicated, private lines are available for the exclusive use of the customer that leases them from a network service provider. For example, large organizations such as the Department of Defense and large pharmaceuticals connect their multistate sites using circuits at 155 million bits per second (OC-3) and greater speeds. These are examples of *wide area networks (WANs)* that run between cities.

Metropolitan area networks (MANs) consist of private lines that connect buildings within a city or metropolitan area. Large hospitals transmit customer records, research files, and radiology images over metropolitan area networks. Major universities also use metropolitan area networks. Dedicated services are available around the clock. This is cost effective for companies that use the dedicated lines for voice, video, and e-mail during the day and bulk data transmissions such as transmissions of sales figures after hours.

Fixed Monthly Fees

Private, dedicated links are priced at flat monthly fees. The fees are not based on minutes used or the amount of data transmitted.

Fixed Routes

Dedicated lines are not flexible. Calls and data can only can be sent between the fixed points to which the lines are connected. Thus, communications with a site not on the network is not possible.

Exclusive Use

Dedicated, private lines are put into place so that voice or data can be sent exclusively by the organization that leases them. For example, organizations with dedicated connections to videoconference equipment can only hold video calls with organizations that are part of their private network.

Voice, Video, and Data

Dedicated lines are suitable for transmission of video, voice, and data. Voice, video, and data can share the same dedicated services, or they can use completely different dedicated lines. Firms often lease T-3 lines that have 672 channels to tie locations together. They can use, for example, 24 of the paths for voice and the rest for data and video.

Fixed Capacity

Dedicated services are leased or built from carriers such as AT&T, BellSouth, NTT, or MCI with a fixed capacity or bandwidth. These speeds range from low 9,600 bits per second (bps) and 19,200bps up to OC-3 (155 megabits) and ATM megabit speeds. They also include T-1 and T-3 and fractional T-1 and T-3 speeds.

Security

An important factor in the decision to use dedicated services is the desire for secure transmissions. Some firms believe that public network services such as frame relay and other virtual private networks are too public or open to hacking for applications such as funds transfer. Organizations concerned about security may place encryption devices on both ends of dedicated services. The encryption device scrambles the transmission when it leaves the sending location and unscrambles it when it arrives at the receiving location.

Voice—Operators and Voice Mail for Multiple Sites

As discussed previously, many companies are planning to move voice services to lower-priced MPLS virtual private networks. Currently, organizations have private lines for the convenience of abbreviated dialing and features that provide one-system functionality between sites. For example:

- Four or five digits instead of the 11 digits used on the public switched network for dialing between sites. Telephones with displays might indicate the name of the person that is calling from another corporate location.

- One set of operators to answer calls for multiple locations, which is a significant cost savings over full-time operators at each location.

- One voice mail system shared by all locations; staff at headquarters maintains the system.

- One speech-activated directory in which callers speak the name of the party they want to reach (the use of speech recognition).

Network Topologies—How Sites Are Connected

The term "topology" refers to the geometric shape of the physical connection of the lines in a network, or the "view from the top." The shape of the network, the configuration in which lines are connected to each other, impacts cost, reliability, and accessibility. Consider the multipoint configuration in Figure 5.4. An application for multipoint design is one used by utilities for communications to monitor the control equipment in their plants. They run fiber on their existing rights of way over which signals are sent. In the mesh configuration in Figure 5.5, if one link is out of service, traffic can be rerouted over other links.

The following are network configurations:

- *Point-to-point*. One line connecting two locations.

- *Multipoint*. One line connecting more than two sites together. This is also referred to as multidrop.

- *Star (hub and spoke) configuration*. All locations connect to, or "hub into," a central site. PBXs and data switches in LANs are configured in star topologies.

- *Mesh design*. All points on the network, nodes, connect to each other in a flat or nonhierarchical manner. Peer-to-peer networks for music sharing are examples of mesh networks. Most wireless community networks based on 802.11 technology use a form of mesh design called partial mesh in which access points with antennas are connected to each other. In partial mesh designs, not all end-user devices are connected to each other (see Chapter 9, "Wi-Fi, Wireless Broadband, Sensor Networks, and Personal Area Networks").

In the star shape illustrated in Figure 5.6, if the main location goes down, all nodes (locations) on the network are out of service. Some virtual private networks have a combination hub and spoke and VPN configuration. Branch offices, remote warehouses, and manufacturing locations are the spokes that access the main location, the hub, via the VPN. The router at the hub sends Internet and e-mail traffic over the hub's access line to the Internet. The VPN service also offers mesh topology—site-to-site connectivity.

Private networks also can be based on mesh design (see Figure 5.5). These are costly but have more reliability than a star arrangement. However, as the network grows, the design, trouble-tracking, and maintenance tasks become increasingly complex. In addition, ownership of private networks requires customer expertise for the initial design and sizing of the dedicated network, ongoing maintenance, and redesign for new applications.

Local and Interexchange Channels

Rates for private lines are based on distance and speed. Higher-speed lines that run over longer distances cost more than slower, shorter circuits. A T-1 line at 1.544 million bits per second is less expensive than a T-3, 44 million bit per second line.

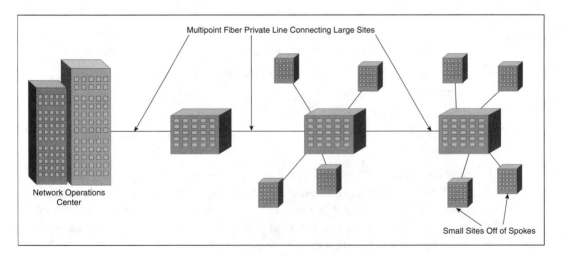

Figure 5.4
Multipoint private lines with hub and spoke for small locations.

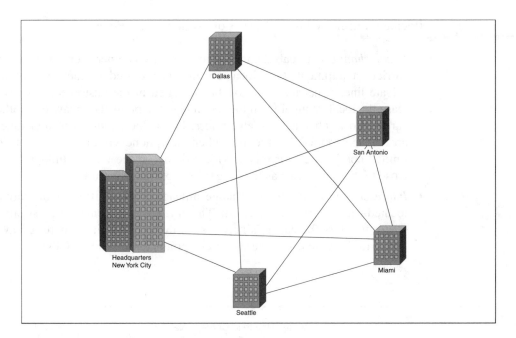

Figure 5.5
Mesh network topology with all-to-all connectivity.

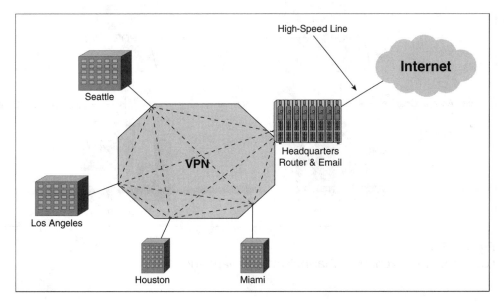

Figure 5.6
Any-to-any mesh design in a VPN; hub and spoke (star) to headquarters for
Internet access.

Pricing for dedicated lines consists of two items (see Figure 5.7):

- *Local channels.* Local channels run from a customer's premises to the carrier's equipment. One local channel is required at each end of the private line. A carrier with no fiber installed in the customer's area will lease the local channel from the incumbent telephone company or another carrier. Local channels are also referred to as local loops. Local channels are often supplied by the incumbent telephone company. Because of limited competition for this service, pricing on these short links is often close to the same price as the longer interexchange circuit.

- *Interexchange miles.* Interexchange mileage is the portion of the circuit located within a carrier's network. The mileage runs from the access point, where it enters the carrier's network, to the egress point, where it leaves the carrier's switch. These are carriers' points of presence (POPs).

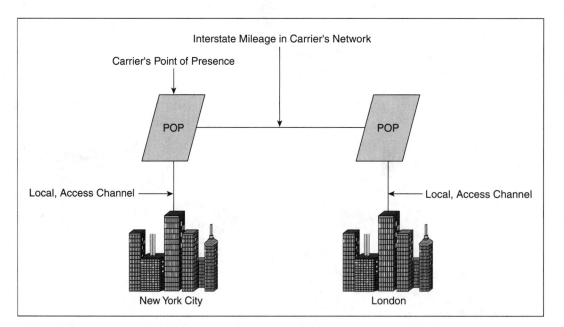

Figure 5.7
Local and interexchange channels of a private line.

REMOTE CONTROL MONITORING OVER RIGHTS OF WAY

Large utilities, railroads, highway authorities, and water and wastewater (sewage) treatment organizations remotely monitor and control water treatment plants and traffic using dedicated communications lines. For example, utilities and waste treatment plants open and close valves (to regulate flows) and operate compressors (to compact gas or waste) based on information gathered at control centers via their private networks. Highway authorities monitor road conditions, congestion, and accidents and issue alerts.

Most organizations lease private lines from telephone companies for private lines. However, large utilities, railroads, highway, and waste treatment authorities own the rights-of-way along their utility poles, tracks, and roads. This is a major advantage. It means that they can economically lay fiber or construct microwave networks for their own infrastructure. Because they own rights-of-way, they don't have to apply to each municipality where they run their network for permission to cross public roadways and/or dig up streets to lay conduit for fiber. This process often delays projects by a year or two and involves the expense of drawing up plans and hiring lawyers and consultants who know the ins and outs of dealing with local public utility commissions.

These organizations often construct private networks at the same time that they are building the infrastructure to, for example, distribute gas and electricity. When they raise the enormous amount of capital for new infrastructure, they add money for fiber or microwave towers. They thus avoid the monthly lease payments to rent high-speed lines from telephone companies.

Thus, many utilities, roadway, and water authorities' private networks are run along rights-of-way. In addition, they supplement higher-speed, backbone portions of their private networks built along rights of way with dedicated lines they rent from telephone companies. One energy company owns a series of point-to-point microwave towers. It leases lines that run from a number of their microwave towers to power plants that are not adjacent to land on the right of way. Thus, the microwave towers act as hubs where signals from a number of power plants are sent over the private network back to control centers. The slower-speed leased lines to power plants are spokes.

T-1—24 PATHS AND T-3-672 PATHS OVER ONE TELEPHONE CIRCUIT ....

T-1 is a multiplexing scheme that enables one circuit to carry 24 voice, video, or data conversations at 64 kilobits per channel. It was made available to retail customers in 1983. Once installed, companies found digital T-1 to be light-years ahead of old analog data lines in terms of reliability and speed.

T-1 is the most prevalent technology for Internet access and access lines connecting customers to their carriers' points of presence (POPs) for long distance. However, large customers now use the higher capacity T-3 (672 channels, 45 megabits) for Internet access, private lines, and access to their carriers. In addition, medium-size customers that previously had one T-1 now have multiple T-1s because of increases in Internet traffic and the desire to have T-1 connections to multiple carriers for backup purposes.

Competition from competitive local exchange carriers (CLECs) led to more price decreases in the late 1990s and early twenty-first century. These price wars have made T-1 affordable for small businesses that combine voice and Internet access on T-1s.

T-1: 1,544,000bps; E-1: 2,048,000bps Speeds

T-1 circuits operate at 1.54 million bits per second. The letters "DS" stand for digital signal level. DS-1 refers to the entire 1.54-megabit T-1 line. The terms DS-1 and T-1 are used interchangeably. The United States, Canada, and Japan use the 1.54 flavor of T-1.

The rest of the world uses E-1, which operates at 2.048 megabits with 32 channels—30 channels for voice or data, one channel for signaling, and one channel for framing and remote maintenance. Organizations that run a T-1 from the United States to an office in Europe need rate-adaptation equipment so that the carrier in the United States can connect the domestic T-1 to the European T-1 line.

DS-0 is the 56Kbps or 64Kbps speed of each of the 24 individual channels of the T-1 or E-1 circuit. The DS-0 speed of 64 kilobits is the same worldwide. (See Table 5.7 in the Appendix section later in this chapter.)

T-3, J-3, and E-3—North America, Japan, and the Rest of the World

DS-3 speeds differ internationally:

- The T-3 North American speed is 44 megabits with 672 channels ($28 \times 24 = 672$)—the equivalent of 28 T-1s.

- The Japanese flavor, J-3, has 32 megabits with 480 channels. This is the equivalent of 20 T-1s.

- The E-3 speed is 34 megabits over 480 channels. E-3 is the equivalent of 16 E-1s. DS-3 is also offered at fractional speeds.

Speeds higher than DS-3 are called *optical carrier (OC)* in North America and *synchronous transfer mode (STM)* in Europe. (See the section on SONET later in this chapter.)

T-3/E-3 Applications—Internet Access and Private Networks

DS-3 service is used mainly for private networks and Internet access. An organization's small sites often access the Internet using the T-3 circuit located at headquarters. This is another example of a hub and spoke configuration in which the headquarters acts as the hub for smaller sites.

T-3/E-3 is also used in large, private networks operated by conglomerates for data communications between sites. They use these links for access to corporate databases and updates on transactions in, for example, large organizations that supply transportation and delivery services. (See the earlier section, "Dedicated, Private Lines.") Internet service providers and small carriers also use T-3 to access the Internet and for connections to other carriers.

T-3 services, the equivalent of 28 T-1 circuits, start to cost less than multiple T-1s when customers have eight to ten T-1s at the same site.

Fractional T-1, T-3, E-1, E-3— Lower-Cost DS-1 or DS-3 Speeds

Customers who require more than 64Kbps but less than a full 1.54 megabit T-1 or E-1 often opt for lower-priced, fractional T-1/E-1. Fractional T-1/E-1 is sold at speeds of, for example, 4 channels at 256, 8 channels at 512, and 12 channels at 768 kilobits per second. Customers don't purchase fractional DS-1 at higher than 8 or 12 DS-0 channels because the price becomes equivalent to the cost of a full T-1.

Fractional T-3 and E-3 service is sold as well. However, customers that need speeds of, for example, 10 megabits or 100 megabits per second are starting to opt for Gigabit Ethernet because of its flexibility in upgrading speed without changing equipment and lower prices for higher speeds.

Common applications for fractional T-1 are Internet access, videoconferencing, and access to virtual private networks.

Signaling and Framing—8,000 Bits Per Second

The total bandwidth of all DS-1 and higher circuits is higher than the sum of all of the channels, or 24 × 64,000, which equals 1,536,000. The total bandwidth of DS-1 is 1,544,000 bps. On DS-1s, these extra 8,000 bits are used for signaling and framing. A frame is a grouping of bits with samples of user data from each of the 24 channels. Data from devices connected to the T-1 are sampled 8,000 times per second, put into frames and sent sequentially on the T-1. Multiplexing on T-1 depends on strict adherence to timing—time division multiplexing.

A Fat Pipe for Data—Unchannelized T-1

T-1 circuits, or a portion of the T-1 circuit used for data, can be ordered from carriers in an unchannelized format. An unchannelized T-1 is a single pipe with more capacity for data than one broken up into 24 channels using T-1 multiplexing. With unchannelized service, the router performs the multiplexing.

Unchannelized T-1 service is used for the following:

- Access to frame relay, the Internet, and virtual private network service
- Packetized, compressed, digitized voice—Voice over IP
- Dedicated lines between locations

Unlike voice carried in VoIP packets, voice carried on T-1 to the public switched telephone network must be channelized, put into DS-0 channels compatible with central office switches.

Integrated Access Devices (IADs)—Affordable T-1

Competitive local exchange carriers (CLECs) were the first telephone companies to offer integrated access devices to small organizations. This innovation greatly increased the affordability of T-1 for small customers by eliminating the need for a separate broadband connection for Internet access in addition to voice lines. RBOCs and smaller incumbents later adopted this strategy. Integrated access for voice and data on one T-1 benefits telephone companies that only need to provision a single four-wire (two-pair) copper line or fiber rather than multiple copper pairs for voice and data.

Integrated access devices (IADs) have multiple functions, including T-1 service, security protection via firewalls, a point for remote monitoring, routing, and frame relay access. IADs enable T-1 circuits to mix voice and Internet access on the same line. If the organization requests 12 voice lines, it has capacity left for 768 kilobits of data plus 8 kilobits for signaling ([1.544 × 8 kilobits of signaling] × [12 × 64] = 768). Their carrier provides an integrated access device (IAD) that drops off a certain number of voice channels to their telephone system and Internet traffic to their local area network. A compatible integrated access device is located at the carrier (see Figure 5.8).

Some integrated access devices are based on asynchronous transfer mode (ATM) technology. (ATM is described later in this chapter.) ATM provides *dynamic bandwidth allocation* on the T-1. Dynamic bandwidth allocation dynamically shifts traffic on the T-1 so that customers don't have to permanently allocate a set number of channels for voice or data. If there are only five channels used for voice, the IAD automatically uses the rest of the "pipe" for data. However, if a sixth outgoing or incoming call is placed, data is shifted to the other channels. Traffic is dynamically reallocated within the entire T-1's capacity. Therefore, the customer uses the T-1 line more efficiently by, for example, having more capacity for data during times of the day or night when voice traffic is low.

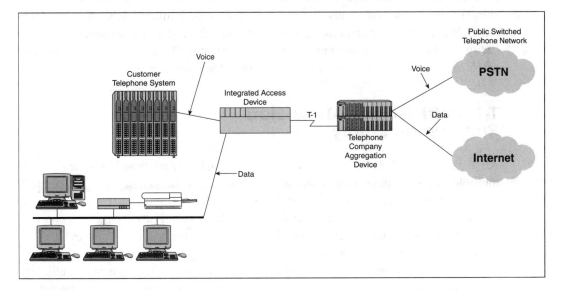

Figure 5.8
Integrated access devices for T-1s carrying voice and data.

Channel Banks—Connecting T-1 to Analog PBXs and Central Offices

Channel banks are the multiplexing devices that connect digital T-1 circuits to older analog private branch exchanges (PBXs) and key systems. (A *circuit* is a path for electrical transmissions between two points.) Decoders within the channel bank perform coding and decoding functions of converting analog voice to digital and vice versa. All new PBXs and key systems are digital, as are the vast majority of central office switches, and channel banks are not required for T-1 connections on these systems.

DS-1: Media Agnostic; DS-3: Fiber, Microwave, and Satellite

DS-1 is media agnostic. It can operate over any medium, including fiber, copper, and microwave. DS-3, however, because of its higher speeds, requires fiber, terrestrial microwave, or satellite-based microwave.

Telephone companies use T-1 and T-3 over microwave for hard-to-cable areas such as across rivers and canyons, and cellular providers use microwave as one choice between antennas and mobile central offices in cellular carriers' networks.

T-1 on fiber is more reliable than T-1 over copper. Because of decreasing costs of fiber and the lower cost to maintain it, telephone companies deploy fiber to new sites. Fiber is now commonly in place directly to medium and large business premises. When fiber is brought into a user's premises, the end user must supply the electricity for the equipment on which the fiber terminates. If there is no backup power, customers lose their T-1/E-1s and E-3/T-3s when they lose power.

T-1 Inefficiencies—Time Slots Running on Empty

All T carrier signals (for example, T-1, E-1, E-3, and T-3) are based on time division multiplexing. Each device that communicates over a T-1 line is assigned a time slot. If there are eight telephones contending for a T-1 circuit, a time slot is saved for each telephone for the duration of the particular telephone call. For example, telephone 1 might be assigned slot A; telephone 2, slot B; and so forth. During pauses in voice conversations, the slot is not assigned to another computer. The assigned time slot is transmitted without any bits. This is why time division multiplexing is not an efficient way to use a wide area network. Pauses in data transmission result in idle time slots. In a network with millions of time slots, this can result in many idle time slots and wasted bandwidth.

CSU/DSUs—Digital Modems: Testing and Clocking

Channel service units (CSUs) and data service units (DSUs) are required to interface with digital T-1, T-3, fractional T-1 and T-3, and 56Kbps lines. CSU/DSUs are supplied in one integrated piece of equipment. The CSU plugs into the network jack. The DSU connects to the customer's equipment, such as the T-1 or E-1 multiplexer. CSU/DSUs are generally cards within multiplexers, integrated access devices, and PBXs rather than standalone, external devices.

Maintenance and performance tests are done from the CSU/DSU to determine if a repair problem is in the equipment, the CSU/DSU, or the telephone line. The CSU also provides clocking and signal reshaping. The clocking function is responsible for sending out bits in an evenly timed fashion. If the clocking is off, the transmission will not work. In this case, the technician might say, "The line is slipping," or "The timing is off." The CSU also provides framing, in which the starting and ending points for each channel are set and monitored. The DSU makes sure the correct positive and negative voltages are present on the signals from the multiplexer to the CSU.

CSUs use mainly extended superframe (ESF) so that T-1 and T-3 circuits can be monitored while a line is in service. Network service providers have extended superframe CSU/DSUs in their networks. Earlier CSUs used superframe (SF), which required taking the circuit out of service for many maintenance functions.

ISDN—INTEGRATED SERVICES DIGITAL NETWORK ....

Integrated services digital network (ISDN) is a worldwide public standard for sending voice, video, data, or packets over the public switched telephone network (PSTN) in a digital format. There are two "flavors" of ISDN: basic rate interface (BRI) and primary rate interface (PRI), which are defined in Table 5.2.

However, manufacturers implemented some forms of ISDN differently from each other. This resulted in some incompatibilities between ISDN in Europe, North America, and Japan.

ISDN is used mainly in enterprise call centers, connections from businesses to local and long distance telephone companies, and videoconferencing. PRI and BRI ISDN use out-of-band signaling to carry dialed digits, caller identification, dial tone, and other signals. It works over existing copper wiring, fiber, or satellite media.

Table 5.2 Basic Rate and Primary Rate ISDN

ISDN Service	Number and Speed of Channels	Total Speed	Number of Pairs of Wires from Telco to Customer Premises
BRI ISDN: 3 channels	2 at 64 kilobits per second 1 at 16 kilobits per second for signaling	144 kilobits per second	1
PRI ISDN: 24 channels	23 at 64 kilobits per second 1 at 64 kilobits per second for signaling or packetized data	1.54 megabits per second	2
PRI ISDN— Europe: 32 channels	30 at 64 kilobits 2 at 64 kilobits per second for signaling	2.05 megabits per second	2

Basic Rate Interface ISDN—Higher Usage in Europe and Japan Than the United States

The most common uses for BRI ISDN in the United States are for dial backup for frame relay and for videoconferencing. Basic rate interface (BRI) consists of two bearer channels for customer voice or data at 64Kbps. In addition, it has one 16Kbps signaling channel. It runs over a single pair of twisted wires between the customer and the telephone company.

Deployment of BRI ISDN is higher in Europe and Japan than in the United States, where it never reached more than 1% penetration. It was complex to install, telephone companies charged usage fees for ISDN data calls, and the initial lack of widespread availability greatly hindered acceptance of ISDN, particularly among consumers.

France, Germany, Japan, and Switzerland are widely acknowledged to have a large base of BRI ISDN customers. In Europe, BRI ISDN is sometimes referred to as ISDN 2 because it has two bearer channels. Consumers in these countries use it for voice calls and Internet access. The absence of flat-rate pricing on switched services made per-unit charges for dial-up Internet access more acceptable.

BRI: Bonding on Videoconferencing and Access to Frame Relay

Because prices of BRI lines are low compared to PRI (24-channel) service, many enterprises use BRI for videoconferencing. To achieve adequate speed for acceptable quality, they bond three or four BRI circuits together (see Figure 5.9). *Bonding* is the combination of multiple lines to increase bandwidth. For example, bonding the two bearer channels provides 128 kilobits of speed (2×64). Most organizations bond three or four circuits together for acceptable video quality at 384 kilobits per second (3×128) or 512 kilobits (4×128).

In bonded circuits, the signaling channel sends bits from each bearer channel sequentially on the ISDN circuits (see Figure 5.10). People viewing the video see a continuous stream of images. To initiate the calls, the video equipment dials the telephone numbers at the remote BRI-equipped video system. Telephone companies charge per-minute fees for these video calls. The conference is ended when one party hangs up. Because it is a switched service, organizations aren't limited to having video calls to sites on their private networks.

Another application for BRI ISDN is backup access to frame relay networks in case the dedicated access line to the frame relay network fails. In these applications,

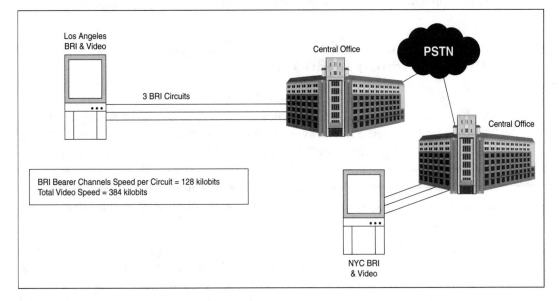

Figure 5.9
Videoconferencing using three bonded BRI ISDN circuits.

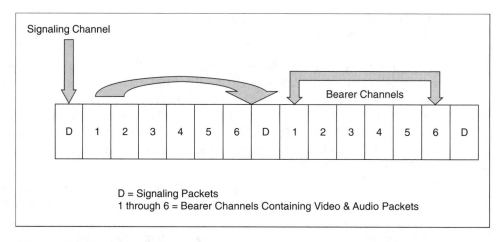

Figure 5.10
A BRI ISDN bonding schematic.

the router usually automatically dials into the frame relay network when it senses that the dedicated access line is down. On data services, BRI equipment is required at both ends of the call. However, BRI-equipped voice services can call anyone on the public switched telephone number. ISDN is not required at each end of voice calls.

Primary Rate Interface ISDN—23 Bearer and 1 Signaling Channel

Primary rate interface (PRI) has 24 64-kilobit channels in the United States and Japan and 30 elsewhere in the world. PRI lines are similar to T-1 because they both have 24 channels. However, PRI ISDN has out-of-band signaling on the twenty-fourth channel. This is different from T-1 circuits, in which signaling is carried in-band, along with voice or data on each channel. On data communications, the signaling channel leaves each of the bearer channels "clear" capacity for all 64,000 bits. PRI does not require any bearer channel capacity for signaling such as call setup or teardown of signals.

PRI is used with PBXs, key systems, and routers for incoming and outgoing voice and data. It is also used by ISPs and CLECs for dial-in modem Internet access. Each PRI supports 23 rack-mounted modems. The signaling channel carries the customer telephone number and the type of modem used. This provides billing and routing information. Moreover, the modems can handle ISDN as well as analog modem traffic.

BRI and PRI ISDN can communicate with each other for data such as videoconferencing and voice. PRI as well as BRI can make and receive voice calls to any device on the public switched telephone network.

PBXs with PRI Trunks

PBXs are used with PRI lines for the following:

- Call centers, to receive the telephone numbers of callers
- Individual telephone users for call screening
- One voice mail system to support multiple PBXs
- Dial-up videoconferencing

Large call centers use PRI ISDN to receive the telephone number of the person calling. With ISDN, the telephone number is sent at the same time as the call. However, it is sent on the *separate D*, or *signaling channel*. This is significant because it enables the telephone system, the PBX, to treat the telephone number information differently than the call. It can send the telephone number to a database that matches the telephone number to the customer account number. The data network sends the account number to the agent's terminal that the call is sent to. It saves agents time by eliminating the need to key in account numbers.

Many corporations use PRI ISDN for incoming voice traffic. The local telephone company sends the caller's name and phone number over the signaling channel. The telephone system captures the information and sends it to the display-equipped telephone. Figure 5.11 illustrates a PRI line for transporting caller ID. Employees who receive heavy volumes of calls from vendors or who only take calls from certain callers use ISDN to screen calls. Unanswered calls are forwarded automatically into voice mail.

PRI ISDN private lines that connect PBXs together enable one voice mail system to be shared between multiple sites. The D channel carries voice mail signals that identify mailbox numbers and instructions to turn message-waiting indicators on or off. It also enables broadcast lists to be made up of users at different sites.

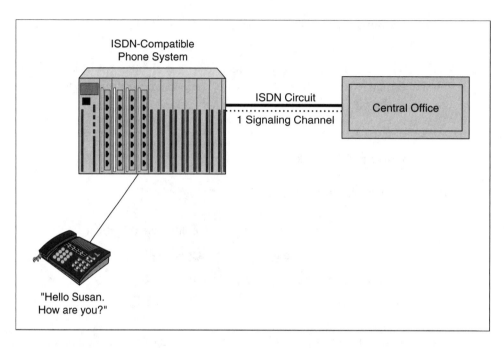

Figure 5.11
PRI ISDN carrying the caller's billed telephone number   automatic number identification (ANI). The ANI is often the same as the customer's telephone number.

Sharing Signaling Channels—Nonfacility Associated Signaling (NFAS)

Companies with multiple PRI trunks can share the twenty-fourth signaling channel among a group of PRI trunks via *nonfacility-associated signaling (NFAS)*. For example, an organization with six PRI trunks might have four of them equipped with 24 channels for voice and data. Two of the six would have 23 channels for user data and one signaling channel each with NFAS to support all six PRI trunks. Having two PRI circuits with signaling provides a backup in case one signaling channel fails. PRI lines don't work without a signaling channel.

NT1s and TAs: Modem-Like Devices for ISDN

ISDN lines need NT1s and terminal adapters to make them compatible with the public network and customer equipment. The network termination type 1 (NT1) provides the electrical and physical connections to the carrier's network. On BRI ISDN services, NT1 devices change the ISDN circuit from two wires that come into the building from the central office to the four wires needed by ISDN equipment. In addition, the NT1 provides a point for line monitoring and maintenance functions.

In the United States, the FCC requires that the customer be responsible for supplying the NT1. In the rest of the world, telephone carriers supply the NT1.

Terminal adapters (TAs) perform the multiplexing and signaling function on ISDN services. Multiplexing enables one line to be used simultaneously for multiple voice or data calls. NTIs and terminal adapters are often built into videoconferencing equipment and routers.

DIGITAL SUBSCRIBER LINE (DSL)— AN INTERIM TECHNOLOGY OR A VEHICLE FOR VIDEO AND IP?................................

Digital subscriber line (DSL) service is used primarily for high-speed Internet access. The most commonly used types of DSL services are listed in Table 5.3. Asymmetric DSL counts for the largest installed base. Asymmetric services have higher download speeds away from the Internet to the customer and slower uploading speeds from the consumer to the Internet. Business customers, for the most part, lease symmetric DSL with equal speeds upstream to the Internet and downstream. Asymmetric DSL shares the same copper cabling already in place for voice. This made it an appealing technology for telephone companies that can, for the most part, use existing cabling to provide broadband access. However, copper cabling is not suitable for carrying video over long distances.

Now, however, newer versions of asymmetric digital subscriber line (ADSL) are available that support television on shorter cabling runs of 5,000 to 8,000 feet. However, DSL works only on copper, not fiber. To create short copper cabling runs, telephone companies extend fiber closer to customers. They convert DSL signals to those compatible with fiber, where fiber connects to the copper cabling carrying DSL signals.

Interest in new DSL standards has been spurred by competition from cable TV, wireless, and Voice over IP (VoIP) providers. Cable TV operators are starting to sell more voice telephony along with Internet access, television, and video on demand. To compensate for lines lost each year since 2001 to competitive services, incumbent telephone companies are putting in place strategies for new infrastructure that will enable them to sell television, voice telephony, and Internet access plus enhanced services.

There is disagreement in the industry about whether DSL is an interim technology and whether fiber should be run to people's homes and businesses. Some telephone companies are planning to bring fiber to every customer location in their territory. They believe that bringing fiber to premises is less expensive in the long run because it is more reliable, less costly to maintain, and supports higher speeds. However, in the short run, the labor involved in digging trenches for fiber and purchasing materials will cost billions of dollars. SBC, BellSouth, and Qwest have announced they will bring fiber closer to customers and use DSL for the last few thousand feet. They will build fiber to premises at new housing developments. Verizon Communications has taken a different tack. They have announced a nationwide initiative to lay fiber to all of their residential and business customers' premises instead of using new ADSL technology to reach customers.

Table 5.3 is an overview of the different flavors of DSL service.

Table 5.3   DSL Speeds and Cable Requirements

Digital Subscriber Line Service	Upstream Data Rate	Downstream Data Rate	Distance from Telephone Company DSL Equipment	Voice	Comments
ADSL (asymmetric DSL)	176Kbps* 640Kbps*	1.54Kbps 9Mbps**	18,000 feet 12,000 feet	Yes	Offered to residential customers. Uses one pair of wires.
ADSL2+	128Kbps* 640Kbps* 800Kbps	192Kbps 4Mbps 15Mbps	18,000 feet 12,000 feet 5,000 feet	Yes	Supports video on demand on short cable runs.
Reach extended ADSL2+	96Kbps 128Kbps 640Kbps 800Kbps	192Kbps 384Kbps 4Mbps 15Mbps	22,000 feet 18,000 feet 12,000 feet 5,000 feet	Yes	Increases reach of ADSL2+.
Bonded ADSL2+	1Mbps** 1.5Mbps	18Mbps 30Mbps	9,000 feet 5,000 feet	Yes	Bonds 2 ADSL2+ lines together to achieve higher speed.

Table 5.3   DSL Speeds and Cable Requirements   (continued)

Digital Subscriber Line Service	Upstream Data Rate	Downstream Data Rate	Distance from Telephone Company DSL Equipment	Voice	Comments
HDSL (high-bit-rate DSL) HDSL2	1.54/ 2.048Mbps	1.54/ 2.048Mbps	12,000 feet	Yes	Carries T-1/E-1. HDSL requires four wires; HDSL2 uses one pair of wires.
SDSL (symmetric DSL)	Up to 2.048Mbps	Up to 2.048Mbps	24,000 feet	No	Requires only one pair of wires. Offered for business customers.
SHDSL	192Kbps 4.62Mbps	192Kbps 4.62Mbps	40,000 feet 6,500 feet	Yes	Single pair of wires; speeds up to 2.3Mb. Two pair; speeds up to 4.62Mbps.
VDSL (very high-bit-rate DSL)	1.5Mbps 2.3Mbps	13Mbps 52Mbps	4,500 feet 1,000 feet	Yes	
VDSL2 (second-generation very high-bit-rate DSL)	1Mbps 3Mbps 20Mbps	14Mbps 30Mbps 100Mbps	6,000 feet 3,000 feet 1,000 feet	Yes	Requires only one pair of wires; specifications not approved.

Kbps = kilobits per second

**Mbps = million bits per second

Table 5.3 courtesy the DSL Forum

Although DSL modems often use the same copper cabling that carries voice, data carried on DSL service is handled separately from voice in carriers' networks. When DSL traffic hits the central office, it is routed on data networks that are separate from the public switched telephone network. Equipment at the central office packetizes DSL traffic and sends it to Internet service providers (ISPs) or other data networks.

The DSL Marketplace

Incumbent telephone companies sell the vast majority of DSL service in the United States. They sell it primarily to residential customers and, to a lesser extent, small businesses. Of the total DSL and cable modem subscribers in the United States, as of September 2004, 19.4 million used cable modems and 12.6 million had DSL-enabled phone lines. The National Cable & Telecommunications Association and the DSL Forum supplied these statistics, respectively. The percentage of cable modems shrank in 2003 and 2004 due to DSL price decreases and increased availability.

In addition, Covad sells mostly wholesale DSL. CLECs AT&T and MCI offer DSL directly to end users, primarily small business customers. Covad reaches a small number of residential customers through Internet service providers such as EarthLink.

Outside of the United States—for example, in Asia Pacific and Europe, particularly in Korea, France, and Germany where cable TV does not have the high penetration rates that it has in North America—DSL is the most common broadband wireline access method. It is also used internationally in conjunction with fiber to deliver television signals. Table 5.4 lists countries with the most lines equipped with DSL modems. The DSL Forum is a worldwide organization that produces specifications for standards and that tests new DSL technologies and equipment.

Table 5.4   *Top 20 Countries: Total DSL Subscribers (Q3 September 2004)*

Ranking	Country	Total DSL Q3 2004	Ranking	Country	Total DSL Q3 2004
1	China	13,700,000	11	Spain	2,227,805
2	Japan	12,739,564	12	Brazil	1,633,700
3	USA	12,594,346	13	Netherlands	1,552,000
4	South Korea	6,717,251	14	Belgium	938,000
5	Germany	5,950,000	15	Australia	910,000

Table 5.4 Top 20 Countries: Total DSL Subscribers
(Q3 September 2004) (continued)

Ranking	Country	Total DSL Q3 2004	Ranking	Country	Total DSL Q3 2004
6	France	5,253,000	16	Hong Kong	774,000
7	Italy	3,680,000	17	Sweden	751,000
8	UK	3,335,000	18	Switzerland	717,000
9	Taiwan	2,900,000	19	Israel	600,000
10	Canada	2,568,351	20	Denmark	594,000

Table 5.4 courtesy of the DSL Forum and Point Topic

Business Class DSL—Static IP Addresses

RBOCs sell higher-speed DSL service to the small and medium-size business and small office home office (SOHO) market segments. These offerings support static IP service. Static IP enables customers with their own domain name to have their Web site hosted by the Internet service provider connected to their DSL service. It also allows them to use their domain name as part of their e-mail address. Dynamic IP service does not support this because IP addresses are assigned at random rather than to the same device consistently.

Until recently, telephone companies sold symmetric DSL to business customers because it was assumed that businesses sent and received large files via the Internet. Symmetric DSL offers the same speeds upstream as well as downstream toward the customer. Most telephone companies now offer asymmetric DSL service to business and residential customers who are within reach of telephone DSL service. These offerings have 3 megabit per second downstream and 384,000 bit per second upstream speeds. They operate with standard ADSL gear. However, customers need to be closer to central offices to be able to reach 3 megabits. BellSouth estimates that over 90% of its customers are eligible for the 3 megabit per second service.

DSLAMs—Digital Subscriber Line Access Multiplexers

Digital subscriber line access multiplexers (DSLAMs) aggregate traffic from multiple DSL modems and combine it into higher speeds before sending it to the Internet or data networks. DSLAMs are located in carriers' central offices or digital loop carriers, also referred to as remote terminals, in neighborhoods (see Chapter 4, "VoIP, the Public Switched Telephone Network, and Signaling") and in the wiring closets of large apartment and office buildings (see Figure 5.12). DSLAMs combine DSL traffic into higher-speed streams. These are, for the most part, ATM speeds of optical carrier level 3 (OC-3), 155 million bits per second, but some DSLAMs use slower DS-3 44-megabits-per-second connections.

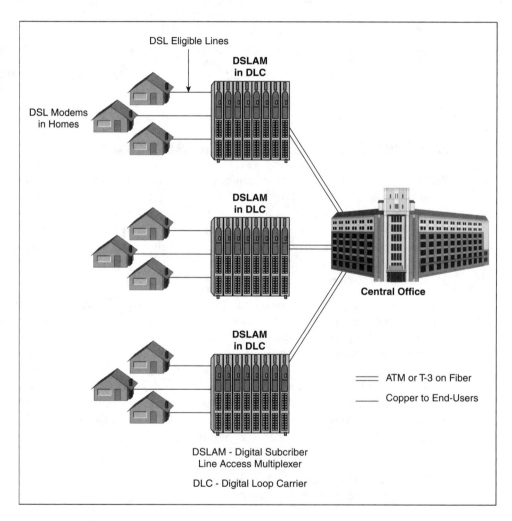

Figure 5.12
DSLAMs located in digital loop carriers (remote terminals).

Table 5.4   Top 20 Countries: Total DSL Subscribers
(Q3 September 2004) (continued)

Ranking	Country	Total DSL Q3 2004	Ranking	Country	Total DSL Q3 2004
6	France	5,253,000	16	Hong Kong	774,000
7	Italy	3,680,000	17	Sweden	751,000
8	UK	3,335,000	18	Switzerland	717,000
9	Taiwan	2,900,000	19	Israel	600,000
10	Canada	2,568,351	20	Denmark	594,000

Table 5.4 courtesy of the DSL Forum and Point Topic

Business Class DSL—Static IP Addresses

RBOCs sell higher-speed DSL service to the small and medium-size business and small office home office (SOHO) market segments. These offerings support static IP service. Static IP enables customers with their own domain name to have their Web site hosted by the Internet service provider connected to their DSL service. It also allows them to use their domain name as part of their e-mail address. Dynamic IP service does not support this because IP addresses are assigned at random rather than to the same device consistently.

Until recently, telephone companies sold symmetric DSL to business customers because it was assumed that businesses sent and received large files via the Internet. Symmetric DSL offers the same speeds upstream as well as downstream toward the customer. Most telephone companies now offer asymmetric DSL service to business and residential customers who are within reach of telephone DSL service. These offerings have 3 megabit per second downstream and 384,000 bit per second upstream speeds. They operate with standard ADSL gear. However, customers need to be closer to central offices to be able to reach 3 megabits. BellSouth estimates that over 90% of its customers are eligible for the 3 megabit per second service.

DSLAMs—Digital Subscriber Line Access Multiplexers

Digital subscriber line access multiplexers (DSLAMs) aggregate traffic from multiple DSL modems and combine it into higher speeds before sending it to the Internet or data networks. DSLAMs are located in carriers' central offices or digital loop carriers, also referred to as remote terminals, in neighborhoods (see Chapter 4, "VoIP, the Public Switched Telephone Network, and Signaling") and in the wiring closets of large apartment and office buildings (see Figure 5.12). DSLAMs combine DSL traffic into higher-speed streams. These are, for the most part, ATM speeds of optical carrier level 3 (OC-3), 155 million bits per second, but some DSLAMs use slower DS-3 44-megabits-per-second connections.

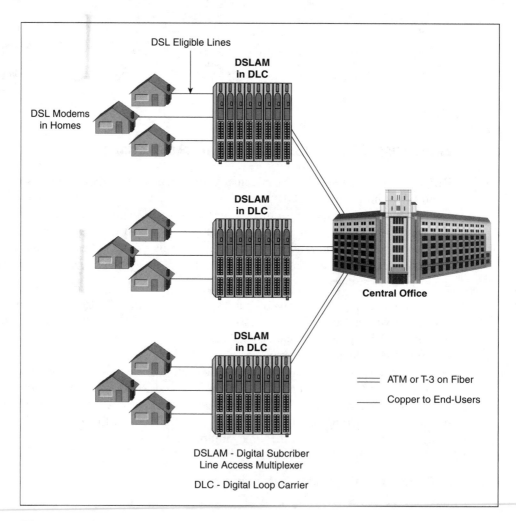

Figure 5.12
DSLAMs located in digital loop carriers (remote terminals).

Customers have dedicated capacity between their DSL modem and the digital subscriber line access multiplexer (DSLAM) that they don't share with other customers. However, capacity between the DSLAM and the Internet or the ISP is shared by data from other customers. The connection between the DSLAM and an Internet service provider is a potential site for network congestion (see Figure 5.13). If not enough capacity is available, a customer might experience delays. DSLAMs are manufactured by Adtran, Alcatel, Catena, Lucent, Paradyne, and Westell.

MiniRAM—Mini Remote Access Multiplexer

A new, lower-cost, smaller DSLAM is being deployed to provide DSL over short copper telephone lines. These mini remote access multiplexers (MiniRAMs) are about the size of two pizza boxes stacked on top of each other. They can be located on telephone poles or in standalone boxes on the ground and serve 10 to 24 customers (see Figure 5.14). Power is fed to MiniRAMs through copper telephone lines on the pole or underground.

Because they are closer to customers, they avoid most of the impairments found on copper lines further from central offices. These impairments are caused by crosstalk, loading coils that boost signals, and bridge taps used to share copper lines among customers. The dilemma is that the closer the fiber and MiniRAMs are to customers, the higher the overall costs. As they get closer to customers, MiniRAMs serve

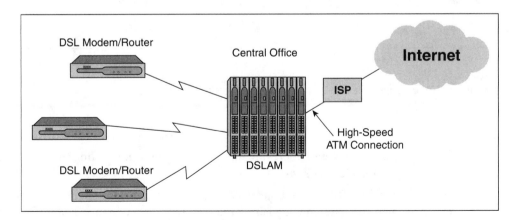

Figure 5.13
DSLAM connections to an Internet service provider.

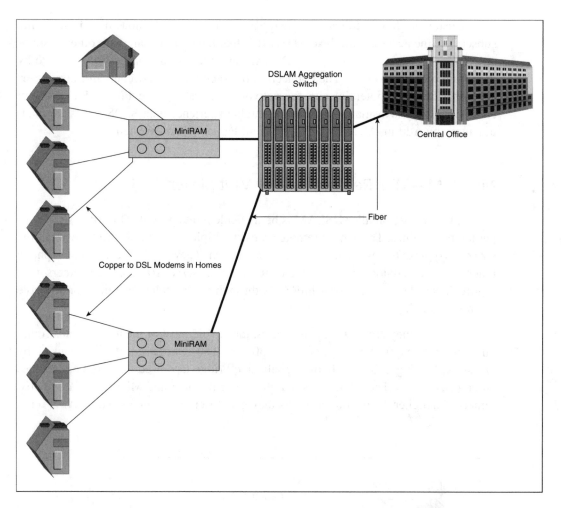

Figure 5.14
Neighborhood mini remote access multiplexers (MiniRAMs).

fewer customers. Overall there are more fiber runs, more MiniRAMs, and more equipment to maintain and install.

Smaller MiniRAMs are connected to central office–based aggregation switches that packetize the data and send it to Internet service providers. Traffic from larger miniRAMs is aggregated in DSLAMs. In the future, switches in the DSLAM will provide more of the aggregation functions.

Edge Architecture to Support Video— Broadband Remote Access Server (BRAS)

Network infrastructure, as well as customer equipment, needs to be upgraded to carry digital television. For example, currently, switches in the central office aggregate (combine) traffic from multiple DSLAMs and from cross connects (connection points) in building and apartment basements. Multistory apartments and businesses using DSL often have fiber from the outside to these cross connects in the basement and DSL over copper inside the building to multiple tenants.

In the future, these aggregation switches will be located in *broadband remote access servers (BRAS)* instead of at central offices. The BRAS, also referred to as *broadband loop carriers*, will provide higher speeds, more suitable to data, than current DSLAMs. Further, they will be the point from which carriers remotely program privileges for customers, depending on the service the customer selects. Security functions such as authentication ("you are who you say you are") will be done at the broadband remote access server.

The BRAS will be connected to multiple DSLAMs and mini remote access multiplexers. In addition to the preceding, speeds from the DSLAM and broadband remote access server will be increased from ATM to Gigabit Ethernet. (See subsequent sections for ATM and Gigabit Ethernet.)

Television Providers—Multicasting to DSL Customers

Multicasting refers to broadcasting from a single source to a group of devices. Incumbent telephone companies will have arrangements with multiple video broadcasters and gaming companies. These content providers will send content over incumbents' MPLS-enabled backbones to addresses of specific groups in broadband remote access multiplexers. The BRAS will send the streams to individual subscribers.

The Vital Role of Advanced Compression

Advanced compression algorithms, such as MPEG-4 and Windows Media 9 developed by Microsoft, dramatically shrink the size of digital television and other multimedia files. Chips with advanced compression are required in set-top boxes and DSL equipment for carriers to supply high-definition television. Older compression used with ADSL2+ or VDSL2 over short loops can handle standard definition television. Standard definition television has higher quality than analog but lower quality than high definition TV.

Turbo Buttons—Sustaining High Speeds and Supporting VoIP

The turbo button is a feature that incumbent telephone companies hope to use to generate revenue and to become a platform for VoIP from other carriers as well as for other services such as games and movies. A *turbo button* appearing on a Web page lets users or providers that select it upgrade their broadband service. It will essentially provide bandwidth on demand.

For example, a provider could use the turbo button feature to select a higher quality of service. The provider would pay the telephone company expedited forwarding for customer xyz. This would ensure higher-quality voice for customers who select higher priced, faster DSL. This would eliminate the congestion possibility if multiple household members simultaneously chat, play interactive games, and make voice calls. It would make VoIP more suitable for second lines and home businesses.

Turbo buttons could also be used by service providers to activate the speeds capable of carrying sustained capacity for movies from, for example, CinemaNow or, in the future, Netflix.

Television over DSL Service— ADSL2+ and VDSL2

ADSL2+ and its variations, ADSL2+ extended reach and ADSL2+ with bonding, are new standards developed for the delivery of digital television over short cable lengths of under 5,000 feet. Bonding uses two pairs instead of one pair of wires to increase speeds even more. However, because they operate on short cable runs only, telephone companies need to place the DSLAM closer to customers. They do this by running fiber into neighborhoods and either placing DSLAM in the equipment cabinet with the fiber or aggregating many small DSLAMs at the fiber node.

In addition to increasing speeds over short distances, ADSL2+ increases the capability of DSL to reach ADSL speeds over longer cable lengths that have disturbances such as loading coils on them. Loading coils boost signals on copper telephone wires that are far from the central office. ADSL2+ is backward compatible with consumers' ADSL modems. For example, carriers can use ADSL2+ cards in their DSLAMs that will interoperate with older ADSL modems. However, higher speeds and other advantages won't be achieved.

VDSL2 is a proposed standard that increases the reach of VDSL. It provides even higher speeds than ADSL2+ but at shorter distances. Unlike ADSL2+ with bonding, it has the advantage of requiring only one pair of wires. Currently, VDSL is used in Asian countries such as South Korea in conjunction with fiber to apartment buildings. The video is distributed to individual apartments over copper from the fiber equipment in the basement-wiring closet.

Telephone companies that provide television service over cabling infrastructure have to receive franchising permission in each city or town in which they wish to offer television.

DSL—No Truck Roll; Self Service

DSL providers do not dispatch a technician to install DSL in homes. Rather, they mail a DSL modem, filters, and software to customers who call the provider's toll-free number if they need technical assistance. Filters are plugged into each telephone jack. Filters screen out data signals above the 4-kilohertz (KHz) range so that interference is eliminated. Not requiring a truck roll dramatically lowers the cost of provisioning DSL service. This is referred to as *self-provisioning*.

Having an older alarm panel or more than five or six telephones may require a splitter at the entry point of telephone lines into the home. The splitter, which is the size of two cigarette packs, separates the low-frequency voice signals from the high-frequency data signals. Splitters and filters are also located at the telephone company equipment.

T-1/E-1 over DSL—HDSL

Most DS-1 (T-1) service that is provisioned on copper uses HDSL and the newer HDSL2 standards. HDSL is a lower-cost way for carriers to provision DS-1 because fewer repeaters that boost signals are required. Customers are not aware of having HDSL because the equipment is located at the central office and matching equipment is located at the demarcation, usually in the building's wiring closet.

GIGABIT ETHERNET ....

Gigabit Ethernet (also referred to as GigE) is a site-to-site and Internet access service that was first introduced in the late 1990s. When used by enterprises, Gigabit Ethernet is intended to increase network access speeds so that they more closely match speeds in local area networks. Gigabit Ethernet operates mainly over fiber-optic cabling. A key advantage is that it uses the same protocol used in LANs, making it less complex to connect to customers' networks and simpler to upgrade to higher speeds.

Gigabit Ethernet is used in enterprises' internal networks, carriers' metropolitan area networks (MANs), and by enterprises to access the Internet or connect to other sites. As an Internet access service for enterprises, Gigabit Ethernet is generally offered at speeds ranging from 10 megabits to 1000 megabits (1 gigabit) per second. Enterprises also use it for point-to-point communications between local area networks in metropolitan areas and for access to national virtual private networks for site-to-site communications. See Figure 5.15 for Ethernet site-to-site service in the metropolitan area. Customers use either a router with an Ethernet port or an Ethernet switch to connect to carriers' Ethernet offerings. Cisco Systems, Extreme Networks, Foundry

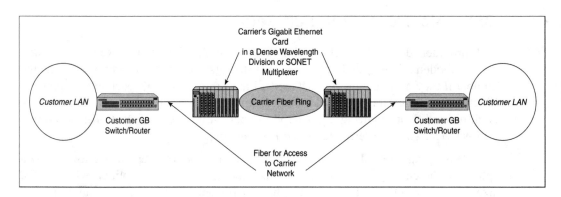

Figure 5.15
Gigabit Ethernet service over fiber-optic cabling and metropolitan fiber rings.

Networks, and Nortel Networks manufacture Gigabit Ethernet switches. Gigabit Ethernet does not require a CSU/DSU (used for T-1 type service), a T-1 multiplexer, or frame relay access device (FRAD).

Ethernet Sales Channels

Regional Bell Operating Companies, MCI, Cogent, OnFiber, Time Warner Telecom, and Yipes are the leading Ethernet providers. Many providers that originally offered Gigabit Ethernet service failed to survive, in large part because they underestimated the cost of running fiber from metropolitan fiber rings to end-user customers. In addition, they were not able to attract sufficient numbers of enterprise and carrier customers. Most Ethernet providers sold capacity on their fiber networks to competitive local exchange carriers (CLECs) as well as enterprises and data center operators. When CLECs went out of business or shrank in size, Ethernet providers lost a share of their customer base.

Challenges to Wider Deployment

A major challenge for Gigabit Ethernet is extending fiber from existing metropolitan fiber rings to enterprises. The process of digging trenches and laying fiber from fiber rings to customers is referred to as building *laterals*. Availability of fiber would enable Fortune 1000 companies with multiple sites to use Gigabit Ethernet from one network provider for service to all of their sites.

Ethernet can also operate over copper and wireless media. However, finding sites eligible for wireless access that are within line of sight of the fiber ring is not always feasible. The Institute of Electrical and Electronic Engineers (IEEE) approved a standard for 10-megabit-per-second Ethernet over copper in June 2004. This requires dry copper cabling, cabling from the central office to customers that is used for no other services. However, for other than RBOCs, dry copper cabling is not always available or easily rented.

In newly developed countries in Africa and Asia, fiber is more prevalent because costs to lay new fiber compare favorably to costs to lay copper. This is because prices for copper have increased, fiber costs have decreased, and labor and installation are the major costs for new cabling. In these countries and in dense cities, Ethernet and Gigabit Ethernet are used on new fiber to homes and businesses. Ethernet is often used in conjunction with passive optical networks (PONs), which are discussed in Chapter 6, "Entertainment, Cable TV, and Last-Mile Fiber Systems." PONs are a lower-cost method of extending fiber to premises and neighborhoods.

Multiplexers Equipped with Reconfigurable Optical Add and Drop Multiplexers (ROADMs)

Ethernet is transported over bidirectional fiber rings located between carriers' central offices or points of presence (POPs) and customers. For the most part, these rings are based on SONET technology. However, SONET was not designed for Ethernet service. Ethernet on SONET wastes capacity because of high overhead (nonuser data for addressing, signaling, and maintenance) and mismatches in frame sizes between SONET and Ethernet. In addition to using bandwidth inefficiently, it is more complex to separate out Ethernet traffic for individual customers on SONET than on newer dense wavelength division multiplexers.

As they carry more IP and Ethernet traffic, some telephone companies are testing dense wavelength division multiplexers (DWDM) equipped with *reconfigurable optical add and drop multiplexers (ROADMs)* cards. DWDM equipment combines up to 768 channels (called wavelengths or colors) of traffic onto a single pair of fiber cabling. Reconfigurable optical add and drop multiplexers enable carriers to more easily add, separate out, and drop off traffic carried on optical rings to and from customers.

ROADM-equipped multiplexers will carry central office–to–central office traffic in addition to Ethernet and IP-based customer traffic. It will encapsulate individual customers' Ethernet traffic on single wavelengths (colors) derived from dense wavelength division multiplexers. Many carriers currently plan to use ROADM equipment on shorter fiber rings with high amounts of IP, Ethernet, and storage area network protocols such as fibre channel traffic. The cost per bit for carrying this type of traffic is lower on DWDM than on SONET.

These DWDM devices will be built as carrier class, fully redundant configurations. Each fiber ring, multiplexer, and power supply will be duplicated. The multiplexers will sense failures and fiber cuts and automatically use the backup ring and multiplexer. This is referred to as automatic failover or *resilient packet ring*. Resilient packet ring (RPR) is an Institute of Electrical and Electronics Engineers (IEEE) standard that is used in SONET and Gigabit Ethernet rings. Luminous Networks and Cisco offer Gigabit Ethernet–based resilient ring products.

SONET will continue to be used on fiber rings that carry less traffic and that aggregate streams of slower speed voice and T-1/E-1 data. Newer providers, such as OnFiber Communications, already carry metropolitan Ethernet traffic on dense wavelength division multiplexers.

Some telephone companies are upgrading SONET to make it more suitable for data rather than planning to transition to DWDM with add and drop multiplexers. See the following sections for next generation and third generation SONET.

SALE OF INDIVIDUAL WAVELENGTHS—IN METROPOLITAN AREAS

As technologies mature and manufacturing costs decrease, technologies initially used only by carriers become cost effective for enterprises. The sale of individual wavelengths is an example. Providers now offer individual wavelengths of fiber-optic capacity to customers at speeds of, for example, 1.5, 2.5, and 10 gigabits per second. One application for wavelengths is disaster recovery for between two to five sites. If one site fails, the other sites will still be in service for functions such as call centers and financial transactions. Enterprises also use individual wavelengths for connections to data centers and storage area networks in the same metropolitan area (see Figure 5.16).

Because access to long distance networks often represents up to 40% of customers' long distance costs, providers with fiber to large enterprises now offer individual wavelengths from enterprises to their long distance provider. The enterprise leases the fiber and is able to send Ethernet or optical carrier (OC) type traffic to its long distance provider. See Table 5.6 for optical carrier speeds. If fiber is available, this is often a less-costly option than purchasing access from incumbent telephone companies.

In addition, Regional Bell Operating Companies and other providers use wavelengths between their metropolitan fiber ring and the customer to provide Ethernet service. Because of distance limitations in the hundreds of kilofeet, wavelength service is a   metropolitan area service.

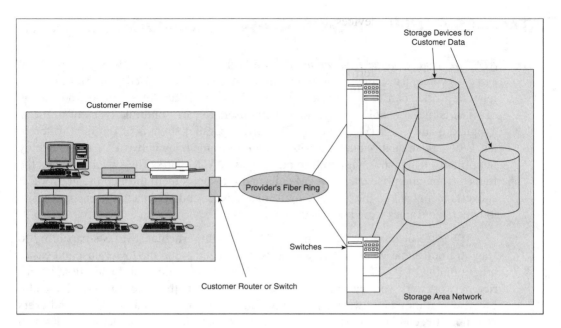

Figure 5.16
Wavelengths between a storage area network and the enterprise in the same metropolitan area.

Ethernet Enterprise Service—Internet, VPN Access, and Private Lines

Internet access is the most widely used Gigabit Ethernet application. In addition, it is offered for point-to-point private lines within the metropolitan area. Large hospitals, universities, and government offices use Gigabit Ethernet. Examples include connectivity between health centers and locations where patient records and imaging files are stored. It is also used for connections to storage area networks that hold organizations' backup files.

Ethernet is also used to access virtual private networks (VPNs). For example, customers might access national MPLS virtual private networks using Ethernet or Gigabit Ethernet speeds, depending on the level of traffic at each of their sites. At remote or smaller sites without fiber connectivity, another service, perhaps T-1 or fractional T-1, might be used.

ATM—ASYNCHRONOUS TRANSFER MODE ....

ATM, or asynchronous transfer mode, is a high-speed switching service capable of carrying voice, data, video, and multimedia images. ATM is used primarily in frame relay networks, carrier networks, and enterprises for private lines. The key advantage of ATM is that it enables providers and end users to carry multiple types of traffic at assigned quality-of-service levels. ATM carries parallel streams of traffic at different levels of service quality over the same circuit. In frame relay networks, carriers deploy multiplatform switches with both frame relay and ATM ports. The switch converts the frames from enterprise sites to ATM cells and transports them through the network. It converts them back to the frame relay format before sending data to the enterprise site to which the frames were addressed.

Because of improvements in IP protocols—in particular, MPLS's capability to "tag" traffic so that voice and video can be prioritized—and the lower cost and easier programming of IP, ATM is becoming displaced by IP equipment. In addition, in carrier networks, IP services achieve higher speeds. On the enterprise side, Gigabit Ethernet and individual wavelengths offer lower-cost options than ATM for end users who need to send large files between sites. However, Gigabit Ethernet and individual wavelength services are still not universally available, and wavelength service has distance limitations.

ATM is expensive and complex for carriers to install and program. As older equipment is depreciated, carriers will transition to IP with MPLS for voice, data, and video traffic.

ATM's Speed Is Due to Three Characteristics

When ATM was developed in the early 1990s, its speed provided a key advantage over T-1 and T-3 services, which are based on time division multiplexing. It was also faster than routers available at that time. ATM's speed is due to its fixed-size cells, switching in hardware, and asynchronous technology, which does not depend on timing. Rather, cells are forwarded based on priority and arrival time.

Fixed-Sized Cells—Less Processing

Asynchronous transfer mode (ATM) packages data into discrete groups called cells. This is analogous to putting the same number of letters into each envelope. Handling fixed-sized cells requires less processing than older routers with variable-sized packets. The ATM switch does not have to look for bits telling it when the cell is over. Each cell is 53 bytes long.

Five of the 53 bytes contain header information. This includes bits that identify the type of information contained in the cell (for example, voice, data, or video) so that the cell can be prioritized. The remaining 48 bytes are the "payload"—user data such as voice, video, or sales proposals.

Switching in Hardware—Less Address Lookup

ATM cells are switched in hardware. This means that an ATM switch does not have to look up each cell's address in software. Rather, an ATM switch sets up a route through the network when it sees the first cell of a transmission. It puts this information into its hardware and sends each cell with the same header routing information down the virtual path previously established. For example, all cells with XXX in the header use route 234. Using the same path for each cell makes ATM a connection-oriented service.

Asynchronous Switching— Improving Network Utilization

With asynchronous switching, every bit of the network capacity is available for every cell. This is different than synchronous multiplexing technologies such as T-1/E1 and T-3/E3. With T-3 multiplexing, every one of the 672 input transmissions is assigned a time slot. If device A has nothing to send, its slot is sent through the network empty. ATM has no synchronous requirements. It statistically multiplexes cells onto the network path based on quality-of-service information in the header. With ATM, network capacity is not wasted forwarding empty cells.

DSLAMs and ATM—Oversubscription

Because not every device connected to a public network sends data all of the time, frame relay and DSL carriers that use ATM have the capability to sell aggregate capacity that is higher than the total available capacity. This is called the capability to *oversubscribe*. For example, DSLAMs that use ATM connections to send DSL data to Internet service providers have a top speed that is lower than the sum of the DSL modems connected to them (refer to Figure 5.13 earlier in this chapter).

Mapping IP and Ethernet Traffic onto ATM

Carriers that haven't upgraded all of their networks to MPLS use their ATM switches to carry IP traffic. The ATM switches read IP routing information in MPLS packets.

The ATM switch puts IP packets into cells and reassembles the cells back into packets at the end of the transmission. This is referred to as *mapping IP onto ATM*. It is also referred to as *interworking*.

ATM is also used to carry Gigabit Ethernet traffic. This is referred to as Ethernet over ATM (EoATM).

Elements of an ATM Network

The ITU has defined the elements of an ATM network. The elements are as follows:

- User network interface
- Quality of service
- Connections between customer locations

These elements are important because they create a common way to prioritize traffic, send traffic between sites, and create connections to ATM networks.

User Network Interface (UNI)—The Physical Connection to the ATM Network

The UNI, or user network interface, is the dedicated digital telephone line connection between the customer and the ATM equipment. The dedicated connection to ATM can be implemented at various speeds, including T-1/T-3, fractional T-3, OC-1 (52 megabits per second), OC-3 (155 megabits per second), and OC12 (622 megabits per second) and higher.

Quality-of-Service Categories— For Different Applications

Quality-of-service (QoS) parameters include availability, information transfer accuracy, priority, and delay. Customers and carriers have the option of deciding which traffic should be given priority and paying for the priority service. If customers want fewer delays on video and voice communications, they select constant bit-rate quality of service. Level-of-service information is communicated to the network in the ATM cell's 5-byte header.

Table 5.5 lists ATM's quality-of-service categories. Constant bit-rate and real-time variable bit-rate services are the highest level, most expensive categories, and unspecified is the lowest, least costly category.

Table 5.5   ATM Quality-of-Service Categories and Descriptions

QoS Category	Description	Typical Applications
Constant bit-rate	Provides the highest priority and lowest delay through a network	Videoconferencing, voice, television, and video on demand
Real-time variable bit-rate	Applications that can tolerate small variations in speed and small losses of cells	Compressed voice and some types of interactive video
Non-real-time variable bit-rate	For bursty, not-constant-in-nature traffic; delay and speed variations can be tolerated	LAN-to-LAN communications, Internet traffic
Available bit-rate	Applications that can tolerate variations in speed and delay	Frame relay traffic
Unspecified bit-rate	For non-time-sensitive applications that take advantage of unused bandwidth	File transfer, e-mail, and message and image retrieval

ATM Permanent Virtual Connections (PVCs)—Multiple Parallel Streams

ATM supports multiple parallel communications. For example, a videoconference can be transmitted on the same line carrying large file transfers. Thus, even though there is only one physical connection, multiple communications are taking place in parallel. This is a major strength of ATM. Predefined paths between network locations are called permanent virtual connections (PVCs). These are the PVCs used in frame relay networks previously described.

Each virtual channel can be assigned a different quality of service. Figure 5.17 illustrates the way ATM is used to carry communications at multiple qualities of service.

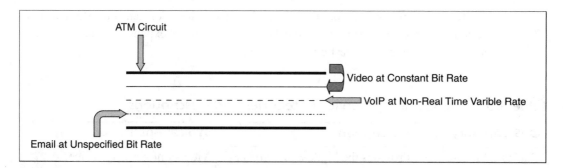

Figure 5.17
Parallel streams in an ATM circuit.

SONET—SYNCHRONOUS OPTICAL NETWORK........

Synchronous optical network (SONET), first introduced in 1994, is a North American standard for multiplexing slower streams of traffic onto fiber-optic cabling and transporting it at optical carrier (OC) speeds. The international standard for the same functions is synchronous digital hierarchy (SDH). SONET/SDH was a major innovation in enabling carriers to carry enormous amounts of voice and data traffic reliably on fiber networks. As SONET equipment prices dropped, large enterprises adopted it as well.

SONET equipment transports high-speed traffic on fiber-optic networks between the following:

- Central offices in metropolitan areas (the *metropolitan core*)
- Remote terminals (digital loop carriers) in metropolitan networks (metropolitan access networks) and central offices
- Long-haul backbone networks and metropolitan areas
- Points of presence (POPs) in long-haul, core networks
- Enterprises and data centers where backup data is stored
- Enterprises and points of presence (POPs) that carry their long distance traffic
- Enterprises to separate central offices for redundancy in case of a central office failure or a fiber cut

SONET also can carry ATM and IP traffic and television signals.

However, as increasing amounts of traffic is data rather than voice and more of the data and a growing percentage of the traffic is IP based, lower-priced gear is becoming available to transport IP traffic more efficiently and at lower costs on redundant fiber rings. These rings found in MPLS networks and some metro-area networks are based on dense wavelength division multiplexing.

BUSINESS CONTINUITY AND STORAGE AREA NETWORKS

As more business processes are computerized, enterprises are storing exact copies of all of their data at remote data centers and storage area networks (SANs). A *storage area network* is a network designed for backup and disk mirroring of large databases. These networks include those used for vital functions such as inventory, accounts receivable, order entry, and accounts payable. *Disk mirroring* is the process of simultaneously writing data to backup and primary servers. Storage area networks provide data restoral in the event of disasters or computer failures. They are located at the same site as the primary servers or at other locations in the metropolitan area or across the country.

A *data center* is a centralized location for corporate data with special environmental controls such as air conditioning, fire alarms, and duplicate power sources. It also has special security provisions regarding who is allowed to enter the center. Data centers can support multiple enterprise sites. Some organizations hire outside organizations to manage their data center either at their site or at a remote site.

Enormous speed is required to transport the massive amounts of data between corporate sites and storage area networks and/or data centers. In some cases, data centers act as backups to each other. *Fibre channel,* also spelled *fiber channel,* is a standard for high-speed connections at between 133 megabits per second and 4 gigabits per second between servers and storage devices. Fibre channel is used as a local physical channel *within* the data center. Because there are many devices in a storage area network, SANs use either hubs or switches to distribute data to devices. Hubs provide a common path between devices, and switches establish dedicated paths. Fibre channel data is transmitted directly to devices' input/output interfaces. Fibre channel operates over most network protocols.

Because of the speed and reliability requirements, organizations typically use Ethernet VPNs, SONET, or leased fiber with an individual wavelength. Individual wavelengths have distance limitations of hundreds of kilometers but are less costly than SONET. Wavelengths are sent to data centers, customers, or storage area networks at speeds of 1.5 gigabits, 2.5 gigabits, or 10 gigabits per second over one pair of fiber.

BUSINESS CONTINUITY AND STORAGE AREA NETWORKS (CONTINUED)

Companies such as eVault and Connected use proprietary compression so that companies can back up select data to data centers using available Internet connections during off-hours when more of the capacity is available on links to the Internet.

Optical Carrier (OC): North American; Synchronous Transport Mode (STM): International

SONET was developed to aggregate (multiplex) and carry circuit switched traffic such as T-1, E-1, T-3, and E-3 as well as slower rates from multiple sources on fiber-optic networks. SONET transports traffic at high speeds called OC (optical carrier). The international version of SONET is synchronous digital hierarchy (SDH). SDH carries traffic at synchronous transport mode (STM) rates. See Table 5.6 for optical carrier and synchronous transport mode speeds. Interfaces in the equipment make SONET and SDH speeds compatible with each other. The same SONET equipment can be used for both OC and SDH speeds.

Europe's time division hierarchy is based on E1 (2-megabit) and E3 (34-megabit) signals. E1 circuits carry 30 channels at 64 kilobits per channel. E3 circuits carry 512 channels at 64 kilobits per channel. Traffic that is carried between cities in Europe or in undersea cables is often referred to as being carried at STM-1 or STM-16 rates.

Table 5.6   SONET/SDH Capacity

Speed	North American Synchronous Transport Signals (STS) Levels	SONET Channels	European Synchronous Transfer Mode (STM) Levels	Synchronous Digital Hierarchy (SDH) Channels
52 megabits	OC-1	28 DS-1s or 1 DS3	STM-0	21 E1s
155 megabits	OC-3	84 DS1s or 3 DS3s	STM-1	63 E1s or 1 E4
622 megabits	OC-12	336 DS1s or 12 DS3s	STM-4	252 E1s or 4 E4s

Table 5.6   SONET/SDH Capacity   (continued)

Speed	North American Synchronous Transport Signals (STS) Levels	SONET Channels	European Synchronous Transfer Mode (STM) Levels	Synchronous Digital Hierarchy (SDH) Channels
2,488 megabits	OC-48	1,344 DS1s or 48 DS3s	STM-16	1,008 E1s or 16 E4s
9,953 megabits	OC-192	5,376 DS1s or 192 DS3s	STM-64	4,032 E1s or 64 E4s
39.812 gigabits	OC-768	21,504 DS1s or 768 DS3s	STM-256	16,128 E1s or 256 E4s

SONET Rings—For Greater Reliability

SONET can run as a straight point-to-point line between sites, or in a ring topology. When fiber in a point-to-point arrangement is cut, service is lost. However, the higher speeds attainable on fiber make reliability critical. When a medium such as copper carries a conversation from one telephone subscriber, a copper cut only impacts one customer. Fiber cuts in networks can put hundreds of businesses, police stations, or hospitals out of service. For this reason, the majority of telephone companies deploy bidirectional ring topology.

In the bidirectional SONET/SDH ring, one set of fiber strands is used for sending and receiving; the other is the protect ring (spare ring). If one set of fiber strands is broken, the spare (protect) ring reroutes traffic in the other direction. Figure 5.18 illustrates this concept. In addition, if one multiplexer on one set of fibers fails, the backup multiplexer on the fiber running in the other direction automatically takes over.

Second Generation—Next Generation SONET

Second generation SONET, also referred to as multiservice platforms, achieved higher speeds (up to OC-192, 10 gigabits), took up less space by supporting more ports on each card, and gave carriers the capability to increase and decrease speeds remotely without taking the ring out of service. They also enabled carriers to drop off lower optical carrier streams to customers for enterprise SONET service previously

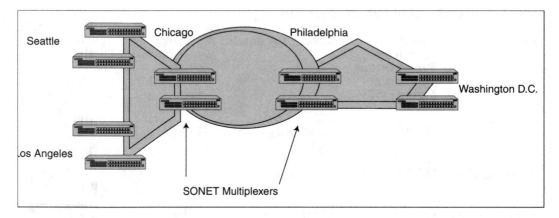

Figure 5.18
SONET bidirectional duplicate rings in a carrier's backbone network.

described. However, next-generation multiplexers do not interface directly to MPLS networks. In addition, although they carry Ethernet and storage area network services, they do so inefficiently, in SONET frames.

Next-generation SONET devices can have internal add and drop multiplexers and digital cross-connect systems.

Add and Drop Multiplexers (ADM)

Add and drop multiplexers add and drop channels from fiber rings at the edge of the network. They drop off and pick up channels to a particular central office or to a small metropolitan area from rings that connect the core to the access network. Add and drop multiplexers are less complex and handle fewer streams of traffic than digital cross connects.

Digital Cross Connects

Digital cross connects rearrange channels of traffic between multiple routes. A digital cross connect system has the same functionality as a switch. For example, multiple rings may connect at a carrier's point of presence (POP) in the core network in the northeast. The digital cross connect sends some of the traffic to, for example, New

York, some to Pennsylvania, and the rest to New Jersey. It also accepts traffic from these states and connects it to other routes.

The newest digital cross connects are all-optical. They switch colors (channels) of traffic without converting light signals carried on fiber to electrical signals and electrical signals back to light. This eliminates the need for conversion equipment in these devices, which leads to lower prices and higher-speed switching.

SONET with Dense Wavelength Division Multiplexing Capability

Manufacturers are combining SONET and wave division multiplexing functions in one piece of equipment. For example, the wave division multiplexer function can be built into a shelf of a SONET device. A wavelength division multiplexer (see Chapter 2, "VoIP Systems, Circuit Switched PBXs, and Cabling") takes SONET streams and sends them out on many different colors of light so that one fiber pair can handle up to 768 times the capacity of a SONET multiplexer. The sending SONET multiplexer couples (connects) light streams to the wave division multiplexing card. At the receiving end of the fiber, the light is demultiplexed into a single color stream by wave division equipment and is sent to the SONET equipment.

Third Generation SONET— Connectivity to Ethernet

Transporting IP voice and Ethernet traffic on SONET-equipped links wastes capacity on carriers' networks. This is because SONET carries traffic in "chunks" at 64 kilobits per second in fixed-size frames called cells. However, IP and Ethernet traffic bits are in variable-size packets. In addition, SONET cells have high overhead (nonuser data such as monitoring and addressing), which adds to its inefficiency because less customer traffic is carried in each cell. This mismatch between frame size results in carriers stuffing zeros into many SONET frames.

Some manufacturers have developed SONET equipment that handles packet traffic more efficiently. For example, newer multiplexers have Gigabit Ethernet ports and ports that can interface directly with telecommunications services used in storage area networks. These SONET multiplexers have the capability to pick up and drop off Ethernet and IP traffic more efficiently at Ethernet speeds. However, they transport traffic to older SONET devices in SONET frames, which wastes capacity.

CONCATENATION

Concatenation puts streams of data into one "fat" or high-bandwidth contiguous stream. For example, optical carrier 1 (OC-1) speeds of 52 million bits per second may be used to carry high-speed broadcast video. In this case, OC-1C, or concatenated OC-1, carries OC-1 streams back-to-back or contiguously. They travel through the network in a continuous stream as long as capacity is available. Concatenated speeds are referred to as OC-1C, OC-3C (155 million bits per second), and so forth. Applications for concatenation are high-speed data and broadcast-quality video.

SONET Offerings for Enterprises

Local telephone companies sell SONET transport for connections between local customers and interexchange carriers. The speeds offered are at OC-3 (155-megabit), OC-12 (622-megabit), and OC-48 (2.5-gigabit) rates. The local telephone companies guarantee 50-millisecond network restoration in the case of a network failure or degradation. They run the SONET service to multiple local central offices. In the case of a failure at one central office, service is immediately available from the backup central office. Matching SONET multiplexers are required at the customer premises and at the telephone company office. Another variation of SONET service protects customers from fiber cuts. This diverse routing scheme offers fiber from separate building entrances to the same central office.

Customers often opt for point-to-point SONET rather than bidirectional rings to save money. The major impediment on sales of these services is the cost to dig trenches for additional fiber runs from the customer to the incumbent carrier's fiber ring. Because it is lower in price, newer Ethernet services at gigabit or lower speeds ranging from 10 megabits to 500 megabits are gaining in popularity for data communications. However, customers with existing SONET service have the option to add Ethernet data that runs at 10, 50, or 100 megabits per second. This uses spare capacity on the SONET multiplexer for perhaps LAN-to-LAN connections in metropolitan areas. (See the section on Gigabit Ethernet service earlier in this chapter.)

SUMMARY

Entrepreneurs, spurred by perceived opportunities for new networks, developed many optical and switching innovations. They envisioned that competition would provide opportunities to sell equipment to new carriers. However, in most of Europe and in the

United States, competitive network providers underestimated the difficulty of competing with incumbents and the expense of building new infrastructure. Moreover, competitors have been hurt by regulators' failure to uniformly enforce low-priced, timely interconnections to incumbent networks. In addition, new carriers have incurred huge loses and large amounts of debt as a result of the high costs of building out their networks. In the short run, capital investment has dried up for the purchase of new equipment for landline networks. It's unclear what that impact will be on the continued development of new technologies.

In the near term, incumbent local exchange carriers (ILECs) that have the largest networks are changing their voice switching architecture very slowly. They are generally conservative and won't adopt a new technology until they see a payback. In particular, they want to make sure their billing, customer care, and inventory-tracking operation support systems (OSS) built over 25 to 30 years can interoperate with any new switching technologies they install.

Countries in which companies are building new infrastructure are more likely to take advantage of new metropolitan optical technologies, particularly if these technologies, such as passive optical networking, are lower in cost to deploy and maintain. Cellular providers that upgrade to higher-speed 3G, next-generation service, are likely to deploy IP service in their backbone networks. Carriers such as Level 3, WilTel Communications, Qwest, and Broadwing, Inc. that have built new networks since the late 1990s are the ones that, if they have the capital, will continue to deploy packet networks.

APPENDIX ....

Table 5.7 Digital Signal Levels

Level	North America		Japan		Europe	
	User Channels	*Speed*	*User Channels*	*Speed*	*User Channels*	*Speed*
DS-0	1	64Kb	1	64Kb	1	64Kb
T-1 (DS-1)	24	1.544Mb	24	1.544Mb	30	2.048Mb
T-2 (DS-2)	96	6.312Mb	96	6.312Mb	120	8.448Mb
T-3 (DS-3)	672	44.7Mb	480	32.06Mb	480	34.368Mb
T-4 (DS-4)	4,032	274.17Mb	5,760	400.4Mb	1,920	139.3Mb

Part III

Advanced Technologies, Cable TV Networks, and the Internet

6 Entertainment, Cable TV, and Last-Mile Fiber Systems

In this chapter:

Cable TV providers and incumbent telephone companies are in fierce competition. Both segments are encroaching into territories previously controlled exclusively by the other. They are investing heavily in infrastructure to support new services that will keep them competitive and increase profits. Cable operators have the lion's share of residential broadband, Internet access customers. However, incumbent telephone companies have mounted a challenge. They started a price war for new customers by cutting prices on new service and offering discounts on bundled services. These tactics, plus the increased availability of DSL, reduced the gap between the installed base of cable modems and DSL modems. Thirty percent of users in the United States have broadband Internet access. For every 15 cable modems, there are about 10 DSL subscribers. However, new subscribers are split evenly between DSL and cable access. Cable providers are also losing market share to satellite TV as viewers defect in response to rate hikes.

Cable TV operators spent billions upgrading their networks with fiber-optic cabling over the last decade. This enormous investment put them in a position to offer high-speed Internet access, Voice over IP (VoIP), digital television, and video on demand. It also provided their networks with higher reliability and their subscribers with improved television reception. However, to help cover these costs plus climbing costs for rights to transmit specialized sports and entertainment networks such as Disney and Home Box Office, they raised their rates and would like to raise them again.

Cable operators are also referred to as MSOs, multiple system operators. Large MSOs and smaller cable operators meanwhile are making their own incursions into the heart of incumbent telephone companies' territory, voice service for residential customers. Their upgraded infrastructure and additional upgrades are platforms from which they provide service to small and medium-size business customers. The name of the game for all providers, telephone companies, and cable providers is to fill up their costly fiber-optic pipes with as many services as possible to reap gains to repay investments. Once the infrastructure is in place, costs to carry additional traffic are minimal, and additional subscribers are highly profitable.

As they steadily lose local telephone lines to competing services, wireline telephone companies are investing in fiber infrastructure capable of carrying interactive television and entertainment services as well as Voice over IP and high-speed Internet access. The costliest portion of their investment is in the local access networks between telephone company equipment and subscribers. Telephone and cable operators are investing in passive optical networks in their access networks.

Verizon Communications, the largest incumbent telephone company in the United States, is making a huge financial bet that their investment in fiber to each one of its customers who chooses its optical service will be rewarded. It has announced its intention to be a broadband and wireless company. To that end, it has announced that it will either sell or spin off millions of local copper lines in rural areas to help finance its investment in fiber to customers' premises.

When television and radio were new media, customers received free service, and sponsors underwrote the costs of developing, purchasing, and transmitting programs. However, as radio and television matured, commercials took up more and more of the broadcast hour, resulting in what is known as commercial clutter. According to "Shill-o-vision: The ads take over TV" by Frazier Moore published in CNN.com™/ENTERTAINMENT on February 18, 2003, about 16 minutes per prime time hour and nearly 21 minutes of each daytime hour are devoted to commercials. These are increases of more than 15% over the last decade. As a result of this clutter and for more program choices, customers are subscribing to new models of radio and television in which subscribers and commercials pay for content. These new methods of distributing entertainment are satellite radio and cable television. There are two tiers of cable television and satellite radio. The lower-cost tiers have commercials. Premium channels of radio and television are entirely subscriber funded, have no commercials, and have higher fees.

Nationwide Broadcasters (ABC, CBS, NBC, FOX, Pax, UPN, and WB) and radio stations are upgrading to digital service to expand their offerings. The resolution and audio will be improved. Because it carries signals more efficiently than analog service, digital spectrum has the capacity for their standard offers plus additional, fee-for-service content. It's unclear if consumers will pay for the new content offerings.

The end result is that residential customers will have choices of much more content and new services on their televisions, radios, and personal computers. However, these will be costly bundles of services costing well over $100 monthly. There is a growing digital divide between those who can and those who cannot afford inclusive packages for telephone, cable TV, and Internet access as well as satellite radio. The days of affordable, universal, high-quality television and radio service are over, and affordable access to high-speed data was never available universally.

CABLE MULTIPLE SYSTEM OPERATORS (MSOS).......

Satellites played a key role in the growth and popularity of cable television. Cable television, which started in the late 1940s, didn't gain national acceptance until pay television channels such as Home Box Office (HBO) began using satellites to transmit content. In 1975, HBO was the first network to use satellite technology to broadcast live television to cable operators, a boxing match between Muhammad Ali and Joe Frazier. Prior to 1975, HBO rented space on AT&T microwave towers to send programs to cable operators. Satellite distribution significantly lowered the cost of distributing programming. As a result, many more channels started becoming available in the late 1980s.

Prior to the transmission of content from satellites, the vast majority of cable TV offerings were rebroadcasts of national networks' (ABC, CBS, NBC) programs. Cable TV customers consisted, for the most part, of people who wanted improved television reception. Many of these consumers lived far from television towers or in valleys where picture quality on terrestrial television was poor. These early systems were community cable systems, hence the name *community antenna television (CATV)*.

During the 1990s, large cable operators such as Comcast and Time Warner Cable purchased many small operators and consolidated their territories into generally contiguous geographic areas. As these mergers took place, cable companies with more than one system became known as *multiple system operators (MSOs)*. This enabled merged entities to have more resources to upgrade facilities and use their large size as purchasing clout for programming and equipment. The five largest cable operators (see Table 6.1) have a 69% share of the 73 million cable subscribers. Comcast alone has close to a 30% market share. One factor in Comcast's growth was its 2002 purchase of the cable arm of AT&T, AT&T Broadband. AT&T Broadband had previously purchased large MSOs, TCI and MediaOne. In 2005 Comcast and Time Warner made a joint bid to purchase bankrupt Adelphia Communications. If the purchases are approved, Time Warner will have about 3.3 million additional customers and Comcast will gain about 2 million customers.

Large MSOs have tremendous purchasing power. Their clout is a reflection of both past and continuing upgrades to facilities as well as expectations of revenue from new Voice over IP, higher-speed Internet access, expansion to more business customers, and interactive, on-demand entertainment.

Table 6.1   Largest Multiple System Operators (MSOs) in the United States

Cable Company	Number of Subscribers
Comcast Cable Communications	21.5 million
Time Warner Cable (part of AOL Time Warner)	10.9 million
Charter Communications	6.2 million
Cox Communications	6.4 million
Adelphia Communications	5.4 million
Cablevision Systems Corporation	2.9 million
Bright House Networks	2.2 million

Source: Kagan Research, LLC; on the National Cable & Television Association Web site (NCTA)

Cable TV Architecture—Upgrades, Capacity, Speed, and Reliability

Cable TV signals were carried as one-way analog signals from the headend to customers over coaxial cabling until the late 1980s when cable operators first began upgrading their infrastructure with fiber optics. A *headend* is the point from which programming is distributed to local customers. These upgrades enabled cable networks to support Internet access, which requires two-way transmissions to the Internet and back to customers.

Analog Cable Systems— Maintenance Costs; Poor Reception

Analog service over coaxial cabling required amplifiers to boost the signal every half-mile. However, in analog systems, amplifiers boost the noise as well as the television signal. Thus, homes farther from cable providers' headends had inferior reception. In addition, an outage in one amplifier disabled service on all amplifiers farther down the cable. Thus, all coaxial cabling systems required expensive maintenance in addition to providing uneven television reception. Cable subscriber growth resulting from additional programming was also putting strains on coaxial systems.

New Fiber Optic Cabling— Investments for the Future

Cable operators invested heavily in fiber-optic cabling during the 1990s. This reduced maintenance expense and prepared their networks for future two-way services such as Internet access and voice. Cable operators' infrastructures are known as hybrid fiber coax (HFC)-based systems. Cable operators run fiber-optic cabling from their distribution centers to neighborhood fiber nodes (see Figure 6.1). Fiber nodes convert optical light signals to electrical signals and vice versa. From fiber nodes, signals are for the most part carried over coaxial cabling to people's homes.

Fiber Nodes—Coaxial Cabling Connections to Fiber

Every optical node provides shared capacity of coaxial cabling to typically 250 to 1,000 homes, depending on the volume of traffic in an area. For example, in neighborhoods where a high percentage of subscribers use cable modems or on-demand

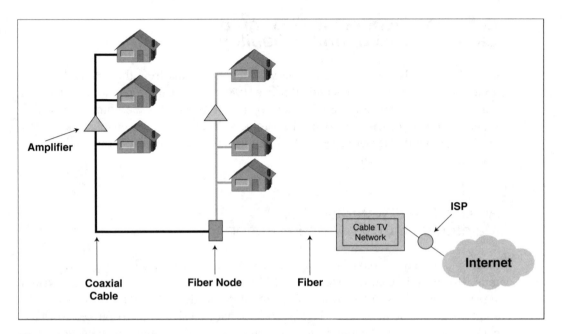

Figure 6.1
Coaxial cable fiber (HFC) for two-way Internet access, improved reception, and added reliability.

digital cable, a fiber node may serve 250 or 500 subscribers. In new subdivisions, fiber nodes generally support 500 homes. To add capacity for newer services or business customers, providers add additional fiber from the fiber node closer to homes using passive optical networks (PONs). See the section later in this chapter for an explanation of PONs.

Two-Way Data Communications—Reverse Channels

The addition of fiber in cable television access networks made the sale of Internet access possible. Broadband cable modem service requires two-way service. Two-way service is created using "reverse" channels.

Reverse channels are created using different frequencies for upstream and downstream transmissions. The upstream channels from the subscriber to the headend use lower frequencies than the downstream headend-to-subscriber channels. Cable TV data communications are asymmetric, with higher speeds in the downstream channel. Splitting the frequencies into different ranges enables the same coaxial cables to be used for both sending and receiving signals. A separate cable does not have to be installed for the reverse, upstream channel because of the high capacity in coaxial cabling.

Cable Modems—Using Cable TV Facilities for Data Communications

The basic functions of cable modems are to convert digital signals from computers or data networks to those compatible with coaxial cabling and to convert radio frequency (RF) from cable networks to digital signals. In cable TV, electromagnetic waves carried on coaxial cabling are referred to as RF signals.

The Cable Modem Handshake, an Agreement Prior to Transmitting

Cable modems also perform a "handshake," an exchange of signals before data is transmitted with cable modem termination systems (CMTAs) located at the cable operator site. (See the section later in this chapter for CMTA equipment.) Complex signaling, use of frequencies, the speed at which to transmit, and authentication are agreed upon between the two devices.

Connecting Cable Modems to Home Networks and Computers

Cable modems plug into either an Ethernet card in computers, a PC's USB port, or a router if multiple computers share the broadband connection. TCP/IP software is required in the computer. Some cable providers also provide applications along with their modem setup software for parental controls and e-mail access. At startup, the network checks the user's login before allowing access to the Web or certain Web sites.

Cable modems are connected by coaxial cabling to an outlet spliced (wired) into an interface box at the side of the house. The cable company provides the interface.

Cable Modem Standards to Lower Costs and Transition to Higher Speeds and Voice

Having uniform standards brings down manufacturing costs because devices can be manufactured in quantity by a variety of companies. This leads to price competition and the capability of operators to "shop around" so that they are not dependent on any one vendor. The cable standards are intended to provide a technology "road map" for cable MSOs to move toward implementing higher-speed IP networks. Implementation of new standards will enable cable MSOs to offer more television and movies that customers can view whenever they choose and new services such as multiplayer games. Cisco, D-Link, Motorola, RCA Thomson, Linksys (part of Cisco), Nortel, Scientific-Atlanta, Toshiba, 3Com, and Zoom supply cable modems.

The cable industry sets modem standards through CableLabs, the research and development arm of the North and South American cable TV industry. These standards are the Data Over Cable System Interface Specifications (DOCSIS®). The European Telecommunications Standards Institute (ETSI) and the International Telecommunications Union (ITU) have approved the standards listed in Table 6.2.

Table 6.2   DOCSIS Standards

Standard	Capabilities
DOCSIS 1.0	Two-way service for Internet access
	Upstream speed of 5Mbps (megabits per second)
	Uniform specifications so that cable modems can be purchased from retail outlets and be compatible with cable operators' infrastructure
DOCSIS 1.1	Increases the upstream speed to 10Mbps (megabits per second)
	Improves security and privacy
	Quality of service (QoS) to enable operators to provide differentiated quality for Voice over IP and interactive services such as real-time multiplayer games
	Tier-based services such as higher speeds to heavy users who use more bandwidth or purchase additional data services
DOCSIS 2.0	Increases upstream speed to 30 megabits per second
	Symmetric services such as those for business customers
	Peer-to-peer such as VPN with site-to-site connectivity (see Chapter 5 for VPN service)

DOCSIS 1.0 and 1.1 modems are widely implemented. DOCSIS 2.0 modems are available and, according to CableLabs, are in field trials. For the most part, migrating from DOCSIS 1.0 to DOCSIS 1.1 requires new hardware. A new standard, DOCSIS 3.0 is in the planning stages. It will support higher speeds of 100 megabits to homes, and be available in five to seven years.

A Shared Medium Based on Ethernet, the Protocol Used on Local Area Networks

Using cable TV for data communications is analogous to being on an Ethernet network. The Ethernet networking protocol is a shared protocol. All messages are broadcast onto the cable connecting devices to the cable network. These neighborhood networks need to be designed carefully without too many heavy users on each network. People using home computers for e-mail and Internet access use different frequencies on the same cable TV facilities as subscribers receiving television signals via cable TV.

Cable Modem Termination System (CMTS)— For IP Traffic

Cable modem termination systems (CMTSs) are located at the cable headend or distribution center. The cable modem termination systems modulate and demodulate digital voice and data signals and place them on cable infrastructure. Modulation is the technique of making digital signals suitable for radio frequencies (electromagnetic waves) that carry signals on cabling infrastructure. CMTSs demodulate signals received from customers to make them suitable for transmission on cable companys' fiber-optic rings connecting smaller hubs (distribution centers) to headend facilities.

Cable modem termination systems monitor the level of traffic at each fiber node so that cable providers are aware when nodes need to be broken into fewer homes per node. In addition, they are responsible for encryption to ensure privacy, security, and conditional access, the determination of whether a customer is entitled to certain features. CMTS devices have built-in routers. The router sends traffic to different destinations such as the Internet, long distance providers, or the cable MSO's VoIP service. These routers have evolved from "best effort," in which packets are discarded if there is congestion, to those that provide differentiated service, important for voice IP service. Refer to Chapter 4, "VoIP, the Public Switched Telephone Network, and Signaling," for more information on Voice over IP in carriers' networks.

Cable Modem Termination Systems to Support Next-Generation Access Architecture

Cable modem termination systems are evolving to support IP access networks that carry voice, video, and data in packets between customers and cable providers' equipment. These IP access networks are referred to as next-generation access architecture. Like other carriers' networks, the core, backbone networks are being converted to IP before last-mile access networks. Upgrading access networks involves many more devices at customer and cable TV locations than core networks.

The driving force behind upgraded access networks is the desire to support more capability for individual selections of video and television. For example, instead of using Wal-Mart's rental service for movies or television reruns, customers could choose from television menus with thousands of selections. These might include archived sporting events or playbacks, HBO reruns, foreign language films, comedies, and children's films.

CMTSs need improved compression to carry this additional video traffic. To support higher speeds, an architectural change from routers to gigabit-speed switches that send packets to headends are being promoted. Refer to Chapter 5 for more on Gigabit Ethernet, which enables providers to carry high-speed traffic in Ethernet packets over fiber-optic rings. Other enhancements to cable modem termination systems would dynamically allocate capacity between upstream and downstream channels. For example, different types of traffic might require more downstream capacity to deliver individual video streams to customers at certain times of day or more upstream traffic if customers initiated frequent videoconferences.

Headends—To Receive and Transmit Programming

The terms "headend" and "hub" are used differently by various MSOs. The site where the cable operator receives content from satellites is referred to as a headend, master headend, or master telecommunications center. A group of satellite dishes that receives content is also referred to as a satellite farm. Central office switches and Voice over IP equipment to support telephone services are also located at headends. Network operations centers capable of monitoring and making programming changes to the network as well as operations support systems may be located here. Headends typically serve seven to ten towns. Multiple hubs are connected to the master telecommunications center (headend), as shown in Figure 6.2.

Hubs—Closer to Subscribers

Hubs, also referred to as distribution hubs, are located closer to customers than master telecommunications centers (headends). Cable modem termination systems are located at hubs. In addition, local programming or frequently downloaded content might be located at a hub, which serves between 10,000 and 50,000 homes. A hub might serve a metropolitan area. Large towns would have two hubs.

Transport Networks—Between Hubs and Headends Using Fiber Rings

Transport networks link cable modem termination systems to headends (refer to Figure 6.2). Currently, hubs transmit traffic to headends over SONET rings that use older technology more suited for circuit switched and slower speeds. (Refer to Chapter 5 for more on SONET.) As cable operators transition to all IP networks, more of them will use 10-gigabit Ethernet based on Resilient Packet Rings (RPRs). The RPR standard specifies backup fiber in the event of a fiber cut or Ethernet equipment failure. Gigabit Ethernet is less costly, simpler to manage, more flexible, and more

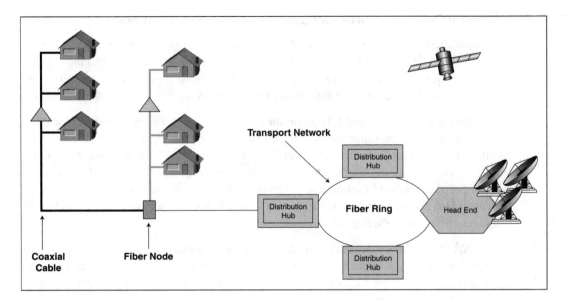

Figure 6.2
Transport networks linking distribution hubs to headends.

suited to IP traffic. Flexibility will enable operators to more easily add and drop traffic between hubs and headends. In addition, dense wavelength division multiplexing is used to increase the number of channels per strand of fiber. Refer to Chapter 2, "VoIP Systems, Circuit Switched PBXs, and Cabling," for an explanation of dense wavelength division multiplexing.

Video and Television on Demand

Cable TV operators provide video on demand, sporting highlights, and some television on demand to customers who can download it to set-top boxes with internal TiVo, like digital video recorders. Subscribers can view selections of hundreds of programs at any time. The industry is working toward making more content available on demand, essentially providing viewers individual streams of television and movies. One vision of on-demand programming is that of storing television and movies that viewers can watch at any time at the cable operator's facilities rather than in set-top boxes. This gives more control of content to operators, which limits copying content and skipping commercials.

Technical Challenges—Network Capacity and High-Speed Retrieval

A major challenge, in addition to network capacity, of supporting video and television on demand is developing servers fast enough to retrieve and send out thousands of different movies and television programs simultaneously to thousands of viewers. The retrieval functions needs to be fast enough so that viewers don't notice delays.

Streaming on-demand television and movies to subscribers requires enormous storage capacity. Streaming refers to the capability of subscribers to start viewing content as it starts to arrive rather than after the entire movie or TV show is received. Content, movies, sports highlights, and reruns of television shows are stored on servers, high-speed, specialized computers. Clusters of these servers are referred to as *server farms*. Management software monitors traffic and holds databases of movies and other content stored on the servers.

Satellite dishes that receive content from cable networks and server clusters are located at either master headends or specialized centers. These facilities distribute on-demand content for an MSO's entire customer base to distribution centers closer to customers. Comcast has a centralized distribution center in Littleton, Colorado, their Comcast Media Center. The media center receives content from cable channels such as HBO and ESPN. For example, it receives 20-minute clips of highlights of professional football games and previous episodes of HBO series. They send these clips, episodes, and other content to distribution centers closer to customers. The Comcast Media Center also has studios in which staff members create digital programming, which they provide to Comcast facilities, other cable multiple system operators, and local stations in the United States, Europe, and Asia. They use both satellite and fiber-optic cabling to deliver the digital content.

Moving to IP—Vendor Independence and Interoperability

To aid cable operators' transition to networks capable of carrying all traffic in IP packets, CableLabs has defined an architecture to carry voice in IP networks. These standards are referred to as PacketCable™. The PacketCable™ architecture has specifications for how voice is carried and also defines how VoIP networks connect to the public switched telephone network. CableLabs enhanced some standard protocols so that they support PacketCable™ architecture. However, softswitch architectures do not need to be modified for cable operators' IP services.

PacketCable™ multimedia defines multimedia architecture for services such as video and games carried as IP packets. Its main purpose is to provide quality of service to devices without inherent QoS, such as those not embedded in cable modems.

PacketCable™ creates a standard way that operators can purchase equipment from multiple vendors that meet PacketCable™ specifications. The PacketCable™ architecture specifies standards for security, quality of service, signaling, provisioning (the process of installing service), billing, and network management. The architecture is similar to that described in Chapter 4 for converged IP networks.

PacketCable™ is intended to work in conjunction with DOCSIS standards and has been approved by the International Telecommunications Union (ITU).

Cable TV Offerings

After spending millions of dollars on infrastructure and experiencing short-term decreases in earnings as a result of these expenses, cable operators now have enormous advantages of owning connections capable of supplying broadband Internet access, Voice over IP, and video to most residences in the United States and Canada. This gives them a tremendous head start in offering even more advanced services as they continue to upgrade their facilities.

Brian Roberts, chief executive of Comcast, made the following statement in an interview printed in *The Wall Street Journal Online* article "Comcast's Big Bet on Content" on September 24, 2004 by Peter Grant:

> *"We're already planning our next suite of products: videophones, video chat, interactive television, Internet search capabilities, and interactive advertising."*

Although their infrastructure gives them an advantage, cable operators face fierce competition from incumbent telephone companies' DSL and satellite television providers. They are planning to expand service to more small and medium-size businesses.

Cable Service for Business Customers

Cable multiple system operators (MSOs) have started to sell additional voice and data service to business customers. They hope to leverage their cabling infrastructure for additional revenue. They often have separate customer service departments for improved service for business customers and promise faster turnaround for repair calls.

For business customers within 2 to 3 kilometers (1.24 to 1.86 miles) from a fiber node, Cox runs dedicated fiber directly to their premises. They use passive optical network (PON) service, which enables them to deploy fiber without having to lay new fiber all the way back to a hub. Rather, they lay new fiber from a fiber node to a business. They sell up to four T-1s on the fiber.

Small businesses generally use standard cable modem service for Internet access. Cox is testing using the hybrid fiber coax plant for single T-1s based on circuit emulation for small businesses. Emulation provides all the features of T-1, which is a circuit switched service, but it runs over a shared cable modem network.

Cable operators also offer secure remote access for teleworkers via virtual private network (VPN) service. Enterprise employees who work at home access corporate files using their cable modem service. The cable company offers security features from its network and routes this traffic over its backbone network to the corporation's Internet access service. (Refer to Chapter 5 for more on VPN service.)

Digital Cable TV—A Way to Add Services

Close to 100% of subscribers are in areas where they can receive digital cable. Customers who sign up for digital cable pay an extra fee and receive set-top boxes with hard drives capable of storing content and playing it back at the users' convenience. Digital cable is the basis for video on demand. Encoders convert analog signals to digital at cable providers' headends where signals are received from satellites.

Digital cable provides more capacity and improved video resolution because there is less interference from noise, which creates snow and shadows that appear on the television screen. Providers can put 10 to 12 channels instead of 1 into each 6-megahertz channel of capacity, thus increasing the number of offerings that can be carried without adding cabling. In addition, because access control is defined in software, cable operators can upgrade and downgrade viewers' service remotely without sending out a technician. Security is higher and cable TV theft is lower on digital service because of improved scrambling (encryption).

Video on Demand Versus Pay-Per-View

With pay-per-view, viewers are offered the opportunity to view a set number of "premium" movies each week. Satellite TV and cable television customers can order particular movies from menus on their television. The movies are offered at set, defined times. Cable subscribers with a hard-drive-equipped set-top box can select a convenient time to play the movie. Once they start the movie, they have 24 hours in which to view it. Satellite TV offers set-top boxes that allow subscribers to store the movie and play it many times as long as there is space on their hard drive.

Video on demand lets subscribers order from hundreds or a few thousand movies without waiting for a scheduled time when a movie will be offered. However, once they start playing one, they generally have only 24 hours in which to watch the entire movie. Video on demand requires digital cable TV because of the capacity required to play so many different movies. Video on demand is not available for satellite TV customers because satellite is a one-way transmission service. See the section later in this chapter for more on satellite direct broadcast service.

The Window Between Film Openings and Availability on Cable

Because of the six-month window between when a movie is first available in theaters and when cable TV offers it, video on demand has to-date not been a popular offering. After their initial run in movie theaters, movies are first distributed to video rental outlets (Blockbuster, Wal-Mart, and so on) and airlines and hotels before they are available to cable MSOs and satellite TV companies.

The biggest single source of revenue to Hollywood studios is DVD and video rentals from retail outlets. These rentals are a multibillion dollar business. All outlets including cable TV, satellite, Netflix, and retailers pay royalty fees to studios based on the number of people who view each movie.

For a Fee, On-Demand All You Can Eat

For a set monthly fee, subscribers to on-demand television have access to all of the programs that a cable operator offers. This includes movies, sports events, all the premium channels, and reruns of televised comedies. This is an offering that requires digital cable and set-top boxes with hard drives. The capability to watch *time-shifted television*, pause the show, and fast-forward is a popular offering. Time-shifted television refers to the capability to watch shows at a user's convenience rather than at a set time scheduled by a network.

Voice Over IP Offerings—Digital Telephone Service

To add to their product mix, cable multiple system operators (MSOs) started offering traditional, circuit switched telephone service in the 1990s. However, costs and the knowledge that Voice over IP was the technology of the future held back large-scale investments in this older technology. Cable operators are in the early stages of offering Voice over IP services to consumers. They refer to their telephone service as digital telephone service. These offerings are different than the Vonage and AT&T type of packages. Rather than mail customers an interface (a terminal adapter) in which to plug their telephones, cable operators dispatch installers with equipment that interfaces with a home's internal wiring.

Unlike Vonage and AT&T service, which can be accessed from any Internet connection, digital phone service is not intended to be portable. In addition, because it is carried over operators' own infrastructure, the cable operators manage the voice quality of packets carrying voice on the cable network. The voice streams carry bits that identify them so they can be handled as separate streams from data. (Refer to Chapter 4 for more on convergence.)

Outsourcing Strategies

As cable operators add Voice over IP, they use some of their own infrastructure and outsource other tasks, mainly back-office transactions to other carriers. For example, packets carrying digital voice are carried from homes to cable modem termination systems (CMTSs) on providers' own hybrid fiber coax plant (see Figure 6.3). The CMTS routes these packets to the headend. At the headend, some providers have their own softswitch components. Others hire carriers—for example, Sprint—to manage equipment at the headend for carrying voice. They also pay carriers to transport their traffic across the country and internationally.

The most complex tasks in voice telephony are back-office services such as 911, directory assistance, and connections to other carriers. To illustrate, 411 directory

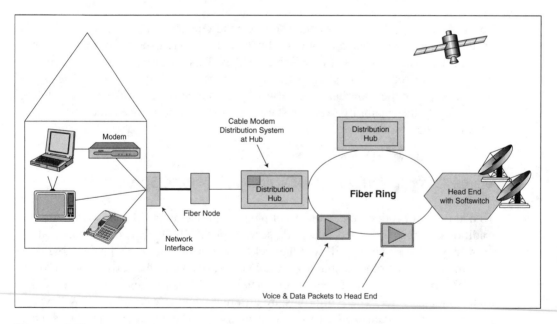

Figure 6.3
A video, voice, and television offering.

assistance requires training and hiring operators, buying listing databases, and investing in technology such as speech recognition. Rather than invest in resources to perform these functions in-house, cable operators often hire other carriers to do them. This leaves cable operators able to concentrate their resources on video and Internet access infrastructure and offerings. AT&T, Level 3, MCI, and Sprint offer these wholesale services to cable operators.

Possible Quadruple Plays

Cable MSOs don't have wireless as part of their triple-play offerings of television, telephone, and Internet access. However, in the future, they may offer wireless on a partnership basis with, for example, Sprint. For instance, new wireless phones are in development, and some are available that work on both 802.11 wireless networks and cellular networks. 802.11 is also referred to as Wi-Fi (see Chapter 9, "Wi-Fi, Wireless Broadband, Sensor Networks, and Personal Area Networks"). A consumer with a combination 802.11/mobile phone and digital telephone service from an MSO could use an 802.11 wireless phone in his or her home. The calls would be linked to the cable network via an 802.11 wireless router built into a cable modem. Outside the home, the phone would operate on the cellular network.

Gary Forsee, chief executive and chairman of Sprint Corp., in an interview published October 21, 2004 in *The Wall Street Journal Online* article, "Turning Sprint Around" by Jesse Drucker, alluded to this future combination of cellular and home telephone service:

> "The typical home will have broadband access from the cable or the phone company. And there will be a device that will work across [networks], so that experience is the same: When the phone gets into the home zone, that phone will work over that broadband facility. . . . We've also been clear about enabling cable companies to have that as part of their consumer strategy."

Set-Top Boxes—Interfaces to Satellite TV and Cable TV

Cable TV *set-top boxes* are interfaces between televisions, satellite TV, subscription television, and cable TV networks for access to television and other services. At the most basic level, they are tuners that filter out all of the channels except the one selected by the viewer. Cable and satellite TV operators remotely administer filters and traps in set-top boxes to allow subscribers access to basic cable TV or premium channels. Set-top boxes also have advanced security functions and contain links to billing systems. The billing system provides information on which channels to allow the subscriber to receive. The security function scrambles and unscrambles TV signals. Credit information is also stored in some set-top boxes. Motorola, Sony, Philips, Nokia, and Scientic-Atlanta manufacture set-top boxes.

Set-top box capabilities also may include the following:

- Advanced programming with 30 days worth of programming information.
- Conversion of digital to analog for people who have analog televisions. The set-top box converts digital cable TV or satellite TV into analog signals compatible with analog television. This capability can be built directly into digital televisions.
- Computer operating systems, software and a hard disc for programming guides, and new services such as picture-in-picture for viewing statistics while watching sports programs.
- An Ethernet outlet on the back of the set-top box so that computers, media storage devices, or home routers can be connected to the set-top box.

Program Guides

Program guides embedded in set-top boxes are the first screens that viewers see when they turn on their televisions. They are analogous to Internet portals. Onscreen interactive program guides are used extensively. Interactive guides include movies on demand as well as two-way consumer information such as entertainment listings.

Personal Video Recorders (PVRs)

Personal video recorders (also called *digital video recorders*) in set-top boxes let people record, store, and play back television programs. They are provided with digital cable and satellite TV. TiVo is offered through retail outlets and DirecTV. The feature that users find attractive is the capability to fast forward through commercials. In addition, each night the PVR downloads the next day's television listings. Users can select shows and have them recorded through a remote control device. TiVo has a version that can be used on personal computers for people who want to download content from the Internet.

Privacy advocates note that these devices send information on customers' viewing habits to the network provider.

Personal video recorders have far-reaching consequences for how companies advertise because many viewers skip commercials. Advertisers depend more heavily on "product placement" within programs in which their products are displayed prominently. For example, lead characters might be prominently displayed drinking a particular brand of soda.

Middleware for Set-Top Boxes

The cable industry's initiative to establish uniform middleware for set-top boxes is called OpenCable Application Platform (OCAP™). Middleware on set-top boxes enables interactive television applications from different developers to work with set-top box hardware from a variety of manufacturers rather than designing applications differently for each set-top box. The middleware translates between the hardware (set-top devices) and network protocols and the applications. Applications include electronic commerce, online chatting, digital radio, and interactive television program guides. Companies that develop and sell middleware include Canal+, Liberte Technologies, Microsoft, OpenTV, and Sun Microsystems. CableLabs is spear heading OCAP™.

Set-Top Boxes for Multiple TVs, Digital Photos, and Music

Digital video recorder software enables set-top boxes to play music, display photos, and offer single-player games. They can also support multiple televisions from one set-top box. DVR software developed by digeo, inc. includes support on the set-top for a CD/DVD player and a USB connection for users to upload digital photographs from cameras. These photos can be displayed on the television. Users have the capability to rip CDs (insert a CD into a drive and export music onto a machine), delete some songs, and create menu driven "jukeboxes" of favorite song titles for easy playback on the television.

The multiple television set-top boxes support two to four televisions. They connect to other televisions over coaxial cabling. In these configurations, the secondary televisions have either a small unit or an older-style set-top box. Ucentric Systems, digeo, and Microsoft supply software that supports multiple televisions. In addition to the preceding, these applications supply program guides from which viewers select programming to watch or record and view later.

To date, these set-top boxes don't have Ethernet interfaces for downloading content such as movies from personal computers or home media-storage devices. There are concerns about copyright issues on content downloaded from the Internet.

The Next Step in Home Networks Supplied by Cable Operators

In addition to networking televisions, the next generation of set-top boxes will support networking a multitude of electronic devices including PCs, game players, music players, and alarm systems. They will also include firewalls and security, parental control options, and enhanced capability for operators to remotely monitor and manage services. These will interface directly with future cable operators' IP networks. Operators plan to use this capability to sell home security, home monitoring, health management, and remote network services. See the section later in this chapter for more about home networking.

DIRECT BROADCAST SATELLITE TV— REACHING CUSTOMERS WIRELESSLY ....

Direct broadcast satellite (DBS) has the advantage of not requiring cabling infrastructure from the satellite provider to each customer. Direct broadcast satellites transmit strong, high-powered signals. For this reason, small, low-cost dishes are able to receive their signals. Satellites broadcast movies, television, games, and sporting events from satellites 22,000 miles above the earth. These satellites are referred to as geosynchronous. Geosynchronous satellites rotate around the earth at the same speed that the earth rotates. Thus, they remain in position to consistently beam signals to the same locations.

Because these satellites are high above the earth, fewer of them are required to cover large regions. This is analogous to a flashlight; as it is raised higher, its beam covers a larger area. Programming is transmitted wirelessly from large dishes at DBS providers' facilities to satellites that broadcast programming to customers. Small dishes are adequate to receive DBS's high-powered, concentrated signals. Each customer's 18-inch-in-diameter dish is wired to set-top boxes with internal tuners.

News Corp's DirecTV and EchoStar's Dish Network are the largest direct broadcast satellite operators in the United States. News Corp also owns Fox Entertainment Group.

Satellite television was initially popular in rural areas where cable TV was not available and reception from standard television was poor because of distances from broadcasters' towers. However, once DBS started carrying local programming such as news in 1999, its popularity grew. It now (as of October 2004) serves close to 23 million customers in the United States, up from 18.2 million as of June 2003. The June numbers are from the FCC's "Tenth Annual Report on Competition in Video Markets." According to A.C. Nielsen Media Research, as of May 2004, there were 73.4 million basic cable customers.

Increases in satellite subscriptions have also resulted from marketing efforts by Regional Bell Telephone Companies and large independent telephone companies and in reaction to price hikes for cable TV. Incumbent telephone companies now offer bundled satellite TV along with their Internet access, wireless, and local service. Cable operators are fighting back with video on demand and bundles of voice and broadband Internet access. (See "Cable TV Offerings" earlier in this chapter.)

For the most part, satellite TV is a one-way transmission. Because the satellites are 22,000 miles above the earth, there are delays when customers send data back to providers. However, satellite operators are creating interactive services. For example, EchoStar set-top boxes have middleware created by OpenTV Corp. The middleware provides menus from which users select features such as weather in their area, news from Reuters or Bloomberg, and certain games created by software developers. OpenTV also developed an application used at EchoStar's studio that shows subscribers a screen-in-screen collage of six stations simultaneously. This is used for coverage of special events such as the Olympics and presidential elections. Subscribers then select the station they want to watch from the screen-in-screen collage.

There are efforts to have satellite work interactively via DSL from telephone companies such as SBC. SBC Communications announced a joint endeavor with EchoStar to develop a set-top box that would provide EchoStar customers with better interactivity such as ordering movies in real time, playing games, and participating in polls. Satellite TV customers can order movies from a nine-day program guide and, if they have a set-top box, store them for as long as they want. However, movies not on the program guide or offered by a cable channel are not available on demand.

BROADCAST, OVER-THE-AIR TELEVISION................

National broadcast television is made up of seven networks that purchase, create, and transmit programming. The national broadcasters transmit programs to over-the-air local stations. Local stations, in turn, broadcast programs to viewers, cable TV, and satellite TV providers. The following is a list of nationwide over-the-air network broadcasters with their owners listed in parenthesis: ABC (Disney), CBS (Viacom), NBC (General Electric), and PBS. PBS is funded by a combination of the government, viewers, and corporate underwriters. In the 1990s, the following four new networks were formed: FOX Network, known as Fox (News Corp.); Warner Brothers Networks, known as WB (Time Warner); United Paramount Network, known as UPN (Viacom); and Pax Network, known as PAX (Paxson Communications and 35% NBC).

Broadcasters receive the bulk of their revenue from advertising. They pay local stations to carry their programs. In return, networks keep the revenue from advertisers. However, competition for advertising dollars from other sources, mainly cable, has decreased broadcast television's total share of advertising revenue. According to media marketing and research firm Universal McCann, in 1980, broadcast television's share of total U.S. advertising dollars was 21.4% versus cable's 0.1%. By year-end 2004, broadcast television's share was 17.5% ($46.3 billion), and cable's share had grown to 8.2% ($21.5 billion). Internet advertising equaled 2.6% ($6.9 billion). These statistics are on the Television Bureau of Advertising Web site at www.TVB.org.

Towers—Terrestrial Wireless Transmissions

Broadcast television is also referred to as over-the-air television because local stations broadcast from land-based (terrestrial) towers. In addition to receiving programs from national broadcasters, local stations also create some of their own programming such as the local news. Local stations transmit programming using spectrum granted to them by the FCC.

Affiliates—Transmitting Programming to Consumers

Affiliates are local stations that contract with national broadcasters to carry a certain number of their programs annually. Because newspaper, radio, and television station cross-ownership rules were relaxed in 1996 and again in 2003, there are few independently owned local television stations. For example, media giants that already owned newspapers in an area can now also own a TV station. For the most part, conglomerates own local affiliated and nonaffiliated stations. Viacom, Paxson, Fox TV (owned by News Corp), and Tribune Co. are examples of conglomerates that own numerous local television stations. National broadcasters NBC (owned by General Electric) and ABC (owned by Disney) own many local stations. Local stations retransmit programming to cable TV providers that pay them fees for these rights. They also retransmit to satellite TV providers.

Copyright Protection for Digital Television— The Do Not Record Flag

In an effort to control piracy of high definition television content, the Federal Communications Commission in November 2003 issued a broadcast flag rule. Broadcast flags are bits designed to control distributing digital TV content over IP networks. The ruling intended that consumers retain the right to copy programs for their own use. Encrypted programs would be viewable only by another display or digital recorder that can also read the flag.

However, on May 8, 2005, the U.S. Court of Appeals for the District of Columbia overturned the FCC's broadcast flag rule stating that the FCC overstepped its authority. It affirmed that the FCC has the right to regulate equipment that broadcasts signals and TVs that receive signals, but no authority to control signals after they are received. In response, industry officials have requested that Congress pass copyright legislation to protect digitally transmitted, over-the-air programs.

The FCC's order was in response to broadcasters who wanted to ensure that their television content was not traded online in a fashion similar to free online music swapping. To counter anticipated copyright protection, a small number of people already distribute digital television shows over the Internet at a quality lower than that on digital televisions. In addition, the Electronic Frontier Foundation, which opposed the ruling and is concerned that manufacturers will add other restrictions to equipment, is distributing instructions on how to add off-the-shelf tuner cards to personal computers. This will allow consumers to record shows and watch or pause them at their convenience. Another issue is the fact that broadcast flags add copyright protection to free programs and noncopyright protected programs. For example, news and public affair shows, which might be used by libraries and educational institutions, will be restricted.

The FCC also endorsed copy protection for cable TV-ready set-top device tuners built into digital televisions. These are referred to as cable plug-and-play devices. Cinemax and HBO instituted their own copy protection software in their television programs. This allows consumers to make only one copy of Cinemax and HBO analog shows and no copies of their on-demand programs.

Digital Television—Less Spectrum Used, Improved Quality

Television and cable TV operators worldwide are transitioning to digital television services that use spectrum more efficiently than analog TV. The additional capacity gained with compression is available for revenue-producing services such as video on demand, games, and contests. Because digital services travel further without needing to be amplified, they are more suitable for two-way services. In addition, digital service provides a more consistent and higher-resolution video quality. With analog services, noise as well as signals is amplified. With digital signals, only the video, not the noise, is amplified, resulting in a "cleaner" picture. See Figure 6.4 for digital television broadcasts.

Digital services are changing the nature of television. The first organization to broadcast digital signals was HBO, which distributed signals digitally via satellite to local cable systems. The impetus for a digital over-the-air standard in the United States came from national broadcasters in 1987. Broadcasters wanted to use advanced television services to compete with other forms of digital entertainment.

High Definition Digital Television— Studio-Quality Video

High definition digital television (HDTV) provides studio-quality video in a wide "letter box" screen format and six-channel, CD-quality, surround-sound audio. It uses spectrum more efficiently (three to four digital channels can be carried over the spectrum required for one analog channel), and it can carry information services such as on-demand sports scores, chat, games, and interactive services. In 1996, the government gave free spectrum to broadcasters for HDTV. The government's goal was to receive back the analog spectrum for other uses. Because digital TV uses spectrum

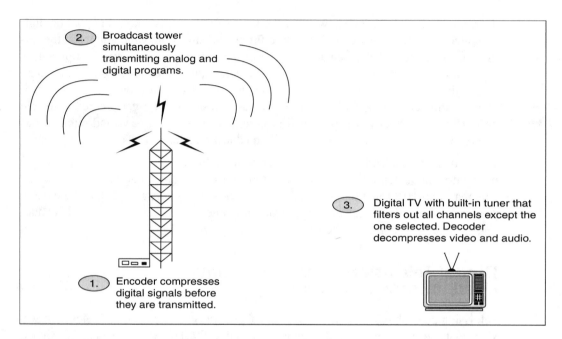

Figure 6.4
Digital broadcasting and compression.

more efficiently, this will give the government 40% more spectrum. In return, broadcasters, hoping to compete with cable and satellite TV using the new spectrum, promised to share 5% of revenues derived from subscription services sold in conjunction with HDTV with the government.

Broadcasters pledged to return the analog spectrum after the transition to digital television. The FCC plans to use close to a third of the returned spectrum for interoperable public safety services so that, in emergencies such as the Oklahoma City bombing in 1995 and the World Trade Center and Pentagon attacks in 2001, emergency providers from different communities and departments can communicate with each other wirelessly using the same frequencies. The government will auction off the rest to cellular carriers.

Over-the-air TV broadcasters must purchase costly transmitters and antennas to carry HDTV signals. ("Over-the-air broadcasters" refers to broadcasters who were granted rights to public airwaves to broadcast programs. They are non-cable TV providers.) According to the National Association of Broadcasters' president and chief executive, Edward Fritts, as reported by Reuters on April 19, 2004, 1,200 television stations are airing digital programs. There are approximately 1,600 broadcasters in the United States. However, of the 1,200 stations' digital programs, fewer than 400 of them are carried as digital signals on cable TV. The National Cable & Telecommunications Association reported in its *2003 Year-End Industry Overview* that cable operators were broadcasting some programming in high definition format in every major metropolitan area. Over 90% of the population in the United States receives its TV programs over cable TV or satellite. Satellite providers are adding HDTV programs at a faster pace than cable TV operators.

Networks are required to return spectrum used for analog television to the federal government by January 1, 2007 if 85% of the households in each broadcasting area have access to local digital broadcasting. Beginning July 1, 2004, televisions with 36-inch or bigger screens must have digital tuners. Due to the high cost of high definition televisions, the fact that TV manufacturers aren't required to include digital tuners in all televisions until July 1, 2007, and slow transition by broadcasters to the high definition digital television format, it is unlikely that the January 2007 deadline will be met. The FCC is thought likely to delay the deadline. Also, some members of Congress have requested that by January 1, 2007, the government seize signals from 75 broadcasters in channels 63, 64, 68, and 69 for public safety organizations.

In addition to the United States, Argentina, Canada, Mexico, South Korea, and Taiwan have adopted the high definition television standard.

NEW REVENUE STREAMS FOR BROADCASTERS USING SPARE DIGITAL SPECTRUM

Steve Lindsley, formerly president of KSL-TV in Salt Lake City, Utah, saw broadcasters' increased cost for infrastructure to carry digital television coupled with the industry's declining share of advertising revenue because of competition with cable TV and satellite TV as an opportunity for a new business model. His vision was to use spare capacity in over-the-air broadcasters' digital spectrum to offer consumers a low-cost pay-TV package of cable channels along with local channels.

U.S. Digital Television, Inc. (USDTV) is the first company to provide subscription-based television using spare digital spectrum. It has formed partnerships with 11 cable networks plus the premium network Starz. USDTV selected 11 networks, such as ESPN 1 and 2, Fox News, and The Food Channel, in different categories for its 11 cable channels.

USDTV pays fees to five or six broadcasters (for example, local affiliates of ABC, CBS, and NBC) in each area that USDTV offers service to distribute the cable channels. Fees are based on the number of subscribers to which the pay television signals are broadcast.

continues

NEW REVENUE STREAMS FOR BROADCASTERS
USING SPARE DIGITAL SPECTRUM (CONTINUED)

Subscribers need a standard VHF/UHF antenna or a special 22-inch antenna developed for U.S. Digital Television. In addition, users receive a USDTV-compatible tuner/receiver that converts digital signals to those compatible with analog televisions and unscrambles cable channel signals. USDTV has announced that it will have a set-top with a hard drive in early 2005 for video on demand, the capability to play back, pause, and fast forward television, and to receive other paid services. Its receivers send HDTV signals and surround-sound audio to customers with digital TVs.

Figure 6.5 illustrates the following steps in sending TV signals to subscribers:

1. Cable content providers beam programs to USDTV's network operations centers via satellite.

2. USDTV sends the channels to local broadcasters with whom they have agreements.

3. The broadcaster transmits programming to customers along with standard local shows.

4. Customers' receivers decode the cable channels.

Service is currently available in Salt Lake City, Albuquerque, and Las Vegas and will be in 30 or more major markets by year-end 2005. In accordance with FCC rules, broadcasters pay the government 5% of fees derived from subscription services carried on digital spectrum. Other educational and entertainment entities have approached broadcasters about leasing digital spectrum. To date, none of these have reached agreements with broadcasters.

Advanced Television Systems Committee (ATSC) Digital Television Standard—Used by Over-the-Air Broadcasters

The digital standard on which high definition television is based is called the Advanced Television Systems Committee (ATSC) Digital Television Standard. An

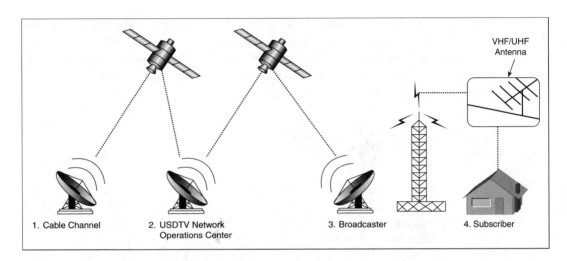

Figure 6.5
USDTV broadcasts. Figure courtesy of USDTV.

industry advisory committee recommended the suite of standards in September 1995, and the FCC approved it in December 1996. It includes 36 different digital standards, all based on Motion Picture Expert Group 2 (MPEG-2) compression. Each of the 36 standards impacts the quality of the picture transmitted. HDTV discards redundant images, sends only changing images, and discards about 60 bits for every bit sent. At the receiver, the signal is re-created (decoded).

The following are the three most commonly transmitted types of Advanced Television Systems Committee (ATSC) Digital Television signals:

- *High definition television (HDTV)*. Transmits high-resolution video and surround-sound audio. HDTV can display enhanced definition television and standard definition television signals.

- Enhanced definition television. Has a lower resolution than high definition television. Enhanced definition televisions cannot display HDTV-quality signals. Only a handful of sets based on enhanced definition television are on the market.

- *Standard definition television*. Usually is better than analog television resolution. It has lower resolution than both enhanced definition television and high definition television.

All televisions with Advanced Television Systems Committee (ATSC) Digital Television Standards tuners and receivers can receive television based on any of the 36 standards. However, the resolution may be degraded. For example, a standard definition television can receive HDTV signals but display them in the lower resolution standard definition format.

Digital Cable TV—Lower Resolution Than HDTV

Digital cable and satellite TV operators implemented digital television in the United States using a different transmission technique than that used in HDTV. Transmission technique (modulation) refers to how bits are carried on airwaves. However, standards used by broadcasters, cable TV operators, and specified by ATSC are all based on MPEG-2 compression, which is a way of encoding and decoding bits before and after they are transmitted. The resolution on cable TV's digital television is lower than HDTV. The cable TV method enables providers to pack up to 10 digital channels and their associated audio and closed-caption services into the same 6-megahertz channel that carries one channel of analog television and its audio. This frees up capacity for more services and television channels.

Cable providers started with this method of digital transmission mode because set-top boxes and upgrade costs were lower than those for HDTV. Some providers that transmit HDTV signals as well as their own digital and analog channels do so in a more compressed format than that specified in the ATSC standard. The compressed signals use up less capacity. However, viewers see a noticeable drop in resolution. Because ATSC and cable and satellite digital television are based on MPEG-2, the costs for using the same tuners and decoders for each service is minimal.

Digital TV Standards Worldwide

There are two digital television standards worldwide in addition to that set in the United States. In addition, another standard is evolving. Digital video broadcasting (DVB) is a standard approved by the European Telecommunications Standards Institute (ETSI). Digital video broadcasting offers a lower resolution than high definition television. The United Kingdom and other European Union countries are phasing in digital video broadcasting. Australia, Singapore, and New Zealand have also adopted DVB. However, Japan has committed to integrated services digital broadcasting (ISDB). Both of these standards are newer and use a more advanced modulation scheme. They can send signals to televisions that are stationary as well as those in moving vehicles. China, meanwhile, is developing its own unique standard. As in the

United States, the majority of digital television is carried via cable and satellite, which may deploy different digital transmission and coding methods.

DIGITAL DELIVERY—ENTERTAINMENT OVER THE INTERNET...

The way movies are delivered will gradually change over the next decade. When television was first available, it was thought that people would stop going to movies, and movie attendance did drop. Video rentals at retail outlets and cable TV offerings of video on demand also made at-home viewing of movies attractive. The development of smaller, higher-quality, lower-cost-to-produce-and-mail digital videodiscs (DVDs) led to postal service movie delivery. The next breakthrough in movie distribution will be downloading movies via the Internet.

U.S. Postal Mail with E-commerce for Movie Delivery

Netflix, Inc. started a major trend in the distribution of movie rentals. Netflix mails DVDs from its network of 20 warehouses located in metropolitan areas throughout the United States. It mails DVDs to customers who place orders online. Netflix has more than 2 million subscribers who pay a monthly fee for the service and has 25,000 titles in its library. Netflix, in turn, pays content providers a royalty fee every time someone orders a DVD. Customers are not charged late fees, but they are limited to no more than two to eight DVDs at a time. The idea was so popular with customers that the customer base grew by word-of-mouth initially rather than through advertising. Now Blockbuster and Wal-Mart are getting into the DVD-by-mail-order business, Amazon.com is expected to enter, and price wars have begun.

The fact that customers order online is a major advantage to these services. In addition to saving money on staffing, the Internet model lends itself to enhancing users' experiences. For example, Netflix has extensive user ratings and offers customers choices based on past selections. Netflix lets subscribers create a queue of movies that will be mailed to them. The queue includes information informing them if movies have been mailed or received back. It also includes dates when new releases will be available.

When asked by *The Wall Street Journal Online* about having Amazon.com as a competitor, Netflix Chief Executive Reed Hastings replied, "We feel like beating Amazon in e-commerce is like beating Brazil in the World Cup. It's a big challenge and incredible glory when you do it." This quote appeared October 20, 2004 in "Netflix's CEO is Mobilizing for Battle with Amazon," written by Carl Bialik.

Using the Internet to Deliver Digital Entertainment

Downloading movies from the Internet to personal computers provides instantaneous access to movies, in contrast to the mail method in which consumers have to plan in advance and wait for postal deliveries. New companies have emerged that enable consumers with broadband Internet connections to download movies. These include the following:

- CinemaNow, Inc. offers films from independent film companies as well as mainstream studios including Warner Brothers, Universal Pictures, MGM, and Disney. They offer their library of 2,000 films as rentals and purchases. They also have a subscription service for independent and soft-core adult films.

- Movielink, LLC offers movies on demand through the Internet. Movielink is a joint venture between MGM, Paramount Pictures, Sony Pictures Entertainment, Universal Pictures, and Warner Brothers. It has 200 movies in its library. Movielink has a partnership agreement with SBC Communications for a co-branded Web site for movie downloads. They are working with Intel to promote digital distribution of movies in home networks.

- Netflix has an agreement with TiVo to deliver movies over the Internet to TiVo-brand digital video recorders (DVRs) starting in 2005.

Although downloading movies or entertainment from the Internet is in its infancy, the following four technologies have made it viable:

- *Lower-cost data storage.* Hard drive storage in cell phones, PCs, and digital recorders has dropped dramatically, making it affordable to store hundreds of hours of movies.

- *Improved compression.* MPEG-4 and Windows Media greatly reduce the time needed to download large files.

- *Wireless networking.* Higher speeds and improved security, together with the ease of installation, make networking devices easier and lower cost than running new wiring throughout homes. However, interference is still an issue in larger homes in which wireless signals can't always penetrate thick walls. In addition, signals may fade in multistory dwellings.

- *Recording technologies.* Personal video recorders have become cheaper and are available in personal computers so that people can record on their PCs.

Home Networks—Transferring Movies from PCs to TVs

For the Internet to become a large-scale viable medium from which to download movies, home networks and storage systems need to be developed that are low-cost, easy-to-install, and based on commonly accepted standards. The biggest barrier to digital delivery of movies over the Internet is the high cost of media equipment to store and send movies to televisions. People prefer watching movies over televisions rather than on personal computers.

The following is a quote from Barry McCarthy, Netflix CFO, from Netflix's third quarter 2004 Earnings Conference Call:

> *"I believe that the downloading market will evolve with slow but steady progress enabled by the availability of low-cost devices which are going to move that content from the Internet to the TV set. We need to be on as many of those devices as we can be, so that will be a core strategy for us. Those devices become relatively inexpensive, like the DVD player did, . . . in the mass-market distribution."*

New devices called media servers will start to be available sometime in 2005 that cost between $500 and $700. They are servers that store about a hundred movies downloaded from the Internet. The servers will be capable of being connected over high-speed home wireless links or coaxial cabling to televisions. This will enable users to download movies from their PCs but view them on their television.

Media players currently on the market do not store movies or photos. Rather, they provide customers with a controller about the size of a book, a remote control device, and menus with lists of movies stored on the personal computer. The media center provides a means for users to select multimedia files on computers and transfer them to a television set for viewing. To date, most wireless standards they are compatible with are too slow to handle quality video. This will change.

DIGITAL RADIO—SUBSCRIPTION VERSUS ADVERTISING SUPPORT ....

Digital radio services, broadcast from land-based (terrestrial) towers or satellites, use compression to squeeze more radio channels into existing airwaves and digitization to improve audio quality. Compressed radio uses about 15 times less spectrum. Digital radio providers hope to take advantage of the digital nature of the service to offer advanced features.

HD Radio—High Definition Radio

AM/FM analog radio is more than 100 years old and is the primary medium over which people receive news and information. Like broadcast television, analog radio is a terrestrial service that uses towers to transmit signals. However, analog radio has uneven audio quality, tends to be noisy (people hear crackling), and stations fade in and out. In addition, analog signals use a large amount of spectrum. Radio listenership has been decreasing slightly in recent years, and broadcasters are concerned about losing the youth market to music downloaded from the Internet for MP3 players and Web-based radio.

WHAT ARE TUNERS?

Set-top boxes, televisions, and radios all have internal, chip-based tuners. Tuners receive all the channels broadcast and filter out all the signals except the correct channel based on users' selections. Satellite television, cable TV, over-the-air broadcasts, analog radio, and digital radio broadcasts all require tuners compatible with their type of service. For digital broadcasts, decoders in the set-top box, television, or radio convert the digital bits to analog signals compatible with the television or radio.

Other tuners in end users' televisions and radios filter signals for interactive services such as programming guides and pay-per-view.

Because each tuner filters only one channel at a time, set-top boxes that are used for more than one television simultaneously require multiple tuners, as do tape-based video cassette recorders (VCRs) that record one program while viewers watch a different program. Personal digital video recorders such as TiVo also have two tuners so that one tuner filters a channel that is being recorded and the other tuner filters the channel currently being viewed.

However, set-top boxes for home networks with multiple televisions will require additional tuners. For example, a viewer in the den may record and watch certain programs while family members in another room are watching and recording different shows.

WHAT ARE TUNERS? (CONTINUED)

HDTV and standard digital television are challenges as well. Set-top boxes will need faster hard drives and more sophisticated compression. Faster hard drives are needed to keep up with the greater number of bits in digital television. Improved compression, MPEG4, and Windows Media 9 will shrink the number of bits that need to be stored on the set-top's hard drive and, importantly, with fewer bits, the speed at which the hard drive needs to read the streams. This is referred to as disk-reading, putting bits onto the drive as they arrive from networks.

In an effort to keep up with competition, add new services, and improve quality, major broadcasters and technology companies formed iBiquity Digital Corporation to design digital technology for radio. iBiquity developed In-Band On-Channel (IBOC), which was approved by the FCC in October of 2002. It is licensed under the brand name HD Radio™, which is capable of transmitting compact disc digital-quality radio signals. Premium-priced radios that can play both analog and digital programs channels are now available.

HD Radio™ operates over the same spectrum used for analog AM and FM programs. In-Band On-Channel (IBOC) has secondary audio channels that can be used for scrolling text such as continuous weather and traffic updates, the name of music titles as they are played, sports scores, and more advanced data services such as graphics and video. With intense data services such as videos and graphics, safety precautions are being considered—not streaming data unless the car is traveling below ten miles per hour or the parking brake is engaged.

The advantages of reusing spectrum for high definition digital service are cost savings for broadcasters who avoid replacing most of their antenna infrastructure, convenience for consumers, and avoidance of acquiring scarce spectrum from the FCC. For consumers who buy digital radios, listening to a digital program will be transparent, as they will not have to change their dial settings. Their radios will automatically pick up digital service where it is available and analog elsewhere.

High Cost of Radios—Slowing Transition to Digital

The high cost of digital radios is holding back stations' transition to digital. According to Scott Stull, executive director of broadcast business development for iBiquity Digital Corporation, of the 14,000 stations in the United States, as of October 2004, 150 broadcast all their programs in digital format, and 250 are in the process of transitioning to digital. Most of these stations are in larger cities, but there are a number of public radio and owner-operated stations in smaller cities and rural areas that broadcast HD Radio™. Three of the largest radio broadcasters, Clear Channel Communications Inc., Cox Radio, Inc., and Entercom have stated that they will broadcast most programs digitally by 2008.

Declining Listenership—Ads and Content

Digital radio solves the quality issue and opens the door to features such as continual weather reports; it does not address the content issue. Listeners are still subject to frequent commercials and often-limited selections of music and content. To address the commercial clutter issue, Clear Channel, the largest owner of radio stations (with 1,200), is urging advertisers to limit their ads from 60 seconds to 30 seconds. Clear Channel also pledged to limit ads to 15 minutes of every hour with 6 or fewer sequential ads.

Digital Radio Worldwide

There are three worldwide digital radio standards in addition to the United States HD Radio. Because there are so many different digital standards, a single radio type cannot be produced that will operate everywhere. The requirement to manufacture and distribute so many radios increases costs. All digital standards provide high-quality audio. Radios that decode digital signals can be equipped with displays for data services such as continuous text weather and traffic reports, song titles, and electronic program guides.

- Much of Western Europe, Israel, Canada, and Singapore are transitioning to the Eureka 147 Digital Audio Broadcasting standard, which uses different spectrum for digital and analog radio. Eureka 147 was developed in Europe by a consortium of broadcasters, government research bodies, and some electronics manufacturers. Most countries outside of the United States have only four or five bands for radio, so more spectrum was needed to add digital stations. Government-owned stations, such as the United Kingdom's BBC, wanted new spectrum so that stations could use the same band nationwide. This makes it possible for listeners to seamlessly hear the same program as they drive without changing stations. Eureka 147 is suitable for both terrestrial and satellite radio.

- Japan uses a digital radio technology called Integrated Services Digital Broadcasting—Terrestrial (ISDB-T) that to-date is unique to Japan. Versions of Integrated Services Digital Broadcasting, ISDB-S and ISDB-C, can be used for satellite and cable television, respectively. ISDB-T will be used for television and radio.

- Digital Radio Mondiale (DRM) is a nonproprietary, international standard partially approved for use outside of North and South America for digital AM radio. China has committed to implementing Digital Radio Mondiale. DRM uses the same frequencies as analog radio and is used mainly in Europe.

Satellite Digital Radio—Pay Radio

Like cable TV and satellite TV, digital satellite radio is a subscription-based service with a paid listenership. XM Satellite Radio Holdings and Sirius Satellite Radio have launched satellites that transmit digital radio signals in the United States. Each sells about 100 channels of specialized programming for about $12.95 per month for basic service with additional fees for premium programs.

Unlike cable TV, in which customers need specialized set-top boxes but keep their televisions, customers that purchase satellite radio service need to buy special radios for each service. A consumer with a radio compatible with XM currently cannot use it for Sirius programs and vice versa. However, the FCC has mandated that they develop radios compatible with each other's programs. Programs are transmitted nationwide, and there is a minimum of advertising. There are four other satellite radio services worldwide, and all of their programs work only on specialized radios. General Motors and Honda have each invested in XM. DaimlerChrysler and Ford have invested in Sirius.

Sirius and XM satellites operate over a portion of the airwaves auctioned to them by the United States government. XM Satellite Radio broadcasts its signals to all of North America from two satellites, which are positioned 22,000 miles from the earth at fixed locations at the eastern and western coasts of the United States. Satellites require line-of-sight. However, in locations such as large cities where tall skyscrapers block line-of-sight, land-based towers are used to supplement the satellites. In these areas, signals are beamed from the satellite to towers that "repeat" them to radios in urban areas (see Figure 6.6). The FCC sold additional spectrum to XM Satellite and Sirius for these terrestrial repeaters.

The Federal Communications Commission regulates both AM/FM and satellite radio stations' rights to use spectrum, ranges of frequencies in airwaves. However, it does not regulate content on satellite radio. In return for granting free rights to spectrum to AM/FM stations, they are prohibited from broadcasting indecent programming. They are also required to make the airwaves available on an equal basis to political candidates running for the same office. Satellite radio is exempt from these content and programming restraints. To increase their subscriber bases, XM Radio and Sirius have hired high-profile radio stars.

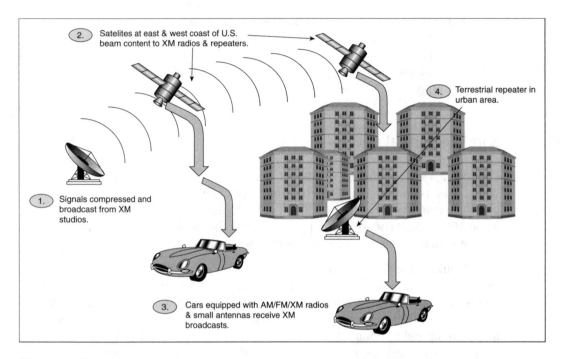

Figure 6.6
Satellite digital radio broadcasts. (Courtesy XM Satellite Radio.)

Competition between digital, "free" radio and satellite radio is similar to competition between over the air broadcasters and cable TV operators—a free service funded by commercials competing with a subscription service subsidized by subscription fees.

PASSIVE OPTICAL NETWORKING ....

Telephone companies and cable operators use passive optical networks to support higher speeds in access networks for digital video, Voice over IP, Internet access, and future interactive services such as multiparty games. Passive optical networks (PONs) are deployed for residential neighborhoods, small and medium-size businesses, as well as office parks to bring high-capacity fiber-optic technology to customers or close to customers. Passive optical network (PON) technologies lower the cost of deploying fiber-optic cabling closer to customers.

One pair of fiber is brought to the neighborhood, and multiple pairs are run from there. Fiber is also used in conjunction with new DSL standards. Copper for DSL is connected to PONs so that carriers can bring DSL closer to customers without digging trenches for fiber to each subscriber. There is a particular interest in PONs in Asia, where much of the infrastructure is being built from scratch. Carriers in Asian countries are interested in bringing fiber to apartments and small businesses using PON electronics. Advanced Fibre Communications, Inc., Alcatel, Inc., Alloptic, Cisco Systems, Inc., FlexLight Networks, Marconi, Nortel Networks, Terawave Communications, Inc., and Quantum Bridge (now part of Motorola) manufacture PON equipment.

PONs—Fiber to the Premises, Curb, Basement, or Neighborhood; FTTx

Passive optical networks (PONs) are devices located in the access network that enable carriers to dynamically allocate capacity on a single pair of fibers to multiple homes, buildings in a campus, apartments, and small and medium-size businesses. Access networks comprise the cabling and infrastructure between the customer and the telephone company or cable operator equipment.

They are used for the following:

- *FTTP*. Fiber to the premises of residential customers
- *FTTN*. Fiber to the neighborhood serving about 100 to 200 homes with copper twisted pair or coaxial cabling from PON equipment in the neighborhood to homes
- *FTTC*. Fiber to the curb, serving 12 or so homes with copper cabling from the PON equipment at the curb to homes
- *FTTB*. Fiber to the basement of multistory dwellings or businesses

The term "FTTx" is used to refer to passive optical networks that terminate in several of the preceding locations.

Telephone companies and cable operators deploy passive optic networks differently. Verizon Communications, independent telephone companies, municipality-controlled utilities in mostly rural areas, and NTT in Japan deploy much of their PON infrastructure to homes and basements of larger buildings. Regional Bell Operating Company (RBOC) SBC and most cable multiple system operators bring fiber to neighborhoods and then use twisted pair or coaxial cabling to serve 125 to 500 customers. The RBOC BellSouth brings fiber all the way to curbside pedestals in much of its territory. These implementations serve only 8 to 12 customers per PON device. In general, PON service closer to customers is more expensive to deploy and provides higher-speed service.

PONs are used to bring fiber all the way to the premises in new "greenfield" developments. They are also the basis for wireline infrastructure in developing countries. This is the result of decreasing fiber costs, which make the cost of new fiber and copper about the same. Qwest is using this strategy and not currently deploying PON in older areas. PONs are being deployed in China and other Asian countries.

PON Components—At the Central Office, Neighborhood, and Premises

The passive optical network switch that sits at the central office or the cable TV headend is called an optical line terminal (OLT). The optical line terminal controls the other PON devices. Splitters in neighborhoods split the fiber's capacity to multiple optical networks units and optical network terminations. Optical network units (ONUs) are connected to coaxial or copper cabling in neighborhoods and basements when providers don't deploy fiber all the way to the premises (see Figure 6.7). Optical network terminations (ONTs) are at the customer's premises if fiber is brought to the building (see Figure 6.8).

The following is an overview of PON devices:

- The *optical line terminal*, located at the central office or headend, has multiple cards, each of which supports up to 32 end users. The optical line terminal has ports for the fiber and backup fiber connected to the splitter. It also interfaces to the network service providers' high-speed backbone network.

- The splitter, at the far end of the fiber from the provider equipment, is like a garden hose that splits the capacity of the fiber among up to 32 end users. Splitters are passive; they don't require electricity.

- The *optical network unit* converts optical signals to those compatible with coaxial cable and twisted pair. It has interfaces for DSL, T1/E1, LANs, cable TV, and plain old telephone service (POTS). It is used for fiber to the curb, the basement of apartments or businesses, or fiber to a neighborhood cabinet.

- The *optical network termination*, which brings fiber to the building, has cards that connect the fiber to customer premise equipment (CPE). These interfaces include T-1 (24 voice and/or data channels) and E-1 (the European version of T-1 with 30 channels), voice ports, coaxial cable ports for video, and Ethernet LAN ports for data. Twisted pair copper, coax, or fiber connections are supported.

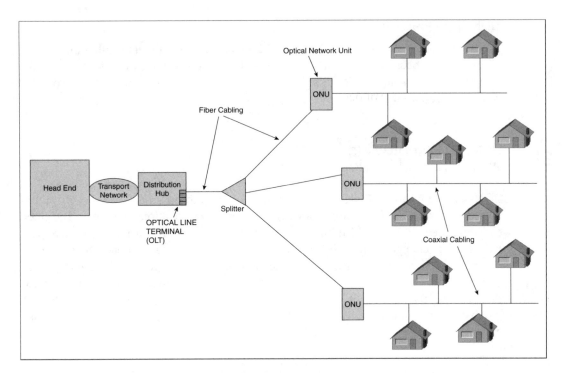

Figure 6.7
A passive optical network with an optical network unit (ONU).

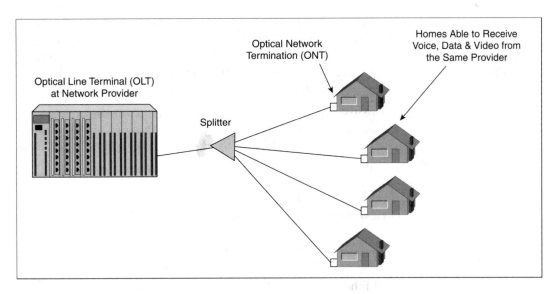

Figure 6.8
A passive optical network with optical network terminations (ONTs).

High-Speed Processing

Processing speed is critical for the optical line terminal (OLT), also called the optical access switch, because it can only communicate with one optical network termination or optical network unit device at a time. Thus, 32 devices contend for service from the central office-based OLT.

PONs—Remote Administration and Bandwidth Allocation

PONs enable up to 32 locations to share the bandwidth on a pair of fibers. If multiplexing is used in conjunction with PONs, even more locations can share the fiber capacity. (See "PONs and Multiplexing" below.) An advantage of passive optical networks is that changes to this allocation of capacity can be made remotely by computer commands rather than by dispatching a technician. For example, bandwidth to particular customers can be increased or decreased through computer control rather than by the more costly method of dispatching a technician. Thus, the programmability of passive optical network devices enables carriers to manage complex networks more efficiently.

Passive Versus Active PON Devices—Low Electrical and Space Requirements Decrease Costs

Passive optical networks have lower space, maintenance, and power requirements than alternative technologies. The term "passive" in passive optical networks refers to the fact that the splitters don't require electricity. Splitters can transmit 32 individual streams of light signals. The other devices in PON networks—at the central office, customers' premises, and neighborhoods—do require electricity.

The small size of the splitters, about the size of a personal digital assistant (PDA), and the fact that they don't require electricity, lowers the cost of PON service. These are key factors because space in the network is at a premium and electrical costs are soaring.

PONs and Multiplexing—Increasing Fiber Utilization

A major advantage of having fiber in access networks is that once the fiber is in place, adding electronics without laying new cable can increase capacity dramatically. Wavelength division multiplexing is often used in conjunction with passive optic network systems (PONs). For example, wavelength division multiplexers split a single fiber pair into 8 to 80 different channels. The wavelength division multiplexers can be separate units or fit into shelves of the optical line terminal (OLT) at the network provider.

When wavelength division multiplexing is used with PON service, each channel on the multiplexed fiber supports 32 end users. These channels are also referred to as colors and lambdas. The term "lambda" comes from the eleventh letter of the Greek alphabet. A lambda represents one wavelength or stream of traffic in a strand of fiber.

Passive Optical Network Standards

There are three sets of PON standards. The ATM PON and broadband PON are both based on ATM. Gigabit Ethernet (GPON) is newer and faster, as is the Ethernet PON (EPON) service. See Table 6.3 for PON standards.

ATM PON and Broadband PON—The Full Service Access Network (FSAN) Standard

Full Service Access Network (FSAN) is an organization of 21 carriers worldwide that has defined a standard for passive optical networks. FSAN is based on asynchronous transfer mode (ATM) technology, and its PON standards are referred to as APON and BPON. ATM is a protocol used to aggregate voice and data traffic for transmission across networks (refer to Chapter 5). ATM differentiates voice, video, and data, but the APON standard is slower than newer Gigabit and Ethernet PON standards. It is also not as well suited to IP and Ethernet traffic.

Gigabit Ethernet (GPON) and Ethernet (EPON) PONs

For the most part, if carriers don't select BPON or APON, they use gigabit passive optical networks service. The Gigabit Ethernet PON standard was approved in February 2004, so some carriers felt that until recently, it has not been a mature standard. GPONs are faster than EPONs and are more flexible. Gigabit Ethernet is suited for both circuit switched traffic such as T-1 and traditional voice as well as IP voice and data. An important advantage of Gigabit Ethernet PONs is that they can be configured in redundant rings. If one ring fails, traffic is rerouted onto a backup ring and backup PON equipment. Gigabit Ethernet is more suited for high-speed digital television and to transport corporate data to storage networks in metropolitan areas. EPON and GPON customer equipment have ports for high-speed optical services.

Table 6.3 Passive Optical Network Standards

	APON ATM PON	BPON Broadband PON	EPON Ethernet PON	GPON Gigabit Ethernet PON
Speed	622Mbps* (OC 12) downstream 155Mbps * (OC 3) upstream	622Mbps* upstream and downstream	1Gbps** upstream and downstream	2.5Gbps** downstream 1.25Gbps* upstream
Comments	Earliest PON standard	A faster version of APON	Newer than APON Not as flexible for handling IP as GPON	Newest standard Most efficient for IP traffic

Megabits per second, optical carrier

**Gigabits per second*

Telephone Company PON Implementations to the Premises

Verizon Communications, municipality-controlled utilities, and many rural independent telephone companies use passive optical networks to bring fiber to consumers and small and medium-size businesses. Bringing fiber to all the premises in a provider's territory is an enormously costly endeavor. The biggest portion of the cost is digging trenches for new fiber. When Verizon brings fiber to towns, fiber is only brought to customers' homes that select the package of services, which includes the high speed Internet access that Verizon offers via its passive optical network. These customers' voice telephone service is moved to the PON network as well, but there is no charge for this. Verizon's Internet access offered on its fiber to the home service is faster than its standard DSL service.

Verizon Communications supplies customers with an optical network termination (ONT) on the side of their house. The ONT is 11" × 13" × 3" and has ports for four telephone lines, an Ethernet dataport for Internet access, and a port for a coaxial cable to support video. To protect the ONT against power outages, it is equipped with a battery that will supply power for about eight hours. The battery has a seven-year life. Verizon installs data cabling inside the house for two or three personal computers.

The top speed on the Internet service is up to 100 megabits per second downstream from the Internet. However, Verizon currently offers speeds ranging from 5Mbps to 30Mbps downstream and 2Mbps to 5Mbps upstream.

The voice service it offers now is based on circuit switched voice. However, as its network is upgraded with equipment (softswitches) to handle Voice over IP, it will transition its PON-based customers to Voice over IP.

Verizon also brings PON service to small and medium-size businesses. It offers 12 to 24 voice channels, a T-1 and Ethernet Internet access, as well as access to frame relay networks.

Verizon selected broadband PON service (BPON) because the company felt it was a more mature standard. However, Verizon has not ruled out changing to GPONs in the future. Verizon selected BPON after issuing a joint request for proposal with two other Regional Bell Operating Companies, BellSouth and SBC. BellSouth and SBC for now are bringing fiber to neighborhoods and to the curb rather than to the premises.

Cable Provider Implementations

Cable operators have been using optical splitters at their headends since they first started using fiber in their networks. These splitters saved money by enabling multiple channels on fibers to share expensive lasers that converted light to radio frequency signals and vice versa. These configurations were less complex and costly than PON service.

Cable multiple system operators (MSOs) now combine the efficiencies of wave-length division multiplexing with passive optical networks to bring higher speeds to neighborhoods and to expand service to business customers. They use optical network units in neighborhoods to convert light signals to radio frequency signals compatible with coaxial cabling and vice versa. They bring fiber to business customers' premises using PON networks. For consumers, they split fiber nodes so that customers share capacity with fewer subscribers.

7 The Internet

In this chapter:

Availability and decreasing costs of high-speed Internet access are the most significant factors in the growth of the Internet. The vast majority of businesses have affordable high-speed Internet access, and their use of the Internet is growing. Firms that initially had only one T-1 connection often have multiple T-1s at 1.54 megabits per second or even a T-3 link at 44 megabits. Competition and price decreases have spurred consumer broadband adoption in parts of Asia (Japan, Hong Kong, South Korea, and Taiwan), Europe (Belgium, the Netherlands, and Scandinavia), and North America (Canada). Recent price decreases have also stimulated increased broadband adoption in the United States. However, the U.S. has less consumer broadband than the preceding countries. As of fourth quarter 2004, over 24% of its adult population had broadband Internet access in their homes.

The Internet was developed in the United States and evolved into a worldwide series of interconnected networks. These networks communicate with each other using the transmission control protocol/Internet protocol (TCP/IP) suite of protocols, which transmits data in "envelopes" called packets. Network operators use high-speed routers to transmit these packets at gigabit speeds over high-speed lines; which are the backbone of the Internet. They carry the greatest amount of Internet traffic. Carriers that operate Internet backbones exchange traffic with each other at peering sites, also referred to as network access points (NAPs).

The Internet became commercially viable with the development of the World Wide Web and browsers, which created user-friendly access to the Internet. When the Internet was first used commercially, e-mail was the most common application. Quality was acceptable from dial-up as well as broadband service because most e-mail did not contain large attachments. Initially, people used dial-up at home for e-mail and faster broadband at work for browsing and shopping. Price decreases led to growth in consumer broadband and use of the Internet more frequently for services that need higher speeds. People now use the Internet more often to access online content such as downloading music, playing online games, gambling, and accessing news than for e-mail. Moreover, activities, which were initially totally subsidized by advertising, are increasingly charging subscription or one-time fees. The first services that successfully charged for content were pornographic. Computers with larger, higher-resolution screens and improved graphics cards have also spurred online activities by enhancing video quality on home computers.

As more businesses and residential consumers use the Internet, sites have increasingly adopted new technology to improve shopping and searching experiences. For example, checkout is smoother at retail sites, and search sites offer a wider array of options such as searching news articles as well as commercial sites. Lines are blurring between sites that formerly offered only searches or portal service (links to other services). In an effort to attract visitors, portals such as Yahoo! and search engines such as Google have expanded their offerings.

The improvement in Web-site-creation software and corporate know-how in building user-friendly Web sites has attracted major retailers to the Web. These retailers, including Wal-Mart and Target, are becoming increasingly sophisticated in creating synergy between their "bricks and mortar" sites and their electronic sites. They are increasing the number of products available online and attracting a growing amount of traffic. Although many of them were late to the Internet, they often avoid the mistakes of some e-commerce pioneers who, in the early days of the Web, created many shipping and ordering snafus because of inexperience in e-commerce.

In addition to e-commerce and information gathering, the Internet is a powerful tool in fostering communities of users around special interests. There are many poignant examples of seriously ill people who find encouragement and important medical information by joining discussion groups sponsored by various nonprofit medical societies. In addition, business staffs join mailing lists and discussion groups built around common equipment such as Cisco, Avaya, and Nortel products. These forums provide details on how others solved equipment problems or whether certain software actually worked in the manner advertised.

Communities of interest are also formed around blogs and instant messaging. Blogs, Web pages created by individuals and used as personal journals, have proliferated as forums around particular topics. Political, technical, and special-interest bloggers exchange ideas around specialized topics. Some blogs have become influential in swaying political opinions. Instant messaging is the capability to exchange e-mail in near real time without typing in an address. Users merely click on an icon representing the user to whom the message is intended and click Submit after typing the messaging. Instant messaging, which only consumers used initially, is now used by commercial organizations that recognize its value.

Security and terrorist attacks, plus copyright issues such as illegal music downloads, have spurred the legal community, governments, and technical companies to seek ways to trace the identity of Web surfers. Questions have been asked about when these activities protect valuable infrastructure and intellectual property and when they interfere with individual rights. They raise important questions about privacy and free speech on the Internet. For example, people don't want their identity stolen in phishing attacks. They also want to be protected from terrorists. However, they don't want their own privacy to surf the Internet breached.

World Wide Web applications for consumers and businesses are still evolving. Applications already in existence will be enhanced with more interactivity. As more applications, including voice and commerce, are carried on the Internet, the criticality of Internet reliability increases. An outage caused by a natural disaster, software glitches, hardware failures, or sabotage has enormous business ramifications. Moreover, utilities and transportation infrastructure are at risk. These organizations run power, water, and electrical plants remotely from network operating centers (NOCs), often using the Internet. If these are compromised, security and welfare are impacted.

THE EVOLUTION OF THE INTERNET ....

The Department of Defense's Advanced Research Projects Agency (DARPA) started the Internet in 1969 with the goal of developing a network secure enough to withstand a nuclear attack. To increase reliability, they based the Internet on packet switching in which packets—"envelopes" with bits for addressing, error checking, and user data— from multiple computers share the same circuit. The vulnerability of any particular site was decreased because in the case of an attack, if one computer crashed, data could be rerouted to other computers in the packet network. This proved to be the case when the World Trade Center towers were attacked September 11, 2001. The Internet was more widely available than the voice networks.

Vinton Cerf and Robert Kahn developed the TCP/IP suite of protocols in 1974. These protocols have been enhanced but are still used on the Internet. TCP/IP is used on the Internet for e-mail, file transfer, and logging onto remote computers. In 1984, as more sites were added to ARPANET, the term "Internet" started to be used. ARPA-NET was shut down in 1984, but the Internet was left intact. In 1987, oversight of the Internet was transferred from the Department of Defense to the National Science Foundation. In 1995, the National Science Foundation turned the management of the Internet backbone over to international commercial organizations. International commercial networks owned by carriers such as Sprint, UUNET (now part of MCI), and NTT carry a large portion of the backbone Internet traffic. Backbones are analogous to highways that carry high-speed traffic.

UNIX, Telnet, and File Transfer Protocol

Prior to the advent of the World Wide Web, people who surfed the Internet did so via services such as *FTP (file transfer protocol)* and *Telnet*. These services relied on users knowing UNIX commands, the computer operating system developed in 1972 by Bell Labs, at that time part of AT&T. Telnet is an Internet service for creating an interactive session with a computer on a different network. Telnet enables users to log onto computers located on the Internet as if they were local terminals. People used Telnet with arcane commands such as `host name`. They had to know the name of the remote computer they wished to log onto. If they wanted to download a file, they used the file transfer protocol (FTP). Telnet and FTP are still used; however, access to them is via menu-driven browsers (such as Netscape Navigator and Internet Explorer).

E-mail access also depended on UNIX commands. UNIX commands include m for Get Mail, j for Go to the Next Mail Message, d for Delete Mail, and u for Undelete Mail. The Internet was not for the timid or for computer neophytes.

World Wide Web—Based on the Client Server Model

The World Wide Web was conceived as a way to make using and navigating the Internet easier. It is a graphical way to navigate the Internet. Moreover, it provides links to information using text and graphic images embedded in documents to "connect" to other Web sites. These links are in the form of highlighted text and graphics. In addition to linking and graphics, the World Wide Web provided Web addresses as text rather than numbers in the form of uniform resource locators (URLs).

Tim Berners-Lee created the World Wide Web in 1989 at CERN, the European Laboratory for Particle Physics. The Web merged the techniques of client-server networking and hypertext to make it easy to find information worldwide. The basic concept is that any type of client, computer, or wireless device, with TCP/IP software, should be able to find information without needing to know particular computer commands or without needing a particular type of terminal. Access is universal.

Browsers—Commercialization of the Internet

The first browser, Mosaic, was created in 1993 by the National Center for Supercomputing Applications at the University of Illinois and Europe's CERN (the European Laboratory for Particle Physics) research laboratory. It was developed as a point-and-click way to access the World Wide Web. This opened up the Internet to users without computer skills. The name of the protocol used to link sites is the hypertext transfer protocol (HTTP). The letters "http" start Web addresses. When a browser sees http, it knows that this is an address for linking to another site.

Mosaic was created with government funding and was intended to be a standards-based Web browser. However, the University of Illinois did not have the staff to provide user support for the browser and gave the license to Spyglass, Inc. to commercialize. In return, the university expected Spyglass to pay it royalties from sales of

Mosaic. Before Spyglass could make a success of the Mosaic browser, Netscape undercut them.

At about the same time that Spyglass was given Mosaic, Jim Clark of Silicon Graphics and people who created the Mosaic browser at the University of Illinois started Netscape Communications. Netscape Navigator eclipsed Mosaic and was a significant step away from government standards and toward commercialization of the Internet. Netscape's strategy was to set its own *de facto* standard by flooding the market with free copies of Netscape Navigator. Netscape envisioned selling Web page design tools later. Netscape Communications also spawned sales of software programs called plug-ins to work with its browser. Examples of plug-ins are Windows Media Player, RealPlayer, and Flash. Plug-ins enable users to hear sound and see color, video, and graphical representations of information.

Browser Wars—Microsoft Versus Everyone Else

Meanwhile, not to be outdone, Microsoft introduced its own browser, Internet Explorer, in 1995. In 1996, Microsoft reached an agreement with AOL in which AOL agreed to use Microsoft's browser software. Furthermore, in an attempt to control the browser market, Microsoft installed Internet Explorer on all of its new Windows™ PCs. In November 1998, AOL announced its intent to purchase Netscape.

Earlier in 1998, the Justice Department sued Microsoft, accusing Microsoft of bundling its browser with the Microsoft Windows operating system and thwarting competition in the Web software market from companies such as Apple Computer, Netscape, Intel Corporation, and Sun Microsystems. The government's case rested on the fact that Microsoft had a monopoly in operating systems and was using it to stifle competition. In November 2002, the courts ruled that Microsoft could continue to include browsers in its operating systems. However, it cannot include restrictive clauses in its software agreements with PC manufacturers. It cannot prohibit hardware makers and ISPs or software companies from making licensing arrangements in which offers from Microsoft's competitors are the first choice that consumers are offered when they first start their computer.

Although Microsoft controls about 90% of browser sales, competition is increasing from free browsers such as Firefox and Avant. Firefox was developed by the Mozilla Foundation, which was spun off from AOL as a nonprofit organization. The Netscape browser is based on Mozilla code. The foundation's goal is to promote the development of software products for Firefox. Nokia has invested in a Mozilla Foundation project to develop a browser for its cell phones.

Internet Advisory Boards

The Internet is made up of networks that use a common set of protocols to carry traffic. Representatives of carriers and academicians participate in a number of international organizations to set standards and agreements on protocols and architectures. The following is an overview of key societies and committees:

- The Internet Society (ISOC) is an international professional society founded in 1991 that promulgates global coordination and cooperation on the Internet. The group is the closest thing to a governing body for the Internet. It was formed in 1992 and is the organizational home of the Internet Engineering Task Force and the Internet Architecture Board.

- The Internet Architecture Board (IAB) is a committee of the Internet Engineering Task Force (IETF) and an advisory body of the Internet Society. It confirms chairs of the IETF and provides architectural oversight for the protocols and procedures used by the Internet. For example, IETF committees manage the evolution of the TCP/IP suite of protocols.

- Internet Corporation for Assigned Names and Numbers (ICANN) is charged with overseeing Internet address allocation and setting rules for domain-name registrations. It oversees the creation of new top-level names. Examples of top-level domain names are .com and .net. ICANN also influences the setting of technical standards. It is a nonprofit organization created in 1998 by various members of the Internet technical, business, and academic community. The U.S. government assigned it to take over from the government-funded Internet Assigned Numbers Authority.

- Internet Engineering Task Force (IETF) is an international standards-setting body. The IETF works under the aegis of the Internet Society (ISOC). It focuses on the evolution of Internet architecture. Working groups cover topics such as routing, transport, and security.

- The World Wide Web Consortium, also known as W3C, was founded in 1994 to develop common standards and e-commerce specifications for the World Wide Web. It is run jointly by the MIT Laboratory for Computer Science; the National Institute for Research in Computer Science and Automation in France, which is responsible for Europe, Africa, and the Middle East; and Keio University in Japan, which is responsible for Asia. MIT is responsible for all other areas. Close to 400 organizations are members.

Peering—To Exchange Data Between Carriers

Carriers, including AT&T, BT, Cable & Wireless, France Telecom, Level 3, NTT, Sprint, Telecom Italia, and MCI, carry Internet traffic over high-speed backbone networks. These carriers, also referred to as network service providers, own the high-speed lines that make up the Internet or lease fiber lines from other carriers such as AT&T and connect their own switches and routers to the leased lines. Network service providers transfer data between each other at peering sites so that users on different networks can communicate with each other. These peering sites are also referred to as Internet exchanges and network access points (NAPs).

Carriers that own *public peering points* charge other carriers for connections to these sites. These peering exchanges are open to any carrier that wants to use the service.

In 1994, the National Science Foundation funded four public peering sites, or network access points, in New Jersey, Washington, D.C., Chicago, and San Francisco. These sites are now run by commercial organizations, and carriers worldwide have established other exchanges. SBC runs the Chicago peering point. MCI runs three public peering sites in the United States. They all use the MAE® designation, such as MAE® East in Virginia. They also operate public peering operations in Paris and Frankfort. MAE was previously defined as *metropolitan area exchange* but is now an MCI registered trademark. Internet service providers lease ports on MCI routers and switches at MAE sites that they connect to their equipment. Examples of European public exchanges are the one in London (London Internet Exchange, or LINX) and the one in Amsterdam (AMS-IX).

In response to concerns about traffic at these peering centers "bogging down" the Internet, network service providers arranged *private peering exchanges*. These "meeting places" where data is exchanged have been set up to avoid possible congestion at the major exchange centers. This direct-exchange method is seen as a more efficient way to exchange data. Moreover, carriers agree on levels of service, amount of data to be transferred, and delay parameters. They feel they can monitor reliability more closely at private peering exchanges. If carriers exchange about the same amount of traffic, they don't charge each other under this arrangement.

Private Internet Networks

Public Internets handle traffic in a "best effort" manner, meaning that if there is congestion, packets are dropped. If there is adequate capacity, all packets are transmitted.

Carriers generally also have private Internets that carriers control end-to-end. These networks offer customers guaranteed levels of service for extra fees. Customers use them to send voice and data between their own sites via high-speed links to the selected carrier. Carriers and customers sign service level agreements (SLA). For set fees, carriers use SLAs to commit to prioritizing customers' traffic. Private Internets offer virtual private network (VPN) service. Many customers share the network infrastructures. However, features of private networks, such as privacy and security, are available. (Refer to Chapter 5, "VPNs and Specialized Network Services," for more on VPN service.)

Hypertext Markup Language (HTML)— Formatting Web Pages

The hypertext markup language, or HTML, is the language that Web page creators use to write Web documents. HTML is the authoring software that controls the "look" of a Web page. Employees who write Web pages for their organizations' home pages use HTML commands. Each hypertext command begins and ends with the <> signs. For example, bolded text is prefaced with <b>. Early users had to know the commands themselves. New HTML word processing software used for creating Web pages has embedded HTML commands. All Web pages are linked together with hypertext links.

The fact that there is a standard way to write code for Web pages is significant. It means that corporations can buy software tools and hire outside software companies to develop Web sites for them that integrate with the rest of their site.

Affordable, Sophisticated Web Sites

Small and medium-size organizations are increasingly supporting and designing sophisticated Web sites. They often hire outside developers who use streamlined methods to produce Web pages at lower costs. Authoring tools are available that simplify Web publishing to add multimedia to Web sites. These tools often have graphical interfaces with "what you see is what you get" (WYSIWYG) capability. With WYSIWYG, Web page developers see what the Web site will look like on the Internet as they write the Web page offline.

Web page designs have become more varied and suited to the Web's medium. They employ video, audio, and streaming music. Software development tools such as Macromedia's Flash and Microsoft's Windows Media 9 Series programs have made site development easier. Some of these products have the capability to query and test end users' Internet connections. If they have slow connections, the audio but not the video is played. Other sites query users about the speed of their connections and play the video according to their responses. Broadvision, Ektron, interactivetools.com, Interwoven, Microsoft, and Vignette sell content-management software used to design and update Web pages.

Dynamic Web Application Servers

Dynamic Web application servers, such as Macromedia's Cold Fusion and BEA System's WebLogic®, interface with databases and operating systems from multiple vendors. They translate between Web servers and customer databases that are in formats such as Oracle and SQL. Web servers hold the actual pages that people see when they visit the site (see Figure 7.1). With dynamic Web application servers, surfers ask for information on certain products in a catalog and receive a Web page with the information. The dynamic Web application server stores templates (forms) that the dynamic Web application server populates with information from the database. They send the filled-in template back to the Web server to be viewed by the customer that initiated the request.

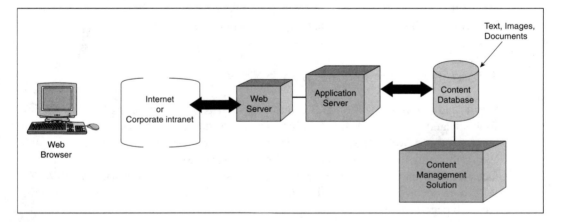

Figure 7.1
Web server, application server, content management software, and content database. (Courtesy of Ektron, Inc.)

Templates include static items such as the corporate logo and elements that are the same for every page. They are stored on the application server, and the changing information elements are stored in the database. This is different than static Web pages with content and logos or page layouts stored in one server. In static Web sites, the content is part of every page. If there is a change made to the logo, company name, or "button" layout, each page on the Web site must be changed.

ISPs: With Software Platforms for Enhanced Offerings

When residential consumers sign up for broadband DSL or cable modem service, they receive ISP service bundled into one package along with Internet access. The Internet access is the physical path to the Internet. ISP (Internet service provider) packages include e-mail plus other optional offerings such as domain registration, spam protection, remote access, Web page hosting, online interactive games, and Web page design. Cable operators, Regional Bell Operating Companies, competitive local exchange carriers (CLECs), Earthlink, AOL, MSN, NetZero, and Yahoo! are examples of Internet service providers. Providing Internet access with ISP services gives these providers direct access to customers for future service offerings.

Major carriers such as AT&T, MCI, and Sprint, as well as smaller competitive local exchange carriers (CLECs), sell Internet access to business and commercial customers. Their Internet access includes optional ISP services such as e-mail servers, firewall protection, domain registration, and hosting. They also sell secure remote access for employees of enterprises with virtual private networks (VPNs). (Refer to Chapter 5 for more on VPNs.)

Cable multiple service operators offer their own ISP service to their cable modem customers. Customers' Web pages, e-mail, and media partners' Internet content, such as sports scores, travel services, games, and shopping information, are stored at cable operators' data centers. Cable backbone networks carry signals from individual headends to cable TV data centers and from the data center to the Internet (see Figure 7.2). Headends are the point from which cable TV operators transmit television signals and operate transmission systems that convert radio frequencies to signals compatible with the Internet. Cable operators own and operate the routers, servers, and optical lines connecting cable company headends with regional or national data centers. The data centers are connected to the Internet.

Regional Bell Operating Companies also include their own ISP function with DSL modem access for residential and small and medium-size business customers. SBC has a partnership with Yahoo! in which Yahoo! provides the software for SBC's

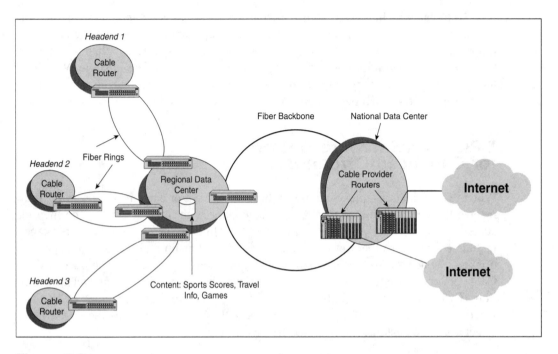

Figure 7.2
Internet access from a cable multiple system operator (MSO).

service. This is essentially a portal, an entrance to the Internet. SBC has announced that it will use Yahoo!'s software as an access point for future cellular, cable television, and Voice over IP functions. For example, customers with Cingular cell phones, SBC cable television, and Voice over IP could use Yahoo! software to check e-mail messages, order TV programming, and set parental controls for the Internet or television. (Refer to Chapter 6, "Entertainment, Cable TV, and Last-Mile Fiber Systems," for more on set-top boxes.) The other large incumbents operate their own ISP service and are in a position to use their DSL platforms for these offerings as well.

ISPs such as AOL, MSN, and EarthLink sell Internet service provider service mainly to customers with dial-up Internet access. Dial-up customers have Internet access that is separate from their ISP service. Their telephone company provides their local telephone service used for Internet access. The increasing percentage of customers opting for broadband access has meant decreases in the preceding ISPs' sales. Some of these ISPs sell consumers both ISP and Internet access over DSL and cable modem facilities. In this arrangement, the ISP purchases Internet access at wholesale prices and resells it along with e-mail and other services. However, this represents a small percentage of broadband consumer Internet access. AOL has some broadband customers, but the company announced that it is no longer marketing that service. AOL does offer a "bring your own access" in which, for a monthly flat fee, customers can log into AOL and access member services.

Hosting—Outsourcing Web Pages

Anyone who wants to can make information available to the Internet community by obtaining a Web address (domain name) and connecting to the Internet. People and organizations "publish" documents on the Web via a Web server. Because of the cost of maintaining reliability, adequate bandwidth in the face of traffic peaks, and security against hackers and viruses, hosting often is done at an Internet service provider, carrier, or hosting company's site.

Residential home pages generally are at Internet service provider sites such as AOL, MSN, or at portals such as Yahoo! or Terra Lycos. Often carriers such as AT&T, MCI, and Sprint and small ISPs offer specialized hosting services to corporate customers. Most telephone companies provide hosting as well as Internet backbone service.

Hosting companies often refer to their locations as *hardened*. The term "hardened" signifies high reliability and security as well as capacity to handle unexpected traffic spikes. For instance, there may be dual power supplies, feeds to duplicate power companies, backup telephone lines, and physical security. For example, entrance to the facility may be limited and monitored, and computers belonging to individual businesses may be locked into cages. As well, buildings may be constructed to improve their capability to withstand hurricanes and tornadoes. Traffic is monitored around the clock. For example, peaks may indicate that someone has hacked into the site.

There are various levels of hosting. For example, a customer can supply the hosting company with text, pictures, and information, and the host company builds the Web pages on the host's computer. In other cases, the customer designs and creates the Web pages on his or her own computer. Large hosting companies use high-speed connections such as OC-3, 155-megabit links to the Internet backbone from their onsite routers (see Figure 7.3). The hosting company monitors the security so that hackers do not compromise the data in the Web pages.

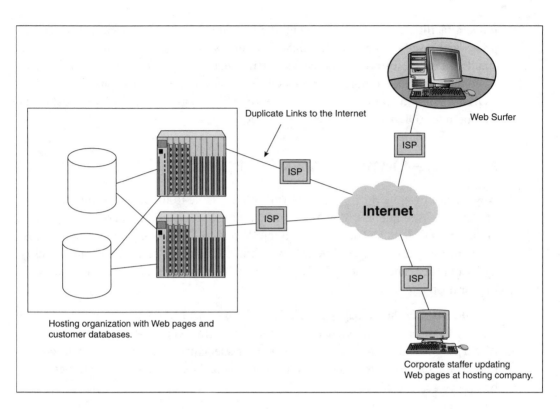

Figure 7.3
Links between hosting companies and the Internet.

MESSAGING AND THE GROWTH OF SPAM.............

E-mail is a major impetus in consumers' decisions to do the following:

- Sign up for Internet access
- Purchase and network multiple computers in homes
- Upgrade to broadband connections

Consumers rather than businesses initially used instant messaging, also referred to as "chat." It is now widely used in businesses as well. Instant messaging has increased the interactivity and spontaneity of e-mail in corporations. Instant messaging is the capability to exchange e-mail in near real time. Instead of typing in an address, users click on an icon representing the user to whom the message is intended and then click Submit after typing the messaging. The recipient replies with a short message and also clicks Submit to send.

Electronic mail (e-mail) is the computer-based storage and forwarding of messages. Text-based electronic mail, without photos and advanced formatting, is based on simple mail transfer protocol (SMTP), which is part of the suite of TCP/IP protocols. SMTP specifies addressing conventions. For example, the @ sign differentiates between the user's name and his or her computer. SMTP also specifies how to address mail to multiple locations, ways to copy other people, and the use of ASCII code. The American Standard Code for Information Interchange (ASCII) translates computer bits into a limited number of characters. Retailers such as Lands' End, small businesses, and corporations routinely send newsletters and promotional material using hypertext markup language (HTML) for advanced formatting and links to their Web sites.

Multimedia Attachments—Photographs, Movies, and PowerPoint

Sending attachments has become the *de facto* way in which people exchange documents and photographs. Companies exchange spreadsheets, photographs, PowerPoint, and word processing documents with consultants, remote employees, and business partners. Consumers transmit photos and videos created with digital cameras, using compression software such as Joint Photographic Experts Group (JPEG). As the number of years that consumers have been using the Internet increases, they become savvier about how to use technology and use it for more applications. Downloading pictures from digital cameras and sending them to family members is a prime example of this trend.

However, attachments are capable of spreading viruses. *Viruses* are software programs written to damage computer files. Straight-text e-mail messages cannot "pollute" PCs with viruses. However, a virus included in attachments can harm files when the attachment is opened from within programs. Viruses can wipe out the entire content of a PC's hard drive. As new viruses are discovered, virus protection software that blocks the transmission of files containing known viruses is updated.

E-mail Formatted in HTML—Another Vehicle for the Spread of Viruses

E-mail sent in the hypertext markup language (HTML) is sent with commands capable of adding special formatting to e-mail. The e-mail messages have commands embedded in the text files for specialized fonts, Web links, color, and placement of images. Thus, e-mail contains links to retailers' sites, JPEG pictures, specialized fonts, and color backgrounds. Some electronic greeting cards, for example, contain synthesized voice messages that speak or sing their message when recipients click on them. E-mail with images for catalog items and corporate logos contain large amounts of data. This makes it slow for people with dial-up Internet access to download e-mail formatted in HTML.

The increased use of broadband among residential and small businesses has enhanced the viability of e-mail sent in HTML. However, e-mail in hypertext markup language has the disadvantage of being able to spread viruses with malicious code hidden in the message. Unlike plain-text e-mail, computers can be infected with viruses without users opening attachments. These e-mail messages also have the capability of adding spyware to computers. See the section later in this chapter on spyware, computer code that tracks users' keystrokes and Web browsing.

Spam—Clogging Inboxes with Junk Mail

Spam is unsolicited mass e-mailing of advertising messages. The International Telecommunications Union (ITU) estimates that spam costs the global community $25 billion annually. *NetworkWorldFusion* published this statistic November 1, 2004 in the article "E-mail at a Crossroads" by Cara Garretson. Estimates on the percentage of e-mail that is spam vary, but there is agreement that it is growing. Message Labs, an e-mail security services firm, estimated that as of April 2004 two-thirds of all e-mail in the United States was spam.

The worldwide increase in the number of people with computers is exacerbating the problem. Spam now originates from locations as diverse as Russia, China, and Belize as well as from developed countries such as the United States, South Korea, and Japan. Because spam is international, any successful solution depends on agreements between lawmakers and international standards bodies. The low cost of spam makes it an attractive business model for sending millions of messages. Spam is profitable when only a low percentage of people buy the offered product or service. Efforts to slow down spam involve user education, technology, and legislation.

One attempt to stop spam is the Controlling the Assault of Non-Solicited Pornography and Marketing Act (CAN-SPAM) law enacted in the United States. CAN-SPAM specifies that unsolicited commercial e-mail must identify itself as advertising and have an opt-out provision, letting recipients opt out of future mailings. CAN-SPAM's effectiveness is hampered because it only affects spammers within the United States, and spammers are located worldwide. Moreover, it is difficult to find spammers because they hide behind false addresses and frequently change their addresses.

Many consumers and ISPs use some form of filter to delete spam. For example, they compile a list of addresses and content with words commonly used by spammers, such as "Viagra" and "low mortgage rates." However, these filters are not perfect and identify some legitimate e-mail as spam.

Protecting Corporations from Spam

Enterprises purchase specialized software and hardware called *appliances* to protect their Internet networks from spam, viruses, worms, and access to certain types of Web sites such as those containing pornography. (Viruses are code that is capable of destroying data on hard drives. Worms can take over computers' e-mail address books and send themselves to each address.) Software on the appliance has lists of known spammers. These messages are deleted as they arrive. However, to prevent deleting important e-mail, they weigh suspicious messages against content and message subject and ascertain the likelihood of these messages being spam. They periodically send these suspicious e-mail messages to recipients who can delete them or put them in a "whiteboard." A whiteboard is a list of approved recipients from whom people want to receive messages. Borderware, CipherTrust, and IronPort sell e-mail security appliances.

To ensure that employees use the Internet for work-related tasks, organizations as well as governments block particular Web sites. They use software that blocks URLs to known pornography, hate/racism, sport, gambling, religion, and weapons sites. Suppliers of Internet filtering software use automated search tools that find sites with pornographic pictures, racist symbols, and Web content related to the preceding topics. Other filtering software screens incoming Web pages or sends warnings to staff that pop up on their computer screens. The message on the screen tells the employee that the site he or she is viewing is not an appropriate work-related site.

Outsourcing Spam Blocks

The most effective spam prevention techniques are expensive and are used primarily by large enterprises. Some of these are outsourced solutions in which business customers pay an upfront fee plus monthly service charges. Brightmail (part of Symantec) offers one of these services. Brightmail installs a filtering computer at each of its customers' sites that screens e-mails based on known spammers' domains. Brightmail identifies spammers by attracting spam to false Web sites and e-mail accounts that it sets up. As spam is sent to the false accounts, Brightmail updates filtering lists every ten minutes at each of its customers' sites.

Antispam Standards

Standards organizations, ISPs, and software companies are working on various solutions that involve verifying the sender's ID or the domain from which the e-mail was sent. A domain is the portion of the e-mail after the @ sign, such as AOL.com. This would cut back on anonymous e-mail. The problem with these systems is that many legitimate e-mail users have different addresses for different purposes. In addition, spammers can frequently register and change domain names, thus making their messages appear to be nonspam. Moreover, there is nothing currently built into e-mail systems that automatically checks on the legitimacy of e-mail addresses. These systems also don't stop types of viruses dubbed Trojan horses or bots, in which hackers take over legitimate users' computers and use them to send messages to everyone in the users' electronic address book. These messages carry the "from" address of the computer taken over by the hacker.

Charging for E-mail to Discourage Spam—Stamps

Microsoft and Yahoo! have stated they support a system in which individuals and commercial organizations would be charged under a penny for each e-mail they send. In this system, small users would get an allotment of free messages, but spammers that send millions of messages would have to pay to mail. The stamps would be in the form of certificates, encrypted strings of bits issued and verified by a trusted organization such as AOL or VeriSign. Fred Goldstein, principal at ionary Consulting, feels that stamps are currently the only solution that will significantly decrease the amount of spam aimed at consumers. Others such as operators of not-for-profit mailing lists feel that electronic stamps would hurt small organizations and that large spammers would be able to afford the fees. However, users could opt to receive unstamped messages from people on a list called a whiteboard. When they sign up for a mailing list, part of the process could be putting the mailing list on their white list.

Phishing—A Form of Online Identity Theft

Phishing is the attempt to deceive people as to the true identity of the organization sending e-mail or sponsoring a Web site. Phishing schemes are used to persuade people to provide user IDs and Social Security, credit card, or account numbers and passwords. Organizations that perform phishing use logos and formatting to create e-mail messages and Web sites that make the copycat sites and e-mail messages look like the financial or retail sites, such as eBay, Bank of America, and PayPal, that they are aping. They generally send e-mail messages purporting to be from bank ABC with links to a site masquerading as a legitimate financial or retail institution. Links within e-mail often display the address of the legitimate bank but actually send the user to the copycat site.

Successful phishing attacks cost banks billions of dollars in unrecoverable charges made from stolen credit cards. Compromised trust in online banking services and in the financial institution itself are bigger problems. Financial institutions save huge costs when people bank online rather than at ATMs or tellers. Moreover, if customers are cheated out of money at bank A and move their assets to bank B, the institutions lose customers and increase its operational expenses.

Phishing is on the rise and is more effective than traditional spam. *The Washington Post* published statistics from the Anti-Phishing Working Group, a coalition of businesses and technology companies, stating that as many as 5% of consumers respond to phishing e-mails and provide private information. The article "'Phishing' on the Rise, But Don't Take the Bait" appeared November 9, 2004 on Page C10. Phishing attacks use many of the same techniques used by spammers to send millions of messages in a short period of time. They also use fake return addresses to make them look like legitimate institutions. Once they glean e-mail addresses, passwords, and credit card numbers, they either sell them to spammers or use them themselves. Many phishing attacks originate in international locations other than the location where the attacks occur.

Because of the magnitude of the problem, there have been suggestions that the government promote programs to educate people about phishing. For example, to avoid phishing attacks, consumers should not click on Internet links in e-mail messages sent from organizations purporting to be a bank. Banks, retail sites, and financial institutions don't send e-mail soliciting confidential information. To ensure the legitimacy of a Web site, users should access their provider's bank directly from their browser rather than from a link in e-mail. The FBI has warned that terrorists could use phishing to raise money for their activities.

Spyware—Tracking Individuals' Web Browsing

Spyware is software unknowingly added to people's computers to track their browsing and their keystrokes. The software is often added when people click on Web links within spam e-mail that sends them to malicious Web sites. Hackers that use spyware often exploit newly discovered weaknesses in Internet Explorer browsers or older versions of the browser without patches for earlier vulnerabilities. Spyware is used to add code to computers, causing them to slow down and malfunction. The United States Federal Trade Commission (FTC) has the authority to file complaints in federal courts against companies and individuals who use spyware to defraud consumers. In October

2004, the FTC filed such a complaint in the United States District Court of New Hampshire against Seismic Entertainment Productions, Smartbot.Net, and Sanford Wallace.

The FTC alleged in its October 12, 2004 press release that these organizations installed malicious software that tracked users' browsing, changed their home pages and search engines, and triggered numerous pop-up ads. The FTC further stated that the defendants offered to sell consumers Spy Wiper and Spy Deleter antispyware to correct problems caused by the defendants' software. The FTC stated that the spyware was able to create this havoc by exploiting a feature of Internet Explorer's Web browser. Because many of the people behind spyware schemes are located outside of the United States, prosecution has limited effect. The U.S. Justice Department is working with foreign governments to coordinate efforts to cut down on cybercrime.

Interactivity Tools: Usenet, Chat, Mailing Lists, and Blogging

The Internet and instant messaging have increased the pace of locating information and communicating. Instant messaging enables co-workers to know when someone is available to respond to messages that require fast answers. This is an improvement over e-mail, which is not suitable for urgent messages because of time delays between sending and receiving a reply. Communities have sprung up around common areas of interest. Groups of people interested in common topics exchange information through Usenet and mailing lists. They establish links to Web logs (blogs), personal Web pages in the form of journals, around common topics of interest.

Usenet—Posting Messages to Newsgroups

Usenet groups were the original communities formed around common interests, news events, and even medical conditions. Usenet, short for UNIX user networks, consists of discussion groups formed around specific topics. Usenet is also referred to as newsgroups. Usenet was created in 1979 prior to the advent of the World Wide Web. Newsgroups were used by computer hobbyists, college faculty, and students and were formed around special interests such as cooking, specialized technology, and lifestyles. Newsgroup topics included science, religion, and gender issues. Users posted articles and personal opinions to servers that sent replies to other servers.

Usenet newsgroups were originally accessed only through newsgroup software, which is part of e-mail programs. Users set up access to Usenet newsgroups through their e-mail and posted messages to Usenet. They read messages from newsgroups through their Usenet software. Google and Yahoo! offer newsgroups on their servers that can be accessed through the Web rather than through Usenet software on e-mail. Groups are organized by topics, which are listed in their abbreviated forms. Some sample topics are alt.anyconceivable topic; comp.hardware, software, or consumerinformation; and talk.currentissuesand.debates. Users who post messages to Usenet select a username that is often a pseudonym.

In 2001, Google purchased Deja.com's Usenet archives, which date back to 1995. Most Usenet groups are now on Google's site. Yahoo! has a significantly smaller number of groups.

Mailing Lists—Non-Real-Time E-mail Around Common Interests

Mailing lists are groups of messages and links to articles sent to groups of people via e-mail. Like Usenet-based newsgroups, mailing lists are based on common areas of interest. However, the groups of e-mails are mailed to users without any logon procedure. For example, people may join lists to stay current on technical subjects in their profession. Messages are automatically e-mailed to people who sign up to be on the mailing list. People join the mailing list by sending an e-mail message to a computer called a list server (listserv) with the word "subscribe" in the subject line. If there is a list moderator, he or she checks for duplicate messages and ensures that messages cover the mailing list's topic. Discussions about subtopics, such as security on a mailing list about computer networks, are called *threads.*

Mailing lists are an example of asynchronous, non-real-time communications. People post messages that are read at a later time. A challenge for mailing list moderators is avoiding spam messages that are advertising or junk e-mail.

Instant Messaging—Real-Time Chats

Instant messaging (IM), also referred to as "chat," is the capability to exchange messages electronically in near real time with other people who are also signed on to the public Internet or private intranets. An intranet is a private Internet within an enterprise with Web-type access to corporate information. With instant messaging, a window pops up on people's computers, letting them know who in their chat group is online. AOL calls people in the same chat group "buddies." Instant Messenger software, AOL's product, works independently of its ISP service. Its ISP-based product is ICQ, short for "I seek you." AOL's two instant messaging systems are incompatible with each other. AOL is the largest provider of instant messaging. The next largest providers of instant messaging software are Yahoo! and MSN's Messenger service.

The high numbers of people using instant messaging has attracted large numbers of advertisers at these Internet sites. Because teenagers are the leading users of public instant messaging, many of these ads are aimed at young people.

Multimedia Chatting—More Traffic, Competition with Traditional Voice

Instant messaging (IM) has expanded from text only to voice, videoconferencing, file transfer, and messaging on cell phones. People who click on an instant messaging button next to a user's name can place a voice phone call to their "buddy." In some systems, users can click on a group of names to initiate a video call if they all have a Web cam, a video camera compatible with their computer. Chat is becoming media independent, compatible with voice, text, and video. These functionalities are adding traffic to the Internet and competing with traditional voice service.

Chat Rooms

Chat rooms, a feature of instant messaging, often are organized around common interests such as travel and music. People come into and out of the chat room using a name (handle) that they select. Users have a split screen, an area for viewing messages, and one for typing messages. After a person types a message and hits the Send button, the text appears on everyone's screen who is participating in the chat. The proliferation of pornography has prompted many parents to ban their children from using some of these free chat rooms.

Presence

Presence is the capability of users to know when someone within their community of users is available for real-time or near-real-time messaging. People indicate their availability via icons on e-mail software on their computer, personal digital assistant, or Internet Protocol (IP) telephone. For example, they can let people know that they are available, on the phone, on a business trip, or on vacation by selecting an icon on their device. Presence is a powerful tool for improving business productivity when employees are located in other offices, buildings, cities, and across the world. It essentially removes barriers to fast access between co-workers, friends, and family.

Presence was first used mainly by residential consumers, but it is now used extensively in business and commercial organizations. For example, if someone is on a telephone call and is asked a question he or she can't answer, the person can IM (instant message) someone he or she knows is available to receive an immediate response. An important function of instant messaging is that it works in real time or near real time. In contrast, voice mail and e-mail are non-real-time applications. People send messages and hope to hear back. Chat is also frequently used by people who multitask. For example, users can simultaneously be on a conference call and engaged in instant messaging with colleagues.

SIP and Presence—Interoperability and Multimedia Capability

Session initiation protocol (SIP) is a prime enabler of presence and is important in developing intersystem compatibility for instant messaging systems. The SIP protocol is designed to set up and tear down sessions between two or more devices. These sessions can be for voice, instant messaging, videoconferencing, and audioconferencing. SIP translates names and locations so that users' devices can "find" each other and be aware of availability. For example, it translates john.doe@company-mail.com to John. If John Doe is working from a remote location and is logged into the corporate network, it translates his new address so that messages reach him. The SIP protocol is device independent. It works with any device or media connected to IP networks, including videoconferencing systems and voice telephones. It also works with wireless devices.

Just as residential chat services let customers make Voice over IP calls as well as text-based chat, products geared to business users are becoming available with the same capability. For enterprises with Voice over IP telephone systems for internal use, presence indicators on telephones and personal computers alert people to the availability of someone to take a call before the call is dialed. These types of telephones are not yet prevalent in corporations.

Instant Messaging in Enterprises

According to the consultancy Osterman Research, Inc., about 92% of North American businesses use instant messaging. This statistic was reported in the July 15, 2004 *Wall Street Journal* article "Microsoft to Link Message System with Yahoo, AOL" by Daniel Nasaw. Instant messaging has become so popular that people commonly use the term "IM" as a readily understood acronym. For example, staff on a phone call can tell a customer or business partner that he or she needs to IM someone for an answer to a question. Systems have lists of names of people with whom staff members communicate. Next to each name is an availability indicator; a red button indicates unavailability, green signifies availability, and half green and half red means do not disturb. Instant messaging is faster than e-mail and less intrusive than a telephone call.

However, many companies still use free residential products from companies such as AOL and MSN. Nevertheless, requirements for security, protection from viruses, and federal laws mandating archiving e-mail messages are prompting adoption of products made specifically for commercial firms. Instant messaging providers often include instant messaging in software that they sell to enterprises. Enterprises that use private instant messaging install servers with the software. The server links to a Lightweight Directory Access Protocol (LDAP) compatible or Lotus Notes list of e-mail addresses. LDAP is a protocol that defines a standard layout for directories and a standard method of accessing them. Broadsoft, Convoq, Inc., Ipswitch, Inc., Jabber, Inc., Microsoft Corp., IBM Corp., and LiveOffice Corp. offer instant messaging to corporations.

Corporate Requirements: Archiving and Security

Institutions in health and financial services are under rules governing privacy and record keeping. Employees who use free, commercial chat service may unwittingly violate these rules. For example, privacy rules may be violated because administrators of external, residential systems have access to these messages. Instant messaging products made for enterprises enable administrators to decide which employees are allowed to use the service, filter content, and track keywords alerting them to the possibility of secrets or confidential information in chat sessions. They also check incoming and outgoing attachments for pornography and viruses. Archival capability is important for public companies that may be asked to produce records in a federal investigation. This capability is also available.

Chat—Training, Sales Support, and Presentations

Online chat software is often integrated into online collaboration, document-sharing tools for distance learning, training, and sales presentations. For example, in online sales presentations, the moderator uses PowerPoint to illustrate products or services. At some point in the presentation, the moderator signals that users can submit comments or questions. Users' comments and moderator responses appear in the bottom portion of the computer screen, and the PowerPoint demonstration is in the top. Chat technology also is used for one-to-one customer service and technical support for e-commerce applications. For example, potential customers browsing a Web site can click a chat button to start an instant messaging dialogue with a customer service representative.

Chat Protocols—Proprietary and Open

The first protocol that supported instant messaging was the Internet relay chat (IRC) protocol developed in 1988 by Jarkko Oikarinen of Finland. Later AOL, Microsoft, and Yahoo! developed proprietary instant messaging services based on the same model as IRC, the client server architecture. The Internet relay chat (IRC) protocol uses "channels" as defined by IRC. A *channel* is the path defined to carry messages to chat rooms or "buddy" lists in which everyone receives the same message. The IRC protocol defines how a group of clients (end-user computers) all receive the same message from the server to which they're all connected. Chat programs relay a message from single users to a predefined group. This is feasible because they are based on TCP/IP, which can deliver packets containing the same message to many computers. Each client that is part of the IRC group of networks downloads special client Internet relay chat software.

Prior to the commercialization of chat by AOL and Yahoo!, chat networks such as EFNet, DALNet, and the Undernet were used by thousands of people who logged on through their Internet service provider. Users of IRC typed computer commands such as **/join#Newbies** to join the Newbies chat group. In the mid-1990s, organizations developed proprietary chat software that was easier to use but did not initially interoperate with each other. Currently, except for AOL, many providers have made their services compatible with each other.

Interoperable Instant Messaging Between Businesses

Businesses take it for granted that they can seamlessly exchange e-mail messages worldwide. This is not the case with instant messaging services. For the most part, current chat software platforms are internal only. Some are also included in Web site products to enable chat between customers browsing a Web site and the company.

The Internet Engineering Task Force (IETF) has approved a SIP-based instant messaging standard called the session initiation protocol for instant messaging (SIMPLE). Instant messaging systems that use SIMPLE are able to communicate with each other. The IETF is developing a standard for presence, which SIMPLE does not address. People using different instant messaging systems would be able to "chat," but they would not have status indicators. The XMPP (extensible messaging and presence protocol) is another protocol with specifications for presence, message routing, and security. It is an open standard that is free and has been ratified by the IETF. It is the basis for the Jabber, Inc. product.

Blogs—Web Logs

Web logging is the capability to create personal, stripped down Web pages, called blogs. Web logs (blogs) can be personal journals, or they can be built around specific topics such as political candidates, technology, and food. Some are a combination of diaries and opinions on topics. For instance, people use them to keep extended family members updated. Blogs often influence public opinion. During the 2004 United States presidential election, certain blogs generated so much traffic that they attracted thousands of dollars in advertising.

Although blogs were used prior to 1999, Blogger, developed by software company Pyra Labs (now part of Google) in 1999, made it easier for people to create and post content to blogs through their browser and from within e-mail. These tools sim-plified adding and tracking content, formatting, linking blogs to other sites, and archiving content. Other software providers developed blog software. Moveable Type and Life Journal are examples. Some of these firms supply hosting as well as soft-ware. Blogs also often have multimedia content such as digital photographs or videos.

In addition, many of the products have a comment facility. People can e-mail com-ments that appear on the blog site. Unlike chat sites, these posts are permanent comments unless the blogger deletes them. In addition, blog sites can accommodate many more people than most discussion groups, newsgroups (Usenet), and mailing lists.

Dan Bricklin, founder of Software Garden and co-creator of the spreadsheet program VisiCalc, has been blogging since 1999, primarily to provide a platform for his writing and additionally to keep his family up-to-date on his activities. Dan made the following comment about blogs on November 8, 2004:

> *"If there's some interesting thing happening, there's probably someone writing about it who knows what they're talking about. There are also many people writing who don't know what they're talking about. Part of blogging's attraction is that we're listening to a real person and over time developing a familiarity with that person. Blogs are continual over time with real people."*

Distributing Content from News Sites and Blogs: Really Simple Syndication (RSS)

Really Simple Syndication (RSS) is a series of software standards that automates feeding updates from news sites such as Forbes.com and blogs to other sites and users. The use of RSS means that people don't have to continually check to see news headlines or updates to blogs. To provide a link to their site, blog owners provide a button on their site that their readers can click to download a program that notifies them when the blog has been updated.

In addition to RSS feeds for individual sites, blog aggregators such as Bloglines use RSS. Aggregators provide links to many different blogs, which are organized by topic. To use Bloglines, users download a small program to their desktop or browser. The program periodically sends queries to Bloglines and notifies users when there are updates to the blogs in which users have expressed an interest. Bloglines has the entire Web log at its site. It doesn't send traffic to individual blogs. In most cases, these links can be provided without users divulging e-mail addresses. People who set up feeds from news sources need an RSS reader program, which is often free.

Wired.com and Forbes.com are examples of news sites that offer RSS feeds. Other sites that want new headlines plus the first few lines of a story on their Web page

click on the RSS button to set up a "feed." Once set up, people browsing the site with the feed (channel), such as Netscape.com, can click on the headline to be transferred to the original story. These are examples of *syndication*, making content available to other providers. The goal of making just the headlines and first few lines available is to increase readership at the primary news site. These news sources can also be put into a format compatible with personal digital assistants (PDAs), mailing lists, wireless phones, and set-top boxes to increase readership even further. RSS is also used to send Internet-based radio programs to portable music players.

Really Simple Syndication (RSS) is based on the extensible markup language (XML). XML is a software language that was developed to make it easy for disparate computers to exchange information. XML uses tags to identify fields of data. The <title> tag tells the site that this is the field with the news headline. The <link> tag notifies the computer that the Web address field is next. The <description> field typically includes the first few lines of the article or blog entry. Using RSS with XML automates the update process in a way that works between different types of computers.

INTERNET ADDRESSES ....

Network routers route messages based on their domain name. Domain names are part of uniform resource locators (URLs) such as www.yahoo.com or e-mail addresses such as *yourname*@earthlink.net. In these two examples, yahoo.com and earthlink.net are domain names. Computers on the Internet called domain name servers translate domain names into Internet protocol (IP) 32-bit IP addresses (such as 123.444.52.323) so that they can be routed to their destination. To avoid duplication, the most common domain names are administered by central organizations.

The Internet Corporation for Assigned Names and Numbers (ICANN) appoints organizations to assign and keep track of domain names and approves the creation of new top-level domain names. Top-level domain names can be generic (such as .com) or country specific (such as .uk for the United Kingdom). There are 242 country code top-level domain names (ccTLDs).

In January 1993, the National Science Foundation had assigned Network Solutions, Inc. (now part of VeriSign) the tasks of registering Internet names, assigning addresses, and managing the database of names. VeriSign manages the master lists of .com and .net. It runs a master directory of Internet sites that route .com and .net traffic. Other companies register names for end users. VeriSign sold the part of Network Solutions that registered names for end users to Pivotal Private Equity. The nonprofit Public Interest Registry (PIR) is the registry operator for .org, the top-level domain name used by nonprofit organizations.

ICANN approves companies to be registries and registrars.

- *Registries* manage the entire database for top-level domain names such as .org. They may also sell domain names to end users. There is only one registry per top-level domain name.
- *Registrars* sell domain names to end-user customers. However, they don't manage the database for all of a particular top-level domain name. There are many registrars for each top-level domain name.

Registries—Management of Entire Top-Level Domains

Registries keep track of and manage databases of domain names. VeriSign manages the database and registry of top-level domain names .net and .com. For example, if an organization or individual requests a particular domain name, the registrar checks the master database for availability. The database contains information about networks, domain names, and the contacts for each domain name. VeriSign's .net registry agreement with the U.S. Department of Commerce expires June 30, 2005.

Other top-level domain names include .edu and .mil for educational and military institutions. .gov is for the government. There are other top-level domain names for businesses: .info, .biz, .us, .name, .coop, .aero, .museum, and .pro. Limited numbers are in use.

Registrars—Assigning Domain Names to Organizations

Registrars have been approved by ICANN to buy banks of names at a discount from registry organizations. Registrars are responsible for gathering the technical information on which each domain name they register is located. They pay fees of about $6 to companies such as VeriSign and NeuLevel for each address they assign within a domain. Customers pay an annual fee to registrars to keep their domain registration up-to-date.

Thirteen Root Servers Worldwide— The Basis for Internet Routing

The *domain naming system* (*DNS*) is the umbrella name of the Internet's capability to translate alpha characters to numeric IP addresses. Carriers and organizations send traffic addressed to locations outside their networks to one of 13 *root servers*, usually the one nearest to them to determine where to route these messages. The root servers, which are massive databases, translate alphabetic hostnames (aol.com) into numeric IP addresses (193.22.1.126) and vice versa. Hostnames are the names of the host computers to which messages are addressed, essentially the domain name.

Each of the 13 root servers is designated by one of the first 13 characters of the Latin alphabet. The University of Maryland operates the D root server, and Reseaux IP Europeens Network Coordination Centre (RIPE) operates the K root server. The root servers are updated from registries' lists of top-level domains and country code domain names, maintained on registries' servers.

The Criticality of Root Servers

The Internet cannot function without root servers. Root servers are critical for reliability, capacity, and survivability, in addition to accurate routing. In 2002, a denial of service attack in which massive numbers of messages were directed at root servers brought down a portion of the Internet. To lessen vulnerability to these attacks, the software on which the domain naming system (DNS) is based has been upgraded.

Each root server has multiple servers at various sites. RIPE, which operates the K root server, has servers in nine cities across Europe and in Qatar. The following is from their January 27, 2004 news release. The section in quotes is from RIPE's Chief Technology Officer Andrei Robachevsky. (Anycast is the protocol that enables the server with the most recent updates from registries' databases to automatically update all servers.)

> *Anycast allows exact copies of the server, including the name and IP address, to be deployed in different locations . . . . "Our strategy is to deploy servers at multiple locations where there is a lot of Internet connectivity."*

The root name server system was developed and implemented in the 1990s. The late Jon Postel developed and oversaw the creation of the root server system. To keep up with growth, many new servers have been added, in particular to locations outside of the United States.

Assignments of Numeric IP Addresses to ISPs and Carriers

Registry bodies such as the American Registry for Internet Numbers (ARIN) assign numeric IP addresses to ISPs and other organizations. ARIN assigns numeric IP addresses in North and South America, the Caribbean, and sub-Saharan Africa. ISPs keep lists of IP addresses. They use them to route traffic to customers who don't have their own domain names (username@AOL.com). Asia Pacific Network Information Center (APNIC) and Reseaux IP Europeens (RIPE) manage numeric IP addresses for Asia and Europe, respectively.

Public and Private IP Addresses

To conserve IP addresses, organizations and ISPs use private IP addresses on their internal networks. (Public IP addresses point to an organization. Private IP addresses specify particular users or devices within organizations.) Private addresses also protect internal devices from hackers who don't know the private address and thus can't reach internal computers without being screened by firewalls.

PORTALS, SEARCH ENGINES, AND E-COMMERCE ....

Portals were developed to act as gateways to other sites on the Internet. In the early stages of the Internet, navigating the Web was crude and finding information laborious. Portals like Lycos (now Terra Lycos) and Yahoo! hoped to attract visitors by providing easily navigated links to resources. The goal was to earn revenue from advertising and a percentage on the sale of goods sold at the portal. Search sites have improved, and some offer services indistinguishable from portals. Both search engines and portals are key vehicles for directing consumers to Web addresses where they can make online purchases of both products and services. Differences between search sites and portals are blurring.

Portals—The Door to the Internet

Web sites that offer a host of services, news, and search capabilities are considered portals, a point from which to surf the Web or use a variety of services. Locations started as strictly search engines and sites begun as portals or home pages for ISPs have many portal functions. For example, Microsoft's Internet Explorer and AOL's Netscape browsers can both function as users' home pages. They, along with Yahoo!, AOL, and Google, attempt to attract large numbers of users and keep them there by offering e-mail, content, discussion groups, search engines, Web hosting, instant messaging, calendaring, and chat services.

Just as search engines are branching out, so too are organizations like Yahoo! and Terra Lycos that started out as portals. Rather than earn all their revenue from advertising, sites now offer services for fees and have purchased companies that specialize in niche areas such as personals and interactive games. However, ad revenues still count for a major portion of revenues. In the second quarter of 2004, 83% of

Yahoo!'s total revenue was from advertising. See the section "Electronic Commerce" later in this chapter for descriptions of key subscription- and fee-based services.

Top Web Sites—Increased Influence of Conglomerates and Large Organizations

In the early days of the World Wide Web, there were many small startups offering innovative services. Many of them have failed or been purchased. However, competition is keeping innovation strong. Just as major corporations control movie studios, broadcast networks, cable networks, newspapers, and telecommunications services, conglomerates now own popular Internet sites (see Table 7.1). Microsoft is the largest software company in the United States. Time Warner owns Time Warner Cable, HBO, Warner Brothers, and Time-Warner Music. Disney owns ABC. Moreover, independent companies such as Yahoo!, Ebay, and InterActiveCorp have each grown by acquisition. For example, eBay purchased e-payment company PayPal plus a string of auction firms. Yahoo! bought HotJobs and Broadcast.com as well as search software firms Keikoo, Overture, and Inktomi plus others. Amazon, Google, Yahoo!, and eBay are major success stories. It is becoming more difficult for a startup to become a major presence on the Internet next to these conglomerates and successful innovators.

Table 7.1 Top 10 Parent Companies, Month Ending October 2004,   Residential Surfers

Parent Organizations	Comments
MSN-Microsoft sites	Software giant Microsoft owns MSN and 50% of MSNBC, which provides news coverage. GE owns most of the rest of MSNBC. MSN is an Internet service provider. Hotmail is its e-mail service. Its premium e-mail, available for a monthly fee, includes access to Microsoft's Encarta encyclopedia.
Time Warner	Time Warner's Internet division, AOL, is the largest provider of dial-up Internet access. It owns Mapquest, Love.com, and Moviefone. AOL offers broadband users ISP service for a monthly fee, which includes Time Warner content such as CNN, music, and HBO. AOL has service in Europe, Latin America, and Japan.
Yahoo!	A global portal provider with 2004 sales of $3.58 billion and subsidiaries that operate portals in Asia, Latin America, and Europe. Its Web-site offerings include Yahoo! autos, search, and personals. Its properties include HotJobs, MusicMatch, and Overture, a search firm.

continues

Table 7.1 Top 10 Parent Companies, Month Ending October 2004, Residential Surfers (continued)

Parent Organizations	Comments
Google	In addition to searching, Google offers blogging, e-mail, and shopping. It licenses its search services to other companies as well as using them at its own site. Its services are offered globally.
eBay	Hosts online auctions and charges fees for listing and selling items. It owns PayPal. PayPal acts as an intermediary between credit card companies and purchasers and sellers so that people aren't required to give credit card information to sellers. eBay has business-to-business auctions and virtual storefronts for retailers.
United States government	Nielson/NetRatings reported that the Mount St. Helens volcanic eruption in October 2004 caused traffic increases at government sites. Popular government sites include the White House, the copyright office, and the federal jobs site.
Amazon.com	The biggest online retailer, it has expanded from books into CDs, DVDs, and videos as well as a variety of other retail products. Customers purchase merchandise from many retailers at Amazon.com. It also runs the Borders and Toys R Us Web sites.
IAC/InterActiveCorp	Owner of Ticketmaster, CitySearch, and travel sites Expedia, Hotels.com, Hotwire, and Interval International. Also owns Evite, Match.com (personals), and Home Shopping Network plus others. IAC is in the process of purchasing Ask Jeeves Inc. Majority owned by Barry Diller, formerly head of QVC and USA Networks.
Ask Jeeves	Operates search sites such as Ask Jeeves, ask.com, and Ask Jeeves for Kids in the United States and other countries. 70% of its revenue is from Google for placement of ads that Google has sold to advertisers. These ads are placed on Jeeves sites. It also owns portals iWon.com, Myway.com, and Excite.com through its acquisition of Interactive Search holdings. Has signed an agreement to be purchased by IAC/InterActiveCorp.
Walt Disney Internet Group	Formerly called Go.com, controls DisneyBlast.com, FamilyFun.com, ESPN.com, ABC.com, ABCNEWS.com, and ToonTown.com. The Internet Group is part of The Walt Disney Company.

Source Nielsen//NetRatings

Search Engines—Vehicles for Advertising Revenue

A search engine is a site that seeks information on the Internet based on words that users enter. The two most popular search engines are Google, which in 2004 handled 36% of Internet searches, and Yahoo!, which handled 29%, according to research firm comScore Media. Many Internet sites originally devoted to other functions, such as yellow pages or retailing, now incorporate search as an added inducement to attract traffic. The capability to attract traffic is the key ingredient of search engines' capability to generate revenue. In addition, because many consumers check out search engines before making purchases, retailers spend millions of dollars determining keywords and phrases to use on their sites that will cause them to be ranked high in search engines so that consumers will click through to them and make purchases.

Competition and Services to Attract Visitors

The field of search has become more competitive as organizations recognize its popularity and capability to attract advertisers. Microsoft first started offering its search service in late 2004. The company plans to integrate its search engine into its browser and e-mail programs. This could increase the number of people using its search engine. In addition, it will be easy for Microsoft to steer users to its own music site, MSN Music. Moreover, increasing competition and a desire for increased revenues has led organizations that initially offered primarily search to branch out to extra offerings. Google has stated that its goal is to organize information for users, such as organizing users' PC desktops and providing e-mail at Google's site.

The following are services offered at various search sites:

- Blogs—Software that users can use to create personal Web-based journals.
- Shopping—Yahoo! and Google offer comparison shopping for specified products and services; Amazon offers access to items from multiple retailers that users can search for and purchase while at Amazon.
- Telephone directories and yellow pages.
- Social networking—Personal listings for matchmaking.
- PC searching—Software that searches users' own computers.
- E-mail—Yahoo!, Google, and Microsoft.
- Photo sharing.

- News—At Google, certain searches trigger an option to scan recent headlines about the topic. Users can click on any headline to view the entire article.

- Local searches—People can search for weather, restaurants, and movie listings for their own localities.

All the major search organizations have sites in countries worldwide. In addition, search results can often be translated into multiple languages.

Paid Inclusions—Fees That Raise Ranking in Search Results Versus Context-Sensitive Ads

Web searching is the most popular online activity after e-mail, according to the November 11, 2004 *Wall Street Journal Online* article "Growth Engine Microsoft, Late to Search Party, Seeks to Capture Google's Turf" by Robert A. Guth and Kevin J. Delaney. Large numbers of consumers select online shopping sites through search engines. Many search engines capitalize on this and charge companies a fee for a high-ranking placement in search results. For example, when someone searches for a retail product, the responses to the query will be listed in descending order depending on fees paid to the search engine. Yahoo! charges for listings but only in its searches for retail products. Some search engines also get paid every time a user clicks on a link to a sponsor's site. Other search engines such as Google do not accept paid listings. They do accept advertising, but their ranking is based on the results of their searches and is independent of the advertising.

In 2002, the FTC (Federal Trade Commission) issued guidelines that called for search sites to clearly distinguish between paid rankings and nonpaid results. A study conducted by *Consumer Reports*' Consumer WebWatch found that the majority of search engines did not follow these guidelines. For example, Yahoo! provided disclosure through a small "about this page" link. The report praised Google for clearly delineating its paid ads. These results were reported in *eWeek* on November 10, 2004 in the article "Study: Paid Search Disclosure Lacks Transparency" by Ryan Naraine.

Google's context-sensitive ads are clearly separate from search results. Google derives a large majority of its revenue from context-sensitive advertising on its own site and on partners' sites. Context-sensitive advertising brings up ads for products and services related to users' searches. These ads appear to the right of the search results. Site visitors who click on ads are sent to the Web site of the sponsoring organization. In context advertising, sponsors select words that trigger their ads when searches are conducted using the selected words.

The Technology Behind Search Engines

Search engines create databases of either the first page of a Web site or all of the sites' pages through automated software programs called spiders or bots (short for robots). (These are different terms for the same process.) A *spider* will "crawl" from site to site looking for key phrases or URLs. When it completes the search, it creates indexes (lists) of the pages. When people do searches, it lists them in a particular order using proprietary algorithms. The order in which pages are listed is called *ranking*. Factors used in ranking include how frequently terms are used, the location of terms within the document (in the title or in the headers and so on), and the number of pages at a site that use the term searched for. Other external factors may be used, such as how many other sites link to the site and how often visitors "click" on a site (visit it). Placement fees discussed previously are also a factor at many sites.

When users request a search, they are often searching Web pages located on search sites' computers. The computers are located in clusters at server farms at hosting sites on the Internet. Search engines "crawl" the Web continuously looking for new and updated Web sites. (*Crawling* is the use of a software program to automatically search the Web.) Google has publicly stated that it has more than 10,000 computers with Web pages.

Search engines use a combination of page ranking, relevancy, and proprietary mathematical algorithms. The page-ranking system looks at other pages that link to particular sites. For example, if someone does a query on restaurants in Spain, the engine looks at and ranks restaurants based partially on how many sites link to it and the type of sites linking to it. For example, a *New York Times* link ranks higher than a link from a personal Web page. The proprietary mathematical equation analyzes the links to the page and looks at the text on the page— the headlines, the bolding, and the proximity of words to each other for relevancy of text or data on the page. This validation is important because it eliminates the possible "spam" effect of sites sending thousands of the same messages to a search site. Ask Jeeves uses relevancy in addition to page ranking. Relevancy-based searches look at the likely credibility of the site to the search. This technology was developed by software firm Teoma, which Ask Jeeves purchased.

Search engines are also meta based and natural language based.

- Meta-based search engines, such as Dogpile.com and MetaCrawler, search multiple search engines and compile them into a list for searchers.

- Spider-based search engines perform searches using automated software programs. Yahoo!, Google, and LookSmart use spiders plus mathematical algorithms.

- Ask Jeeves and Microsoft's Underdog services use a natural language search engine in which people can ask questions in everyday sentences or phrases. Microsoft uses its own Encarta encyclopedia as one source for its answers.

ELECTRONIC COMMERCE ....

Advancements in and development of electronic commerce depend to a great extent on the adoption of broadband Internet access. Although it is possible to surf the Internet and use e-mail with a dial-up connection, response times are so slow that shopping, searching, and getting news online can be tedious. Having high-speed access helps makes the Internet part of how people communicate, get their news, and shop. Companies that have attracted the most customers on the Internet have added something unique that's not available at bricks-and-mortar retail sites. For example, Amazon.com enhances its site with purchasers' reviews. In addition, it offers, as do many e-retailers, the capability to easily sort offerings by topic and listen to short music clips. Amazon.com also developed unique offerings such as the capability to search text inside books for key terms and to read sample pages of books. Web-based personals didn't gain mass appeal until digital cameras made it simple for people to post their photographs so that people could see what potential dates look like. Match-making sites are now starting to accept video clips. These enhancements clearly demonstrate the power of electronic commerce.

Advertising on the Web—
Instant Access to Offers

In the early days of the World Wide Web, experts believed that the Web would operate similarly to television in which ad revenue paid for programming. That model certainly applies to search sites and portals like Google and Yahoo!. According to the November 18, 2004 *Wall Street Journal* article "Microsoft Targets Web-Ad Business" by Kevin J. Delaney and Robert A. Guth, search-related ads generated $1 billion in the second quarter of 2004. The article stated that this is the fastest growing segment of online advertising.

While still only a little more than 3% of total U.S. ad spending in 2004, online advertising is growing at double-digit rates. According to research firm eMarketer, Inc., online ad spending grew at 28.8% in 2004 while the overall ad industry grew at 7.7%. These statistics reflect industries' recognition of the increasing significance of the Internet in purchasing decisions. According to *BusinessWeek Online*'s November 22, 2004 Special Report article "The Online Ad Surge" by Stephen Baker, Ford Motor has moved 10% of its ad budget to the Internet. Large consumer goods producers

Procter & Gamble, Kellogg, Kraft Foods, and Nestle are also moving some of their ad dollars to the Internet.

The Advantage of Being Electronic

In addition, the Internet has a key advantage over newspapers, current television, and magazines. It is interactive and immediate. Consumers can make impulse purchases the moment they see an ad or receive a promotional e-mail with links to retailers' sites. Television and print media depend on raising consumers' brand awareness by repeating advertising in multiple media outlets over time. However, a compelling Internet ad can prompt an immediate purchase without risking a consumer changing his or her mind before acting on an impulse by calling a toll-free number or visiting a retail outlet.

The Internet also provides a way for sponsors to measure the effectiveness of advertising campaigns even if they are not conducted over the Internet. For example, corporations can track the number of people who visit their sites (the number of hits) when they embark on new print, television, or radio campaigns. The effectiveness of ads placed on the Internet at search firms and portals can be calculated by the amount of traffic generated. These measurements provide virtually instantaneous feedback. Prior to the Internet, enterprises often had to manually track response rates in the form of telephone calls and mail-in response cards.

Impact of Technology on Entertaining Ads

Improved compression, higher rates of broadband adoption, and more capacity in Web servers have increased the viability of multimedia advertising. Web-based advertising, which first appeared in 1994, is using more creativity to engage surfers to "click-through" to sponsors' sites. Advertisers such as American Express, BMW, and Ford Motor have hired top directors to produce entertaining short films. These films, made expressly for the Web, attempt to hold viewers' attention for longer than the length of standard television commercials. Amazon.com is featuring short films on its site. People who purchase items mentioned in the film receive a 5% discount on these purchases. Ads with animation and video are referred to as *rich-media* ads. The first multimedia ad to gain nationwide attention was sponsored by Victoria's Secret, which promoted it during the 1999 Super Bowl. The response to the ad, which featured scantily clad models, was so high that the ad's site could not keep up with the traffic. In addition, the slow dial-up Internet connections prevalent at that time resulted in poor video quality and small images.

Popular E-commerce Sites

The percentage of purchases made over the Web is small compared to the number of transactions at stores. However, according to Gartner Group, at least 40% of shoppers research products, especially electronics, online before they make a purchase. Thus, the Internet influences purchasing decisions. In addition, people spend money on services such as subscriptions, online games, gambling, and pornography. The Internet is a vehicle for new types of purchases such as auctions and purchases of used books. The presence of major retailers, including Wal-Mart, Dell, Target, Best Buy, and Sears, is indicative of the realization by retailers that the Internet is an important sales channel. These retailers are developing synergy between their Web sites and stores. For example, many of them make coupons available online and allow people to purchase items online and pick them up or return them at stores.

Table 7.2 illustrates the most popular retail sites.

Table 7.2   Most Popular U.S. Web Retailers in October 2004

Web Site	Visitors in October
eBay	60,327,000
Amazon.com	37,488.000
Wal-Mart	19,050,000
Dell	12,944,000
Target	12,863,000
Overstock.com	12,287,000
Hewlett-Packard	10,158,000
Apple Computer	10,137,000
Best Buy	8,179,000
Sears (includes Lands' End)	7,640,000

Source: comScore Networks, Inc. published in the November 25, 2004 washingtonpost.com article "The Sites Before Christmas" by Leslie Walker.

Gambling

Because of the compulsive nature of gambling, online gamblers are often more likely to spend money than people who shop online. According to the June 8, 2004 article "More Gamblers Flock to the Web" by Peter Grant in the *Wall Street Journal Online*,

Christiansen Capital expects 2004 worldwide revenue to be $7.46 billion. Other than horse racing, which is legal in 18 states, most gambling sites are controlled outside of the United States. Laws in the United States are unclear. The 1961 Wire Wager Act prohibits the use of telephone lines for gambling. Most courts have interpreted this act to apply to the Internet. However, in 2001 a federal appeals court said that this act does not apply to casino bets placed on the Internet. The United States Department of Justice is appealing the decision. Meanwhile, some credit card companies do not accept payments for gambling. The largest percentage of gambling is in conjunction with sporting events. The 2004 National Basketball Association playoffs attracted about $85 million alone.

Pornography

Online pornography was the first application on the Internet to generate profits through subscription-based services. In the United States, online pornography, which generated $1 billion in 2000, doubled in the short time span of only two years to $2 billion in 2003. The 2003 statistics were published in *USA Today* on March 9, 2004 in "Online porn often leads high-tech way" by Jon Swartz. The paper's source was *Adult Video News*. The year 2000 statistics were published April 24, 2001 in *AlterNet* in its article "All Porn, All the Time" by Don Hazen. In addition, in the United States, adult content receives more traffic, 18% of all Web traffic, than search sites. *Web optimizer* published these statistics on June 7, 2004 in the article "Online porn 'more popular than search engines'." No author was listed. The statistic was attributed to Hitwise, a California-based online measurement company.

In addition to generating revenue and drawing traffic, adult programming sites pioneered the use of multimedia and electronic-billing technologies as well as antipirating software to protect their content from thefts. Pornography sites not only charge monthly fees, they also assess per-minute charges for video clips. This innovative fee structure could potentially be copied by mainstream entertainment venues. For example, offering visitors movie clips of classic movies.

Interactive Online Games

According to DFC Intelligence, a market research firm specializing in interactive entertainment, the worldwide market for online games will be $2.2 to $2.3 billion in 2004 and is expected to grow significantly, spurred by growth in broadband Internet access. The country with the highest penetration of broadband, South Korea, is the leader in online game purchases. Online gaming grew slowly until broadband was more widely deployed in the early 2000s. High-speed Internet is required for acceptable video quality on interactive features in which players compete against each other.

Broadband access enables *massively multiplayer online games (MMOGs)* to be played by thousands of players simultaneously. Many players use headsets to speak with other players during games.

When online games were first available, the only way to access them was from a personal computer. Online games can now be played directly from a personal computer or from a game console with a network adapter (Ethernet port) and cable connected to a DSL or cable modem. A game console is a proprietary hardware platform with software used only for games developed and/or licensed by particular corporations such as Sony, Microsoft, and GameCube. Sony Online Entertainment, with its PlayStation, and Microsoft, with XBox consoles, are the leading publishers of games. Companies such as Electronic Arts develop games for consoles; however, they pay royalties to make them compatible with and used on particular consoles.

Whether accessed from a personal computer or a console, playing games requires the purchase of gaming software plus monthly subscription fees. Game software is sold online in downloadable formats and at retail outlets. It often includes a free one-month trial online subscription. Playing games online changes the experience from an individual effort to one that can be played in teams and with thousands of other players.

The online game market has similarities to book publishing. Distribution is key in both markets for gaining recognition and market share. Yahoo! sells both subscription-based games and downloadable game software. RealNetworks is expanding into games, and AOL and MSN distribute games. Many broadband providers such as Deutsche Telecom, Comcast, RCN, and Bell Canada make online games available on their sites as well. Broadband and portal providers are recognizing the importance of content in attracting users. For example, AOL and Comcast are two of the largest investors in new online game developer Exent.

In a manner similar to the book industry, individual games can be blockbusters that deliver continuing revenue streams. According to David Cole, president of DFC:

> *"Online games can earn more than a big budget movie. For over five years, Sony Online Entertainment's game EverQuest has had 400,000 to 500,000 subscribers. Customers purchase the software for $50, buy add-ons, and pay monthly subscription fees of $13 for the online-only game."*

Start-up NCsoft earns over $100 million annually in sales of its game *Lineage* in South Korea. Teenagers are the mainstay of online games, and they tend to play for long periods of time.

In addition to games that require special software, there are games for adults who tend to be casual users. These attract adults, particularly women, to games such as Scrabble, solitaire, poker, card games, and Mah Jong. Some of these are subsidized by advertising, and others charge fees to play in a competitive setting. These are often developed using multimedia Java-based software such as Flash or Shockwave and require Java-based browser plug-ins. Java is a computer language developed by Sun that can be used on any computer platform. The plug-ins are software code that enable the computer to use the online game.

Corporations and the military are in the early stages of using simulations to incorporate online games for training that involves problem-solving challenges. Rather than having adults passively read or attend class, this software challenges adults to use critical thinking to solve real-world problems. They do this by enacting real-world challenges to which players respond by developing strategies and tactics.

Privacy Concerns, Commerce, and National Security

The war against terrorism, copyright protection, and e-commerce market research often conflict with privacy and free speech on the Internet. The nature of the Internet is such that people who send e-mail and surf the Internet leave an electronic trail of sorts. In addition, Internet service providers have access to servers in which they store many (but not all) of their customers' messages. Online service providers also keep data logs for anywhere from a few days to a month that help them bill for usage and track network troubles. In most cases, these logs track the date, time, and information identifying users associated with each online session. Governments can request that providers give them access to these messages and logs through subpoenas, warrants, or court orders. Various congressional acts define circumstances—for example, suspected terrorism, copyright infringement, or hacker attacks—that give governments rights to this information.

Moreover, governments, in their fights against terrorism, often develop large databases in which they compile profiles of people. The United States government also is working with Internet network providers to develop ways to eavesdrop on suspects' e-mail and instant messages. Citizens worldwide hope that these government activities are performed in good faith against true enemies and not political opponents. Individual corporations have also used the courts to investigate, prosecute, and fire employees who send malicious e-mail messages about the company, give away corporate secrets, or publish unfavorable Web pages about the business.

Concerns about privacy can have a negative impact on e-commerce. When people use credit cards to make purchases on the Internet (or in retail outlets), sellers have the capability to establish large databases with information that tracks people's purchasing history. Credit card companies also keep huge databases with purchase histories and personal identities. These databases, if not secure, can be hacked into.

Consumers are aware that computer systems are vulnerable to hackers and are sometimes leery of leaving private information on the Internet. The following are examples of and explanations of some of the ways personal information can be tracked:

- *Cookie software.* Sites visited by a user can add a small text file to the visitor's browser that identifies the user's unique browser to the site. The cookie is used for password authentication so that people are not required to type in passwords each time they visit sites to which they subscribe. Other information, along with the cookie, is recorded at sites. This includes users' Internet address, date and time, and browser type. In addition, the URL of every page visited, which at search sites includes the information searched for, is recorded. For the most part, however, cookies do not divulge site users' e-mail addresses. If a corporate user's Internet address includes her e-mail address, then the site knows the user's identity.

- *Online registration and contest form*s. Telephone numbers, e-mail addresses, and home and business addresses are collected from online forms. This information is associated with the preceding cookie information, and these sites can associate people's real identities, if they fill out registration forms truthfully, with their cookie. Depending on privacy policies at Web sites, these are frequently put into demographic databases by companies and sold to direct marketers.

- *Set-top boxes with TiVo-like capability.* Cable TV and satellite TV providers have the capability to monitor and capture information about the viewing habits of their customers who have personal video recorders. Personal video recorders are set-top devices with hard discs that let users schedule recording of television shows and play back the shows minus the commercials. (Refer to Chapter 6 for more information on personal video recorders.)

- *HTML e-mail.* E-mail "bugs" can be embedded in HTML e-mail (described previously), which enables marketers to send e-mail with the look and feel of Web pages with multimedia formats. The software bugs tell marketing companies if users opened the e-mail message. The bugs also send marketing firms copies of the e-mail and comments added to it if it is forwarded to others. The bug also can be planted in e-mail that looks like it is plain text only. (Users can disable this JavaScript feature in their Netscape or Explorer browsers, but they will lose the capability to receive mail in the HTML format.)

- *Powerful databases.* Customer information technology firms offer online services in which, for a fee, direct marketers purchase lists built around certain types of consumers.

- *The "wired" universe.* People hack into computers containing personal information. As systems acquire more sophisticated security, hackers increase their own break-in capabilities. For example, in 2005 hackers broke into files at major retailers, a college, a stock broker, credit companies, and a compiler of consumer credit ratings.

IP GEOLOCATION TO ENABLE TARGETED MARKETING, FRAUD PREVENTION, AND REGULATORY COMPLIANCE

Unlike telephone numbers used on circuit switched networks, IP addresses do not provide geographic information about the origination of traffic. This makes it difficult for Web sites that cover large countries or international markets to target advertising to particular localities and to adhere to tax and gambling regulation variations. It also makes it hard to track the source of phishing schemes and fraudulent credit card purchases.

IP geolocation software traces the physical location down to the metropolitan area of the 1.4 billion IP addresses, many of them continually changing, used in core routers. These IP addresses do not disclose a person's identity. Knowing the physical location of people's IP addresses lets governments and corporations do the following:

- Display content in the correct language automatically without asking users to click on a particular language.

- Offer only particular drugs that are legal in the potential customer's country; for example, certain drugs are legal in Canada but not in the United States.

- Do further checks on online purchases made from suspicious locations; for example, someone using a California credit card attempting to make a purchase from Florida, Russia, or Nigeria, or people using the same card within a few minutes of each other in different locales.

- Help governments find phishing rings. Banks that know they were recently hit by phishing attacks collect IP addresses of users that usually access accounts locally but that now access them from a different locale. Banks can spot activity hotspots, which often indicate locations of fraud rings.

continues

IP GEOLOCATION TO ENABLE TARGETED MARKETING, FRAUD PREVENTION, AND REGULATORY COMPLIANCE (CONTINUED)

Banks gather IP addresses associated with suspected fraud and give governments the Internet service providers from which these attempts originated. The ISP can check its data logs to help identify credit fraud and identity theft perpetrators. Data logs contain the time and date and usually the identity of surfers. Phishing schemes are used to steal credit card and other user identity information by sending e-mails pretending to be from legitimate financial and retail institutions. (Refer to previous sections for information on ISPs' data logs and phishing.)

IP geolocation software firms such Quova, Inc. essentially create maps of the Internet with the location of IP addresses assigned to each carrier worldwide. They do this in a number of ways. They gather addresses from registries that give out domain names. In addition, Quova traces routes that bits take by sending out multiple data bits that return to Quova. The returned bits indicate all the routers through which they traveled and addresses associated with these routers.

Quova also gathers information on how different carriers label their routers and structure their network. They use this information to create mathematical algorithms to perform these tasks. Staff analyze the results. Quova's systems are well over 99.9% accurate at the country level and about 94% accurate at the state level. Its software is located on servers at customers where it is automatically updated daily. Akamai and Digital Envoy also supply IP geolocation software, as do smaller startups.

Freedom of Speech, Access to Information, and Protection of Children

In 1998, the United States Congress passed the Child Online Protection Act (COPA), which makes it a crime to place commercial objectionable material on the Web where a child might view it. The law specifies that the material may be on the Web but that sites must require users to use a credit card or access number as proof of age to view the material. The law has never been put into effect. The American Civil Liberty Union challenged the act on the basis of constitutional freedom of speech issues. A lower court granted the ACLU's request to prevent COPA taking effect. However, the United States Supreme Court ruled for a fuller reconsideration of the act and sent the case back to the lower court. In the meantime, the Supreme Court kept COPA from taking effect until the lower court's fuller interpretation is complete.

In 2000, the United States Congress passed another act in which freedom of speech and access to content intersects with protecting children from pornography. It is the Children's Internet Protection Act (CIPA). CIPA only affects schools and libraries. It requires schools and libraries that participate in certain federal subsidy programs to install "technology protection measures" to block access to obscenity, child pornography, and material harmful to minors on all of their terminals used by children to access the Internet. The act also requires Internet safety policies preventing minors from accessing e-mail, unlawful activities online, and chat. The American Library Association (ALA) and the Freedom to Read Foundation challenged the constitutionality of CIPA on the basis that it does not allow libraries to make information freely available to patrons. The case went all the way to the U.S. Supreme Court, which on June 23, 2003 declared Children's Internet Protection Act (CIPA) constitutional. Lower courts had declared it unconstitutional as it applied to libraries.

Libraries and schools that don't implement filtering will lose certain federal subsidies. However, the Supreme Court justices in their written opinions and the United States Solicitor General specifically stated that libraries should unblock computer access for any adult patron who requests it. Solicitor General Theodore Olsen opened his remarks at the Supreme Court hearing by stating that any adult can ask that the filter be disabled and the librarian will comply. In addition, Justice Anthony M. Kennedy stated that he would not have approved CIPA if it applied to adults as well as to children. The following is a quote published June 23, 2003 from Justice Kennedy's opinion in United States et al. v. American Library Association, Inc., et al.:

> *"The interest in protecting young library users from material inappropriate for minors is legitimate and even compelling. . . . Given this interest, and the failure to show that adult library users' access to the material is burdened in any significant degree, the statute is not unconstitutional on its face. If some libraries do not have the capacity to unblock specific Web sites or to disable the filter or if it is shown that an adult user's election to view constitutionally protected Internet material is burdened in some other substantial way, that would be the subject for an as-applied challenge."*

INTRANETS AND EXTRANETS.................................

An *intranet* is the use of World Wide Web technology within single-site and multi-site organizations. *Extranets* extend the reach of intranets from internal-only communications to sharing documents and information for business-to-business transactions. Online education is an example of an extranet.

Intranets—Web Technology for Corporate Access

In essence, an intranet is a private Internet with a browser interface to corporate information. Employees use browsers on their PCs for applications such as collaboration on projects and looking up employee extension numbers. An intranet provides employees with access to internal information and applications. However, unlike the Internet, outside users cannot access intranet applications. Security is built into intranets so that only authorized users have access to the internal databases, applications, and documents.

Without intranets, many new applications for personal computers need to be added one at a time to each user's computer. In large corporations, this is cumbersome. Intranets have enabled enterprises to add new software without distributing the client (personal computer) piece of the software to each desktop (each PC). For example, users click on applications located on Web servers to access the program. This makes it faster for IT staffs to add applications.

Portals are available for enterprises that organize information content for users in a fashion similar to public portals. In addition, enterprises with vast amounts of information available to employees provide commercial search tools on their portals. However, access to corporate information is controlled by software restriction. Not everyone has access to all files.

Intranets are one of the applications that have added traffic to commercial, government, and nonprofits' internal networks. Browsers are "bandwidth hogs." They have color, sound, and graphics capabilities. They add traffic to local area networks (LANs), campus connections between LANs in, for example, hospitals and universities, and connections between LANs across countries and worldwide. Intranets used in multisite organizations that are available remotely use virtual private networks (VPNs) to connect remote locations to the intranet at headquarters. Virtual private networks use public data networks to provide features of private networks. These public networks are shared by multiple organizations. However, only traffic from designated users is routed to each organization. Refer to Chapter 5 for more information on VPNs.

Extranets—Web Access for Customers, Partners, and Vendors

Typically, extranet transactions are conducted with suppliers, vendors, and trading partners. They allow more limited access to applications than intranets because they are used with outside partners. Specific vendors or partners have access to only specific applications. Placing orders is one application for extranets. Access to extranets is generally password protected or password plus token. A token is a small device, usually small enough to be attached to a key ring, that generates different random numbers. Users key in the number displayed on their token plus their password to access applications.

Online banking is an example of an extranet service. Customers transfer money between accounts, pay bills, and gain instant, graphical interfaces to the status of their accounts. In addition, financial institutions save money by eliminating the need to process paper checks.

Repair reporting and online billing are examples of extranet functions. Large organizations give customers the capability to report repair problems via the Internet. After a customer logs in with his customer ID and password, he fills out a form, a trouble ticket, describing the repair problem. The trouble ticket assigns him a trouble ticket number for tracking purposes. The trouble ticket is automatically sent to the dispatch staff to be resolved. Major corporations use online billing for telecommunications services because it enables them to sort and manipulate information to determine usage patterns and often to charge back various services. For example, online billing for audioconferencing enables customers to sort bills by accounting codes that identify departments or clients. When firms send only electronic bills, they eliminate enormous costs in mailing and printing bills.

A concern with extranets is security. Extranet applications give outside organizations access to portions of organizations' databases. Authentication, integrity checks, and encryption are among the security tools for organizations that host extranets. (Refer to Chapter 5 for more information on security topics.)

- Authentication assures receivers that senders are who they claim to be and not hackers.

- Integrity checks assure the sender that no third party has inserted third-party data such as viruses that damage corporate data. Integrity checks ensure that the data is what it claims to be and not something that can harm computer files.

- Encryption scrambles the data sent so that no one except the intended recipient can read the data.

Because of these security concerns, many extranets are located at Web hosting sites. The customer has its own computer or a host-supplied computer located at the hosting company. High-speed T-3 or various OC-speed lines connect the hosting company to the Internet backbone. Often companies remotely upload or download information to their host-located computer via T-1 lines, T-3 lines, or OC (optical carrier) lines (see Chapter 5). Carriers such as NTT, AT&T, Sprint, and MCI offer hosting and extranet services. Distance learning is an example of extranet service. It provides Web-type access to educational material for school staff and customers (students). In addition to supplying extranet software, distance-learning companies offer to host the application at their own site.

DISTANCE LEARNING—THE IMPACT OF THE INTERNET ON HIGHER EDUCATION

The availability of the Internet and robust networks within universities will have a major impact on the availability of and access to learning resources worldwide. Large portions of nations' economies are used for education, and education has a major impact on innovation and workforce development. According to Matthew Pittinsky, chairman of educational online software developer Blackboard, Inc., 10% to 12% of the United States gross domestic product (GDP) is spent on education. GDP is the measure of domestic spending plus exports less imports. Online learning has the potential to enrich education, make it more widely available, and expand availability of instructional resources.

Distance learning, also called online learning, is the capability to put course materials and announcements online. For example, syllabi, course schedules, instructors' notes, grades, and exams can be added to schools' intranets and extranets. Although many U.S. colleges and universities—70% according to EDUCAUSE Center for Applied Research in Education (ECAR)—use online learning to supplement classroom teaching. The creative use of the technology to enrich education is still in its infancy. According to Karen Gage, VP for marketing at e-learning software company WebCT, most professors use the new technology to do the old tasks more efficiently. As distance learning matures, it will be used more often to improve education.

Pittinsky made the following comments in a telephone interview on November 11, 2004 about the potential of and technological challenges for online learning:

DISTANCE LEARNING—THE IMPACT OF THE
INTERNET ON HIGHER EDUCATION (CONTINUED)

"All we're talking about now is, in this world, people are busy; they're constantly moving around. There are many more demands on people's time. The classroom can only be there for 90 minutes once a week. With an online environment, you are creating a much truer vehicle for that network learning environment concept. It's a very age-old value of community.

"By network learning environment, we mean getting to a point where any teacher can access resources anyplace. It could be students posting questions at 11 p.m. on a discussion board about a reading that they don't understand, and another student sees that and responds even faster than the instructor typically does.

"Amazing digital resources are available that help teachers teach concepts in ways that telling about them can't. I saw Electoral College simulations that showed how a small shift in the popular vote in different states could create an entirely different election outcome and, when mapped with demographics, allowed a political science course to really start creating different theories and hypotheses on how elections are going to move.

"I think the number one way that technology is holding us back is multimedia and bandwidth. The experience that one can create an online environment in terms of emerging experiences such as virtual reality and other types of experiences is still limited. Just because someone has network access may not mean they have a very powerful machine. It may not be a very fast connection. The connection breaks from time to time. There's still a lot about the technology that disrupts the concept of the network, but it wouldn't even be conceivable without the network."

Distance learning is used most often as a supplement to classroom instruction rather than to replace the classroom. For example, many institutions, particularly public colleges and universities, can't accommodate all the students that need certain required courses. As a result, for many of these students, it takes more than four years to take enough of the classes they need to get a degree. Distance learning helps make courses available to more students. For example, to free up space, students can attend classes once a week instead of twice weekly and participate online for the other session.

continues

DISTANCE LEARNING—THE IMPACT OF THE INTERNET ON HIGHER EDUCATION (CONTINUED)

A major thrust in online learning is expansion worldwide. There is a tremendous potential for online learning in developing countries and other parts of the world. For example, in China, there are more students than university space to accommodate them. Once a country has a broadband network infrastructure, it can use it to expand the availability of educational resources.

Distance learning application programs are Web based and run on schools' application servers. They are generally written in common languages such as Java, which was developed by Sun. The power of Java is that any browser with a Java reader can read programs written in Java. This includes most browsers. Schools' servers access large databases containing items such as course content, tests, and grades. The application programs provide ways for professors to organize courses. E-learning programs support discussion forums and links to massive stores of online resources at libraries as well as links to other universities and community resources.

Educational software companies also have offerings in which a school's applications and databases with course material are hosted by the vendor rather than by the school. The software supplier is, in essence, an application service provider (ASP). An application service provider manages applications at colocation sites for customers. As of year-end 2004, Blackboard has more than 300 customers that pay it to install the Blackboard software on servers Blackboard manages. Each of the 300-plus schools has a dedicated server at a secure, colocation facility where Blackboard leases space. The fact that the application is at a hosted location rather than the school is transparent to students and faculty who access course material via the Internet (see Figure 7.4).

Public and Private Keys and Digital Certificates—Encryption

Unless a specific action is taken, data travels across the Internet in an unprotected, unscrambled manner. Encryption scrambles data, and decryption unscrambles it. Credit card numbers and other financial transactions need special encryption and decryption tools to protect them from being stolen.

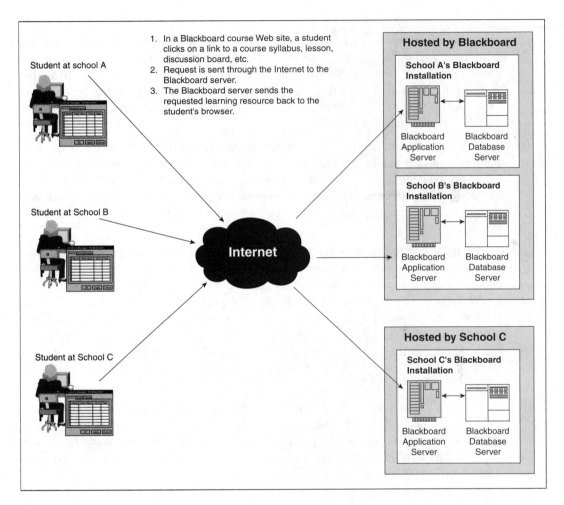

Figure 7.4
Distance learning company hosting applications and course material for schools.
Figure courtesy Blackboard, Inc.

These tools are public key encryption, private key encryption, and digital certifi-cates. *Digital certificates* verify that the vendor is who it says it is. *Private* and *public key encryption* ensure that only the intended recipient can read confidential informa-tion such as credit card numbers.

Encryption scrambles documents using mathematical algorithms so that only the intended recipient can decrypt and read the document. Algorithms are complex mathematical formulas. Public and private key encryption work together to create and read secure documents. Complementary mathematical algorithms called public and private keys are used to encode documents. Public keys are made generally available. A document scrambled by a private key can only be read by a recipient with the complementary public key. A public key can't read a document created by the same public key, and a private key can't decipher a document created by the same private key. Thus, public with private key encryption is asymmetric. Different keys perform the encoding and the decoding.

When someone shops, for example, at Amazon.com, Amazon.com sends the shopper a unique public key that scrambles the user's credit card number and order. The Amazon.com site uses its complementary private key to decode the order. The advantage of asymmetric public key encryption is that the public key can be given out freely without corrupting the security because only the owner of the key has the private key.

Digital certificates with digital signatures are used to authenticate vendors. Web sites contain digital certificates that verify that the vendor is who it claims to be. The digital certificate is provided by a trusted third party that has done a background check on the vendor. The digital signature verifies that people are who they claim to be by sending a digital summary of the data sent. The receiving end receives the digital signature and makes a mathematical summary of it. If the receiving end's summary exactly matches the sending end's summary, the identity of the sender is verified. Security software made by VeriSign, Inc. and installed on browsers reads the digital certificates that authenticate vendors.

Trusted third parties also provide proof that sites use strong encryption. Browsers normally have an open padlock icon that shuts during a secure transaction. This is extremely important because the padlock indicates that the site uses encryption technology such as secure sockets layer (SSL), which uses a 128-bit code for encryption. This means it uses a code-based 2^{128} encoding technique.

Part 4

Wireless Service

8 Mobile Services

In this chapter:

Competition between mobile network operators, and the desire for more robust networks, have led to implemention of third generation (3G) digital networks by major mobile operators. These networks are capable of carrying vastly increased amounts of voice traffic and high-speed data traffic, which enables them to support a variety of applications such as music downloading, messaging, and video-on-demand services. Meanwhile, enhancements to the international specifications have already been defined, and suppliers are delivering software and hardware that will enable transmission of higher-speed mobile data and entertainment services over broadband mobile networks. The cellular industry did not always coordinate standards on a worldwide basis.

When first generation (1G) cellular technology was first implemented in Japan, Europe, and the United States in the early 1980s, only the United States, where AT&T, which at that time set *de facto* standards, implemented uniform analog service, known as advanced mobile phone service (AMPS). Thus, all mobile telephones worked on all analog cellular networks in the United States. Interestingly, there were seven different, incompatible analog types of cellular service implemented at the time in Europe. Japan implemented yet another incompatible analog service.

When competition led to decreased prices in the late 1990s, analog cellular services became so popular that capacity, particularly in metropolitan areas, was inadequate. Thus, carriers began to install second generation (2G) digital services.

In the United States, because AT&T no longer set standards nationwide, two different, incompatible digital standards, time division multiple access (TDMA) and code division multiple access (CDMA), were implemented. However, in Europe, standards bodies specified one compatible digital cellular technology, global system for mobile communications (GSM), for the continent. Thus, in Europe, people could use their handset in whichever European country they traveled. Many other countries adopted GSM, making it the dominant 2G standard worldwide. However, carriers saw in the late 1990s that these networks lacked the capacity to handle increased voice traffic and were not adequate for supporting twenty-first century mobile data services.

Manufacturers, governments, and network operators recognized the importance of mobility and foresaw continued increases in cellular traffic. They knew that large corporations conducted business worldwide, and productivity depended on the capability for people to easily communicate on a mobile phone on a worldwide basis. They were also aware of the impact that more spectrally efficient networks would have on reducing tariffs and increasing global penetration of mobile services. Spectral efficiency refers to the capability to handle more traffic over a given amount of airwaves.

The International Telecommunications Union (ITU), in conjunction with key industry representatives, developed third generation (3G) standards for networks capable of supporting more voice traffic and broadband mobile multimedia (speech, audio, text, graphics, and video) services. Although they had set out to specify one compatible standard, they developed five different standards in response to pressure from competing governments, operators, and suppliers. Currently, the most prevalently adopted standard is CDMA2000, with more than 145 million subscribers as of the end of 2004, and the second most prevalent one is WCDMA, with around 16 million subscribers. However, this will change because, for the most part, GSM carriers are implementing WCDMA, and CDMA carriers are implementing CDMA2000. However, chips in handsets will enable people to use their 3G cell phones globally on both types of networks.

Government policies are one of the most significant factors in the speed of innovations in telecommunications. Governments determine the level of competition, allocate access to airwaves (spectrum), and have the resources to promote research and development for infrastructure. For example, in Europe, cellular network operators paid billions of euros for the right to use airwaves suitable for third generation networks. This made it difficult for many of them to raise capital to add the network equipment needed for upgrades. It was also a factor in market consolidation, resulting in the formation of large conglomerate carriers. Smaller carriers just didn't have the resources to both acquire spectrum and upgrade their networks. (Another factor in the mergers was the cutthroat pricing that resulted in lower margins, and decreased smaller carriers' ability to fund upgrades.) In other countries, notably South Korea, Japan, and Indonesia, governments made spectrum available to carriers based on capabilities. In addition, they invested in or subsidized upgrades and set policies for development of uniform, compatible network technologies.

To create additional revenue by targeting specific market segments, 3G network operators such as Sprint PCS resell their network capacity to mobile virtual network operators (MVNOs) such as Virgin Mobile and ESPN. MVNOs typically brand their service to appeal to particular segments of the population. For example, ESPN will promote its service to sports fans and Virgin Mobile to youth. Some resellers offer cellular as a way to round out their offerings to existing customers. For example, cable TV providers in the United States are expected to resell mobile video services to their customer base.

Because upgrading to third generation cellular adds capacity for voice, it enables carriers to satisfy the demand for affordable voice services. However, the road to success in selling 3G applications has a number of possible potholes. Creating easy-to-use, multifunctional handsets and batteries with long lives, producing compelling applications, and overcoming security threats from hackers are major hurdles facing the industry as 3G networks evolve from those carrying mostly voice and short text messages to those that support new applications such as multiplayer games for consumers and business applications for enterprises. Ease of use is particularly thorny because handsets will have a growing number of features including streaming music, TV tuners, interactive 3D games, FM radios, cameras, camcorders, and multimedia messaging. This is analogous to the development of personal computers in which the user interface on early computers was extremely complex, and consumers did not purchase PCs in large numbers until Netscape introduced an easy-to-use Web browser and high-speed access to e-mail became affordable. Also, because both cell phones and personal computers have connections that are "always on" and open to the Internet, security is a major worry whether customers access the Internet from landline phones or wireless devices. Nevertheless, the mobile industry has learned from the PC industry and is determined to not repeat its mistakes.

Despite these challenges, growing revenue opportunities have fueled continued interest in developing mobile services. Decreasing equipment prices, reduced tariffs, free night and weekend long distance phone calls, bundling of broadband mobile data services, and significant handset improvements have all led to a substantial growth in the demand for mobile services. Total spending in the United States is higher for mobile services than for landline, traditional home telephone lines. According to the FCC, Americans spent approximately $24 billion on wireless services in the second quarter of 2004 and about $20 billion on landline service. Matt Richtel and Ken Belson reported these statistics in the December 20, 2004 *New York Times* online edition article "Fewer Cellular Carriers, but Not Fewer Services." Revenue disparities between cellular and landline services are larger in parts of Africa, China, India, and Latin America where the vast majority of people will make their first phone call using a mobile telephone.

Most of the U.S. adult population uses a mobile phone. However, only about 6% of Americans use their mobile phone, instead of a personal landline phone, as their primary means to communicate. However, the percentage of young singles in metropolitan areas that relies totally on a mobile phone to communicate is much higher than in the general population. As these young people age, more of the population will rely on mobile service. The introduction of calling party pays (CPP) would facilitate reliance on mobile service, and being able to move landline phone numbers to mobile telephones (wireless local number portability) makes it more convenient to drop landline service all together. Nevertheless, incomplete coverage on mobile networks hinders strict reliance on mobile services.

Many subscribers are deterred from dropping home phone service because of poor reception inside residences. In addition, there are areas in large cities where tall buildings and congestion lead to calls being dropped or blocked. Another problem is that rural areas have sparse coverage because the return on investment for most operators to install base stations in low-usage areas isn't justified. In addition, many providers worldwide operate cellular and landline networks in the same country. This deters them from promoting cellular as customers' only voice service in these areas, as this would shrink their landline revenues even more.

Growing use of 802.11 and interest in WiMAX mobile services threaten to cut into 3G mobile revenue. However, to date it's not clear what their impact will be on

3G mobile service revenues. Although they both offer higher speeds than current third generation technologies with sufficient backhaul capacity, their business case for producing recurring revenue from public areas is still unproven. 802.11, also called Wi-Fi service, is used primarily from fixed locations such as hotspots and inside private homes, campuses, and businesses. WiMAX is a potential high-speed wireless service that may be used for fixed and portable last-mile Internet access in markets that are not already being adequately served by broadband fiber, cable modems, DSL, 3G, and Wi-Fi. WiMAX covers a larger area than 802.11. However, WiMAX standards for mobile service have not been finalized. 3G's advantage is that it is suitable for mobile applications when users are in moving vehicles or walking and is more widely deployed. It is likely that all of these technologies will be deployed depending on applications and network availability. More information on fixed wireless technologies can be found in Chapter 9, "Wi-Fi, Wireless Broadband, Sensor Networks, and Personal Area Networks."

Geosynchronous and medium earth orbiting (MEO) satellites are widely deployed for military surveillance and television and radio broadcasts. However, low earth orbiting (LEO) satellite phones capable of carrying voice and data traffic never attracted the number of users envisioned by those companies that invested in such satellites. Geosynchronous and medium earth orbiting satellites are located further from the earth than low earth orbiting satellites. Nevertheless, satellite phones are critical in some applications. Satellites have the advantage over cellular and landline services of reaching remote areas. Thus, they are used in shipping, on offshore facilities, and by travelers in regions so remote that they have no mobile service. Moreover, they are used in war zones and areas hit by disasters where infrastructure to support mobile and landline networks has been destroyed.

THE DEVELOPMENT OF CELLULAR NETWORKS.....

All wireless services use spectrum, frequency bands, which are portions of airwaves, to carry either analog or digital communication signals. Spectrum consists of the multitude of invisible frequency bands that surround the earth and are used to transmit segregated radio waves. Radio waves carry signals as electrical energy on unseen waves. These waves are grouped by frequency. High frequencies carry short wavelengths; more of them can be sent in a given amount of time. Lower frequencies carry longer-length waves; fewer of them can be transmitted in a given amount of time. AM radios use the low-frequency portion of spectrum, and microwave service uses high frequencies. There is a finite amount of spectrum, and governments regulate its allocation and use.

Wireless services were first used for voice communications in the United States in 1921 by the Detroit police department. These first systems had no connections to the public switched telephone network. Police could only communicate within their own department. The first two-way systems with connections to public networks were implemented in 1946. Analog cellular service, implemented in the 1980s, uses spectrum more efficiently by enabling networks to reuse the same frequencies in different cells within cities and towns. Prior to cellular service, entire cities had to share the same frequencies (see Figures 8.1 and 8.2).

Cellular, Wireless, Cordless, and Mobile

The terms "cellular," "wireless," "cordless," and "mobile" have different meanings. However, some services fall into multiple definitions. For example, services can be cellular, mobile, and wireless. Here are the definitions:

- *Cellular*. Any service in which the spectrum allocated to a carrier is broken up into geographic areas called cells. Cells next to each other use different frequencies, but ones not contiguous to each other reuse the same frequencies.

- *Wireless*. Any service that uses radio waves instead of wires or fiber optics to carry electrical signals.

- *Cordless*. A service that uses unlicensed spectrum and is restricted to a small coverage area within a home or private premise.

- *Mobile Wireless*. Service that can be used over a wide distance as people move around on foot or in cars and public transportation.

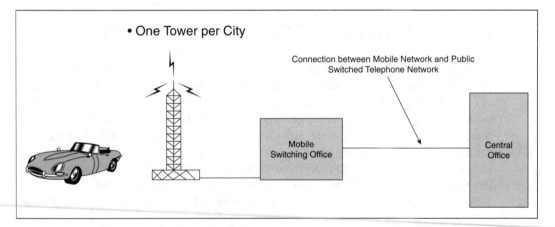

Figure 8.1
Precellular mobile service.

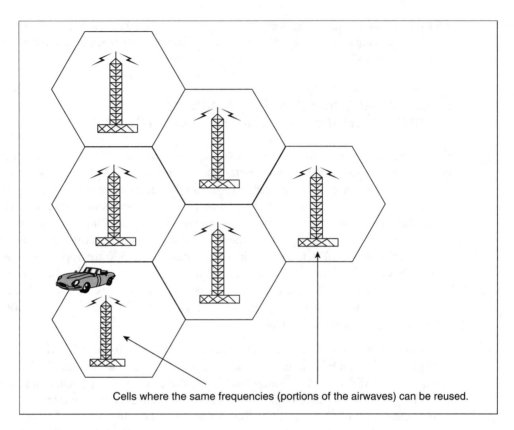

Cells where the same frequencies (portions of the airwaves) can be reused.

Figure 8.2
Cellular service.

When new digital cellular networks were first deployed in the United States in the 1990s, some carriers referred to their networks as wireless, mobile, or personal communications service (PCS) networks to distinguish them from earlier analog cellular networks. However, these networks, in fact, use cellular technology to deploy spectrum more efficiently. The terms "mobile," "wireless," "PCS," and "cellular" can be correctly used to refer to these networks.

Precellular Mobile Networks

The first mobile telephone network with connections to the public switched telephone network was started in 1946 in St. Louis, Missouri. Mobile systems were later deployed throughout the United States. The local telephone company in each city operated these networks. One transmitter and receiver covered the entire area, and all users shared the spectrum (see Figure 8.1). This meant that only a limited number

(25 to 35) of simultaneous calls could be placed on each city's mobile system. In addition to limited capacity, the quality of service was spotty with considerable static and breaking up of calls.

First Generation Analog Cellular— Advanced Mobile Phone Services (AMPS)

The first generation of cellular service used analog equipment. The first analog cellular service in the United States, advanced mobile phone service (AMPS), was installed in 1984. Cellular service increases capacity of mobile technology because it reuses frequencies in small areas, represented by hexagonal-shaped cells in Figure 8.2. AT&T's Bell Laboratories (now part of Lucent Technology) originated the concept of cellular telephone service. In the early 1980s, the FCC set aside radio spectrum for cellular service at 825MHz to 890MHz and decided that each of the 306 metropolitan statistical areas (MSAs) and 428 rural service areas (RSAs) were to have two cellular providers. The local wireline telephone company was assigned the B block of frequencies, and a nontelephone company was assigned the A block. The FCC hoped to foster competition by having two providers in each area.

Other than the 30 largest metropolitan areas, cellular frequencies in the A block were given out by an FCC lottery to qualified operators such as McCaw Cellular (later purchased by AT&T) and CellularOne. Thus, there were two network operators in each city. However, with limited competition between only two operators per area, per-minute rates were high. Initially, businesses leased cellular service for salespeople and business executives who justified paying high rates with their ability to use their time more effectively. Although usage fees were high, handset costs dropped. Telephones were often provided at no cost or at a minimal fee to attract new customers.

When carriers need more capacity, they split cells into smaller sizes and reuse frequencies in the newly created cells. More cells equal more capacity. However, adding small cells has its problems. Smaller cells lead to more dropped calls and dead areas where calls cannot be made because of problems of overlapping into adjacent cells.

WIRELESS HANDSETS—RADIOS FOR TWO-WAY COMMUNICATIONS

All wireless handsets are in reality radios with antennas that convert signals to and from formats compatible with the airwaves. When antennas receive radio frequencies, they translate them into electrical signals. To transmit voice, data, or video, antennas convert signals into airborne waves, radio frequencies.

Second Generation Digital Mobile Air Interfaces

In the early 1990s, carriers started upgrading their analog networks to second generation (2G) digital networks to gain more capacity. Meanwhile, the FCC announced its plans to hold auctions for additional spectrum and to introduce increased competition. Operators also wanted to be able to offer services such as caller ID and voice mail message notification, not available on analog cellular service.

All digital wireless services use multiplexing access techniques to carry more calls than analog cellular service on the same amount of spectrum. When used in wireless networks, multiplexing techniques are referred to as *air interfaces* that are used to access (share) spectrum between the wireless device and the provider's base station and antennas. The air interface in the customer's device must match the one used in the carrier's cell site. Thus, while all digital services have more capacity than analog cellular, the ways they added capacity were incompatible with each other. That is why U.S. digital mobile service subscribers cannot necessarily use their cellular telephones when they travel abroad.

The three most prevalent 2G air interfaces in the world, in order of worldwide subscriber use, are global system for mobile communications (GSM), code division multiple access (CDMA), time division multiple access (TDMA), and Motorola's proprietary digital technique iDEN, which Nextel uses.

TDMA, CDMA, iDEN, and GSM operate in many frequencies, portions of the world's spectrum. See Table 8.3 later in this chapter for additional information on these frequencies. U.S.-based carriers still have analog service in addition to their digital offerings because the Federal Communications Commission requires that carriers keep some analog cellular service operational until February 2008. Because of declining digital handset costs and discontinued analog handset production, very few people have analog handsets. However, there are still pockets of analog-only service in rural areas.

Privacy and Advanced Features

All digital cellular services improve privacy. Snoopers with scanners can easily listen in on analog cellular signals. Eavesdropping on digital transmissions is more difficult because the digital bits are scrambled when they are transmitted over the air between handsets and operators' equipment.

Digital mobile service supports many new services like caller ID, alphanumeric paging, voice mail notification, short messaging, and enhanced services such as call return. In addition, batteries in handsets last longer before they need recharging. Digital signal processors in handsets decode the digital bits representing caller ID numbers and paging messages into alphanumeric characters displayed on handsets' liquid crystal displays. Digital signal processors (DSPs) are specialized, very-high-speed computer chips. The DSPs also code and decode the voice signals, converting them from analog to digital at the sending end and from digital to analog at the receiving end.

Digital Air Interfaces—Between Handsets and Mobile Networks

Carriers and standards bodies worldwide selected the following second generation digital air interfaces to increase the amount of traffic they previously supported with analog service on a given amount of spectrum.

GSM Service

GSM (global system for mobile communications) is the most widely used air interface worldwide. According to the GSA (Global mobile Suppliers Association), as of June 2004, there were 1.1 billion subscribers worldwide. GSM's strength lays in its wide penetration worldwide, which enables people to use their telephones when they travel. GSM phones have clip-on subscriber identity module (SIM) cards that contain a microchip that stores user identity and other information such as speed-dial lists. The SIM card encrypts voice and data before they are transmitted.

GSM (global system for mobile communications) uses a form of time division multiplexing. GSM was first used in Europe in the 900MHz frequency band and then later in the 1800MHz band. T-Mobile USA and Cingular operate GSM networks in the United States using the 850MHz and 1900MHz frequency bands. GSM is the digital cellular standard that was originally decided on by European governments and was first deployed in 1992. GSM divides channels of 200-kilohertz spectrum into eight time slots. Seven of the time slots carry traffic, and the eighth carries control signals. The control channel also carries short message service (SMS), which is brief text messages.

GSM operates in four ranges of frequencies listed in Table 8.3 later in this chapter.

TDMA Service

TDMA (time division multiple access), also referred to as digital advanced mobile service (D-AMPs), is based on a different form of time division multiplexing than GSM. Each call is assigned a time slot. Cingular Wireless and other networks in the Americas originally used TDMA for their second generation digital service. At the time TDMA was adopted, most carriers in all of the Americas that did not implement CDMA adopted TDMA. At that time, GSM was not yet the most predominate second generation air interface. Many of these operators are transitioning their customers to their GSM service.

CDMA Service

CDMA (code division multiple access) divides up the airwaves by associating a unique code to each call. It is a "spread spectrum" technology. Each conversation transmitted is spread over a 1.25MHz frequency channel as it is sent. Use of this technology gives CDMA more capacity than GSM and TDMA. United States–based technology company Qualcomm pioneered CDMA in the commercial sector.

CDMA supports more phone calls and data sessions per cell than any other 2G air interface. CDMA also employs a soft *handoff* to transfer (hand off) calls from cell to cell. This is superior to TDMA's handoff. With a soft handoff, a call is rarely dropped during the handoff. For a short period of time during the handoff or transfer, the call is held as it is received and as the cell hands it off. The decision to use this superior multiplexing method cost many carriers in the United States a high price in lost compatibility to GSM. However, it enabled them to offer voice and data services at a lower cost and easily upgrade their networks to 3G.

According to the CDMA Development Group, as of second quarter 2004, there are more than 227 million subscribers worldwide who use CDMA technology. Verizon Wireless, Sprint PCS, and other carriers use it in over 60 countries worldwide, including China, Japan, South Korea, Canada, Russia, Taiwan, Israel, India, Australia, and Africa. It is also used in Eastern Europe, Southeast Asia, and the Americas.

IDEN—Nextel and Telus and Others

Nextel and Canadian carrier Telus use iDEN (integrated digital enhanced network) for their air interface. A key strength of iDEN is that it had the first push-to-talk offering in the industry that could be used on cellular handsets. Push-to-talk using iDEN enables individuals and groups of people to reach each other in under a second. See the section later in this chapter on push-to-talk, which is a walkie-talkie type service.

IDEN breaks each 25-kilohertz channel into up to six time slots able to carry voice, paging traffic, data, and dispatch messages in a packetized format. Packetizing data results in fewer delays and enables more flexibility in slow-speed data offerings such as e-mail via handsets. Nextel is in the process of upgrading its network to WiDEN. WiDEN stands for wide integrated digital enhanced network. It is a software enhancement for data service that supports higher data speeds of 20 to 80 kilobits per second via improved compression. After its merger with Sprint PCS, Nextel is expected to upgrade its network to 3G.

Compatibility Throughout Europe:
A Mix of Standards in the United States

When analog cellular was developed in the United States, one organization, AT&T, set de facto standards for all telecommunications services. However, in the 1990s when carriers in the United States upgraded to digital services, AT&T had been divested of the local telephone companies. The Regional Bell Operating Companies (RBOCs) from which they were divested were free to select different standards. Also, new cellular companies, which purchased spectrum at a government auction, chose various air interfaces. Initially, RBOCs chose code division multiple access (CDMA) because of CDMA's superior capacity.

However, due to its complexity, Qualcomm, the developer of CDMA, was late delivering CDMA software, and since TDMA was standardized by the Telecommunications Industry Association (TIA) before CDMA, Southwestern Bell Mobility (now Cingular) chose to commercialize TDMA. Southwestern Bell Mobility's parent company, SBC, purchased Ameritech and PacBell, and converted them to TDMA as well. Cingular, a partnership between BellSouth and SBC, became a mostly TDMA operator. In addition, AT&T Wireless chose TDMA. Prior to the Cingular and AT&T Wireless merger in 2004, both companies had also installed GSM technology alongside their TDMA service. GSM-compatible service was sold to business customers so that they could use their handsets when they traveled internationally. GSM was also intended to be part of their transition to high-speed 3G service able to support more voice, video, and high-speed data.

Meanwhile, European standards bodies adopted a uniform technology, GSM, for all of Europe. Europe at the time had a mix of incompatible analog technologies. The presence of a uniform air interface made using the same mobile handset across the continent convenient. Other countries worldwide adopted GSM because of roaming compatibility. Roaming is the capability to use the same mobile handset in different carriers' networks.

To gain capacity and compatibility with GSM worldwide, many operators, including Cingular Wireless, are transitioning customers to GSM service and plan to discontinue TDMA technology in the near future. This will enable them to support fewer types of equipment, gain additional capacity, and provide GSM handsets that operate worldwide. They will no longer purchase handsets with TDMA air interfaces. Networks in which the spectrum is not split up between multiple access types can carry more traffic than those that must carry multiple types of air interfaces.

SPECTRUM AND RIGHTS TO AIRWAVES ....

Because spectrum is a valuable asset, governments' policies in awarding spectrum, whether making it available at low prices, giving it away based on capabilities, using lotteries, or selling it to the highest bidder, impact a nation's development of advanced wireless services. The term *spectrum* refers to airwaves, which are composed of ranges of frequencies. Frequency refers to the type of airwave as measured by wavelength. Governments allocate portions of the airwaves, frequencies, for particular applications such as satellite or mobile service. Adequate spectrum is critical to carriers. It is an important factor for adequate capacity for growth and new services.

Efficient ways to carry wireless traffic are also crucial. This is called *spectral efficiency*, the capability to use the same amount of spectrum to carry more voice or data services. For example, 3G wireless technologies capable of carrying high-speed wireless data, video, and voice are more spectrally efficient than 2G services. They can carry more voice, data, and video within an equal amount of spectrum.

Frequency

Frequency can also be thought of as how frequently an entire wave completes a cycle. A *frequency* is the number of times in each second that each radio wave completes a cycle. As mentioned in Chapter 1, "Basic Concepts," each cycle looks like a resting letter S. A cycle is complete when energy passes through an entire radio wave from the highest to the lowest portions of the wave. The term *hertz* refers to one cycle of a radio wave. Thirty MHz means that each wave has 30 million hertz, or cycles per second; energy passes through 30 million resting Ss in one second.

Ranges of Frequency—Spectrum Blocks

Governments allocate spectrum in chunks of frequency bands such as 15 megahertz, 25 megahertz, or 30 megahertz. Determining the amount of spectrum, the bandwidth, is done by subtracting the bottom frequency of the range of frequency from the top frequency (highest frequency minus lowest frequency). For example, when someone is granted the right to use 15 megahertz, if their top frequency is 800 megahertz, then the bottom of the range would be 785 megahertz. In addition, spectrum bands set aside for specific services are divided into blocks designated by letters of the alphabet. For example, the B block refers to a different block or range of frequencies within a larger range of frequencies than the G block. The B block might be allocated to one carrier and the G block to a different carrier to offer competing services.

Rights to these blocks are strategic assets enabling carriers to offer new, competitive services. Rights to spectrum are argued about in the courts, before the FCC, and in Congress. For example, the FCC awarded Nextel 10 megahertz of spectrum in the 1.9 gigahertz G block of spectrum suitable for 3G high-speed data. In return, Nextel agreed to give up other spectrum in lower frequencies that interfered with public safety equipment. Negotiations with the FCC took three years. In the final agreement, Nextel will pay the government $4.8 billion for the cost of the spectrum plus expenses of at least $2.8 billion for moving equipment using the spectrum to other portions of the radio waves. The government will give Nextel more than $2.06 billion in credit toward the preceding expenses for the spectrum it is returning. Verizon Wireless and the Cellular Telecommunications Industry Association (CTIA) objected to the FCC's award of spectrum to Nextel without a public auction.

Spectrum Caps—Limiting the Amount of Spectrum Per Carrier

Governments often establish policies limiting the amount of spectrum that any one carrier can have rights to in any single area. These caps are created to promote competition by splitting up air rights among carriers. At one time, the FCC had a spectrum cap of 45 megahertz for cell phone companies. They raised this cap 22% in 2001 and completely eliminated it in 2003. Elimination of the cap is a significant factor in mergers between AT&T Wireless and Cingular and the merger between Nextel and Sprint in the United States. It also is a factor in Verizon's purchase of additional spectrum from other carriers in frequencies suitable for 3G, third generation mobile services.

Allocation

Spectrum allocation is administered on both an international and national level. The International Telecommunications Union (ITU) manages the allocation of spectrum for services such as satellite and television because these services cross national borders. Individual countries allocate spectrum for other services. The Federal Communications Commission (FCC) and the National Telecommunications and Information Association (NTIA), part of the Commerce department, jointly manage spectrum allocation in the United States. The FCC has broken up spectrum into bands and assigned it for particular purposes. For example, citizens band radio is assigned to the 27MHz, 462MHz, and 467MHz, or million hertz, bands. Television, mobile carriers, police, and fire are also assigned specific bands.

Implication of Spectrum Ranges

Frequencies used for wireless service have important implications in costs and capabilities. Services carried on high frequencies require more equipment to support them than those on lower frequencies. This is because high frequencies have shorter wavelengths. (A *wavelength* is the distance between the highest point in one wave to the highest point in the next wave.) For example, a 1.9GHz wavelength has a shorter wavelength than an 800MHz wavelength. Short wavelengths are more susceptible to rain and weather conditions. A rain droplet can destroy a smaller wave more easily than a larger one. In addition, higher frequencies fade over shorter distances and cannot penetrate walls as well as lower frequencies.

Therefore, towers and antennas for high frequency networks must be closer together. This is the reason that wideband CDMA (WCDMA) 3G networks that use higher frequencies (2100MHz) need many more cellular towers and associated equipment (cell sites) than GSM 2G networks operating at lower frequencies (900MHz). When carriers add high-frequency spectrum to networks made up of lower frequencies, their major expense is adding cell sites, which are the additional antennas and the equipment associated with each antenna.

Interference—When Signals from Devices Obstruct Each Other

When transmissions use the same airspace (frequencies) in the same areas, they may interfere with each other. For example, when people install Wi-Fi wireless equipment and cordless telephones that both operate at 2.4 gigahertz, they often have operability problems. These problems are caused by interference. Newer wireless technologies have the capability to hop between channels when they sense that other signals are in the same channel. Concerns about interference often lead to political conflicts between factions. For example, when the FCC announced it was planning to auction blocks of spectrum previously assigned to satellite service for high-speed 3G mobile service, Sprint PCS and Nokia voiced concerns that mobile data in these frequencies would cause interference.

Spectrum for Higher-Speed 3G Services

The World Radiocommunication Conference (WRC) 2000 of the International Telecommunications Union identified three bands of spectrum on which third generation cellular (3G) service should operate. (3G services for advanced voice, video, and data services are reviewed later in this chapter.) European countries held auctions in which carriers bid billions of dollars. Other countries, such as Japan, held beauty contests and awarded spectrum based on capability. The United States made spectrum available through auctions. However, much of the spectrum designated for 3G services is or was, until recently, used by military, analog television, and educational television as well as other services.

In the United States, some small carriers and business owners who won PCS spectrum auctions in 1996 to introduce digital second generation services never used them and subsequently filed for bankruptcy. However, bankruptcy courts did not allow the FCC to repossess this spectrum. Following the court's decision, Cingular and Verizon Wireless purchased unused spectrum from NextWave, one of the bankrupt carriers. The bankrupt companies worked out agreements to share revenue from spectrum sales with the FCC and to return the rest of the unused spectrum. The FCC will auction the enormous amount of unused spectrum from the 1996 auction in January 2005.

The following spectrum is expected to be auctioned later in 2005 and 2006:

- Analog spectrum used for television. Broadcasters that were given free additional spectrum for digital TV, promised to return UHF spectrum used for analog TV, but are now trying to delay returning it. The spectrum is scheduled to be returned when 85% of users have televisions capable of receiving high definition digital television (HDTV). Negotiations are underway to require that UHF TV and cable operators transmit all national network programs in digital as well as analog. This would speed up progress toward meeting the 85% rule, as most people receive TV over cable. Because it's not clear when the spectrum will be cleared, few mobile carriers have bid for it. An exception to this is the 700 megahertz band (Channel 55) that was purchased by Qualcomm to offer mobile video multicasting services nationwide. Multicasting is the capability to send the same message to many users simultaneously.

- 90 megahertz of spectrum now used mostly by the military and federal government. A fund will be created from money raised at the auction to pay for relocating the military's equipment to different frequencies.

- 20 megahertz of spectrum now used by satellites.

- 3G spectrum. The FCC intends to auction advanced wireless services licenses in the 1710MHz to 1755MHz and 2110MHz to 2155MHz frequency bands as early as June 2006.

Once spectrum from these auctions is available, it is thought that carriers will own sufficient capacity for new advanced mobile services. Some of this spectrum is also suitable for high-speed, fixed wireless broadband alternatives to cable modems and DSL.

Paired Banding—Different Bands for Sending and Receiving

Many wireless services use a higher frequency for the downlink, from the base station to the customer, than for the uplink, from the customer to the wireless network. The use of different frequencies for the uplink and downlink is referred to as *paired spectrum*. Higher frequencies, which fade at shorter distances, are deployed for the downlink because power at base stations can be more easily raised to increase the range. Increasing power on mobile devices drains batteries.

Cellular and 3G technologies based on frequency division duplexing (FDD) use paired spectrum to prevent interference between downlink and uplink signals. A frequency separation of 20 and 85 megahertz is used for cellular and 3G FDD technologies, respectively. Frequency division duplexing carries traffic from multiple users on slightly different frequencies. However, time division duplex (TDD), a 3G technology, does not use paired spectrum. The TDD air interface splits up traffic from multiple devices into brief time slots. Thus, it can use the same frequency band for sending and receiving. This makes more efficient use of the spectrum. It is spectrally efficient because if less bandwidth is used for sending, it can be used for the receiving. On paired spectrum, idle capacity on the uplink cannot be used by the downlink.

Geographic Licensing Schemes

In Europe and many other locations, when governments offer spectrum to carriers, they offer it in country-wide swaths. However, in the United States spectrum auctions for mobile service only cover portions of the geographic region. Part of the reasoning is that this encourages competition. In addition, the United States is so large that purchasing nationwide coverage could be cost prohibitive for entrepreneurs. As a result, in the United States, no carrier's network provides complete geographic coverage.

U.S. Metropolitan Statistical Areas (MSAs) and Rural Service Areas (RSAs)

For cellular (800MHz) mobile coverage, the regions are broken up into metropolitan statistical areas (MSAs) and rural service areas (RSAs) as follows:

- 306 metropolitan statistical areas (MSAs), which are large population areas that include the major U.S. metropolitan cities and their adjacent communities (a county).
- 428 rural services areas (RSAs), which are rural regions outside of the metropolitan areas made up of multiple, smaller cities or towns that do not cross state borders.
- Frequencies used in MSAs and RSAs are auctioned off in two 10MHz frequency blocks, identified as A and B blocks.
- MSAs are defined by the U.S. Office of Management and Budget.

U.S. Basic Trading Areas (BTAs) and Major Trading Areas (MTAs)

For PCS (1900MHz) mobile coverage, the regions are broken up into basic trading areas (BTAs) and major trading areas (MTAs) as follows:

- 493 basic trading areas (BTAs).
- 51 major trading areas (MTAs), which are regions that include multiple cities or states. Each major trading area is made up of multiple, smaller basic trading areas.
- MTA and BTA frequencies are auctioned off in blocks such as A, B, C, D, E, and F blocks. Each block is a portion of a larger band of frequencies often designated for 3G or PCS services.
- MTAs and BTAs are based on the *Rand McNally Commercial Atlas & Marketing Guide*.

Unlicensed Spectrum for 802.11 and WiMAX

Governments specify portions of the airwaves for unlicensed services such as 802.11 Wi-Fi services. Bluetooth and ultra-wideband (UWB) services also use unlicensed spectrum. In many countries but not all, spectrum for 802.16, otherwise referred to as WiMAX, is also available on an unlicensed basis. Unlicensed spectrum is available free to companies who do not have to apply for a license to use it. This significantly lowers the cost of deploying service, but it doesn't mean the government does not regulate the spectrum. Most governments will issue certification, signal spreading, and power limitation rules to protect adjacent licensed spectrum bands from egregious interference from transmissions within the unlicensed spectrum. However, there are no assurances that congestion from many networks in the same unlicensed airspace will not interfere with each other or overwhelm capacity. 802.11, Bluetooth, ultra-wideband, and 802.16 (WiMAX) services are covered in Chapter 9.

PCS—Personal Communications Services

The term "personal communications services" originally referred to mobile telephony in the higher 1.9-gigahertz frequency band (UL: 1850–1910MHz/DL: 1930–1990MHz) auctioned by the FCC in 1996. Uplink (UL) is the link from the subscriber to the wireless network; downlink (DL) is the link from the network to the subscriber. PCS services were conceived as a way to provide a low-cost, feature-rich mobile telephone service. Pricing was to be low enough for the service to be affordable to a wide segment of the population (see Table 8.3, later in this chapter). Networks worldwide offer PCS services. In Europe, PCS offered in the 1.8-gigahertz band is known as digital cellular system (DCS).

The U.S. government's goal in auctioning PCS spectrum in 1996 was to promote new uses of the airways by encouraging competition. It also hoped to raise money for the U.S. Treasury. The government auctioned the PCS spectrum off in six blocks of frequencies so that each area could have four PCS competitors plus the two existing cellular providers. Competition from PCS services has driven prices down for all cellular service and has encouraged growth in new wireless services. Operators who owned the original analog cellular networks such as Bell Atlantic Mobile, Air-Touch, and GTE (now Verizon Wireless) later acquired PCS spectrum through a combination of acquisition of other carriers, spectrum purchases from other carriers, and subsequent auctions.

PCS (or DCS in Europe) is now used in the industry to refer to all second generation cellular access technologies such as GSM, TDMA, and CDMA.

Multiband Versus Multimode

Handsets that operate in more than one frequency have multiband capability. For example, handsets that operate on 800-megahertz and 1.9-gigahertz frequencies are dual band. Devices that operate on multiple air interfaces—analog, CDMA, TDMA, GSM, as well as various 3G standards—have multimode, as well as multiband, capabilities. Since carriers often have networks made up of two or more frequencies and air interfaces, it is important that handsets and data devices operate in more than one set of frequencies and air interfaces. Customers need handheld devices that match both the air interface and the frequency for compatibility throughout the carrier's network. Also, when networks are upgraded to next generation, 3G service, they may be deployed in pockets of the network and need to fall back on the 2G services for continuity. In addition, people who roam to other networks may need multiband and possibly multimode handsets.

Multiband Devices—Operability on Various Frequencies

Each handset needs to be designed to operate over specific frequencies. As mobile telephony grew in popularity, countries expanded the amount of airspace available for the service. In doing so, they opened new frequencies for voice and data service. The European Union decreed that all countries in the Union use the same frequencies. Thus, European countries provisioned GSM in the same portions of the airways, and manufacturers developed multiband devices compatible with the frequencies that were allocated. For example, most GSM phones are either dual or triple bands and are capable of operating on various GSM frequencies, 900MHz, 1800MHz, and 1900MHz.

In the United States, carriers such as Cingular and Verizon Wireless offer multiband handsets for their lower 800MHz frequency and higher 1900MHz PCS frequencies.

Multimode Devices—Operability with Various Air Interfaces

Most digital mobile handsets are dual mode and in the future will be trimode or quadruple mode. Dual-mode phones operate with two air interfaces, such as CDMA and analog. Trimode phones operate with three different air interfaces such as CDMA, GSM, and analog. When callers are in analog areas, they lose caller ID and other advanced features associated with digital cellular. Nextel offers a dual-band, dual-mode GSM and 900-megahertz TDMA Motorola telephone that operates in more than 60 countries in which it has roaming agreements. Nextel sells service directly and through Nextel Partners, an affiliate that sells in small to medium-size markets in 30 states within the United States.

Once the merger between Sprint and Nextel is completed, multimode, multiband devices for customers to use their handsets on both networks will be required that operate on the former Nextel iDEN and the former Sprint CDMA air interfaces and frequencies. Motorola has stated its intention to do this.

MOBILE CARRIERS ....

Worldwide, there are intense, competitive pressures in most markets that are keeping prices low. At the same time, operators are searching for new revenue sources and are upgrading their infrastructure to support additional voice capacity and to enable new data services such as multiplayer games, audio download, and mobile enterprise services. In addition, operators are considering expansion into developing and newly developed areas such as India, China, Africa, Latin America, and Eastern Europe where there are more opportunities for growth. These upgrades, expansions, needs for capital, and competitive pressures have fueled the desire by carriers to grow by acquisition. Many operators are huge conglomerates (see Table 8.1). The top 10 mobile carriers provide service for over half of the world's mobile customers. Many of them are subsidiaries of or were formerly owned by landline carriers.

Table 8.1   The Largest Mobile Operators in the United States

Cellular Provider	Number of Customers as of December 2004*	Comments
Cingular Wireless	47 million customers	SBC owns 60% and BellSouth owns 40%. Cingular purchased AT&T Wireless in 2004 to increase coverage. Prior to the purchase, AT&T Wireless was the third largest carrier. The network is based on a mix of analog, TDMA, GSM, GPRS, EDGE, and WCDMA. Plans to begin rollout of HSDPA 3G broadband technology in 15 to 20 cities by year-end 2005.
Verizon Wireless	42 million customers	Vodafone, second largest wireless company worldwide, owns 45% of Verizon Wireless. It is scheduled to complete its nationwide rollout of its CDMA2000 1xEV-DO network for mobile broadband data services by the end of 2005. Verizon has been adding capacity to keep up with subscriber growth by purchasing spectrum nationwide. It is the fastest growing cellular company in the United States.

continues

Table 8.1 The Largest Mobile Operators in the United States   (continued)

Cellular Provider	Number of Customers as of December 2004*	Comments
Sprint PCS	25 million customers plus 3 million through affiliates	Part of Sprint Corporation. In 2004, announced plans to acquire Nextel. The combined company will have a customer base of 38.5 million, more access to business customers, and broader nationwide coverage. Uses CDMA technology. Rolling out a nationwide CDMA2000 1xEV-DO broadband network, which it plans to complete by 2006. Sprint and Nextel also own nationwide spectrum capable of supporting fixed wireless WiMAX service in the MMDS 2- to 3-gigahertz range. 50% of Sprint's geographic territory, rural areas, is served by affiliates that receive roaming fees to carry Sprint traffic. Sprint is also the largest provider of MVNO services.
T-Mobile USA	16.3 million customers	Part of the T-Mobile International subsidiary owned by German carrier Deutsche Telecom. T-Mobile's entire network is based on GSM, which it has upgraded to GPRS and EDGE packet data communications services, which are slower than 3G services. After EDGE it will upgrade to HSDPA, a 3G high-speed downlink packet access standard.
Nextel Communications	13 million customers plus 1.5 million for Nextel Partners	Nextel has international holdings in Canada, Latin America, and Asia/Pacific. Nextel owns 31% of Nextel Partners and will likely purchase the rest after the merger with Sprint PCS. Nextel has the highest average revenue per user (ARPU) due primarily to its share of business customers and push-to-talk offerings.

The United States

Competition has benefited customers by triggering price decreases and wider availability of services. In most metropolitan areas in the United States, there have been six major carriers from which to purchase mobile service. However, in 2004, the number of nationwide carriers decreased because of mergers between Cingular and AT&T Wireless, Alltel and US Cellular, and Sprint and Nextel. See Table 8.1 for a list of the major carriers in the United States. These mergers were triggered by the desire to improve coverage, spread overhead among more customers, and improve the capability to raise capital. Cellular service is extremely capital intensive, and larger organizations have better opportunities to raise money. Unlike much of Europe and Asia, which have dense populations, the United States is a large country with vast, sparsely populated areas. In addition, the FCC has granted spectrum only within metropolitan and rural areas. Thus, no one carrier owns spectrum that covers the entire country.

For some carriers, phone number portability, poor coverage, and capacity issues have resulted in up to 2.5% average monthly churn, the process of customers changing carriers. Customers, in particular residential customers, are also motivated by lower rates at other carriers. Churn is a problem because it costs carriers about $400 in marketing, activation, and handset expenses to add each new customer. By merging, carriers hope that expanded coverage will cut down on churn. They also hope that having fewer carriers will cut down on price wars, which in some cases cause operators to price services below cost. However, in the short run, merging is tremendously complex. Sales, operations, and administrative departments must be reorganized, billing and operational services platforms need to be unified, and network infrastructure must be combined.

Table 8.2 Annualized Wireless Industry Survey in the United States, June 1988 to June 2004

Date	Estimated Total Subscribers	Total Service Revenues (in $000s)	12-Month Roamer Revenue (in $000s)	Number of Cell Sites	Average Monthly Bill
1988	1,608,697	$1,558,080	NA	2,789	$95.02
1989	2,691,793	$2,479,936	$210,699	3,577	$85.52
1990	4,368,686	$4,060,494	$365,549	4,768	$83.94
1991	6,380,053	$5,075,963	$565,989	6,685	$74.56
1992	8,892,535	$6,668,302	$838,077	8,901	$68.68

continues

Table 8.2 Annualized Wireless Industry Survey in the United States, June 1988 to June 2004 (continued)

Date	Estimated Total Subscribers	Total Service Revenues (in $000s)	12-Month Roamer Revenue (in $000s)	Number of Cell Sites	Average Monthly Bill
1993	13,067,318	$9,008,700	$1,124,493	11,551	$67.31
1994	19,283,306	$12,591,947	$1,552,382	14,740	$58.65
1995	28,154,415	$16,460,516	$2,173,003	19,844	$52.45
1996	38,195,466	$21,525,861	$2,737,177	24,802	$48.84
1997	48,705,553	$25,575,275	$2,858,432	38,650	$43.86
1998	60,831,431	$29,637,742	$3,166,656	57,674	$39.88
1999	76,284,735	$37,214,819	$3,837,994	74,157	$40.24
2000	97,035,925	$45,295,550	$4,134,626	95,733	$45.15
2001	118,397,734	$58,726,376	$3,698,683	114,059	$45.56
2002	134,561,370	$71,117,599	$3,872,035	131,350	$47.42
2003	148,065,824	$81,185,272	$3,874,788	147,719	$49.46
2004	169,467,393	$95,515,593	$3,956,823	174,368	$49.49

Source: The CTIA Semi-Annual Wireless Industry Survey. Used with permission of CTIA.

The nationwide mobile carriers are in various stages of upgrading to higher-speed cellular networks. (See Table 8.3 for Mobile Services Worldwide.) In addition to providing higher-speed services such as news headlines, short video clips, and e-mail, they are upgrading to achieve higher capacity for voice traffic. Currently, revenues from data are under 10%, with Sprint PCS reporting that in its second quarter 2004 revenue, 7% of average revenue per user was for data services. Other providers reported data revenues at 5% or less of average bills. However, most of the data revenue was from short messaging services (SMS), which do not require high-speed networks. Short messaging services are text messages of 160 characters or less.

In 2004, annual revenue for mobile service was over $95 billion (see Table 8.2). While mobile service is capital intensive—there are around 200,000 cell sites in the United States alone—it generates large cash flows of close to $50 per subscriber.

However, growth in mobile phone service to adults has been limited because 80% of the adult population already has service. Thus, providers have promoted service to teens and families in an attempt to increase market penetration. For example, Nextel started a division called Boost Mobile LLC to target the youth market for its walkie-talkie service. Sprint PCS has also offered Virgin Mobile and ESPN the capability to offer youth-centric MVNO services on its PCS network. As growth in numbers of subscribers becomes limited, operators hope to sell more services to existing customers over networks with adequate coverage and capacity. Many of these services are attractive because once the basic infrastructure is in place, costs to add value-added services such as high-speed data, push-to-talk, and multimedia messages are minimal.

Resale—Mobile Virtual Network Operators (MVNOs)

Not all cellular companies own the networks over which they sell mobile service. Providers that sell mobile service over other companies' mobile networks are called *mobile virtual network operators (MVNOs)*. Virtual operators buy mobile airtime in bulk at discount rates. They mark up and resell airtime and mobile services to their own customers. MVNOs bill customers and provide customer service for repair and billing issues. Virgin Mobile, a unit of UK-based Virgin Group, is known as a *mobile virtual network operator*. It supplies service but has none of its own mobile network infrastructure. Virgin Mobile, for example, resells services over the United Kingdom's T-Mobile UK's (formerly One 2 One) network, Sprint PCS infrastructure, and over the Optus network in Australia. Virgin Mobile targets the youth market. One of its popular services is music downloads to mobile phones.

Operators launch virtual network offerings as an avenue for content they produce or as a complement to their landline service. For example, in the United States, Qwest Communications, a Regional Bell Operating Company, offers mobile service to enterprises over the Sprint PCS network. In addition, cable TV operators in the United States are expected to launch mobile services on a resale basis to round out their offerings. In the United Kingdom, incumbent telephone company BT announced that it will sell MVNO 3G mobile services to enterprises on Vodafone's network. At one point, both Qwest and AT&T owned their own mobile networks. AT&T spun off AT&T Wireless, which later merged with Cingular. Qwest Communications sold its wireless spectrum and infrastructure to Verizon Wireless in 2004. For many companies, it costs less to offer mobile services on a resale basis than to build and maintain a nationwide network. Other resellers include AAPT Limited in Australia and Yes Telecom in the United Kingdom.

ESPN, a unit of Disney, is an example of a company using resale to promote its own content. ESPN announced a resale agreement with Sprint PCS in which ESPN will offer ESPN-branded phones with easy access to sports scores, highlights, and headlines. Its parent company Disney has also announced its intention to enter into an MVNO agreement and offer its content on Disney-branded handsets.

Increasing competition for mobile services is causing prices to fall in many developed nations. This puts a squeeze on virtual operators' profits because it decreases the revenue per minute sold. For example, if an operator charges 15¢ per minute to retail customers, it might charge 12¢ to virtual operators, which then can only mark up services a few pennies. Achieving profits in resale requires strong marketing skills or specialized services such as those that ESPN offers. Resale is a way for network owners to recoup some of their investments associated with building 3G networks. Sprint, for example, sells unused capacity to virtual operators. It is able to "fill up more of its pipes" and earn revenue, even though it's at a lower per-minute rate, on their facilities.

The emergence of resale in mobile services is reminiscent of the resale market for landline services in the United States, where AT&T and MCI sold capacity to resellers and other carriers. However, as prices for voice dropped to under 6¢ per minute, profits for resale fell through the floor. With resale, network owners often compete with companies to whom they sell service for resale. For example, Sprint PCS competes with Qwest for business customers' wireless, mobile data services.

Table 8.3 Mobile Services Worldwide

Technology	Frequencies	Features	Comments
First Generation Cellular Service			
Advanced mobile phone service (AMPS)	UL: 824MHz to 849MHz DL: 869MHz to 894MHz	Analog, first type of cellular technology. Provided basic calling and voice mail. Implemented in the late 1980s. More capacity than previous noncellular services.	Two providers, the local telephone company and a competitor, originally served each metropolitan area. All telephones were compatible with all services.

Table 8.3 Mobile Services Worldwide (continued)

Technology	Frequencies	Features	Comments
Nordic mobile telephone (NMT)	Between 410MHz to 490MHz (varies by country) Band A (most used): *UL: 425.5MHz to 457.475MHz *DL: 462.5MHz to 467.475MHz	Analog technology and service offered in Europe. Provides basic calling and voice mail.	CDMA450 is being licensed and deployed within the NMT frequency bands.

Second Generation Cellular Service

Technology	Frequencies	Features	Comments
Digital cellular service (CDMA, TDMA, GSM, and iDEN)	UL: 824MHz to 849MHz DL: 869MHz to 894MHz	Digital service has more capacity than analog service. Provides advanced features such as caller ID and short message service.	CDMA, TDMA, iDEN, and GSM are considered digital cellular air interfaces.
Personal communications service (PCS)	UL: 1850MHz to 1910MHz DL: 1930MHz to 1990MHz	PCS service added more digital spectrum, competitors, and innovative services, driving prices down.	PCS refers to higher-frequency 1.9GHz services. CDMA, TDMA, and GSM service are considered PCS air interfaces.
Global system for mobile communications (GSM)	UL: 890MHz to 915MHz DL: 935MHz to 960MHz	A cellular digital technology. The same handsets can be used in all countries that use GSM multiplexing.	Standard used in Europe, the Far East, Israel, New Zealand, and Australia. Also used by T-Mobile and Cingular Wireless in the United States.
Digital cellular system (DCS)	UL: 1710MHz to 1785MHz DL: 1805MHz to 1880MHz	DCS service added more digital spectrum for most existing carriers and a few new entrants.	DCS refers to higher-frequency 1.8GHz services in Europe. GSM is considered a DCS air interface.

continues

Table 8.3 Mobile Services Worldwide (continued)

Technology	Frequencies	Features	Comments
Enhanced specialized mobile radio (ESMR)	UL: 806MHz to 821MHZ DL: 851MHz to 866MHz	Offerings include packet data from Velocity Wireless (formerly Cingular Interactive), Motient Corporation, and Nextel.	Originally used for analog, two-way voice dispatch services. Nextel and other SMR operators use iDEN technology developed by Motorola to support voice, paging, push-to-talk, and messaging on the same telephone.
2.5 generation services (2.5G)		*Many GSM mobile operators have deployed these packet data services as an interim to 3G. They use the same spectrum as GSM. A lower-cost solution than 3G but with less efficient spectrum utilization.*	
GPRS	Same as GSM, DCS, and PCS	General packet radio service.	Appropriates voice channels for data; 40 to 60 kilobits per second.
EDGE		Enhanced data rates for GSM evolution.	Data speeds of about 110 kilobits per second. Requires fewer voice channels for data than GPRS.
Third generation services (3G)		*Third generation services pack more services into a given amount of spectrum than 2.5G technology. 3G networks will evolve to all-IP, converged networks.*	

Table 8.3 Mobile Services Worldwide   (continued)

Technology	Frequencies	Features	Comments
WCDMA, also called UMTS CDMA2000 1X CDMA2000 1xEV-DO UMTS TDD TD-SCDMA	**IMT2000 bands:** *UMTS:* *UL: 1885MHz to 2025MHz (in the U.S.: 1710MHz to 1755MHz) *DL: 2110MHz to 2170MHz (in the U.S.: 2110MHz to 2155MHz) *CDMA2000:* 450MHz (NMT), 800MHz, 1700MHz (Korea), 1900MHz (PCS), and 2100MHz (UMTS) *UMTS TDD:* 1885MHz to 1920MHz or 2010MHz to 2025MHz (primary), plus 2300MHz to 2400MHz (secondary) *TD-SCDMA:* TBD (China)	More capacity for voice, higher speed data, acceptable video, low latency applications, and so on. Standards bodies have specified all of these frequency bands for 3G services.	Carriers are launching value-added 3G services to generate higher revenues. CDMA2000 1xEV-DO (data optimized) is always combined with CDMA2000 1X (voice and data) on a single chip. WCDMA is normally combined with GSM on a single chip for voice services. UTMS TDD uses one frequency band for uplink and downlink data transmissions. The Chinese government is interested in commercializing TD-SCDMA, a home-grown version of UMTS TDD.

*UL = uplink
*DL = downlink
*2.5G and 3G services are explained in more detail at the end of this chapter.

Europe

Europe has excellent cell phone coverage and, for the most part, uses GSM service in which people take for granted the capability to use their cell phone throughout the continent. However, due to the saturation of cell phones in Western Europe, carriers are looking to expand by offering service in Eastern Europe and Latin America. Most

European countries upgraded from GSM to GPRS and EDGE for higher-speed packet data. They offer short messaging service, e-mail, and news headlines. However, these networks are not fast enough to support video or satisfactory Web browsing.

Hutchison Whampao (known by the brand "3") was the first carrier to implement 3G technology in the United Kingdom in March 2003 and initially focused on selling low-cost mobile voice minutes in addition to offering high-speed Internet access or other data services. In 2004, other carriers such as Vodafone, Telecom Italia, Orange, and T-Mobile followed suit by offering competitive 3G voice services, but they focused more on offering high-speed wireless data PC cards that fit into laptops for business travelers and enterprises.

The following largest cellular carriers in Europe offer service throughout the continent. They are all large conglomerates, offer services internationally, and are among the 10 largest carriers worldwide:

Vodafone Group PLC—The Second Largest Mobile Carrier Worldwide

UK-based Vodafone is the second largest carrier worldwide, after China Mobile, with 133 million subscribers. It and Hutchison are among the few carriers of Europe's largest mobile operators to offer only mobile service. This gives it the advantage of not losing revenue on its fixed-line revenues when customers drop or decrease usage on home telephone services. Vodafone has aggressively offered new services and innovations. In Europe, it offers services in Belgium, France, Germany, Greece, Italy, Poland, Romania, Spain, Switzerland, and the UK. Vodafone branded its GPRS service Vodafone Live! and has used it to successfully sell additional enhanced services such as ring tones and other content. Vodafone has noncontrolling stakes in many operators including Verizon Wireless and providers in Germany, Italy, Greece, and France. The total number of subscribers in mobile companies in which it has a controlling stake is 108 million.

T-Mobile Deuschland—The Largest Mobile Provider in Germany

Germany's incumbent telephone company, Deutsche Telekom, owns T-Mobile International, their wireless subsidiary. T-Mobile International has more than 61 million subscribers worldwide, including those of T-Mobile USA. It offers service in Germany, Austria, the UK, Poland, and Russia.

Orange SA

Orange is owned by France Telecom, which purchased it in 2000. Orange sells mobile service in the UK, Switzerland, and France. It has 49 million mobile customers worldwide, with controlling interest in nine carriers including ones in Romania, Slovakia, Egypt, and Belgium. It has partial ownership in other operators, many of which are in developing countries. UK cable TV operator NTL has announced that it will resell wireless service over Orange's network.

Telecom Italia Mobile

Telecom Italia Mobile, also referred to as TIM, is the largest mobile operator in Italy. Fixed-line operator Telecom Italia owns TIM and is in the process of purchasing the 44% it doesn't own. This is expected to result in Telecom Italia more closely integrating its fixed-line and wireless operations. TIM is expected to benefit from large cash flows from operations in Italy and, as a result of the integration, will be in a position to offer packages of service to customers that include home phone service, wireless, and Internet access. Telecom Italia Mobile has 48 million subscribers. In Europe, it has service in Greece and Turkey. It also has large holdings in South America. It has announced plans to expand internationally in southern Europe and South America.

Telefónica Moviles, SA

Telefónica is the largest mobile provider in Spain and the second largest mobile provider after America Móvil in Latin America. It is owned by incumbent telephone company Telefónica and has 50 million subscribers. It is in the process of purchasing BellSouth's Latin American holdings. It also holds 3G licenses in Germany, Italy, and Switzerland and has joint mobile offerings with Portugal Telecom in Brazil and Morocco. Although Spain counts for well over half of its revenue, mobile growth in Latin America is increasing faster than that in Europe.

China

China has a population of 1.3 billion people and has 120 cities with over 1 million people. The Chinese government recognized in the 1990s that it needed telecommunications infrastructure to become a leading technology country and undertook a major push to develop this infrastructure in China, starting with the eastern coastal region.

According to Dixon Doll, the co-founder and managing general partner of early stage venture capital firm Doll Capital Management:

> *"The Chinese government recognized right from the beginning (and they were very, very savvy to do this) that for their economy to thrive and prosper, they needed a world class telecommunications infrastructure in place, and they did a great job of taking all the investment and planning steps necessary to achieve this goal.*

> *"In the information economy we live in today, if you can't get connectivity to your business, you're in a very tough spot. There are a lot of studies about macroeconomics that talk about the critical success factors for an emerging market economy. You have to have ample supplies of energy and a good communications system. A good communications system facilitates speed, volume of business transactions, and more than anything else facilitates the substantial amounts of productivity increases, which are central to a thriving economy."*

Because of the cost of digging trenches and laying cabling to its large population, most of whom had no landline telephone service, China concentrated on building out its cellular infrastructure. For large businesses, it developed Ethernet-based IP networks rather than investing in older circuit switched technology. In some areas, IP-based networks use the same fiber-optic lines and other infrastructure as the backhaul network connecting antennas and controllers in cellular base stations to mobile switching offices.

There are still gulfs between rural and urban areas in the level of infrastructure. However, Chinese manufacturers are moving to rural areas in the western parts of the country to take advantage of low wages. As they relocate, it is expected that infrastructure will be built out in these areas as well. In addition, in outlying areas, the backhaul network is not connected to high-speed backbone networks that have links to international networks and countrywide high-speed lines. This hinders communications between sections of China.

The Chinese mobile market is highly competitive, and carriers are adding 4 million to 8 million customers per month. The two largest mobile operators in China are China Mobile, the largest mobile carrier in the world, and China Unicom, the third largest mobile carrier worldwide. Both are majority owned by the government, although there is private investment in each of them. China Mobile has grown from just 45.1 million subscribers in 2000 to 202.7 million subscribers by December 2004. China Unicom has 115 million total subscribers, consisting of 85 million GSM subscribers and 30 million CDMA subscribers. According to *Bloomberg*'s April 2004 article "China Mobile to Buy Parent's Networks for $3.65 Bln (Update 2)" by Kenneth Wong and Charles Bickers, 20% of the population has a mobile handset.

Most cellular carriers operate GSM networks. However, China Unicom operates a second generation CDMA and is trialing a third generation CDMA2000 1xEV-DO network. About 10% of China Unicom's CDMA handsets are multimode, capable of functioning on both GSM and CDMA networks. China Unicom implemented its 3G service to gain capacity for voice. In addition to the approximately 320 million cellular customers, there are 65 million customers who use personal handyphone service (PHS), a lower-cost option to full cellular service. These phones can be used only within limited areas such as an individual town. Traditional landline operators offer PHS service.

India

India, with its population of 1.1 billion, is the second most populous country in the world after China. During 2003 and 2004, the telecom sector grew 35% to 40% annually to a point at which 8.37% of the population had either a fixed-line or mobile phone. Mobile phones outnumber fixed-line phones. These statistics were published January 03, 2005 in the article "India has 90 Million Phones Now" in *India Telecom News Weekly*. As of January 2004, only 3% of the population had cellular service. Eighty-one percent of mobile handsets operate on GSM technology and the rest on CDMA, but GSM service is growing faster than CDMA, spurred in large part by the number of well established GSM carriers, their willingness to decrease phone tariffs in response to the CDMA competition, their access to more spectrum than the CDMA carriers have, and because of upper classes' desire to take their phones with them when they travel abroad. Along with the growth, there are many challenges including low prices, large investments in infrastructure needed to keep up with growth, and the fact that electronic processes for doing business are not yet widespread.

India's mobile industry is highly competitive, with 13 mobile carriers as of year-end 2004. However, the government has loosened restrictions on foreign ownership and companies' abilities to merge with other carriers. With these changes, the number of carriers should decrease. For example, Hutchison has made offers to purchase Aircel and merge it into its other holdings in India. Although the standard of living is improving due to increased industrialization, there is still a high level of poverty and low prices for cellular service. Plans that include some minutes of usage cost about $10 per month, and airtime is often just below 2¢ per minute. In addition, carriers are spending money to build up infrastructure, modernized operational support, and billing systems.

Reliance Group, Bharti Cellular Limited (which does business as AirTel), Bharat Sanchar Nigam, Ltd (BSNL), and BPL Mobile are the largest mobile providers in

India. The Indian government owns BSNL, which also operates fixed-line networks. In addition, the Indian government has a majority ownership in Mahanagar Nigam Telecom Ltd. (MTNL), which also offers cellular service. Besides their GSM service, carriers such as Reliance, MTNL, and BSNL started offering CDMA service with limited mobility within local towns as a lower-cost alternative to cellular service for people without landline phones. With the issuance of universal service licenses, two of the largest wireless operators in India, Reliance and Tata Teleservices, now offer full mobility services with roaming facilities anywhere in India. Meanwhile, MTNL and BSNL have started upgrading their 2G CDMA network to 3G CDMA2000 1X. Other mobile providers are Idea Cellular, Tata, Hutchison Max, and Aircel.

THE STRUCTURE OF SECOND GENERATION DIGITAL MOBILE NETWORKS.................................

Although wireless networks don't require the labor-intensive process of laying copper or fiber cabling to individual homes and businesses, they are highly capital-intensive businesses. Mobile networks are made up of cell sites, switching equipment, and connections to other networks as well as peripheral billing, operations and maintenance, and enhanced services components. Second generation cellular networks are composed of the following services and equipment:

- Cell sites, also referred to as base stations, contain antennas and base transceiver stations (BTSs) that convert wireless traffic from customers to signals compatible with landline protocols and vice versa. Cell sites also have connections to mobile central office switches and controllers that manage many cell sites.

- Controllers that assign calls to specific frequencies in each cell site.

- Mobile central office switches that route traffic within mobile networks and to other networks. They have connections to

  - Databases for billing and roaming

  - The public switched telephone network

  - Switches and databases that support features such as push-to-talk and ring tones

  - Cell sites and controllers

  - Other mobile switches

  - Signaling networks

Base stations are the most expensive portions of mobile carriers' networks. In rural areas, cell sites might cover up to 30 miles. However, in densely populated cities with high concentrations of traffic, a cell site may cover less than a mile. Cingular alone has 5,000 cell sites, including those belonging to the former AT&T Wireless. Therefore, network upgrades to, for example, next generation mobile service or acquisition of different spectrum that requires additional base stations or upgrades to existing cell sites can cost carriers billions of dollars.

In addition to the wireless parts of their networks, used by customers to access the network, wireless carriers operate vast landline networks. These connect cell sites and controllers to mobile switches. They also connect cellular networks to the Internet, to other cellular networks, and to the public switched telephone network. Links between their switches may be within the same country or international to other countries. Their networks are made up of microwave, wireless links, twisted pair copper, and fiber-optic cabling. As cellular operators carry more video, voice, and data traffic, these links will have to be upgraded as well. See Figure 8.3 for base stations and mobile switches.

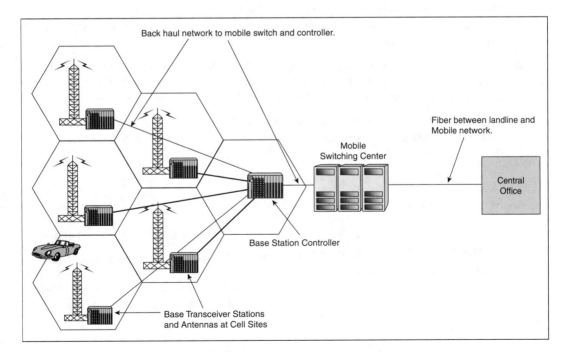

Figure 8.3
The mobile telephone switching office (MTSO) connects the cellular network to the public switched telephone network. The backhaul network connects cells to the mobile switch.

A Cell Site—Connections Between Customers and Mobile Networks

A cell is the physical area in which a set of frequencies is used. Each cell site has a base transceiver station (BTS) and antenna. Initially, when most mobile traffic originated from cars, cell sites were located near heavily trafficked highways. With the increase in pedestrian use of mobile telephones, more cell sites are located in shopping malls and downtown areas. Carriers often share space at cell sites to save costs. For example, a large operator may lease space on a tall water tower for its antenna and on the ground for ancillary equipment. Companies specialize in building towers and leasing space for cell sites. For example, rather than a single mobile carrier owning a tower or the land around the tower, a third-party company builds the tower and leases space on the tower as well as space for the rest of the equipment at base stations. This spares carriers from investing capital in towers and real estate.

Mobile handsets and data devices are connected to cellular networks by the base transceiver station. The base transceiver station (BTS) is connected to the antennas by coaxial cabling. It transmits and receives mobile calls from the cell site's antennas and amplifies (strengthens) signals. It also performs the conversion of signals between over-the-air radio frequency formats, such as GSM and CDMA, to those compatible with landline networks and visa versa.

The base station controller (BSC) is the traffic cop of the mobile network. It does the precall setup, meaning it assigns calls to radio channels in the base station transceiver, sends ringing to the correct channel, and measures signal strength.

For analog service, the base station controller must be located at the base station. For digital cellular service, one controller can manage many base transceiver stations (BTSs).

Power Requirements at Cell Sites

Each cell site needs local power for equipment at the site. Maintaining service during electrical outages can be a critical issue, and loss of power is one of the reasons that mobile phones don't operate in disasters. However, not all carriers have adequate backup. Some have battery backup for momentary power glitches and short outages lasting a few hours. Installation of generators that operate for a few days is uneven.

Backhaul—Connecting Base Stations to Switches

In addition to managing vast amounts of cellular traffic, carriers operate large landline networks between their cell sites and the rest of their equipment. The links between cell sites, controllers, and mobile switches are referred to as backhaul. Traffic from many cell sites is backhauled to a central location—the operator's mobile switch. Depending on the amount of traffic, backhaul networks use the following:

- T1/E1 (1.54 megabits/2.05 megabits) on copper cabling
- Microwave (a wireless transmission service at T1/E1) or T3/E3 (44 megabits/34.4 megabits) speeds
- Optical carrier speeds of 155 megabits per second on fiber cabling

Switching and Signaling

The *mobile switching center (MSC)*, also called the *mobile telephone switching office (MTSO)*, is analogous to a PBX or central office switch. It switches calls between cellular networks and the public switched telephone network. Mobile switches have Signaling System 7 (SS7) links to databases that contain billing and roaming information (see Figure 8.4). Short message service, information displayed on handsets, and enhanced features such as caller ID, voice-activated dialing, and repeat dialing are made possible by Signaling System 7 links to databases. (Refer to Chapter 4, "VoIP, the Public Switched Telephone Network, and Signaling," for more information on SS7.) Older mobile switches control up to 255 cell sites, and new ones control up to 1,024 sites.

The following databases are linked to mobile switches by Signaling System 7.

- *Databases.* Home location registers (HLRs) contain information services and billing information on subscribers. The HLR also keeps track of the status and location of subscribers within its area. Visitor information is located in the visitor's location register (VLR). There are other databases that store telephone identities and authentication codes for digital phones. The United States has a nationwide Signaling System 7 cellular network operated by a consortium of cellular companies. It was started by AT&T.

- *Messaging centers.* These databases and processors handle short messaging services (SMS), which are short text messages. More advanced systems store multimedia messages.

- *Connections to the public switched telephone network.* Mobile telephone switching offices are connected to landline public networks by high-speed, 44-megabits-per-second (Mbps) T-3 links and higher-speed links. In large networks, multiple mobile switches connect to a centralized trunking switching center, which provides high-speed links to other networks.

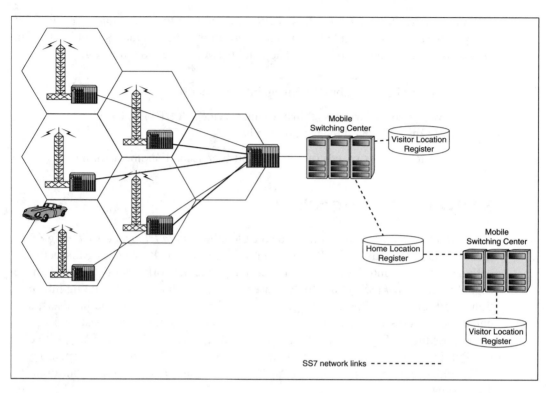

Figure 8.4
Mobile switching center, Signaling System 7 (SS7), and registers containing subscriber databases.

Coverage Gaps—Rural Locales, Inside Buildings, and Congested Metropolitan Areas

Providing adequate capacity and coverage is a major challenge, particularly in competitive markets where flat revenues make it difficult to allocate capital for infrastructure. Coverage gaps are most noticeable in rural areas, inside buildings, and in congested city centers. Carriers concentrate their efforts where there are the largest pools of potential customers and fill in gaps later. However, the increased use of mobile phones for voice and text messaging by pedestrians and workers within office buildings has increased traffic within cities and buildings.

Mobile service reliability and availability have strategic and safety implications. The biggest problem of inadequate capacity is felt during natural disasters or other crises. Traffic more than doubles during these peak periods. People rely on cellular service during crises to call for help when tradition landline networks are out of service. Emergency providers, such as police and firefighters, also use cellular handsets to communicate with other departments or cities.

In the aftermath of the December 2004 tsunami that affected India, Indonesia, Sri Lanka, parts of Africa, and Thailand, many people were able to send text messaging from their cell phones to let loved ones know they were safe. Short text messages were often successfully transmitted even when the voice part of the cellular network was congested. Text messages, which are sent on the control channel used for signals such as ringing and caller ID, are sent in packets interspersed with control signals and other text messages. In addition, if there is congestion, they can be held for short periods of time until capacity becomes available.

Coverage Inside Buildings and Tunnels

Large buildings, airports, concrete parking lots, and tunnels are particularly hard places in which to provide coverage. It's extremely difficult to penetrate walls without turning up power on antennas too high. The height of buildings also is a problem. Putting antennas in top stories gives coverage there, but the signal is too weak to reach the street. One solution is to install a cell site within buildings with small antennas on every floor or every few feet in tunnels. Many systems can support multiple air access methods simultaneously (such as TDMA, GSM, Nextel, paging, and CDMA). Some carriers install these systems and lease capacity to other carriers.

Number Portability—Wireless to Wireless and Wireline to Wireless

Wireless local number portability enables subscribers to keep their mobile telephone number when they change wireless providers within a local area. Wireless local number portability, as instituted in the United States, mandates that carriers also provide wireline-to-wireless and wireless-to-wireline portability. This increases the number of people who drop their landline service in favor of mobile service because it eliminates the problems associated with changing telephone numbers. By the end of the first year of portability, November 2004, the FCC reported that 8.5 million people changed providers using local number portability (LNP). The FCC further reported that close to 850,000 of them dropped their home lines for wireless service. In the United States, prior to wireline-to-wireless portability, about 7.5 million people relied on wireless service for all their voice telephony. There are close to 183 million landlines in the United States. Internationally, Australia, the United Kingdom, and Hong Kong have wireless local number portability.

The way portability works is that the mobile identification number (MIN) is no longer always the same as users' 10-digit mobile telephone number. Under wireless number portability, when someone calls the mobile number, the wireless carrier performs a "data dip" at a national database. The database correlates the 10-digit directory number to a 10-digit mobile subscriber identification number, which identifies the mobile carrier assigned to the directory number.

Wireless Service As a Replacement for Landlines

About 6% of telephone users in the United States use cellular service for all their voice service. Problematic service inside homes and apartment buildings is a major impediment to dropping wireline service for wireless service. Signals often don't penetrate walls in residential dwellings. To overcome this problem, as well as the problem of using cellular service from multiple phones, Sprint offers a docking station with a high-powered antenna that improves coverage inside buildings. The docking station plugs into any telephone jack and converts the cellular signal to that compatible with home wiring and vice versa. Thus, people with this service can use all their home phones to make and receive mobile calls as long as the cell phone is plugged into the docking station.

Another way in which users will solve the problem of service within buildings is with wireless 802.11 technologies, also dubbed Wi-Fi, and wireless local area networks (WLANs). WLANs use wireless voice over IP to carry voice traffic on local area networks inside buildings. For example, manufacturers offer wireless handsets that operate on both wireless mobile networks covering large areas and WLAN networks inside homes, businesses, and hotspots. *Wireless mobility* refers to using wireless services when driving, walking, or other places where users can move from area to area without dropping their connections. The point of having chips in handsets that operate on WLAN and cellular networks is to enable people to talk on either type of network and have their conversations continue automatically without dropped calls when they move out of or into 802.11 or cellular coverage areas. WLAN services are covered in Chapter 9.

Another challenge of using wireless for all voice service is protection from power outages. Circuit switched service usually operates during these outages because power is supplied at most of the telephone company equipment. In addition, when people dial 911 in an emergency, public service access providers may not know the address from which people are calling. See the section later in this chapter for E911 on mobile service.

In addition, the fact that, in the United States, people pay for calls they receive as well as those they make is an impediment to using mobile service for all calls. In Europe and much of the rest of the world, people who place calls to mobile phones pay for the call. This is referred to as *calling party pays (CPP)*. Calling party pays limits customers' costs, making the price of mobile service closer to or on a par with landline service.

The Impact of Wireless LNP in Enterprises

As more businesspeople rely on mobile service, being able to keep their numbers when they change carriers becomes critical. Highly mobile business customers tend to put their mobile telephone number on their business card. Therefore, wireless local number portability removes an important barrier to corporate clients changing carriers. Because a single large enterprise customer often has thousands of cellular numbers for employees, retaining these business customers is critical to carriers. In addition, these customers tend to be heavy users and take advantage of profitable services such as roaming, e-mail, and data communications. As high-speed 3G data offerings mature, carriers will focus major resources on retaining these customers.

Roaming Using Mobile Devices in Other Networks

Roaming is the capability to use voice or mobile data devices in other carriers' networks. These networks are usually in other countries or, for U.S.-based customers, in other states. Roaming is important because no one carrier has coverage everywhere. Calls made and received while roaming are more expensive than those in people's home territory. People with GSM service often have different SIM (subscriber identity module) modules for countries to which they frequently travel to save on roaming fees. People who travel tend to be high-end customers who use more mobile services. Thus, inbound roamers from other networks are profitable sources of revenues worldwide.

Links Between Wireless Carriers

Agreements between carriers are required for every region in which roaming is enabled. Roaming agreements spell out costs, billing, and payment terms. To illustrate the complexity of roaming arrangements, most carriers have agreements with 200 to 250 other carriers. Some carriers use brokers who already have agreements worldwide and share revenue with the broker.

Once the agreement has been signed and the service tested, roaming is activated. Carriers lease high-speed links from their network to other carriers from international carriers such as MCI, France Telecom, and Belgacom. These links carry voice traffic. Signaling links are also established to perform functions such as the handshake between the handset and the user's home carrier. The handshake verifies that users are legitimate customers of the originating network and have roaming privileges. Because parts of the world use incompatible flavors of Signaling System 7, gateways are used to translate between incompatible SS7 types.

Enhanced Roaming—Making Away Seem Like Home, Boosting Roaming Revenues

Often when people travel, they are frustrated because features they use in their home networks don't work. For example, dialing codes to access voice mail, speed dialing, directory assistance, and emergency services may be different or inoperable. In addition, mobile devices may not receive calling line ID (CLID), the identity of the person calling them, if the international fixed-line carrier has stripped the digits out. To provide feature transparency and boost roaming revenues, mobile carriers are taking the following steps:

- Requesting that the fixed-line international carrier, which connects cellular carriers to each other, retain CLID because CLID increases call completion rates and promotes additional outbound calling.

- Looking at calls that don't complete, guessing the correct access codes, and inserting them. For example, many countries use different short codes to access emergency service (911, 112, 111); also speed dialing often doesn't work because the number is programmed without the international access code (for example, zero plus one or zero).

- Routing calls between users roaming in the same network and from the same home network directly to each other without sending the call back to the home network.

- Intercepting roaming registration so that callers use subsidiaries of the parent company or operators with whom the carrier has the most favorable agreement for their roaming service.

Push-to-Talk—Mobile Walkie-Talkie Service

Push-to-talk is a walkie-talkie service in which users push a button on their telephone to reach others in their predefined group. Push-to-talk (PTT) service provides a second channel on handsets for quick connections to individuals or predefined groups. It's a half duplex service—only one person at a time can talk—but everyone on a group call can hear the conversation. Traditional voice calling is full duplex, which supports simultaneous two-way transmissions. With full duplex service, both people on calls can talk at the same time.

Nextel is the first carrier that deployed push-to-talk. Nextel customers that make a cellular call push the "Send" button rather than the push-to-talk button on the side of the telephone. To call an individual rather than a group, people generally dial the last four digits of the person's telephone number if they are in the same organization. Alternatively, users can select a person from their address book and then press the push-to-talk button.

In addition to Nextel, other carriers such as Orange (a French carrier with service in nine countries) and T-Mobile (a German cellular provider) offer push-to-talk service. Sprint, Alltel, and Verizon Wireless plus some smaller carriers also offer it in the United States. However, some of the early services had noticeable delays in connecting callers. All push-to-talk services require handsets that interoperate with the push-to-talk service installed in operators' networks. Some of the services are standards based and some are proprietary.

Nextel Push-to-Talk

Nextel was the first carrier to offer push-to-talk and cellular service on the same network. The company initially offered it to small contractors, truckers, and companies with dispatch requirements. Push-to-talk became so popular that large companies started using it to stay in touch with staff—for example, at conventions or for standard connectivity within departments. Nextel also sells service to residential customers, but their customers are mainly businesses. The Nextel service operates over iDEN technology developed by Motorola. Canadian wireless and fixed-line provider Telus also uses Motorola's technology for push-to-talk service on its mobile network and handsets.

How iDEN Push-to-Talk Works

Motorola's proprietary technology, integrated digital enhanced network (iDEN), transmits voice and data in packets over dedicated channels. When users activate push-to-talk, the iDEN network sends a paging message through its signaling network to locate the called person. The called party hears a short "chirp" and presses his or her push-to-talk (PTT) button if he or she wishes to take the call. The iDEN network then sets up a wireless channel for the call. These calls do not use the public switched telephone network (PSTN). Therefore, during PSTN outages, push-to-talk still works if Nextel equipment is up and running. Nextel states that its walkie-talkie calls are set up in less than a second.

Because the iDEN network is proprietary, only Motorola handsets are compatible with Nextel service. The disadvantage of the iDEN network is that it does not support high-capacity 3G service.

IDEN Nationwide Push-to-Talk Coverage

When Nextel first offered push-to-talk, it was limited to customers' local geographic area. Nextel increased the reach of its walkie-talkie service by making it available nationwide and to carriers in other countries that operate iDEN networks. It did this by connecting Nextel networks to other localities through its nationwide asynchronous transfer mode (ATM) data network. ATM is a packet network protocol that supports parallel voice, video, and data sessions. Connections between sites use permanent virtual circuits (PVCs) to carry traffic from many sources. No single PTT or data session requires a dedicated path in the network (see Figure 8.5).

Push-to-Talk from Other Carriers— Voice Instant Messaging

Carriers wishing to emulate Nextel's success with push-to-talk have started offering their own push-to-talk service, which they also refer to as voice instant messaging. Manufacturers have taken differing approaches in their offerings. Kodiak Network's

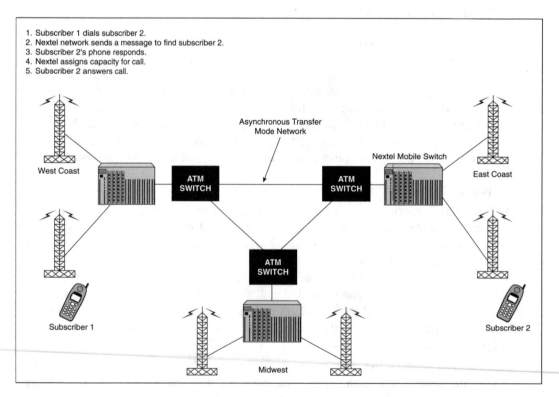

1. Subscriber 1 dials subscriber 2.
2. Nextel network sends a message to find subscriber 2.
3. Subscriber 2's phone responds.
4. Nextel assigns capacity for call.
5. Subscriber 2 answers call.

Figure 8.5
The Nextel nationwide push-to-talk service used for nationwide service.

design is similar to iDEN's in that both use the same channels for voice and push-to-talk. In both systems, push-to-talk traffic between geographically separate networks is carried over packet networks. In contrast to Nextel's push-to-talk, which operates only with Motorola iDEN equipment, the Kodiak packet switch interoperates with all over-the-air protocols. One Kodiak packet switch can support an entire network and connects to other networks over private IP networks as well as circuit switched protocols such as T-1/E-1 (see Figure 8.6).

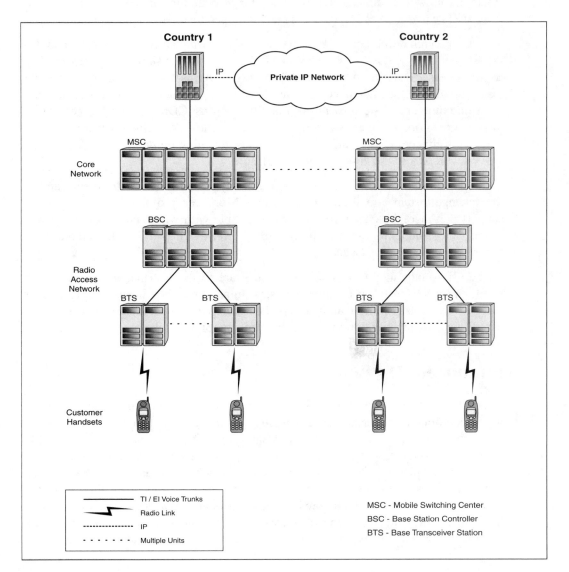

Figure 8.6
Kodiak push-to-talk between cellular networks. Figure courtesy of Kodiak Networks.

Other manufacturers, such as Fastmobile, Inc., Motorola (through their purchase of Winphoria), and Sonim sell systems based on the Push-to-Talk over Cellular (PoC) specifications. PoC was developed for GSM operators by a consortium of carriers and manufacturers. These systems operate over 2.5G and third generation networks. However, when used on slower-speed 2.5G networks, noticeable delays may be introduced between requesting and connecting calls. It's not clear whether these latency (delay) problems will be solved when they're installed on advanced third generation WCDMA networks implemented by many GSM operators. In standards-based systems, users can use voice instant messaging with people on different networks.

Qualcomm developed BREWChat and QChat, which are push-to-talk technologies supported by CDMA2000 1xEV-DO Release 0 and Revision A, respectively. The second release, Revision A of CDMA2000 1xEV-DO, is a third generation protocol that is optimized for low-latency IP transmissions. Low-latency networks reduce the call setup time experienced by push-to-talk users. Most CDMA2000 third generation mobile operators such as Verizon Wireless, Sprint PCS, China Unicom, VIVO (Brazil), Reliance, KDDI, and SK Telecom are planning on deploying CDMA2000 1xEV-DO Rev A in the 2006 to 2007 timeframe.

In addition to voice instant messaging, many manufacturers offer the capability to exchange instant e-mail and instant video. Moreover, protocols specified for 3G support presence, the capability to know if people with whom customers exchange instant voice and text messages are available. Refer to Chapter 7, "The Internet," for more information on presence.

Push-to-talk suppliers license their software to handset manufacturers, which pay them fees to install it on their handsets. In addition, they license rights to their software to infrastructure manufacturers. For example, Kodiak has licensed its product to Lucent, which will provide it as part of its mobile switches.

Enhanced 911

Over 30% of all calls to 911 are from cellular telephones, and the percentage is growing. According to the National Emergency Number Association (NENA), as of November 2003, there were 100,000 calls daily from mobile phones. However, people who call 911 often can't tell emergency operators their exact location because they're driving in new places, choking, or having a heart attack. Cases have been documented in which a lack of location information caused people in fires, drowning, or in the midst of a heart attack to die before emergency personnel reached them. To solve this problem, the FCC mandated enhancements to the information that cellular carriers are required to transmit to public safety access points, the people and equipment that handle emergency 911 calls. This order makes enhanced 911, the capability for public safety agencies to receive caller ID and location information, mandatory by December 2005. This deadline did not take into account the lack of required location databases needed by people who answer emergency calls. These snags to wireless E911 functionality, which are outside the FCC's control, are listed in the next section.

Phase 1 of the FCC order on enhanced 911, which commenced on April 1, 1998, ordered that callers' numbers and the section of the cell site from which the call is sent must be transmitted. The cellular number is sent so that the public safety group can call back the cellular phone if the call is dropped. As of December 2004, this phase was 65% complete. Part of the delay resulted from T-Mobile, Cingular, and the former AT&T Wireless changing technology because their initial network-based service did not perform adequately.

The two main types of technology that support wireless enhanced 911 (E911) services are handset- and network-based systems. In handset-type systems, chips in the handset communicate with the global positioning system satellites (GPS) and network-based servers. The servers analyze the time it takes GPS signals to reach handsets to calculate location. The federal government launched 24 GPS satellites for military tracking purposes and later made them available for commercial use.

CDMA2000 operators such as Verizon Wireless, Sprint PCS, China Unicom, KDDI, Reliance, and Alltel use the handset-based approach. These operators use the gpsOne handset-based position location technology that is inserted within all Qualcomm chip sets to satisfy the FCC's E911 mandate. gpsOne is a hybrid technology that uses both GPS satellites and network triangulation algorithms to provide the most accurate position location data possible for both outside (5m–10m) and inside of buildings (50m–75m). In network-based systems, the intelligence is in the provider's cell site. Base stations communicating with handsets determine callers' locations. TDMA and GSM operators such as Cingular and T-Mobile use the less-accurate network-based solution. The handset-based services make it possible for users to opt to have only their E9ll calls tracked for location. This ensures privacy for customers who prefer that carriers not track customers' locations except when they call 911.

Because of possible interference in tunnels, within buildings, and by foliage, the FCC does not require 100% accuracy. Depending on the technology used, accuracy must be within a 164-foot (50 meters) to 984-foot (300 meters) radius of the caller.

These rules apply to calls made while roaming as well as in home territory. They also apply to in-car navigation systems such as GM's OnStar service, which enables people to call for help if they have a problem on the road.

Stumbling Blocks to E911—Software Upgrades and Databases

As of December 2004, only 18% of emergency answering locations were compatible with E911 from cellular callers. When mobile networks provide location information to public safety access providers (PSAPs), it is by longitude and latitude and not street address. Mapping software with spatial location databases is required to translate latitude and longitude information into street names so that public safety staff can dispatch police, fire departments, and ambulances. This requires costly town-by-town or metropolitan area upgrades to locations that answer 911 calls.

Another challenge is directing the call to the correct PSAP. There are 6,000 nationwide. When people dial 911, the cellular network sends the call over a landline connection to the PSAP. At times, these calls are directed to the incorrect public safety access provider because of incorrect dialing or inferior connections to landline networks.

The following is a November 11, 2003 quote from *E911 Mapping* by John Fisher that appeared on the National Emergency Number Association (NENA) Web site:

> *"With some notable exceptions, government has not met the challenge of creating and maintaining the spatial databases necessary for E911 operations. An interesting observation arising out of the NENA conference was that, in many cases, there were private sector spatial databases that were far better than the government ones, but they were not being utilized."*

The article went on to list information needed on these databases such as the closest major intersection, nearby landmarks, directions to the site, and the best route to the site. Other information required includes the location of the nearest hospital. To pay for new databases with mapping information, some states instituted E911 fees on cell phone bills. However, many of them, including California, North Carolina, and New York, used E911 funds for other purposes. To help finance PSAP upgrades, the Senate and the House of Representatives in December 2004 voted to establish a $250 million fund for grants for upgrades. However, Congress still has to appropriate money to fund the program. Grants can't be given to states that used E911 taxes for other purposes.

Killing Lost or Stolen Portable Computers Using GPS and Other Technologies

A major source of security lapses occurs when corporate laptops and personal digital assistants such as Blackberries are lost or stolen. Confidential corporate information and private e-mail messages are often stored on these devices. Currently, mobile carriers have the capability to remotely disable personal digital assistants (PDAs) when corporations report them lost.

In addition, according to research firm IDC, 50% of new PDAs in Western Europe are equipped with GPS chips. The GPS chips enable organizations to find missing devices so that data can be recovered from them. In addition, Nokia is working with partners on ways to use GPS chips in Nokia handsets and data cards in laptops to kill missing or stolen devices. As carriers upgrade to 3G, they will be more likely to implement GPS technology because 3G networks depend on GPS satellites to synchronize the timing in their networks. Hutchison's 3G networks in Europe and Southeast Asia support GPS tracking, as do most networks in Japan and some in Korea. One possible application is for parents to keep track of children or spouses who have GPS chips in their handsets.

Privacy Concerns

Location-based services raise privacy concerns. Databases located in carriers' networks track location information about users when their cellular phones are turned on. Privacy experts are concerned that if carriers share tracking information, marketing organizations will know people's shopping habits and driving routes and collect this information in a database. These worries are not limited to information gathered from cellular telephones. They cover tracking habits of people that use Blackberry e-mail pagers, in-car navigation systems such as GM's OnStar, personal digital assistant devices, and laptops equipped with radio modems.

The Criticality of Mobile Networks— Emergency Preparedness

People depend on wireless service for more than casual conversation. They use their handsets to call for help, report accidents, and stay in touch with family during emergencies. Moreover, mobile service is an essential feature of complex rescue efforts in national disasters. During terrorist attacks, wireless infrastructure is a matter of national security. Emergency responders, the military, and the executive branch of governments rely on wireless service to communicate from remote locations. In addition, landline networks are often not operational in emergencies.

Accountability in Disasters

Governments hold wireless carriers that receive licenses for telecommunications services and airwaves accountable for the quality of their networks. These need to deliver
the following:

- Reliability in the absence of acts of aggression under normal operating
  conditions

- Sustainability in the event of an attack or emergency utilizing hardware
  and software redundancy

- The capacity to handle at least double the call volumes in emergencies

- The security to prevent unauthorized people or organizations from gaining
  access to and damaging networks

PORTABLE EQUIPMENT FOR COVERAGE IN EMERGENCIES AND SPECIAL EVENTS COWS AND COLTS

One of the major advantages of cellular networks is that portable equipment can be deployed quickly in disasters such as hurricanes when infrastructure including cell sites and switches are destroyed. In addition,
portable equipment can be deployed to provide added capacity for special events such as the Olympics, major sporting events, and presidential
conventions. The main ways to provide temporary infrastructure is
through the use of cell-sites on wheels (COWs) and cell-sites on light
trucks (COLTs). The difference between a COW and a COLT is that COWs
are mounted on flat-bed trailers that need to be hooked up to trucks.
COLTs are on light trucks and can be immediately driven to locations.

COLTs and COWs have their own batteries or generators, so they can
operate independent of the local electric supply. They also have one or
two towers that communicate back to the mobile switch. Some of them
also have small offices, extra fuel, food and water, and cots for technicians. Cell-sites on light trucks (COLTs) are intended for rapid deployment in the event of disasters because they don't need to be hooked up
to trucks.

EXTENDING CAPACITY INTO BUILDINGS

Extra capacity often is needed inside convention centers and hotels, as was the case during the 2004 Republican and Democratic national conventions. In these instances, repeaters make spectrum available inside buildings from nearby "donor" cell sites. Repeaters within radio range of the "donor" cell site are located at the building to provide more capacity. The repeater redirects and extends signals from the nearby "donor" site into the building.

Priority Access Service—Increasing Mobile Availability for Officials During Emergencies

One way the United States government reserves capacity on cellular networks is by selecting certain carriers to provide priority access in emergencies. Priority access gives designated public and private officials higher priority to cellular service in emergencies. For example, authorized emergency preparedness officials and government officials can gain access to the next available wireless channel by dialing a special code. There are five different levels of priority. Dialing the code does not interrupt a call in progress. However, the use of priority access reduces availability of cellular networks for consumers. For example, when people try to make calls and there are fewer channels (wireless capacity), the available channels are assigned to people dialing the priority code. Priority access service increases availability for officials. It does not add overall capacity. Rather, it decreases availability for citizens' emergency calls to hospitals and police. Getting through for these calls can make a difference in saving lives. In the United States, Nextel and T-Mobile USA have been awarded priority access service contracts by the government.

EVOLVING TO THIRD GENERATION PACKET NETWORKS ....

The main drivers behind evolving to standards-based third generation mobile networks are a desire for more capacity and the capability for operators to offer revenue-producing services that require advanced, third generation (3G) networks. Standards are one way to control equipment costs because they foster competition among suppliers. Network equipment built around standards is meant to be interoperable. Interoperability enables carriers to purchase equipment from a wide choice of manufactures. This promotes competition, driving down prices and reducing dependence on a single supplier. However, standards-based equipment may not be as feature rich because manufacturers adhere to standards that sometimes make it difficult to create innovations, which might differ from established standards.

The International Telecommunications Union started an effort called IMT-2000 (international mobile telephone) to define one advanced digital standard for next-generation voice and high-speed data on cellular networks. Unfortunately, due to political pressure from operators and manufacturers, who wanted standards to more closely match the equipment they produced and used in their networks, the International Telecommunications Union (ITU) subcommittees endorsed several third generation techniques. Third generation standards have various evolutions, referred to as releases or revisions, that increase speeds, capacity, and suitability for converged networks capable of carrying voice, video, and data. These upgrades also improve quality and the capability to prioritize voice, video, and data (see Tables 8.4 and 8.5). The peak and attainable data rates associated with these services vary because of a number of factors, including distance from antennas, congestion within the cell, and weather conditions.

Comparing Third Generation Technologies

Third generation standards are collectively known as IMT-2000 international mobile telecommunications. The most widely implemented third generation standards are WCDMA and CDMA2000.

The following is a list of third generation technologies:

- WCDMA (wideband CDMA) is the third generation standard that most GSM cellular providers have stated they will use. WCDMA is also known as the universal mobile telecommunications system (UMTS).

- TD-SCDMA (time division-synchronous CDMA) is a standard that the Chinese government has suggested because it favors Chinese manufacturers. However, the government has left it up to operators to make their own choice on third generation technology and has made spectrum available for the three main 3G standards. It reaches peak data rates of 2Mbps. There are currently no TD-SCDMA-compatible handsets in commercial deployment.

- CDMA2000 is the standard that most CDMA providers and some providers in newly developing countries such as China (China Unicom Ltd.) use. Verizon Wireless and Sprint use CDMA2000. CDMA2000 was the first IMT-2000 standard deployed commercially, in October 2000 by SKT in South Korea.

- UMTS TDD, also known as TDD (time-division duplex) and TD-CDMA, was initially used for broadband wireless access but is now used for mobile services as well. TDD supports downlink speeds toward the customer of up to 3 megabits per second. IPWireless supplies most of the TDD equipment that is on the market. Mobile TDD is being used by Maxis in Malaysia and Clix/Optimus/Sonaecom in Portugal and is being trialed in Japan and Asia. IPWireless systems are sold on an OEM basis through suppliers such as Alcatel. TDD uses unpaired spectrum. Mobile operators deploy it as an overlay technology for high-speed data.

- EDGE is used as a transition to 3G by operators such as Cingular and the former AT&T Wireless that used TDMA for their second generation digital services. The 3G version of EDGE has never been deployed.

The Transition to WCDMA— GPRS and Then EDGE

Most GSM operators implemented general packet radio service (GPRS) and EDGE before WCDMA, which supports higher data rates and more capacity for voice. See Table 8.4. They took these steps first for the following reasons:

- WCDMA equipment was not stable until 2004.

- Small, lightweight 3G handsets were not widely available prior to 2004.

- Installing GPRS and EDGE delayed the large expenses to upgrade to WCDMA.

- Handsets for GPRS and EDGE were readily available.

- GPRS and EDGE operate on the same frequencies as GSM, thus upgrades are less costly.

Handset availability is a critical factor in network upgrades. Handsets need to be equipped with chips containing matching air interfaces to operate on all cellular networks. Thus, handsets must to be equipped for 3G, GPRS, or EDGE for customers to use these networks. In addition, attractive, feature-rich mobile devices attract customers.

Table 8.4   Transitional 2.5G and 3G Cellular Services

Carriers with GSM and TDMA networks implement these technologies before installing more costly WCDMA networks.

Service	Other Designations for the Service	Comments
GPRS (general packet radio services)		64Kbps peak data rate; achievable rate of about 30Kbps*
		Packet data—takes capacity from voice in GSM networks and dedicates it to data
EDGE (enhanced data rates for global evolution)	UWCC-136 Universal Wireless Communications Consortium	Peak data rate of 384 kilobits; achievable rate of 100Kbps*
		More efficient way than GPRS to transmit packetized data, as channels are dynamically shared between voice and data

Kbps = kilobits per second
Mbps = megabits per second

GPRS—Data Carried As Packets in 2.5G Networks

When operators added GPRS service, they envisioned expanding their offerings. Many of them hoped to emulate Japanese wireless carrier DoCoMo's success with its iMode offerings that included short messaging service, financial information, and downloading cartoon characters. GPRS did enable GSM operators to offer new services, although the vast majority of their revenue remains voice. For example, Vodafone branded its GPRS-enabled service Live!, which offers features such as photo swapping between Live! handsets and access to content. GPRS is inadequate for high-bandwidth applications like surfing the Internet.

GPRS is a data overlay network that operates on GSM networks and uses the same backhaul network between base stations and mobile switches as voice traffic. To implement GPRS, software and hardware are added to base transceiver stations and base station controllers, and software is loaded into mobile switches. A major disadvantage of GPRS is that it uses voice capacity for data, which is a problem in congested areas. Carriers such as Cingular in the United States added GSM service to their TDMA networks and then installed GPRS. Breaking up their spectrum into these separate chunks for different services resulted in less efficient use of spectrum and more congestion. Large chunks of capacity for few air interfaces result in more efficient utilization of network capacity. This phenomenon is similar to many lines at banks and post offices to access a limited number of clerks. It takes less time to get served when there is one combined queue for all customers than where there is a separate queue for each clerk. With one or two air interfaces, the "pool" of capacity increases.

GPRS is a packet data service for GSM networks. GPRS is a data-only service. Interference, noise, prioritization of voice capacity, availability of time slots, and possible network congestion cause the typical speed to be about 10Kbps to 40Kbps. GPRS service supports "always on" capability. Thus, whenever their handsets are on, users receive their messages without having to dial into the network to receive messages.

EDGE-Enhanced Data Rates for Global Evolution— Faster and More Efficient Than GPRS

As of December 2004, 106 operators worldwide have implemented EDGE technology, 46 of them in the Americas. EDGE is considered a 2.5G technology or a 3G technology, depending on the type of EDGE service deployed. However, the 3G version of EDGE has not been implemented. In addition to being slower than WCDMA, EDGE provides less capacity for voice. As other carriers implement WCDMA and CDMA2000 1xEV-DO networks with higher data rates and more voice capacity, carriers will be under competitive pressure to also upgrade to WCDMA, particularly as the greater voice capacities enable operators with WCDMA to reduce their prices on calling plans (see Table 8.5 for a comparison of 3G technologies). In Europe, Telecom Italia Mobile has implemented EDGE, and Cingular introduced EDGE in the United States. T-Mobile USA announced its intention to introduce EDGE in 2005, and other carriers use it in Asia.

Most carriers considering EDGE plan to use it as an intermediary service for higher-speed data. Enhanced data rates for global evolution (EDGE) offers higher-speed data rates than general packet radio services (GPRS). The average data throughput typically is between 60–120 kilobits per second, depending on network conditions. In addition, it uses up less network capacity because it dynamically assigns voice and data to channels as they become available instead of dedicating part of the network to voice and part to data. Upgrading to EDGE can be relatively low cost for carriers with base stations that are only two to three years old. The acronym EDGE originally stood for enhanced data rates for GSM evolution.

WCDMA—Wideband Code Division Multiplexing

WCDMA, also called universal mobile telecommunications system (UMTS), is the 3G service that most GSM operators install. The Japanese carrier NTT DoCoMo was the first carrier to implement WCDMA in October 2001. Vodafone KK in Japan was next in December 2002 with Hutchison's 3 subsidiary, following in Italy and the UK in March 2003. Because of the enormity of the change, WCDMA implementations experienced rocky starts with spotty coverage and technical glitches (since resolved) such as calls dropped when callers moved from cell to cell and handsets overheating because of high power consumption. Upgrading from GSM and from the Japanese cellular technology was a technical challenge and involved a completely different air interface.

Carriers are moving ahead with WCDMA implementations for its added voice capacity and expectations of future applications. According to umts-forum.org, as of December 2004, there were 57 WCDMA networks worldwide. The Web site 3gtoday.com noted that there are 13.3 million WCDMA subscribers worldwide, most of them in Japan, as of December 2004. However, in Japan, for example, NTT DoCoMo and Vodafone K.K. lost many customers to KDDI, which smoothly evolved to 3G straight from its earlier second generation CDMA services.

Upgrades to WCDMA from GSM— Enormous Spectrum and Equipment Costs

European operators invested enormous amounts of money in spectrum and equipment for 3G services based on their desire for more capacity for voice and for higher achievable data rates. They collectively spent $109 billion Euros for 3G spectrum licenses. Market research firm iSuppli predicts that they will spend roughly the same amount building 3G networks between 2001 and 2007. These statistics were published on September 2, 2004 in *Economist.com*'s article "Vision, meet realty" from the *Economist* print edition. No author was listed.

Japan, like other parts of Asia, did not hold auctions for spectrum for 3G services. Rather, many governments awarded spectrum based on "beauty contests" of carriers' qualifications. The lack of requirements to spend huge sums on spectrum has left Asian companies with more resources to upgrade their networks.

The largest expense in moving to WCDMA from GSM is new base stations. The higher-frequency spectrum needed for 3G means that many more base stations are needed because antennas for high frequencies cover smaller areas than those used in 2G and 2.5G networks. GSM in Europe operates on 900 megahertz and WCDMA on

2.1 gigahertz. Because WCDMA is based on code division rather than time division access, upgrades on GSM networks (based on time division) to full 3G services require new infrastructure equipment. In addition, hardware and software upgrades for mobile switching offices are needed as well as new billing and back office systems.

NTT DoCoMo, one of the largest mobile network operators with 46 million subscribers in Japan, initially implemented 3G based on WCDMA FOMA, a standard used only by DoCoMo. The company is now upgrading to WCDMA-compliant service that will make its handsets compatible with other networks when customers travel and will also provide them with a greater choice of handsets. Japanese mobile customers are sophisticated mobile users who more and more frequently use their handsets to send e-mail, download ring tones and cartoon characters, and exchange photographs. In metropolitan areas with heavy pedestrian traffic, people are often seen speedily sending each other text messages via their handsets. In most of the rest of the world, except South Korea, which already has many CDMA2000 1xEV-DO high-speed networks, customers use 3G service for lower-cost voice and text messaging. Enterprise customers with mobile employees and applications such as vehicle tracking and asset tracking in hospitals are expected to adopt 3G data applications earlier than consumers.

The Evolution to CDMA2000 1X (Voice and Data) and CDMA2000 1xEV-DO (Data Optimized—High Data Rate)

The transition to third generation CDMA2000 from second generation CDMA networks is less costly and complex than the transition from GSM networks to WCDMA. This is because second generation CDMA networks are already based on code division multiple access so that massive technical changes aren't required. In addition, the handoff between cells in CDMA2000 networks is very reliable. It is a soft handoff (a make-before-break type of handoff) in which, for a brief period, both the old cell (from which the call is moving) and the new cell hold onto the call so that it won't be dropped. CDMA2000 operates on the same spectrum as second generation CDMA. Thus, these operators were not required to add new base stations.

Like GSM operators, the major incentive for upgrading to third generation CDMA2000 is the increased voice capacity as well as the desire for a network capable of handling advanced applications. Because of the ease of implementation, there are many more CDMA2000 subscribers than WCDMA, but this is expected to change as more operators worldwide implement WCDMA. As of December 2004, there are more than 145 million subscribers on CDMA2000 third generation networks.

CDMA2000 1X—Doubled Voice Capacity

The first phase of third generation CDMA2000, CDMA2000 1X (also referred to as 1X), provides "always on" data rates anywhere from 60Kbps to 100Kbps plus doubled voice capacity. SK Telecom, the largest wireless carrier in South Korea, achieves an average data rate of 91Kbps. All that is required for upgrades to 1X are new cards in the base transceiver system and software in the mobile switching center. Routers, billing, authentication and authorization systems, and connections to IP networks are necessary for the data services.

Carriers in South Korea implemented the first release (IS-2000 Rel 0) of CDMA2000 in October 2000. In the United States, Sprint PCS, Verizon Wireless, and smaller cellular operators such as AllTel upgraded to CDMA2000 1X in 2001–2004. Other international carriers such as China Unicom, VIVO (Brazil), Telstra (Australia), and Reliance (India) also upgraded to 1X, and most of them have already announced their plans to upgrade their networks to include the higher data capacity, data optimized (DO) technology.

CDMA2000 1xEV-DO (Data Optimized or Data Only)

Network providers who already have the first stage CDMA2000 can upgrade to higher data speeds by adding software and channel cards to their base stations for high data rate (HDR). High data rate service is a data-only enhancement with higher downlink speeds. No capacity is gained for voice traffic. In Japan, where KDDI implemented DO technology, customers are experiencing download speeds (from the network to their wireless devices) of close to 1 megabit per second, far faster than current WCDMA speeds of 384 Kbps. The faster speeds that 1xEV-DO provides within a single 1.25MHz carrier (like CDMA2000 1X) are significant when compared to the speeds offered by WCDMA, which uses 5MHz of bandwidth. However, there are paths for both types of 3G service to evolve to higher speeds. (See the section later in this chapter for more information on IP converged networks.) Data optimized (DO) is backwards compatible with 1X and can be mixed with 1X equipment so that only areas with high demand for data need to be upgraded.

3G Compatible Handsets— Multimode Capabilities for Roaming

Handsets are a major expense in upgrading cellular networks and an important marketing tool in attracting status-conscious customers. All 3G networks require handsets with chips compatible with 3G air interfaces. The majority of carriers subsidize handsets that they sell to subscribers as a way to attract customers. For example, a carrier might pay $350 for a handset that it offers to customers for $250. The rationale is that usage revenue will offset handset costs and that customers will gravitate to operators offering new hip handsets.

In the future, improvements in roaming capabilities and multimode chips will enable people with WCDMA and CDMA2000 service to use their handsets with increasing feature transparency worldwide and within their own provider's network. For example, a network may have WCDMA capability in large cities and only GSM or GPRS elsewhere. Mobile workers and vacationers assume that they can use their handsets when they travel. The following chips for handsets are available or planned:

- Triple mode; WCDMA/GSM/GPRS available now
- Triple mode for CDMA2000 networks; 1X/GSM/GPRS available now
- Quadruple mode for CDMA2000 networks; 1X/GSM/GPRS/1xEV-DO available in 2005
- Quintuple mode for CDMA2000 and WCDMA networks, 1X/GSM/GPRS/1xEV-DO/WCDMA available in 2007

If carriers have roaming agreements, CDMA2000 subscribers with the last two types of chips in their handsets will be able to roam on GSM and GPRS networks. Because eventually there will be more WCDMA networks than CDMA2000, this multimode capability and roaming agreements are crucial to ensure that CDMA2000, as well as users on WCDMA networks, can use their service worldwide.

Multifunctional Handsets— Ease of Use and Battery Life

As manufacturers add complexity to handsets, ease of use will become a critical factor in user acceptance of advanced features. Features already included in handsets include MP3 players, digital cameras, Bluetooth capability (for wireless connections to headsets, printers, and computers), video cameras, and FM radio receivers. Advanced handsets are, in effect, multimedia computers, some with 3D engines for video and stereo speakers plus voice and high-speed data capabilities.

Many 3G handsets have multimedia processors and additional memory, and plans are being developed to add more. For example, Motorola and Apple announced in December 2004 that they are working together to develop an iTunes-enabled wireless handset that will have improved memory for storing music. One challenge in adding music, video, and high-resolution displays to handsets is that they drain battery life faster than voice and noncolor screens. New high-resolution screens are being developed that use less power because they take advantage of existing light to reduce power requirements and extend battery life.

The shape and size of phones is called *form factor*. Because of high power requirements and the need for multiple chips, early WCDMA handsets were heavy and large. New ones now are around 110 grams (3.85 ounces) to about 130 grams (3.9 ounces), and a few are lighter. NTT DoCoMo is introducing a handset aimed at businesspeople. It is the size of a business card. Developing small handsets is a major technical endeavor. These handsets require more chips with the capability to complete instructions faster and more complex software than handsets that operate on earlier-generation digital networks.

In addition, there are various ways that manufacturers are adapting handsets to text messaging such as e-mail and short messaging services. For example, T9 software predicts the words that people want to spell based on the context of the other words they've already entered. This eliminates the necessity to, for instance, press the 2 number button, which represents ABC, three times to select C. Japanese 3G subscribers are known to be adept at quickly typing e-mail and short messages on handsets with T9 software. Other handsets are equipped with standard computer keyboards that can be slid into slots when not in use.

The Path to IP Converged 3G Networks

Although converged cellular networks won't be implemented until around 2006, partnership projects are specifying interoperable protocols and architectures (the way devices are connected together and interoperate) in future converged core mobile networks. The collaborative group Third Generation Partnership Project (3GPP) is a collaboration agreement formed by European, Asian, and North American telecommunications standards bodies to jointly develop technical specifications for maintaining GSM, GPRS, and EDGE and for evolving WCDMA networks. The Third Generation Partnership Program 2 (3GPP2) is an analogous group working on developing technical specifications for CDMA2000 networks. The goal of these groups is to ensure that networks are able to interconnect seamlessly and that subscribers can roam globally while maintaining feature transparency.

Table 8.5 lists the 3G standards that were initially available as well as further releases and revisions. Achievable speeds are estimates that vary according to factors including congestion, distance from the base station, and weather. Subscribers who are stationary have higher data rates than those that are walking or in moving vehicles.

Table 8.5 Releases and Revisions to 3G Cellular Services

The following is a list of the major 3G standards. The releases and revisions are upgrades.		
Name of Service and Release	Downlink Data Rates: From the Network to the Subscriber	Uplink Data Rates: From the Subscriber to the Network
CDMA2000 Releases (1.25MHz Channel Bandwidth)		
CDMA2000 1X (Release 0) Doubles voice capacity.	Peak data rate 153.6Kbps* Average data rate 64Kbps	Peak data rate 153.6Kbps Average data rate 64Kbps
CDMA2000 1xEV-DO (Release 0) Data optimized. High data rate (HDR). Release 0 currently deployed.	Peak data rate 2.4Mbps* Average data rate 500Kbps to 1Mbps*	Peak data rate 384Kbps Average data rate 144Kbps
CDMA450 Same features as other CDMA standards but operates in lower frequencies so that fewer base stations are needed.	Same as 1X and 1xEV-DO	Same as 1X and 1xEV-DO
CDMA2000 1xEV-DO (Revision A) or CDMA2000 DO Rev A Expected deployment 2006. Supports IP voice and low-latency data in a single 1.25MHz channel.	Peak data rate 3.1Mbps Average data rate 1.8Mbps	Peak data rate 1.8Mbps Average data rate 630Kbps per sector (std) Average data rate 1,325Kbps per sector (with 4-way receive diversity)
WCDMA Releases (5MHz Channel Bandwidth)		
WCDMA (Release 99) Current release.	Peak data rate 2Mbps Average data rate 220Kbps*	Peak data rate 384Kbps Average data rate 64Kbps

continues

Table 8.5   Releases and Revisions to 3G Cellular Services   (continued)

The following is a list of the major 3G standards. The releases and revisions are upgrades.

Name of Service and Release	Downlink Data Rates: From the Network to the Subscriber	Uplink Data Rates: From the Subscriber to the Network
WCDMA (Release 4) Currently available. Enables operators to prioritize data services per customer subscription.	Peak data rate 2Mbps Average data rate 384Kbps	Same as WCDMA (Release 99)
WCDMA (Release 5) HSDPA (high speed downlink packet access). IP voice and data. Laptop data cards will be available in 2005; handsets in 2006.	Peak data rate 14Mbps Average data rate 2Mbps	Same as WCDMA (Release 99)
WCDMA Release 6 HASUPA (high speed uplink packet access). Doubles the uplink speed. Infrastructure available 2006 or 2007; no dates on user devices.	Same as WCDMA (Release 5)	Standard not defined Expected peak data rate 5Mbps Expected average data rate 1.4Mbps per sector (std) Expected average data rate 3.4Mbps per sector (with 4-way receive diversity)

*Kbps = kilobits per second; Mbps = megabits per second

Infrastructure Components of Converged IP Mobile Networks

Cellular networks have transitioned from circuit switched data to packed switched technology for data. However, for the most part, voice is carried separately using circuit switched technology, which saves a path for the entire voice call. As the proportion of data and video increases, links to base stations, controllers, mobile central offices, and other networks will evolve to more efficient Internet protocol (IP) based networks. These networks will be capable of transporting larger amounts of traffic from base stations to the Internet. Mobile switching centers (central offices) will also evolve to standardized platforms, softswitches, to carry voice, data, and video in IP packets.

In a fully converged infrastructure, the air interface as well as core networks will be upgraded from circuit switched for voice to IP-based platforms for all traffic. Figure 8.7 illustrates the Third Generation Partnership Project (3GPP) specified architecture for WCDMA mobile networks as they evolve to IP, high-speed networks. These networks are backward compatible with earlier GSM and 2.5G networks. IP, second generation, as well as 2.5G traffic can all be transported on the same core (backhaul) facilities.

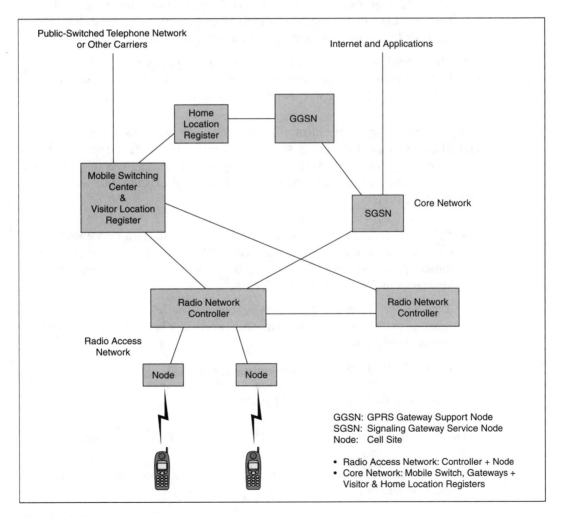

Figure 8.7
Third generation network architecture as defined by the 3GPP.

3GPP has designated names for devices in converged networks (see Figure 8.7) for various functions:

- The *radio network controller* sends messages to radio base stations to manage devices' access to spectrum. It is connected to other network controllers and to radio base stations.

- *Nodes* are the base stations, antennas, and radio base stations, also referred to as base transceiver stations, that translate between radio frequencies (signals carried over the air) and landline frequencies and vice versa.

- The *GPRS gateway support node (GGSN)* converts universal mobile telecommunications system (UMTS) data packets to those compatible with GPRS, the Internet, and other data networks and vice versa.

- The *signaling gateway service node (SGSN)* transmits data signals between radio network controllers and network databases, applications, and billing systems. Also communicates with the GPRS gateway.

3GPP2 has defined specifications for converged networks for CDMA2000, which will have similar architectures to those defined by 3GPP. 3GPP2 specifies backward compatibility to earlier CDMA technology so that carriers can mix older and newer cellular technologies using the same spectrum and existing base stations and mobile switching centers.

- *CDMA packet data service node (PDSN)* transmits data traffic between the core network and applications in CDMA2000 networks. It also converts unlike protocols into formats readable by other applications. It is analogous in function to the GGSN.

- The *Internet protocol base station controller (IP-BSC)* is similar in function to the radio network controller except that both voice and data are carried as IP packets.

- CDMA2000 uses upgraded *base transceiver stations* (described previously) for second-generation cellular networks to convert traffic between radio frequencies and landline signals.

The following terms apply to both CDMA2000 and WCDMA networks:

- *Air interface.* The wireless portion of the network between user devices and base stations.

- *Core network*. Radio network controllers, signaling gateways, home location registers, visitor location registers, and mobile switches.

- *Radio access network (RAN)*. The base transceiver station and the base station controller in CDMA2000 networks and the radio network controller and radio base stations in WCDMA networks.

- *Transport network*. A generic term for links between equipment such as base stations, controllers, signaling devices, and switches in mobile networks. The transport network includes links to other networks.

In a similar fashion to landline and enterprise telephone networks, converged mobile networks will separate switching and call processing functions onto separate devices. For more information on convergence, refer to Chapter 4. The goal, as the percentage of multimedia and data traffic increases, is to provide higher capacities for voice, data, and video by carrying all traffic in IP packets. In addition, the networks should support applications from multiple vendors using interoperable protocols.

Voice Over IP in the Core—For Less Costly Mobility in Developing Countries

The number of mobile subscribers in Africa and other developing areas is increasing at a fast pace. However, because of poverty and low income levels, rates need to be kept low to attract customers. To keep up with this growth and to provide low-cost voice services, carriers in developing countries, such as Africa and Mexico, often find it less costly when they install new cellular networks to implement 3G services, which provide higher capacity for voice calling. They also install IP infrastructure in their core networks. The core is the portion of the network where traffic from many radio controllers is connected to mobile switches. The core also has connections to the Internet and the public switched telephone network. Carriers save money on mobile switches by purchasing softswitches based on standard computer platforms. Softswitch architecture handles both voice and data so that separate devices in the core are not needed for voice and data.

Although all the links between the base stations and mobile switches, as well as the switching platforms, often use IP for all traffic, the air interfaces still employ circuit switching for voice traffic. This is because air interfaces that prevent noticeable delays are not available for acceptable voice over IP in the radio access network.

QUALITY OF SERVICE FOR VOICE AND DATA

For voice over IP in mobile networks to be acceptable to customers, it is critical that users not perceive delays in voice conversations. Landline networks have largely solved this with quality of service (QoS) protocols that are able to prioritize voice and video. They assign a priority level to traffic based on traffic type, such as voice or e-mail. In addition, priority levels can be assigned based on users' subscription choices (for example, games or e-mail) that carriers offer customers. Mobile networks have the added challenge of requiring robust enough over-the-air interfaces as well as protocols to support adequate voice over IP. For example, traffic may be prioritized over the landline portion of mobile networks, but if the wireless interface introduces latency (delay), the user will perceive that delay as a poor-quality-voice call.

Mobile networks are evolving to the capabilities already present in backbone landline networks. For some traffic, voice, push-to-talk, and video, protocols are required that can look into packets to determine priority levels. In other instances, carriers determine the type of data application such as Web browsing versus short messaging. WCDMA has defined quality of service for data applications. However, Release 4 does not have QoS for voice. Release 5 defines end-to-end quality of service across all users to recognize voice and video packets so that they can be prioritized.

CDMA2000 1X has the capability to apply various quality-of-service modes to data traffic based on customer subscription and customer profiles in network databases (home location registers) for parameters such as data rates and delay. CDMA2000 1xEV-DO can look at certain bits in packets to distinguish between packets carrying voice and video and those carrying e-mail. CDMA2000 1xEV-DO will also prioritize data by application used.

The WCDMA Evolution

WCDMA Release 5 includes *high-speed downlink packet access (HSDPA)*, which provides higher-speed data, increased capacity, and quality of service for data applications. It triples downlink throughput (the rate at which actual user data is carried) to the subscriber. Achievable throughput is expected to be 2 million bits per second. In addition, Release 5 is expected to double capacity for voice traffic. Many operators have announced 2005 implementations of HSDPA because they want to maintain competitive capabilities against CDMA2000 1xEV-DO data rates of 1 megabit per second and WiFi speeds of roughly 5 to 10 megabits per second in hotspots. (Wi-Fi, 802.11 wireless service, is only suitable for access from fixed locations.) The original availability date of HSDPA was expected to be in the 2007 or 2008 timeframe.

High-speed downlink packet access (HSDPA), because of its high downlink rates, will enable applications such as music downloads, Web browsing, and e-mail with large attachments. HSDPA-equipped data devices (referred to as terminals) such as modem cards for laptops will be available in the second quarter of 2005. However, handsets won't be available until mid-year 2006 because technology has to be developed that does not drain battery power when handsets transmit at high speeds. In addition, handset manufacturers have expressed concern about consumers' desire for HSDPA handsets. Data terminals have larger power supplies, so the power problem is easier to solve. Data is carried as IP packets between the base transceiver stations and the radio network controller. Release 5 also enables multimedia messaging such as receiving voice mail and e-mail on laptops.

Release 6 includes *high-speed uplink packet access (HSUPA)*, which doubles the throughput on both the uplink and downlink transmissions. HSUPA doubles throughput by using multiple input multiple output (MIMO) technology. MIMO antennas send multiple streams within single channels. Thus, HSUPA is suitable for IP voice and data. Commercial deployment is slated for 2005. However, no dates have been announced for handset and terminal availability. Interworking between Wi-Fi and WCDMA will be supported in Release 6 so that customers can seamlessly roam between mobile networks and Wi-Fi networks without dropping their connections.

The CDMA2000 Evolution

The next release of CDMA2000 1xEV-DO service is Revision A, also referred to as Rev A. The Rev A air interface will support packet switched voice (VoIP) and packet switched data in the same over-the-air channel. Because of its real-time capabilities, it will support applications such as Voice over IP, multiplayer games, push-to-talk, and videoconferencing in which latency must be minimal. Uplink speeds will increase to a peak of 1.8 million bits per second and downlink speeds to a peak of 3.1 megabits. Revision A will be commercially deployed in 2006. Enhancements to CDMA2000 1xEV-DO include multicasting, which is the capability to transmit the same multimedia streams (for example, radio and video) to many users simultaneously. Availability of the next release that Qualcomm is developing, Revision E, hasn't been announced.

Carriers are also implementing CDMA using the lower-frequency 450-megahertz bands. This is referred to as *CDMA450*. The motivation is that CDMA450 costs less because fewer base stations are needed at lower frequencies where longer wavelengths travel further before fading. Operators are interested in using CDMA450 in rural areas. In addition, cellular providers in developing countries use CDMA450. Data rates are lower at these frequencies. CDMA450 refers only to the frequency band. It can be implemented using any of the CDMA technologies if manufacturers make it available.

802.20: IP Mobile Broadband Wireless Access—MobileFi

The goal of new IP mobile technology developers is to provide users with local area network speeds wirelessly at their desk and when they are mobile. One of these technologies is the proposed 802.20 standard, also referred to as *MobileFi*. Flarion and ArrayComm backed the original 802.20 proposals that the IEEE is studying in its Mobile Broadband Wireless Access (MBWA) Working Group. The IEEE formed the Working Group in 2002 to develop specifications for packet-based, all-IP service using licensed spectrum in the under 3.5GHz frequencies. In 2002, the IEEE stated its intention to provide mobility in vehicles such as trains traveling up to 150 miles or 250 kilometers per hour and to support higher data rates and more users than the technologies currently available.

Flarion uses a form of orthogonal frequency division multiplexing (OFDM) in its equipment called FLASH-OFDM™. FLASH is short for fast, low-latency access with seamless handoff. According to Flarion, in addition to hopping between frequencies, FLASH-OFDM™ spreads signals over a wider range of frequencies and at a faster rate than OFDM. In addition, Flarion service includes handoffs between Wi-Fi and FLASH-OFDM™ networks so that users can use Wi-Fi when it is available and Flarion service when it is not.

Flarion's technology supports Voice over IP, and it includes the capability to prioritize traffic. In addition, the technology promises fast enough handoffs between cells to preclude latency (delay, which results in poor voice quality). Although the service is designed to be able to carry voice, FLASH-OFDM™ is intended primarily for high-speed data with achievable speeds of about 200 to 375 kilobits per second for uplink to the network and 1 to 1.5 megabits for downlink toward the user. Because it operates in spectrum licensed for 3G service, IP mobile wireless can be deployed as an overlay service. Overlay wireless networks use the same frequencies currently used and co-exist with in-place base stations. The existing base stations and associated equipment would still be used for voice and slow-speed data. Because of the low latency, it is also suitable for applications such as multiparty games and push-to-talk, a walkie-talkie-type voice service.

The Flarion service is not expected to reach wide deployment until about 2008. T-Mobile, Vodafone, and TIME dotCOM in Malaysia are conducting trials of the Flarion equipment. Until its merger with Sprint was announced, it was thought that

Nextel would use Flarion for high-speed data services. However, because Sprint uses different technologies, CDMA2000 1xEV-DO and CDMA2000 1X, for its third generation cellular service, this is unlikely. The combined Sprint Nextel is expected to take advantage of economies of scale by purchasing the same third generation equipment in its entire network.

The other main early proponent of 802.20, ArrayComm, has developed smart antenna systems that extend the range and capacity of cell sites. ArrayComm has licensed its antenna technology to equipment manufacturers Kyocera in Japan and LG Electronics in Korea. ArrayComm also offers base stations in conjunction with smart antennas for residential high-speed mobile Internet access. This service is being trialed in Australia.

The 802.20 standard-setting committee has new leadership, and it's not certain if the standard will be ratified or what the specifications will be if it is ratified. The new leadership is from organizations that manufacture and use 3G cellular and WiMAX equipment. These manufacturers produce third generation cellular equipment that will potentially compete with Flarion and ArrayComm equipment. Because it is not currently based on an international standard, it is unlikely that Flarion's equipment will be manufactured in large quantities. Without large-scale production, Flarion's equipment could be more costly than competitors' gear.

There are other obstacles to widespread adoption. Most carriers worldwide have invested heavily in third generation mobile service. In addition, in response to competition from other technologies, mobile cellular equipment suppliers have speeded up development and availability of technologies that provide higher speeds and greater capacities than previous 3G technologies.

Mobile Networks for Video— Using Incompatible Technologies

Supporting many simultaneous, high-quality video streams on cellular networks requires enormous bandwidth and sophisticated technology. Current offerings over GPRS and CDMA2000 1X networks have poor video and audio. This is because video requires *sustained* capacity with no breaks between sessions. This is different than most voice and data applications in which pauses in conversation or e-mail messages enable packets from other sessions to be transmitted. To illustrate this, SK Telecom, South Korea's leading mobile operator, offered low-cost video-on-demand in which short movies were transmitted to subscribers' handsets. The popularity of the service overwhelmed SK's DO network. It subsequently raised prices to decrease demand. SK now offers a hybrid satellite cellular service with video and audio channels. The entertainment is broadcast via satellite to new handsets equipped with satellite TV receivers. Users' selections are transmitted over SK's cellular network.

Using satellite avoids overwhelming network capacity with video. In February 2005, Verizon Wireless debuted a video offering of short, two- to five-minute video clips, 3-D games, and music video over its CDMA2000 1xEV-DO.

To solve the problem of adequate capacity, some companies are building separate broadcast networks for TV and radio, which they will make available to carriers in exchange for a percentage of the entertainment revenue. Operators who build these networks are referred to as overbuilders. Their service operates along with carriers' cellular networks. *Overbuilders* use the existing operator's network for some functions and supply their own equipment and leased spectrum for other service. Qualcomm and Nokia are building specialized networks for entertainment.

Qualcomm started a subsidiary called MediaFLO USA (where FLO refers to "forward link only") to deliver video to mobile devices nationwide using a section of the 700 megahertz UHF spectrum. Meanwhile, Nokia is teaming up with tower company Crown Castle to deliver similar services. The Nokia/Crown Castle service will be offered on the 5 megahertz of spectrum in the 1670 frequency band throughout the United States on which Crown Castle has rights. With both networks, the carrier will bill the customer, promote the service, and provide customer service. In addition to building the network, the overbuilder will negotiate with content providers for music and video rights. Satellite radio provider Sirius Radio is testing sending video broadcasts to mobile handsets.

Qualcomm purchased spectrum in the United States in the UHF Channel Number 55 (716MHz to 722MHz) TV band for its MediaFLO network. Using a low frequency enables Qualcomm to build fewer base stations to multicast short 5 to 10 minute video clips and music to mobile phones. For example, in Denver, just two towers are sufficient to cover the entire city. Customers who subscribe to MediaFLO will have satellite TV–like program guides on their handsets from which to choose content such as soccer highlights from ESPN, soap opera clips, music videos, or access to TV channels for continuous viewing on handsets. Content will be modified to be suitable for handsets with chips with TV tuners. MediFLO is deployed as an overlay network that will be compatible with all 3G networks (CDMA2000 and WCDMA) that provide the uplink (handset to network) connectivity used for selecting channels, purchasing content, and requesting services. The MediaFLO service will be made available globally. The service is expected to be commercially available in 2006. Qualcomm is also developing a capability for its BREW middleware software to interface with billing systems so that carriers can charge for selected MediaFLO features such as forwarding clips to others. Middleware software converts applications to formats compatible with handset operating systems and vice versa. It can also contain its own applications.

Both Qualcomm and Nokia plan to use *orthogonal frequency division multiplexing (OFDM)* for their mobile multimedia networks. OFDM supports sustained video

transmissions because it splits up signals from a single session among many narrow frequencies and sends bits simultaneously, in a parallel fashion, within channels. It's a complex technology that requires sophisticated base stations able to support multiplexing at high data rates. Using it only for one-way service, to forward links to subscribers, lessens the chance for interference, which can occur with OFDM.

Security

As mobile devices access the Internet and gain the capability to download software wirelessly, they become vulnerable to the same viruses that attack landline networks connected to the Internet. Developers are aware of security when they develop software and operating systems for mobile devices. They write tighter code so that there are fewer areas of vulnerability. However, these measures don't eliminate viruses altogether. For example, in 2004, a trojan horse virus attacked Symbian-based Nokia phones. Trojan horse viruses hide in software downloaded from the Internet in e-mail and programs such as games. They do malicious damage to computers or can be used to relay viruses to other devices. This one replaced icons with skulls and locked phones so that they could not make or receive calls.

Because people often use mobile personal digital assistants (PDAs) and laptops in corporate networks, viruses in mobile devices have the potential to spread to corporate networks. There are firewalls and other specialized software available to protect handsets that access the Internet from viruses. Like virus protection for broadband landline networks, these need to be updated periodically for protection from new viruses.

Bluetooth, the wireless technology that operates over distances of 30 feet or less, has known flaws that make it vulnerable to hackers. For example, nearby devices can connect to Bluetooth-equipped devices and use them to place calls and spread viruses. This is known as Bluejacking or Bluesnarfing. Manufacturers are working on fixes to these flaws.

Carriers are concerned about security and use the same measures—including authentication, digital signatures, digital watermarks, and encryption—used in landline carriers' networks. These methods attempt to ensure that mobile commerce and networks are protected from hackers.

- *Authentication* verifies that users are who they claim to be.
- *Digital signatures* provide proof that particular people made transactions by encrypting messages with a message sender's individual private encryption code that the recipient unscrambles with a matching public key decoder.

- *Digital watermarks* are code that verifies content ownership.
- *Encryption* scrambles data so that it remains private.

Refer to Chapters 2 and 4 for additional information on security in computer networks.

Spam in Short Message Services, E-mail, and Mobile Instant Messaging

In some networks, spam accounts for well over the majority of short message services (SMS). According to UK market research firm Canalys, 80% of Japanese and 20% of American SMS is spam. Short message services are brief messages that can contain 160 Latin characters or 70 non-Latin characters such as Chinese and Arabic. SMS can be sent to and from most digital telephones.

SMS subscribers, like people who use cable modems, DSL modems, and other landline access, have developed ways to spoof (hide) their identity behind false addresses, making it difficult to track their identity. Suppliers are developing filters to block spam. However, these filters have the same problem as spam filters on landline networks. They do not always distinguish legitimate messages from spam. As more customers use e-mail and instant messaging on mobile networks, spam is expected to spread to these services. Unlike e-mail on landline networks, people pay for messages they receive on mobile networks, making spam more troublesome to customers.

MOBILE COMMERCE, ENHANCED SERVICES, AND OPERATING SYSTEMS ....

Application developers are moving ahead with new services designed for 3G networks that they believe will gain acceptance, particularly from the business community. They are hoping to generate additional revenues from these services. To date, short messaging is the most popular data application for cellular devices.

Other than in Asia, uptake of 3G applications by consumers is unproven. Data-enabled wireless devices provide the means for users to access computer data and Internet information from remote locations. Revenue sharing models vary by country, but generally operators bill users for the service. In Japan, DoCoMo receives 10% for services for which it bills. In China, China Mobile receives 15%. However, carriers in Europe and the United States operators are trying to receive a 40% share of revenue from applications, which may dampen development of applications. In addition, some services require higher speeds than those generally available. For example, music downloads require higher-speed CDMA2000 1xEV-DO or HSDPA. CDMA2000 1xEV-DO is widely available in South Korea and is being implemented in the United States. However, HSDPA handsets won't be deployed until 2006. For markets with speeds capable of downloading acceptable-quality music, handsets with integrated music players are available. Users select an icon or button to access a music site and click on links to individual titles to make a selection.

The Battle for Operating System Dominance

Symbian Ltd. is the leading provider worldwide of operating systems for mobile computing devices. Microsoft Corp. is next, and Palm has the third largest market share. (Nokia, L.M. Ericsson, and Siemens AG back Symbian.) Operating systems are used for functions such as organizing information and determining how applications are viewed on computer "desktops." Research in Motion supplies the operating system for Blackberry devices. Mobile computing devices such as smartphones and personal organizers use operating systems for Internet access as well as other functions. Smartphones combine the features of PDAs with cell phones. Examples include the Treo, which is based on the Palm operating system, and the Blackberry.

Operating systems are important because applications are developed to work with specific operating systems. Thus, Symbian, Microsoft, and Palm make enormous efforts to attract developers, hoping they will create applications that will entice people to purchase cell phones with these applications. Supplying operating systems is growing in importance, particularly in nations such as India and China where more subscribers have mobile devices than personal computers.

Microsoft has an advantage in the potentially lucrative enterprise market because of the dominance of its e-mail servers in corporations. Carriers often supply phones with its operating system to enterprise customers. Rivals have accused Microsoft of designing its e-mail server software to work better for cell phones using Microsoft's operating system. One fear is that handsets will become commodities dominated by operating system suppliers, particularly Microsoft. This would be analogous to what happened following Microsoft's dominance of operating systems for personal computers. To date, that has not happened.

To access the Internet, mobile devices also need special microbrowsers such as those offered by Psion and Openwave, which are optimized for wireless devices by using code from standard browsers.

Camera Phones

It's often difficult for analysts and network operators to predict which applications will become popular. For example, multimedia messaging, in which people pay to send photos or video messages to each other, has not caught on. However, camera phones are hugely popular. In the third of quarter 2004, according to UK-based market research firm Canalys, two-thirds (just under 40 million) of mobile handsets shipped in Europe, the Middle East, and Africa were equipped with cameras. Falling prices are a factor in popularity. In addition, digital cameras were already popular, and the convenience of having one device with both functions appeals to subscribers who like always having a camera handy. Some camera phones also have Bluetooth capability that enables them to wirelessly send photos to personal computers for a hard copy, long-term storage, or transmission via e-mail.

Ring-Back Tones—Mobile Music Instead of Ringing

According to the consulting firm Yankee Group, wireless carriers earned $2.3 billion worldwide from ring-tone sales in 2003. With customized ring tones, when subscribers' phones ring, they hear preselected music instead of standard ringing. The popularity of ring tones has spurred a new service, ring-back tones. Ring-back service is similar to ring tones in that both services were originally targeted to the youth market and both involve user selection of media, usually music, to replace ringing tones.

However, with ring back, a relatively new service first implemented in 2002 in South Korea by SK Telecom, the calling party hears the music, hears customized messages from the called party, or views a video clip. The potential popularity of ring-back tones is good news for mobile network operators. According to ring-back supplier NMS Communications, operators who use NMS equipment receive average monthly revenue of about $2 per month per subscriber. Unlike customized ring tones, ring-back service is device independent and works on all phones.

Appeal of ring-back tones is spreading from mostly a youth market to adult consumers and businesses. The service can be used by enterprises to play commercials and information about their company to people who call their employees' cell phones. In the United States, multinational corporations have issued requests for proposals (RFPs) to mobile network operators for ring-back tones. In addition to carriers in Asia, many operators in Europe and the United States have announced or already offer ring-back service.

Companies that supply equipment for both ring tones and ring-back service license music from record companies and other sources of content. Because content for ring-back service is not downloaded, piracy is not an issue. The infrastructure to support these services includes gateways to carriers' signaling systems and mobile central offices and databases with audio or video content and subscriber information. These systems also integrate with operators' billing and operation support systems (OSS). OSS platforms are software applications used to manage installation, repair, and service changes for carriers. In addition to NMS, Comverse and WiderThan offer ring-back equipment and service.

Mobile Commerce—Mobile Devices to Make Purchases

Mobile commerce is the capability to use mobile devices for purchases and entertainment. Slow networks and lack of consumer interest have held it back. However, with the proliferation of 3G networks, mobile commerce is expected to grow. New methods of paying for services are being devised to eliminate users having to key in credit card information. For example, e-wallet sites have been set up to hold a consumer's credit card information. The e-wallet is used to make online purchases without entering credit card data. For all of these applications, gateways called mobile servers are located at the edge of the Internet to convert cellular protocols to those compatible with the Internet.

DoCoMo offers phones in Japan that act as electronic wallets with chips that let people make purchases by pressing buttons on their phones. The chips store personal information such as credit card information and personal identification. In addition, the phone can store money in electronic formats. When customers make a purchase, they hold their phone near special sensors. Either funds are withdrawn from bank accounts or charges are applied against credit cards. The phones can be used for other applications, including purchasing concert tickets and buying items from vending machines. The manufacturer, Fujitsu, has the capability to electronically disable phones reported stolen. DoCoMo has announced that it plans to license the technology, with Sony, to other carriers. The electronic wallet requires agreements with retailers to accept payment in this manner.

The IP Multimedia System and Interoperable Multimedia

In 3G networks, IP multimedia systems (IMS) refers to the equipment and software that will make it possible to store, transmit, administer, transform (for example, from text to voice), and bill for multimedia services. Examples of multimedia services are games, audio and video clips and photos as attachments to e-mail messages, downloading entertainment, and Web-based shopping. Both 3GPP and 3GPP2 have defined specifications for IP multimedia systems in IP networks. These specifications define how devices for content storage, billing, and application support will be connected to networks and which protocols will be used. IMS is intended to support whatever means the user uses to accesses the IP network including broadband landlines, fixed wireless (802.11 or WiMAX), and mobile services.

However, IMS-compliant systems won't be installed until 2007 as mobile networks evolve to IP. IP multimedia systems will be similar to infrastructure for enhanced services in converged landline networks. However, the nomenclature differs. For example, 3GPP calls a media server a *media resource function (MRF)*. A media server provides functions to applications that include playing announcements and collecting digits that users enter. IP multimedia systems will contain applications servers, which hold applications and databases with, for instance, video clips.

In addition to the 3GPP and 3GPP2 efforts, carriers in Europe and the United States are working on ways to develop interoperability earlier so that users can send photos and video mail and add sounds and photos to messages that they exchange with people from different networks. In the United States, the Cellular Telecommunications and Internet Association (CTIA) announced in October 2004 that carriers have agreed on guidelines for interoperability.

In Europe, carriers such as Vodafone and Orange are developing a single standard to which handset-software suppliers should adhere so that multimedia applications interoperate. Orange has already announced interoperability on its "video answerphone"' service in which callers with 3G handsets have the option of leaving a ten-second video message rather than a voice mail message with users with non-3G as well as 3G handsets. The service interoperates with other 3G networks.

3G Applications for Enterprises

Many carriers are focusing marketing efforts for their 3G-empowered applications on enterprises. This is because a substantial percentage of corporate employees travel for business and have already demonstrated a need for remote computing and access to e-mail and other applications when they are away from the office. In addition, many corporations regularly manage large fleets, delivery services, and remote technicians as part of their core business. These are the types of applications that lend themselves to 3G services. For example, location-based services similar to those used in conjunction with E911 services can be used to track the location of vehicles so that they can be deployed in the most economical way.

A major hurdle to sales to enterprises is ensuring that applications are secure. According to research conducted by market research firm NOP World, 44% of U.S. companies stated that security is their top concern in deploying mobile data services for their employees. This study was cited in the *RCR Wireless News* December 30, 2004 article "Wireless in the Enterprise Still Hindered by Security Concerns" by Colin Gibbs. The article quoted NOP World Vice President for Market Research Richard March:

> *"The more access you have on a wireless basis, the more you open yourself up. No business wants to be on the front page because they were hacked into."*

In addition, IT staff may not have the resources to manage complex wireless applications and numerous mobile devices. Many providers offer end-to-end, turnkey service to manage mobile data services. These offerings include managing applications for corporations, such as security, asset tracking, and over-the-air configuration. Over-the-air configuration is the capability to remotely add features or applications to mobile modem cards in laptops, personal digital assistants, and handsets. Carriers will also add and delete service for new hires and employees no longer working for the customers. If a mobile device is reported stolen or lost, the carrier will remotely "kill" it, making it inoperable.

SPECIALIZED MOBILE RADIO—SLOW-SPEED PACKET DATA AND PUSH-TO-TALK ....

Push-to-talk, walkie-talkie service was originally used in private mobile voice networks, such as those used by construction workers, that had no links to the public switched telephone network or public cellular networks. People pushed a button on their microphone to talk to a central site. These services operated in the 800MHz to 900MHz range of *specialized mobile radio* spectrum. This is the same spectrum that Nextel Communications uses for most of its current digital services.

ARDIS (now part of American Mobile Satellite Company) and Cingular Wireless's former Mobitex packet data network (now Velocita Wireless) also use the 800MHz to 900MHz spectrum for slow-speed packet data. Velocita Wireless offers e-mail and Blackberry access over its Mobitex data network. Organizations that provide delivery services, field service and installation, and transportation services use these services for mobile employees. European operators offer similar services in the 400-megahertz range. They primarily use a circuit switched technology called TETRA (trans-European trunked radio).

Specialized Mobile Radio—Packetized Data Networks for Two-Way E-mail and Field Services

Specialized mobile radio networks cover the major urban centers in the United States and are also used in Europe and Canada. They operate at a top throughput speed of 14.4Kbps over their given spectrum. Companies often lease specialized mobile radio networks from companies such as Velocita Wireless and Motient Corporation for use with remote monitoring and other mobile applications, including trucking, field service, and dispatch. The underlying packet technology used in the Motient network is called DataTAC (total access communications). The availability of portable computers, hand-held devices, and scanners for data entry helped spur the use of radio networks for mobile workers.

In the late 1970s, companies started using radio frequency networks to transmit data from mobile workers to headquarters. A prime example of an organization using wireless for private data communications is FedEx. FedEx's early implementation of its private data communications network gave it a major edge over competitors. The service is used to track the location of packages. Each package has a bar code; when the package is picked up or dropped off for delivery, its bar code is scanned into FedEx's computer system at the drop-off site or by a driver's hand-held device. The hand-held device transmits the bar code to FedEx's computers. The scanning is repeated at each strategic point in the delivery system and is transmitted to FedEx's computers over the radio frequency network; thus, FedEx knows where each package is in each step of its journey.

Packet Access for Personal Digital Assistants (PDAs) and Blackberry Devices

In the late 1990s, Research in Motion (RIM) developed a radio modem for a pager to support two-way electronic mail and Internet access over packet networks in specialized mobile radio frequencies. Other manufacturers also developed integrated internal radio modems for personal digital assistants like Palm and Handspring. Unlike early Palm devices, the RIM device was an "always on" device. E-mail was automatically sent when there were messages. The Blackberry wireless device is used with the Motient packet networks in the United States and Canada as well as the Bell Mobility data network in Canada. Blackberries are small, hand-held devices with small displays and keyboards. The Blackberry devices sold to enterprises include servers integrated with enterprise e-mail systems such as Lotus Notes and Microsoft Exchange. Blackberries are available internationally.

Upgrades to the original Blackberry include interfaces to most cellular networks and the addition of voice capabilities. Research in Motion receives royalties on Blackberries sold to network providers. Interestingly, like Nextel's push-to-talk service, the RIM devices operating on the older paging networks and carriers' packet networks with no connections to public switched networks or cellular networks continued to function after the September 11, 2001 attacks at the World Trade Center in New York City.

SATELLITES AND PAGING ....

Geosynchronous satellites orbit 22,300 miles above the earth's surface. Because they are so high in the sky, the area to which each satellite is capable of beaming signals is large. Therefore, less equipment is required to cover large areas. Paging service revenues have been declining since the advent of lower-priced mobile phones and improved mobile coverage.

Satellite Networks

Satellite networks are composed of a hub, satellites, and receiving antennas on dishes. Receiving antennas also are called *ground stations*. Receivers on antennas convert airborne signals to electrical signals. The transmitter on the antenna converts electrical signals to airborne (radio frequency) signals. The point from which broadcasts originate is the hub. The hub has a large dish, routing equipment, and fiber links to the enterprise's headquarters for commercial customers. All communications broadcast from the hub travel up to the satellite and then down to the ground stations, the satellite dishes.

Satellites are used to broadcast television and paging signals and to transmit positioning information to aircraft and air traffic controllers. Governments also use satellites for surveillance in military and national security applications.

Satellite Telephones—
For Emergencies and Remote Areas

Because they are so high, geosynchronous satellites introduce a few-seconds delay on voice and data transmissions. People who placed calls to international locations in the 1970s and 1980s often experienced clipping and delay. If two people on a telephone call spoke at the same time, parts of words were "clipped" off. The quality of these calls was notably degraded by delays in transmission. Low earth orbiting satellites (LEOs) solve the delay problem because they are positioned only 435 to 1,500 miles above the earth. LEOs cover a smaller area than geosynchronous satellites because they are lower in the sky. Thus, more of them are needed for worldwide coverage.

The phones associated with these services are larger, heavier, and more expensive than cellular phones and per-minute rates are high. However, during national disasters such as hurricanes and wars, they are sometimes the only service operational because of destroyed cell towers and lack of electricity at cell sites. For example, they were used during the 2003 Iraqi and 2002 Afghanistan conflicts. They are also used on tankers, fishing vessels, and geology expeditions where cellular service is not available. The two largest companies that offer voice service in the United States using low earth orbiting satellites are Globalstar and Iridium Satellite LLC.

VSAT Service—Small Satellite Dishes

Very small aperture terminals (VSATs) are small satellite dishes that contain antennas that receive and transmit signals between computers and satellites. The dishes range in size from 24 inches high by 36 inches wide for VSATs used for data communications to 18 inches wide for those used for direct broadcast television. Their small size is possible because of highly focused beams generated from antennas on satellites and the fact that the service is offered at high frequencies, which have shorter wavelengths.

The development of VSAT technology in the late 1980s made satellite service affordable for commercial applications in which many branch locations transmit back to a central location. These applications include gas stations for transmission of credit authorizations and daily receipts and retail chains for inventory, pricing updates, and sales results. The implementation of VSAT networks obviated the need for organizations such as retail chains and postal services to main complex networks of private lines. However, many retailers have replaced VSAT service with virtual private networks (VPNs). VPNs also connect large numbers of sites without the expense of dedicated lines to each site, but they have more robust two-way capabilities. (Refer to Chapter 4 for more information on virtual private networks.)

Paging Services

From the time they were introduced in 1956, pager sales grew until the late 1990s when competition in the cellular industry caused prices for cellular phones to drop, and customers began substituting mobile telephones for pagers. People found that they could carry one device capable of paging, short messaging, and two-way telephoning. In 1997, for the first time, the number of cellular telephones exceeded the number of pagers in service. By the late 1990s and early 2000s, paging companies were merging and declaring bankruptcy. The two largest paging companies in the United States, Arch Wireless, Inc. and Metrocall, merged in 2004 and formed USA Mobility, Inc. Both had previously emerged from bankruptcy.

Two-Way Paging Using Narrowband PCS

Two-way paging uses two narrow slices of the PCS spectrum that the FCC started auctioning off in 1994. One channel is used for sending the page and the other for responding to pages. Paging companies were interested in narrowband paging, not only for its two-way capability but also for its capability to provide additional capacity. Paging companies had hoped that advanced services such as e-mail would revive paging. However, two-way paging using PCS spectrum has experienced disappointing sales, and for the most part, customers who want two-way messaging use Blackberrys, Treos, or wireless handsets with text messaging.

9 Wi-Fi, Wireless Broadband, Sensor Networks, and Personal Area Networks

In this chapter:

When Wi-Fi, wireless local area networks based on 802.11 technology, were first introduced to the consumer market, people immediately understood the benefit of not having to cable their homes to share DSL and cable modem type Internet access among computers. In addition, low equipment cost, and easier installation spurred sales. Benefits were not so readily apparent in industries other than those in healthcare, education, retailing, and warehousing. In addition, security concerns, changing standards, and complex implementation and support hindered adoption. However, newly ratified security standards and maturing technology, as well as expectations of using wireless local area networks (WLANs) for voice, are stimulating corporate interest.

Hotspots offer higher-speed Internet access than most cellular networks' data offerings and cost less to build than cellular base stations. Hotspots are public areas such as cafés and airports that offer Internet access using 802.11 technologies. However, they are not as widely available as cellular data services, which cover entire metropolitan areas. In spite of lower infrastructure expense, for the most part hotspots are not yet profitable. They have high backhaul costs, the mostly landline links from hotspots to the Internet. In addition, they have expenses faced by other startups: infrastructure such as billing systems and customer acquisition expenses. Hotspot operators also compete with free services offered by various retailers and community networks being constructed by cities and towns. Nevertheless, coverage is increasing, and aggregators are emerging that offer service to thousands of hotspots that enable customers to use the same password and user ID nationwide and sometimes internationally.

In addition to high-speed wireless data service within buildings and public areas, new wireless broadband access services are available that offer Internet access speeds that match wireline broadband services such as cable modems, DSL, and T-1/E-1. Whereas cellular networks were originally designed for voice and are only recently being upgraded for data, many of these technologies are designed primarily for data and will add voice later. One of these, Worldwide Interoperability for Microwave Access (WiMAX), is based loosely on 802.16 technologies for fixed wireless service. WiMAX fixed wireless service requires an antenna attached to customers' buildings. The service is wireless from the customer to the carrier but not within the building or metropolitan area. The key standard for fixed wireless service was approved in 2004, and the WiMAX Alliance has stated its intention to initiate a certification program similar to that of the Wi-Fi Alliance. Most of the manufacturers that offer fixed, wireless, WiMAX-type equipment have stated their intention to meet the specifications.

Other wireless broadband services are based on third generation (3G) cellular technologies. Some, such as universal mobile telecommunication system time division duplex (UMTS TDD), provide portability within buildings or cell sites or full mobility within a carrier's coverage area. Others do not. Most of these are marketed to residential customers. Carriers offer a mix of primarily Internet access or voice, data, and facsimile service. The ones that offer voice, data, and facsimile are used instead of a wireline local loop, particularly in rural areas and developing countries where wireless services cost less to deploy than running a cable to each resident. In some countries, these wireless local loops compete directly with third generation cellular offerings, particularly for voice service. However, small businesses do benefit from facsimile service, which is not generally available on cellular service.

In addition to wireless services for Internet and plain old telephone service (POTS), there are wireless services that replace cable clutter in offices, track inventory, and monitor heating, security, and electricity. These services include wireless personal area networks (PANs), which include Bluetooth, RFID, and ultra-wideband. Another wireless protocol, ZigBee, was recently ratified and is being promoted for sensor networks. These services are based on a number of ratified and proposed standards.

- *Bluetooth* links cellular handsets to headsets, keyboards and mice to PCs, and mobile handsets to computers to exchange content.
- *Radio frequency identification (RFID)* uses inexpensive antennas to automate toll collection at tollbooths and for inventory tracking in enterprises, the government, and healthcare.
- *Ultra-wideband (UWB)* supports higher data rates than RFID and can be used in some of the same applications such as tracking assets in hospitals. It is also used by the military and by governments for tracking and for finding people trapped under rubble.
- The *ZigBee* protocol, which currently operates on network technology that is slower than ultra-wideband, is used in sensor networks for monitoring heating and lighting controls and other types of equipment.

RFID and sensor networks that are installed in corporations collect large amounts of information. Integrating the data gathered by these networks in enterprise-level software is costly and complex. These are factors in delaying implementation of some RFID services. A snag holding up deployment of ultra-wideband technology is the lack of ratification of a standard for the service. Manufacturers developing two different UWB chips and equipment have lobbied the IEEE, which to date has not ratified either proposal.

Standards are critical to the success of new technologies. For enterprises and carriers, they provide some assurance that the products they purchase won't be made obsolete by new standards or that customers will not be forced to purchase all the equipment from one supplier. The one supplier may charge high prices for its proprietary equipment.

Often, when approvals for standards are delayed, vendors don't wait for the approval process to be completed because they don't want to miss out on the window of opportunity. Thus, they develop prestandard products. Large companies and blocks of companies with complementary products attempt to influence standards bodies to ratify standards that match their products. In addition, companies often pledge to make their prestandard products match standards when they are approved.

802.11 WIRELESS LOCAL AREA NETWORKS (WLANS) ....

802.11 wireless networks were originally intended to provide wireless computing for staff within businesses and commercial organizations. However, residential customers adopted Wi-Fi more quickly than enterprises because of the simplicity of these networks, fewer concerns about security, and the immediate benefit of avoiding the expense of cabling. Wi-Fi is also sold extensively to hotspot operators, particularly for hotels, convention centers, cafés, and airports. 802.11 networks are spreading out from separate hotspots at airports, hotels, and cafés to community-wide networks.

802.11 wireless standards are based on Ethernet protocols that define ways for people to use laptops, personal digital assistants, and computers wirelessly in the preceding areas. While new standards are being developed to improve security, the size of area covered, and quality of service to support voice, the main standards are 802.11a, 802.11b, and 802.11g. The Institute of Electrical and Electronics Engineers (IEEE) approved the 801.11a and 802.11b standards in 1999 and the 802.11g standard in 2003. See Table 9.2 in the Appendix section at the end of this chapter for an overview of various 802.11 standards.

The Terms 802.11, WLAN, and Wi-Fi

802.11 refers to the family of IEEE standards around which most wireless local area networks (WLANs) are built. Wi-Fi is short for wireless fidelity. The Wi-Fi Alliance tests equipment in its labs and certifies that it meets various 802.11 standards for interoperability. Thus, 802.11 is a technology, Wi-Fi is a certification, and wireless local area network (WLAN) is a generic term applicable to any wireless LAN technology. Because 802.11 is the predominate WLAN technology, people use the terms 802.11, Wi-Fi, and WLAN interchangeably. In addition, 802.11a is sometimes referred to as Wi-Fi5 because it operates on part of the 5-gigahertz band.

The Criticality of Standards

The proliferation of 802.11 wireless networks worldwide can be attributed directly to the presence of internationally accepted standards. There were other wireless LAN techniques available prior to the 802.11 standards; however, high costs and complex installation held back sales. Once the 802.11b standard was agreed upon, an increasing number of products became available and prices dropped. Consumers, drawn to the low prices and retail availability, began purchasing the gear to network computers together to share broadband Internet access in homes. However, with the exception of certain sectors, sales to enterprises have not met with the same level of acceptance.

802.11 gear with the Wi-Fi Certified™ logo on the package has been certified by the nonprofit Wi-Fi Alliance to meet the IEEE standards for interoperability. All Wi-Fi Certified™ 802.11b as well as 802.11a and 802.11g certified devices are supposed to interoperate with each other. 802.11a products interoperate with each other as well. However, because interoperability requires matching security protocols, interoperability is not always achieved. In addition, enterprises that use nonstandard switches on their LANs to manage their wireless networks are required to purchase switches and antennas (access points) from the same manufacturer. The main wireless LAN standards are shown in Table 9.1.

Table 9.1 802.11 Wireless Local Area Network Standards

Standard	Top Speed	Achievable Speed	Number of Channels	Frequency Band
802.11a	54 megabits per second	24 megabits per second	24	5 gigahertz
802.11b	11 megabits per second	5 megabits per second	3	2.4 gigahertz
802.11g	54 megabits per second	12 to 24 megabits per second	3	2.4 gigahertz

The Main Standards: 802.11a, 802.11b, and 802.11g

Although 802.11a was developed before 802.11b, 802.11b is less complex and its equipment was available first. Most new base stations have 802.11b and g chips that operate in the 2.4-gigahertz frequencies. Many base stations (also referred to as access points) sold to enterprises have chips with all three standards: 802.11a, b, and g. These multiband devices operate in both the 2.4- and 5-gigahertz frequencies. However, laptop interfaces are just beginning to support all three standards. Laptops with 802.11a capabilities are required to benefit from higher speeds associated with

802.11a-capable access points. 802.11a and 802.11g operate at higher speeds because they use orthogonal frequency division multiplexing (OFDM). OFDM splits a high-speed stream into several parallel, slower streams at different frequencies. Because data arrives at different times, receivers can decode transmissions as they arrive rather than all at one time. This lets them handle more traffic faster.

In a similar manner to cellular service, achievable speeds are always lower than the top, theoretical speeds. These speed variations relate to congestion, distance from antennas, and overhead. Congestion impacts data rates because when there is a limited amount of capacity, some wireless devices will experience delay when multiple users attempt to send or receive simultaneously. In addition, the area covered by each of these standards can vary. For example, 802.11b and g cover a range of about 100 to 150 feet, and 802.11a covers about 75 feet. However, interference from thick walls or other material decreases ranges. For example, a university installed a WLAN in its library, but interference from the books caused problems. Overhead is the number of bits required for nonuser data such as addressing, acknowledging receipt of messages, and controlling errors.

802.11a: Higher Speeds, Smaller Coverage, and More Channels

802.11a is the only 802.11 standard that operates at 5 gigahertz. Use of the 5-gigahertz band eliminates possible interference from microwave ovens, Bluetooth-equipped devices, and many cordless telephones, which operate at 2.4 gigahertz. When 802.11 devices sense another session in the same frequency using a different protocol, they become inoperable or slow down considerably until the other device is turned off.

A disadvantage of the 5-gigahertz spectrum is that signals fade faster than at 2.4 gigahertz. Thus, more antennas, which cover only about 75 feet, are required to cover the same area. For the most part, 802.11a gear is sold to enterprises that want the greater capacity offered by 802.11a, which supports more simultaneous users per access point (antenna plus transceiver) because it has up to 24 channels rather than only 3. Enterprises that use 802.11a need to equip their employees' laptops with 802.11a network interface cards or chips to gain extra capacity. This costs about $50 per laptop. To date, most enterprises have 802.11b and 802.11g services, but that may change as more equipment is equipped with 802.11a and enterprises need to support more users.

In addition to enterprise equipment, 802.11a capabilities are included in most of the new residential media centers. This equipment is designed to wirelessly transmit music and video between televisions and personal computers in homes and apartments.

802.11b

When they were first available, 802.11 network equipment was equipped with only 802.11b chips. Now, however, most residential and enterprise equipment includes 802.11b and g, which both operate at 2.4 gigahertz and are designed to interoperate. However, because home broadband connections are slower than 802.11 networks, no advantage is gained with this combination. In addition, most hotspots use the 802.11b standard because Internet access at most hotspots is slower than 802.11g.

802.11g: Higher Data Rates Using 2.4-Gigahertz Bands

802.11g operates at 2.4 gigahertz but supports higher data rates than 802.11b. However, when 802.11b-equipped end-user devices are used on the same network with 802.11g base stations, data rates on 802.11g devices are degraded to 12 megabits or lower.

Because of their higher data rates, 802.11g and 802.11a chips are both installed in home media centers. The higher speeds and capacity associated with 802.11g and 802.11a are also required to support voice over IP on WLANs.

802.11n—Improving Range (Area Covered), Capacity, and Data Rates

802.11n is a proposed Wi-Fi standard that will be backward compatible with 802.11a, b, and g networks. For example, laptops with 802.11g chips will interoperate with access points based on 802.11n. 802.11n enables wireless local area networks to cover larger distances by overcoming a certain amount of interference. It also increases achievable speeds (actual throughput) and supports more users per access point. Improvements in spectral efficiency, the number of users supported in a given amount of airspace, are critical as the number of users and applications on wireless local area networks increases. For example, growth in hotspot usage could strain existing capacity. In particular, voice and multimedia applications are expected to make current capacity inadequate.

Although, the IEEE has not approved the 802.11n standard, prestandard access points and laptop cards are available. The IEEE is expected to finalize the 802.11n standard in late 2006 or early 2007. The proposals are backward compatible; they interoperate with 80211a-, b-, and g-equipped devices. However, for laptops without 802.11n chips, range improvements are much less than when access points and user devices have 802.11n capability.

Improved Antennas and Battery Life on 802.11n

Improvement in antennas is the reason 802.11n uses spectrum more efficiently and overcomes many dead spots. A dead spot is an area that access points don't cover because of interference from building materials or distance. 802.11n antennas use *multiple input multiple output (MIMO)* technology. MIMO antennas simultaneously transmit multiple streams at different frequencies within a single channel. This improvement is analogous to increasing capacity on a multilane highway versus a road with a single lane. MIMO uses multiple antennas to transmit several streams from a single access point. The receiving equipment puts the streams back into the proper order. In networks based on 802.11b and g, 802.11n equipment is expected to support data rates of 27 megabits to 40 megabits, depending on distance from the access point.

802.11n is also expected to improve battery life in user devices. Like other new technologies, 802.11n devices cost more than equipment based on older standards in which manufacturing efficiencies have resulted in low pricing and commodity-like products. This is particularly true in the residential market.

WLAN Infrastructure: Access Points and Switches

All wireless local area networks (WLANs) have base stations (access points) and user radios also referred to as the user interface. The air interfaces used in the base station must be compatible with that in the user device. In addition, networks with multiple base stations often have switches or controllers that direct traffic to particular base stations, can be used to remotely change access point configurations, and monitor traffic on the wireless network.

User Interface

In WLANs, the air interface can be in network interface cards in computers, personal digital assistants, or laptops. Most new laptops now come with 802.11 chips preinstalled. This is a significant factor in increased adoption.

Access Points (APs)

An access point has an antenna and chips with 802.11a, 802.11b, or 802.11g air interfaces. Access points also translate between radio frequencies and Ethernet signals for cabled networks. An access point has similar functions to base stations for cordless home phones and cell stations in cellular networks. Access points for the residential market also have routers and hubs included in them with ports to which Ethernet cables can be connected. The router functionality enables the access point to aggregate traffic and send it to the Internet via dial-up, DSL, and cable modems. Access points for corporations plug into local area network connections (data jacks).

Switches

In enterprise networks, access points connect to switches. The switch sends packets addressed to the Internet to corporate routers connected to the Internet. Switches also direct traffic to and from corporate databases and applications such as e-mail. These switches are either standard LAN switches or switches designed to manage wireless networks. Workgroup switches manage traffic within the same floor.

Wi-Fi switches make it easier to manage multiple access points. For example, they monitor traffic on each access point and pinpoint interference. Wireless switches are able to react to interference by moving traffic to other channels and raising or lowering power. They are used to plan where to place access points using their integrated radio frequency tools in conjunction with floor plans. Corporations must purchase switches and access points from the same manufacturer because of proprietary switch capabilities. However, laptops and other portable devices don't require Wi-Fi chips or network interface cards from the same manufacturer, although user devices do need the matching security used by the enterprise. In the future, Wi-Fi switch capability will be incorporated into standard LAN switches.

Core Switches

Core switches are used in large, enterprise WLANs to manage traffic between workgroup switches located on individual floors. Core switches send traffic to workgroup switches based on addresses and network congestion. See Figure 9.1 for switches and access points in enterprises. Cisco (through its Airespace subsidiary), Symbol, 3Com, and Trapeze supply WLAN switches. Airespace OEMs its products to Alcatel and Nortel, which put their own brand name on the Airespace switch.

WLAN Gateways (Access Controllers)

Gateways, also referred to as access controllers, can be part of core switches or separate devices. If separate devices, they sit between the wireless and wired part of

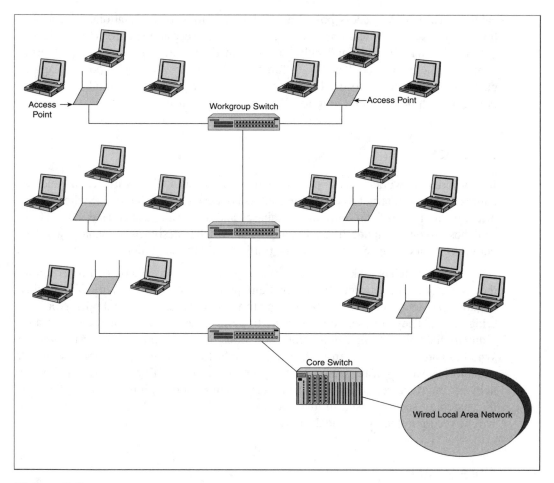

Figure 9.1
Workgroup switches (which are on individual floors), access points, and a core switch in an enterprise network.

networks. They act as gateways to the network, allowing access to only certain users. They often allow access to particular applications on a per-user basis. In addition, gateways authenticate users and access points.

In Enterprises

WLAN services are deployed most frequently in organizations with many mobile employees within a campus or building and by small businesses in new offices. Many employees in these organizations work at various locations within institutions rather than at a fixed desk. Moreover, they require access to corporate shared applications and databases as they perform their job. WLANs for these organizations are deployed in the following common areas: conference rooms, cafeterias, patient floors, outside areas between buildings, manufacturing areas, and warehouses.

These are some of the vertical industries most likely to use Wi-Fi:

- *Education*. To provide Internet access to students and teaching staff in classrooms, student centers, and common areas. Large universities often offer free Internet access to campus visitors and nearby residents as well.

- *Warehousing*. For scanning stock and updating inventory levels wirelessly.

- *Healthcare*. To enable nurses and physicians to electronically update patient charts and records using handheld devices in inpatient areas.

- *Retailing*. To provide sales staff with the capability to take calls and check merchandize availability using Voice over IP on Wi-Fi networks. They also use Wi-Fi to update inventory records using portable data devices.

In addition to productivity improvements for mobile employees within a campus, saving money on cabling is a key motivating factor in implementing 802.11 networks. For example, rather than paying an electrician to wire a new office, businesses install a wireless network. This is particularly true of small businesses and branch offices. In remote offices, central switches located at headquarters can remotely manage access points in branch offices.

Universities and elementary and high schools avoid the expense of cabling when they enable students to use laptops in classrooms, quadrangles, and other facilities wirelessly. Wi-Fi is also used in locations such as libraries to supplement wired outlets for the convenience of students who prefer to work wirelessly because their laptops are already set up that way for their home wireless networks. In addition, large enterprises avoid cabling when they add Wi-Fi in conference rooms and cafeterias to provide access to shared applications.

Stumbling Blocks to Wider Enterprise Deployment— Security and Perception of Need

Enterprise adoption of WLAN networks has been held back by concerns about security, support costs, lack of perceived need, and speed. New security standards have been approved; however, equipment that meets these standards is expensive and time intensive to implement and manage. In addition, security devices don't necessarily address the problem of rogue access points (APs). Rogue access points are nonauthorized APs installed within the building or outside (for example, in the parking lot). Rogue access points use the institution's network for Internet access or hacking purposes.

In addition to security, support by information technology (IT) staff is a major issue. For example, once cabling is in place, little support is required other than arranging for moves. However, with wireless connections, there is a concern that the nature of wireless media will lead to additional calls to help-desk personnel about problems setting up secure connections, complaints about degradation from interference and unacceptably low speeds resulting from traffic peaks, or from people logging on when they are out of range of access points. In terms of speed, WLANs are perceived as adequate for e-mail and logging onto shared applications within campuses but not necessarily as replacements for desktop connections. They don't currently reach the 100 megabits per second currently supported on wired LANs.

Moreover, medium-size or small organizations that have already invested in cabling infrastructure don't necessarily perceive the value of wireless capability within their organization. If they have already put cabling in conference rooms and offices, their only savings occur when offices are rearranged and cabling needs to be moved. In addition, in some small and medium-size establishments, staff mostly work at their desks and perceive little or no value in mobility within the office.

NORTHEASTERN UNIVERSITY'S WIRELESS NETWORK

Northeastern University , which is located in Boston, Massachusetts, is a large urban university with more than 20,000 full-time students. Northeastern has an 802.11b network connected to its 20,000-port wired network. Each port represents a data jack into which a data device can be connected. Access points with antennas are plugged into wired network outlets in common areas such as the library. The wireless network is available, free of charge, for Internet and e-mail access to anyone within range of the antennas. In addition, students are able to browse the school's student intranet for information such as class schedules. However, they can't print or access shared network storage or the school's business applications.

Northeastern University's Wireless Network (continued)

According to Bob Weir, vice president of information service:

"We're like a Starbucks. We're an extremely sophisticated Internet service provider for students, faculty, and campus visitors. We manage a large hotspot for a population of over 20,000 students, faculty, and staff. We have no objection to sharing this resource with the community. We also run conferences and symposiums. People who attend these conferences want to access the Internet wirelessly while they're here, and we provide that as a service to support that business."

Within the next few months, Northeastern will offer certain faculty and staff wireless access to any secure file they can access from their office. To provide security, the university will distribute virtual private network (VPN) client software for these users' computers. The software will provide encryption to make it more difficult for hackers to eavesdrop on transmissions. In addition, faculty and staff will be required to enter their user identification and password.

The information technology department at Northeastern thinks that in the future wireless technology will eclipse wired service. However, before that happens, they think that wireless networks need to be faster, cheaper, more secure, and easier to manage. They also would like to see standards solidified so that institutions that invest in WLANs will not be forced to replace equipment every two years to keep up with technology. Currently, Northeastern's replacement cycle is five years for wired local area network equipment. However, because of rapid changes in WLANs, they would need to replace wireless technology every two years to stay current.

Hotspots—Wi-Fi Inside Public Places

A wireless local area network hotspot is a public area where people with Wi-Fi-equipped laptops or personal digital assistants can access the Internet. Access may be free or available for monthly or daily rates. In addition, some cities and towns offer wireless LANs. The Wi-Fi hotspot business is multilayered and includes aggregators, cellular providers, and companies that supply "back office" services such as billing, roaming, and secure access to corporate networks from hotspots. Hotspot operators are also referred to as wireless Internet service providers (WISPs). Hotspots are available worldwide.

The Mobile Professional

Large numbers of people in the work force, such as consultants, salespeople, and high-level executives, travel extensively for their jobs. Moreover, some corporations no longer routinely assign all employees a desk in an office. In addition, people with heavy travel schedules expect to be able to work wherever they can to accomplish their work goals. These workplace changes are major factors in the increasing use of high-speed wireless computing and Internet access. Both cellular and Wi-Fi availability will increase to accommodate mobile professionals. According to Frank D. Hanzlik, director of the nonprofit Wi-Fi Alliance:

> *"There is an expectation that people are always connected. You can't say, 'I'm leaving the office for six hours; don't bother me.' As a result, the concept of the office is changing and becoming more nebulous. Now, the office is wherever you happen to be."*

The preceding quote appeared in the October 24, 2004 article "Citywide Wi-Fi Link Considered" by Matt Viser in *The Boston Globe*'s online edition at Boston.com.

In addition, many people work in isolated home offices. Moreover, people in urban areas worldwide live and work in cramped spaces. For many of these professionals, working at cafés is a social experience, an opportunity to meet others. It also provides a change of scenery for people who no longer have a permanent desk at a company office. A market research consultant who lives and works in New York City made the following comment about working at Wi-Fi-enabled cafés:

> *"A ton of people in the city work at home, and it's great to have people around when you're working. It's actually less distracting. I'm less likely to procrastinate, and it's more social just having bodies around. I know that Wi-Fi draws folks to Starbucks. The coffee shops in Manhattan and Brooklyn are full of people working and writing on their computer. It's quite a scene."*

Inside a Hotspot

The structure of a small hotspot such as a café is similar to those in homes and small businesses with the exception that they generally use more robust access points. A wireless router with an integrated access point provides wireless service within buildings. The wireless router connects to the Internet using a broadband connection such as DSL or a T-1 line. Thus, although service inside the hotspot is wireless, for the most part connections from the hotspot to the Internet use fiber or copper cabling. Airports and other large hotspots have multiple access points connected via a local area network to either a switch or a router.

The switch manages the assignment of individual devices to access points. The LAN is connected to the Internet by a high-speed data link. In small and large hotspots, a wireless Internet service provider (WISP) manages security, billing, and authenticated logon to the wireless network. As in enterprise and cellular networks, the cabling between base stations and switches (the backhaul) accounts for a major part of the expense of building a large wireless network.

The two largest hotspot operators in the United States are Wayport and T-Mobile USA. Both are aggregators. Aggregators install hardware and Internet access for hotspot services and resell it to other providers who provide billing, marketing, and customer service to end users. Wayport, the largest hotspot supplier, for the most part does not sell directly to end users. As of January 2005, it provided Wi-Fi networks at 6,300 locations including McDonald's, Hertz car rental, 700 hotels, and 12 airports. For a fixed monthly fee per location, they license companies such as SBC, Sprint, and MCI to sell Wi-Fi access at certain locations such as McDonald's.

T-Mobile's hotspot locations include Starbucks, Borders Books & Music, FedEx, some airports, and Kinko's. They sell service to end users and also provide infrastructure to resellers.

Boingo is an aggregator that provides no infrastructure. Rather it resells service from small wireless Internet service providers, from about a third of Wayport's hotspots, and from STSN systems, which are mostly in hotels. STSN builds Wi-Fi networks and arranges Internet access for hotels. Boingo's customers download client software that enables them to have single-billing and single-sign-on Wi-Fi access from hotspots worldwide.

Hotspots As Supplements to Other Services— Cellular, DSL, Broadband, and Consulting

With the exception of airports and convention centers, most hotspots cover small areas and don't support a large number of customers. In addition, many hotspots compete with free services offered by municipalities, hotels, and retailers. Thus, by themselves, except for airports, most hotspots tend to generate low total revenues. In addition, they have high startup costs. However, operators may offer them to entice customers to their cafés, and retailers use them to attract customers. Other hotspot operators supplement revenue with sales of other services. The following are examples of hotspot services offered along with cellular and wired services or subsidized by complimentary offerings:

- T-Mobile USA, which as yet has no 3G cellular services, offers its Wi-Fi service as a high-speed wireless data enhancement to its cellular offerings.
- SBC offers its DSL subscribers Wi-Fi service at thousands of locations including Barnes & Noble bookstores, Avis, United Parcel Service, and McDonald's sites.
- South Korean telephone company KT Corp. offers its residential DSL customers access at 12,000 hotspots for less than $1 monthly.
- Wayport earns additional revenue from its wireline broadband connections such as those that connect hotels to the Internet.
- The Cloud, a UK aggregator with service in Europe, consults on building Wi-Fi networks to cable and cellular operators. It also offers Wi-Fi infrastructure to these operators.

To boost revenues, operators are testing or considering services such as voice calling, movies, local printing, and music over Wi-Fi networks.

Public Access Gateway—Single Sign-On, Security, and Billing

Hotspot operators are widening their coverage in attempts to make it comparable to cellular networks by reselling Wi-Fi from many hotspots. In addition, hotspot owners expand their coverage areas by making global roaming agreements with each other. In some of these arrangements, wireless Internet service providers (WISPs) hire companies to supply security, authentication, usage tracking, access control, and connections to the Internet uniformly from many sites. Customers are essentially roaming between multiple hotspots but receiving a single bill. Subscribers also use single sign-on, the same password and user identification, to sign on at different hotspots.

Billing is often provided at *clearinghouses*. A clearinghouse is a neutral third-party entity that settles payments between multiple carriers. For example, if WISP One owes WISP Two $10 and WISP One owes $5, the clearinghouse bills the difference, $5, and sends reports to each operator so that it can bill its customers appropriately (see Figure 9.2).

In addition, support organizations have hardware and software at a central site that authenticates customers to verify that they are who they claim to be. The equipment to support security is often a remote access dial-in user service (RADIUS) device.

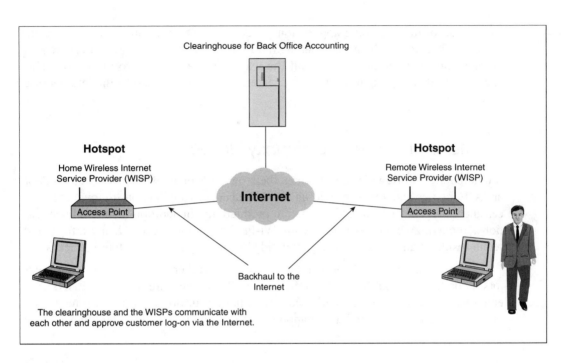

Figure 9.2
A gateway for public access.

Remote Access Aggregators for Enterprises— Single Sign-On, Security, and Billing

A key feature of remote access aggregators is secure access to corporate virtual private networks (VPNs). iPass, STSN, GoRemote (formerly GRIC Communications, Inc.), Fiberlink Communications, and Infonet sell this service to enterprises to support customers who travel globally. Each employee who uses the service receives client software that enables him or her to log on securely for remote access to corporate e-mail and other files. The aggregator arranges for access from diverse Wi-Fi and wired public Internet cafés and designated hotels. In addition to remote access from hotspots, some of these aggregators offer remote access via cellular services as well. The enterprise receives a single bill, and users have the convenience of a uniform way to sign on to services remotely.

For example, NTT DoCoMo offers its customers roaming on other cellular networks, Wi-Fi in 33 countries, and DoCoMo's 3G network in Japan. All of these services are charged for on one bill. Hotspot aggregator and remote access provider iPass manages authentication for DoCoMo at hotspots.

In all of the preceding applications, security software creates a tunnel of extra bits around the data transmitted, making it difficult for hackers to capture the data as it is transmitted. The tunnel extends all the way from the Internet to the laptop. This encrypts the data stream at the hotspot or Internet café as well as over the Internet (see Figure 9.3).

In Cities and Towns—Community Networks

Municipalities worldwide are building their own Wi-Fi networks to cover outdoor areas. For cities and towns, providing wireless access to applications to town employees and emergency providers is a boon to productivity. In addition to internal applications, modernizing infrastructure with Wi-Fi for Internet access helps attract and retain residents and lessens the digital divide by creating affordable Internet access.

Municipalities have large numbers of remote workers, including health inspectors, department of public works staff, police officers, and firefighters. WLANs give employees who work in the field access to important information on town networks. For example, many towns have mapping applications that include building layouts

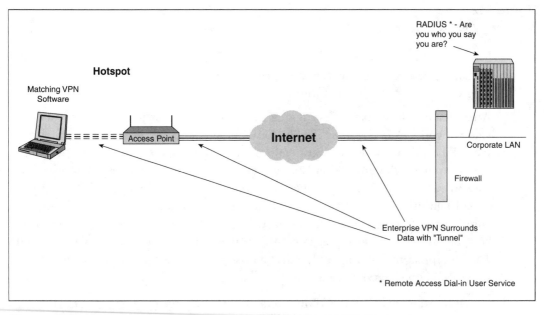

Figure 9.3
A secure virtual private network (VPN) connection between hotspots and enterprises using tunneling.

with entrances, exits, and the existence of hazardous material inside commercial structures. Fast access to this information can help save the lives of firefighters and people trapped in burning buildings. In emergencies such as hurricanes and major snowstorms, fire, police, snowplows, and ambulances can quickly communicate important information back to a central emergency center. In addition, some Wi-Fi equipment made for community networks includes location-tracking software that can be used to trace town vehicles and improve utilization of expensive equipment. Wi-Fi devices on the vehicles beam their location to multiple antennas (access points), which use the strength of the signal to determine their location.

Once networks are implemented for municipal applications, there is a minimal cost to extend their use to town residents and visitors for Internet access at no cost or for low monthly fees of $10 to $16. For example, in poor neighborhoods, local businesses may be allowed to use the WLAN for alarm systems that the police monitor. In exchange, the businesses offer free or low-cost Internet access to customers living in the neighborhood. This is a way for towns to offer upgraded services that benefit residents. Most towns don't want to offer in-home Internet access to town residents who can afford to purchase it at market rates.

There are other motivations for building town-wide Wi-Fi networks. Some towns that depend on tourist revenues build Wi-Fi networks to attract visitors. They feel it adds an extra incentive for people to visit their city. In rural areas without broadband service, wireless LANs are deployed to provide reasonably priced high-speed Internet access to homes and businesses. They are often installed by municipally owned utility departments in conjunction with outside firms that manage the network, connect the Wi-Fi service to a fiber link for Internet access, bill for the service, and share revenue with the utility.

In addition to municipalities, enterprises that use wireless networks to cover large campuses use the same technology, mesh networking, for its added redundancy and savings on cabling costs.

Regulatory Issues Around Community Networks

Lobbying efforts by powerful telephone companies may stem the creation of low-priced community networks. Incumbent telephone companies and cable operators have mounted lobbying campaigns trying to make it illegal for municipalities to sell telecommunications services. The campaigns are aimed at state governments because the United States Supreme Court granted them the power to regulate municipal creation of networks that charge fees to users. The telephone and cable companies have taken the position that tax money should not be used to compete against private companies.

As a result of these lobbying efforts, the Pennsylvania legislature required that municipalities give incumbents the right of first refusal on municipl broadband projects such as Wi-Fi service for which they intend to charge a fee. However, in a deal brokered with the legislature, Verizon promised not to block a network being planned for the city of Philadelphia. Lobbying campaigns are being waged in other states including Utah, Louisiana, and Florida where cities are starting to plan networks. A number of states already have regulations limiting the creation of municipal networks.

Mesh Networking—To Create Community Wi-Fi Service

Most community-wide networks use some type of *mesh* networking for their Wi-Fi connections. Mesh networks are also referred to as *multipoint-to-multipoint* networks. In multipoint-to-multipoint configurations, all devices are connected to each other. The two most common topologies (the way devices are connected) are infrastructure and client mesh networks.

- In *infrastructure mesh networks*, all of the access points pass packets to each other and ultimately to the Internet or municipal LAN. Infrastructure mesh networks are also referred to as fixed mesh networks because the access points, the devices that pass messages across the network, are in fixed locations. Cities and towns most commonly implement fixed mesh networks.

- In a *client mesh network*, every Wi-Fi-equipped user device transmits packets from other users across the network. This is also referred to as *ad hoc networking*.

See Figure 9.4 for a comparison of the two topologies.

Mesh networks are complex and require sophisticated software to route packets between user devices or access points. This is more complex than standard Wi-Fi networks in which every access point merely routes packets to switches or routers. In essence, access points or user devices act as repeaters. They repeat signals to other devices to or from the Internet or LAN. Moreover, because there may be many links, mesh networks may introduce latency (delay) if they are not designed properly. Motorola (through its MeshNetwork subsidiary), Nortel Networks, Tropos, Firetide, BelAir, and Alvarion provide mesh networks for municipalities. Enterprises also use mesh networks but in fewer numbers.

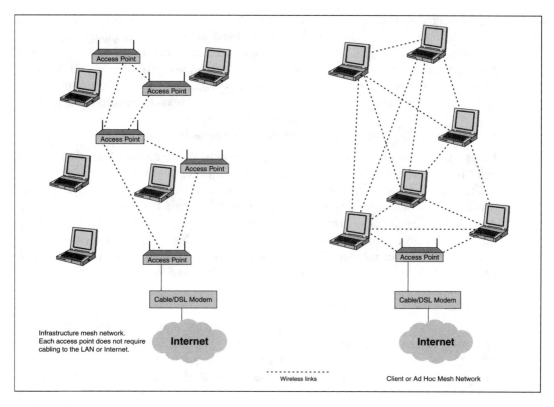

Infrastructure mesh network.
Each access point does not require
cabling to the LAN or Internet.

- - - - - - - - - -
Wireless links

Client or Ad Hoc Mesh Network

Figure 9.4
Mesh WLAN networks.

Line of Sight and Redundancy

Line of sight is required by some high-frequency wireless technologies including Wi-Fi. Line of site occurs when there are no obstructions between devices that communicate with each other wirelessly. For example, in nonmesh designs, obstructions between an access point and a user device may block the transmission. However, in mesh networks, signals can be transmitted via a different route when the nearest device cannot be seen because a tree or building blocks visibility.

Thus, organizations that install 802.11 networks don't have to plan for line of sight because paths are dynamically created when there are obstructions. This is important in outdoor installations where there are many trees and no high buildings where antennas can be placed higher than nearby trees or other buildings. Because town installations are outdoors where these conditions often occur, not requiring designs based on line of sight is important.

Because of their reliability and the fact that they don't need line of sight, the first mesh networks were designed for the military. Mesh networks are reliable because they dynamically reroute signals if an access point or device is not turned on. Thus, during battles, if nodes (access points or user devices) are destroyed, the network still operates. In addition, networks can be quickly deployed because site surveys are not needed to determine line of sight. Moreover, mesh networks can be installed regardless of terrain.

Savings on Cabling—In the Backhaul Between Access Points

Infrastructure mode networks save money on backhaul, the cabling from each access point to a central switch, because fewer access points are cabled to switches. Rather, traffic is carried wirelessly from access point to access point until it reaches its destination. The destination can be switches, routers, or end-user portable computing devices. The backhaul is composed of wireless media rather than cabling. This is important because cabling backhaul traffic back to LANs is a major expense in large 802.11 networks. In most mesh networks, a central switch manages traffic between access points and is wired to the local area network or router.

Mesh Networks for Telemetry

Mesh networks are also used for telemetry. In telemetry, they are used to control manufacturing processes, electrical usage, and alarm systems. ZigBee, which is based on the 802.15.4 standard, is a newly standardized protocol for wireless sensor networks that use mesh topology. For more information on ZigBee networks, see the section later in this chapter.

Free Open-Source Software for Mesh Networks

In the United States, the government recognized the importance of telephone service and created universal service policies that promised affordable telephone service to consumers. No such policy has been created to make Internet access affordable for residential customers. There are U.S. government Internet access subsidies for education, libraries, and rural hospitals but none for individual users. Recently, a worldwide grassroots movement has developed to create free or low-cost Internet access using Wi-Fi networks.

One of these groups, the Champaign-Urbana Community Wireless Network (CUWiN), was awarded several grants to create and test free open-source software for mesh networks. The software was created by a core group of 25 developers, many of whom worked as volunteers. The software created is used with off-the-shelf access points to create low-cost networks. One of the goals is to make it available for developing countries.

The city of Urbana, Illinois, which is the test bed for the software, was able, for a small amount of money, to fund an entire wireless network covering much of the downtown area. The idea for the simple algorithm for routing traffic grew out of a research paper published by BBN, which developed mesh networking for the military. The CUWiN developers consulted researchers at MIT and other groups active in the community wireless movement: the Bay Area Wireless Users Group (BAWUG) in San Francisco, FreiFunk in Berlin, and Seattle Wireless.

In Homes—To Avoid Running Cables

A number of factors resulted in the widespread residential uptake of Wi-Fi. Low prices, increased broadband Internet access, and easier installations are the major ones. (Wi-Fi is used inside homes, and broadband services such as cable modems connect users to the Internet.) When Wi-Fi was first available, people often had to ask more technical friends for help installing software on their computer and connecting the access point to their modem or router. As the devices matured, single devices became available with access points and routers and suppliers made installation easier.

However, as in enterprises, interference is an issue. In large multistory homes, the signal may not reach every room in the house, resulting in dead spots. Availability of products with prestandard 802.11n chips will improve coverage for customers willing to pay for improved coverage. In addition, customers have the option of purchasing repeaters to extend signals to dead spots. The repeater is an antenna that picks up weakened signals, strengthens them, and repeats them over an extended area.

The fact that broadband providers now supply access points, routers, and modems in one device and offer to mail combination wireless routers and access points along with their modem is a factor in the growing use of wireless gear for home networks. These network operators, for the most part, mail the 802.11 gear and provide a help line to assist with installation. Siemens, Cisco (through its Linksys subsidiary), Netgear, D-Link, Belkin, and ZyXEL sell gear for the residential market.

Home Networks—Sharing Content

Wireless home entertainment networks move content between personal computers, music systems, and televisions. This enables subscribers to view movies, view photographs snapped with camera phones or digital cameras, and hear music downloaded from the Internet on their televisions, stereo systems, or cell phones. Home networks will also enable users to share games among computers and televisions. Although there are products on the market called media centers that perform these functions, there are still hurdles to overcome for widespread adoption of home networks for sharing multimedia files. Chief among these are differing formats for audio, images, and video files and inadequate speed on home networks. As well, copy protection software in content received over the Internet is not always compatible with copy protection on devices that play the content.

In addition, consumers for the most part still don't have fast enough broadband links to receive high-quality video from the Internet. Within homes, 802.11n is adequate to support streaming-broadcast-quality video, but to date it has not been widely adopted by residential customers. Streaming refers to the capability to play content as it is received rather than waiting for the entire file to be downloaded. Furthermore, setting up a home entertainment network is complex.

Differing Standards for Audio, Video, and Images

Most video is still received via set-top boxes provided by cable TV operators or satellite TV networks. Incumbent telephone companies are starting to offer subscription television also. All of these providers are developing different, incompatible standards to share content over home networks. To date, satellite operators have not published details about possible home networking for their services.

CableLabs®, the research and development consortium of cable operators in North America, is developing the OpenCable™ Applications Platform (OCAP™). OCAP™ is middleware software that converts applications such as interactive games created by outside developers to a format compatible with set-top boxes and televisions with internal set-top boxes. The OpenCable™ Applications Platform also supports portability for content throughout a home. To date, no networking devices on the market support OCAP™. However, Sun has stated its intent to incorporate it in its products.

Incumbent telephone companies are settling on a different, incompatible standard, the DSLHome™ initiative, which was developed by the DSL Forum, an industry consortium of DSL providers and suppliers. The DSLHome™ standard was developed to support high-speed broadband DSL service capable of carrying telephone companies' subscription digital television offerings, Voice over IP, and Internet access. The DSLHome™ initiative specifies a gateway and DSL modem, usually in a single device. The gateway will contain middleware that will format content so that it can be shared with televisions, IP telephones, and printers.

Components of Home Entertainment Networks—Media Servers

In the future, subscription-based content from companies such as Netflix, CinemaNow, and Movielink will be downloaded to personal computers over the Internet. When broadband services to homes support this and content is made available for streaming over the Internet, customers are likely to want to view movies downloaded from the Internet on televisions rather than PCs. Home network devices now on the market support sharing content downloaded from the Internet onto PCs with televisions or stereo systems. These systems are not compatible with OCAP™ or DSLHome™.

Microsoft's XP Media Center software for personal computers is intended to enable a PC to transmit content to televisions and stereos. XP Media Center has a TV receiver, compression software, and the capability to be remotely controlled and to record TV shows to hard drives. Media servers are adjuncts to personal computers in home networks. They have built-in 802.11 networking and the capability to convert content to various audio (MP3 and so on), image (GIF, TIFF, and so on), or video (MPEG4, QuickTime, RealVideo, Windows Media Video, and so on) standards. In addition, they are compatible with various analog and digital television formats.

These systems include a remote control device with menu selections that appear on the television screen for photos, songs, movies, or home videos stored on PCs or separate hard drives. Media centers can also stream music and Internet radio to stereo systems and record television shows. For now, most media centers connect to stereo systems and televisions by coaxial cabling and to PCs wirelessly. This is because 802.11 protocols do not support adequate speeds for real-time television viewing.

HomePlug AV—Using a Home's Electrical Cabling Between TVs and Media Centers

Faster wireless protocols such as HomePlug AV would enable media centers to be wirelessly connected to televisions. With HomePlug AV, the base station plugs into a standard electrical outlet and beams signals to devices such as televisions. Signals from the base station to media centers are carried on existing electrical wiring. However, to date, HomePlug AV is not widely available or supported.

Wi-Fi Networks for Voice Over IP (VoIP)

Voice over IP can be carried in wired as well as wireless networks, and there is a great deal of interest in using 802.11 networks for packetized voice as well as data. (See Chapter 2, "VoIP Systems, Circuit Switched PBXs, and Cabling," and Chapter 4, "VoIP, the Public Switched Telephone Network, and Signaling," for VoIP in wired networks.) Using 802.11 for voice is also referred to as *Voice over wireless LAN (VoWLAN), (VoFi),* and *(VoWi-Fi).* The interest revolves around the following advantages:

- Hotspot infrastructure costs less than equipment that supports cellular access.

- Enterprises are considering wireless voice over 802.11 to save money on cellular fees for employees away from their desk but within campuses.

- If handsets support both Wi-Fi and cellular access, users can use the same telephone both at home to replace wireline home phones and away from home instead of cellular where Wi-Fi is available.

There are a number of technical and business hurdles to overcome before voice on wireless local area networks is adopted on a large scale. Hurdles include the following:

- Seamless roaming between WLAN and cellular networks when calls are in progress

- Providing adequate quality and capacity on Wi-Fi networks

- Improving battery life on telephones

- Competition from cellular providers, which are developing and implementing higher speed, more widely deployed technologies in anticipation of competition from Wi-Fi and other fixed wireless services

- Ensuring that there are no delays when roaming between access points within the same WLAN

- Setting up billing and roaming agreements between providers worldwide

Skype, Vonage, BT Telecom (British Telecom), and Net2Phone plus other broadband VoIP operators are in various stages of testing or offering 802.11 handsets for voice in conjunction with their broadband Internet service. Cable TV and incumbent telephone companies are also looking at supplying Wi-Fi handsets that in the future will operate on cellular and WLAN networks.

Quality and Capacity on Wi-Fi Home and Hotspot Networks

Ethernet, on which Wi-Fi networks are based, was designed for data and drops packets in the event of congestion. Voice requirements are different than data. When there is congestion in networks and packets are dropped, voice quality sounds choppy. Also, most Wi-Fi networks don't have adequate capacity to support voice. In addition, many hotspots still use 802.11b, which has less capacity than 802.11a and 802.11g. The newly emerging 802.11n increases capacity. However, it is not widely installed.

In addition to greater capacity, wireless networks need to prioritize voice so that packets are not dropped if there is congestion. To that end, the IEEE specified the Wi-Fi multimedia (WMM) subset of the *802.11e* standard in October 2004. The WMM has provisions for prioritizing packets based on type of service, such as voice or video. For example, voice and video have a higher priority than packets carrying e-mail or other data applications. In addition to being used for voice, the 802.11e Wi-Fi multimedia standard is intended to prioritize video traffic in home entertainment networks.

Roaming Between Cellular and Wi-Fi Networks

Efforts are underway to promote both cellular and Wi-Fi networks for data applications. With the existing agreements between cellular carriers and Wi-Fi operators, customers can use their laptops at both Wi-Fi-enabled airports and locations with cellular access. However, roaming that enables customers to continue voice conversations as they move between Wi-Fi and cellular networks is more complex to accomplish.

Seamless roaming between cellular networks and Wi-Fi networks is more important for voice calls than for data communications because people often shut down their computer or other portable data device when they leave a hotspot or cellular network. However, with voice calling, subscribers tend to keep speaking as they walk or ride. Thus, it's desirable to transfer calls between these networks without dropping calls.

Fixed-Mobile Convergence: One Handset for Calls Over Wi-Fi and Cellular Networks

Network operators that both supply VoIP over broadband and operate cellular networks are in the planning stages of offering a seamless handover of voice calls between cellular networks and Wi-Fi networks in residences and hotspots. This will give their customers one-number service and a single handset to use in homes and remotely. It is also a way to attract customers to bundles of service. Cable TV operators as well as incumbent telephone companies are considering these offerings. Cable TV operators would resell capacity on other cellular networks for these offerings.

Complex business and technical issues must be resolved for seamless roaming between cellular and Wi-Fi hotspots. These include the following:

- Roaming agreements
- Uniform billing
- Uniform access
- Compatible signaling protocols
- Equipment, such as access controllers, to support interoperable roaming between networks

Authentication, the process of proving the subscriber's identity, is a problem because of the patchwork of different authentication systems used at hotspots. Customers are used to signing on differently from laptops but not for telephone calls. When users with Wi-Fi handsets are at hotspots, the hotspot needs to authenticate the device in less than 50 milliseconds to avoid the subscriber perceiving a delay.

British Telecom (BT), which operates 1,500 hotspots, mostly in the UK and Ireland, has announced that it will provide the capability for customers to use a new service called Bluephone that lets callers use existing local telephone service in homes and businesses and cellular service when they are out of range of homes and enterprises. The base station has a range of 25 meters and is connected to customers' local telephone lines. When they are out of range of the base station, the Motorola dual-mode handset will connect customers to BT's mobile service. The mobile service operates on Vodafone's wireless network. BT is a mobile virtual network operator and resells mobile service on Vodafone's network. The goal is to provide one bill and one voice mailbox for cellular and home/business telephone service.

BT's Bluephone service is based on the unlicensed mobile access (UMA) specification developed by the Unlicensed Mobile Access Consortium composed of a number of network operators and equipment suppliers. The UMA has specified a gateway to connect IP networks to mobile networks. Bluephone will be available by spring 2005 and will involve new billing, operation, and management software, special access points, and new handsets. It is also designed for enterprise customers who will have special hardware and software to administer the service. UMA is intended to work with Bluetooth, WiFi, and WiMAX networks. See the sections later in this chapter that discuss Bluetooth (a wireless short distance technology) and WiMAX.

Initially, Bluephone will use a Bluetooth-equipped base station and a Bluetooth/GSM cordless/cellular handset. Inside homes, the phone will operate like a cordless phone. However, BT has stated its intention to use dual Wi-Fi and GSM handsets later. Motorola is developing Wi-Fi infrastructure for enterprises for Bluephone. This service should be capable of operating over BT's hotspots for voice. Mobile carrier Orange has also announced a converged product for 2005 in the United Kingdom. However, that one will be based on Wi-Fi and GSM-capable handsets. In addition to the Bluephone telephone handset, manufacturers including Motorola, Samsung Electronics, and Nokia are beginning to offer dual-mode cellular and WiFi handsets with, for example, GSM-Wi-Fi, CDMA-Wi-Fi, and UMTS-Wi-Fi dual-access capabilities. See Chapter 8, "Mobile Services," for cellular standards and mobile virtual network operators.

Using the Same Data Device in Wi-Fi and Cellular Networks

Portable data devices often include capabilities to access Wi-Fi and mobile cellular networks. However, using these services often entails corporations managing at least two different bills, one from their cellular carrier and at least one for WLAN service. Users also access the networks using a different interface on their computer. Various types of integration options are becoming available. For example, Vodafone and T-Mobile USA offer a data card with 3G, GPRS (cellular service slower than 3G), and Wi-Fi access.

The T-Mobile USA service automatically connects data users to whichever is the fastest service available.

VoIP in Enterprises

Voice calls carried on Wi-Fi networks are referred to as VoIP, Voice over WLAN (VoWLAN), or Voice over WiFi (VoWi-Fi). The desire to carry voice on WLANs is a major application driving adoption of WLANs in enterprises. In addition, corporations that already have Wi-Fi networks would like to maximize their investment in wireless networks by adding voice. For the most part, enterprises have not yet added voice to their wireless networks. However, manufacturers are readying products that will overcome past hurdles including security, unacceptable quality caused by delays, short battery life, and lack of capacity.

As previously noted, the IEEE approved part of a standard for quality of service in late 2004 that prioritizes voice traffic so that one source of delay, other traffic, is minimized. Spectralink, which currently has the largest market share of enterprise WLAN VoIP customers, offers its prestandard, proprietary quality-of-service software in conjunction with its service.

Two other problems that manufacturers are just resolving are delays introduced when calls are handed over between access points and security. When people use portable data devices on LANs, they enter passwords and user IDs. However, with voice, this is not practical. Therefore, system administers create separate local area networks, virtual LANs. This lets the network identify voice users and authenticate them without requiring passwords.

Scalability, the capability to grow and handle more traffic, is also a concern. However, standards such as 802.11g, 802.11a, and 802.11n address some of these concerns. In addition, as the technology matures and becomes accepted, more businesses will use sophisticated switches to manage traffic and to alert administrators to the need to add access points in the event of congestion. See Figure 9.5 for voice on a wireless local area network.

Integration of PBX, Cellular, and 802.11 Service in Enterprises

New service is available that provides some integration between PBXs, GSM cell phones, and 802.11 networks in enterprises. One example of this is a partnership between PBX manufacturer Avaya, Wi-Fi provider Proxim, and wireless phone manufacturer Motorola. Motorola supplies a dual-mode Wi-Fi/GSM handset for the service. The integration enables employees to publish just their work telephone number but receive calls to that number on the Wi-Fi service at their company WLAN and the cellular network. Unanswered calls to desk phones are first passed to the campus

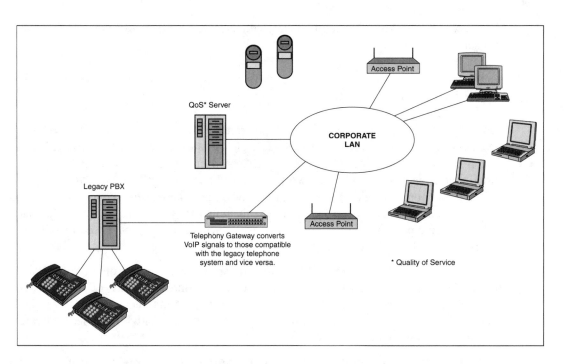

Figure 9.5
Voice over IP carried on corporate 802.11 wireless networks.

802.11 networks and then to the cellular network. When people on calls on 802.11 networks move out of range of an antenna, calls are seamlessly handed over to the GSM network.

This is similar to a service that NTT DoCoMo offers enterprise customers. Business customers can receive calls on their corporate WLAN or the cellular network on dual-mode Wi-Fi mobile handsets. However, neither service currently allows customers to receive or make calls at public hotspots.

Managing Security on WLANs

The broadcast nature of 802.11 networks makes them vulnerable to hackers. Access points continually broadcast their network's service set identifier (SSID) and Wi-Fi-enabled devices respond to these broadcasts. These broadcast messages are vulnerable to eavesdroppers and attempted logon by unauthorized users. This is the phenomenon that enabled "war drivers" to drive down streets and into parking lots looking for and finding insecure networks. In addition, unlike wired networks, there are no natural boundaries, cables. Thus, in apartment buildings and businesses, signals often easily leak into adjacent units and outside areas. In addition to early Wi-Fi products with the following security problems, early customers did not implement security safeguards properly:

- Encryption was easily cracked.

- There was no authentication.

- Businesses and residential customers often did not and many still don't do the following:

  - Turn on security

  - Change factory-set, commonly known passwords

  - Turn off factory-set, commonly known service set identities broadcast by access points that make it easier for others to log into WLANs

This increases vulnerability to eavesdroppers and hackers.

New security standards have been ratified that provide stronger encryption and authentication. The newer standards are Wi-Fi Protected Access (WPA), which is a subset of the IEEE-specified 802.11i standard. The full 802.11i standard is available and is referred to as WPA2. However, many older networks haven't upgraded to WPA, many enterprises don't trust the new standard, and administering it is time consuming and complex. Also, security products and outsourced services are costly. Simpler, less-complex versions are available for homes and small businesses.

Four layers of security are required for WLAN service. These should be in the following:

- Users' devices with the following:

  - VPN software that enables the network to treat wireless devices differently

  - Personal firewalls to prevent hackers from accessing data on laptops, notebooks, and personal digital assistants

- Access points

- The local area network

- Applications

The complexity is due to the fact that software on the user device, the access point, switches, and security servers must all match. In addition, enterprises have the following tasks:

- Distribute client software to each user's device.
- Check for rogue access points.
- Enter names in databases.
- Monitor usage.
- Make sure that portable devices don't spread viruses to the corporate network that they may have picked up in hotspots.

When corporations use Wi-Fi Protected Access (WPA), employees' laptops won't be compatible with corporate networks unless their home 802.11 networks also use WPA, which most now don't.

Compared to 3G: Mobility, Coverage, and Data Rates

Wi-Fi service, which costs less to implement than cellular networks, has the potential to compete with mobile networks for data service. In addition to lower equipment costs, spectrum is free, and for the most part Wi-Fi is faster than cellular data service. Wi-Fi offers the biggest advantages over mobile networks where Internet access is slower than dial-up service. Mobile operators recognize this and have speeded up their timetable for 3G, high-speed implementation. Operators are also choosing to implement higher-speed versions of new 3G technologies and to upgrade existing 3G networks to those that support more users and higher data rates. These upgrades will create cellular data speeds that match or are close to WLAN speeds.

Some operators, such as Sprint, Vodafone, and T-Mobile USA, are supplementing their cellular offerings with lower-cost Wi-Fi service, particularly inside congested buildings and skyscrapers. Wi-Fi is most suitable for densely populated areas such as airports where mobility is not required. It costs less to add capacity by adding additional access points than by installing more cellular base stations. In addition, as the technology evolves, users will have laptops and handsets with Wi-Fi and cellular service. Mobile cellular operators may then be able to automatically switch traffic to their cellular spectrum, if there is congestion on the free Wi-Fi spectrum in a given airport or building.

However, hotspot coverage is spotty. For example, it's available inside airports but not on the drive into the airport. Cellular has wider coverage than WLAN services with seamless handovers between base stations. Wi-Fi provides primarily portability within buildings, but cellular offers mobility over entire cities and countries. Thus, users can often access the Internet anywhere within the territory, assuming speeds are adequate. Moreover, seamless mobility means that people in moving vehicles, such as subways and trains, can use cellular service.

For consultants, technicians, and salespeople who require Internet access while conducting business at customer locations, depending on Wi-Fi can be problematic. Many enterprises have security enabled that allows only employees' virtual private network (VPN) software on their devices to use the corporate WLANs for Internet access. For visitors, high-speed mobile wireless (cellular) service is often the only way they can access their company's applications or e-mail.

BROADBAND WIRELESS ACCESS.............................

Broadband wireless access provides similar capabilities as DSL, cable modems, T-1/T-3/E-1/E-3, and other broadband technologies using wireless media rather than cabling. Some of these technologies, such as WiMAX and universal mobile telecommunications system time division duplex (UMTS TDD), may in the future provide *mobile wireless broadband service* for pedestrians, persons in moving vehicles, and people within buildings. However, most of the current implementations are for less-complex wireless services between fixed locations or for wireless service with Internet access and portability within a service provider's coverage area.

Some of the services discussed in this section are for low-cost wireless local loops for voice as well as data. These are intended primarily for developing countries, which don't have extensive cabling to end users' locations. Broadband wireless access provides coverage to sites over wide metropolitan and rural areas. However, currently no portability is provided within buildings. In contrast, Wi-Fi is primarily a wireless local area network technology.

WiMAX: Broadband Access, Based on 802.16

Although worldwide interoperability for microwave access (WiMAX) is referred to as a service, it is actually a WiMAX forum whose goal is to certify interoperability of equipment based on 802.16 standards for high-speed, broadband wireless service. Future versions may be used for mobile wireless service. (See Table 9.3 in the Appendix section at the end of this chapter for the various 802.16 standards, some of which operate in the 10GHz to 66GHz bands. Others operate in the 2GHz to 11GHz bands.) Proponents claim that WiMAX supports data rates of 70 megabits per second at shorter distances of two to three miles in non-line-of-sight environments. However, this has not been tested, and actual speeds are expected to be a great deal slower. As in other wireless technologies, the farther signals travel, the lower the data rates achieved. The main standard, which the IEEE ratified in 2004, is for fixed, high-speed non-line-of-sight wireless service. The standard specifies point-to-multipoint service in which one base-station antenna mounted on a building rooftop or a tower is connected wirelessly to multiple subscribers who have smaller, eight-inch-square antennas on rooftops or outside windows. Later product versions may support portable Internet access within buildings via laptop PCs equipped with WiMAX antennas. The laptops will communicate directly with carriers' base stations.

Background—Microwave Point-to-Point Service

Fixed wireless services to connect stationary sites to each other have been used since after World War II. Improvements in multiplexing increased their capacity, and as lower frequencies became crowded, technologies were developed for higher-frequency, microwave services. Microwave refers to wireless services with short wavelengths that operate in the frequency range of about the 890-megahertz to 60-gigahertz bands. Utilities, railroads, and carriers implemented microwave service, many along rights-of-way they owned. This enabled utilities and railroads to avoid the expense of leasing private lines from telephone companies. Carriers used wireless services to avoid laying cables in areas such as across canyons and beneath lakes and rivers. Microwave links were used by only the very largest enterprises for private networks because of the costs and delays incurred by site surveys and FCC licensing. In addition, microwave is limited to point-to-point configurations. One antenna can only communicate with one other antenna, not to multiple antennas.

Comparisons to Earlier 802.16 Services

WiMAX, which also uses high-frequency microwave spectrum, is based on earlier versions of the 802.16 standard developed following passage of the Telecommunications Act of 1996. At that time, CLECs such as WinStar, Teligent, and Advanced Radio Telecom (ART) purchased spectrum for new fixed wireless technologies such as microwave multipoint distribution system (MMDS) service. These wireless services were intended as low-cost alternatives to providing local telephone service in developing countries as well as in Europe and the United States. Like earlier microwave service, they required a line of site and costly licensed spectrum. In addition, the equipment was expensive, and the standard was not ratified until 2001, after most of the companies had already failed.

WiMAX service is based on an improved version of IEEE 802.16 designed to lower costs of deploying fixed wireless service through interoperable multivendor equipment. This standard specifies both licensed and unlicensed spectrum for non-line-of-sight service in the 2GHz to 11GHz bands. In addition, WiMAX is used primarily for data and thus does not necessarily require interconnections with incumbent

telephone companies. Moreover, it can carry any protocol including Ethernet, Internet protocol (IP), and asynchronous transport mode (ATM). This makes it flexible for enterprise customers to deploy.

Although a standard was ratified in June 2004 for fixed mobile service, no equipment has been made available to meet the standard. As of January 2005, all pre-WiMAX equipment is proprietary, and once a carrier purchases equipment, carriers are tied to a particular vendor unless they change all of their equipment. However, the WiMAX Forum, an alliance of carriers and manufacturers that supports WiMAX, plans to create a WiMAX certification program similar to the Wi-Fi Alliance's program in 2005. Thus, once equipment is built to comply with the latest WiMAX standard for fixed wireless broadband access, it can be certified as WiMAX compliant. If this happens, carriers that purchase the equipment will know that they can use a mix of suppliers. It is hoped that this will drive prices down.

Many suppliers have stated their intention of building equipment compliant with the WiMAX standard. Airspan Networks, Alcatel, Alvarion, Aperto Networks, Beam-Reach, Motorola, NextNet, Proxim, Siemens, and Redline supply WiMAX type equipment.

WiMAX Services—Fixed and Mobile

WiMAX is a broadband wireless service able to operate at high data rates without line of sight in lower frequencies because it uses orthogonal frequency division multiplexing (OFDM). OFDM is the same type of multiplexing specified in the Wi-Fi 802.11a and 802.11g standards. OFDM minimizes interference because it sends bits over multiple frequencies within the same channel. These parallel lower-frequency bits (subcarriers) offer higher immunity from interference from objects in their paths because bits at these lower frequencies have longer wavelengths. Longer wavelengths are more immune to interference than shorter wavelengths because they are often larger or of a longer duration than the interference. Reduced interference results in higher data rates.

The two main amendments to IEEE 802.16 standards for WiMAX are:

- 802.16d, also known as 802.16-2004, which was approved in 2004
- 802.16e, which has not been approved, is for mobile wireless service

802.16d: Designed for Fixed Wireless Service

Fixed wireless services are deployed between stationary points. A fixed wireless connection between enterprises and Internet service providers is an example of fixed wireless service. The service is wireless between the dish at the enterprise and the provider's antenna but not inside the building.

802.16e: A Proposed Amendment for Mobility

Mobile wireless supports applications in which people can use their service on a portable basis inside buildings and on a mobile basis while walking or in moving vehicles. It is being developed to compete with 3G cellular services. Mobile wireless provides wireless capability to users' devices via PCMCIA cards or chips built into laptops or wireless handsets. 802.116e is a mobile wireless standard intended for pedestrians and use in vehicles such as cars and trucks with speeds up to 120km/hour (74.4 miles/hour). It is not designed for use in high-speed trains.

WiMAX for mobility is an unproven technology. The requirement to hand over traffic between towers as people move between coverage areas adds to its complexity. In addition, picking up signals at long ranges when antennas are hidden in laptops is more problematic than when antennas are in fixed locations, mounted on the outside of buildings. Moreover, it's likely that 3G cellular technologies will have higher data rates through enhancements and wide availability by the time equipment is on the market. Chip makers such as Intel are working directly with carriers such as Sprint and NTT DoCoMo on R&D for mobile 802.16 gear.

Unlicensed Versus Licensed Spectrum; Possibility of Congestion and Lower Startup Costs

Because WiMAX operates in both licensed and unlicensed spectrum, startup costs are lower for carriers that offer the service in unlicensed frequencies. However, there are potential drawbacks. Use of unlicensed spectrum could lead to uncontrollable interference and traffic bottlenecks, particularly in densely populated urban areas. For example, other carriers might cause interference by offering service using the same spectrum.

This is analogous to what is happening in airports in the United States, where airlines have implemented wireless systems for applications such as luggage handling. The radio frequencies used by these systems often interfere with airports' Wi-Fi networks installed by airports for passengers in waiting areas. Analogous phenomena can occur with WiMAX in cities.

Small carriers that decide to use licensed spectrum will have to contend with the fact that large providers such as Sprint Nextel, T-Mobile USA, and SBC already own large chunks of the licensed spectrum specified for WiMAX. In addition, Hispanic Information Television Network (HITN) owns a chunk in the Educational Broadband Service (EBS) 2.5GHz band.

Support for Voice Over IP

The current prestandard WiMAX installations support primarily data. However, that may change as new applications are added to the standard or as vendors add proprietary functions. The current IEEE 802.16 standard specifies primarily Layer 1 and

Layer 2 functions. This functionality includes how devices access the network, the type of media used, error correction, and multiplexing techniques. The WiMAX Forum is planning to develop support for applications such as Voice over IP and video.

In addition, quality of service and the capability to prioritize services are built into the standard, which strengthens WiMAX's capability to support Voice over IP.

Security Built into the Standard

An advantage of WiMAX is that security provisions are included in the standard so that organizations that implement it don't have to either wait for upgraded security standards or purchase proprietary security products. The current 802.16 standards support privacy and authentication. Privacy is ensured with encryption, or scrambled bits. Authentication is a way to confirm that only legitimate users log into the service.

WiMAX: DSL and T-1 Replacement, Hotspot and Cellular Backhaul, Underdeveloped Areas

Regulatory changes drive the adoption of new technologies. Competitive local exchange carriers often purchase single switches that cover an entire town or a large section of a city. Although some carriers provide their own fiber to their largest customers, for the most part they lease last-mile connections from incumbents for T-1 and DSL services. Many also lease fiber from incumbents' central offices to their switches. However, regulatory changes have caused leasing rates for these connections to increase, and the result is that leasing facilities is often not a viable business strategy. Internet service providers and competitive local exchange carriers (CLECs) have responded to these changes by using pre-standard WiMAX equipment to deploy wireless T-1/E-1 services to enterprises without renting high-priced facilities from incumbent telephone companies or laying their own fiber.

In these wireless deployments, master base stations with antennas wirelessly communicate with outdoor dishes attached to customer buildings. The master base station has connections to an Internet service provider or to the Internet for data or Voice over IP service. In addition, carriers provide redundancy by having overlapping wireless coverage in the event that one base station (antenna and associated equipment) is out of service (see Figure 9.6). If they provide voice service, they have connections to tandem central offices.

Most large corporations use multiple high-speed T-1 circuits for Internet access services. For these customers, wireless service is one choice for an alternative route for their increasingly business-critical data services. In the event of an outside cable

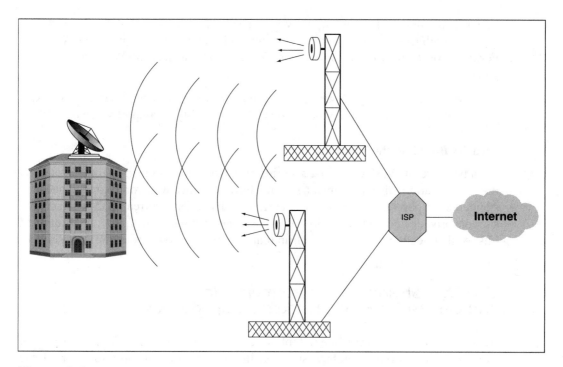

Figure 9.6
WiMAX service with overlapping wireless coverage for redundancy.

cut, the wireless service is operational. In addition, prices are often less than for comparable services. Carriers that supply wireless access are referred to as wireless Internet service providers (WISPs). These include TowerStream, Clearwire, Digiweb (in Ireland), U.S. Wireless Online, Inc., Speakeasy, and Xplore (in Canada). Moreover, large long distance companies such as Sprint and MCI are testing WiMAX, and AT&T, before its announced acquisition by SBC, announced plans to deploy it. There are many other small WISPs worldwide.

Broadband wireless access is also positioned to compete with DSL and cable modem broadband service. However, in urban developed areas in countries such as in Europe, South Korea, and North America, much of the infrastructure for broadband is already in place, and prices are fairly low. In addition, for most residential customers, changing providers entails the inconvenience of changing e-mail addresses. However, incumbent telephone companies are looking at WiMAX for locations far from central offices where DSL is costly to deploy and not yet available. For example, BellSouth and Verizon are testing the service, and Qwest has announced plans to deploy it.

The following are additional applications:

- Basic voice for consumers. Fax traffic and Internet access for small businesses in developing countries with no cabling in place to much of the population.
- Backhaul from base stations to mobile switches in rural cellular carriers' networks.
- Linking enterprise buildings together in either a campus or cities.
- Connecting access points to each other in Wi-Fi mesh networks in communities.
- Linking hotspots to the Internet.
- Broadband Internet access for residential consumers in rural areas where long distances between customers and central offices make providing DSL and laying cabling expensive.

Hurdles to Wider Deployment

Although WiMAX for fixed wireless access is growing, it is still in its infancy, and the systems that are installed are proprietary pre-standard WiMAX versions of the 802.16 standard for fixed service. In addition to competing with other, already-installed broadband services as well as other newly developed wireless broadband offerings, there are technical complexities and differing spectrum specified for the service worldwide.

Differing Spectrum and Power-Level Requirements Worldwide

Each country specifies the technologies that can be used on particular frequency bands and differing power levels allowable per service. This is because higher power levels are more apt to interfere with other signals. (Higher power levels enable signals to travel further.)

To ensure that equipment meets power, frequency, and other specifications, countries require that electronic equipment be certified so that it meets their rules before it can be sold in their country. This is true for equipment used both in licensed and unlicensed bands. The result is that manufacturers are required to manufacture electronic equipment to meet different specifications.

The most commonly used bands for WiMAX services are 2.5GHz, 3.5GHz, and 5.8GHz. In the United States, the 2.5GHz band is licensed for Broadband Radio Service (BRS) and some of the 3.5GHz and 5GHz bands are specified for unlicensed use. WiMAX is a Broadband Radio Service. Other countries make different bands in the

3.5GHz bands available for Broadband Radio Service on a licensed basis. However, many countries have not authorized the 5GHz band for this service.

The WiMAX Forum has formed a Regulatory Working Group whose goal is to work with regulatory agencies worldwide toward agreement on using the same frequency and power regulations everywhere. These efforts are referred to as harmonizing the rules. Harmonization helps manufacturers achieve manufacturing economies of scale to produce chips and base stations in enough quantities to lower manufacturing costs and ultimately purchase prices. This is one way to stimulate adoption of WiMAX. The WiMAX Forum expects the adoption of 5GHz to proceed quickly, but the other bands could take three or more years.

Complex Standard

The 802.16-2004 standard, upon which fixed WiMAX service is based, is complex, and as of January 2005, no equipment meeting the standard has become available. For example, the standard specifies that equipment operate over multiple frequency bands. It also includes security provisions for complex encryption and authentication plus definitions for transmitting voice traffic. Because of its complexity, it's not clear when equipment will be available that meets all of the security and other specifications. However, various manufacturers are developing products to meet the standard.

In addition, the fact that 802.16-2004 is point-to-multipoint adds complexity. The master base station has to quickly sample data from multiple remote antennas and sort them out as they are received. There are also three options for how bits are modulated and multiplexed in the over the air interface. *Modulation* refers to the process of changing the shape of individual wavelengths to carry signals. Advanced modulation schemes enable individual wavelengths to carry more bits and achieve higher data rates.

Adapting 3G for Wireless Broadband Access: UMTS TDD and WCDMA

Time division duplex (TDD) is a 3G technology used for fixed and mobile broadband wireless access. TDD is also referred to as universal mobile telecommunication system time division duplex (UMTS TDD) and time division-code division multiple access (TD-CDMA). IPWireless manufactures equipment based on UMTS TDD.

SOMA Networks supplies equipment for residential wireless local loop service based on a modified version of WCDMA. Both services are intended to lower carriers' costs of deploying high-bandwidth data service between fixed locations. Neither service requires a line of sight to operate. In addition, both operate on licensed spectrum.

TDD for Broadband Wireless Access

IPWireless deploys time division duplex (TDD) for fixed wireless access in licensed spectrum in the 2.5GHz and the 3.4GHz bands and is developing a product for the 2.3GHz band. (When used by cellular operators, it is used in other 3G specified frequencies as well.) TDD achieves high data rates in part by using unpaired spectrum, the same frequency band for sending and receiving. This is spectrally efficient because idle capacity not used for sending can be used for receiving and vice versa. TDD CDMA uses a combination of CDMA and time division for its air interface. Time division divides up capacity into multiple time slots. Each group of bits is assigned a time slot. CDMA is a form of spread spectrum that assigns a unique code to each session and spreads the signals over multiple frequencies.

For high-speed data, each desktop device or laptop uses a TDD-compatible modem with its own antenna and interface to the network. No external antenna is required on the building. Second-tier telephone companies and Internet service provides in Europe and Asia sell the service to residential and small office, home office (SOHO) customers. The service is a replacement for DSL and cable modem service. IPWireless customers include Airdata in Germany, Woosh in New Zealand, and Netcom in Nigeria. The company also has customers in Africa, the United Kingdom, Australia, Sweden, Malaysia, and Kazakhstan.

Portability and Voice Over IP

Although most carriers initially purchased IPWireless equipment for fixed wireless broadband, the service is actually portable, and many customers use it that way. For example, customers with laptops are able to use their computers portably within their home and in their providers' total coverage area. If a carrier is licensed to only provide fixed service, it has the option to turn off the handoff capability within the base stations so that customers can't use their service on a mobile basis within the coverage area.

IPWireless has also announced support for Voice over IP. The equipment will dedicate channels to voice so that voice and data will not have to contend with each other for bandwidth.

WCDMA Modified for Wireless Local Loops

SOMA Networks provides a packetized wireless local loop service that is a replacement for broadband cable and DSL service. The service is designed for circuit switched voice and fax as well as high-speed data. The equipment operates in the 1.9GHz, 2.3GHz, and 2.6GHz licensed frequency bands. SOMA sells primarily to carriers in developing nations where there is a scarcity of cabling to residential and small office, small home (SOHO) customers. It also sells to carriers in rural areas as a way to extend the reach of its service. Customers purchase an integrated 6" × 3" × 6" gateway about the size of a large book. The gateway has an antenna, 2RJ11 jacks for voice or facsimile connections, and Ethernet and USB connections for internal LANs. The capability to transmit faxes over SOMA's packetized network is an important service because, in developing countries, facsimile is a huge part of business transactions.

The self-installable gateway, which can be purchased at local electronics stores, provides the conversion between landline and radio frequency signals. SOMA, which has been developing its service since 1999, modified third generation WCDMA technology to provide end-to-end quality of service and multimegabit data speeds. SOMA supplies base stations in addition to integrated customer gateways. The base stations cover large areas that are 30 square miles in size. Carriers select their own switches and routers as well as gateways for connections to the Internet and the public switched telephone network. SOMA tests its equipment with the gateways to ensure compatibility.

The SOMA service is not portable or mobile. However, it is rolling out an integrated Wi-Fi handset for portable voice within homes. Jaring, the largest ISP in Malaysia, plus a number of rural carriers in the United States, use SOMA equipment.

PERSONAL AREA NETWORKS (PANS) ....

Personal area networks are those that operate over small areas within rooms and buildings. Of all of the technologies discussed in the following sections, Bluetooth has the largest installed base, spurred by the increasing use of cell phones and wireless headsets. However, ultra-wideband and RFID have the potential to grow and provide lower-priced connections for home networks and inventory tracking.

Bluetooth

Bluetooth is a collection of standards for special software on low-cost, low-powered radio chips that enables devices to communicate with each other over a short-range wireless link. Bluetooth eliminates cable clutter between computers and peripherals in offices and supports wireless peripherals for mobile handsets. According to Mike Dano's article "Convergence—back with a vengeance," which appeared in the December 30, 2004 online issue of *RCR Wireless News*, 20% of all wireless handsets have Bluetooth capability. The article predicts that this percentage will grow.

The following are examples of connections between Bluetooth-enabled devices:

- Headsets and wireless phones
- Personal digital assistants and computers to synchronize information
- Stereo music systems and headsets or speakers
- Hands-free speakerphone kits preinstalled in cars that work with cellular handsets
- Cell phones and computers to update speed-dial lists or to download photos
- Keyboards/mice and personal computers
- Base stations and cordless phones
- Printers and computers
- MP3 players and stereo systems
- Cellular phones and laptops for Internet access without a data card

Each of the preceding applications uses one of over 20 protocols called *profiles*. Each Bluetooth profile supports communications between particular types of devices such as headsets with cell phones and music systems with headsets or speakers. Bluetooth-equipped devices emit high-frequency radio signals so that other Bluetooth-equipped devices within range of these signals can communicate with each other by recognizing a range of addresses defined by a profile. The goal of defining profiles is to enable devices from different manufacturers to communicate with each other.

Bluetooth operates at low speeds of less than 1 megabit per second over distances of up to 10 meters (32.8 feet). A new specification, Bluetooth Version 2.0 + Enhanced Data Rate (EDR), doubles this speed. Bluetooth uses the same frequency, 2.4GHz, as 802.11 wireless LANs and some cordless phones. To minimize interference, Bluetooth hops between frequencies 1,600 times per second and uses low power. Low power also conserves battery life and limits the range of transmission, the distance signals travel before fading. In addition, hopping between frequencies mitigates interference because signals use each frequency band for only a small fraction of a second.

Like other technologies, when Bluetooth products first appeared on the market in about 2001, chip prices were high, and some early Bluetooth keyboards and mice did not operate consistently. Since that time, Bluetooth chip prices have decreased, and the standard has been upgraded and functions reliably.

Some mobile network operators, however, have disabled particular Bluetooth functions in the handsets they offer. This is because, in some instances, using Bluetooth eliminates cellular airtime charges. For example, consumers with Bluetooth-enabled personal computers and handsets can download photographs snapped on their camera phones to their computers and synchronize their address books with their cell phones using Bluetooth instead of cellular minutes. The carriers who disable Bluetooth transmissions between cell phones and computers hope to generate revenue when people send each other photographs over the cellular network. In addition, although people can download pictures to computers via a cable connected to universal serial bus (USB) ports on the handset and computer, using a Bluetooth wireless connection, while slower, is more convenient.

There are two drawbacks to Bluetooth. The initial setup can be complex for users to implement. Subsequent setup times—the "handshake," for example—between a Bluetooth-enabled mouse and the computer or between a PDA and a computer are also slow. In addition, Bluetooth devices are battery operated, and batteries need to be changed every few months.

Radio Frequency Identification (RFID)

Radio frequency identification (RFID) is a non-line-of sight wireless technology used to control, detect, and track objects. Two common applications are merchandise tracking and automated tollbooth collection. RFID systems are made up of the following:

- Interrogators, which are "readers"
- Transponders with integrated antennas on chips

Transponders are either passive or active and are attached to the items being tracked, such as an automobile or merchandise.

- *Active transponders* have batteries and are larger and more costly than passive transponders. However, they can be read at further distances from readers.
- *Passive transponders* have no batteries, are about the size of a dime, and are "woken up" momentarily by magnetic induction from interrogators. Passive transponders are also referred to as tags.

All transponders have unique codes, identifiers either preset at the factory or user set. Readers broadcast a steady stream of radio signals to detect transponders, collect identifying codes, and transmit them to databases.

While RFID devices are relatively low cost, software and networks to support them are complex and expensive. Software called middleware is required to reformat information gathered by interrogators to make it compatible with databases and management information systems that hold information gathered by RFID equipment. The database management software responds to data gathered by readers to, for example, make automated decisions about reordering inventory. In addition to middleware costs, there are costs to attach tags to items and the expense of network connections to interrogators. Wi-Fi connections are sometimes used because no new cabling to readers is required and because these are low-bandwidth applications.

RFID tags have electronic product codes (EPCs), which are similar to bar codes. Electronic product codes are more advanced than bar codes. RFID readers don't have to come in contact with them for scanning, RFID tags hold more information than bar codes, and multiple EPC tags can be read simultaneously. For example, rather than just identifying a style of shoe and manufacturer, EPCs can store information about where the item was manufactured and when it was purchased or received into inventory.

Applications

Applications for RFID include security, healthcare, and retailing. Some of these applications are as follows:

Retailing

- Companies such as Wal-Mart, Target, and Albertsons require suppliers to put RFID tags on merchandise containers so the retailers can track inventory levels and reduce delivery errors.
- The Department of Defense has mandated that suppliers use RFID tags so that the department can improve the way it tracks inventory to reduce loss.
- The tire industry tracks purchases of tires so that manufacturers can notify purchasers if tires they've purchased are recalled.

Agriculture and Transportation

- Ranchers use RFID to track cattle.
- Highway authorities use RFID to automate toll collection with readers at tollbooths that scan transponders attached to vehicles.

Healthcare

- Hospitals track wheelchairs, beds, and other assets so that they know where equipment is and how much of everything they have. This cuts down on excess inventory. See Figure 9.7 for a sample RFID network in a hospital.
- RFID labels are placed on surgery patients to make sure correct procedures are performed.

Security

- RFID is used to track containers with hazardous material on trucks or ocean freighters.

- The United States requires RFID chips on new passports starting mid-2005. Tags will transmit a traveler's name, address, and photo to a nearby reader. This is intended to decrease passport fraud.

- The theme park Legoland in Denmark offers parents bracelets with embedded RFID tags for children. Parents send a short message to the park if they want to find their child, and the network returns a message with the child's location.

- Nokia has released a cell phone with an embedded RFID reader. The reader enables customers to purchase items with tags by scanning them. The charges appear on customers' mobile phone bills.

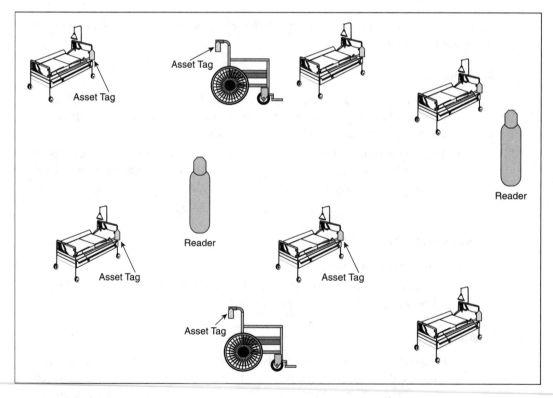

Figure 9.7
RFID service in hospitals to manage assets.

Super RFID for Sensor Networks

Initial development is underway to use radio frequency identification for sensors that monitor conditions and record data. This will require intelligent tags and readers that record conditions being monitored and set off alarms if the condition monitored—such as temperature—exceeds a preset limit. The reader could, for example, have the intelligence to send a message to a mobile phone, alerting someone that a threshold has been exceeded. These networks could also monitor transportation systems such as rail cars.

RFID Standards for Codes Embedded in Transponders

The lack of uniform standards is a prime factor holding back more widespread implementation of RFID technology. Currently, there are two parallel standards efforts. One effort by the EPCglobal Hardware Action Group specifies 96-bit electronic product codes in its Gen2 specification for the UHF 868MHz to 953MHz band. This band is considered most suitable to warehouse environments.

The International Standards Organization (ISO) recommends a different standard. To resolve the differences, the EPCglobal Hardware Action Group, which guides the industry toward achieving worldwide adoption and standardization of EPC technology, has recommended adding header bits to EPCs that would indicate to the reader whether the tag used an EPC- or ISO-specified code. The International Standards Organization is considering this option. However, as of January 2005, this is still an open issue.

Spectrum Bands Used by RFID Systems

Radio frequency identification systems operate in low-frequency 30KHz to 500KHz and high-frequency 850MHz to 950MHz and 2.4GHz to 2.5GHz ranges. Range is generally inversely proportional to frequency. However, in RFID systems, low-frequency systems have shorter ranges because they are used with passive, low-power transponders. For example, lower-frequency systems are less costly and have shorter ranges than higher-frequency systems. High-frequency systems have ranges of about 90 feet. The 2.4GHz systems can interfere with Bluetooth and Wi-Fi gear, many of which operate in the same band.

Technical Issues

When RFID announcements, such as those by the Department of Defense and Wal-Mart, were first made about mandating suppliers' use of RFID technology, many people had visions of RFID tags being affixed to individual items that people purchased. However, these announcements and ones made later by other retailers specified that cartons and pallets, not individual pieces of machinery or clothing, will be tagged.

Even at the container level, as in most new technologies, there were technical issues to resolve. These include the inability to "read" all of the cases on a pallet and the inability to read tags in metal or foil packages. For example, RFID interrogators can't read tags that are perpendicular to them. In the future, reading more tags and tags perpendicular to the reader may be improved by having multiple antennas in readers.

Due to these issues and the cost and complexity of setting up networks and information systems that support RFID, many organizations scaled back or delayed their RFID implementations. It is estimated that it will take three to four years for RFID tags to be used on individual pieces of equipment or clothing.

Privacy—Fears of Being Tracked

Concerns about privacy are a major issue in certain RFID applications. For example, initial concerns focused on consumers purchasing clothes or other items with embedded RFID chips that would enable manufacturers to know precisely who purchased the item. Although this capability won't actually be available in the near future, it reflects consumer fear that companies can track their behavior or sell lists of codes identifying buyers to other firms. Once a consumer leaves the store, their movements cannot be tracked unless they are near the store's RFID readers or if RFID readers are located in outside areas.

There are more immediate ramifications to fears about loss of privacy. For example, German retailer Metro Group ended its plans to embed RFID tags in its frequent shopper cards because of poor publicity about invasion of privacy. Moreover, the Utah state legislature enacted a law requiring retailers to let consumers know if RFID tags are in merchandise they purchase and to destroy the tags before consumers leave the store with their purchases. With the trend toward retail chains owning many stores, there are fears that tags embedded in clothes could be used to track customers' shopping and browsing patterns in many different retail locations.

In the meantime, because of its convenience, consumers are purchasing transponders for automated tollbooth collection systems. This is true even though the transponders track where and when they drive on highways equipped with interrogators that scan their transponders.

Ultra-Wideband—High-Speed, Short Distance Links

Ultra-wideband (UWB) is a high-speed, short-range wireless technology that works by transmitting low-power signals over a wide range of frequencies. Because it sends signals at a low noise level, conventional radio transceivers are not supposed to be able to perceive the signals. Thus, it is designed to not interfere with other wireless communications services in the area. However, some in the industry feel that this is unproven. UWB uses time-shifting technology to transmit 2 million to 40 million pulses per second. Zeros are transmitted at shorter time intervals and ones at longer intervals; thus, it is the time between signals that determines if they represent a one or a zero (see Figure 9.8). In addition, ultra-wideband signals are able to penetrate walls. Morever, because of its low power, UWB devices do not drain batteries quickly.

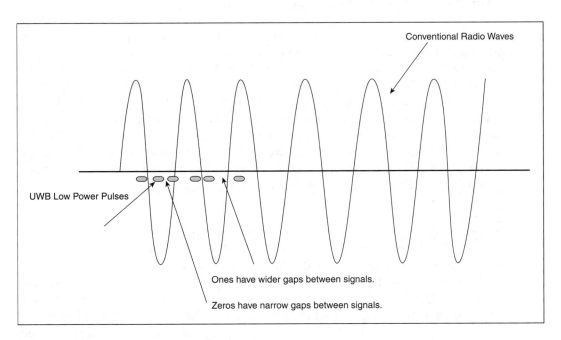

Figure 9.8
Ultra-wideband (UWB) low-power signals.

Ultra-wideband can be used to link consumer electronics for home entertainment networks, for asset tracking in hospitals, and by governments and the military for other types of tracking. UWB is faster than Bluetooth and Wi-Fi. Although products are expected by 2006, as of May 2005, no ultra-wideband products are on the market for consumer applications such as linking high definition TV to PCs and audio systems to speakers. The lack of a uniform standard is holding back ultra-wideband sales.

There are location-based UWB products available. The majority of nongovernmental products target the healthcare market. In these networks, receivers determine assets' locations by triangulating the distance from the two closest transmitters. The transmitters are on credit-card-size tags attached to assets such as wheelchairs and hospitals beds. This is valuable in hospitals, particularly during an emergency, when institutions need to quickly determine the location of important resources. In addition, the radar-like capability of ultra-wideband makes it valuable to the military and to governments, which have used it for decades. Radar determines distance by multiplying the time it takes signals to travel by the rate at which the signal is reflected back (is seen) to the point of origin.

Standards for Ultra-Wideband—802.15.3a

Adoption of ultra-wideband technology has been severely hampered by a lack of agreement on specifications of a standard. Ultra-wideband will eventually be based on the IEEE 802.15.3a standard. However, the IEEE Task Group is deadlocked. Two different groups of companies are lobbying for standards that differ in whether spectrum is treated as a continuous band or broken into three bands. The Multiband OFDM Alliance (MBOA) faction, which is spearheaded by Texas Instruments and Intel, has no chips on the market and only received a waiver from the FCC in March 2005 for a license. The waiver was needed because its chips do not hop between frequencies. Motorola spearheads the other group. Its technology is referred to as direct sequence UWB (DS-UWB), and it treats the spectrum as one large band.

Federal Communications Commission Rules

Ultra-wideband coexists over a wide range of the same frequencies that other wireless services use. No spectrum license is required, but equipment does need to be certified under Part 15 or Part 90 of the FCC rules in the United States. In February 2002, the FCC issued rules limiting UWB to higher frequencies of 3.1-gigahertz to 24-gigahertz ranges. It also imposed limits on power. The original low-power requirements limited UWB's use in search-and-rescue operations for which it is suitable because of its capability to penetrate obstructions such as rubble and burning walls. However, in February 2003, the FCC raised power limits on Part 90 rules pertaining to imaging equipment such as radar, surveillance, and medical imaging devices so that clearer images can be obtained for applications such as locating utility pipes underground and finding people trapped under rubble.

Not everyone agrees that UWB signals, particularly equipment less than a few meters from ultra-wideband equipment, do not interfere with other services such as cell phones. In March 2003, the UK's Radiocommunications Agency's commissioned report concluded that UWB service could interfere with WCDMA handsets. In addition, cellular companies, the Pentagon, the Department of Transportation, and the National Association of Broadcasters have expressed concerns about the possibility of interference.

SENSOR NETWORKS— THE 802.15.4 STANDARD.......................................

Wireless sensor networks are an emerging technology to monitor conditions in buildings, gather intelligence for the military, and control manufacturing systems. Until now, large-scale sensor networks have been prohibitively expensive because sensors required costly wired connections to each other and to the local area network. The new networks being developed will send information between sensors wirelessly. Sensor networks will use one of two types of wireless mesh technology: full mesh or partial mesh topology. In *full mesh topology*, each sensor is connected wirelessly to every other device. With *partial mesh topology*, some nodes are connected to all others, and others are connected only to nodes with which they exchange the most information.

802.15.4 is a slow-speed, 20Kbps to 250Kbps, non-line-of-sight protocol suitable for sensor networks based on a mesh topology. The protocol is designed to support multiyear battery life. Long battery life is achieved because devices are in sleep mode, where they don't use battery power, until a transmission signal from other sensors or the equipment they are monitoring wakes them up for a split second to pass on a message. The protocol specifies bands unlicensed worldwide. These are 2.4GHz worldwide, 915MHz in the Americas, and 868MHz in Europe. The range varies from 10 meters (328 feet) to 75 meters (246 feet).

802.15.4 differs from Bluetooth in application, the number of devices supported, and speed. It is slower than Bluetooth's 1 megabit speed, supports more devices (255 compared to 8 for Bluetooth), and is designed for monitoring, not exchanging, information. Bluetooth is primarily a cable-replacement technology between devices and peripherals such as cell phones and headsets and between PCs and keyboards or mice. Bluetooth is also intended for exchanging photos and contact information between handheld mobile devices and personal computers. However, 802.15.4 is intended as a standard for transferring status information with few bits, not content requiring more bandwidth. An amendment to 802.15.4, 802.15.4a, is being developed to specify higher speeds. In the future, sensor networks based on 802.15.4a will be able to support higher speeds, more intelligence in sensors, and additional sensors. These could be used to, for example, monitor electrical use in entire skyscrapers rather than just homes and buildings that require only 255 sensors per network. Monitoring energy use could have an important impact on conserving limited resources.

ZigBee—A Protocol for Sensor Networks

The ZigBee™ specification, which is based on the 802.15.4 standard, was developed by the ZigBee Alliance, which was formed to define higher-level protocols that will operate over networks using the IEEE 802.15.4 standard. As specifications are developed, the ZigBee Alliance will implement a certification program similar to the Wi-Fi Alliance program to certify interoperability among products that meet its specifications. The first specification, ZigBee 1.0, was announced in December 2004, and a certification program will follow in 2005.

In the future, the alliance might develop protocols for other, faster networks such as those based on 802.15.5, which to date has not been ratified. See Table 9.4 in the Appendix at the end of this chapter for 802.15 standards. ZigBee is a lightweight routing protocol for mesh networks that adds security and additional mesh networking functions to 802.15.4. The intent of the ZigBee Alliance is to create a specification for a simple, easily implemented protocol. The term "lightweight" refers to the fact that the protocol specifies few bits, 28 thousand bytes, so that ZigBee-certified devices won't need capacity to store many bits.

The following are some of the functions that the ZigBee Alliance defined:

- Ways to manage encryption keys (passwords) for security
- How sensor networks route messages between nodes (sensors)
- How to route messages if a node is out of service
- How mesh networks add new nodes (sensors)
- Definitions of certain applications (lighting controls and so on)
- Application programming interfaces (APIs) capable of translating between applications and other ZigBee software instructions

ZigBee Partial Mesh Topology

ZigBee specifies a partial mesh topology and defines three types of devices. Each ZigBee network has one coordinator that can communicate with all devices. The coordinator selects the frequency and the unique code that is the network identifier. ZigBee networks also have routers, which are used to extend the size and range of the network. Routers can be connected to other routers as well as sensors. They relay information between devices that are out of range of each other. See Figure 9.9 for devices on a ZigBee network. Thus, every device does not need to communicate with every other device. This enables networks to grow (scale) more efficiently. ZigBee routers give out addresses to end devices (sensors).

ZigBee networks are in the shape of a tree with branches extending from the coordinator, which is essentially the trunk of the tree. Each branch is made up of a few routers and many end devices, sensors. Signals can hop from sensor to sensor to reach their destination, or they can hop from one branch to another if that reduces the

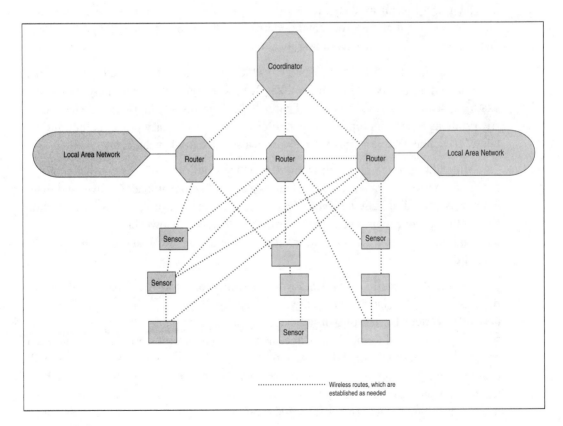

Figure 9.9
A ZigBee partial mesh network.

distance required to reach their destination. To simplify the network, routers can direct end devices to any branch that provides the closest route. This is intended to lessen congestion as well as simplify the network.

Initial ZigBee Applications

ZigBee has the potential to control alarms, monitor electricity, and provide status from smoke detectors, thermostats, and hot water tanks in commercial and residential buildings. Moreover, it can monitor windows to determine if they're open or closed. Initial products are expected to enable builders to install portable light switches, thermostats, and security systems. ZigBee, with its slow speeds, is not intended for home entertainment networks. Rather, its target applications include remote controls, many of which now use infrared technology that requires a line of sight. Zigbee could also be included in cell phones for remote control functions such as opening garage doors and making purchases from vending machines.

In contrast to Wi-Fi for consumers (which, when it first appeared, was the only low-cost wireless networking choice), ZigBee faces competition on many fronts. For example, security firms such as ADT already have an installed base of wireless security products based on proprietary technology. Other proprietary products for building controls such as WirelessUSB from Cypress also have market share.

In addition to competition from proprietary solutions, there is another protocol for sensor networks, Z-Wave™. Denmark's Zensys Inc. developed Z-Wave, and manufacturers including Leviton Manufacturing, Intermatic Corp., and Wayne Dalton Corp. are building equipment to Z-wave specifications. However, one of ZigBee's advantages is that major home automation suppliers Honeywell and Phillips back the standard.

While it generally takes years for new technologies to reach large-scale adoption, as the ZigBee specifications are upgraded, applications such as citywide sensor networks to detect bioterrorism attacks may become possible. In addition, the networks could be used to monitor bridges and to help authorities prioritize bridges that are most in need of repairs. For these applications to be possible, sensor networks will have to scale to support thousands of sensors. In addition, installation and maintenance costs have to decrease. Moreover, like RFID networks, there are still challenges in integrating manufacturing software and building automation software with sensor networks.

APPENDIX ....

Table 9.2   802.11 Standards

802.11 Standard	Description
802.11d	Proposed standard that supports the capability for Wi-Fi devices to operate in different countries that require different power levels and frequencies. Enables equipment to be adjusted according to each countries' rules.
802.11e	A quality-of-service standard, the Wi-Fi multimedia (WMM) section of 802.11e that defines prioritizing voice and video was approved October 2004.
802.11f	A proposed standard that supports the capability for access points from different manufacturers to interoperate in the same WLAN.
802.11h	A proposal that defines ways for 802.11a networks to dynamically assign packets to other channels if there is interference with other access points and services such as radar, medical devices, and satellite transmissions. In some countries, radar and satellite use the same frequencies as 802.11a.
802.11i	A standard for improved security. It's also referred to as wireless protected access 2 (WPA2).
802.11k	A proposed standard to make information for radio measurements, such as roaming requests by access points, statistics on device usage, and traffic levels in channels, available to WLAN management systems so that they can balance traffic between access points.
802.11n	A proposed standard to increase throughput—actual user data transmitted and the range covered by each access point. Improvements achieved through enhancements in antennas that decrease effects of interference.
802.11r	When the standard is approved, it will define ways for switches to quickly hand off sessions between access points so that users don't have to be authenticated again. It is important to avoid delay for voice on WLANs.

continues

Table 9.2   802.11 Standards (continued)

802.11 Standard	Description
802.11s	A proposed mesh networking standard. It will define how access points forward packets between each other.
802.11x	A proposed security standard for authentication and security to prevent unauthorized packets from entering wired LANs from Wi-Fi networks. It's an alternative to creating virtual private networks.
Control and provisioning of wireless access points (CAPWAP)	A proposal for WLAN switches to control access points by centralizing intelligence in one device, a controller. Will be used to standardize roaming between cellular and Wi-Fi networks.
Unlicensed mobile access (WMA)	A way to route cell phone traffic over Wi-Fi networks. The cellular network maintains control of calls so that it can bill for traffic.
Wi-Bro (formerly HPi)	A Korean version of 802.11e. The Wi-Bro standard is not currently recognized by the IEEE, but it is possible that a compromise will be reached between the IEEE and the Korean government.

Table 9.3   802.16 Standards for WiMAX Service

Name of Standard	Description
802.16a	Intended to be used in carriers' backhaul networks. Based on earlier 802.16 fixed wireless technologies. Added the capability for non-line-of-sight in the 2GHz to 11GHz frequency bands.
802.16c	Added the higher-frequency 10GHz to 66GHz bands.
802.16d (also known as 802.16-2004)	An enhancement to 802.16a. Intended for fixed wireless applications and lower-cost applications. No line-of-sight required if used in 2GHz to 11GHz frequency bands.
802.16e	A proposed standard for mobile applications in licensed frequency bands of 2GHz to 6GHz. Supports handing over traffic between base stations for mobility.

Table 9.3   802.16 Standards for WiMAX Service   (continued)

Name of Standard	Description
HIPERMAN	The European Telecommunication Standard Institute (ETSI) standard for fixed broadband wireless, which is similar to 802.16 (WiMAX). HIPERMAN only covers the 2GHz to 11GHz range. Standards bodies are working to ensure compatibility between WiMAX and HIPERMAN.

Table 9.4   802.15 Personal Area Network (PAN) Standards

Name of Standard	Description
802.15.1	The version of the standard to which many Bluetooth devices adhere.
802.15.2	Recommended practices suggested by the IEEE to lessen interference between Bluetooth devices and Wi-Fi 802.11b and 802.11g networks that operate in the 2.4GHz frequencies.
802.15.3 (also known as WiMedia)	A standard to increase speeds to 55 megabits per second on networks that distributes multimedia content such as television, photos, and music. It is intended for home networks. It includes Quality of Service specifications.
802.15.3a	Proposed amendment to 802.15.3 that increases speeds on ultra-wideband technology. 480 megabits per second over one meter (3.28 feet) and 110 megabits per second over ten meters (32.8 feet).
802.15.4	The standard intended for low-data-rate, low-complexity mesh networks for ZigBee devices to operate over. Specifies multimonth to multiyear battery life. Intended for sensor networks, interactive toys, smart badges, remote controls, and home automation such as turning lights and devices on and off.
802.15.5	Being developed for simplifying mesh network addressing and access to the network.

Glossary

2G (second generation cellular service)

Second generation cellular services are based on digital access to cellular networks. GSM and CDMA are second generation cellular technologies.

3G (third generation cellular service)

Third generation (3G) mobile standards specify techniques that are capable of supporting more voice traffic and broadband mobile multimedia (speech, audio, text, graphics, and video) services. There are five third generation services, including WCDMA, CDMA2000, and UMTS TDD. *See 3GPP and 3GPP2.*

3GPP (Third Generation Partnership Program)

The collaborative group Third Generation Partnership Project (3GPP) is developing an agreement to jointly develop technical specifications for maintaining GSM, GPRS, and EDGE and for evolving W-CDMA networks. European, Asian, and North American telecommunications standards bodies formed the 3GPP.

3GPP2 (Third Generation Partnership Program 2)

The Third Generation Partnership Program 2 (3GPP2) is an analogous group to 3GPP but is working on evolving technical specifications for CDMA2000 networks.

5ESS

A digital central office formerly manufactured by Lucent Technologies for use in the public switched telephone networks.

10BASE-T

An IEEE specification for unshielded twisted-pair cabling for Ethernet local area networks, which transmit at 10 million bits per second. The distance limitation on 10 base-T networks is 100 meters.

100BASE-T

An IEEE standard compatible with 10base-T for transmitting at 100 megabits over twisted pair cabling on local area networks.

802.11

A set of IEEE standards for local area networks. 802.11a, 802.11b, and 802.11g are the most common ones and are used in homes to share Internet access, in enterprises, and in hotspots.

802.15.4

The IEEE standards upon which the ZigBee Alliance tests and certifies equipment and adds functions to sensor networks.

802.16

The IEEE standards upon which WiMAX is based.

802.20

A proposed set of IEEE standards for wireless technology based on OFDM. Flarion builds pre-802.20 equipment.

8YY toll-free numbers

8YY is an abbreviation describing the format of the North American Numbering Plan for toll-free numbers. The first three digits of toll-free telephone numbers must be the number 8 followed by 0 or 2 through 9 for the second and third numbers. When central office switches see the 8YY format, they request a database check to determine where the toll-free number should be routed.

access fees

Carriers pay access fees to local telephone companies for transporting long distance traffic to and from local customers. The FCC sets access fees for interstate traffic, and state utility commissions set access fees for intrastate traffic. They are intended to offset the costs that local phone companies incur in providing links to local customers, but they have been decreasing, and residential and business customers are paying some of these costs in the form of monthly charges called subscriber line charges (SLCs). VoIP traffic is exempt from access fees.

ACD (automatic call distribution)

Equipment and software that distribute calls to agents based on parameters such as the agent that has been idle the longest. ACDs are part of telephone systems or adjuncts to telephone systems. ACDs are also referred to as contact centers. *See contact centers.*

ANI (automatic number identification)

The business or residential customer's billing number. Customers such as call centers pay for callers' ANIs to be sent to them simultaneously with incoming 800 and 888 and other toll-free calls.

AP (access point)

Access points have antennas and chips with 802.11a, 802.11b, or 802.11g air interfaces for 802.11 wireless local area networks. Access points translate between radio frequencies and Ethernet signals for cabled networks. An access point has similar functions to base stations for cordless home phones.

applet

A small Java program that can be executed on any Java-capable browser regardless of PC model. Animation in Internet ads uses applets. Document sharing programs work by sending Java applets to the participants in the document sharing session.

architecture

Architectures define how computers are tied together. Some vendors refer to the architecture of their equipment in terms of the growth available in their systems and the hardware and software needed to grow.

ATM (asynchronous transfer mode)

A high-speed switching technique that uses fixed-size cells to transmit voice, data, and video. A cell is analogous to envelopes that each carry the same number of bits.

backbone

A segment of a network used to connect smaller segments of networks together. Backbones carry high concentrations of traffic between on and off ramps to networks.

backhaul

The term "backhaul" is used mostly to describe the links between antennas at base stations and mobile central offices in cellular networks. Traffic and signaling information is backhauled from where it enters the network to the mobile switching center and vice versa.

bandwidth

The measure of the capacity of a communications channel. Analog telephone lines measure capacity in hertz, the difference in the highest and lowest frequency of the channel. Digital channels measure bandwidth in bits per second.

BGP (border gateway protocol)

A routing protocol with more than 90,000 addresses. Used by carriers to route packets on the Internet. BGP enables routers to determine the best routes to various destinations.

bill and keep

A billing approach being considered by the FCC as a way to eliminate access fees in which carriers that bill the end customer for the call keep all of the money. Currently, in most cases, local telephone companies and other carriers bill other carriers to transmit calls to local customers. For Wi-Fi-based hotspots, bill and keep is used by billing companies to only bill carriers that carry less traffic than carriers with whom they exchange traffic.

bit error rate

The percentage of bits received in error in a transmission.

blade

Circuit boards are often referred to as "blades" when they are dense, such as when they have many ports (connections) or software for a specialized application such as security.

Bluetooth

Bluetooth is a set of standards for special software on low-cost, low-powered radio chips that enables devices to communicate with each other over a short-range wireless link. Bluetooth eliminates cable clutter between computers and peripherals in offices and supports wireless peripherals for mobile handsets.

BOC (Bell Operating Company)

One of the 22 local Bell telephone companies owned by AT&T before 1984. Examples of Bell operating companies are Michigan Bell, Illinois Bell, and Pac Bell. Bell Operating Companies are now part of Regional Bell Operating Companies (RBOCs), such as BellSouth, Qwest, SBC Communications, and Verizon Communications.

border elements

Another name for media gateways. *See media gateways.*

bps (bits per second)

The number of bits sent in a second.

BRI (basic rate interface)

The ISDN (integrated services digital network) interface made up of two B channels at 64 kilobits each and a signaling channel with a speed of 16 kilobits.

bridge

A device that connects local or remote networks together. Bridges are used to connect small numbers of networks. Bridges do not have routing intelligence. Organizations that want to connect more than four or five networks use routers.

broadband

A data transmission scheme in which multiple transmissions share a communications path. Cable television uses broadband transmission techniques.

broadband wireless access

Broadband wireless access provides similar capabilities as DSL, cable modems, T-1/T-3/E-1/E-3, and other broadband technologies using wireless media rather than cabling. WiMAX is a broadband wireless access service.

broadcast

A message from one person or device forwarded to multiple destinations. Voice messaging and e-mail services have broadcast features whereby a user can send the same message to multiple recipients.

BTA (basic trading area)

A BTA is a relatively small area in which the FCC allocates spectrum. There are 491 basic trading areas in the United States.

CAP (competitive access provider)

Originally provided large and medium-size organizations with connections to long distance providers that bypassed local telephone companies. CAPs are now often referred to as competitive local exchange carriers (CLECs). They sell local and long distance telephone and Internet service.

CCIS (common channel interoffice signaling)

A signaling technique used in public networks. Signals such as those for dial tone and ringing are carried on a separate path from the actual telephone call. CCIS allows for telephone company database queries used in features such as caller ID, call forwarding, and network-based voice mail. CCIS channels are also used for billing and diagnosing public network services.

CDMA (code division multiple access)

CDMA is an air interface used to transmit digital cellular signals between handheld devices and cellular carriers' networks. CDMA assigns a unique code to every voice and data transmission using a channel of a particular carrier's airwaves. CDMA is a spread spectrum technology that is used by Verizon Wireless, Sprint, and South Korean carriers such as SKT.

CDMA2000 (code division multiple access 2000)

CDMA2000 is a third generation technology for carrying high-speed data and multimedia traffic on cellular networks.

CDMA2000 1X (code division multiple access 2000)

CDMA2000 1X is the earliest version of the CDMA2000 third generation technology for carrying high-speed data and multimedia traffic on cellular networks.

CDMA2000 1X 1xEV-DO (code division multiple access 2000 data optimized or data only)

CDMA2000 1X 1xEV-DO is a later, higher data rate version of CDMA2000 1X third generation technology for carrying high-speed data and multimedia traffic on cellular networks.

central office

The site with the local telephone company's equipment that routes calls to and from customers. It also has equipment that connects customers to Internet service providers and long distance services.

Centrex (central exchange)

Centrex, like private branch exchanges, routes and switches calls for commercial and nonprofit organizations. However, local telephone companies manage Centrex service. The computerized Centrex equipment is most often located at a telephone company's central office rather than at a customer premise.

channels

A path for analog or digital transmission signals. With services such as ISDN, T-1, and T-3, multiple channels share the same one or two pairs of wires or fiber.

CIC code (carrier identification code)

The four-digit code (previously three digits) assigned to each carrier for billing and call-routing purposes. AT&T's CIC code is 0288. If someone at a pay telephone dials 1010288 and then the telephone number he or she is calling, the call is routed over the AT&T network.

CIR (committed information rate)

A term used in frame relay networks to indicate the speed of the transmission guaranteed for each customer on the frame relay network.

circuit switching

The establishment, by dialing, of a temporary physical circuit (path) between points. The path (circuit) is terminated when either end of the connection sends a disconnect signal by hanging up.

CLEC (competitive local exchange carrier)

A competitor to local telephone companies that has been granted permission by the state regulatory commission to offer local telephone service. CLECs compete with the incumbent telephone company. CLECs are also simply called local telephone companies.

CLID (calling line ID)

Calling line identification is the number that identifies the telephone number from which a call was placed. For most residential customers, the calling line ID is the same as their billing number, their automatic number identification (ANI).

CO (central office)

The location that houses the telephone company switch that routes telephone calls. End offices are central offices that connect end users to the public network.

compression

Reducing the size of the data, image, voice, or video file sent over a telephone line. This decreases the capacity needed to transmit files.

concatenation

The linking of channels in optical networks so that voice or video is transmitted as one stream. This is done to ensure that there are no breaks in the transmission.

connectionless service

The Internet protocol is connectionless. Each packet travels through the network separately. If there is congestion, packets are dropped. Packets are reassembled at their destination.

contact centers

Another term for ACD. The term "contact center" implies that call centers have the capability to respond to e-mail and facsimile as well as voice calls.

convergence

Convergence is the use of one network for voice, data, and video. It also refers to the use of a single wireless handset to access wired landline and wireless mobile networks.

cordless

Cordless telephones are those that provide portability mainly within homes and apartments.

core networks

Core networks are the portions of carrier networks that carry the highest percentage of traffic and where switches and routers connect to other switches and routers rather than to customers. High-speed core routers are located in core networks.

CPE (customer premise equipment)

Telephone systems, modems, terminals, and other equipment installed at customer sites.

CSU/DSU (channel service unit/data service unit)

A digital interface device that connects customer computers, video equipment, multiplexers, and terminals to most digital telephone lines.

CTI (computer telephony integration)

CTI software translates signals between telephone systems and computers so that telephone systems and computers can coordinate sending call routing and account information to agents in contact centers.

CWDM (coarse wavelength division multiplexing)

Coarse wavelength division multiplexing is a multiplexing technology standard that enterprises and carriers deploy to connect corporate sites to public networks and to bring the capacity of fiber closer to residential neighborhoods. CWDM carries up to eight channels of traffic on a single fiber pair.

dark fiber

Fiber optic cables without any of the electronics (that is, multiplexers and amplifiers). Carriers can lay dark fiber and add SONET, Gigabit Ethernet, and wavelength division multiplexers later.

DCE (data circuit-terminating equipment)

A communications device that connects user equipment to telephone lines. Examples are modems for analog lines and CSUs (channel service units) for digital lines.

dedicated line

A telephone line between two or more sites of a private network. Dedicated lines are always available for the exclusive use of the private network at a fixed monthly fee.

DID (direct inward dialing)

A feature of local telephone service whereby each person in an organization has his or her own ten-digit telephone number. Calls to DID telephone numbers do not have to be answered by onsite operators. They go directly to the person assigned to the ten-digit DID telephone number.

DiffServ (differentiated services)

Used in routers to tag frames. The tags request a particular level of service on the Internet and other Internet protocol (IP)-based networks.

digital loop carriers (DLCs)

Digital loop carriers (DLCs) are used to economically bring fiber closer to customers. Carriers run fiber cabling from central offices to DLCs, and they lay twisted pair copper cabling from DLCs to customers.

Divestiture

Divestiture, in January 1984, deregulated long distance service in the United States. It separated AT&T from its 22 local Bell telephone companies. Agreement on Divestiture was reached by the Justice Department, which negotiated an antitrust settlement with AT&T called the Modified Final Judgment.

DMS 100

A digital central office switch formerly manufactured by Nortel for use in circuit switched public networks.

DNIS (dialed number identification service)

The service used to identify and route toll-free and 900 numbers to particular agents or devices within a customer site. For example, if a customer has multiple 800 numbers, the network provider routes each toll-free number to a different four-digit number at the customer's telephone system. The onsite PBX, key system, or Centrex system then routes the call to a particular group of agents, voice response system, or department.

domain name

Everything after the @ sign in an e-mail address. It includes the host computer, the organization's name, and the type of organization (for example, *com* for commercial and *edu* for educational). .com and .edu are top-level domain names. The domain name can also designate the country, such as .bo for Bolivia. A domain name is part of the TCP/IP addressing convention.

DoS attack (denial of service)

A denial of service attack occurs when hackers bombard networks with thousands of packets, which are intended to disrupt the capability of the attacked network to function.

downloading

Downloading refers to receiving an entire file from, for example, the Internet or an intranet. When music is downloaded, the entire music file must be downloaded before the music can be played.

DS-0 (digital signal level 0)

The digital signal level 0 is 64 thousand bits per second. It refers to one channel of a T-1, E-1, E-3, T-3, fractional T-1, or fractional T-3 circuit.

DS-1 (digital signal level 1)

The T-1 transmission rate of 1.54 million bits per second. There are 24 channels associated with DS-1 or T-1.

DS-3 (digital signal level 3)

The T-3 transmission rate of 44 million bits per second with 672 channels. (T-3 is equivalent to 28 T-1s.)

DSP (digital signal processor)

DSPs compress (shrink the number of bits required) voice and video, perform digital-to-analog and analog-to-digital voice conversions, and packetize voice and video in realtime speeds in IP networks.

DTE (data terminal equipment)

Devices that communicate over telephone lines. Examples are multiplexers, PBXs, key systems, and personal computers.

DVB (digital video broadcasting)

Digital video broadcasting (DVB) is a standard approved by the European Telecommunications Standards Institute (ETSI). It has lower resolution than high definition television (HDTV).

DWDM (dense wavelength-division multiplexing)

A way of increasing the capacity of fiber optic networks. DWDM carries multiple colors of light, or multiple wavelengths, on a single strand of fiber. Also known as WDM or wavelength-division multiplexing.

E-1

The European standard for T-1. E-1 has a speed of 2.048 megabits with 30 channels for voice, data, or video, plus one channel for signaling and one for diagnostics.

E-3

The European standard for T-3. E-3 has a speed of 34.368 megabits with 480 channels. It is equivalent to 16 E-1 circuits.

E-911 (enhanced 911)

E-911 is the capability for agents who answer 911 calls to receive callers' phone numbers and locations.

EDGE (enhanced data rates for GSM evolution)

EDGE mobile services offered by cellular carriers have higher data rates than second generation cellular networks. EDGE is often used by carriers as they transition to higher data rate, third generation mobile service.

end offices

End offices are the central offices that are connected to end users and to tandem central offices. Most end offices are based on circuit switching, but they are slowly being converted to softswitch technology to carry voice over IP.

endpoints

Endpoints are any device connected to local area networks, such as PCs, printers, and voice over IP telephones.

Ethernet

Ethernet, which is based on the 802.3 standard approved by the Institute of Electrical and Electronics Engineers (IEEE), defines how data is transmitted on and retrieved from local area computer networks. It is used by devices such as personal computers to access the LAN and to retrieve packets carried on the LAN.

FDDI (fiber distributed data interface)

An ANSI-defined protocol in which computers communicate at 100 million bits per second over fiber-optic cabling. FDDI may be used on backbones that connect local area network segments together. It is not widely used.

fiber-optic cable

A type of cable made from glass rather than copper. The key advantage of fiber-optic cabling is that it is nonelectric. Thus, it is immune from electrical interference and interference from other cables within the same conduit. Fiber-optic cabling can be used for higher-speed transmissions than twisted pair copper cabling.

fibre channel protocol

Fibre channel protocols are used in storage area networks and data centers for gigabit-speed, highly reliable, short-distance access to devices such as disks, graphics equipment, video input/output devices, and storage devices that hold massive amounts of data.

firewall

A firewall is software and hardware that prevents unauthorized access to an organization's network files. The intention is to protect files from computer viruses and electronic snooping.

fixed mobile convergence

The capability to use the same handset or portable computer for landline as well as mobile voice and data sessions. For voice calls, it is the capability to continue the call when moving, for example, from a hotspot or home to a cellular network.

fixed wireless

Wireless service between fixed points. Generally, these are between an antenna on a tower and a dish on a business or residential customer's building.

fractional T-1

Fractional T-1 lines are cheaper and have a fraction of the 24-channel capacity of T-1 lines. The most common capacities are 2 channels = 128 kilobits, 4 channels = 256 kilobits, and 6 channels = 384 kilobits.

fractional T-3

Fractional T-3 lines have a fraction of the 672-channel capacity of T-3 lines. For example, they might have the capacity of six T-1s or 144 channels. Fractional T-3s are cheaper than a full T-3 line.

frame relay networks

Public data networks commonly used for local area network to local area network communications and Internet access. Customers connect to frame relay services over telephone lines from each of their locations to the frame relay network. Frame relay services require less maintenance, hardware, and upkeep than traditional private-line data communications services for customers with more than about four locations.

FTP (file transfer protocol)

A part of the TCP/IP suite of Internet protocols. It is software that lets users download files from a remote computer to their computer's hard drive.

gateway

A gateway device allows equipment with different protocols to communicate with each other. For example, gateways are used when incompatible video systems hold a video-conference.

GGSN (GPRS gateway support node)

GPRS gateway support nodes convert third generation data packets to those compatible with GPRS, the Internet, and other data networks and vice versa.

Gigabit Ethernet

Gigabit Ethernet is a high-speed service used in metropolitan area networks and in enterprise internal networks. These networks operate at one or ten billion bits per second.

gigabits

Billions of bits per second. Fiber-optic cables carry signals at gigabit or billions of bits per second. Gbps is short for gigabits per second.

GPRS (general packet radio services)

A cellular data packet network service. Upgrades to digital cellular networks are required to provision the service. This is an "always on" data service that users do not have to dial into to access. Its data rates are lower than EDGE and third generation (3G) networks.

GPS (global positioning system)

GPS satellites are used for tracking purposes. For example, many wireless E911 systems are based on GPS satellites along with equipment at carriers' cell stations and special handsets.

GSM (global system for mobile communications)

GSM is the most widely deployed cellular service worldwide. It is a digital service that was first used in Europe in the 1990s.

H.320

The standard for enabling videoconference equipment from multiple vendors to communicate with each other using ISDN service.

H.323

An ITU-based standard for sending voice via the Internet protocol (IP). H.323 was originally developed for videoconferencing.

H.324

An ITU (International Telecommunications Union) standard for sending video, voice, and data between devices over a single analog, dial-up telephone line using a 28,800 bit per second modem. Compression is used on the voice, video, and data.

headend

The control center of a cable television system where incoming video signals are received and converted into a format compatible for transmission to subscribers and combined with other signals onto the cable operators' fiber infrastructure.

HDTV (high definition television)

High definition television (HDTV) is a standard for digital high-resolution television video and surround sound audio.

home page

A home page is the default first page of a World Wide Web site that users see when they visit an organization's Web site. A home page is analogous to the first page and table of contents of a book.

hotspot

A hotspot is a public area where people with Wi-Fi-equipped laptops or personal digital assistants can access the Internet. Access may be free or available for monthly or daily rates.

hub

Each device (such as computers and printers) on a local area network is wired to the hub, generally located in the wiring closet. Hubs enable local area networks to use twisted pair cabling rather than more expensive, harder to install and move coaxial cabling. Hubs are sometimes referred to as concentrators.

ILEC (incumbent local exchange carrier)

ILECs refer to the Bell and independent telephone companies that sell local telephone service. This term differentiates telephone companies that were the providers of telephone service prior to the Telecommunications Act of 1996 and new competitors such as CTC, MCI, and AT&T. The Telecommunications Act of 1996 decreed that local Bell telephone companies could sell interstate telephone service when they met FCC guidelines for connecting competitors to their networks.

IMS (IP Multimedia System)

In 3G networks, IP Multimedia System (IMS) refers to the equipment and software that will make it possible to store, transmit, administer, transform (for example, from text to voice), and bill for multimedia services. Examples of multimedia services are games, audio and video clips and photos as attachments to e-mail messages, downloading entertainment, and Web-based shopping.

Indefeasible Right of Use (IRU)

IRUs are long-term leases for fiber-optic cable runs. They are analogous to condominium arrangements. One organization lays the cable and leases it to another carrier for its exclusive use.

independent telephone company

An incumbent local telephone company other than a Regional Bell Operating Company. Examples of independent telephone companies are Alltel Corporation and Cincinnati Bell, Inc.

Instant messaging

Instant messaging is the ability to exchange e-mail in near real time without typing in an address. Users merely click on an icon representing the user to whom the message is intended and click Submit after typing the message.

intermodal competition

Competition between services based on different media and technology. For example, mobile services compete with wireline services for local and long distance calling. Cable TV companies compete with Regional Bell Operating Companies such as Bell South and SBC.

Internet

The Internet, with a capital I, is composed of multiple worldwide networks tied together by a common protocol, TCP/IP.

intranet

An intranet is the use of World Wide Web technologies for internal operations. Intranets are used by organizations as a way to make corporate information readily accessible by employees. An example is a corporate telephone directory accessed by a browser.

inverse multiplexer

Instead of combining individual channels into one "fat" pipe, which is what a multiplexer does, an inverse multiplexer separates out channels into smaller "chunks." Inverse multiplexers are used for videoconferencing, where the 24 channels may be transmitted in groups of 6 channels at a speed of 386,000 bits per second.

IP (Internet protocol)

The part of TCP/IP that performs the addressing functions for networks. Each device on an Internet network is assigned a 32-bit IP address.

IPSec (Internet protocol security)

The IPSec protocol establishes a secure, encrypted link to a security device at the carrier or the enterprise. It is used for remote access to corporate services (such as e-mail) in conjunction with virtual private networks (VPNs).

ISDN (integrated services digital network)

ISDN is a digital network standard that lets users send voice, data, and video over one telephone line from a common network interface.

ISP (Internet service provider)

An Internet service provider connects end users to the Internet via telephone lines. The ISP has banks of modems and devices such as ISDN interfaces for its own customers to dial into, and these are connected to telephone company central offices. Some Internet service providers, such as UUNET (part of MCI), also own Internet backbone networks. ISPs supply services such as voice mail, hosting, and domain name registration.

IXC (interexchange carrier)

Interexchange carriers are the long distance companies that sell toll-free 800, international, data networking, and outgoing telephone service on an interstate basis. They now also sell local telecommunications services.

Java

A programming language created by Sun Microsystems. Multiple types of computers can read Java programs. They increase the power of the Internet because programs written in Java can be downloaded temporarily by client computers. They do not take up permanent space on the client hard drive. Interactive games can use Java programs.

key system

Key systems are onsite telephone systems geared to organizations with fewer than 100 telephones. Like PBXs, they switch calls to and from the public network and within users' premises.

LAN (local area network)

A local area network is located on an individual organization's premises. It enables computer devices such as personal computers, printers, alarm systems, and scanners to communicate with each other. Moreover, LANs allow multiple devices to share and have access to expensive peripherals such as printers, firewalls, and centralized databases.

LATA (local access transport area)

At Divestiture in 1984, LATAs were set up as the areas in which Bell telephone companies were allowed to sell local telephone services. LATAs cover metropolitan statistical areas based on population sizes. For example, Massachusetts has two LATAs and Wisconsin has four, but Wyoming, which has a small population, has one LATA. The rules of Divestiture decreed that long distance telephone companies such as AT&T, Sprint, and MCI were allowed to carry calls between LATAs but that Bell telephone companies such as Illinois Bell could carry calls only within a LATA.

Layer 4

Layer 4 devices can route and prioritize packets based on the source of the packet, the destination port number, the protocol type, and the application. For example, Layer 4 devices can prioritize voice and video so that networks using the Internet protocol for voice and data can handle voice without the delays and lost packets associated with lower-level protocols.

LDAP (lightweight directory access protocol)

LDAP is a directory protocol that describes a uniform way of organizing information in directories. Examples of LDAP directories are the address books in Netscape Communicator 7 and Microsoft Outlook Express browsers. LDAP enables companies to use one central directory to update multiple corporate directories. They also facilitate single sign-on to access different applications on corporate intranets.

leased line

A leased line is analogous to two tin cans and a string between two or more sites. Organizations that rent leased lines pay a fixed monthly fee for the leased lines that are available exclusively to the organization that leases them. Leased lines can be used to transmit voice, data, or video. They are also called private or dedicated lines.

LEC (local exchange carrier)

Any company authorized by the state public utility commission to sell local telephone service.

LMDS (local multipoint distribution service)

A high-speed, fixed wireless service used to provision local telephone service without laying fiber to individual customer sites. Some competitive local exchange carriers employ LMDS as a way to provision local telephone, high-speed Internet access, and video service.

local loop

The local loop is the telephone line that runs from the local telephone company to the end user's premises. The local loop can be made up of fiber, copper, or wireless media.

MAN (metropolitan area network)

A metropolitan area network is a network that covers a metropolitan area such as a portion of a city. Hospitals, universities, municipalities, and large corporations often have telephone lines running between sites within a city or suburban area.

Mbps (million bits per second)

A transmission speed at the rate of millions of bits in one second. Digital telephone lines measure their capacity or bandwidth in bits per second.

media gateways

Media gateways contain digital signal processors (DSPs) that compress voice traffic to make it smaller so that it can be carried more efficiently. In addition, media gateways are equipped with circuit packs with ports for connections to traditional circuit switched analog and T-1 trunks. Thus, they are used to link converged IP networks to public switched telephone networks.

media server

Media servers are specialized computers that play announcements and generate ring tones in corporate telephone systems and converged public networks. In corporate VoIp systems, they control call processing.

media server for homes (home server)

PCs or separate devices that store content, music, photos, movies, or TV shows, that can be distributed over home networks to home entertainment equipment.

mesh networks

Mesh networks are networks in which every device is connected to every other device. Community wireless networks and sensor networks often use variations of mesh networks, as does the military when it sets up communications facilities in war zones. Mesh networks are also referred to as multipoint-to-multipoint networks.

microwave wireless service

Microwave refers to wireless services with short wavelengths that operate in the frequency range of about the 890 megahertz to 60 gigahertz bands. It is a fixed point-to-point wireless technology used to connect two points together. Line of sight is required between microwave towers. For example, if there is a tree blocking the view between the towers, the service is inoperable.

middleware

Middleware is software used to translate between unlike systems. When used in set-top boxes, middleware translates between the hardware (set-top devices) and network protocols and the applications in satellite TV and cable TV networks. Middleware on set-top boxes enables interactive television applications from different developers to work with set-top box hardware from a variety of manufacturers. Thus, applications don't have to be designed differently for each type of set-top box.

millimeter wireless services

Millimeter wireless services operate at microwave and higher frequencies. They include LMDS (local multipoint distribution service) and MMDS (multipoint multichannel distribution service). Millimeter refers to the very short wavelengths of high-frequency services. The wavelength is the distance from the highest or lowest point of one wave to the highest or lowest point of the next wave.

MIMO (multiple input multiple output) antennas

MIMO antennas simultaneously transmit multiple streams at different frequencies within a single channel. This improvement is analogous to the increased capacity on a multilane highway versus a road with a single lane. MIMO antennas are starting to be used on 802.11 (Wi-Fi) wireless local area networks.

MMDS (multipoint multichannel distribution service)

MMDS is a fixed wireless technology for high-speed data, video, and voice. It is a way to provide high-speed Internet access without laying fiber or cable to each customer. It was originally conceived as a way to supply cable TV services. WorldCom is investing in companies that supply MMDS gear. MMDS uses a lower frequency than LMDS and has less capacity than LMDS. MMDS has a larger range than LMDS; the dishes can be up to 35 miles apart.

mobile wireless services

Mobile wireless services, such as cellular services, provide mobility over wide areas, such as in cities, states, nations, and in some instances, internationally.

MPLS (multiprotocol label switching)

The MPLS protocol is used to increase routers' speed and prioritize packets. Short, fixed-length "labels" tell routers how to route each packet so that the router does not have to examine the entire header of each packet after the first point in the carrier's network. Voice and video can have tags that classify them with a higher priority than data bits.

MSOs (multiple system operators)

MSOs are large cable TV operators, such as Comcast and Time Warner Cable, with cable franchises in many cities.

MTA (major trading area)

Major trading areas are regions that include multiple cities or states. They are made up of some of the 491 basic trading areas (BTAs). The FCC auctions off spectrum in both BTAs and MTAs.

MTSO (mobile telephone switching office)

Mobile telephone switching offices are central offices used in mobile networks. They connect cellular network calls to the public switched telephone networks and vice versa.

multicasting

Multicasting is the transmission of the same message from a single point to multiple nodes.

multiplexing (muxing)

Multiplexing is a technique in which multiple devices can share a telephone line. With multiplexing, users do not have to lease individual telephones for each computer that communicates. T-1 multiplexers enable many devices to share one telephone line.

MVNOs (mobile virtual network operators)

MVNOs such as Virgin Mobile, BT in Britain, and ESPN resell cellular service on cellular carriers' networks.

NEBS (network equipment building standards)

Requirements published in a Bellcore (now Telcordia) technical reference for products placed in a central office environment. Bellcore is the former Bell Telephone central research organization. There are eight standards referring to issues such as environmental, electrical, and cabling requirements as well as resistance to natural disasters such as earthquakes.

network

A network is an arrangement of devices that can communicate with each other. An example of a network is the public switched telephone network over which residential and commercial telephones and modems communicate with each other.

Non-blocking

Non-blocking switches have enough capability so that each device can communicate at the same time up to the full speed of the port to which it is connected.

NT1 (network termination type 1)

The NT1 device sits between an ISDN line and an ISDN terminal adapter. The NT1 plugs into the ISDN jack. It provides a point where the network provider can test the ISDN line. The NT1 also converts the ISDN line from the telephone company's two-wire to four-wire cabling. The four wires are the portions of the cabling inside the customer's premises.

number pooling

Allows local carriers to share a "pool" of telephone numbers within the same exchange. Number pooling is a way to allocate scarce telephone numbers more efficiently. Without pooling, a single local telephone company has rights to the entire 10,000 block of telephone numbers, but it might only use a portion of the block.

OSS (operation and support service)

Hardware and software that carriers use for billing, maintenance, and changes to customers' features.

packet switching

A network technique that routes data in units called packets. Each packet contains addressing and error-checking bits as well as transmitted user data. Packets from a transmission can be routed individually through a network such as an X.25 or frame relay network and be assembled at the end destination.

PANs (personal area networks)

Personal area networks are those that operate over small areas within rooms and buildings. Bluetooth and RFID are examples of PANs.

PBX (private branch exchange)

PBXs are computerized, onsite telephone systems located at commercial and nonprofit organizations' premises. They route calls both within an organization and from the outside world to people within the organization and vice versa.

PCMCIA (portable computer memory card industry association)

An industry group that has developed a standard for peripheral cards for portable computers. PCMCIA cards are used for functions such as modems, Wi-Fi services, and for additional memory.

PCS (personal communications service)

PCS originally referred to second generation digital mobile services that use spectrum in the higher frequencies. PCS (or DCS in Europe) is now used in the industry to refer to all second generation cellular access technologies.

peer-to-peer networks

Peer-to-peer networks distribute intelligence over devices in the network instead of relying on central computers. Peer-to-peer networks are often used to download free music and movies from the Internet. In addition, companies such as Skype, Peerio, and Free World Dialup use the technology for voice calls and other services.

photonics

All of the elements of optical communications. This includes fiber, lasers, and optical switches and all elements involved in transmitting light over fiber.

ping (packet internetwork groper)

A software protocol used to test communications between devices. To "ping" means to send a packet to another device or host to see if the device sends back a response. The ping also tests round-trip delay, the time it takes to send a message to another device.

plug-and-play digital television [digital cable-ready (DCR)]

Plug-and-play digital televisions are televisions that can be plugged directly into cable systems without the need of a set-top box. They are also referred to as digital cable-ready TVs. For these sets to work, cable operators need to supply customers with CableCards, which are PC cards that fit into slots in the back of plug-and-play televisions. CableCards have security functions and unscramble premium services based on customer subscriptions.

PON (passive optical network)

Passive optical networking technologies are deployed to extend fiber to homes, businesses, and neighborhoods. Passive optical networks (PONs) use nonelectrical devices located in the access network that enable carriers to dynamically allocate capacity on a single pair of fibers to multiple homes, buildings in a campus, apartments, and small and medium-size businesses.

POP (point of presence)

A POP refers to a long distance company's equipment that is connected to the local telephone company's central office. The POP is the point at which telephone and data calls are handed off between local telephone companies and long distance telephone companies.

POTS (plain old telephone service)

Telephone lines connected to most residential and small business users. POTS lines are analog from the end user to the nearest local telephone company equipment. People using POTS service for data communications with modems are limited in the speed at which they can transmit data.

power over Ethernet

Power over Ethernet is a standard that defines how power can be carried from wiring closets on floors to the PCs and other LAN-connected devices using the same cabling that transmits voice and data. Thus, every device does not need its own power or backup power.

Presence

Presence is the ability of users to know when someone within their community of users is available for realtime or near real time messaging.

PRI (primary rate interface)

PRI is a form of ISDN (integrated services digital network) with 23 paths for voice, video, and data and one channel for signals. Each of the 24 channels transmits at 64 kilobits per second.

protocol

Protocols define how devices and networks communicate with each other. For example, a suite of protocols, transmission control protocol/Internet protocol (TCP/IP), spells out rules for sending voice, images, and data across the Internet and in corporate networks.

proxy server

Proxy servers authenticate callers to make sure they are who they say they are before they are sent to their destination. They serve as intermediaries between callers and applications or endpoints, telephones, and other devices connected to the LAN. For instance, a proxy server in a voice over IP environment ensures that external devices requesting to communicate with an IP telephone are who they say they are.

PSAP (public safety answering point)

Public safety answering points are groups of agents that answer and dispatch 911 and E911 calls for their town, county, or cluster of towns. They are often located at police stations.

push-to-talk

Push-to-talk is a walkie-talkie type service pioneered by Nextel in which customers can reach each other by pushing a button on the side of their phone. They also dial an abbreviated telephone number. Push-to-talk can be used to reach individuals or pre-defined groups.

QSIG

A standard for networking PBXs from different vendors together over ISDN PRI trunks. The signaling channel of the ISDN circuit carries signals such as those allowing users connected to different PBXs to dial each other using only their three- or four-digit extension number. Signals can also be used to turn voice mail message lights on and off so that different sites can share the same voice mail system.

radio

A wireless device with an antenna that converts signals to and from formats compatible with the airwaves. Wireless handsets are radios.

RBOC (Regional Bell Operating Company)

At Divestiture in 1984, the Justice Department organized the 22 Bell telephone companies into seven Regional Bell Operating Companies. Examples of RBOCs are Qwest and BellSouth. Since Divestiture, Pacific Telesis and Ameritech have merged with SBC, and NYNEX merged with Bell Atlantic. There are now four RBOCs. Before Divestiture, AT&T owned all of the Bell telephone companies.

reverse channel

In cable TV systems, the reverse channel carries signals from the customer to the cable operator's equipment. Reverse channels are required for Internet access, on-demand TV, and VoIP.

RFID (radio frequency identification)

Radio frequency identification (RFID) is a non-line-of-sight wireless technology used to control, detect, and track objects. Two common applications are merchandise tracking and automated tollbooth collection.

roaming

Roaming in mobile networks is the capability to use the same handset on another carrier's network. Carriers set up roaming agreements to define terms such as per-minute fees that carriers charge each other.

router

A device with routing intelligence that connects local and remote networks together. Routers are also used to forward packets in the Internet.

RSS (really simple syndication)

A series of software standards that automates feeding updates from news sites such as Forbes.com and blogs to other sites and users. The use of RSS means that people don't have to continually check to see news headlines or updates to blogs.

RTP (realtime transport protocol)

Realtime transport protocol is an Internet Engineering Task Force (IETF) standardized protocol for transmitting multimedia in IP networks. RTP is used for the "bearer" channels, the actual voice, video, and image content.

SDH (synchronous digital hierarchy)

A world standard of synchronous optical speeds. The basic SDH speed starts at 155 megabits, also called STM-1 (synchronous transport mode-1) in Europe. SONET (synchronous optical network) is a subset of SDH.

SDT (standard definition television)

Standard definition television is digital TV that usually has better-than-analog television resolution. It has lower resolution than high definition television.

server

A server is a specialized, shared computer on the local area network with corporate files such as electronic mail. It can also be used to handle sharing of printers, email, and other applications.

set-top box

A device that is connected to a television and that allows access to various content, including pay-per-view. Set-top boxes can be used to distribute content to other TVs and devices. New ones contain hard drives and multiple tuners. They can be used to watch one program while recording a different show and to pause and rewind programs.

signaling gateway

A signaling gateway is a type of media gateway that converts signaling from IP networks to that compatible with traditional, circuit switched networks and vice versa.

SIP (session initiation protocol)

SIP is a signaling protocol used to establish sessions over IP networks, such as those for telephone calls, audio conferencing, click-to-dial from the Web, and instant message exchanges between devices. It is also used to link IP telephones from different manufacturers to SIP-compatible IP telephones. It is used in landline and mobile networks.

SLA (service level agreement)

SLAs are often provided to customers by frame relay, virtual private network, and ATM carriers. The SLA defines service parameters such as uptime and response time.

SMS (short message service)

Short, 160-character (including header address information) text messages that can be transmitted between digital cellular telephones.

SMTP (simple mail transfer protocol)

The electronic mail protocol portion of the TCP/IP protocol used on the Internet. Having an electronic mail standard that users adhere to enables people on diverse local area networks to send each other e-mail.

softphone

Softphones are telephone functionality on a personal computer in Voice over IP systems. People with softphone-equipped laptops can use their VoIP remotely.

softswitch

Softswitches are used in converged enterprise and carrier networks that carry Voice over IP traffic. Softswitches are built on standard computer processors and use standards-based protocols, which make them less costly than proprietary switches based on circuit switched technology. Softswitches manage and control traffic in IP networks.

SONET (synchronous optical network)

SONET is a standard for multiplexing high-speed digital bits onto fiber optic cabling. SONET converts electronic impulses to light impulses and vice versa. Telephone companies use SONET to transmit data from multiple customers over the same fiber cables.

spectrum

Spectrum is made up of frequency bands or airwaves that carry either analog or digital wireless signals. Spectrum consists of the multitude of invisible frequency bands that surround the earth and are used to transmit segregated radio waves. Radio waves carry signals as electrical energy on unseen waves.

SSL (secure socket layer)

Secure socket layer is a newer type of security for virtual private networks (VPNs) than IPSec. It is embedded in browsers so that organizations aren't required to install special client software in each user's computer.

statistical multiplexing

Statistical multiplexers do not save capacity for each device connected to it. Statistical multiplexers assume that not all devices are active all the time. They operate either on a first come, first serve basis or on a priority basis in which certain streams of traffic have higher priority than others.

streaming video and audio

A means of starting to play a message while the rest of it is being received. Streaming uses compression to make the voice, video, and data files smaller so that it can be transmitted in less time. Streaming video and audio are used in broadcasting video and audio over the Internet.

Switched 56

A digital "dial-up" data communications service. It was used at one time for video-conferencing but is now considered too slow for adequate resolution.

switching

Equipment, with input and output ports, that transmits traffic and sets up paths to destinations based on digits dialed or addressing bits.

T.120

The ITU-defined standard for document sharing and white boarding. People using T.120-adherent software can participate in document-sharing conferences with each other over the Internet. For example, vendors can demonstrate their products to potential customers via computers connected to the Internet at dispersed sites.

T-1

A North American and Japanese standard for communicating at 1.54 million bits per second. A T-1 line has the capacity for 24 voice or data channels.

T-3

A North American standard for communicating at speeds of 44 million bits per second. T-3 lines have 672 channels for voice and/or data. Fiber optic cabling or digital microwave is required for T-3 transmissions.

TA (terminal adapter)

Terminal adapters are used for residential and small business VoIP service. They compress, packetize, and convert analog voice streams to digital voice and vice versa. They are also used with BRI ISDN service. The terminal adapter sits between the PC or the telephone and the ISDN, cable, or DSL modem and the broadband access line. Often the modem and TA are combined into one device.

tandem central offices

Tandem central offices are used in the core of traditional, public switched telephone networks. Tandem central offices switch traffic between central offices. End users are not connected to tandem offices. Tandem central offices are being replaced by lower cost, more efficient softswitches.

TCP (transmission control protocol)

Includes sequence numbers for each packet so that the packets can be reassembled at their destination. The sequence numbers ensure that all of the packets arrive and are assembled in the proper order. If some packets are discarded because of congestion, the network retransmits them. The numbering and tracking of packets make TCP a connection-oriented protocol. Router-based LAN internetworking uses TCP.

TCP/IP (transmission control protocol/Internet protocol)

The suite of protocols used on the Internet and also by organizations for communications between multiple networks.

TD-SCDMA (time division synchronous code division multiple access)

The Chinese government is interested in commercializing TD-SCDMA, which is a home-grown version of UMTS TDD, a third generation mobile protocol.

TDMA (time division multiple access)

TDMA is one way that carriers transmit digital cellular signals between handheld devices and cellular carriers' networks. It assigns a time slot to every voice or data transmission.

throughput

Throughput is the actual amount of user data that can be transmitted on a telecommunications line or on wireless networks. Throughput does not include, for example, bits used for addressing, error correction, or prioritizing packets with voice and data bits.

tier 1 provider

A loosely defined term for Internet service providers that own Internet backbone fiber optic facilities in addition to ISP services such as hosting and e-mail. Examples include

Cable & Wireless, Sprint, MCI, UUNET (which is part of MCI), and AT&T.

time division multiplexing

Time division multiplexers, such as T-1/E-1 equipment, save capacity for each device that is transmitting.

topology

Refers to the geometric shape of the physical connection of the lines in a network, or the "view from the top," which is the shape of the network, the configuration in which lines are connected to each other.

trunking gateway

Trunking gateways convert packet network circuits to those compatible with the public switched network (such as T-1/E-1 and T-3/E-3) and vice versa so that voice traffic can be transferred between IP networks and traditional, circuit switched networks.

trunks

Trunks are the circuits (electrical or fiber paths) between telephone companies and enterprise telephone systems and between central office switches. A T-1 is a trunk.

tuner

Tuners are used in televisions, radios, and set-top boxes to filter out all channels (frequencies) except the particular one at the frequency the tuner is designed to accept. The tuner then adapts the frequency to ones compatible with the TV or radio. Newer set-top boxes are equipped with multiple tuners so that one channel can be recorded while another is being viewed.

tunneling

Tunneling is a method of securely transferring data between sites connected by networks such as a virtual private network, the Internet, an intranet, or an extranet. Tunneling puts a new header in front of the data.

This is a way of separating data from multiple companies using the same network.

UDP (user data protocol)

Part of the TCP/IP suite of protocols. UDP protocols have less overhead because they do not have bits with packet numbers and acknowledgments. UDP is considered a connectionless protocol because packets arrive at their destination independently from various routes without sequence numbers. There is no assurance that all of the packets for a particular message arrive. The header is smaller with UDP than TCP because UDP headers do not have sequencing and acknowledgment bits. UDP is suited for applications such as database lookups, voice, and short messages.

UMTS (universal mobile telecommunications system)

UMTS is a European standard for third generation mobile wireless networks that GSM networks generally use when they are upgraded. WCDMA is a UMTS technology.

UMTS TDD (universal mobile telecommunications system time division duplexing)

A high-speed wireless technology used for third generation cellular and broadband wireless access to the Internet. It is also referred to as TD-CDMA. It uses the same channel for sending and receiving, with small time slots to separate the sending and receiving streams rather than the larger guard band used in other 3G technologies.

UNE (unbundled network element)

Unbundled network elements are parts of the incumbent local telephone company infrastructure that it is required to lease out to other local exchange carriers. Examples of unbundled network elements are the copper lines to customers' premises. Many UNE requirements have been eliminated.

unicasting

Unicasting is the transmission of one message from a single point to another point. This is also referred to as point-to-point communications.

unified messaging

Unified messaging is computing platforms that contain voice mail, facsimile, e-mail, and sometimes video mail on a single system. Users can access all of these services from either their computer or telephone.

unlicensed spectrum

Governments specify portions of the airwaves for unlicensed services at no charge to companies. 802.11 services are an example. Most governments issue certification, signal-spreading, and power-limitation rules to protect adjacent licensed spectrum bands from harmful interference from transmissions within the unlicensed spectrum.

URL (universal resource locator)

An address on the World Wide Web. The address is made up of strings of data that identify the server, the folder location, and other information indicating the location of information on the Internet.

USF (universal service fund)

The USF is used to fulfill the United States' commitment to affordable universal telephone service to all residential consumers. The Telecommunications Act of 1996 expanded universal service to rural health-care organizations, libraries, and educational institutions for Internet access, inside wiring, and computers. The library and educational subsidies are a part of universal service known as the e-rate. Every interstate carrier, cell phone, and paging company must pay a percentage of its interstate and international revenues to the fund. Broadband, affordable Internet access for residential customers is not included in the USF.

UTP (unshielded twisted pair)

Most inside telephones and computers are connected together via unshielded twisted pair copper cabling. The twists in the copper cables cut down on the electrical interference of signals carried on pairs of wire near each other and near electrical equipment.

UWB (ultra-wideband)

A wireless service that supports higher data rates than RFID and can be used for some of the same applications. However, widespread adoption is held up by a lack of an agreed-upon standard. It is also used by the military and by governments for tracking and for finding people trapped under rubble.

VLANs (virtual local area networks)

VLANs are groups of devices programmed in Layer 2 switches for special treatment in enterprise networks. They are not grouped together in physical networks; rather, they are grouped together in software for common treatment and programming purposes. They are "virtual" networks that act as if they were separate LANs.

VoIP (Voice over Internet Protocol)

VoIP is the process of sending voice traffic in packets on IP-based data networks. VoIP digitizes analog voice, compresses it, and puts it into packets at the sending end. The receiving end does the reverse. Unlike circuit switching, no path is saved for the duration of the voice session. However, voice packets can be prioritized.

VPIM (voice profile for Internet mail)
VPIM is an IP-based digital networking standard for sending voice mail and fax messages as attachments to e-mail messages.

VPNs (virtual private networks)
VPNs provide the functions and features of a private network without the need for dedicated private lines between corporate sites or between corporate sites and remote users. Each site connects to the network provider's network rather than directly to another corporate location.

VRUs (voice response units)
Voice response units (VRUs) provide information to callers based on callers' touch-tone or spoken commands. VRUs query computers for responses and "speak" them to callers. For example, people often can call their bank or credit card company to find out their balance or to learn if a payment has been received.

WAN (wide area network)
Wide area networks connect computers that are located in different cities, states, and countries.

WAP (wireless application protocol)
A protocol that defines how Internet sites can be displayed to fit on cellular devices' screens and how devices access and view these sites.

WCDMA (wideband code division multiplexing)
WCDMA is the 3G service that most GSM operators install.

WDM (wavelength division multiplexing)
Also known as dense wavelength division multiplexing, this enables multiple colors or frequencies of light to be carried on single pairs of fiber. WDM greatly increases the capacity of network providers' fiber optic networks.

Wi-Fi (wireless fidelity)
Wi-Fi refers to wireless networks that are based on 802.11 IEEE standards. The Wi-Fi Alliance tests and certifies that products meet IEEE 802.11 standards.

WiMAX (worldwide interoperability for microwave)
WiMAX is a forum whose goal is to facilitate interoperability of equipment based on 802.16 standards for high-speed fixed wireless service using the 2GHz to 11GHz frequency bands. Future versions may be used for mobile wireless service. Currently, no WiMAX-compliant equipment is available. Pre-WiMAX fixed wireless service is used for Internet access and for backhaul networks, which connect cellular towers to mobile central offices.

wire speed
The capability of switches to forward packets equal to the full speed of their ports. Ports are the interfaces to which cabling is connected. Wire speed is achieved with powerful switch processors, the computers that look up addresses and forward packets.

wireless local loop
With wireless local loops, wireless media is used to bring telephone service to customers' premises rather than copper or fiber cabling.

WISP (wireless Internet service provider)
A WISP provides Internet access from hotspots.

WLAN (wireless local area network)
Local area networks in which devices are connected to other devices or the LAN

wirelessly rather than with cabling. 802.11-based Wi-Fi networks are WLANs.

worms

Worms are viruses that are programmed to start infecting networks and other computers at a predetermined future time and date. These time-released viruses are also referred to as bots.

WWW (World Wide Web)

The World Wide Web has multimedia capabilities. It links users from one network to another when they "click" on highlighted text. It was developed in 1989 to make information on the Internet more accessible. A browser is required to navigate and access the World Wide Web.

X.25

An ITU-defined packet switching protocol for communications between end users and public data networks. X.25 is slower and older than frame relay service.

XML (extensible markup language)

A software language that was developed to make it easy for disparate computers to exchange information. XML uses tags to identify fields of data. XML is like a data dictionary in that uniform "tags" are attached to elements so that diverse programs can read the tags. For example, tags can be used to identify elements such as prices, model numbers, product identities, or quantities ordered.

ZigBee

ZigBee is based on the IEEE 802.15.4 standard for wireless networks with devices that operate at low data rates and consume small amounts of power. The ZigBee alliance is developing specifications for higher-level services to be used in sensor networks such as those that monitor and control heating and electrical systems.

Bibliography

Bedell, Paul. *Wireless Crash Course.* New York: McGraw-Hill, 2001.

Crystal, David. *A Glossary of Netspeak and Textspeak.* Edinburgh: Edinburgh University Press, 2004.

Dornan, Andy. *The Essential Guide to Wireless Applications, Second Edition.* Upper Saddle River, New Jersey: Prentice Hall PTR, 2002.

Geier, Jim. *Wireless Networks First-step.* Indianapolis: Cisco Press, 2005.

Gralla, Preston. *How the Internet Works, Seventh Edition.* Indianapolis: Que, 2004.

Harte, Lawrence; Levine, Richard; Kikta, Roman. *3G Wireless Demystified.* New York: McGraw-Hill Telecom, 2002.

Maufer, Thomas. *A Field Guide to Wireless LANs for Administrators and Power Users.* New Jersey: Prentice Hall PTR, 2004.

Morais, Douglas H. *Fixed Broadband Wireless Communications.* New Jersey: Prentice Hall PTR, 2004.

Muller, Nathan J. *Wireless A to Z.* New York: McGraw-Hill, 2003.

Newton, Harry, with Contributing Editor Ray Horak. *Newton's Telecom Dictionary, 20th Edition.* New York: CMP Books, 2004.

O'Driscoll, Gerard. *The Essential Guide to Digital Set-Top Boxes and Interactive TV.* New Jersey: Prentice Hall PTR, 2000.

Panko, Raymond R. *Business Data Networks and Telecommunications, Fourth Edition.* New Jersey: Prentice Hall, 2003.

Weisman, Carl J. *The Essential Guide to RF and Wireless, Second Edition.* New Jersey: Prentice Hall PTR, 2002.

Index